April 10–13, 2012
Bern, Switzerland

**Association for
Computing Machinery**

Advancing Computing as a Science & Profession

EuroSys'12

Proceedings of the
EuroSys 2012 Conference

Sponsored by:
ACM SIGOPS

Supported by:
**VMWare, Microsoft Research, Crédit Suisse, Google,
SI, MICS, Telefonica, and byte.nl**

Organized by:
EuroSys, Universität Bern, & Université de Neuchâtel

In cooperation with:
USENIX

**Association for
Computing Machinery**

Advancing Computing as a Science & Profession

The Association for Computing Machinery
2 Penn Plaza, Suite 701
New York, New York 10121-0701

Notice to Past Authors of ACM-Published Articles

ISBN: 978-1-4503-1223-3

Additional copies may be ordered prepaid from:

ACM Order Department
PO Box 30777
New York, NY 10087-0777, USA

Phone: 1-800-342-6626 (USA and Canada)
+1-212-626-0500 (Global)
Fax: +1-212-944-1318
E-mail: acmhelp@acm.org
Hours of Operation: 8:30 am – 4:30 pm ET

ACM Order Number: 534123

Printed in the USA

Foreword

It is our great pleasure to present the proceedings of the *7th ACM European Conference on Computer Systems*. Ever since the first EuroSys conference in 2006, EuroSys has gained and maintained a reputation as one of the premier systems conferences in the world. This year is no exception. The program is thought-provoking, high quality, and very broad—with topics ranging from kernels to clouds; from storage to security; and from energy to multicore. In addition, the program includes 8 co-located workshops, 3 tutorials, posters and demos. We are thrilled to announce that Steve Furber (University of Manchester), one of the original designers of the BBC Micro and the ARM 32-bit RISC processor, will give the keynote about Biologically-Inspired Massively-Parallel Computing.

With an acceptance rate of just 15%, the bar for papers to be accepted was exceptionally high. All papers in the program were first reviewed and subsequently heavily discussed at the PC meeting, and in the end, we admitted only the best and most interesting ones. The reviewing process was double-blind. Authors' identities were revealed only after the PC meeting.

So far, these PC discussions and the motivations for accepting or rejecting a paper at the PC meeting have remained hidden from the audience, and attendees have to figure out by themselves what motivated the program committee to accept or reject a certain paper. As we know from experience that such information is interesting, this year we decided to make the audience privy to the deliberations of the program committee. For this reason, we sent a summary of the PC discussions to the authors of rejected papers and publish not only the accepted papers themselves, but also a summary of the reviews and the discussions on the conference web site.

It is not the only novelty in this year's conference. To cope with the growing number of submissions, we decided to follow the model of some of the other top venues in growing the program committee and splitting it up in a PC light and a PC heavy. There is no distinction between the two, except that only heavies participated in round 3 of the reviewing process and attended the PC meeting in person. Incidentally, we are happy to report that several of the PC members "graduated" from the Shadow PCs of yesteryear!

Growing the PC proved to be wise, because with 179 papers submitted, EuroSys 2012 sets a new record in terms of submissions. All on-topic papers received at least 3 reviews in round 1. Of the original 179, no fewer than 96 made it to round 2, where they received at least two more reviews. The PC discussed all of these in person at the PC meeting. In addition, papers in round 2 with strongly diverging reviews received an extra review in round 3. All in all, the PC members wrote more than 750 reviews!

In addition to the regular PC, this year's EuroSys ran a shadow PC, consisting of talented young researchers that, hopefully, will provide the community the next wave of high quality PC members and scientists. The shadow PC was led by Rodrigo Rodrigues (MPI-SWS) who put in an admirable amount of time and energy to make the experience for everyone both useful and enjoyable. Moreover, the shadow PC was an excellent opportunity for authors to receive even more feedback on their work.

Finally, the authors had an opportunity to rebut some of the reviewers' comments, which the PC also took into account for their final decision. When the dust settled at the PC meeting in Amsterdam, the EuroSys PC had selected 27 papers. All of the papers were shepherded by a PC member.

Putting together EuroSys 2012 was a tremendous amount of work and our gratitude goes out to those who did most of the heavy lifting: the incredibly professional and hard working PC members, the secondary reviewers, and the authors. Without their diligence, punctuality and willingness to work well beyond the call of duty, this conference would not have been possible.

We also thank Eddie Kohler for the HotCRP conference management system—don't organise a conference without it—and Andrei Bacs for running the system. Special thanks to Etienne Rivière who managed the process of shepherding and finalizing. Finally, we would like to thank ACM SIGOPS and the EuroSys steering committee for their continued support and guidance.

EuroSys 2012 takes in Bern, Switzerland, in the historical building of the University of Bern. The organization of the conference was more than a year-long team effort, and we were blessed to work with some incredibly talented, hard-working people. It would not have been possible without the dedication of all the members of the organization committee. We would particularly like to thank Torsten Braun, Peter Kropf, Ruth Bestgen, and Daniela Schroth for their prodigious work in handling local arrangements, Alain Sandoz for his professional management of the conference's budget, and Etienne Rivière for his extensive work on the conference logistics. We are also indebted to the University of Bern for providing room space and technical support, to the University of Neuchâtel for handling registrations and finances, and to the volunteer students for working extra-time during the week of the conference.

We gratefully acknowledge the generous support of our sponsors who allowed us to award a number of grants to students and junior researchers for attending the conference.

We hope that you will find the program interesting and thought-provoking and that the conference will provide you with a valuable opportunity to share ideas with other researchers and practitioners from institutions around the world.

EuroSys 2012 Program Co-chairs   EuroSys 2012 General Chair

Frank Bellosa   **Herbert Bos**   **Pascal Felber**

KIT   *VU University Amsterdam*   *University of Neuchâtel*

Table of Contents

Session 10: Cores Galore

EuroSys 2012 Conference Organization

General Chair:	Pascal Felber *(University of Neuchâtel, Switzerland)*
Program Chairs:	Frank Bellosa *(KIT, Germany)*
	Herbert Bos *(VU University Amsterdam, The Netherlands)*
Local Chairs:	Torsten Braun *(University of Bern, Switzerland)*
	Peter Kropf *(University of Neuchâtel, Switzerland)*
Finance Chair:	Alain Sandoz *(University of Neuchâtel, Switzerland)*
Workshops & Tutorials Chairs:	Benoît Garbinato *(University of Lausanne, Switzerland)*
	Fernando Pedone *(University of Lugano, Switzerland)*
Poster Chairs:	Gilles Muller *(INRIA, France)*
	Christian Tschudin *(University of Basel, Switzerland)*
Shadow PC Chair:	Rodrigo Rodrigues *(MPI-SWS, Germany)*
Publication Chair:	Etienne Rivière *(University of Neuchâtel, Switzerland)*
Publicity Chairs:	Cesare Pautasso *(University of Lugano, Switzerland)*
	Romain Rouvoy *(University of Lille 1, France)*
Grant Chairs:	Desislava Dimitrova *(University of Bern, Switzerland)*
	Vivien Quéma *(Grenoble Institute of Technology, France)*
Webmaster:	Markus Anwander *(University of Bern, Switzerland)*
Secretariat:	Daniela Schroth *(University of Bern, Switzerland)*

Additional reviewers:

Deniz Altinbüken
Silviu Andrica
Jeremy Andrus
Hitesh Ballani
Radu Banabic
Pramod Bhatotia
Alex Böttcher
Silas Boyd-Wickizer
Stefan Bucur
Dhruva Chakrabarti
Davide Cherubini
Vitaly Chipounov
Austin Clements
Patrick Colp
Björn Döbel
Aggelos Economopoulos
James Elliott
Benjamin Engel
Robert Escriva
David Fiala
Pedro Fonseca
Davide Frey
Daniel Fryer
Alex Garthwaite
Inigo Goiri
Tim Harris
Marius Hillenbrand
Wanja Hofer
Timo Hönig
Baris Kasikci
Johannes Kinder
Elisavet Kozyri
Volodymyr Kuznetsov
Adam Lackorzynski
Jean-Sébastien Légaré
Jinyang Li
Cheng Li
Daniel Lupei
Xiaosong Ma
Dutch Meyer
Konrad Miller
Robert Morris

Sape Mullender
Arjun Narayan
Jad Nous
Alex Pesterev
Daniel Porto
Dan Ports
Shriram Rajagopalan
Arash Rezaei
Michael Roitzsch
Nuno Santos
Abhik Sarkar
Dan Schatzberg
Fabian Scheler
Ji-Yong Shin
Asia Slowinska
Julian Stecklina
Isabella Stilkerich
Michael Stilkerich
Jan Stoess
Reinhard Tartler
Hendrik Tews
Peter Ulbrich
Sudharshan Vazhkudai
Nicolas Viennot
Bimal Viswanath
Marcus Völp
Sergii Vozniuk
Jonas Wagner
Chao Wang
Carsten Weinhold
Alexander Wieder
Dirk Wischermann
Xing Wu
Cristian Zamfir
Nickolai Zeldovich
Mingliang Zhai
Jidong Zhai Liu
Mingchen Zhao
Haoqiang Zheng
Haoqiang Zheng
Wei Zheng
Christopher Zimmer

Shadow Program Committee: Lorenzo Cavallaro *(Royal Holloway, University of London, UK)*
Allen Clement *(Max Planck Institute for Software Systems, Germany)*
Paolo Costa *(Imperial College, UK)*
Tobias Distler *(University Erlangen-Nuremberg, Germany)*
Simon Duquennoy *(Swedish Institute of Computer Science, SICS)*
Petros Efstathopoulos *(Symantec Research, USA)*
Joshua Ellul *(Imperial College, UK)*
Eva Kalyvianaki *(Imperial College, UK)*
Manos Kapritsos *(University of Texas at Austin, USA)*
Stephen Kell *(Oxford University, UK)*
Rodrigo Rodrigues *(MPI-SWS, Germany)* **(chair)**
Etienne Rivière *(University of Neuchâtel, Switzerland)*
Yao Shi *(National ICT, Australia / University of New South Wales, UK)*
Asia Slowinska *(VU University Amsterdam, The Netherlands)*
Jens Teubner *(ETH Zürich, Switzerland)*
Tim Wood *(George Washington University, USA)*

EuroSys 2012 Sponsor & Supporters

Sponsor:

Platinum Supporter:

Gold Supporters:

Bronze Supporters:

Organized by:

In cooperation with:

STM in the Small: Trading Generality for Performance in Software Transactional Memory

Aleksandar Dragojević

I&C, EPFL, Lausanne, Switzerland
aleksandar.dragojevic@epfl.ch

Tim Harris

Microsoft Research, Cambridge
tharris@microsoft.com

Abstract

Data structures implemented using software transactional memory (STM) have a reputation for being much slower than data structures implemented directly from low-level primitives such as atomic compare-and-swap (CAS). In this paper we present a specialized STM system (SpecTM) that allows the program to express additional knowledge about the particular operations being performed by transactions—e.g., using a separate API to write transactions that access small, fixed, numbers of memory locations. We show that data structures implemented using SpecTM offer essentially the same performance and scalability as implementations built directly from CAS. We present results using hash tables and skip lists on machines with up to 8 sockets and up to 128 hardware threads. Specialized transactions can be mixed with normal transactions, allowing fast-path operations to be specialized for greater performance, while allowing less common cases to be expressed using normal transactions for simplicity. We believe that SpecTM provides a "sweet spot" for expert programmers developing scalable data structures.

Categories and Subject Descriptors D.1.3 [*Programming Techniques*]: Concurrent Programming—Parallel Programming

Keywords Lock-Free Data Structures, Parallel Programming, Transactional Memory

1. Introduction

Over recent years a great deal of attention has been paid to the design and implementation of transactional memory systems. Transactional memory (TM) allows a program to make a series of memory accesses appear to occur as a single atomic operation [16, 17, 29].

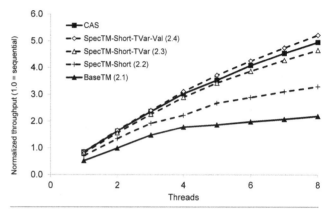

Figure 1. Throughput of operations on a hash table (90% lookups), normalized to optimized sequential code.

Atomicity can simplify the design of shared memory data structures. Unfortunately, data structures rarely perform well when built using software implementations of transactional memory (STM) [2, 8]. Figure 1 illustrates this for a hash table benchmark (in Section 2 we return to the details of the particular experimental setting). The figure shows the throughput of operations for a hash table built using a state-of-the-art STM system (labeled BaseTM), and an implementation built directly from atomic compare-and-swap (labeled CAS). With a single thread the performance of the baseline STM system is less than half that of sequential code. The CAS-based implementation is both faster than the STM-based implementation, and it scales better.

STM and CAS can be seen as two points in a spectrum of programming abstractions. On the one hand, STM can be relatively easy to use, but perform relatively poorly. On the other hand, CAS can be extremely difficult to use, but can perform extremely well. In this paper we examine intermediate points in this spectrum. Compared with STM, how much simplicity do we lose in order to achieve good performance? Compared with CAS, how much performance do we lose in order to make programming appreciably simpler?

Our main contribution is to show that data structures built using specialized STM systems can match the performance and scalability of existing CAS-based data structures. We call our system SpecTM. We explore three kinds of specialization (Section 2):

First, SpecTM provides specialized APIs for short transactions. These APIs shift responsibilities from the STM's implementer to the STM's user: for instance, the STM's user must provide sequence numbers to their data accesses (one function for the first read in a transaction, a different function for the second, etc.). This shift in responsibility removes book-keeping work from the STM implementation.

Second, SpecTM provides specialization over the placement of STM meta-data, allowing pieces of meta-data to be located on the same cache lines as the application's data structures. In contrast, traditional STM systems often use an automatic hash-based mapping from data to meta-data, requiring multiple cache lines to be accessed.

Third, SpecTM provides a value-based validation mechanism in which the per-word meta-data is reduced to a single bit reserved in each data item. Requiring a "spare" bit for the use of the STM system restricts the kind of data that the STM can work over. However, on a 64-bit machine, the remaining 63 bits can nevertheless accommodate typical integer values, and pointers to aligned data structures. We show how, for many workloads, we can use value-based validation without needing to maintain shared global version numbers.

Importantly, specialized transactions can be mixed with normal transactions that use a traditional STM interface. This enables SpecTM to be used in two ways. First, specialized transactions can be used to build a new data structure, with the knowledge that long transactions are available as a fall-back for any cases that are difficult to write. Second, a data structure can be built using ordinary transactions, and then SpecTM can be used to optimize the common cases. Section 3 illustrates this using a detailed example. We show how SpecTM is used in building a skip list, using specialized transactions for the most common forms of insertion and deletion, and normal transactions for more complex cases.

The kind of specialized interface we provide in SpecTM is not appropriate for all settings. We are explicitly giving up some of the generality of TM as a synchronization mechanism in order to achieve better performance than existing implementations. In effect, we are returning to the original application of TM in building shared memory data structures, as espoused by Herlihy and Moss [17], and explored in the first STM design [29]. Another way to view SpecTM is that it provides a little bit more than early implementations of multi-word compare-and-swap (CASN) [13, 22]. Unlike CASN, SpecTM transactions are dynamic (allowing a transaction to atomically read a series of locations, rather than specifying all of the locations in a single function call). In addition, unlike early CASN implementations, SpecTM transactions can be mixed with traditional transactions.

Section 4 describes the implementation of SpecTM, and evaluates its performance and scalability. In this paper we focus on building data structures such as the hash tables and skip lists. The motivation for this focus is the central role of these data structures in key-value stores and in-memory database indices. The evaluation uses two systems: a 16-core machine and a larger 128-core machine. Our experiments show that specialized STM performs almost as well as existing lock-free algorithms, with slowdowns of less than 5%. Also, specialized STM scales as well as the lock-free algorithms on the 128-core machine even when the contention is high.

We describe related work (Section 5) and conclude (Section 6).

2. Specializing the TM Interface

In this section we introduce the interfaces exposed by SpecTM. We illustrate the use of SpecTM using the running example of a simple double-ended queue (dequeue). This queue supports `PushLeft`, `PopLeft`, `PushRight`, `PopRight` operations to add and remove items to either end. We focus on `PopLeft` and sketch how it would be written using a traditional STM (Section 2.1), and then how it would be written using SpecTM (Sections 2.2–2.4). (We use a basic dequeue as a concise example: a scalable implementation would be more complex [18].)

To give a feeling for SpecTM's performance, Figure 1 shows how some variants scale on 1–16 cores. The baseline TM system (BaseTM) follows the TL2 algorithm of Dice *et al.* [4], extended with timebase extension from Riegel *et al.* [27], and the hash-based write-set design of Spear *et al.* [30]. The CAS-based hash table is implemented from Fraser's design [11]. All the implementations use epoch based memory management, also following Fraser's design.

Building on BaseTM, we discuss the contributions of each form of specialization in the corresponding sections below (Section 2.2–2.4). In Section 4 our main results consider more combinations of design choices, and they examine scalability on larger machines.

2.1 Traditional STM (BaseTM)

Here is the `PopLeft` operation implemented using the traditional STM interface exposed by BaseTM:

```
void *Items[QUEUE_SIZE] = { NULL };
int LeftIdx = 0;
int RightIdx = 0;

void *PopLeft(void) {
  void *result = NULL;
  TX_RECORD t;
  do {
    Tx_Start(&t);
    int li = Tx_Read(&t, &LeftIdx);
    void *result = Tx_Read(&t, &Items[li]);
    if (result != NULL) {
      Tx_Write(&t, &(Items[li]), NULL);
      Tx_Write(&t, &LeftIdx, (li+1)%QUEUE_SIZE);
    }
  } while (!Tx_Commit(&t));
  return result;
}
```

The queue is built over an array which holds the items at indexes `LeftIdx–RightIdx-1` (wrapping around the array, modulo the queue size). Queue elements must be non-NULL, allowing NULL values to be used to indicate the presence of empty slots (and to distinguish a completely empty queue from a completely full queue). Consequently, PopLeft starts by reading the left index, and reading the array item at that index. If the item is non-NULL, then the left index is advanced, and the array slot is cleared.

Compared with a sequential implementation, the STM adds three main costs: (*i*) book-keeping required when starting a transaction (e.g., recording a snapshot of the processor state so that the transaction can be restarted upon conflict), (*ii*) managing the transaction record on each read and write (e.g., incrementing read/write pointers into the transaction's logs, and, in the case of reads, ensuring that they see any earlier writes in the same transaction), (*iii*) visiting meta-data locations to perform concurrency control.

Our interface for short transactions (Section 2.2) addresses the first two of these costs. The third cost is addressed by our interface for explicit transactional data (Section 2.3), and for integrating meta-data within application data structures (Section 2.4).

2.2 Short Transactions

The key ideas for SpecTM's interface are to require the programmer to indicate the sequencing of operations within a transaction, and to require the programmer to avoid write-to-read dependencies within a transaction. Here is PopLeft re-implemented using SpecTM:

```
void *PopLeft(void) {
  void *result = NULL;
  TX_RECORD t;
restart:
  int li = Tx_RW_R1(&t, &LeftIdx);
  void *result = Tx_RW_R2(&t, &Items[li]);
  if (!Tx_RW_2_Is_Valid(&t)) goto restart;
  if (result != NULL) {
    Tx_RW_2_Commit(&t, (li+1) % QUEUE_SIZE, NULL);
  } else {
    Tx_RW_2_Abort(&t);
  }
  return result;
}
```

Compared with the previous section, there are five main changes: (*i*) The read operations include sequence numbers in the function signature (_R1 for the first read, _R2 for the second, etc.). The first read implicitly starts the transaction. (*ii*) Transactions can access only a small number of locations (four in our implementation, which can be increased in a straightforward manner). (*iii*) Each access must be to a distinct memory location. (*iv*) The processor state is not saved implicitly at the start of a transaction and restored upon conflict; the programmer is responsible for calling . . ._Is_Valid to detect conflicts, and for restarting the transaction if needed. (*v*) The commit function signature includes the total number of locations accessed, along with the new values to be stored at each of them.

This example illustrates the trade-off we are studying. The specialized interface requires the programmer to be able to provide sequence numbers on their accesses (and so it

```
typedef void *Ptr;
// Single read/write/CAS transactions:
Ptr Tx_Single_Read(Ptr *addr);
void Tx_Single_Write(Ptr *addr, Ptr newVal);
Ptr Tx_Single_CAS(Ptr *addr, Ptr oldVal, Ptr newVal);

// Read-write short transactions:
Ptr Tx_RW_R1(TX_RECORD *t, Ptr *addr_1);
Ptr Tx_RW_R2(TX_RECORD *t, Ptr *addr_2);
...
bool Tx_RW_1_Is_Valid(TX_RECORD *t);
bool Tx_RW_2_Is_Valid(TX_RECORD *t);
...
void Tx_RW_1_Commit(TX_RECORD *t, Ptr val1);
void Tx_RW_2_Commit(TX_RECORD *t,
                    Ptr val_1, Ptr val_2);
...
void Tx_RW_1_Abort(TX_RECORD *t);
void Tx_RW_2_Abort(TX_RECORD *t);
...
// Read-only short transactions:
Ptr Tx_RO_R1(TX_RECORD *t, Ptr *addr_1);
Ptr Tx_RO_R2(TX_RECORD *t, Ptr *addr_2);
...
bool Tx_RO_1_Is_Valid(TX_RECORD *t);
bool Tx_RO_2_Is_Valid(TX_RECORD *t);
...
// Commit combined read-only & read-write transactions:
bool Tx_RO_1_RW_1_Commit(TX_RECORD *t, Ptr val1);
bool Tx_RO_1_RW_2_Commit(TX_RECORD *t,
                        Ptr val_1, Ptr val_2);
...
// Upgrade a location from RO to RW:
bool Tx_Upgrade_RO_1_To_RW_2(TX_RECORD *t);
...
```

Figure 2. SpecTM API for short transactions.

would be ill-suited to a series of reads performed in a loop). In addition, SpecTM requires all of the writes to be deferred until commit-time. Imposing these restrictions reduces the book-keeping required by the STM. To see why, consider the operation of a typical STM system using deferred updates [16] (similar optimizations are possible when compared with STM systems using eager updates, but we omit the details for brevity). With deferred updates, the STM must log the new values written by a transaction, and copy them to target memory locations only upon successful commit. This logging means that transactional reads need to search the update log so that they see early writes by the same transaction. SpecTM's restrictions mean that: (*i*) There is no need for an update log, because the values being written are provided at commit-time. (*ii*) For the same reason, read-after-write checks are no longer necessary. (*iii*) For read-write transactions, the implementation can eagerly acquire a write lock at the time of the read, eliminating the need for commit-time read-set validation. (*iv*) Focusing on short transactions means that the set of all locations accessed can be held in a fixed-size array inline in the TX_RECORD. Similarly, there is no need to track operation indices, as they are provided by statically the program. This is in contrast to traditional STM systems which must track indices dynamically.

Figure 2 shows the full API for writing short transactions. In addition to the short read/write transactions that occur in this example, SpecTM provides:

Single-operation transactions. The `Tx_Single_*` functions perform transactions that access a single location: either read, write, or compare-and-swap. These operations synchronize with concurrent transactions—e.g., a `Tx_Single_Read` will not read uncommitted writes. More generally, the `Tx_Single_*` operations are linearizable [19] and so if read r_1 sees a value written by a transaction Tx_A then a subsequent read r_2 must see all Tx_A's writes. The single-operation API enables further optimizations, completely eliminating any logging to an explicit transaction record.

Short read-only transactions. As with the RW transaction in the `PopLeft` example, SpecTM provides short read-only transactions. We distinguish read-only transactions from read-write transactions so that an implementation can handle the two kinds of transaction differently (e.g., using encounter-time locking for locations in a short read-write transaction, but invisible reads for read-only transactions [16]).

A read-only transaction is started with a call to `Tx_RO_R1`, which also performs the first read. Subsequent reads are performed using `Tx_RO_R2, . . .` . The `Tx_RO_*_Is_Valid` functions test whether or not the transaction is currently valid, with variants specialized to the size of the read set. There are no explicit commit or abort functions. Successful validation serves in the place of commit. If a program wishes to abort a read-only transaction then it can simply discard the transaction record.

As with read-write transactions, short read-only transactions avoid the need to dynamically allocate logs and maintain log indices.

Combining read-only and read-write transactions. A single transaction may mix the `Tx_RO_*` operations for the locations that it only reads, and the `Tx_RW_*` operations for the locations that it both reads and writes. The two sets of locations must be disjoint. A set of commit functions with names such as `Tx_RO_x_RW_y_Commit` is provided to commit these transactions: x refers to the number of locations read, and y to the number of locations written. As with the `Tx_RW_*_Commit` functions, the values to write are supplied to the commit operation.

Finally, if a transaction wishes to "upgrade" a location from read-only access to read-write access, then the function `Tx_Upgrade_RO_x_To_RW_y` function indicates that index x amongst the transaction's existing reads has been upgraded to form index y in its writes—x may be any of the locations read previously, and y must be the next write index.

This form of upgrade is used when the value read from one location determines whether or not another location will be updated. For instance, consider a double-compare-single-swap operation which checks that two locations `a1` and `a2` hold expected values `o1` and `o2` respectively and, if they do, writes `n1` to `a1`. This function can be written:

```
bool DCSS(void **a1, void **a2,
          void *o1, void *o2,
          void *n1) {
  TX_RECORD t;
restart:
  if (Tx_RO_R1(&t, a1) == o1 &&
      Tx_RO_R2(&t, a2) == o2 &&
      Tx_Upgrade_RO_1_To_RW_1(&t)) {
    if (Tx_RO_2_RW_1_Commit(&t, n1)) return true;
  } else if (Tx_RO_2_Is_Valid(&t)) return false;
  goto restart;
}
```

This `DCSS` function reads from `a1` and `a2`. If the values seen match `o1` and `o2` then it upgrades `a1` to be the first location in the write set. If this upgrade succeeds, then `DCSS` attempts to commit the short transaction, with 2 entries in the read set and the single location in the write set.

Building data structures using short transactions. Our implementations of data structures using short transactions can be seen as a mid-point between building directly from CAS and building with a traditional TM interface. On the one hand, when compared with traditional TM, SpecTM burdens the programmer with adding sequence numbers to their reads and writes, and ensuring that the read-set and write-set remain disjoint. On the other hand, when compared with CAS, SpecTM provides the programmer with an abstraction for making multi-word atomic updates.

In practice, when using SpecTM, we start by splitting operations into a series of short atomic steps, each of a statically-known size. As we show in the case study in Section 3, in our skip list implementation we use short RW transactions to atomically add and remove an item when it appears only at level-1 or level-2 in the skip list. We use general purpose transactions for the (rarer) cases of nodes that appear at higher levels. Short and general purpose transactions can be mixed as they use the same STM meta-data. Our hash table and skip list implementations are more complex than ones built using traditional TM implementations. However, they are simpler than the equivalent lock-free algorithms as the use of multi-word atomic updates simplifies the most complex parts of these data structures.

Code complexity. Using short SpecTM transactions interface from Figure 2 can easily result in mistakes by programmers (e.g. using a wrong function name or a wrong index). Incorrect uses of the SpecTM interface can typically be detected at runtime. For performance, we do not implement such checks in non-debug modes. Furthermore, short transactions do not compose as well as traditional transactions, as they require static operation indices. Short transactions are intended for performance critical code and programmers are often willing to sacrifice composability of such code, so this is not a major limitation. For example, code using CAS or locks is routinely used when performance is important, despite its poor composability.

Performance. The "SpecTM-Short" line in Figure 1 shows the impact on performance of using short transactions. In particular, note how short transactions remove much of the

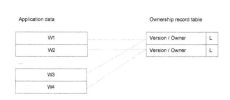

(a) Meta-data held in a table of ownership records, indexed by a hash function.

(b) Meta-data co-located with application data in `TVars` (Section 2.3).

(c) One lock-bit of meta-data held in each data item (Section 2.4).

Figure 3. Different ways of organizing STM meta-data in variants of SpecTM.

overhead at 1-thread without harming scalability. This follows from our focus on designing the SpecTM API to remove much of the book-keeping of typical STM systems: we are performing the same synchronization work.

2.3 Explicit Transactional Variables

The second way in which SpecTM specializes the STM interface is to allow transactional data to be located alongside meta-data. Typical STM systems for C/C++ are built without control over data structures, and instead place their meta-data in a table of ownership records ("orecs" [17]), using a hash function to map from a location in the heap to the orec used for that location. This traditional design means fetching two cache-lines on each data access. It can also introduce false conflicts when distinct data items can hash to the same orec. Even with a few false conflicts, this traditional design can increase book-keeping overheads, as more complex data structures need to be used for handling updates to several locations that map to the same orec.

With SpecTM, we follow STM-Haskell [15] in using a `TVar` data type which encapsulates both (*i*) the meta-data required by the TM system, and (*ii*) a word of the application's data. If the `TVar` is aligned to a 2-word boundary, then the complete structure will be held on a single cache line.

`TVars` do not significantly change the short transaction API in Figure 2: the calls simply take addresses of `TVars` instead of memory words. However, using `TVars` reduces the cache miss rates thus improving STM's performance and scalability. Also, as each memory location maps to a single orec, the book-keeping overheads are reduced.

Figure 3 illustrates these different approaches. Figure 3(a) shows the use of a table of ownership records, with application data words `W1` and `W3` both mapping to the first ownership record, and `W2` and `W4` to the second. In contrast, in Figure 3(b), each `TVar` includes an application word and the ownership record.

Performance. The "SpecTM-Short-TVar" line in Figure 1 shows the impact on performance of using short transactions and `TVars` in the hash table workload. The difference between these results and the earlier "SpecTM-Short" results follows from the placement of the orecs within `TVars`, and the consequent changes in cache behavior.

2.4 Combined Meta-Data with Value-Based Validation

The final form of specialization in SpecTM is to combine the STM's meta-data with the application's own data. From the point of view of the SpecTM API, data structures are still maintained using `TVars`. However, rather than having each `TVar` include two words, each `TVar` now consists of a single word of the application's data, within which one bit is reserved for the use of the STM (Figure 3(c)). Eliminating the additional orec word further reduces STM overheads. For example, traditional STMs need to perform a sequence of three reads (orec, data word and then orec again) to get a correct snapshot of data and the corresponding orec [16]. When data and meta-data are held in the same word, this sequence becomes a single atomic read. Similarly, at commit-time, the entire `TVar` can be updated by an atomic write.

Reserving a bit restricts the programmer to storing pointers to aligned addresses (where the alignment guarantees that some low-order bits are spare), or storing small integer values (shorter than a full word). These restrictions would not be palatable in general-purpose code, but they can be accommodated in our pointer-based data structures.

Validation with Version Numbers. Before introducing how SpecTM operates using a single bit per word, we briefly summarize how BaseTM works when using full orecs (Figure 3(a)–(b)). With full orecs, as with TL2 and other STM systems [16], the orecs combine a lock-bit and either a version number or a reference to a transaction record. If the lock-bit is set then the orec is locked by a transaction that is writing to the orec's data (and the body of the orec points to this owning transaction). Otherwise, if the lock-bit is clear, then the body of the orec contains a version number that is incremented whenever a transaction commits an update to the orec's data. As in other STM systems, these version numbers are used for validating locations that are read by a transaction: a transaction records the version numbers of orecs when first reading from them, and it validates by checking that these version numbers are unchanged.

Version-Free Validation. We use the single bit of meta-data as a lock-bit: it is locked by the `Tx_RW_*` operations in read-write transactions, and during the commit phase of normal transactions. To acquire the lock, a transaction atomically tries to set the lock bit and to replace the rest of the word with a pointer to the owner's transaction record. As in other STM systems, deadlock is avoided conservatively by aborting if the lock is not free.

However, having only a single bit of meta-data introduces a problem when handling transactions that read from a location but do not wish to write to it. The problem is that, without version numbers, a transaction cannot check for conflicting writes to the locations that it has read from. In general, it is incorrect for it to simply re-read the values in each of these locations and to check that each of these matches the values seen by the transaction. This is because there is no guarantee that these reads see a consistent view of memory, given that there may be concurrent writes in progress.

Our observation is that, although the general case of version-free validation is incorrect, we can identify a series of special cases in which it can nevertheless be employed safely:

- Many read-modify-write transactions update all of the locations that they read. In SpecTM these transactions are expressed using the Tx_RW_* API. Version numbers are not needed in these transactions because all of the orecs are locked before making the updates. For instance, a transaction to add a node into a doubly-linked list will lock and update all four of the locations involved.

- "Mostly-read-write" transactions read from only one location that they do not update—e.g., in the skip list in Section 3, an insertion must read from a location that records the maximum height of the list nodes. For these transactions it is correct to validate their single read-only access with a value-based comparison. The transaction proceeds by locking the locations being updated, checking that the value in the location read has not changed, and then making the updates and releasing the orecs. The single read forms the linearization point.

- Finally, some locations satisfy a "non-re-use" property in which a given value is not stored in a given location more than once. In this case, if a transaction reads values $v_1, v_2, \ldots$ from a series of locations $a_1, a_2, \ldots$, and then it subsequently sees these same values upon validation, then the non-re-use property means that the complete set of values was present at those locations at the instant of the start of the validation. In effect, the values themselves are taking the place of version numbers. This kind of non-re-use property often occurs when the values are pointers to dynamically allocated data managed by mechanisms such as those of Herlihy *et al.* [21] and Michael [25].

These three special cases cover many of the transactions used in shared memory data structures; indeed they cover all of the cases that occur in our hash table and skip list workloads. In fact, we initially identified these cases after we were surprised that value-based validation worked correctly for our workloads, even though it should not work in general.

Exploiting these special cases requires care on the part of the programmer—the first two cases can be checked automatically by the SpecTM implementation, but we have not yet investigated checking tools or proof methods for the non-re-use property. In order to support general-purpose transactions that do not fit in any of these special cases, a global version number can be used to track the number of transactions that have committed. This can be used, as Dalessandro *et al.* show [3], to make value-based validation safe without requiring a non-re-use property.

If this general-purpose case occurs rarely then, rather than having a single, shared, version number on which each thread contends, each thread can maintain a separate version number. These per-thread numbers are updated on each transactional commit on the given thread. This design makes it fast to (logically) increment the shared counter, at the cost of reading all of the threads' counters in the general case.

Performance. The "SpecTM-Short-TVar-Val" line in Figure 1 shows the impact on performance of using short transactions, with TVars, and with value-based validation exploiting the three special cases described above. For this workload, the additional performance above the "SpecTM-Short-TVar" line is slight; however, it closes the gap with the performance of the CAS-based implementation.

3. SpecTM Case Study

To illustrate the use of SpecTM in more detail, we now show how it can be used to implement a skip list (Figure 4). For brevity, we simplify the skip list to store only integer values and to provide search, insert, and remove operations (the pseudo-code shows only the former two). We also omit memory-management code—many now-conventional techniques can be used [11, 21, 25].

Each skip list node stores an integer value, and an array of forward pointers, with one pointer for each level of the skip list the node belongs to (line 2). The skip list is represented by a head node that points to the first node in each level of the list (line 7). To iterate the list, a window of pointers for all skip list levels is used (line 10).

The function for searching the skip list (line 15) traverses the nodes by reading their forward pointers (line 19). It starts at the highest level in the skip list, moving successively lower whenever the level would skip over the integer being sought. As in lock-free linked list and skip list implementations [11, 18], a "deleted" bit is reserved in all of a node's forward pointers to indicate that the node has been deleted. The search function ignores deleted notes (line 20). The search terminates once it reaches the bottom level.

Adding a new node (line 30) starts with a search for the value being inserted (line 35). The skip list does not permit duplicate elements, so false is returned if the value is found (line 36) Otherwise, the search returns an iterator that can be used for the insertion. The level of the new node is generated randomly, with the probability of node being

```
1   const int MAX_LEVEL = 32;
2   struct Tower {
3     int id;
4     TmPtr next[MAX_LEVEL]
5     int lvl;
6   };
7   struct Skiplist {
8     Tower head;
9   };
10  struct Iterator {
11    Tower *prev[MAX_LEVEL];
12    Tower *next[MAX_LEVEL];
13  };
14
15  Tower *Skiplist::Search(int id, Iterator *it, int lvl)
         {
16    Tower *curr, *prev = &head;
17    while(--lvl >= 0) {
18      while(true) {
19        curr = Tx_Single_Read(&(prev->next[lvl]));
20        curr = Unmark(curr);
21        if(curr == NULL || curr->id >= id)
22          break;
23        prev = curr;
24      }
25      it->prev[lvl] = prev;
26      it->next[lvl] = curr;
27    }
28    return curr;
29  }
30  bool Skiplist::Add(Tower *data) {
31    Iterator it;
32    bool restartFlag;
33  restart:
34    int headLvl = PtrToInt(Tx_Single_Read(&head.lvl));
35    Tower *curr = Search(data->id, &it, headLvl);
36    if(curr != NULL && curr->id == id)
37      return false;
38    data->lvl = GetRandomLevel();
39    if(data->lvl == 1)
40      restartFlag = !AddLevelOne(data, &it))
41    else
42      restartFlag = !AddLevelN(data, &it);
43    if(restartFlag)
44      goto restart;
45    return true;
46  }
47  bool Skiplist::AddLevelOne(Tower *data, Iterator *it) {
48    TmPtrWrite(&(data->next[0]), it->next[0]);
49    return Tx_Single_CAS(&iter->prev[0]->next[0],
50      it->next[0], data) == it->next[0];
51  }
52  bool Skiplist::AddLevelN(Tower *data, Iterator *it) {
53    bool ret;
54    STM_START_TX();
55    int headLvl = STM_READ_INT(&(head.lvl));
56    if(data->level > headLvl) {
57      STM_WRITE_INT(&(head.lvl), data->level);
58      for(int lvl = headLvl;lvl < data->level;lvl++) {
59        it->prev[lvl] = head;
60        it->next[lvl] = NULL;
61      }
62    }
63    for(int lvl = 0;lvl < data->level;lvl++) {
64      Ptr nxt = STM_READ_PTR(&win->prev[lvl]->next[lvl]);
65      if(nxt != it->next[lvl]) {
66        ret = false;
67        STM_ABORT_TX();
68      }
69      STM_WRITE_PTR(&(it->prev[lvl]->next[lvl]), data);
70      TmPtrWrite(&(data->next[lvl]), win->next[lvl]);
71    }
72    ret = true;
73    STM_END_TX();
74    return ret;
75  }
```

Figure 4. Skiplist implementation using SpecTM.

assigned a level l equal to $\frac{1}{2^l}$. The node is then inserted atomically into all of the lists up to this level. The nodes with level one are inserted using a short specialized transaction (lines 40) and the nodes with higher levels are inserted using an ordinary transaction (line 42). If the insertion does not succeed due to the concurrent changes to the skip list, the whole operation is restarted (line 44). Otherwise, the insert succeeds and `true` is returned to indicate its success.

Removals proceed in a similar manner to insertions. The node is first located using the search function. A single transaction is used to atomically mark the node at all levels, and to remove it from all of the lists it belongs too. Removal of nodes at level one is performed using a short specialized transaction, and the removal of nodes with higher levels is performed using ordinary transactions.

These insertion and removal operations typify the way we use SpecTM. The common cases are expressed using short transactions, and less frequent cases are expressed with more general, but slower, ordinary transactions. If developers see the need to further improve performance, they can further specialize the implementations. The skip list implementation used in our evaluations uses short transactions for levels 1–2, leaving only 25% of insert and remove operations to be executed using ordinary transactions.

Code Complexity. The code of the SpecTM skip list is clearly more complex than a traditional transactional implementation. However, it is simpler than the code of the lock-free skip list based on CAS, such as one by Fraser [11]. There are two main reasons for this simplicity:

First, because specialized transactions can co-exist with ordinary transactions, the more complex operations can still be expressed as ordinary transactions. This limits the amount of code that must be written using SpecTM.

Second, although the API for SpecTM is more complex than for traditional transactions, conceptually it still provides the abstraction of atomicity. Experience with the bounded-size Rock Hardware TM [5, 6, 9] has shown that short transactions are simpler to use than CAS—e.g., without multi-word atomic operations, Fraser's CAS-based skip list must handle nodes which are partially-removed and partially-inserted.

4. Evaluation

In this section we evaluate the performance of SpecTM. We first describe the details of the implementation (Section 4.1), and summarize the different STM systems that we use in our evaluation (Section 4.2). We then examine the performance of SpecTM in single-threaded executions (Section 4.3). This lets us assess the sequential overheads of different approaches. Then, we evaluate the performance and scalability of hash table and skip list data structures implemented using SpecTM, and compare it to lock-free implementations (Section 4.4). We do so on two systems that support 16 and 128 hardware threads respectively.

4.1 Implementation

Our implementation of SpecTM operates on 64-bit systems. Consequently, we ignore the possibility of version number overflow. Existing techniques could be used to manage overflow on 32-bit systems if needed [10, 14].

We use a conventional epoch-based system for memory management, based on that described by Fraser [11]. This mechanism ensures that a location is not deallocated by one thread while it is being accessed transactionally by another thread. Epoch-based reclamation works well in our setting. However, it would be straightforward to use alternatives such as tracing garbage collection, or lock-free schemes [21, 25].

Our baseline STM implementation uses the TL2 algorithm [4], timebase extension [27], and hash-based write sets [30]. The approach is typical of C/C++ STM systems [4, 7, 10, 28, 30]. It performs well for our workloads, matching the performance reported by Dragojević *et al.* [8].

BaseTM provides opacity [12], guaranteeing that a running transaction sees a consistent view of the heap. BaseTM provides weak isolation, meaning that it does not detect conflicts between concurrent transactional and non-transactional accesses to the same location (if strong isolation is needed, then many implementation techniques exist [16]). BaseTM does not provide privatization safety (barriers such as those of Marathe *et al.* [24] could be added, if needed).

As illustrated in Figure 3(a), we use a global table of ownership records, indexed by a hash function. We use commit-time locking (CTL), where orecs are locked only during commit, rather than during a transaction's execution. We use invisible reads (so the implementation of Tx_Read does not write to any shared data). We use deferred updates (meaning that updates are held in a write log during execution, and flushed to the heap on commit). We use a simple contention manager: upon conflict, a transaction aborts itself, and waits for a randomized linear time before restarting (as in the first phase of SwissTM's two-phase contention manager [7]). With BaseTM, all transactions executed by the same thread use the same per-thread transaction descriptor that is allocated and initialized at thread start-up.

BaseTM can use two version management strategies. Both strategies are conventional, but they offer different performance characteristics:

Global version numbers. We can use a global version number, held in a 64-bit integer that is incremented by non-read-only transactions. As with TL2, we sample the global version number at the start of a transaction, and obtain opacity by ensuring that all orecs accessed by the transaction have versions no later than this starting number.

Local (per-orec) version numbers. Alternatively, we can use per-orec version numbers, without reference to a global version. This avoids contention on a shared global counter, but instead requires read-set validations after every read in order to ensure opacity.

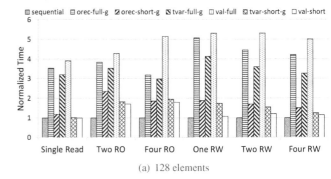

(a) 128 elements

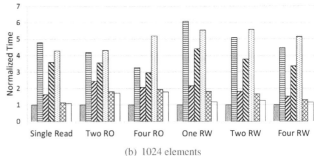

(b) 1024 elements

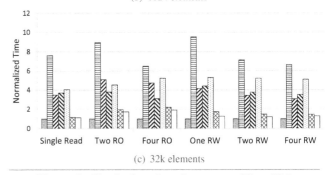

(c) 32k elements

Figure 5. Single thread performance of SpecTM.

4.2 STM Variants

We summarize the labels used on our graphs:

sequential is optimized sequential code; it is not safe for multi-threaded use, but it provides a reference point of the cost of an implementation without concurrency control.

lock-free are lock-free implementations of the data structures, based on the designs from Fraser's thesis [11].

*orec-** implementations use a shared table of orecs, as shown in Figure 3(a).

*tvar-** implementations use per-data-item ownership records, as shown in Figure 3(b).

*val-** implementations use per-data-item lock-bits with value-based validation, as shown in Figure 3(c).

-full- implementations use the normal STM interface (Section 2.1).

-short- implementations use specialized interfaces for short transactions (Section 2.2).

**-g* implementations use a global version number.

**-l* implementations use local (per-orec) version numbers.

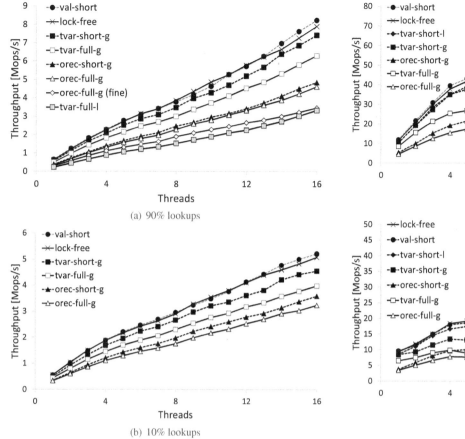

Figure 6. Skip list, 64k values, 16 cores.

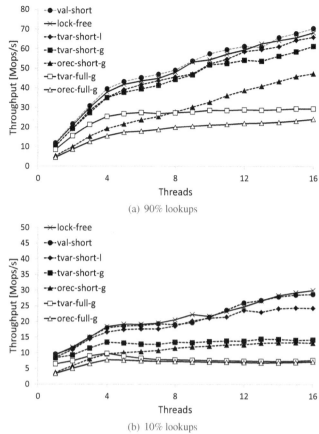

Figure 7. Hash table, 64k values, 16k buckets, 16-cores.

For instance, *orec-full-g* denotes our BaseTM implementation using a TL2-style global version number, whereas *tvar-short-g* denotes an implementation using specialized short transactions, without an orec table. Our experimental harness explores the full set of variants. However, we omit some of the lines from the graphs for clarity.

4.3 Single-Threaded Performance

We evaluate single-threaded performance using a synthetic workload on a single-socket system with a 2.26GHz Intel Xeon E5520 quad-core CPU.

The synthetic workload allocates an array of pointers, with each pointer aligned to a L2 cache-line boundary. We then measure the time needed to execute a large number of short transactions on randomly chosen items in the array. We repeat the experiment for `Tx_Single_Read` transactions, read-only (RO) transactions that access 2 and 4 consecutive items in the array, and read-write (RW) transactions that access 1, 2, and 4 consecutive items. (The *val-full* RO transactions assume the non-re-use property from Section 2.4 and perform value-based validation.) We run the experiments with different sizes of the array, thereby controlling how much of the array fits in data caches, and consequently how frequently cache misses occur.

Figure 5 shows the normalized execution time of the different STM implementations for array sizes of 128 elements (half the size of 32KB L1 cache), 1024 elements (half the size of 256KB L2 cache) and 32 768 elements (half the size of 8MB L3 cache). We normalize the read-only results against sequential code that reads from 1, 2, and 4 items using ordinary load instructions. We normalize the RW results against sequential code that performs a single-word CAS instruction on each of the 1, 2, and 4 items. Comparison with these baselines illustrates the costs that SpecTM implementations add in order to obtain transactional guarantees.

Comparing the *sequential* bars with BaseTM (*orec-full-g*) shows a 3x–10x overhead for the baseline transactions compared with sequential code. Most variants of SpecTM out-perform BaseTM. The exception is *val-full* in which the read-set validation costs incurred on each transactional read dominate execution time.

The best performing SpecTM variants are those that use short transactions. Comparing *orec-short-g* (Figure 3(a)), *tvar-short-g* (Figure 3(b)), and *val-short* (Figure 3(c)), the value-based implementation is slightly faster because it avoids the atomic increment on a shared global timestamp.

For a single read, the fastest SpecTM variants are comparable to sequential code. For RW transactions, the overhead of *val-short* is 10%–30% on 1-item, and 15%–30% on 2 or 4 items. This is substantially less than the 3x-10x overheads of BaseTM. The overheads of RO transactions are higher than those of RW transactions; we believe this is due to the more complex control flow in by validation.

When cache misses are rare (Figure 5(a)), the use of short transactions helps more than the use of TVars and value-based validation. This is because the meta-data remains resident in the L1 cache, and so the reduced number of instructions executed is significant. In contrast, for workloads which are not L1-resident, the use of more compact meta-data is as important as the use of short transactions.

4.4 Multi-Threaded Performance

We evaluate scalability using integer set benchmarks, with threads performing a random mix of lookups, insertions and removals. For each of the operations, threads pick a key uniformly at random from a predefined range. In the experiments, we used the range 0–65 535, and we varied the mix of operations to control the contention between threads. Before the experiment starts, the set is initialized by inserting half of the elements from the key range. In order to keep the size of the set roughly constant, the ratio of insert and remove operations is equal. During the execution, about half of the insert operations fail because the value they are trying to insert is already in the set. Similarly, about half of the remove operations fail because the value they are trying to remove is not in the set.

We use hash table and skip list integer set implementations in our experiments. By default, we set the number of bucket chains in the hash table to $16k$, which makes the average length of the bucket chain 2. We set the maximum height of the skip list nodes to 32.

We use two different multi-core systems. First, a machine with 4 quad-core AMD Opteron 8374HE CPUs clocked at 2.2GHz. Second, a machine with 8 Intel Xeon x7560 CPUs clocked at 2.26GHz. Each of the CPUs has 8 cores and each core can run 2 hardware threads; hence the entire system supports 128 hardware threads. Both systems run Windows Server 2008 R2 Enterprise operating system. Our results are the mean of 6 runs with the lowest and the highest discarded.

In each of the figures below, we omit the implementations that do not perform well to improve readability. In particular, we do not include results for all **-g* implementations where the impact of contention on the shared global version is high. This typically occurs with short transactions and systems with many hardware threads. Likewise, we do not include results for all **-l* implementations where the cost of incremental validation is high. This typically occurs with longer transactions and systems with fewer hardware threads.

4.4.1 Performance on the 16-way system.

Skip list. Figure 6 shows the throughput of the skip list experiment on the 16-way machine with a read-mostly workload (90% lookups) and write-heavy workload (10% lookups).

Figure 6(a) shows the read-mostly workload. The *val-short* implementation performs as well as the lock-free implementation, and it outperforms BaseTM *orec-full-g* by 60%–80%. The *tvar-short-g* implementation is slightly slower than the lock-free algorithm (7–10%). For this workload, the use of the *val-** and *tvar-** variants is more important than the use of short transactions (note that *orec-short-g* is only slightly faster than *orec-full-g*). The *tvar-full-l* implementation performs poorly because of the cost of incremental read-set validations to ensure opacity without a global version number.

Figure 6(a) also shows the performance of a skip list implementation using BaseTM, but splitting each lookup/insert/remove operation into a series of fine-grained transactions that are implemented over the ordinary STM interface rather than using short transactions. This is labeled *orec-full-g (fine)*. Comparing this fine-grained implementation with the ordinary *orec-full-g* implementation shows that we do not obtain performance benefits by using fine-grain transactions *without* the specialized implementation for them in SpecTM: without the specialized implementation, the overheads of the fine-grain transactions are prohibitive.

Figure 6(b) shows performance under the write-heavy workload. The overall performance is lower than the read-mostly workload. However, the relative performance of different variants is approximately the same (in the figure we omit some of these lines for clarity). The *val-short* results perform roughly the same as the lock-free implementation, and outperform base SpecTM by 60–70%.

To summarize, we get a slight benefit from splitting larger transactions into fine-grain short transactions (*orec-full-g* to *orec-short-g*), but in doing so we enable the specializations from *orec-short-g* to *val-short*, that let us achieve the same level of performance as the CAS-based implementation.

Hash table. Figure 7 shows the throughput of various hash table implementations on the 16-way machine.

If a hash table is lightly loaded, as in our setup, then operations on it are much shorter than those on a skip list. Consequently, the hash table workload stresses SpecTM in a different way to the skip list because the use of centralized data has a higher impact on scalability.

The impact of the shared global counter in the **-g* variants is apparent in the read-mostly workload (Figure 7(a)), and even more so in the write-heavy workload (Figure 7(b)). On this machine, we see little scaling beyond 4 threads for the **-g* variants without specialized short transactions. (With more than 4 threads, two or more CPUs must be used, which significantly increases the cost of cache-misses.)

In the read-mostly workload (Figure 7(a)), the *val-short* results match the performance of the lock-free hash table. This implementation outperforms the baseline *orec-full-g* implementation between 2.5 and 3 times and the baseline

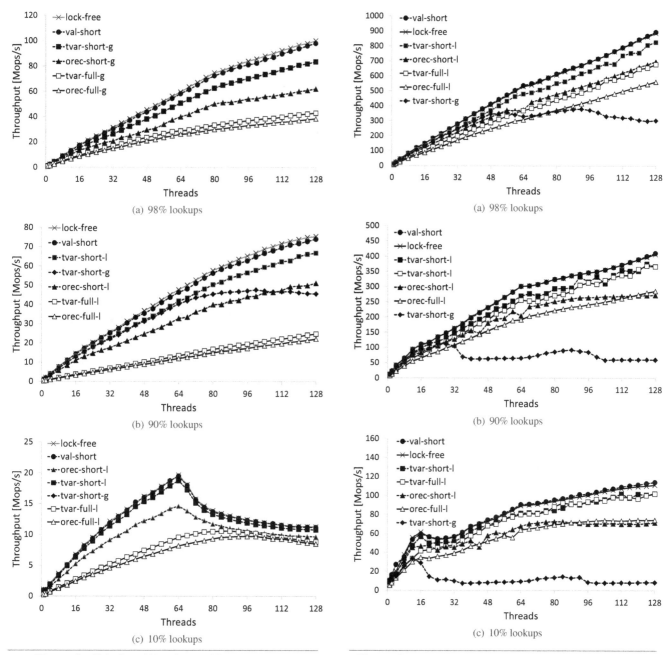

Figure 8. Skip list, 64k values, 128-way system.

Figure 9. Hash table, 64k values, 16k buckets, 128-way.

implementation with local per-orec timestamps *orec-full-l* between 1.6 and 3.5 times (not shown in the figure). The *tvar-short-** results are slightly lower than the *val-short* results. The other SpecTM variants perform and scale less well. The **-l* variants typically have lower single-threaded performance (due to incremental validation), but scale better than the **-g* variants.

In the write-heavy workload (Figure 7(b)) the *val-short* implementation matches the performance of the lock-free implementation, despite a much higher update rate. The main difference between the read-mostly and write-heavy results is that the *orec-** and *tvar-** implementations with

shared timestamp scale poorly because of contention on the shared timestamp.

4.4.2 Performance on the 128-way system.

Skip list. Figure 8 shows the results of the skip list experiment on the 128-way system with 98%, 90% and 10% lookup operations.

With 98% lookups (Figure 8(a)), the rate of update operations is not high enough for contention on the shared timestamp counter to be significant. The most notable difference from the previous experiments is that *val-short* performs slightly less well than the lock-free implementation:

11

it achieves 95%–97% of the lock-free skip list's throughput, and it outperforms the baseline STM by 2–2.5 times. Unlike the 16-way case, the *tvar-short-g* is less competitive with the lock-free algorithm and with *val-short*. Interestingly, also unlike the 16-way case, the use of short transactions helps significantly, even when a shared table of orecs is used (comparing *orec-full-g* and *orec-short-g*).

With 90% lookups (Figure 8(b)), contention on the shared timestamp counter results in the *-l* variants outperforming *-g* variants. For this reason, we focus on *-l* variants in the figure. Once again, the *val-short* and *tvar-short-l* implementations have the best performance and scalability.

With 10% lookups (Figure 8(c)), all implementations scale poorly—including the lock-free implementation. Nevertheless, the relative performance of the SpecTM variants follows that of Figure 8(b).

Hash table. Figure 9 shows the hash table results on the 128-way machine with 98%, 90% and 10% lookups.

Figure 9(a) shows the performance with 98% lookups. The *val-short* implementation matches the performance of the lock-free hash table implementation, and it outperforms BaseTM between 60% and 70%. We see roughly equal gains from co-locating data and meta data, and from using the API for short transactions.

Figure 9(b) shows the performance with 90% lookups. With more update operations the scalability is slightly impacted for all hash table variants (including the lock-free variant). As in previous experiments, *val-short* matches the performance of the lock-free algorithm.

Figure 9(c) shows performance with only 10% lookups. As contention increases, the performance of *orec-short-l* drops to offer little or no benefit above *orec-full-l*. The main reason for the lower scalability of SpecTM variants with short transactions is the use of encounter-time locking (ETL) in short RW transactions, when compared with commit-time locking (CTL) in long transactions. As the contention increases, the ETL implementation leads to more locks being acquired by later aborted transactions, whereas the CTL implementation does not acquire the locks in the first place.

Finally, we examined the performance of the hash table under workload with short chains of buckets (0.5 entries per bucket on average), and with long chains of buckets (32 entries per bucket on average). Figure 10(a) shows the short-chain results, and Figure 10(b) shows the long-chain results. The overall result, that *val-short* matches the performance of the lock-free implementation, remains from the earlier experiments. With longer chains, the *-full-l* variants scale poorly: their read sets become large, increasing costs of incremental validation.

4.5 Summary

We evaluate a number of SpecTM variants across a range of workloads on two parallel systems. In all cases, the best performing SpecTM variant was *val-short*. It either matched

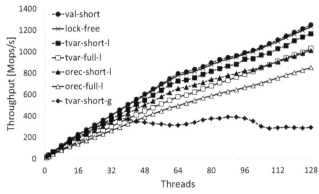

(a) 98% lookups, 64k buckets (0.5-entry chains)

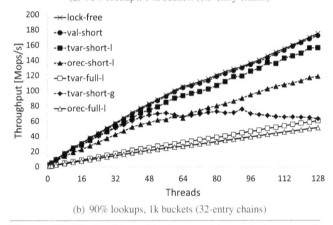

(b) 90% lookups, 1k buckets (32-entry chains)

Figure 10. Hash table, with short and long chains in each bucket, 128-way system.

the performance of the lock-free implementations of the same data structure or was marginally slower (typically 3%–5%). It also outperformed BaseTM substantially across all workloads.

The results suggest that both the specialized API for short transactions, and the control over the STM meta-data, are very useful in achieving good performance. Exactly how much each type of specialization helps depends on the workload and on the target system. In addition, the performance gain of the variants that use both types of specialization is often higher than the simple combination of the performance gains by each type of specialization in isolation. This is because the co-location of STM meta-data with application data allows the implementation of short transactions to be further simplified.

5. Related Work

Transactional memory was first proposed by Herlihy and Moss [17] as a way to simplify lock-free programming by allowing programmers to define short, customized, read-modify-write operations. The first STM of Shavit and Touitou [29] had a similar aim, albeit a simpler, static interface. The first dynamic STM in which transactions do not have to access predetermined sets of objects was STM by

Herlihy *et al.* [20]. Dynamic STMs are more flexible than the static ones as the transactions can choose which object to access based on the values read in the current transaction; this flexibility motivates our use of a dynamic interface for short transactions. Harris *et al.* provide a recent survey of TM implementations [16]. Our BaseTM implementation builds on many techniques from previous work, particularly those of Dice *et al.* [4], Riegel *et al.* [27], and Spear *et al.* [30].

Current hardware typically implements single-word synchronization primitives, such as compare-and-swap (CAS), load-link/store-conditional (LL/SC), fetch-and-add, and similar. Lock-free algorithms are often much easier to develop if less restrictive forms of the synchronization primitives are available.

The restrictions of current hardware have led researchers to investigate software implementations of multi-word atomic primitives, such as multi-word compare-and swap (e.g. [13, 22]), and k-compare-single-swap primitive [23]. Our view is that it is easy to implement CASN over short transactions, but it is difficult to implement short transactions over CASN: Our interface for short transactions is dynamic (unlike typical interfaces for CASN), and it provides the programmer a consistent view of the heap during a transaction. Unlike CASN implementations, our implementations support inter-operation with general-purpose STM.

Recently, HTM systems have started to emerge from industry [5, 26]. Typically, these support limited forms of transactions to enable practical implementations in hardware. The HTM feature of the Rock CPU from Sun Microsystems [5] supports only "best-effort" transactions, where each transaction can fail repeatedly for implementation-dependent reasons. The recently announced Intel TSX [26] instructions support a "restricted transactional memory" mode that is subject to implementation-defined size constraints. Despite weak guarantees, short and simple transactions make it possible to use HTM to simplify and speed-up concurrent code [6, 9].

As with these HTM systems, SpecTM promotes the use of short transactions. Because of the short maximum size of SpecTM's transactions, most algorithms developed for SpecTM can be run on the bounded HTMs and vice-versa. This means that SpecTM allows us to better understand how to design algorithms for the future HTMs, but it also enables us to benefit from these new algorithms even before HTMs are widely available.

Attiya recently examined the complexity of TM systems from a theoretical viewpoint [1] and proposed the use of "mini-transactions" in which a data structure's implementation would be built over a series of small transactions. Attiya's arguments are motivated by complexity lower bounds on implementations of general purpose transactions. However, the proposal matches our practical experience that a series of optimized short transactions can perform better than a single, longer transaction.

6. Conclusions and Future Work

We developed SpecTM to explore the use of optimized short transactions and the co-location and specialization of STM meta-data with application data. These specializations trade the generality of traditional STMs for performance. The target users of SpecTM are experienced programmers that can exploit it in their algorithms to atomically access a handful of locations instead of developing more complex algorithms based on the synchronization primitives available today in hardware. Our experience shows that this ability of SpecTM can result in much simpler algorithms, and our results suggest that the most specialized version of SpecTM (*val-short*) lets us write concurrent hash table and skip list algorithms that perform and scale as well as the lock-free versions of the same algorithms on systems with up to 128 hardware threads.

Our work on SpecTM opens several interesting directions for future work. One direction is to use SpecTM to implement new, efficient, concurrent data structures—for instance, looking at structures such as B-Trees which are more complex than those studied in typical research on lock-free algorithms. This work would let us better understand the kinds of trade-offs STM designers can make when building support for efficient concurrent data structures.

It is possible that some of the techniques used in SpecTM could be employed automatically by STM compilers to optimize transactions, and that software checking tools could be used to ensure that programmers correctly follow the requirements for using SpecTM.

We certainly have not explored the full space of specialized STM designs. For instance, it might be beneficial to explore pointer-only STM designs which use additional spare bits in the pointers as orecs (typically, in 64 bit systems, the processor or OS does not support virtual address spaces that exploit the entire 64-bit space). In addition, a value-based STM that locks words when reading could be used to simplify the programming model in our designs which use value-based validation. Of course, more sophisticated contention managers could improve the performance in some workloads.

Finally, developing algorithms using SpecTM has important implications as HTM systems become available [26]. With the exploration of HTM support in CPUs, it is worthwhile considering the integration of SpecTM and HTMs—both to accelerate aspects of SpecTM, and to provide a software fall-back path for use with best-effort HTMs.

Acknowledgements

We would like to thank the anonymous reviews and our shepherd Bryan Ford along with Richard Black, Austin Donnelly, Miguel Castro, Cristian Diaconu, Steven Hand, Orion Hodson, Paul Larson, Dimitris Tsirogiannis, and Marcel van der Holst for their feedback on earlier drafts of this paper, and for their assistance with conducting the experiments.

References

[1] H. Attiya. Invited paper: The inherent complexity of transactional memory and what to do about it. In *Distributed Computing and Networking*, volume 6522 of *Lecture Notes in Computer Science*, pages 1–11. 2011.

[2] C. Cascaval, C. Blundell, M. Michael, H. W. Cain, P. Wu, S. Chiras, and S. Chatterjee. Software transactional memory: why is it only a research toy? *Communications of the ACM*, 51(11):40–46, Nov. 2008.

[3] L. Dalessandro, M. F. Spear, and M. L. Scott. NOrec: Streamlining STM by abolishing ownership records. In *PPoPP '10: Proc. 15th ACM Symposium on Principles and Practice of Parallel Programming*, pages 67–78, Jan. 2010.

[4] D. Dice, O. Shalev, and N. Shavit. Transactional locking II. In *DISC '06: Proc. 20th International Symposium on Distributed Computing*, pages 194–208, Sept. 2006. Springer-Verlag Lecture Notes in Computer Science volume 4167.

[5] D. Dice, Y. Lev, M. Moir, and D. Nussbaum. Early experience with a commercial hardware transactional memory implementation. In *ASPLOS '09: Proc. 14th International Conference on Architectural Support for Programming Languages and Operating Systems*, pages 157–168, Mar. 2009.

[6] D. Dice, Y. Lev, V. J. Marathe, M. Moir, D. Nussbaum, and M. Oleszewski. Simplifying concurrent algorithms by exploiting hardware transactional memory. In *SPAA '10: Proc. 22nd Symposium on Parallelism in Algorithms and Architectures*, pages 325–334, June 2010.

[7] A. Dragojević, R. Guerraoui, and M. Kapałka. Stretching transactional memory. In *PLDI '09: Proc. 2009 ACM SIGPLAN Conference on Programming Language Design and Implementation*, pages 155–165, June 2009.

[8] A. Dragojević, P. Felber, V. Gramoli, and R. Guerraoui. Why STM can be more than a research toy. *Communications of the ACM*, 54(4):70–77, April 2011.

[9] A. Dragojević, M. Herlihy, Y. Lev, and M. Moir. On the power of hardware transactional memory to simplify memory management. In *PODC '11: Proc. 30th ACM SIGACT-SIGOPS Symposium on Principles of Distributed Computing*, PODC '11, pages 99–108, June 2011.

[10] P. Felber, C. Fetzer, and T. Riegel. Dynamic performance tuning of word-based software transactional memory. In *PPoPP '08: Proc. 13th ACM SIGPLAN Symposium on Principles and Practice of Parallel Programming*, pages 237–246, Feb. 2008.

[11] K. Fraser. *Practical lock freedom*. PhD thesis, Cambridge University Computer Laboratory, 2003. Also available as Technical Report UCAM-CL-TR-579.

[12] R. Guerraoui and M. Kapałka. On the correctness of transactional memory. In *PPoPP '08: Proc. 13th ACM SIGPLAN Symposium on Principles and Practice of Parallel Programming*, pages 175–184, Feb. 2008.

[13] T. Harris, K. Fraser, and I. A. Pratt. A practical multi-word compare-and-swap operation. In *DISC '02: Proc. 16th International Symposium on Distributed Computing*, pages 265–279, Oct. 2002.

[14] T. Harris, M. Plesko, A. Shinnar, and D. Tarditi. Optimizing memory transactions. In *PLDI '06: Proc. 2006 Conference on Programming Language Design and Implementation*, pages 14–25, June 2006.

[15] T. Harris, S. Marlow, S. Peyton Jones, and M. Herlihy. Composable memory transactions. *Communications of the ACM*, 51(8):91–100, Aug. 2008.

[16] T. Harris, J. Larus, and R. Rajwar. *Transactional Memory, 2nd edition*. Morgan & Claypool, 2010.

[17] M. Herlihy and J. E. B. Moss. Transactional memory: architectural support for lock-free data structures. In *ISCA '93: Proc. 20th Annual International Symposium on Computer Architecture*, pages 289–300, May 1993.

[18] M. Herlihy and N. Shavit. *The art of multiprocessor programming*. Morgan Kaufmann, 2008.

[19] M. Herlihy and J. M. Wing. Linearizability: a correctness condition for concurrent objects. *TOPLAS: ACM Transactions on Programming Languages and Systems*, 12(3):463–492, July 1990.

[20] M. Herlihy, V. Luchangco, M. Moir, and W. N. Scherer III. Software transactional memory for dynamic-sized data structures. In *PODC '03: Proc. 22nd ACM Symposium on Principles of Distributed Computing*, pages 92–101, July 2003.

[21] M. Herlihy, V. Luchangco, P. Martin, and M. Moir. Nonblocking memory management support for dynamic-sized data structures. *TOCS: ACM Transactions on Computer Systems*, 23(2):146–196, May 2005.

[22] A. Israeli and L. Rappoport. Disjoint-access-parallel implementations of strong shared memory primitives. In *PODC '94: Proc. 13th ACM Symposium on Principles of Distributed Computing*, pages 151–160, Aug. 1994.

[23] V. Luchangco, M. Moir, and N. Shavit. Nonblocking k-compare-single-swap. In *SPAA '03: Proc. 15th Annual Symposium on Parallel Algorithms and Architectures*, pages 314–323, June 2003.

[24] V. J. Marathe, M. F. Spear, and M. L. Scott. Scalable techniques for transparent privatization in software transactional memory. In *ICPP '08: Proc. 37th International Conference on Parallel Processing*, Sept. 2008.

[25] M. M. Michael. Hazard pointers: safe memory reclamation for lock-free objects. *IEEE Transactions on Parallel and Distributed Systems*, 15(6):491–504, June 2004.

[26] J. Reinders. Transactional synchronization in Haswell, Feb. 2012. http://software.intel.com/en-us/blogs.

[27] T. Riegel, C. Fetzer, and P. Felber. Time-based transactional memory with scalable time bases. In *SPAA '07: Proc. 19th ACM Symposium on Parallelism in Algorithms and Architectures*, pages 221–228, June 2007.

[28] B. Saha, A.-R. Adl-Tabatabai, R. L. Hudson, C. Cao Minh, and B. Hertzberg. McRT-STM: a high performance software transactional memory system for a multi-core runtime. In *PPoPP '06: Proc. 11th ACM SIGPLAN Symposium on Principles and Practice of Parallel Programming*, pages 187–197, Mar. 2006.

[29] N. Shavit and D. Touitou. Software transactional memory. In *PODC '95: Proc. 14th ACM Symposium on Principles of Distributed Computing*, pages 204–213, Aug. 1995.

[30] M. F. Spear, L. Dalessandro, V. J. Marathe, and M. L. Scott. A comprehensive strategy for contention management in software transactional memory. In *PPoPP '09: Proc. 14th ACM SIGPLAN Symposium on Principles and Practice of Parallel Programming*, pages 141–150, Feb. 2009.

Improving Server Applications with System Transactions

Sangman Kim*   Michael Z. Lee*   Alan M. Dunn*   Owen S. Hofmann*
Xuan Wang†   Emmett Witchel*   Donald E. Porter†

*The University of Texas at Austin   †Stony Brook University

{sangmank,mzlee,adunn,osh,witchel}@cs.utexas.edu   {wang9,porter}@cs.stonybrook.edu

Abstract

Server applications must process requests as quickly as possible. Because some requests depend on earlier requests, there is often a tension between increasing throughput and maintaining the proper semantics for dependent requests. Operating system transactions make it easier to write reliable, high-throughput server applications because they allow the application to execute non-interfering requests in parallel, even if the requests operate on OS state, such as file data.

By changing less than 200 lines of application code, we improve performance of a replicated Byzantine Fault Tolerant (BFT) system by up to 88% using server-side speculation, and we improve concurrent performance up to 80% for an IMAP email server by changing only 40 lines. Achieving these results requires substantial enhancements to system transactions, including the ability to pause and resume transactions, and an API to commit transactions in a pre-defined order.

Categories and Subject Descriptors D.1.3 [*Programming Techniques*]: Concurrent Programming; D.4.7 [*Operating Systems*]: Organization and Design

General Terms Design, Performance, Security

Keywords System Transactions

1. Introduction

Server applications must process requests as quickly as possible. Because some requests depend on earlier requests, there is often a tension between increasing throughput and maintaining the proper semantics for dependent requests. For example, if a user is modifying messages in his mailbox, the email server might delay the delivery of a new message; this strategy reduces throughput to avoid race conditions that could result in lost user modifications.

Server applications often use operating system (OS) services, such as the file system and inter-process communication (IPC). But once application data migrates to the OS, the application loses the ability to balance tradeoffs between semantics and concurrent throughput. The POSIX API provides few options for managing concurrency.

Operating system transactions [34], or system transactions, make it easier to write reliable, high-throughput server applications because applications can transactionally execute non-interfering operations in parallel, even if the operations include OS state like file data. Transactions are useful because they detect interfering requests dynamically, based on the actual data access patterns of a request. For most realistic servers, the request dependencies are highly data dependent and can only be determined at runtime.

OS transactions are also valuable to distributed systems because they provide a convenient path to deterministic parallel execution. Some distributed systems, like Byzantine Fault Tolerant (BFT) replication systems, rely on deterministic execution for correctness, and thus must sacrifice performance and simplicity to ensure determinism. By executing requests in transactions with a specified commit order, developers of these replicated servers can easily implement deterministic parallel request execution.

This paper demonstrates that operating system transactions can improve server applications with few modifications to those applications. To demonstrate this principle, we modify the UpRight BFT library [12] and the Dovecot IMAP server [2], changing less than 200 lines of code to adopt system transactions. The applications require few changes because transactions are easy to use. We increase throughput for UpRight by up to 88%, and improve Dovecot throughput by up to 80% while eliminating mail delivery anomalies.

During the execution phase of a BFT system, multiple ordered requests induce state changes on the replicated data. Parallelizing this execution phase has been a long-standing challenge for BFT systems. This challenge arises because of the complexity of detecting dependencies between requests and rolling back server state on misspeculation (see Section 3 for more discussion of previous systems). Most BFT systems execute requests serially to ensure consistent replication. Serial execution throttles performance on increasingly common multi-core systems by preventing parallel execution of independent requests. Even if an application developer understands the application-level semantics enough to manually parallelize the code, reasoning about state that leaks into the OS via system calls (e.g., files, IPC) is intractable without better OS support.

EuroSys'12, April 10–13, 2012, Bern, Switzerland.
Copyright © 2012 ACM 978-1-4503-1223-3/12/04...$10.00

The Internet Message Access Protocol (IMAP) is a widely used protocol for accessing email messages [13]. IMAP is supposed to support concurrent clients accessing an inbox, such as a user accessing email on her phone and laptop at the same time. Unfortunately, OS API limitations cause disturbing artifacts in many IMAP implementations, such as temporarily lost messages during concurrent use. IMAP stores the definitive versions of email messages in folders on a server, and an email client acts as a cache of these emails. The `maildir` server storage format for IMAP is designed to be lock-free [6]. Unfortunately, the POSIX API is insufficient for an IMAP server to guarantee repeatable reads of a `maildir` inbox, so IMAP implementations, such as Dovecot, have reintroduced locks on back-end storage [1]. When server threads terminate unexpectedly without releasing locks, for instance due to a bad client interaction, users experience unpredictable email behavior; email may be lost or messages may not be able to be marked as read. System transactions can guarantee repeatable reads without locks, providing strong semantics, more reliable behavior, and higher performance for concurrent clients.

This paper describes the largest workloads for a transactional OS reported to date. Supporting applications of this magnitude requires substantial enhancements to the recent TxOS design [34], including more careful interfaces for composition of synchronization primitives, separation of application transactions from internal JVM or `libc` state, and a number of design and implementation refinements. Fortunately, the transactional interface remains simple and easy to use for the application-level programmer, and system-level software (such as `libc`) requires only a small number of simple modifications, which are encapsulated from the application programmer.

The contributions of this paper follow.

1. The design and implementation of operating system transactions sufficient to support large, distributed applications written in managed languages like Java (§5). This work requires substantial extensions and improvements over the recently published TxOS design [34].

2. The design and implementation of Byzantine fault tolerant replication that allows the server to speculate on the order of requests (§3).

3. The design and implementation of a Dovecot IMAP server that features true lockless operation without behavioral anomalies and high performance for write-intensive workloads. (§4).

4. A careful study of how to compose transactions with other application synchronization primitives, including `futex`-based locks (§6).

2. Operating system transactions

This section reviews operating system transactions, describing the properties most relevant to supporting distributed systems. We refer the reader to previous work for a more complete description of system transactions [33, 34]. Our implementation is derived from the publicly available TxOS code version 1.01[1]. We call our modified system TxOS+.

System transactions group accesses to OS resources via system calls into logical units that execute with atomicity, consistency, isolation, and durability (ACID). System transactions are easy to use: programmers enclose code regions within the `sys_xbegin()` and `sys_xend()` system calls to express consistency constraints to the OS. The user can abort an in-progress transaction with `sys_xabort()`. Placing system calls within a transaction alters the semantics of when and how their results are published to the rest of the system. Outside of a transaction, actions on system resources are visible as soon as the relevant internal kernel locks are released. Within a transaction, all accesses are isolated until the transaction commits, when changes are atomically published to the rest of the system. System transactions provide a simple and powerful way for applications to express consistency requirements for concurrent operations to the OS.

System transactions provide ACID semantics for updates to OS resources, such as files, pipes, and signals. System transactions are serializable and recoverable. Only committed data are read, and reads are repeatable; this corresponds to the highest database isolation level (level 3 [19]). We call a kernel thread executing a system transaction a transactional thread. A transactional system call is a system call made by a transactional thread.

Conflicts. To ensure isolation, a kernel object may only have one writer at a time, excepting containers, which allow multiple writers to disjoint entries. Two concurrent system transactions **conflict** if both access the same kernel object and at least one of them is a write. The kernel detects and arbitrates conflicts. The arbitration logic might abort one of the conflicting transactions or it might put one of the transactions to sleep until the other commits. The latter policy is often called stall-on-conflict, and resembles condition synchronization. where the condition is a transaction commit.

Transactions and non-transactional system calls serialized. TxOS ensures serializable execution among transactions and between transactions and non-transactional system calls (sometimes called strong isolation [7]). Isolating transactions from non-transactional system calls simplifies the programming model. The programmer can think of each individual system call as its own mini-transaction. For example, if one thread is enumerating a directory's contents in a system transaction while another thread does a rename in that directory, the contents listing will contain only the old or the new name, never both. Note that in Linux, the concurrency guarantees for system calls vary: `rename` is atomic, whereas concurrent `read` and `write` calls can return partially interleaved results. When transactions are not

---

[1] http://code.csres.utexas.edu/projects/txos

involved, TxOS provides the same concurrency guarantees as Linux.

Managing user memory. System transactions primarily provide ACID semantics for system state; the application programmer has several options for managing state in the application's address space. For single-threaded applications, an option to `sys_xbegin()` will make the address space copy-on-write, which allows the OS to revert the application's memory state if the transaction aborts. However, for multi-threaded programs, the OS cannot and does not manage user state. For multi-threaded Java code, pages mapped in response to a transactional allocation request stay mapped on an abort, but any allocated objects are garbage collected by the JVM.

System vs. memory transactions. System transactions are a transactional model for operating system objects. Transactional memory [21, 41] is a transactional model for updating memory objects. Database transactions [19] are a transactional model for a data store. All of these systems are independent realizations of a simple interface for the same ideas: version management and conflict detection. In particular, system transactions do not require transactional memory (though system transactions and transactional memory can interact symbiotically [34]). System transactions are implemented on current, commodity hardware.

Incremental adoption. Concurrency problems are often localized to particular sections of code, and system transactions can be applied to those sections without large-scale redesign. Table 2 shows the magnitude of source code changes (less than 200 lines) to add system transactions to substantial code bases.

3. Replication and Byzantine Fault Tolerance

Distributed systems often replicate services in order to tolerate faults. If one replica behaves incorrectly, others can mask the incorrect behavior until the replica is corrected.

The canonical approach to replicating a service is to design the server as a replicated state machine [38]. The key principle behind replicated state machines is that if the same set of inputs are presented to each replica in the same order, each deterministic replica will produce the same outputs and have the same internal state—yielding identical replicas. Note that inputs in this model include inputs both from a client connected over the network and from the OS, such as a file's contents or the output of a random number generator. However, the OS API is insufficient even to prevent race conditions, including in the file system [10] and signal handlers [49]; concurrent, deterministic execution of arbitrary system calls is impossible.

We examine a Byzantine fault tolerant system, in which a faulty replica can exhibit arbitrary and possibly malicious behavior [26]. The role system transactions play is applicable to any failure model in replicated systems, and is not specific to BFT.

3.1 BFT summary

Byzantine Fault Tolerance (BFT) is a replicated systems framework, which can handle a wide range of faults, including crashes and deliberate misbehavior of a bounded number of faulty servers. When the total number of agreement replicas is n, a typical BFT system based on replicated state machine can tolerate up to $(n-1)/3$ faults, more commonly written as $3f + 1$, where f is the number of faults [8, 25]. Note that this bound is for agreement replicas, and the bound for execution replicas can be as low as $2f + 1$, depending on the protocol [48].

Replicated state machine-based BFT protocols generally process requests in a pipeline consisting of authentication, ordering, and execution phases [12, 48]. When a request arrives from a client, it is first authenticated to ensure that it came from a legitimate client and is well-formed. The ordering phase then imposes a global order on each accepted request. Replicas can execute requests after ordering completes, or speculatively before the ordering [23]. Their responses are generally checked by the client; responses that diverge indicate existence of a faulty node or misspeculation. Each of these phases must be performed by a quorum of replicas (the precise minimum varies by implementation).

3.2 Parallelizing BFT execution with transactions

A key drawback of many BFT systems is their inability to execute requests in parallel. Because multi-threading introduces non-determinism, BFT servers generally cannot leverage the increasingly abundant parallelism of commodity multi-core hardware in the execution phase of the system. This decreases throughput and increases request processing latency. System transactions can provide deterministic, optimistic concurrency to speed up the execution phase. Speeding up execution also speeds up recovery, where one replica must catch up with its peers.

Optimistic parallel request execution for BFT systems has seen limited use because of the complexity of detecting dependencies between requests and rolling back server state on misspeculation. Replicated databases like HRDB [45] or Byzantium [18] rely on transaction support from off-the-shelf database systems to tolerate Byzantine faults inside databases. However, this approach cannot be extended to most other applications, as they do not have a built-in transaction facility. If such applications need BFT, parallelization of replica execution requires very intimate application-specific knowledge about requests and their execution [24], which is infeasible for complex systems. Any attempt to parallelize execution without system-wide concurrency isolation will likely introduce divergence due to non-determinism, which can degrade throughput significantly [42].

Recent research OSes allow deterministic parallel execution [4, 5], but their overheads are substantial. BFT does not actually require a deterministic OS; consistent states on each replica are sufficient, which can be efficiently provided by transactions serialized according to the same schedule.

Parallel execution in replication-based fault tolerant systems also accelerates their recovery. When a failed replica is replaced with a new correct node (or the same node repaired), the new replica's state must be brought up to date with the other replicas. The typical strategy for recovery is for replicas to take periodic checkpoints of their state and to keep a log of subsequent requests. The new replica fetches the most recent checkpoint and replays the log until it catches up. During recovery, requests are processed sequentially, and new requests are buffered. Assuming that some requests can execute safely and concurrently (which is common), optimistic execution can accelerate recovery.

4. IMAP email server

The Internet Message Access Protocol (IMAP) is a widely used protocol for accessing email messages [13]. IMAP stores the definitive versions of email messages in folders on a server, and an email client acts as a cache of these emails. IMAP provides features missing from the previous Post Office Protocol [29], including seamless offline email operations, which are later synchronized with the server, and concurrent email clients (e.g., a laptop, desktop, and smart-phone can simultaneously connect to an inbox).

A key feature advertised by IMAP is concurrent access by multiple clients, yet the protocol specifies very little about how the server should behave in the presence of concurrency. There is no protocol-level guarantee about what happens if two clients simultaneously modify a message or folder. If something goes wrong while moving a message to a sub-folder, the outcome depends on the client and server implementations: the message can be lost or duplicated.

Allowing a wide range of IMAP client and server implementations to dictate ad hoc concurrency semantics leads to practical challenges. For instance, if a user leaves a mail client running at home that aggressively checks for new email messages, the implementation-specific locking behavior on the server may deny the user's client at work the ability to delete, move, or mark new messages as read. This denial of service can result from either aggressive polling by the client (i.e., lock fairness), or "orphaned" file locks from an improper error handling of a client request. This erratic behavior stems from the limitations of the underlying OS API with respect to concurrency and durability.

4.1 Backend storage formats and concurrency

Although the specific storage formats can vary across IMAP server implementations, there are two widely-used storage formats: mbox and maildir. The storage format dictates much of the concurrent behavior of the server; servers that support both backends will behave differently with each.

mbox. The mbox format stores an entire email folder as a single file. Most mbox implementations also have a single file lock, which serializes all accesses to a particular mail folder. If a server thread fails to release a file lock on a user's inbox, perhaps because it received a malformed client message, *all* clients can be locked out of the mailbox until the lock is manually cleaned up by an administrator.

maildir. The maildir format [6] was created to alleviate the issues with stale locks in mbox. Maildir is designed to be lock-free. Maildir represents a mail folder as a directory on a file system, and each message as a file. Mail flags and other metadata are encoded in the file name.

Although maildir is lock-free, the design does not provide repeatable reads for a user's inbox. Reading a user's inbox is typically implemented by a series of `readdir` system calls, which get the names of each file in the inbox, and a series of `stat` or `open/read` system calls, which extract other metadata about the message. If another client is concurrently marking a message as read (by `rename`-ing the file to change its flags), the first client cannot distinguish the change in flags from a deletion, leading to disturbing artifacts such as lost messages. The lack of repeatable reads in maildir led a major IMAP implementation, Dovecot, to reintroduce file locking for its maildir backend [1].

File locking in both storage formats introduces substantial portability issues, as Unix systems have multiple, mutually incompatible file locking regimes, including `flock` and `fcntl` locks. The system administrator must understand the low-level details of the OS and file system in configuring the mail server. Moreover, this proliferation of locking mechanisms diffuses bug fixing effort in the kernel, increasing the likelihood of bugs in specific locking mechanisms. For instance, a Dovecot bug report indicates that using `flock` on Linux triggered a race condition that was eliminated by switching to `fcntl` locks; no bug in the Dovecot source was identified to explain the problem [15].

Because Dovecot's locking scheme is non-standard, a mail client that accesses the backend storage directly, such as `pine`, could still introduce similar anomalies *even if locks are enabled*. This is because lock files are a cooperative primitive—if any application doesn't cooperate, the OS cannot prevent these race conditions.

4.2 Opportunities for system transactions

System transactions should provide a range of benefits to IMAP implementations: eliminating anomalous behavior like freezes and non-repeatable reads, simplifying administration by eliminating lock files, and increasing performance under contention. System transactions give IMAP developers a better interface for managing system-level concurrency.

At a high level, TxOS+ and lock files give the same safety guarantees for Dovecot—the appearance of serial execution.

Dovecot on TxOS+ gives these guarantees with generally higher concurrent performance, as it can execute safe requests concurrently. In contrast, locking always executes requests serially, whether they need to be or not. Strictly speaking, TxOS+ actually gives slightly stronger guarantees than locking: even if a client that does not cooperate in the directory locking protocol tries to access these back-end files non-transactionally, the OS will ensure that Dovecot has repeatable mailbox reads.

Stale lock files left by a server thread that terminates abruptly can prevent other clients from updating their view of a mail folder. System transactions obviate the need for lock files. System transactions allow a consistent read of a directory, even if files in that directory are being added or renamed. System transactions also provide repeatable reads, as the transactions are serializable[2]. Repeatable reads eliminate the disturbing artifacts where messages disappear or spontaneously change state. Finally, because there is no need to lock the mail folder, updates and reads may proceed concurrently, increasing throughput under load.

5. Improving system transactions

This section explains the shortcomings present in the initial TxOS system transaction model and how we addressed them to support large, server applications in TxOS+. The guiding principle for TxOS+ is to keep the application programming interface for transactions as simple as possible.

Many of the challenges that motivated these changes arose from composing transactions with large bodies of middleware code, such as the Java Virtual Machine (JVM) and `libc`. For instance, the JVM issues system calls on behalf of the application, as well as those for its own internal bookkeeping; automatically rolling back part of the JVM's internal state on an application-level transaction abort can corrupt the JVM. Similarly, we faced challenges in composing application-level transactions with synchronization mechanisms encapsulated in middleware code. We extend TxOS+ to address these and other challenges, and demonstrate that the vast majority of this complexity can be sequestered in expert-written, middleware code at a small number of locations, maintaining simplicity at the application-level interface. We emphasize that this complexity arises not from programming with transactions *per se*, but from adapting a large body of already complex code, written with no concept of transactions, to use transactions.

5.1 Managing middleware state

We initially expected user-initiated system transactions to naturally isolate middleware state. For example, if a Java program starts a transaction, then reads from an object bound to a file, it is the JVM that actually issues the `read` system call, which should be isolated as part of the transaction.

---

[2] Serializability is also known as degree 3 isolation [20], which guarantees repeatable reads.

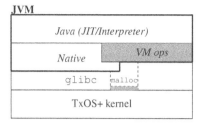

Figure 1. Block diagram of the Hotspot JVM on TxOS+. Shaded regions are where system transactions are paused, including JVM-internal operations and when `malloc` adds pages to a heap.

Some middleware state, however, should not be isolated by a user-initiated system transaction. For instance, if the JVM happens to add pages to a memory allocator while running a transactional thread, portions of this page can be safely allocated to other threads without compromising transactional isolation. Moreover, if the transaction fails, simply unmapping this page is the wrong undo action, as it will cause memory faults in threads uninvolved with the failed transaction. To address this issue, we extended the original TxOS nesting model.

5.2 Nesting model

The **nesting model** for a transaction system defines the semantics of what happens if a transaction executes inside of another. If function A begins a transaction and calls function B, which also begins a transaction, the two transactions must interact in some clearly defined way. The original TxOS nesting model is simple flat nesting. Any inner transaction (e.g., the one started by B) becomes a part of the enclosing transaction (e.g., the one started by A). The inner transaction can see all in-progress updates, and even after it commits, the inner transaction's state (B) is not visible to other threads until the enclosing transaction commits (A). Flat nesting is sufficient to compose many transactions, and its behavior closely matches the naive programmer's intuition.

We extended the nesting model in TxOS+ to allow the JVM to differentiate user-initiated action and middleware-initiated action. System calls issued directly for application operations become part of a system transaction, whereas the JVM or `libc` can *pause* the transaction before issuing system for internal operations. Figure 1 shows a block diagram for a JVM running on TxOS+. A thread can be executing user code, (the Java box), native support code called directly from the Java code, (the Native box), glibc code, (`glibc` box), or kernel code in response to a system call (TxOS+ kernel box). In addition, the JVM sometimes needs to perform operations on behalf of all threads (the VM ops box).

Java source code	`SysTransaction.begin();`
	`r = graphAddEdge(v1, v2);`
	`SysTransaction.end();`	

	(1) without VM ops	(2) with VM ops

Java execution	`sys_xbegin()`
	`graphAddEdge()` native
	Java Interpreter/JIT
	`sys_xend()`
		`sys_xbegin()`
		`graphAddEdge()` native
		
		`tx = sys_xpause()`
		VM operations
		`sys_xresume(tx)`
		
		Java Interpreter/JIT
		`sys_xend()`

Figure 2. A system transactions code example depicting Java source code, and execution inside the JVM. Any active system transaction is paused during VM operations.

5.3 Designing pause/resume for TxOS+

TxOS+ effectively solves this middleware state problem by providing a transactional **pause** and **resume** primitive. When a transaction is paused, the OS treats the thread as if it were running non-transactionally: any system calls the thread issues will be visible to other threads immediately, the thread can conflict with the parent transaction, and the thread can start a new, independent transaction.

We modified the JVM and `glibc` to pause the running transaction before performing internal bookkeeping, such as adding or removing pages to the heap or updating VM bookkeeping, and to resume the transaction afterwards. We discuss the uses of transactional pause in Section 7.1.

The `sys_xpause` system call returns a unique identifier for a transaction, which is passed as an argument to `sys_xresume`. The kernel tracks the association of a transaction with the participating task(s) for security and garbage collection. A thread may only resume a transaction it previously participated in. When the last task with a reference to a paused, uncommitted transaction exits, the transaction is aborted, rolled back, and freed. Pause and resume are only intended for use in system software, they are not intended for use in applications.

Figure 2 shows an example of how Java source code that creates a system transaction is executed. The JVM adds the system calls to start the transaction, but it also pauses the transaction if necessary to perform internal VM bookkeeping. Many JVMs already save time and space by "borrowing" an already existing thread for JVM bookkeeping, rather than creating a dedicated internal thread; the pause and resume primitives make this safe.

It is a reasonable concern that a more complex nesting model erodes the simplicity benefits of system transactions. Novice programmers may struggle to reason about the interactions of paused and transactional system calls. Our experience is that pause and resume are only required for the JVM and `libc`, which are maintained by experts. All refactored application code, even the 138,000 line IMAP server, only uses the simple transaction calls and flat nesting.

5.4 Ordered transactions

Historically, BFT replicas have serially executed requests that issue system calls. Replicas must be deterministic; in sowing system-level concurrency, one often reaps non-determinism. Using **ordered transactions**, TxOS can execute requests in parallel, but commit them using a pre-defined order. For low-contention workloads, ordered transactions should provide performance from parallelism while preserving safety for BFT replicas.

In the original TxOS implementation, OS transactions were serialized according to *some* schedule. The schedule is a result of a configurable, kernel-wide policy that implements performance or fairness heuristics, such as the oldest or highest priority transaction wins a conflict.

We augment these kernel-wide policies with the ability for applications to prescribe the serialized order of their transactions with integer sequence numbers. Transaction ordering is enforced at the granularity of a process group: multi-threaded or multi-process applications can use this feature, but unrelated applications cannot use this mechanism to interfere with each other.

We add an optional `sequence_number` argument and two flags to `sys_xbegin`—one which specifies that the transaction is in an ordered sequence, and one which resets the sequence counter (for loading application checkpoints). The ability to reset the sequence numbers means that sequence numbers are purely a cooperative primitive, they will not constrain arbitrary or malicious code (other work [22] uses system transactions to sandbox potentially malicious code). The sequence counter for a process group is always initialized to zero. Applications that use ordered transactions may need to detach from the current process group to prevent interference from another application using ordered transactions.

Ordered commit is an interface change for transactions. The programmer must decide if *any* commit order is sufficient, or if a specific one is necessary. The nature of the programming problem should make it clear which is needed, for example, deterministic re-execution requires ordered commit, while processing independent requests does not.

6. Composing synchronization mechanisms

Composing synchronization primitives, even of the same type, is a historically fraught problem. In the Linux kernel, for instance, acquiring a blocking lock (e.g., a semaphore or mutex) while holding a spinlock can deadlock the entire system. Transactions are an easy to use synchronization primitive because they guarantee serial behavior and because they compose easily with each other. However, when transactions interact with other synchronization primitives they can inherit the other primitives' complexity.

As we add system transactions to larger code bases, the transactions interact with the application's existing synchronization. Although some mechanisms can be subsumed by transactions, some serve an independent purpose and must compose with transactions, such as locks on state in `libc`. After puzzling over different interactions, we decided to investigate how to compose all existing kernel-visible Linux synchronization primitives with system transactions.

We identify a set of "best principles" that prevent unintended synchronization errors in conscientiously written applications. These principles are derived from both experience with larger application development on TxOS+, as well as a set of small, carefully-written test cases, summarized in Table 1. In writing these test cases, we set out with the goal of both capturing behavior we had seen in practice, and exploring other common design patterns.

6.1 Futexes

First we describe how system transactions interact with the Linux fast userspace mutex, or `futex` [16]. The `futex` system call provides a wait queue in the kernel, which can be used by blocking application-level primitives, such as a mutex or semaphore. Consider a mutex that is implemented using atomic instructions on a lock variable in the application's address space. Rather than spin and waste CPU cycles, threads that fail to acquire the lock will call `futex` to wait for the lock to be released. When a thread releases the lock, it must also call `futex` with different arguments to wake up one or more of the blocked threads.

In futex-based locks, waiting threads are blocked on a kernel-visible queue, but the kernel cannot infer which thread actually has the user-level lock. The state of the user-level lock is completely contained within the application's address space. When a thread is blocked on a futex, the kernel knows that it does not hold the corresponding user-level lock. That is all the kernel knows for sure. To avoid deadlock, TxOS puts transactional threads that block on a futex in "deferential mode" until they wake up. In deferential mode, a transaction takes the lowest possible priority in all conflict arbitration. Therefore, the waiting thread will lose any transactional conflict with the thread that holds the user-level lock, assuring system progress.

Moreover, upon entering deferential mode, the transaction wakes up any threads that were waiting on it to commit. As explained in Section 2, when a transaction (or nontransactional system call) loses a conflict, it generally waits on the winning transaction to commit before retrying (or restarting). When a transaction is blocked on a futex, it wakes up any waiting transactions and allows them to retry early—just in case one of them has the user-level lock.

6.2 Principles for composing transactions with other synchronization

Avoid circular wait. A number of OS primitives, including pipes, sockets, and futexes, can block waiting on an action taken by a different process. Similarly, lower-priority transactions can stall on a conflict (§2), thus blocking while a higher-priority, conflicting transaction completes. These blocking primitives can deadlock each other. For instance, transaction A can block on pipe input after stalling process B on an unrelated conflict (e.g., a write to another file), yet B is the process responsible for providing the pipe input. The `pipe` test in the table represents this case; the `goodfutex` test exhibits a similar pattern.

TxOS+ avoids deadlocks where the deadlocking primitives are all OS-visible abstractions. Instead of doing costly cycle-detection, the OS simply prevents any tasks from waiting on a transaction to commit if that transaction is itself waiting. This policy prevents circular wait, a necessary precondition for deadlock.

Well-formed nesting and non-blocking transactions. To successfully mix application-level locks and transactions, the lock must be both acquired and released either outside a system transaction, or within it, but not both. Synchronization succeeds when one primitive is consistently nested in the other. If nested outside of a transaction, the application lock simply provides mutual exclusion to the transaction; if nested inside, even a failed transaction will still release the lock. Acquiring a lock and holding it while beginning a transaction requires a special non-blocking flag to `sys_xbegin` to prevent the transaction from blocking while holding a lock.

Moreover, the nesting hierarchy must be strict—one thread should not acquire and release a lock inside of a transaction and another thread nest a transaction inside of a lock acquire and release. If thread A cannot commit its transaction until it acquires a lock, and thread B cannot release the lock until thread A commits, the threads can deadlock. "Deferential" futexes cannot prevent this problem in all cases, and only convert it from a deadlock to a livelock. In the example above, deferential mode will abort thread A's transaction if it conflicts with B while waiting on a futex; however, deferential futexes cannot prevent thread A from restarting its transaction and repeatedly conflicting with thread B on other data. This cycle of repeated conflicts between A and B can prevent thread B from ever committing and releasing the lock. In this case the lack of a well-formed nesting discipline in the presence of conflicting transactions creates a race condition that can livelock. The `badfutex` test experiences this livelock.

Explicit ordering for well-structured, deterministic synchronization. When using well-structured or deterministic synchronization paradigms, such as an internal producer/consumer, explicit transaction ordering communicates the programmer's intention to the OS, which helps the OS make better scheduling decisions. The `ordered-p/c` test simulates such an application-level producer/consumer paradigm, using ordered transactions combined with a local semaphore to ensure that consumers follow producers for variables stored in a local array.

In general, one should not mix deterministic and nondeterministic primitives, as a non-deterministic primitive

Test	Description	Comments
goodfutex	Use a raw `futex` call to simulate blocking on one futex inside of a transaction and a second outside of a transaction.	Works with transactions, as it follows a well-formed nesting discipline.
badfutex	Combine a `futex` call with conflicting transactions to simulate acquiring the same lock inside of a transaction and outside of a transaction.	Livelocks because it violates a well-formed nesting discipline.
orderedfutex	Combine a `futex` call with ordered transactions to simulate mixing non-deterministic and deterministic synchronization primitives.	Hangs because of a fundamental determinism mismatch.
mutex	Use a `pthread` mutex lock inside and outside of a transaction, similar to goodfutex.	Works with transactions, as it follows a well-formed nesting discipline.
ordered-p/c	Use ordered transactions and `pthread` semaphores to coordinate access to a local array; consumers write outputs to a file in order.	Transaction ordering is sufficient to coordinate the producers and consumers.
pipe-p/c	Use ordered transactions and an OS-level pipe to implement a producer/consumer pattern; consumers write outputs to an file in order.	Transaction ordering is sufficient to coordinate the producers and consumers.
lockfile	Wait on a lockfile to be created inside of a transaction inside of a polling loop.	Can deadlock with file creator; use scheduling priority to defer to the file creator.
pipe	A pipe reader conflicts with the pipe writer on a file access.	Deadlock is prevented by lowering the reader's priority while waiting and waking up any transactions blocked on the reader.

Table 1. Summary of test cases for composing transactions and other synchronization primitives.

permits many schedules that the deterministic primitive will not. The `orderedfutex` test hangs because it mixes deterministic and non-deterministic synchronization.

Scheduling priority for unstructured synchronization.
When using ad hoc synchronization, application developers may not be able to specify an ordering. For example, the `lockfile` test waits inside of a transactional polling loop for a new file to be created by another task that does not cooperatively order transactions. If the waiting transaction has enumerated the directory contents, degree 3 isolation should prevent it from seeing newly created entries, which TxOS enforces with read isolation on the directory's child list. When the other task attempts to create the file, it will cause a conflict; if the OS arbitrates in favor of the waiter and blocks the file creator, the application will deadlock.

We address this issue with OS scheduling priorities. The default contention management policy in TxOS uses scheduling priorities to arbitrate conflicts. Before entering a polling loop, the transaction should use `nice` or `setpriority` to defer to the process it is waiting on. In each iteration of the loop, the polling transaction can incrementally lower its priority until it defers to the creating transaction. Similarly, the file creator can set the non-blocking flag and incrementally raise its priority until the transaction completes.

7. Implementation

This section both describes our improvements to system transactions and discusses some non-obvious interactions of the system implementation with system transactions. To create TxOS+, we forked TxOS 1.0.1, which is based on the Linux 2.6.22.6 kernel. Our distribution was Ubuntu 8.10, including glibc 2.8.90, OpenJDK Icedtea6 1.9.7.

7.1 Using pause/resume in TxOS+

Pausing and resuming application-initiated transactions is vital to insulate state in the JVM or in libc. We review how pause/resume is used in TxOS+ starting with examples that have been suggested by other researchers, like bookkeeping state and debugging, then moving on to more subtle cases like dynamic linking and `mprotect` calls.

Bookkeeping state. Pause and resume are useful for managing JVM bookkeeping state (an activity we refer to as VM operations). Bookkeeping state does not need to be rolled back on a failed transaction, because the JVM does not rely on it being completely correct. For example, the JVM maintains file-backed shared memory (`perfdata`) containing the total thread count, JIT compiled methods, and the last JIT compilation failure. Updates to this data by different transactions cause spurious conflicts that would throttle transactional throughput. By pausing any active system transaction before VM operations, the code no longer causes spurious transactional conflicts.

Debugging. Another useful application of pause/resume is debugging messages. While developing an application on TxOS, program writers may want to use consoles or log files for debugging purposes. Since these channels are treated as files in many operating systems, changes to them are not written out until the transaction is committed. This kind of behavior may not be desired by program writers, especially when they want to look at user state changes in multi-threaded applications regardless of transaction commit or abort. Log messages written while a transaction is paused will be written out without delay.

Dynamic linking. C and Java link and load dynamic libraries lazily, deferring the memory mapping overheads until the library is actually used by the application. The application is not aware of when linking and loading happens, and it might occur during a transaction. When a library is loaded the linker modifies the application and library to reflect the library's placement in the application's address space.

TxOS+ should not undo any dynamic linking that occurs during a system transaction, since that would simply be wasted work. Therefore, we pause the current transaction before the dynamic linking done by libc or by the JVM.

mprotect. The JVM and libc use mprotect aggressively. malloc within glibc internally uses mprotect for minor changes in heap space size with multiple threads, making calls to mprotect on behalf of malloc more frequent than calls to mmap.

The JVM uses mprotect to implement *safepoints* where the JVM will stop threads for garbage collection and other purposes like locking bias adjustment [35], and implementing light-weight memory barriers [14]. It is possible to eliminate some uses of mprotect. For example, the JVM can use CPU memory barrier instructions instead of mprotect with the -XX:+UseMemBar option. When our JVM can avoid using mprotect it does, but completely eliminating the use of mprotect in the JVM would be too invasive a change. To avoid spurious conflicts on these frequent mprotect calls, we modify libc and the JVM to suspend the current transaction before the call.

brk. The sys_brk system call is a relic from the era of segmented virtual memory. It extends the heap portion of the data segment towards the stack. While Linux and other modern systems don't use segmentation any longer, they retain this abstraction. Many memory allocators, including the default glibc allocator, still use brk to allocate heap space, even though mmap could easily serve the same purpose.

Because brk-based allocators expect the initial heap region to be contiguous, and the address of the heap end is stored in the kernel, TxOS+ only allows one transaction to modify the process heap boundary at a time. Although extensions of the heap commute, rolling back one modification could leave holes, which would break contiguity.

One minor problem with brk is that glibc caches the current brk value, and this cache can get out of sync with the kernel's brk value. If glibc has an outdated brk value, then a subsequent sys_brk call could result in a non-contiguous heap. Initially, we attempted to reload the cached brk value after a transaction abort; we ultimately found it simpler to pause the current transaction around a sys_brk.

7.2 Page locking and transaction abort

If, in the course of servicing a transactional system call, the transaction cannot safely make progress, the TxOS strategy is to use a longjmp-like mechanism to immediately exit the system call. This mechanism was adopted because safely unwinding the stack on a transaction abort would require a massive amount of new error-handling code. The longjmp approach requires undo logging of certain operations, such as lock acquisition or temporary memory allocation. Although this approach works in general, we found it did not interact well with disk I/O.

Synchronization for pages locked for disk I/O is complicated. These pages are protected by a per-page lock, but each page also has an "up-to-date" flag that must be set once a disk read completes. Some kernel code paths may detect that this flag is not set, and spin until the disk read completes—without ever acquiring the page lock.

These two independent synchronization mechanisms interact negatively when a transaction aborts holding a page lock for I/O. In the original TxOS prototype, a transaction could begin an I/O on a page, then lose a conflict and jump out of the stack without properly handling the I/O completion. Subsequent requests for the page would hang waiting for this I/O completion, ultimately hanging the system.

We addressed this problem by preventing the transaction from jumping up the stack until it correctly releases all page locks and handles any I/O completions. We also added a debugging mode that asserted that the longjmp code is never executed with a page lock held. This debugging mode allowed us to quickly pinpoint a small number of code paths that needed explicit abort error handling code.

7.3 File descriptor table

The file descriptor table is a complex, contended kernel data structure that we redesigned for TxOS+. The file descriptor table translates file descriptors to opened file objects. The table provides an efficient means for accessing a file without doing repetitive security checks once a file is opened.

In the Linux kernel, the file descriptor table is implemented as a single array that is expanded when entries are filled. One trivial way to manage the file descriptor table in transactions is to consider the whole table as an object. This coarse-grained approach (taken in TxOS) simplifies implementation, but any open or close from two transactions create unnecessary conflicts.

We added a file descriptor object to TxOS+, and restructured the table to be a linked list of segments. The file descriptor objects supports transactional semantics, and can be committed or rolled back individually. To avoid synchronizing a file descriptor table that has changed location (because it changed size), TxOS+ expands the table by linking in a new segment and leaving the old table in place. Accessing an entry can require additional indirections, but each segment allocated is twice the length of the previous segment and the system defines a limit on per-process file descriptors bounding the number of indirections needed to a small number (less than 2 indirections for all of our experiments including system configuration during boot).

7.4 Data structure reorganization

The TxOS prototype design decomposed kernel objects such as the `inode`, `dentry`, and `file` objects into two main components: a stable header for static or kernel-internal bookkeeping, and a data object for fields that could change during the course of the transaction. We found that many of the fields of the `inode` and `super_block`, specifically, were needlessly included in the data object. For instance, the `inode` data object includes several fields that do not change for the life of the inode, such as the inode number and the operations pointer. A more subtle example is the inode `stat` word, which includes some bits that encode the type (which doesn't change) and other bits that include the permissions, which can change in a transaction.

We migrated several of these static fields into the object header, which has both performance and correctness implications. In terms of performance, looking up whether an object is in the transaction's working set is relatively expensive, and adding the object to the transaction's workset is even more expensive. There were a number of cases where these checks can now be elided. Above (§7.2), we describe how to handle transaction aborts during disk I/O safely. Many of the places where a transaction could abort when requesting disk I/O came from accessing needlessly isolated fields, such the type of an inode, or the file system configuration options. This reorganization substantially reduced the amount of code that needed to be rewritten with explicit error handling.

7.5 Releasing isolation on disk reads

When part of the file system directory tree is not in the in-memory cache (`dcache`), it must be read from disk, creating new `inode` and `dentry` data structures to represent these files. If the disk read occurs during a transaction, the original TxOS prototype would add these objects to the transaction's workset. If the transaction aborts, these cached entries are discarded and re-read from disk on the next access.

In TxOS+, we immediately release isolation on these newly created data structures, as they contain only previously committed state. Though the data was read during a transaction, by releasing isolation, the system treats the files as if they were read outside of a transaction. If the trans-

Application		LOC	LOC changed
BFT	UpRight library	22,767	174 (0.7%)
	Graph server	1,006	18 (1.8%)
Dovecot (IMAP)		138,723	40 (0.0003%)
glibc		1,027,399	826 (0.0008%)
IcedTea JVM		496,305	384 (0.0008%)

Table 2. Lines of code changed to add system transactions.

action modifies any of the files, then TxOS+ creates transactional copies (as it does for all modified kernel objects). If the transaction fails and rolls back, data from clean disk reads are kept in the memory cache. This change eliminates costly and needless disk reads, and reduces the bookkeeping complexity needed to track this special case behavior through the life of the transaction.

8. Evaluation

We present measurements of our prototype in this section. Table 2 shows the number of lines we changed to add system transactions to a set of large applications and libraries. The number of changed lines is very small both in absolute terms and relative to the code size of these projects. We also modified around 17,000 lines of TxOS source code to create TxOS+. The number of modified kernel lines is high because we modified structure definitons to avoid spurious conflicts.

8.1 BFT and System Transactions

Previous BFT systems were generally evaluated using services where dependencies between requests could be easily reasoned about *a priori*, such as a distributed file system (running a simplified workload) or a directory service. Many realistic workloads are not so simple. Thus, we created a new challenge workload for BFT that has opportunities for concurrency but does not lend itself to trivial dependency analysis.

Our challenge workload for fault-tolerant replication stores backend data for a network router, where nodes are machines and edges are network links. We tested this workload with two kinds of graph datasets, which have different graph density. The denser dataset contains a randomly generated graph with 5,000 vertices and 3,174,615 edges (density is 0.254), and the sparser graph has 10,900 vertices and 31,180 edges (density is 0.000525). The sparse graph is sampled from graph data from the Oregon-2 dataset [27] and is comprised of network routes between autonomous systems inferred from RouteViews [3] and other routing information. Both graphs are undirected. Graph data is stored in a file, which allows it to be larger than memory. The application accesses the data using `pread` and `pwrite` calls, and allows the OS to cache the file data.

The server can handle four types of queries from clients: edge addition, edge deletion, edge existence, and shortest

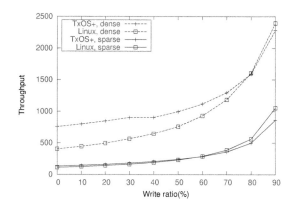

Figure 3. Throughput (higher is better) for UpRight graph server application on TxOS+ and Linux. The x-axis shows different ratios of write requests to shortest path (read) requests.

Dataset			Tput (ops/s)	Latency (ms)	Aborts
Dense graph	0% write	Linux	404.4	96.4	-
		TxOS+	759.1	50.7	0.0 %
	50% write	Linux	760.0	50.4	-
		TxOS+	994.9	40.3	0.43 %
	100% write	Linux	3601	9.49	-
		TxOS+	3360	10.2	0.19 %
Sparse graph	0% write	Linux	114.1	334	-
		TxOS+	132.9	298	0.0 %
	50% write	Linux	232.5	162	-
		TxOS+	239.8	164	3.6 %
	100% write	Linux	3638	9.41	-
		TxOS+	3340	10.0	0.34 %

Table 3. Throughput (higher is better) and latency (lower is better) for the BFT graph service on TxOS+ and Linux. TxOS+ uses server-side speculation to parallelize request processing. The percentage of aborted requests is given for TxOS+ and is highest with 50% write mix.

path between two vertices. The first two operations can modify the graph, while the other two only read it. The shortest path operation takes significantly longer than the others and includes much more data in its transaction, increasing the probability and penalty for a transaction abort (misspeculation). Each modify request first tests for the existence of the edge it seeks to modify, and does no more work if it is trying to add an existent edge or delete a non-existent edge. Dependencies between requests are data dependent and cannot be predicted before execution.

This application runs on the Upright BFT library with TxOS+, our modified JVM and our modified glibc. In our BFT application evaluation, we use 3 execution replicas with 4 threads for each. All the execution replicas run on Dell Optiplex 780 machines with Intel Core2 Q9400 quad-core 2.66 GHz CPU, 3 GB memory. Because this experiment focuses is on concurrent isolation, we use the `ext2` file system, which does not guarantee atomic disk updates, but does simplify kernel debugging. The experiment configuration also has 4 ordering replicas, 4 request quorum replicas, and 40 clients connected over a gigabit network. The clients saturate our execution servers due to the large amount of work in finding a shortest path. All experiments first warm-up the JVM at the replicas [9]. We only consider throughput for requests after the initial 20,000 requests to eliminate transient effects from system startup.

Throughput and Latency Fig 3 shows the throughput of the BFT graph server on TxOS+ with different mixes of read/write requests, compared with the throughput of the server with serial execution on Linux. With read-only requests, the parallelized BFT graph server on TxOS+ achieves 88.3% (dense) or 10.9% (sparse) higher throughput than execution on Linux. TxOS+'s throughput improvements from increased parallelism are offset by bookkeeping that TxOS+ must do to track file I/O. These overheads are

lower for denser graphs, which have shorter shortest paths, and hence fewer file reads and subsequent bookkeeping.

Table 3 provides a cross section view of Figure 3, illustrating noteworthy characteristics of the workload. First, write operations are significantly faster than read operations (10× with dense graphs, 35.5× with sparse graphs), as shown by comparing the latencies of the 0% write and 100% write rows. This is because a read operation actually computes a shortest path—reading many edges and performing a substantial computation. Second, shortest path operations on sparse graphs have a larger read set than those on dense graphs. This larger read set causes an order of magnitude more aborts in the sparse 50% write workload (0.4% to 3.6%). Even with substantially more aborts, TxOS+ shows comparable performance to Linux. Finally, the 100% write test has similar latency in both graphs because each write operation simply updates a given vertex. The 100% write workload on TxOS+ has a 7–9% reduction in throughput compared to Linux, which is attributable to the very short write requests (9.4–10.2 ms) not amortizing thread coordination costs. Recall that the Linux baseline is single-threaded, while TxOS+ uses transactions to execute the writes concurently.

Figure 4 compares time to recover a failed graph server node on TxOS+ and Linux. In this experiment, a server is stopped at 36 seconds and restarted at 53 seconds (17 seconds later). The recovering server re-executes all intervening requests until it has caught up. By executing recovery requests in parallel, TxOS+ recovers 29.9% faster than Linux.

8.2 IMAP

We modified the Dovecot email server, version 1.0.10, to use system transactions. Dovecot is a production-quality email server, shipped as a standard feature in many mainstream Linux distributions, supporting a range of protocols, includ-

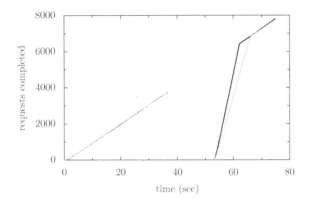

Figure 4. Comparison of time to recover a BFT server in TxOS+ (black) vs. Linux (grey). The x-axis shows time and the y-axis is in 1000's of requests completed. The dotted line tracks the correct execution nodes. In both cases, a node stopped at 36 seconds and restarted at 53 seconds. In this experiment, TxOS+ recovers 29.9% faster than Linux.

Clients	OS	% Writes				
		0	**10**	**25**	**50**	**100**
1	Linux	0.15	0.29	0.63	1.20	2.30
	TxOS+	0.14	0.28	0.62	0.96	2.08
2	Linux	0.12	0.42	0.95	1.47	2.83
	TxOS+	0.10	0.34	0.74	1.38	1.92
4	Linux	0.14	0.60	1.37	2.45	4.80
	TxOS+	0.13	0.38	0.80	1.40	2.66

Table 4. Execution time in seconds of an IMAP client microbenchmark comparing transactional Dovecot on TxOS+ with Unmodified Dovecot on Linux, with varying write fractions and concurrent clients. Lower is better. Work scales with the number of clients, so the same value for a write fraction across more clients indicates perfect scaling.

ing IMAP, and a range of back-end mail storage formats. Specifically, we changed its `maildir` backend storage format [1, 6], to use transactions instead of directory lock files. We use unmodified `maildir` as our baseline, and replace lock files with system transactions for safety. We test with the IMAP client protocol, which touts concurrent client support as an explicit, but often problematic, feature.

We note that `maildir` was originally designed to be lock free. Due to race conditions between a sequence of `readdir` system calls and `rename` calls, Dovecot has reintroduced lock files at the directory granularity [15]. We performed an experiment where we disabled this lock file and confirmed qualitatively that we could reproduce disturbing anomalies attributable to unrepeatable mailbox reads, including temporarily lost email messages when another client marks a message as read.

To evaluate the impact of adding transactions to Dovecot, we also wrote a client test application in Python 2.6.5, using the `imaplib` IMAP client library. This script uses a single test account, and launches a configurable number of concurrent clients (1–4 in our experiments), accessing a shared mailbox with an initial size of 1500 messages. Each client performs 100 operations on randomly selected messages; a configurable fraction are message reads and the rest are randomly chosen between creating a new message and deleting a random message.

We run our IMAP server on a Dell PowerEdge T300 server, with a quad-core Intel Xeon X3363 CPU at 2.83 GHz and 4 GB of RAM. We ran the client script on a SuperMicro SuperServer, with 4 quad-core Intel Xeon X7350 CPUs (16 cores total), at 2.93 GHz with 48 GB of RAM. As with the BFT experiments, our focus is on concurrent isolation, so we use the `ext2` file system for debugging simplicity.

Table 4 reports a sample of measured performance data at a range of write fractions and concurrent clients. Each

value is the average of at least three runs. On single-client or read-only workloads, Dovecot on TxOS+ and Linux perform comparably, indicating that transactions do not harm baseline performance. With two clients, performance improves on TxOS+ by 7–47%, with four clients, the improvement increases from 8–80%. We attribute these performance gains to both the elimination of work creating and deleting lock files, as well as improved block allocation and write scheduling (commensurate with previous results [34]).

9. Related Work

System Transactions. A number of historical research operating systems have provided OS-level transactions, either as a general-purpose programming abstraction [37, 46], or to help isolate untrusted OS extensions [40]. These systems essentially applied database implementation techniques to the OS; TxOS [34] innovated by selecting concurrency management techniques more appropriate for an OS kernel. This work innovates by substantially refining these mechanisms and evaluates them on the largest transactional OS workloads to date (to the best of our knowledge).

Transactional file systems are deployed as part of Windows 7 [36], and they exist in several research prototypes [17, 39, 43]. It is possible that a transactional file system is sufficient to run the workloads described in this paper; but to our knowledge, integrating such large applications with file system transactions has not been explored. Based on our experience, there are a number of complications that arise when OS-level primitives outside the file system are not rolled back on a transaction abort. For instance, the IMAP implementation was simplified by automatic rollback of a file descriptor, which would require more cumbersome application code on a transactional file system.

Speculative Execution in the OS. Speculator [30] extends the operating system with an application isolation and rollback mechanism that is similar to transactions in many respects, improving system performance by speculating past high-latency events. The primary difference is that speculations are not isolated from each other; when two speculations touch the same OS data, they are automatically merged. The initial motivation for Speculator was to hide the latency of common NFS server requests. Speculator has also been extended to hide latency of synchronous writes to a local file system [32], security checks [31], and to debug system configuration [44].

Most relevant to this work, Speculator has been used to hide BFT access latency on the **client**, speculating that it knows the likely answer all replicas will give [47]. Speculator is insufficient to parallelize execution of BFT **servers**, as speculations are not isolated. Concurrent speculations will be merged, doing nothing to prevent non-determinism. Transactions can isolate independent requests on the server and serialize them according to the prescribed order. Thus these similar systems provide related, but distinct guarantees; the differences in their isolation properties dictate what problems they can solve.

High-throughput BFT Systems. BFT systems achieve high availability through replication. This comes at a throughput cost, so improving throughput is a focus of BFT research.

Batching requests increases throughput and is used in PBFT [11] and Zyzzyva [23]. Although batching reduces communication overhead, replicas still must execute requests in a serial order. To parallelize request execution, Kotla and Dahlin [24] suggested using application-specific knowledge to find independent sets of requests in an ordered batch that can be parallelized. Checking dependencies among requests requires complete foreknowledge of their execution behavior—difficult to obtain in practice, especially when the OS is involved.

HRDB [45] and Byzantium [18] are BFT replicated databases that use that use use database transactions to parallelize request processing. These systems use weaker concurrency isolation guarantees: HRDB ensures one-copy serializability while Byzantium relies on snapshot isolation.

These systems, as well as TxOS+, use transactions as a tool for maximizing BFT concurrency. TxOS+ extends the concurrency from structured tables to unstructured OS operations, supporting a wider range of applications. Unlike TxOS+, which uses ordered transactions, these systems order commits by deferring the database commit, harming performance. Ordered system transactions provide a simpler route for applications to use transactional semantics.

Pausing transactional memory. User-level hardware transactional memory systems have proposed similar pausing [50] or open nesting [28] mechanisms to keep libc and OS state out of user-level transactions. In these systems, a program would pause its transaction before calling `malloc` to avoid hardware rollback of libc bookkeeping; in our libc, `malloc` might pause the transaction to keep its state out of the OS. To the best of our knowledge, these pausing mechanisms have not been evaluated on substantial code bases. Because software transactional memory is usually implemented *above* the JVM or libc, pausing is not necessary; pausing is needed only for lower-level transactional mechanisms.

10. Conclusion

This paper takes a promising idea, system transactions, and applies them to server applications that have struggled to balance high throughput with strong safety and concurrency guarantees due to a crippled OS interface. This paper contributes new ideas about the right OS interfaces for these applications and supporting middleware, validated with substantial workloads. In the process of supporting applications that are larger than previously studied, we improved a number of aspects in the design and implementation of system transactions. This work is an important step in a line of research towards OSes that efficiently provide strong guarantees, leading to better applications.

11. Acknowledgments

We thank the anonymous reviewers, Prince Mahajan, and our shepherd, Rodrigo Rodrigues, for valuable feedback and suggestions. We also thank Allen Clement, Manos Kapritsos, and Yang Wang for help with the UpRight code.

This research was supported by the Office of the Vice President for Research at Stony Brook University, NSF Career Award 0644205, NSF CNS-0905602, Samsung Scholarship, and an Intel equipment grant.

References

[1] Dovecot mailbox format - maildir. http://wiki.dovecot.org/MailboxFormat/Maildir. §1, §4.1, §8.2

[2] Welcome to the dovecot wiki. http://wiki2.dovecot.org/. §1

[3] University of oregon route views project. http://www.routeviews.org/, 2000. §8.1

[4] A. Aviram, S.-C. Weng, S. Hu, and B. Ford. Efficient system-enforced deterministic parallelism. In *OSDI*, pages 1–16, 2010. §3.2

[5] T. Bergan, N. Hunt, L. Ceze, and S. D. Gribble. Deterministic process groups in dOS. In *OSDI*, pages 1–16, 2010. §3.2

[6] D. J. Bernstein. Using maildir format (the original specification), 1995. http://cr.yp.to/proto/maildir.html. §1, §4.1, §8.2

[7] C. Blundell, E. C. Lewis, and M. M. K. Martin. Deconstructing transactions: The subtleties of atomicity. In *WDDD*. Jun 2005. §2

[8] G. Bracha and S. Toueg. Asynchronous consensus and broadcast protocols. *JACM*, 32(4):824–840, 1985. §3.1

[9] J. Bull, L. Smith, M. Westhead, D. Henty, and R. Davey. A benchmark suite for high performance java. *Concurrency - Practice and Experience*, 12(6):375–388, 2000. §8.1

[10] X. Cai, Y. Gui, and R. Johnson. Exploiting unix file-system races via algorithmic complexity attacks. In *Oakland*, pages 27–41, 2009. §3

[11] M. Castro and B. Liskov. Practical byzantine fault tolerance and proactive recovery. *ACM Transactions on Computer Systems (TOCS)*, 20(4):398–461, Nov. 2002. §9

[12] A. Clement, M. Kapritsos, S. Lee, Y. Wang, L. Alvisi, M. Dahlin, and T. Riché. Upright cluster services. In *SOSP*, pages 277–290, 2009. §1, §3.1

[13] M. Crispin. INTERNET MESSAGE ACCESS PROTOCOL - VERSION 4rev1. RFC 3501 (Proposed Standard), March 2003. Obsoletes by RFC 2060. §1, §4

[14] D. Dice, H. Huang, and M. Yang. Asymmetric dekker synchronization, July 2001. http://home.comcast.net/ pjbishop/Dave/Asymmetric-Dekker-Synchronization.txt. §7.1

[15] Dovecot maildir and racing. http://www.dovecot. org/list/dovecot/2006-March/011811.html. §4.1, §8.2

[16] H. Franke, R. Russel, and M. Kirkwood. Fuss, futexes and furwocks: Fast userlevel locking in Linux. In *Proceedings of the Ottawa Linux Symposium*, 2002. §6.1

[17] E. Gal and S. Toledo. A transactional flash file system for microcontrollers. In *USENIX*, pages 89–104, 2005. §9

[18] R. Garcia, R. Rodrigues, and N. Preguiça. Efficient middleware for byzantine fault tolerant database replication. In *EuroSys*, pages 107–122. ACM, 2011. §3.2, §9

[19] J. Gray and A. Reuter. *Transaction Processing: Concepts and Techniques*. Morgan Kaufmann, 1993. §2, §2

[20] J. N. Gray, R. A. Lorie, G. R. Putzolu, and I. L. Traiger. Granularity of locks and degrees of consistency in a shared data base. *Modeling in Data Base Management Systems*, pages 364–394, 1976. §2

[21] M. Herlihy and J. E. Moss. Transactional memory: Architectural support for lock-free data structures. In *ISCA*, pages 289–300, 1993. §2

[22] S. Jana, D. E. Porter, and V. Shmatikov. TxBox: Building secure, efcient sandboxes with system transactions. In *Oakland*, Oakland, CA, May 2011. §5.4

[23] R. Kotla, L. Alvisi, M. Dahlin, A. Clement, and E. Wong. Zyzzyva: Speculative byzantine fault tolerance. *SOSP*, pages 45–58, 2007. §3.1, §9

[24] R. Kotla and M. Dahlin. High throughput Byzantine fault tolerance. In *DSN*, pages 575–584. IEEE, 2003. §3.2, §9

[25] L. Lamport. Lower bounds for asynchronous consensus. *Distributed Computing*, 19(2):104–125, 2006. §3.1

[26] L. Lamport, R. Shostak, and M. Pease. The byzantine generals problem. *TOPLAS*, 4(3):382–401, 1982. §3

[27] J. Leskovec, J. Kleinberg, and C. Faloutsos. Graphs over time: densification laws, shrinking diameters and possible explanations. In *SIGKDD*, pages 177–187. ACM, 2005. §8.1

[28] M. J. Moravan, J. Bobba, K. E. Moore, L. Yen, M. D. Hill, B. Liblit, M. M. Swift, and D. A. Wood. Supporting nested transactional memory in LogTM. In *ASPLOS*, pages 359–370, 2006. §9

[29] J. Myers. Post Office Protocol - Version 3. RFC 1939 (Standard), May 1996. Obsoletes by RFC 1725. §4

[30] E. B. Nightingale, P. M. Chen, and J. Flinn. Speculative execution in a distributed file system. In *SOSP*, pages 191–205, 2005. §9

[31] E. B. Nightingale, D. Peek, P. M. Chen, and J. Flinn. Parallelizing security checks on commodity hardware. In *ASPLOS*, pages 308–318, 2008. §9

[32] E. B. Nightingale, K. Veeraraghavan, P. M. Chen, and J. Flinn. Rethink the sync. In *OSDI*, pages 1–14, 2006. §9

[33] D. E. Porter. *Operating System Transactions*. PhD thesis, The University of Texas at Austin, December 2010. §2

[34] D. E. Porter, O. S. Hofmann, C. J. Rossbach, A. Benn, and E. Witchel. Operating systems transactions. In *SOSP*, pages 161–176. ACM, 2009. §1, §1, §2, §2, §8.2, §9

[35] K. Russell and D. Detlefs. Eliminating synchronization-related atomic operations with biased locking and bulk rebiasing. *ACM SIGPLAN Notices*, 41(10):263–272, 2006. §7.1

[36] M. Russinovich and D. Solomon. *Windows Internals*. Microsoft Press, 2009. §9

[37] F. Schmuck and J. Wylie. Experience with transactions in QuickSilver. In *SOSP*, pages 239–253. ACM, 1991. §9

[38] F. B. Schneider. Implementing fault-tolerant services using the state machine approach: A tutorial. *ACM Comput. Surv.*, 22(4):299–319, 1990. §3

[39] M. I. Seltzer. Transaction support in a log-structured file system. In *IDCE*, pages 503–510, 1993. §9

[40] M. I. Seltzer, Y. Endo, C. Small, and K. A. Smith. Dealing with disaster: Surviving misbehaved kernel extensions. In *OSDI*, pages 213–227, 1996. §9

[41] N. Shavit and D. Touitou. Software transactional memory. In *PODC*, pages 204–213, 1995. §2

[42] A. Singh, T. Das, P. Maniatis, P. Druschel, and T. Roscoe. BFT protocols under fire. In *NSDI*, pages 189–204, 2008. §3.2

[43] R. Spillane, S. Gaikwad, M. Chinni, E. Zadok, and C. P. Wright. Enabling transactional file access via lightweight kernel extensions. In *FAST*, pages 29–42, 2009. §9

[44] Y.-Y. Su, M. Attariyan, and J. Flinn. AutoBash: Improving configuration management with operating system causality analysis. In *SOSP*, pages 237–250, 2007. §9

[45] B. Vandiver, H. Balakrishnan, B. Liskov, and S. Madden. Tolerating byzantine faults in transaction processing systems using commit barrier scheduling. In *SOSP*, pages 59–72. ACM, 2007. §3.2, §9

[46] M. J. Weinstein, J. Thomas W. Page, B. K. Livezey, and G. J. Popek. Transactions and synchronization in a distributed operating system. In *SOSP*, pages 115–126, 1985. §9

[47] B. Wester, J. Cowling, E. B. Nightingale, P. M. Chen, J. Flinn, and B. Liskov. Tolerating latency in replicated state machines. In *NSDI*, pages 245–260, 2009. §9

[48] J. Yin, J.-P. Martin, A. Venkataramani, L. Alvisi, and M. Dahlin. Separating agreement from execution for byzantine fault tolerant services. In *SOSP*, pages 253–267, 2003. §3.1

[49] M. Zalewski. Delivering signals for fun and profit, 2001. http://lcamtuf.coredump.cx/signals.txt. §3

[50] C. Zilles and L. Baugh. Extending hardware transactional memory to support non-busy waiting and non-transactional actions. In *TRANSACT*. ACM, 2006. §9

Where is the energy spent inside my app?
Fine Grained Energy Accounting on Smartphones with Eprof

Abhinav Pathak

Purdue University

pathaka@purdue.edu

Y. Charlie Hu

Purdue University

ychu@purdue.edu

Ming Zhang

Microsoft Research

mzh@microsoft.com

Abstract

Where is the energy spent inside my app? Despite the immense popularity of smartphones and the fact that energy is the most crucial aspect in smartphone programming, the answer to the above question remains elusive. This paper first presents *eprof*, the first fine-grained energy profiler for smartphone apps. Compared to profiling the runtime of applications running on conventional computers, profiling energy consumption of applications running on smartphones faces a unique challenge, asynchronous power behavior, where the effect on a component's power state due to a program entity lasts beyond the end of that program entity. We present the design, implementation and evaluation of *eprof* on two mobile OSes, Android and Windows Mobile.

We then present an in-depth case study, the first of its kind, of six popular smartphones apps (including Angry-Birds, Facebook and Browser). *Eprof* sheds lights on internal energy dissipation of these apps and exposes surprising findings like 65%-75% of energy in free apps is spent in third-party advertisement modules. *Eprof* also reveals several "wakelock bugs", a family of "energy bugs" in smartphone apps, and effectively pinpoints their location in the source code. The case study highlights the fact that most of the energy in smartphone apps is spent in I/O, and I/O events are clustered, often due to a few routines. This motivates us to propose bundles, a new accounting presentation of app I/O energy, which helps the developer to quickly understand and optimize the energy drain of her app. Using the bundle presentation, we reduced the energy consumption of four apps by 20% to 65%.

Categories and Subject Descriptors   D.4.8 [Operating Systems]: Performance–Modeling and Prediction.
General Terms   Design, Experimentation, Measurement.
Keywords   Smartphones, Mobile, Energy, Eprof.

1. Introduction

Smartphones run complete OSes which provide full-fledged "app" development platforms, and coupled with "exotic" components such as Camera and GPS, have unleashed the imagination of app developers. According to a new report [1], the app market will explode exponentially to a $38 billion industry by 2015, riding the huge growth in popularity of smartphones. Despite the incredible market penetration of smartphones and exponential growth of the app market, their utility has been and will remain severely limited by the battery life. As such, optimizing the energy consumption of millions of smartphone apps is of critical importance. However, the quarter million apps [2] developed so far were largely developed in an energy oblivious manner. The key enabler for energy-aware smartphone app development is an energy profiler, that can answer the fundamental question of *where is the energy spent inside an app?* Such a tool can be used by an app developer to profile and consequently optimize the energy consumption of smartphone apps, much like how performance profiling enabled by *gprof* [3] has facilitated performance optimization in the past several decades.

Designing an energy profiler for modern smartphones faces three challenges. First, it needs to track the activities of *program entities* at the granularity that a developer is interested in. For example, some developers may be interested in energy drain at the level of threads, while others may desire to understand the energy breakdown of an app at the granularity of routines, which are the natural building blocks following the modular programming design principle.

Second, energy accounting requires tracking of power draw activities of various smartphone hardware components. Third, the power draw and consequently energy consumption activities need to be mapped to the program entities responsible for them. Performing the above two tasks for smartphones faces several major challenges. First, modern smartphones do not come with built-in power meters. Second, and more importantly, smartphone components exhibit asynchronous power behavior, *i.e.*, the instantaneous power draw of a component may not be related to the current utilization of that component. Such asynchronous behavior include: **(a) Tail power state:** Several components (GPS, WiFi, SDCard, 3G) have tail power states [4, 5]; **(b) Per-**

sistent power state wakelocks: Smartphone OSes employ aggressive CPU/Screen sleeping policies and export wakelock APIs for use by apps to prevent them from sleeping. In a typical usage, the power drain due to a wakelock persists beyond a program entity (*e.g.,* a routine); **(c) Exotic components:** Newer components like camera and GPS start consuming high power once switched on in one entity, and often continue till switched off by some other entity [4, 6]. Such asynchronous power behavior pose challenges to correctly attributing the energy consumption of the whole phone to individual program entities.

In this paper, we study the problem of energy profiling and accounting of smartphone apps and make three concrete contributions towards enabling *energy-aware app development* on smartphones. First, we present the design of *eprof*, the first (to the best of our knowledge) fine-grained energy profiler for modern smartphones, and its implementation on two popular mobile OSes, Android and Windows Mobile. Our design leverages a recently proposed fine-grained online power modeling technique [4], which accurately captures complicated power behavior of modern smartphone components in a system-call-driven Finite State Machine (FSM). *Eprof* design focuses on energy accounting policies: how to map the power draw and energy consumption back to program entities. We explore alternate accounting policies and adopt in *eprof* the *last-trigger* policy which attributes lingering energy drain (*e.g.,* tail) to the last trigger, as it more intuitively reflects asynchronous power behavior in mapping energy activities to the responsible program entities.

Second, we report on our experience with using *eprof* to analyze, for the first time, the energy consumption of six of the top 10 most popular apps from Android Market including AngryBirds, Android Browser, and Facebook. *Eprof* exposes many surprising findings about these popular apps: (a) third-party advertisement modules in free apps could consume 65-75% of the total app energy (*e.g.,* AngryBirds, popular chess app); (b) clean termination of long lived TCP sockets could consume 10-50% of the total energy (*e.g.,* browser doing google search, CNN surfing, AngryBirds, NYTimes app, mapquest app), (c) tracking user data (*e.g.,* location, phone stats) consumes 20-30% of the total energy (*e.g.,* NYTimes). In a nut shell, *eprof* shows that, in most popular free apps, performing the task related to the purpose of the app (*e.g.,* chess algorithms in chess apps) consumes only a small fraction (10-30%) of the total app energy.

Our experience with profiling these popular apps using *eprof* revealed several key observations. (1) Our experience confirms with ample evidence that smartphone apps spend a major portion of energy in I/O components such as 3G, WiFi, and GPS. This suggests that compared to desktop apps, optimizing the energy consumption of smartphone apps should have a new focus: the I/O energy. This is especially true since CPU energy optimization techniques have been well studied and mature techniques like frequency scaling have already been incorporated in smartphones. (2) The asynchronous power behavior of smartphone I/O compo-

nents is indeed triggered often in smartphone apps, in fact in all 21 apps we tested, including popular ones such as Angrybirds and the Android browser. (3) Over the duration of an app execution, there are typically a few, long periods of time when I/O components continuously stay in some high power state, which we term as *I/O energy bundles*. (4) Further, the I/O energy of an app is often due to just a few routines that are called by different callers in the app source code, most intuitively a consequence of modular programming practice for I/O operations. This is in stark contrast with CPU time profiling (*e.g.,* using *gprof*) where all routines in the app consume some CPU time. Together observations (3) and (4) suggest that there are often only a few routines that are responsible for I/O bundles.

The above observations suggest that a flat per-entity energy split presentation (similar to time split reported by *gprof*) does not immediately help the programmer to curtail the app energy. A presentation that is more informative and constructive, which aims to reduce I/O energy consumption, is to identify each I/O energy bundle and present its I/O energy profile. In the third part of the paper, we develop such an energy accounting presentation which captures the routines and their causal execution order within each energy bundle. We show how such a bundle-oriented presentation facilitates quick understanding of the energy consumption of an app beyond individual routines and exposes ways of program restructuring to optimize the app's energy consumption. Using the bundle accounting information, we restructured a few apps running on the two OSes, reducing their energy consumption by 20-65%.

2. Accounting Granularity

Energy accounting for smartphone apps answers the essential question for energy optimization and debugging: *where is the energy spent inside an app?* In answering this question, we need to (1) break an app into energy accounting entities, (2) track the power draw and energy activities of each hardware component, and (3) map the energy activities to the entities responsible for them. We discuss the first task of how to track entities in this section.

Granularity of Energy Accounting. The granularity of accounting entities depends on the level at which a developer desires to isolate the energy bottleneck and optimize energy drain, *e.g.,* by restructuring the source code. An entity could be one of the four conventional, well-understood program entities, a process, a thread, a subroutine, and a system call. In principle, an entity can be made more elaborate by the programmer, *e.g.,* a collection of above program entities (*e.g.,* all routines doing networking). In this paper, we focus on the four conventional program entities and leave accounting for more general entity definitions as future work.

Energy accounting at the system call or routine granularity directly exposes the root causes for energy consumption to the developer. Splitting energy among various threads of a process is also important as modern smartphone apps often consist of a collection of code written by third-party service providers (*e.g.*, AngryBirds runs the third-party Flurry [7] program as a separate thread for data aggregation and advertisement.) Finally, per-process accounting is relevant as all new smartphone OSes support multitasking and concurrently running apps affect each other's energy consumption.

Tracking Program Entities. Since system calls are what trigger I/O components into different power states, the key to tracking all four program entities for energy accounting is to log I/O system calls (which is already done by the online power modeling scheme [4]) and their call stacks which allow us to map a system call to the calling routine, thread, and process during postprocessing. To enable accounting for CPU energy drain at the routine level, we use instrumentation to either log the exact routine boundaries or sample the stack periodically to estimate CPU utilization per routine [3]. Finally, we need to log the process and thread ids at each CPU context switch to enable CPU accounting per thread and per process.

3. Asynchronous Power Behavior

Modern smartphones come with a wide variety of I/O hardware *components* embedded in them. Typical components include CPU, memory, Secure Digital card (sdcard for short), WiFi NIC, cellular (3G), bluetooth, GPS, camera (may be multiple), accelerometer, digital compass, LCD, touch sensors, microphone, and speakers. It is common for apps to utilize several components simultaneously to offer richer user experience. Unlike in desktops and servers, in smartphones, the power consumed by each I/O component is often comparable to or higher than that by the CPU.

Each component can be in several operating modes, known as *power states* for that component, each draining a different amount of power. Each component has its own base state which is the power state where that particular component consumes zero power (irrespective of other components). A component can have one or more levels of productive power states (*e.g.*, low and high for WiFi NIC), and the tail power state, which typically consumes less power than a productive power state, *e.g.*, WiFi, sdcard, 3G radio.[1] Finally, the idle power state corresponds to the *system-wide* power state where the phone drains near zero power: the CPU is shut off, the screen is off, and all other components are turned down, except the network components which respond to periodic beacons.

Modern smartphones exhibit *asynchronous power behavior* where an entity's impact on the power consumption of the phone may persist until long after the entity is completed.

Tail energy. Several components, *e.g.*, disk, WiFi, 3G, GPS, in smartphones exhibit the tail power behavior [4–6], where activities in one entity, *e.g.*, a routine, can trigger a component to enter a high power state and stay in that power state long beyond the end of the routine. This is in stark contrast

with the execution time metric profiled by *gprof* which ends promptly when the routine returns.

Wakelocks. Smartphone OSes apply aggressive sleeping policies which make smartphones sleep after a brief period of user inactivity, and export APIs which apps need to use to ensure the components stay awake, irrespective of user activities, so that apps can perform their intermittent activities in the background (*e.g.*, network sync). Figure 1 shows the power state changes due to wakelocks [8] on Android on passion (Table 1 lists the mobile phones we use throughout the paper). For example, when wakelock PARTIAL_WAKE_LOCK exported by the PowerManager class in Android is acquired, the CPU is turned on, consuming 25mA.[2]

Wakelocks thus present another example of asynchronous power behavior of smartphones. A wakelock acquired by a caller entity,[3] *e.g.*, a routine, triggers a component into a high power state. The component continues to consume power after the entity is completed and other entities start using the component. The component is returned back to the idle power state when the wakelock is released, possibly by another entity. Correctly accounting energy due to wakelocks is particularly important as it can help to track down wakelock bugs [9] (*e.g.*, Facebook bug [10], Android eMail bug [11, 12], and Location Listener bug [13]).

Exotic components. Today's smartphones contain several exotic components, such as GPS, camera, accelerometer, and sensors, which consume energy differently than traditional components like CPU [4, 6]. Once these components are switched on by an entity, they continue to drain power until the moment they are switched off, often by another entity.

The above asynchronous power behavior pose challenges to the second task of developing an energy accounting tool, *i.e.*, tracking energy activities of the components. We overcome these challenges by leveraging a recently proposed online power model for smartphones [4], which captures the above intricate asynchronous power behavior of modern smartphones in a finite state machine (FSM). The FSM consists of power states as the nodes and system calls as the triggers for transitions among the power states. Using the FSM power model, system calls issued during the app execution drive the FSM to different power states. For a productive power state, linear regression is used to correlate the duration the component stays in that state with the parameters (workload) of the system call that drove the FSM to the state, and energy consumption at that state is deduced [4]. The duration and hence the energy consumed at tail states and states due to wakelock acquires and releases are straight-forward.

---

[1] Special cases such as CPU frequency scaling and wireless signal strength are handled by altering the magnitude of the power consumed in the respective states as a function of these state parameter values.

[2] In this paper, for power measurement we directly report the current drawn in milli-Amperes (mA). The actual power consumed would be the current drawn multiplied by 3.7V, the voltage supply of the battery. Similarly, for energy we directly report micro Ampere Hours (μAH); the actual energy would be the μAH value multiplied by 3.7V. The smartphone batteries are rated using these metrics and hence are easy to cross reference.

[3] Usually wakelocks are held by framework entities in Android, which control the inactivity timeouts, based on user level policies.

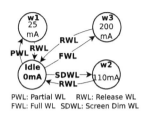

PWL: Partial WL   RWL: Release WL
FWL: Full WL   SDWL: Screen Dim WL

Fig. 1: Wakelock FSM (passion /Android).

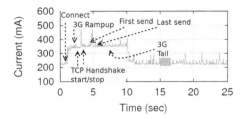

Fig. 2: Send happens right after connect.

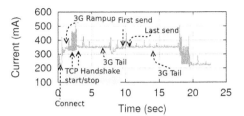

Fig. 3: Send happens 5 seconds after connect.

Table 1: Mobile handsets used throughout the paper.

Name	HTC-	MHz	OS (kernel)
magic	Magic	528	Android 2.0 (Linux 2.6.34)
tytn2	Tytn II	400	WM6.5 (CE5.2)
passion	Passion	1024	Android 2.3 (Linux 2.6.38)

4. Accounting Policies on Smartphones

In this section, we first use an example to show how the above asynchronous power behavior of smartphones poses unique challenges to the third task of energy accounting, *i.e.*, how to attribute energy activities to the responsible program entities. We discuss alternate accounting policies and then present the energy accounting policy used in *eprof*.

4.1 Accounting Policy Challenge: A Simple Example

The accounting policy complications due to the three asynchronous power behavior share the same nature: how to attribute an energy activity that persists beyond the triggering program entity or entities. We focus on the tail energy behavior, to illustrate the complication and design choices.

Consider a simple app that connects (in routine `net connect()`), and uploads data via five sends with 10KB each (in routine `netsend()`), to a server over the 3G network. Figure 2 plots the current draw of passion running Android during the app execution. The app consumes a total of 314 μAH of energy. The moment the connect system call is issued, the 3G radio ramps up [5, 14] power draw for 2.5 seconds before the TCP handshake is started. The rampup consumes 61 μAH (19.5% of the entire app energy). After the handshake which consumes 11 μAH (3.5%), routine `netconnect()` is completed, `netsend()` starts and performs the five sends (which together consumes 55 μAH (17.5%)), and the app is completed. However, even after the app completion, the device continues to draw high power due to the 3G radio staying in the tail power state for 6 seconds, consuming 187 μAH, 59.6% of the total app energy.

Figure 3 plots the power draw of the same app except a single difference, the `netsend()` routine is performed 5 seconds after `netconnect()`. This program consumes 520 μAH (65% more than the original version) with the following energy breakdown: rampup (60 μAH, 11.53%), connect (15 μAH, 2.88%), tail 1 (183 μAH, 35.19%), send (60 μAH, 11.53%), and tail 2 (200 μAH, 38.46%).

The above examples show that the tail energy in Figure 2 would have existed even if the second routine did not exist, and hence intuitively the first routine should be held accountable for the tail energy somehow. One simple policy is to split the tail energy among the two routines either equally or weighted based on the workload generated. Such a policy faces several problems: (1) It is not always easy to define the weights based on the workload generated, *e.g.*, in this app, should the weight assigned to `netconnect()` be 3 handshake packets and to `netsend()` be 5*10KB of packets? (2) This splitting policy becomes more complicated to implement and more obscure in understanding the profiling output in the presence of intermittent component accesses which result in interleaved productive states and tail states. (3) Splitting the tail energy may misinform the developer that if a certain entity, *e.g.*, `netsend()`, is removed, its part of tail energy could be saved.

An alternative accounting policy, termed last-trigger policy, is to account the tail energy to the last entity, out of all the entities, each of which *would have* triggered the tail, *i.e.*, routine `netsend()` in the case of Figure 2. This approach avoids the first two problems above, which makes it not only easier to implement, but more importantly, much easier to understand by the programmer. However, this approach still may misinform the developer that if the last trigger, *e.g.*, `netsend()`, is removed, the tail energy would be removed. In reality, the same amount of tail energy would have been consumed irrespective of whether the last trigger existed. For example, in Figure 2 if `netsend()` did not exist, `netconnect()` would have also been followed by a similar 3G tail.

We also considered other possible policies such as first-trigger, which accounts the tail energy to the first entity, out of all the consecutive entities, each of which *would have* triggered the tail. Such a policy shares with last-trigger in encouraging triggers to draft behind each other to save energy, and in misleading developers that removing the first trigger would remove the tail. Out of the two, last-trigger appears slightly more intuitive; the developer can start with optimizing the last trigger.

Finally, we argue this last "misinforming" problem exists no matter what accounting policy is used. Hence ultimately, for an accounting tool to be informative to the developer, the profiling output needs to make explicit how the energy due to asynchronous power behavior such as tail energy

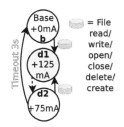 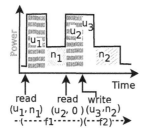

Fig. 4: Sdcard FSM for tytn2 on WM6.   **Fig. 5: Assign energy to last system call.**

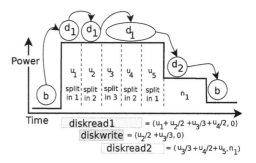

Fig. 6: Splitting energy of a component among concurrent system calls.

is accounted, and the developer needs to understand such asynchronous power behavior to make meaningful use of such energy accounting tools.

4.2 Accounting Policies for Asynchronous Power

Following the above discussion, we adopt the last-trigger policy in *eprof*: always account the energy lingering beyond a program entity due to asynchronous power behavior (*e.g.,* tail energy) to the last entity, out of all the entities that *would have* triggered the power behavior. The policy will be stated explicitly in the profiling output.

4.2.1 Tail Power State

Since tail energy is wasted as the component is not doing any productive work, many potential optimizations (*e.g.,* aggregation [5]) are being studied to reduce tail energy. For this reason, *eprof* explicitly separates tail energy from the rest, and reports an "energy tuple" (u, n), where u and n represent the utilization energy and the tail energy consumption, respectively, in its profiling output.

We illustrate how the accounting policy is applied to the tail power state behavior using an example. Figure 4 shows an example of the tail power state in the FSM power model of sdcard on the tytn2 phone. Any file operation sends sdcard into a high power state $d1$ followed by a tail state $d2$ which continues until 3 seconds of disk inactivity and then sdcard returns to the base state. Figure 5 shows an example containing two entities f1 and f2. Entity f1 invokes the first *read* call which sends the component to state $d1$, consuming u_1 energy, followed by a tail consuming n_1 which is cut short by a *read* call, which again sends the component to $d1$, consuming u_2. Right after entity f1 ends, f2 starts and invokes a *write* call, causing the component to stay in state $d1$, consuming u_3, followed by a tail state consuming n_2. The tail state lasts beyond the completion of f2.

It is clear (u_1, n_1), u_2 and u_3 should be accounted to the first *read* call, second *read* call and the *write* call, respectively. Following the last-trigger policy, n_2 is charged to the last system call before the tail state, *i.e., write*. In summary, the three system calls get energy tuples (u_1, n_1), $(u_2, 0)$ and (u_3, n_2), respectively.

4.2.2 Wakelocks and Exotic Components

WakeLocks and exotic components exhibit similar asynchronous energy drain patterns. Each of them has an on/off switch which when turned on (a wakelock is acquired or GPS/camera is started) starts draining energy and the energy drain stops only when it is switched off (*e.g.,* the wakelock is released). We discuss accounting for wakelocks below. Accounting for exotic components is similar.

Figure 1 shows the FSM that models the power state transitions due to wakelocks on passion running Android. An entity that acquires a wakelock triggers a component into a high power state, which can persist after the entity exits and another entity starts, until the wakelock is released by this other entity. Following the last-trigger policy, the energy consumed by the component during the period when the wakelock was held is attributed to the entity that acquired the wakelock. Accounting this way helps the developer to track "wakelock bugs", an important class of energy bugs in mobile apps [9] due to missing wakelock releases (§7.3).

4.3 Concurrent Accesses

When multiple threads access a component, there can be concurrent system calls issued to the component. Figure 6 shows an example where three threads simultaneously access sdcard for reading and writing files. $diskread1$ triggers a power state change from base to $d1$. While the component is serving this request, two other threads invoke two more requests $diskwrite$ and $diskread2$.

To perform energy accounting, we first apply linear regression inside each productive power state to estimate the total duration that component stays in that state based on the total workload of all system calls. We then divide up the total energy in that state among the multiple system calls as follows: we first estimate the completion time of each system call assuming they have the same rate of making progress, then split the whole duration into intervals, each with a different number of concurrent system calls, and then split the energy consumed in each interval evenly among those system calls. Such a policy is justified as follows. First, we observed using microbenchmarking that the time to complete I/O system calls are roughly proportional to their workload, suggesting the hardware component is mostly fair in carrying out concurrent system calls. Second, smartphone hardware does not export internal information about workload processing order and hence it is difficult to develop a more refined policy.

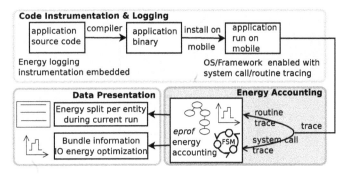

Code Instrumentation & Logging

application source code → compiler → application binary → install on mobile → application run on mobile

Energy logging instrumentation embedded

OS/Framework enabled with system call/routine tracing

Data Presentation

Energy split per entity during current run

Bundle information IO energy optimization

Energy Accounting

eprof energy accounting ← routine trace ← trace ← system call trace

FSM

Fig. 7: *Eprof* architecture overview.

Following the above split policy, the duration while in power state $d1$ is split into five intervals with varying numbers of active system calls, and $d1$ is split evenly within each interval. The tail energy is charged to the last system call served by the component. The final accounting of sdcard energy consumption for the three calls is shown in Figure 6.

4.4 Accounting for High Rate Components

The FSM power model [4] does not cover RAM and Organic LED screen (OLED) since these components are accessed at much higher rates (and hence called high rate components) resulting in high overheads in event based modeling. Traditionally RAM power is modeled using LLC (Last Level Cache) Misses [15, 16], periodically polled from hardware (CPU registers). Power draw of OLED screens is dictated by pixel colors and hence can be modeled by periodically scrapping the screen buffer and computing the energy using sampled pixels [17]. However, the HTC magic does not export LLC Misses information to the kernel, and perf_events [18], the Linux performance counter system which is still new on ARM architectures, does not yet support the HTC passion handset. Also, Google stopped shipping developer phones with OLED screen in 2011 due to a supply shortage [19]. Hence, we leave RAM/OLED accounting as future work.

5. *Eprof* Implementation

We describe *eprof* implementation at the routine granularity. Accounting at the thread and process granularities follows naturally.

5.1 *Eprof* Operations

Figure 7 shows the three components of *eprof*: (1) code instrumentation and logging, (2) power modeling and energy accounting, and (3) profile presentation. In the first phase, the app source code is instrumented for system-call tracing and routine tracing. We also discuss in §5.2 how apps built on top of the Android SDK can be logged without source code. The instrumented binary is then run on the smartphone OS/framework with system call logging enabled, to gather both detailed routine invocation trace and system call trace at runtime. During the second phase, the routine invocation trace is played back while at the same time the system call trace is used to drive the FSM power model to replay the

energy activities. The energy activities are mapped to the routines according to the accounting policy described in §4. Finally, *eprof* outputs the energy profile.

5.2 Implementation

We have implemented *eprof* on two smartphone OSes: Android and Windows Mobile 6.5 (WM6). Due to page limit, we only describe our implementation on Android below.

SDK Routine Tracing. Routing tracing logs routing invocations and the time spent per invocation. Apps written with the Android SDK run inside the Dalvik VM. For such apps, Android provides a routine profiling framework [20] which *at runtime* marks routine boundaries with timestamps and calculates the runtime of each routine. To reduce the overhead of retrieving timestamps, we modified the current profiling framework to only count all caller-callee invocations, and perform periodic sampling to log the routine call stack and the time at each sampled interval, just as in *gprof* [3].

NDK Routine Tracing. Android also provides developers with Native Development Kit (NDK) using which they can run performance critical parts of their apps outside the VM. For the NDK part of apps, we used the *gprof* port of NDK profiler [21] to perform routine tracing, which requires linking with the Android *gprof* library.

System-Call Tracing. System-call tracing logs the time and the call stack of each system call. This is performed in the framework, the bionic C library, and the kernel. First, apps written with SDK invoke both traditional system calls such as network and disk and special framework events, *e.g.*, sensors, location tracking, and camera. We log such system calls by inserting ADB (Android Debugger) logging APIs where they are implemented in the framework code [22] to log the calls (time and parameters) and call stacks. Second, apps written with NDK only use traditional system calls. However, since Arm Linux does not support userspace backtracing from inside the kernel [23], we log the calls and call stacks at the bionic C library interface. Finally, for both SDK and NDK apps, we log CPU (sched.switch) scheduling events in the kernel using Systemtap [24].

Logging without Source Code. In general, a recompile is required after instrumentation for routing tracing. For the evaluation in this paper, we modified the framework to automatically start and stop *eprof* routine and system-call tracing for the SDK part of all apps. This allows us to perform energy profiling without needing a recompile and hence the source code which is often not available (*e.g.*, the Angrybirds app). The source code is still required for the NDK part of apps.

Accounting. The logs collected during an app run are postprocessed for accounting. We extended Traceview [25] in Android SDK, which currently performs runtime accounting, to perform energy accounting and data presentation. We added 3K LOC to the existing 5K LOC in Traceview.

Data Presentation. *Eprof* outputs energy tuple per entity in the sorted order (with inclusive/exclusive energy for hierarchical entities). When routines are the entities, *eprof* be-

Table 2: Apps used throughout the paper.

App	Description	App	Description
Windows Mobile (on tytn2)		Android (on magic)	
sd	Skin Detection [26]	syncdroid	Mobile file sync
lchess	Local Chess [27]	streamer	Photo streaming
pup	Upload photo albums	andoku	Sudoku game [28]
cchess	Cloud Chess (offload)	goOut	Location app
pdf2txt	PDF to text [29]	k9mail	Email Client
pslide	Photo Slide show	wordsrc	Game [28]
fft	speech recog. [30]	andtweet	Twitter client [28]
Android (on passion)			
browser	Google on Browser	cnn	CNN on Browser
fb	Facebook	pup	Photo uploading
ab	AngryBirds	mq	MapQuest
nyt	New York Times app	fchess	Free Chess [31]

comes a call-graph energy profiler; it mimics the output of *gprof* [3] by replacing each time value with a (time, energy) value tuple. It also outputs a breakdown of the total energy consumed into per-component energy consumption.

6. Evaluation

In this section, we compare *eprof*'s accuracy with previous accounting approaches and measure its overhead.

Applications. Table 2 lists the set of 21 apps used in the rest of the paper. Some of them are among the top 10 most popular apps in Android Market while others were downloaded from several open-source projects [26–30].

6.1 Related Work: Previous Accounting Approaches

The energy accounting problem has been previously studied in different context. We summarize the two best known policies proposed: split-time and utilization-based.

The split-time energy accounting scheme simply splits the time into fine-grained time bins, and accounts the energy spent (typically obtained directly from a power meter) in a bin to the sampled running entity (process/thread/routine) in that bin. Powerscope [32, 33] measures power using an external power meter and accounts energy for mobile systems like laptops at the routine granularity using split-time accounting. Li *et al.* [34] use split-time to account OS energy on commodity hardware, using a system-wide cycle accurate power model to estimate instantaneous power consumption. Quanto [35] also uses the split-time policy to measure and account system-wide energy in sensor networks for programmer defined entities.

The recently proposed Cinder [36] and PowerTutor [6, 37] also perform smartphone energy accounting. They differ from *eprof* in several aspects. First, they support processes as the finest accounting granularity. Second, both systems use utilization-based power models to model and account energy of each component to the processes. As shown in [4], utilization-based power models do not capture asynchronous power behavior found in modern smartphones.

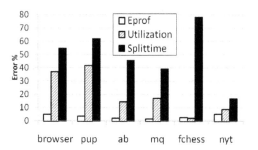

Fig. 8: Accuracy of different accounting policies.

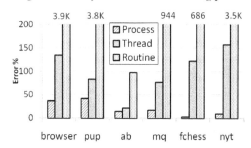

Fig. 9: Accuracy of utilization-based model at different granularities.

6.2 Accounting Accuracy

It is difficult to measure per-entity accounting accuracy since there is no easy way to measure the ground truth in the presence of asynchronous power behavior. We expect the per-entity accounting accuracy of *eprof* to be the same as that of the system-call-based power model it is based on, since the triggers for the power model, system calls, also form the finest granularity among the four program entities that *eprof* profiles (§2). To compare different accounting schemes, we compare their aggregate accounting accuracy: how does the sum of per-entity energy breakdown under different accounting schemes approximate that of the ground truth, *i.e.*, the total energy spent as measured using a power meter [38]? We define accounting "error" as the percentage difference of the sum of all entity energies except process 0 (which does not use any hardware component) with ground truth energy measured.

Figure 8 plots the accounting error of the three schemes, at the process granularity, for a few apps from Table 2 on Android on passion (results are similar for others). We see that the error in *eprof* is under 6% for all apps while that of utilization-based accounting ranges from 3% to 50% and of split-time ranges from 15% to 80%. The higher error for utilization-based accounting is a direct consequence of the error in utilization-based power models [4]. Split-time accounting, which though utilizes direct power meter readings, performs the worst since it accounts most of the energy due to asynchronous power behavior to PID 0 (the null process), which performs no hardware activity and should be attributed zero energy.

For system-wide energy accounting at the thread and the routine granularities, split-time and *eprof* report the same errors as at the process granularity, because split-time is largely oblivious to the accounting granularity as it divides the time into fixed-sized bins and accounts each bin energy to the sampled entity, and *eprof* accounts energy at the system-call level, which is finer-grained than at the routine/thread level. In contrast, utilization-based accounting shows larger error when estimating energy at finer granularities, as shown in Figure 9, since utilization-based power models incur larger errors in finer-grained estimation [4].

6.3 Logging Overhead

Measuring the logging overhead of *eprof* on the smartphone app runtime and energy consumption is tricky since smartphone apps are interactive, *i.e.,* their execution involve periods of inactivities waiting for human input. To prevent such inactivity periods from diluting the measured overhead, for each app in Table 2, we isolated its core part performed in-between human interactions in calculating the logging overhead, *e.g.,* the code in lchess that corresponds to computing each `computer_move`, in between the `moves` made by the human. The logging overhead of *eprof* falls between 2-15% for the apps on WM6 and between 4-11% for the apps on Android on the two handsets, out of which about 1-8% is due to system call tracing alone. Microbenchmarking reveals that logging each entry in *eprof* (syscall or routine) consumes $2.5 \pm 0.5 \mu s$ on passion (1GHz CPU), including $1.5 \pm 0.2 \mu s$ overhead of `getClock()`, and consumes $30 \mu s$ on tytn2 (400MHz CPU) with $10 \mu s$ for reading the clock. Since the logging only incurs overhead on CPU and memory, the energy overhead for logging is the runtime overhead multiplied by the CPU power, which comes down to 0.69-12.99% for the apps on WM6 and between 0.40-7.35% for the apps on Android. Finally, the logging rate (including system call tracing) for the apps varies between 60-70 KB/s.

7. Applications

We report on our experience with using *eprof* to understand the energy consumption of the 21 apps in Table 2. Due to page limit, we first briefly summarize the energy bottleneck of all the apps identified by *eprof*, and then present an in-depth analysis of the most popular 5 apps.

7.1 Identifying Energy Hotspots

Figure 10 shows the percentage time and energy of the energy hotspot routine in each of the 14 apps in Table 2, listed under WM (tytn2) and Android (magic). Already, this summary exposes several interesting observations about the energy consumption of these apps. (1) There is a stark contrast in the percentage runtime and the percentage energy drain for some of the hotspot routines, *e.g.,* goOut spends over 20% of its energy on GPS routine `attachlistener` which runs for under 3% of runtime. (2) The energy consumption behavior of two versions of the same app differ significantly. Specifically, lchess which runs purely on mobile consumes 30% of its energy in checking the human

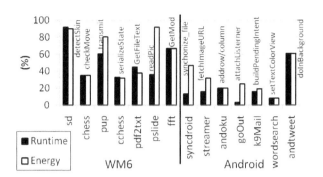

Fig. 10: Percentage runtime and energy consumption of energy hotspots.

Table 3: Session description for the apps used in case study.

App	Session Description
browser	User opens browser, performs a Google search, scrolls the HTML page and closes the app.
angrybirds	User plays a full game of AngryBirds hitting all three birds and then closes the app.
fchess	User plays two moves of chess game with computer.
nytimes	User opens the NYTimes app, app downloads and displays contents, user scrolls the front page.
mapquest	User starts app, app finds location, fetches map tiles and renders, user then clicks "gas station" button.

move, while cchess spends 27% energy packing and unpacking program state for offloading the computation to the cloud (as in [39, 40]). (3) The profiling results of andoku and wordsearch, each containing thousands of routines, reveal that their energy bottleneck routines are for building the UI, *i.e.,* `setTextColorView()` and `AddRow()`, respectively.

7.2 Case Studies

We now present an in-depth analysis of 5 popular apps running on Android on passion. All the apps were run on 3G; we skip the WiFi runs due to page limit. Table 3 describes the session scenario of each app used in the case study. Table 4 summarizes the statistics of the profiling runs and where most of the energy is spent in these apps as identified by *eprof*. It shows that running these apps for about half a minute can invoke 29–47 threads, many of which are third-party modules, and 200K–6M routine calls. The complexity of these apps is daunting; without *eprof*, it would be difficult to understand their energy profile. Overall, the about 30-second run of these apps drain 0.35%-0.75% of a full battery charge, a rate which could discharge the entire battery in a couple of hours.

7.2.1 Android Browser – Google Search vs. CNN

Google search. The Android browser comes with Android and is arguably one of the most frequently used apps on Android. We first profiled a 30-second run of the browser for one dominant usage: Google search, where the user opens the browser, performs a Google search over 3G, and closes

Table 4: Summary of energy drain of 5 popular apps.

App	Run-time	#Routine calls (#Threads)	% Battery	3rd-Party Modules Used	*Where is the energy spent inside an app?*
browser	30s	1M (34)	0.35%	-	38% HTTP; 5% GUI; 16% user tracking; 25% TCP cond.
angrybirds	28s	200K (47)	0.37%	Flurry[7],Khronos[41]	20% game rendering; 45% user tracking; 28% TCP cond.
fchess	33s	742K (37)	0.60%	AdWhirl[42]	50% advertisement; 20% GUI; 20% AI; 2% screen touch
nytimes	41s	7.4M (29)	0.75%	Flurry[7],JSON[43]	65% database building; 15% user tracking; 18% TCP cond.
mapquest	29s	6M (43)	0.60%	SHW[44],AOL,JSON[43]	28% map tracking; 20% map download; 27% rendering

the browser. The Google search page triggers the GPS to determine user location. The browser process consumes a total of 2000 μAH out of which about 53%, 31%, and 16% are spent in CPU, 3G, and GPS, respectively.

The browser forks a total of 34 threads, including 4 http worker threads, a main thread, and a Webviewcore thread besides GC (garbage collector), DNS resolver, and other threads. Less than 500KB of data is transfered over 3G. Figure 11(a) plots the split of the total browser energy among different threads with each thread's energy consumption further split by phone components. We gain the following insight into how the energy is spent in the browser. (1) Thread http0 consumes the most energy (28%), 24% of which is spent in 3G tail. This thread performs the bulk of http I/O (request and response). Thread http1 consumes another 10% energy. Together, the two http threads consume 38% energy. (2) Two generic Android threads, HeapWorker and IdleReaper, consume 14% and 10% energy respectively. Most of their energy are spent in 3G tails as follows. IdleReaper reaps idle TCP connections after a configured timeout, each of which leads to a 3G tail. HeapWorker cleans up each network connection upon app exit by sending a TCP FIN packet, which also often leads to an isolated 3G tail. The two threads are used in any apps that access the web, and we term them *TCP conditioning* utilities. (3) Threads main and Webviewcore are responsible for loading the browser and building its GUI. The main thread consumes 10% energy which is entirely CPU. Webviewcore, which also starts GPS to track user location, consumes 24% of the total energy, with 11% and 5% spent in GPS and GPS tails, respectively. Webviewcore spends most of its energy (24%) in routine `JavaWebCoreJavaBridge.handleMsg()` (18%).

To understand where the energy is spent at the routine level, we plot in Figure 11(b) *per-routine* energy breakdown for a few selected routines. The energy includes that of callee routines to better capture the whole function performed by the routine. The per-routine profiling clearly shows the energy breakdown among the 3 major steps of a Google search. (1) Routine `android/net /http/Connection.processRequests()` which processes network requests on behalf of the browser and hence involves networking, consumes 35% of the browser energy (7% in CPU for processing http). (2) Processing compressed http response after downloading consumes 15% energy, out of which 5% is spent in decompressing the compressed html response (routine `java/util/zip/GZIPInputStream`

`.read()`). (3) Routines from class `android/view/ViewRoot.java` which renders GUI consume about 5% energy.

Browsing a CNN page. When the user surfs CNN, the browser spawns 30 threads, and consumes a total of 2400 μAH out of which about 40%, 60%, and 0% are spent in CPU, 3G and GPS, respectively. Figures 12(a)-12(b) again plot the per-thread and per-routine energy split, which draw contrast with the Google search scenario. (1) Surfing the CNN page results in higher data download (1200 KB) and invokes four different http threads to share downloading and parsing, which consume 26%, 9%, 11% and 8% energy, respectively, for a total of 54%, higher than the 38% by http0 and http1 in Google search. (2) Thread IdleReaper, which reaps idle TCP connections through routine `IdleCache .IdleReaper.run()`, consumes more energy (15%) than in Google search due to reaping more sockets. (3) Webviewcore consumes only 10% energy in CPU, as it no longer starts GPS to track user location.

These profiling results of the Android browser suggest that TCP *conditioning* (reaping and proper shutdown) over 3G can waste significant energy in 3G tails. We discuss strategies to reduce this energy drain in §8.3.

7.2.2 AngryBirds

We next profiled one of the most popular smartphone games, downloaded over 50M times from Android Market, angrybirds. In the profile run, the user plays a single instance of the game over 3G, and the app spawns 35 threads. The "GLThread" thread handles gameplay and the touch events, and invokes the third-party Khronos EGL interface [41] to paint the screen for game events. It also comes bundled with Flurry [7], a third-party mobile data aggregator and ad generator. Flurry runs as a separate thread, collects various statistics about the phone including its location, OS, and software version, and uploads the data to its server. Later, it downloads and renders ads during gameplay.

Figures 13(a)-13(b) show the energy breakdown of the top 5 threads and routines, which provides the following insight. (1) The core part of the app, thread GLThread, though CPU intensive, consumes only 18% of the total app energy. Within the thread, the Khronos API consumes 9% energy over 1K calls made to the API routine, and the rovio renderer spends another 9% energy in over 1K calls. Rendering the ad consumes 1% energy. (2) The Flurry thread consumes most of the energy (45%). Within the thread, GPS location tracking consumes 15% energy and its tail consumes addi-

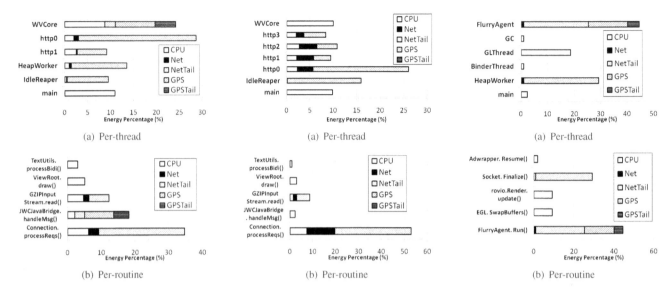

Fig. 11: Google search on browser.   Fig. 12: CNN on browser.   Fig. 13: AngryBirds.

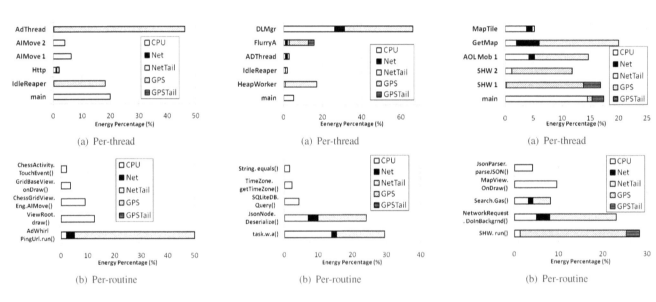

Fig. 14: Free Chess.   Fig. 15: NYTimes.   Fig. 16: MapQuest.

tional 4% energy; collecting the handset information consumes less than 1% energy (CPU only); uploading the information and downloading the ads consume 1% energy with only under 2KB data transfered over 3G; but the 3G tail consumes 24% energy. (3) When the app is closed, thread HeapWorker performs cleanup, closing an unclosed socket as part of the finalize method (Figure 13(b)), which creates a 3G tail consuming 28% of the app energy.

7.2.3 Free Chess

We next profiled the most popular free chess game [31] on Android Market, downloaded over 10M times. Like angry-birds, this app downloads ads over 3G which consumes most of its energy. It spawns 37 threads during the 33-second

profile run. The main thread is responsible for the game-play, AdThread fetches ads over the network, and IdleReaper reaps remote server TCP connections after timeout.

Figures 14(a)-14(b) show a clear four-way energy break-down. (1) AdThread which runs third-party AdLibrary AdWhirl [42] through routine com/adwhirl/PingUrl .run(), consumes 50% energy, almost entirely spent in 3G tail. (2) The main thread which paints the board consumes only 20% energy entirely in CPU through routines android /view/ViewRoot.draw() and uk/co/aifactory/fireball /GridBaseView.onDraw(). The user plays 2 moves which are responded by the computer's AIMoves. (3) The AIMoves are computed through two different threads (AIMove1 and AIMove2), each calling routine uk/co/aifactory/chessfree

`/ChessGridView.Eng.AIMove()`, consuming a total of 10% energy. (4) IdleReaper consumes 18% energy, again almost entirely in 3G tail.

The above energy profiling provides an important insight: free apps like fchess and angrybirds spend under 25-35% of their energy on gameplay, but over 65-75% on user tracking, uploading user information, and downloading ads.

7.2.4 NYTimes

We next profiled the Android app nytimes which has been downloaded over 10M times and is representative of the family of publisher provided viewing apps. The app spawns 29 threads during the profile run to fetch news and display the news. It uses Proguard [45] to obfuscate its class and method names. As a result, understanding *eprof* output was slightly complicated.

Figure 15(a) shows a clear four-way energy breakdown. (1) The main thread which activates GUI and displays the news downloaded, consumes only 5.2% energy. (2) The DownloadManager thread consumes the bulk of the app energy (65%). It downloads about 1MB of data over 3G and stores it in a local SQL database. Interestingly, we observe after the main thread finished displaying the news, until when the app consumed only 25% of its total energy, DownloadManager continues to utilize CPU and network, draining the remaining 75% energy. (3) Like angrybirds, nytimes also runs Flurry consuming 16% of the app energy. (4) Heapworker consumes 15% energy, again mostly in 3G tail.

Figure 15(b) shows the energy split for the top 3 energy consuming routines inside DownloadManager. The app spends 30% of its energy in routine `task.w.a()`, which has an obfuscated name and hence we could not infer its function, 24% in deserializing the fetched content (Jackson JSON library), and 7% in the SQL database.

7.2.5 MapQuest

Finally we profiled the MapQuest location tracking app, which is representative of the family of location-oriented search apps. Upon starting, the app locates user location using the third-party SkyhookWireless (SHW) [44] engine, downloads and deserializes (using Jackson JSON [43]) map tiles, and renders the map. The user then searches for gas stations nearby. The app consumes a total of 3600 μAH energy, split as 28%, 42%, and 30% among CPU, 3G and GPS, respectively. Figures 16(a)-16(b) show that SHW consumes 29% energy via two threads through routine `SkyHook.run()`, the main thread consumes 18% energy performing GUI and map rendering (via routine `MapView.OnDraw()` and JSON parsing), and routine `search.gas()`, invoked when the user clicks the gas station search button, consumes 8% of the app energy, 4% of which is spent in its own 3G tail.

The energy breakdown reveals that the ratios of 3G and GPS energy over their tails differ drastically: 3G spends 82% in its tail while GPS spends only 15% in its tail. The cause of such different tail energy footprint is the way these components are used. GPS is used for continuous tracking and is typically turned on once to start tracking, and turned off to stop tracking, generating one GPS tail. Network transfers are often performed via intermittent sending/receiving small amount of data, incurring many tail periods in between.

7.3 Detecting Energy Bugs

We show how *eprof* helps to find an instance of the class of wakelock energy bugs [9] in FaceBook (FB). As discussed in §3, apps with background services typically use the wakelock acquire/release APIs exposed by the smartphone OS to keep the phone awake, *e.g.,* to perform intermittent I/O activities. A wakelock energy bug happens when a wakelock is held longer than necessary due to a missing lock release.

`facebook.katana.HomeActivity` is one of the main activities of the FB app. In a typical run of the app, the user launches the app, HomeActivity downloads and displays the FB home page, while the user navigates. When using *eprof* to profile a 30-second run of the FB app (v1.3.0, released Oct 2010), which spawned 50 threads, including background services, with over 2M routing calls, and consumed a total of 1200 μAH energy, we observed from the per-routine profiling output of *eprof* that routine `com/facebook/katana/service/FacebookService.onStart()` which starts the background service consumed 25% of the app energy, out of which 18% was attributed to routine `com/facebook/katana/binding/AppSession.acquireWakeLock()`. This much energy due to a wakelock is suspiciously high and is typically a symptom of wakelock bugs. A close look at the call-graph output of *eprof* shows the service routine never called the release API to release the wakelock until the app completion. Apparently the wakelock held by the app continued to drain power even after the app termination, by not allowing the CPU to sleep.

We decompiled the FB installer to Java source code using ded [46], and confirmed that indeed the said routine acquired the wakelock and never released the wakelock due to a programming error. FB fixed the bug in its next release (v1.3.1) which we verified as by inserting a release call of the wakelock as indicated by *eprof*.

8. Optimizing I/O Energy using Bundles

Our experience with profiling popular apps using *eprof* reveals several key observations about the energy consumption of modern smartphone apps. The observations motivate us to propose a new, aggregate accounting presentation called I/O *energy bundle*, which is at a higher level than the default per-entity output of *eprof*, yet more concisely captures *where the energy is spent in a smartphone app and more importantly, why?* Such a presentation offers more direct help to the developer in optimizing the app energy.

8.1 Observations

Our extensive experience with profiling popular apps using *eprof* in §7 reveals the following key observations.
(1) I/O consumes the most energy. Most of the energy in an app is spent in accessing I/O components, and tail energy

Table 5: Energy breakdown summary per app.

App	Total I/O Energy	Bundles	#I/O Routines /total routines
Handset:tytn2 running WM6.5			
pslide	92%	3 (3 Disk)	2/21
pup	57%	3 (3 NET)	3/32
Handset:magic running Android			
syncdroid	50%	4 (1 NET, 3 DISK)	8/0.9K
streamer	31%	3 (3 NET)	4/1.1K
Handset:passion running Android			
browser	69%	3 (2 Net, 1 GPS)	5/3.4K
angrybirds	80%	4 (3 NET, 1 GPS)	5/2.2K
fchess	75%	2 (2 NET)	7/3.7K
nytimes	67%	2 (1 NET, 1 GPS)	16/6.8K
mapquest	72%	3 (2 NET, 1 GPS)	14/7.1K
pup	70%	1 (1 NET)	3/1.1K

typically accounts for the largest fraction of the I/O energy. CPU consumes a small fraction of the app energy, most of which is spent in building up the GUI of the app. The second column of Table 5 shows that most apps spend 50-90% of their energy in I/O.

(2) I/O energy is spent in a few bundles. We observe that apps typically consume I/O energy in a few, distinct lumps. Within each lump, an I/O component actively and continuously consumes power, *i.e.*, it stays in a high power state or the tail power state. For example, Figure 2 shows a lump which consists of several network events – a connect and 5 sends which together drive the 3G FSM from the base state to active states, and back to the base state. The 3G energy spent in the lump consists of ramp-up energy (for connect), energy consumed for TCP handshake and sends, and tail energy. Similarly, in browser performing a Google search (§7.2), there are two overlapping I/O lumps, one of 3G consisting of network connects and sends by the http threads, and the other of GPS consisting of GPS start/stop.

We define an I/O *energy bundle* as a continuous period of an I/O component actively consuming power, which corresponds to the duration in traversing from one instance of the base power state to the next in the component's power FSM. Table 5 (third column) shows that the high I/O energy of apps is typically spread across very few (1 to 4) bundles.

(3) Very few routines perform I/O. We further observe a stark contrast between the way the CPU and I/O components are utilized by smartphone apps: CPU usage is typically split between thousands of routines of an app, though with varying amount, whereas I/O activities arise from very few routines, called by many callers. The intuition behind this finding is that modular programming dictates implementing a few generic routines to perform I/O activities, rather than dispersing them throughout the code. For example, in event based I/O programming with *select()*, the routine containing the select loop performs nearly all the network I/O of the app. In MapQuest, routine `runRequest()` in `com/mapquest/android/util/HttpUtil.java` per-

forms all the HTTP requests. Table 5 (last column) shows that the number of routines performing I/O versus the total number of routines called by each app (on Android this includes framework routines called by the app). We observe that very few routines, between 4 to 8, are responsible for driving I/O components. MapQuest and NYTimes show higher numbers as third-party threads perform their own I/O.

8.2 Bundle Presentation

The above three observations reveal a key insight into how energy is spent in an app: I/O energy accounts for the bulk of an app's energy, and it arises in a few bundles, each of which involves a few I/O performing routines. This insight suggests that a more direct way of helping a developer to understand and optimize the energy consumption of an app is to focus on its I/O energy bundles. We thus propose a bundle-centric accounting presentation which consists of an FSM of the I/O component for each bundle during the app execution, annotated with the relevant routines triggered during that bundle. We show in our case study below that one FSM often captures multiple occurrences of identical bundles.

The bundle presentation is generated as follows. For each bundle captured during the app execution, the productive power states of the FSM of the component are first annotated with the syscall events and hence routines that drove the FSM to those states. Since very few routines are responsible for I/O activities, it is easy to visualize this small set of routines in the annotated FSM. Next, for each instance the component spends in the tail state, we annotate the tail state with the routines called by the app during that period, including routines that use other components, usually CPU. Since the app can call several (possibly thousands) routines during a tail state, we only include the top three most time-consuming routines during the tail state.

8.3 Case Studies

Now understanding the I/O energy of an app boils down to two questions: why are there so many bundles and why is each bundle so long? We have used the bundle accounting presentation to quickly gain insights to these questions and consequently hints on how to optimize the I/O energy of nearly all the apps in Table 5. Due to page limit, we present our experience with four apps below.

8.3.1 Why is a bundle Long?

Pup. Figure 17 shows the bundle presentation for pup during a 30-second app run, which consists of a single 3G bundle that lasts 25 seconds, consuming 70% of the app energy. The bundle presentation clearly shows *why* the bundle consumes 70% energy. It shows that once one photo is sent (in Net High state), the FSM returns to the 3G tail state, during which time it reads the next photo, computes a hash for it, and again uploads it over the network. The app performs CPU computation during the 3G tail which elongates the 3G tail; the tail could have been shorter if the app uploaded the next photo sooner. Further, the above interleaving of network and computation activities happens three times. Such

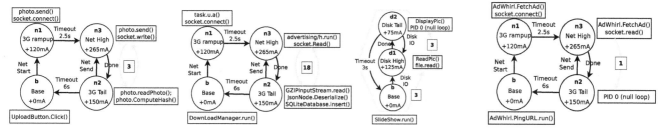

| Fig. 17: Bundles in Pup. | Fig. 18: Bundles in NYTimes. | Fig. 19: Bundles in PSlide. | Fig. 20: A bundle in FChess. |

information gives the programmer the hint that the app's I/O energy can be cut down by aggregating network activities which would reduce the three 3G tails into one.

NYTimes. Figure 18 shows the single 3G bundle of DownloadManager thread. Similarly as pup, this bundle performs periodic I/O and computation 18 times to build its database. In each iteration, it reads one chunk of data and stores it into its database after deserializing.

8.3.2 Why Are There So Many bundles ?

Pslide. Figure 19 shows three similar looking bundles during the app run. Routine `ReadPic()` reads a photo from sdcard which triggers sdcard into a high power state followed by the tail state consuming 75mA. During the tail state, the app displays the photo and sleeps for 5 seconds, during which (after 3 seconds) the FSM returns to the base state. This process is repeated three times. The bundle presentation shows that the three separate bundles waste three tail energies. The three bundles could be merged into one which incurs only one tail by aggregating the reading of sdcard photos.

FChess. Figure 20 shows the first bundle where app component Adwhirl [42] fetches ads over 3G. Once the ad is fetched and displayed, the thread goes to sleep and the 3G FSM returns to tail. The second bundle (not shown) involving IdleReaper and its 3G tail (§7.2.3) can be avoided if this thread cleans up its TCP connections.

8.3.3 Optimizing I/O Energy

The case studies above show how bundle analysis gives hints on restructuring the source code to minimize the number of bundles and the length of each bundles. For the apps for which we had source code, we reorganized the code structure by following these hints. Rerunning the restructured apps shows pslide, pup, streamer, and syncdroid reduced their total energy by 65%, 27%, 23% and 20%, respectively,

9. Related Work

Application profilers. Performance profiling is a long studied topic. Running time profiling has been proposed at the application level [3, 47, 48] to monitor the call graph trace and estimate the running time of routines, for object oriented languages [49, 50], and at the kernel level [51]. *Eprof* is concerned with profiling energy consumption which is not linear as time. Several energy profiling schemes have been proposed for desktops [34], for mobile devices [52], and for sensor networks [53]. These schemes estimate the energy consumption of a routine based on strict time boundaries of the

routines and hence can incur significant error when applied to profiling smartphone apps (§6).

Characterizing smartphone energy consumption. Carroll and Heiser [54] measured the power consumed by different phone components under different application loads by hardwiring individual power meters to different phone components. Shye *et al.* [55] and Zhang *et al.* [6] built linear regression based models for modeling app level power consumption and profiled several apps including Google Map and Browser. All these work measure per-app or per-component energy drain on smartphones. *Eprof* is capable of measuring intra-app energy consumption and gives insights into energy breakdown per thread and per routine of the app.

Mobile energy optimization. Finally, a number of specialized energy saving techniques on mobiles have been proposed, *e.g.,* for specific applications on mobile systems [56, 57], for a specific protocol [58, 59], via offloading [39, 40], and via delaying communication [60]. *Eprof* is a general-purpose fine-grained energy profiler that directly assists an app developer in the app energy optimization cycle.

10. Conclusion

This paper makes three contributions towards answering the ultimate question faced by millions of smartphone users and developers today: *Where is the energy spent inside my app?* We first present *eprof*, the first fine-grained energy profiler for smartphone apps and its implementation on Android and Windows Mobile. *Eprof* adopts the last-trigger accounting policy to most intuitively capture asynchronous power behavior of modern smartphone components in mapping energy activities to the responsible program entities. We then present an extensive, in-depth study using *eprof* to gain insight of energy usage of smartphone apps using a suite of 21 apps. Finally, we propose bundles, a new presentation of energy accounting, that helps app developers to quickly understand and optimize the I/O energy drain of their apps.

Eprof opens up new avenues for studying smartphone energy consumption. It can be readily used to compare the energy efficiency of different implementations of the same app (*e.g.,* Firefox vs. the Android browser). The energy accounting engine of *eprof* can be combined with compiler techniques such as static analysis to develop energy optimizers that automate the process of restructuring app source code to reduce their energy footprint, and with the OS scheduler to develop energy-aware process scheduling algorithms.

Acknowledgments

We thank the reviewers for their helpful comments, and especially our shepherd, George Candea, whose detailed feedback significantly improved the paper and its presentation. Abhinav Pathak was supported in part by a 2011 Intel PhD Fellowship.

References

[1] "Mobile app internet recasts the software and services landscape." URL: http://tinyurl.com/5s3hhx6

[2] "Apples app store downloads top 10 billion." URL: http://www.apple.com/pr/library/2011/01/22appstore.html

[3] S. L. Graham, P. B. Kessler, and M. K. McKusick, "gprof: A call graph execution profiler," in *Proc. of PLDI*, 1982.

[4] A. Pathak, Y. C. Hu, M. Zhang, P. Bahl, and Y.-M. Wang, "Fine-grained power modeling for smartphones using system-call tracing," in *Proc. of EuroSys*, 2011.

[5] N. Balasubramanian and et.al., "Energy consumption in mobile phones: a measurement study and implications for network applications," in *Proc of IMC*, 2009.

[6] L. Zhang and et.al., "Accurate Online Power Estimation and Automatic Battery Behavior Based Power Model Generation for Smartphones," in *Proc. of CODES+ISSS*, 2010.

[7] "Flurry: Mobile analytics." URL: http://www.flurry.com/

[8] "Android powermanager: Wakelocks." URL: http://developer.android.com/reference/android/os/PowerManager.html

[9] A. Pathak, Y. C. Hu, and M. Zhang, "Bootstrapping energy debugging for smartphones: A first look at energy bugs in mobile devices," in *Proc. of Hotnets*, 2011.

[10] "Facebook 1.3 not releasing partial wake lock." URL: http://geekfor.me/news/facebook-1-3-wakelock/

[11] "Email 2.3 app keeps awake when no data connection is available." URL: http://www.google.com/support/forum/p/Google+Mobile/thread?tid=53bfe134321358e8

[12] "Email application partial wake lock." URL: http://code.google.com/p/android/issues/detail?id=9307

[13] "Using a locationlistener is generally unsafe for leaving a permanent partial_wake_lock." URL: http://code.google.com/p/android/issues/detail?id=4333

[14] F. Qian, Z. Wang, A. Gerber, Z. Mao, S. Sen, and O. Spatscheck, "Characterizing radio resource allocation for 3g networks," in *Proc of IMC*, 2010.

[15] A. Kansal, F. Zhao, J. Liu, N. Kothari, and A. Bhattacharya, "Virtual machine power metering and provisioning," in *Proc. of SOCC*, 2010.

[16] F. Rawson, "MEMPOWER: A simple memory power analysis tool set," *IBM Austin Research Laboratory*, 2004.

[17] M. Dong, Y. Choi, and L. Zhong, "Power modeling of graphical user interfaces on OLED displays," in *Proc. of DAC*, 2009.

[18] "perf: Linux profiling with performance counters." URL: https://perf.wiki.kernel.org/

[19] "Android debug class." URL: http://en.wikipedia.org/wiki/Nexus_One#Hardware

[20] "Android debug class." URL: http://developer.android.com/reference/android/os/Debug.html

[21] "Android ndk profiler." URL: http://code.google.com/p/android-ndk-profiler/

[22] "Cyanogenmod." URL: http://www.cyanogenmod.com/

[23] "Introducing utrace." URL: http://lwn.net/Articles/224772/

[24] "System tap." URL: http://sourceware.org/systemtap/

[25] "Profiling with traceview." URL: http://developer.android.com/guide/developing/debugging/debugging-tracing.html

[26] "Skin recognition in c#." URL: http://www.codeproject.com/KB/cs/Skin_RecC_.aspx

[27] "C# micro chess (huo chess)." URL: http://archive.msdn.microsoft.com/cshuochess

[28] "Open source Android app." URL: http://en.wikipedia.org/wiki/List_of_open_source_Android_applications

[29] "itextsharp." URL: http://itextsharp.sourceforge.net/

[30] "Exocortex.dsp: C# complex number and fft library for microsoft .net." URL: http://www.exocortex.org/dsp/

[31] "Chess free: Ai factory limited." URL: https://market.android.com/details?id=uk.co.aifactory.chessfree

[32] J. Flinn and M. Satyanarayanan, "Powerscope: A tool for profiling the energy usage of mobile applications," in *Proc. of WMCSA*, 1999.

[33] F. Jason and S. Mahadev, "Energy-aware adaptation for mobile applications," in *Proc. of SOSP*, 1999.

[34] T. Li and L. John, "Run-time modeling and estimation of operating system power consumption," *SIGMETRICS*, 2003.

[35] R. Fonseca, P. Dutta, P. Levis, and I. Stoica, "Quanto: Tracking energy in networked embedded systems," in *OSDI*, 2008.

[36] A. Roy, S. M. Rumble, R. Stutsman, P. Levis, D. Mazieres, and N. Zeldovich, "Energy management in mobile devices with the Cinder operating system," in *Proc. of EuroSys*, 2011.

[37] "Power monitor for Android." URL: http://powertutor.org/

[38] "Monsoon power monitor." URL: http://www.msoon.com/LabEquipment/PowerMonitor/

[39] E. Cuervo, B. Aruna, D. ki Cho, A. Wolman, S. Saroiu, R. Chandra, and P. Bahl, "Maui: Making smartphones last longer with code offload," in *MobiSys*, 2010.

[40] B.-G. Chun and P. Maniatis, "Augmented Smartphone Applications Through Clone Cloud Execution ," in *HotOs*, 2009.

[41] "Khronos: Egl interface." URL: http://www.khronos.org/

[42] "Adwhirl by admod." URL: https://www.adwhirl.com/

[43] "Jackson: Json processor." URL: http://jackson.codehaus.org/

[44] "Skyhook: Location positioning, context and intelligence." URL: http://www.skyhookwireless.com/

[45] "Android proguard." URL: http://developer.android.com/guide/developing/tools/proguard.html

[46] "Decompiling apps." URL: http://siis.cse.psu.edu/ded/

[47] G. C. Murphy, D. Notkin, W. G. Griswold, and E. S. Lan, "An empirical study of static call graph extractors," *ACM Trans. Softw. Eng. Methodol.*, vol. 7, April 1998.

[48] J. Spivey, "Fast, accurate call graph profiling," *Software: Practice and Experience*, 2004.

[49] M. Dmitriev, "Profiling Java applications using code hotswapping and dynamic call graph revelation," in *Proceedings of the 4th International Workshop on Software and Performance*. ACM, 2004, pp. 139–150.

[50] D. Grove, G. DeFouw, J. Dean, and C. Chambers, "Call graph construction in object-oriented languages," *ACM SIGPLAN Notices*, vol. 32, no. 10, pp. 108–124, 1997.

[51] "Oprofile." URL: http://oprofile.sourceforge.net/news/

[52] K. Asanovic and K. Koskelin, "EProf: an energy profiler for the iPAQ," MS Thesis, MIT 2004.

[53] T. Stathopoulos, D. McIntire, and W. Kaiser, "The energy endoscope: Real-time detailed energy accounting for wireless sensor nodes," in *IPSN*, 2008.

[54] A. Carroll and G. Heiser, "An analysis of power consumption in a smartphone," in *Proc. of USENIX ATC*, 2010.

[55] A. Shye, B. Scholbrock, and G. Memik, "Into the wild: studying real user activity patterns to guide power optimizations for mobile architectures," in *Proc. of MICRO*, 2009.

[56] Y. Wang, J. Lin, M. Annavaram, Q. Jacobson, J. Hong, B. Krishnamachari, and N. Sadeh, "A framework of energy efficient mobile sensing for automatic user state recognition," in *Proc. of Mobisys*, 2009.

[57] S. Kang, J. Lee, H. Jang, H. Lee, Y. Lee, S. Park, T. Park, and J. Song, "Seemon: scalable and energy-efficient context monitoring framework for sensor-rich mobile environments," in *Proc. of Mobisys*, 2008.

[58] Y. Agarwal, R. Chandra, A. Wolman, P. Bahl, K. Chin, and R. Gupta, "Wireless wakeups revisited: energy management for voip over wi-fi smartphones," in *Proc. of Mobisys*, 2007.

[59] F. Qian, Z. Wang, A. Gerber, Z. Mao, S. Sen, and O. Spatscheck, "Profiling resource usage for mobile applications: a cross-layer approach," in *Proc. of Mobisys*, 2011.

[60] M. Ra, J. Paek, A. Sharma, R. Govindan, M. Krieger, and M. Neely, "Energy-delay tradeoffs in smartphone applications," in *Proc. of Mobisys*, 2010.

Energy Efficiency for Large-Scale MapReduce Workloads with Significant Interactive Analysis

Yanpei Chen, Sara Alspaugh, Dhruba Borthakur*, Randy Katz

University of California, Berkeley, *Facebook

(ychen2, alspaugh, randy)@eecs.berkeley.edu, dhruba@fb.com

Abstract

MapReduce workloads have evolved to include increasing amounts of time-sensitive, interactive data analysis; we refer to such workloads as *MapReduce with Interactive Analysis* (MIA). Such workloads run on large clusters, whose size and cost make energy efficiency a critical concern. Prior works on MapReduce energy efficiency have not yet considered this workload class. Increasing hardware utilization helps improve efficiency, but is challenging to achieve for MIA workloads. These concerns lead us to develop BEEMR (Berkeley Energy Efficient MapReduce), an energy efficient MapReduce workload manager motivated by empirical analysis of real-life MIA traces at Facebook. The key insight is that although MIA clusters host huge data volumes, the interactive jobs operate on a small fraction of the data, and thus can be served by a small pool of dedicated machines; the less time-sensitive jobs can run on the rest of the cluster in a batch fashion. BEEMR achieves 40-50% energy savings under tight design constraints, and represents a first step towards improving energy efficiency for an increasingly important class of datacenter workloads.

Categories and Subject Descriptors   D.4.7 [*Organization and Design*]: Distributed systems; D.4.8 [*Performance*]: Operational analysis

Keywords   MapReduce, energy efficiency.

1.   Introduction

Massive computing clusters are increasingly being used for data analysis. The sheer scale and cost of these clusters make it critical to improve their operating efficiency, including energy. Energy costs are a large fraction of the total cost of ownership of datacenters [6, 24]. Consequently, there is a concerted effort to improve energy efficiency for Internet datacenters, encompassing government reports [52], standardization efforts [50], and research projects in both industry and academia [7, 16, 19, 27–29, 32, 33, 43, 48].

Approaches to increasing datacenter energy efficiency depend on the workload in question. One option is to increase machine utilization, i.e., increase the amount of work done per unit energy. This approach is favored by large web search companies such as Google, whose machines have persistently low utilization and waste considerable energy [5]. Clusters implementing this approach would service a mix of interactive and batch workloads [14, 35, 40], with the interactive services handling the external customer queries [32], and batch processing building the data structures that support the interactive services [15]. This strategy relies on predictable diurnal patterns in web query workloads, using latency-insensitive batch processing drawn from an "infinite queue of low-priority work" to smooth out diurnal variations, to keep machines at high utilization [5, 14, 40].

This paper focuses on an alternate use case—what we call *MapReduce with Interactive Analysis (MIA)* workloads. MIA workloads contain interactive services, traditional batch processing, and large-scale, latency-sensitive processing. The last component arises from human data analysts interactively exploring large data sets via ad-hoc queries, and subsequently issuing large-scale processing requests once they find a good way to extract value from the data [9, 26, 34, 54]. Such human-initiated requests have flexible but not indefinite execution deadlines.

MIA workloads require a very different approach to energy-efficiency, one that focuses on decreasing the amount of energy used to service the workload. As we will show by analyzing traces of a front-line MIA cluster at Facebook, such workloads have arrival patterns beyond the system's control. This makes MIA workloads unpredictable: new data sets, new types of processing, and new hardware are added rapidly over time, as analysts collect new data and discover new ways to analyze existing data [9, 26, 34, 54]. Thus, increasing utilization is insufficient: First, the workload is dominated by human-initiated jobs. Hence, the cluster must be provisioned for peak load to maintain good SLOs, and low-priority batch jobs only partially smooth out the workload variation. Second, the workload has unpredictable high spikes compared with regular diurnal patterns for web queries, resulting in wasted work from batch jobs being preempted upon sudden spikes in the workload.

MIA-style workloads have already appeared in several organizations, including both web search and other businesses [9, 26, 34]. Several technology trends help increase the popularity and generality of MIA workloads:

- Industries ranging from e-commerce, finance, and manufacturing are increasingly adopting MapReduce as a data processing and archival system [23].

- It is increasingly easy to collect and store large amounts of data about both virtual and physical systems [9, 17, 27].

- Data analysts are gaining expertise using MapReduce to process big data sets interactively for real-time analytics, event monitoring, and stream processing [9, 26, 34].

In short, MapReduce has evolved far beyond its original use case of high-throughput batch processing in support of web search-centric services, and it is critical that we develop energy efficiency mechanisms for MIA workloads.

This paper presents BEEMR (Berkeley Energy Efficient MapReduce), an energy efficient MapReduce system motivated by an empirical analysis of a real-life MIA workload at Facebook. This workload requires BEEMR to meet stringent design requirements, including minimal impact on interactive job latency, write bandwidth, write capacity, memory set size, and data locality, as well as compatibility with distributed file system fault tolerance using error correction codes rather than replication. BEEMR represents a new design point that combines batching [28], zoning [29], and data placement [27] with new analysis-driven insights to create an efficient MapReduce system that saves energy while meeting these design requirements. The key insight is that although MIA clusters host huge volumes of data, the interactive jobs operate on just a small fraction of the data, and thus can be served by a small pool of dedicated machines; whereas the less time-sensitive jobs can run in a batch fashion on the rest of the cluster. These defining characteristics of MIA workloads both motivate and enable the BEEMR design. BEEMR increases cluster utilization while batches are actively run, and decreases energy waste between batches because only the dedicated interactive machines need to be kept at full power. The contributions of this paper are:

- An analysis of a Facebook cluster trace to quantify the empirical behavior of a MIA workload.

- The BEEMR framework which combines novel ideas with existing MapReduce energy efficiency mechanisms.

- An improved evaluation methodology to quantify energy savings and account the complexity of MIA workloads.

- An identification of a set of general MapReduce design issues that warrant more study.

We show energy savings of 40-50%. BEEMR highlights the need to design for an important class of data center workloads, and represents an advance over existing MapReduce energy efficiency proposals [27–29]. Systems like BEEMR become more important as the need for energy efficiency continues to increase, and more use cases approach the scale and complexity of the Facebook MIA workload.

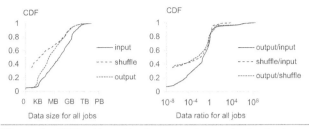

Figure 1. CDFs of input/shuffle/output sizes and ratios for the entire 45-day Facebook trace. Both span several orders of magnitudes. Energy efficiency mechanisms must accommodate this range.

2. Motivation

Facebook is a social network company that allows users to create profiles and connect with each other. The Facebook workload provides a detailed case study of the growing class of MIA workloads. This analysis motivates the BEEMR design and highlights where previous solutions fall short.

2.1 The Facebook Workload

We analyze traces from the primary Facebook production Hadoop cluster. The cluster has 3000 machines. Each machine has 12+ TB, 8-16 cores, 32 GB of RAM, and roughly 15 concurrent map/reduce tasks [8]. The traces cover 45 days from Oct. 1 to Nov. 15, 2010, and contain over 1 million jobs touching tens of PB of data. The traces record each job's job ID, input/shuffle/output sizes, arrival time, duration, map/reduce task durations (in task-seconds), number of map/reduce tasks, and input file path.

Figure 1 shows the distribution of per-job data sizes and data ratios for the entire workload. The data sizes span several orders of magnitude, and most jobs have data sizes in the KB to GB range. The data ratios also span several orders of magnitude. 30% of the jobs are map-only, and thus have 0 shuffle data. Any effort to improve energy efficiency must account for this range of data sizes and data ratios.

Figure 2 shows the workload variation over two weeks. The number of jobs is diurnal, with peaks around midday and troughs around midnight. All three time series have a high peak-to-average ratio, especially map and reduce task times. Since most hardware is not power proportional [5], a cluster provisioned for peak load would see many periods of below peak activity running at near-peak power.

To distinguish among different types of jobs in the workload, we can perform statistical data clustering analysis. This analysis treats each job as a multi-dimensional vector, and finds clusters of similar numerical vectors, i.e., similar jobs. Our traces give us six numerical dimensions per job — input size, shuffle size, output size, job duration, map time, and reduce time. Table 1 shows the results using the k-means algorithm, in which we labeled each cluster based on the numerical value of the cluster center.

Most of the jobs are small and interactive. These jobs arise out of ad-hoc queries initiated by internal human analysts at Facebook [9, 51]. There are also jobs with long du-

# Jobs	Input	Shuffle	Output	Duration	Map time	Reduce time	Label
1145663	6.9 MB	600 B	60 KB	1 min	48	34	Small jobs
7911	50 GB	0	61 GB	8 hrs	60,664	0	Map only transform, 8 hrs
779	3.6 TB	0	4.4 TB	45 min	3,081,710	0	Map only transform, 45 min
670	2.1 TB	0	2.7 GB	1 hr 20 min	9,457,592	0	Map only aggregate
104	35 GB	0	3.5 GB	3 days	198,436	0	Map only transform, 3 days
11491	1.5 TB	30 GB	2.2 GB	30 min	1,112,765	387,191	Aggregate
1876	711 GB	2.6 TB	860 GB	2 hrs	1,618,792	2,056,439	Transform, 2 hrs
454	9.0 TB	1.5 TB	1.2 TB	1 hr	1,795,682	818,344	Aggregate and transform
169	2.7 TB	12 TB	260 GB	2 hrs 7 min	2,862,726	3,091,678	Expand and aggregate
67	630 GB	1.2 TB	140 GB	18 hrs	1,545,220	18,144,174	Transform, 18 hrs

Table 1. Job types in the workload as identified by k-means clustering, with cluster sizes, medians, and labels. Map and reduce time are in task-seconds, i.e., a job with 2 map tasks of 10 seconds each has map time of 20 task-seconds. Notable job types include small, interactive jobs (top row) and jobs with inherently low levels of parallelism that take a long time to complete (fifth row). We ran k-means with 100 random instantiations of cluster centers, which averages to over 1 bit of randomness in each of the 6 data dimensions. We determine k, the number of clusters by incrementing k from 1 and stopping upon diminishing decreases in the intra-cluster "residual" variance.

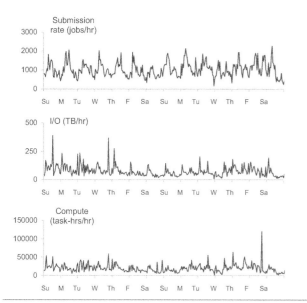

Figure 2. Hourly workload variation over two weeks. The workload has high peak-to-average ratios. A cluster provisioned for the peak would be often underutilized and waste a great deal of energy.

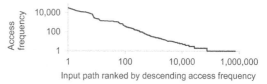

Figure 3. Log-log plot of workload input file path access frequency. This displays a Zipf distribution, meaning that a few input paths account for a large fraction of all job inputs.

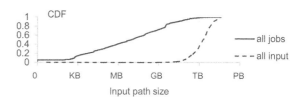

Figure 4. CDF of both (1) the input size per job and (2) the size per input path. This graph indicates that small input paths are accessed frequently, i.e., data sets of less than 10s of GBs account for over 80% of jobs, and such data sets are a tiny fraction of the total data stored on the cluster.

rations but small task times (map only, GB-scale, many-day jobs). These jobs have inherently low levels of parallelism, and take a long time to complete, even if they have the entire cluster at their disposal. Any energy efficient MapReduce system must accommodate many job types, each with their own unique characteristics.

Figures 3 and 4 show the data access patterns as indicated by the per-job input paths. Unfortunately our traces do not contain comparable information for output paths. Figure 3 shows that the input path accesses follow a Zipf distribution, i.e., a few input paths account for a large fraction of all accesses. Figure 4 shows that small data sets are accessed frequently; input paths of less than 10s of GBs account for over 80% of jobs, but only a tiny fraction of the total size of all input paths. Prior work has also observed this behavior in other contexts, such as web caches [10] and databases [21]. The implication is that *a small fraction of the cluster is sufficient to store the input data sets of most jobs*.

Other relevant design considerations are not evident from the traces. First, some applications require high write throughput and considerable application-level cache, such as Memcached. This fact was reported by Facebook in [9] and [51]. Second, the cluster is storage capacity constrained, so Facebook's HDFS achieves fault tolerance through error correcting codes instead of replication, which brings the physical replication factor down from three to less than two [45]. Further, any data hot spots or decreased data locality would increase MapReduce job completion times [2].

Table 2 summarizes the design constraints. They represent a superset of the requirements considered by existing energy efficient MapReduce proposals.

2.2 Prior Work

Prior work includes both energy-efficient MapReduce schemes as well as strategies that apply to other workloads.

2.2.1 Energy Efficient MapReduce

Existing energy efficient MapReduce systems fail to meet all the requirements in Table 2. We review them here.

The covering subset scheme [29] keeps one replica of every block within a small subset of machines called the covering subset. This subset remains fully powered to preserve data availability while the rest is powered down. Operating only a fraction of the cluster decreases write bandwidth, write capacity, and the size of available memory. More critically, this scheme becomes unusable when error correction codes are used instead of replication, since the covering subset becomes the whole cluster.

The all-in strategy [28] powers down the entire cluster during periods of inactivity, and runs at full capacity otherwise. Figure 2 shows that the cluster is never completely inactive. Thus, to power down at any point, the all-in strategy must run incoming jobs in regular batches, an approach we investigated in [13]. All jobs would experience some delay, an inappropriate behavior for the small, interactive jobs in the MIA workload (Table 1).

Green HDFS [27] partitions HDFS into disjoint hot and cold zones. The frequently accessed data is placed in the hot zone, which is always powered. To preserve write capacity, Green HDFS fills the cold zone using one powered-on machine at a time. This scheme is problematic because the output of every job would be located on a small number of machines, creating a severe data hotspot for future accesses. Furthermore, running the cluster at partial capacity decreases the available write bandwidth and memory.

The prior studies in Table 2 also suffer from several methodological weaknesses. Some studies quantified energy efficiency improvements by running stand-alone jobs, similar to [43]. This is the correct initial approach, but it is not clear that improvements from stand-alone jobs translate to workloads with complex interference between concurrent jobs. More critically, for workloads with high peak-to-average load (Figure 2), per-job improvements fail to eliminate energy waste during low activity periods.

Other studies quantified energy improvements using trace-driven simulations. Such simulations are essential for evaluating energy efficient MapReduce at large scale. However, the simulators used there were not empirically verified, i.e., there were no experiments comparing simulated versus real behavior, nor simulated versus real energy savings. Section 5.8 demonstrates that an empirical validation reveals many subtle assumptions about simulators, and put into doubt the results derived from unverified simulators.

These shortcomings necessitate a new approach in designing and evaluating energy efficient MapReduce systems.

2.2.2 Energy Efficient Web Search-Centric Workloads

MIA workloads require a different approach to energy efficiency than previously considered workloads.

In web search-centric workloads, the interactive services achieves low latency by using data structures in-memory, requiring the entire memory set to be always available [32]. Given hardware limits in power proportionality, it becomes a priority to increase utilization of machines during diurnal troughs [5]. One way to do this is to admit batch processing to consume any available resource. This policy makes the combined workload *closed-loop*, i.e., the system controls the amount of admitted work. Further, the combined workload becomes more *predictable*, since the interactive services display regular diurnal patterns, and with batch processing smoothing out most diurnal variations [5, 19, 32].

These characteristics enable energy efficiency improvements to focus on *maximizing the amount of work done subject to the given power budget*, i.e., maximizing the amount of batch processing done by the system. Idleness is viewed as waste. Opportunities to save energy occur at short time scales, and requires advances in hardware energy efficiency and power proportionality [5, 7, 16, 19, 32, 33, 48].

These techniques remain helpful for MIA workloads. However, the open-loop and unpredictable nature of MIA workloads necessitates additional approaches. Human initiated jobs have both throughput and latency constraints. Thus, the cluster needs to be provisioned for peak, and idleness is inherent to the workload. Machine-initiated batch jobs can only partially smooth out transient activity peaks. Improving hardware power proportionality helps, but remains a partial solution since state-of-the-art hardware is still far from perfectly power proportional. Thus, absent policies to constrain the human analysts, improving energy efficiency for MIA workloads requires *minimizing the energy needed to service the given amount of work*.

More generally, energy concerns complicate capacity provisioning, a challenging topic with investigations dating back to the time-sharing era [3, 4, 46]. This paper offers a new perspective informed by MIA workloads.

3. BEEMR Architecture

BEEMR is an energy efficient MapReduce workload manager. The key insight is that the interactive jobs can be served by a small pool of dedicated machines with their associated storage, while the less time-sensitive jobs can run in a batch fashion on the rest of the cluster using full computation bandwidth and storage capacity. This setup leads to energy savings and meet all the requirements listed in Table 2.

3.1 Design

The BEEMR cluster architecture is shown in Figure 5. It is similar to a typical Hadoop MapReduce cluster, with important differences in how resources are allocated to jobs.

The cluster is split into disjoint interactive and batch zones. The interactive zone makes up a small, fixed percentage of cluster resources — task slots, memory, disk capacity, network bandwidth, similar to the design in [4]. The interac-

Desirable Property	Covering subset [29]	All-In [28]	Hot & Cold Zones [27]	BEEMR
Does not delay interactive jobs	✔		✔	✔
No impact on write bandwidth		✔		✔
No impact on write capacity		✔	✔	✔
No impact on available memory		✔		✔
Does not introduce data hot spots nor impact data locality	✔	✔		✔
Improvement preserved when using ECC instead of replication		✔	✔	✔
Addresses long running jobs with low parallelism				Partially
Energy savings	9-50%[1]	0-50%[2]	24%[3]	40-50%

Table 2. Required properties for energy-saving techniques for Facebook's MIA workload. Prior proposals are insufficient. Notes: [1] The reported energy savings used an energy model based on linearly extrapolating CPU utilization while running the GridMix throughput benchmark [22] on a 36-node cluster. [2] Reported only relative energy savings compared with the covering subset technique, and for only two artificial jobs (Terasort and Grep) on a 24-node experimental cluster. We recomputed absolute energy savings using the graphs in the paper. [3] Reported simulation based energy *cost* savings, assumed an electricity cost of $0.063/KWh and 80% capacity utilization.

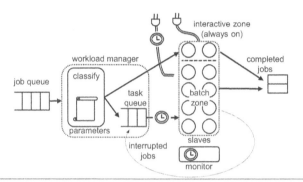

Figure 5. The BEEMR workload manager (i.e., job tracker) classifies each job into one of three classes which determines which cluster zone will service the job. Interactive jobs are serviced in the interactive zone, while batchable and interruptible jobs are serviced in the batch zone. Energy savings come from aggregating jobs in the batch zone to achieve high utilization, executing them in regular batches, and then transitioning machines in the batch zone to a low-power state when the batch completes.

tive zone is always fully powered. The batch zone makes up the rest of the cluster, and is put into a very low power state between batches [25].

As jobs arrive, BEEMR classifies them as one of three job types. Classification is based on empirical parameters derived from the analysis in Section 2. If the job input data size is less than some threshold `interactive`, it is classified as an interactive job. BEEMR seeks to service these jobs with low latency. If a job has tasks with task duration longer than some threshold `interruptible`, it is classified as an interruptible job. Latency is not a concern for these jobs, because their long-running tasks can be check-pointed and resumed over multiple batches. All other jobs are classified as batch jobs. Latency is also not a concern for these jobs, but BEEMR makes best effort to run them by regular deadlines. Such a setup is equivalent to deadline-based policies where the deadlines are the same length as the batch intervals.

The interactive zone is always in a full-power ready state. It runs all of the interactive jobs and holds all of their associated input, shuffle, and output data (both local and HDFS storage). Figures 3 and 4 indicate that choosing an appropriate value for `interactive` can allow most jobs to be classified as interactive and executed without any delay introduced by BEEMR. This `interactive` threshold should be periodically adjusted as workloads evolve.

The interactive zone acts like a data cache. When an interactive job accesses data that is not in the interactive zone (i.e., a cache miss), BEEMR migrates the relevant data from the batch zone to the interactive zone, either immediately or upon the next batch. Since most jobs use small data sets that are reaccessed frequently, cache misses occur infrequently. Also, BEEMR requires storing the ECC parity or replicated blocks within the respective zones, e.g., for data in the interactive zone, their parity or replication blocks would be stored in the interactive zone also.

Upon submission of batched and interruptible jobs, all tasks associated with the job are put in a wait queue. At regular intervals, the workload manager initiates a batch, powers on all machines in the batch zone, and run all tasks on the wait queue using the whole cluster. The machines in the interactive zone are also available for batch and interruptible jobs, but interactive jobs retain priority there. After a batch begins, any batch and interruptible jobs that arrive would wait for the next batch. Once all batch jobs complete, the job tracker assigns no further tasks. Active tasks from interruptible jobs are suspended, and enqueued to be resumed in the next batch. Machines in the batch zone return to a low-power state. If a batch does not complete by start of the next batch interval, the cluster would remain fully powered for consecutive batch periods. The high peak-to-average load in Figure 2 indicates that on average, the batch zone would spend considerable periods in a low-power state.

BEEMR improves over prior batching and zoning schemes by combining both, and uses empirical observations to set the values of policy parameters, which we describe next.

3.1.1 Parameter Space

BEEMR involves several design parameters whose values need to be optimized. These parameters are:

Parameter	Units or Type	Values
totalsize	thousand slots	32, 48, 60, 72
mapreduceratio	map:reduce slots	1 : 1, 27 : 14, (≈ 2.0), 13 : 5 (≈ 2.6)
izonesize	% total slots	10
interactive	GB	10
interruptible	hours	6, 12, 24
batchlen	hours	1, 2, 6, 12, 24
taskcalc	algorithm	default, actual, latency-bound

Table 3. Design space explored. The values for `izonesize` and `interactive` are derived from the analysis in Section 2.1. We scan at least three values for each of the other parameters.

- `totalsize`: the size of the cluster in total (map and reduce) task slots.
- `mapreduceratio`: the ratio of map slots to reduce slots in the cluster.
- `izonesize`: the percentage of the cluster assigned to the interactive zone.
- `interactive`: the input size threshold for classifying jobs as interactive.
- `interruptible`: task duration threshold for classifying jobs as interruptible.
- `batchlen`: the batch interval length.
- `taskcalc`: the algorithm for determining the number of map and reduce tasks to assign to a job.

Table 3 shows the parameter values we will optimize for the Facebook workload. For other workloads, the same tuning process can extract a different set of values. Note that `totalsize` indicates the size of the cluster in units of task slots, which differs from the number machines. One machine can run many task slots, and the appropriate assignment of task slots per machine depends on hardware capabilities.

Another parameter worth further explanation is `taskcalc`, the algorithm for determining the number of map and reduce tasks to assign to a job. An algorithm that provides appropriate task granularity ensures that completion of a given batch is not held up by long-running tasks from some jobs.

BEEMR considers three algorithms: *Default* assigns 1 map per 128 MB of input and 1 reduce per 1 GB of input; this is the default setting in Hadoop. *Actual* assigns the same number of map and reduce tasks as given in the trace and corresponds to settings at Facebook. *Latency-bound* assigns a number of tasks such that no task will run for more than 1 hour. This policy is possible provided that task execution times can be predicted with high accuracy [20, 36].

3.1.2 Requirements Check

We verify that BEEMR meets the requirements in Table 2.
1. Write bandwidth is not diminished because the entire cluster is fully powered when batches execute. Table 1 indicates that only batch and interruptible jobs require large write bandwidth. When these jobs are running, they have access to all of the disks in the cluster.

2. Similarly, write capacity is not diminished because the entire cluster is fully powered on during batches. Between batches, the small output size of interactive jobs (Table 1) means that an appropriate value of `izonesize` allows those job outputs to fit in the interactive zone.

3. The size of available memory also remains intact. The memory of the entire cluster is accessible to batch and interruptible jobs, which potentially have large working sets. For interactive jobs, the default or actual (Facebook) `taskcalc` algorithms will assign few tasks per job, resulting in small in-memory working sets.

4. Interactive jobs are not delayed. The interactive zone is always fully powered, and designated specifically to service interactive jobs without delay.

5. BEEMR spreads data evenly within both zones, and makes no changes that impact data locality. Nonetheless, Figure 3 suggests that there will be some hotspots inherent to the Facebook workload, independent of BEEMR.

6. BEEMR improves energy efficiency via batching. There is no dependence on ECC or replication, thus preserving energy savings regardless of fault tolerance mechanism.

7. Long jobs with low levels of parallelism remain a challenge, even under BEEMR. These jobs are classified as interruptible jobs if their task durations are large, and batch jobs otherwise. If such jobs are classified as batch jobs, they could potentially prevent batches from completing. Their inherent low levels of parallelism cause the batch zone to be poorly utilized when running only these long jobs, resulting in wasted energy. One solution is for experts to label such jobs a priori so that BEEMR can ensure that these jobs are classified as interruptible.

3.2 Implementation

BEEMR involves several extensions to Apache Hadoop.

The job tracker is extended with a wait queue management module. This module holds all incoming batch jobs, moves jobs from the wait queue to the standard scheduler upon each batch start, and places any remaining tasks of interruptible jobs back on the wait queue when batches end. Also, the scheduler's task placement mechanism is modified such that interactive jobs are placed in the interactive zone, and always have first priority to any available slots.

The namenode is modified such that the output of interactive jobs is assigned to the interactive zone, and the output of batch and interruptible jobs is assigned to the batch zone. If either zone approaches storage capacity, it must adjust the fraction of machines in each zone, or expand the cluster.

The Hadoop master is augmented with a mechanism to transfer all slaves in the batch zone in and out of a low-power state, e.g., sending a "hibernate" command via `ssh` and using Wake-on-LAN or related technologies [30]. If batch intervals are on the order of hours, it is acceptable for this transition to complete over seconds or even minutes.

Accommodating interruptible jobs requires a mechanism that can suspend and resume active tasks. The current Hadoop architecture makes it difficult to implement such a mechanism. However, suspend and resume is a key component of fault recovery under Next Generation Hadoop [38]. We can re-purpose for BEEMR those mechanisms.

These extensions will create additional computation and IO at the Hadoop master node. The current Hadoop master has been identified as a scalability bottleneck [47]. Thus, it is important to monitor BEEMR overhead at the Hadoop master to ensure that we do not affect cluster scalability. This overhead would become more acceptable under Next Generation Hadoop, where the Hadoop master functionality would be spread across several machines [38].

4. Evaluation Methodology

The evaluation of our proposed algorithm involves running the Facebook MIA workload both in simulation and on clusters of hundreds of machines on Amazon EC2 [1].

The Facebook workload provides a level of validation not obtainable through stand-alone programs or artificial benchmarks. It is logistically impossible to replay this workload on large clusters at full duration and scale. The high peak to average nature of the workload means that at time scales of less than weeks, there is no way to know whether the results capture transient or average behavior. Enumerating a multi-dimensional design space would also take prohibitively long. Any gradient ascent algorithms are not possible, simply because there is no guarantee that the performance behavior is convex. Combined, these concerns compel us to use experimentally validated simulations.

The simulator is optimized for simulation scale and speed by omitting certain details: job startup and completion overhead, overlapping map and reduce phases, speculative execution and stragglers, data locality, and interference between jobs. This differs from existing MapReduce simulators [37, 53], whose focus on details make it logistically infeasible to simulate large scale, long duration workloads. The simulator assumes a simple, fluid-flow model of job execution, first developed for network simulations as an alternative to packet-level models [31, 42]. There, the motivation was also to gain simulation scale and speed. Section 5.8 demonstrates that the impact on accuracy is acceptable.

Simulated job execution is a function of job submit time (given in the trace), task assignment time (depends on a combination of parameters, including batch length, and number of map and reduce slots), map and reduce execution times (given in the trace), and the number of mappers and reducers chosen by BEEMR (a parameter). Figure 6 shows how the simulator works at a high level.

We empirically validate the simulator by replaying several day-long workloads on a real-life cluster (Section 5.8). This builds confidence that simulation results translate to real clusters. The validation employs previously developed

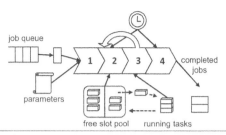

Figure 6. A high-level view of the simulation algorithm. For each simulated second, the following executes: 1. The simulator dequeues newly arrived jobs (arrival pattern given in the trace), classifies the job as interactive, batch, or interruptible, and applies the task granularity policy. 2. The simulator checks for available map or reduce slots, checks the batch policy to see which jobs can be run at the present time, and assigns slots to jobs in round robin, fair scheduler fashion. 3. The simulator removes completed tasks and returns the corresponding slot back to the free slot pool. For each active job, it checks to see if the job has more tasks to run (go back to step 2) or is complete (go to step 4). 4. The job is marked complete and the job duration recorded.

methods to "replay" MapReduce workloads independent of hardware [12]. The techniques there replays the workload using synthetic data sets, and reproduces job submission sequences and intensities, as well as the data ratios between each job's input, shuffle, and output stages.

We model the machines as having "full" power when active, and negligible power when in a low power state. Despite recent advances in power proportionality [5], such models remain valid for Hadoop. In [11], we used wall plug power meters to show that machines with power ranges of 150W-250W draw 205W-225W when running Hadoop. The chattiness of the Hadoop/HDFS stack means that machines are active at the hardware level even when they are idle at the Hadoop workload level. The simple power model allow us to scale the experiments in size and in time.

Several performance metrics are relevant to energy efficient MapReduce: (1) Energy savings: Under our power model, this would be the duration for which the cluster is fully idle; (2) Job latency (analogous to "turn around time" in multiprogramming literature [18]): We measure separately the job latency for each job class, and quantify any trade-off against energy savings; (3) System throughput: Under the MIA open-loop workload model, the historical system throughput would be the smaller of `totalsize` and the historical workload arrival rate. We examine several values of `totalsize` and quantify the interplay between latency, energy savings, and other policy parameters.

Table 3 shows the parameter values used to explore the BEEMR design space.

5. Results

The evaluation spans the multi-dimensional design space in Table 3. Each dimension illustrates subtle interactions between BEEMR and the Facebook workload.

5.1 Cluster Size

Cluster size is controlled by `totalsize`. Underprovisioning a cluster results in long queues and high latency during workload peaks; overprovisioning leads to arbitrarily high baseline energy consumption and waste. Over the 45-days trace, the Facebook workload has an average load of 21029 map tasks and 7745 reduce tasks. Since the workload has a high peak-to-average ratio, we must provision significantly above the average. Figure 7 shows the detailed cluster behavior for several cluster sizes without any of the BEEMR improvements. We pick a one-to-one map-to-reduce-slot ratio because that is the default in Apache Hadoop, and thus forms a good baseline. A cluster with only 32000 total slots cannot service the historical rate, being pegged at maximum slot occupancy; larger sizes still see transient periods of maximum slot occupancy. A cluster with at least 36000 map slots (72000 total slots) is needed to avoid persistent long queues, so we use this as a baseline.

5.2 Batch Interval Length

Energy savings are enabled by batching jobs and transitioning the batch zone to a low-power state between batches. The ability to batch depends on the predominance of interactive analysis in MIA workloads (Section 2.1). We consider here several static batch interval lengths. A natural extension would be to have dynamically adjusted batch intervals to enable various deadline driven policies.

We vary `batchlen`, the batching interval, while holding the other parameters fixed. Figure 8 shows that energy savings, expressed as a fraction of the baseline energy consumption, become non-negligible only for batch lengths of 12 hours or more. Figure 9 shows that map tasks execute in near-ideal batch fashion, with maximum task slot occupancy for a fraction of the batch interval and no further tasks in the remainder of the interval. However, reduce slot occupancy rarely reaches full capacity, while "dangling" reduce tasks often run for a long time at very low cluster utilization. There are more reduce tasks slots available, but the algorithm for choosing the number of task slots limits the amount of parallelism. During the fifth and sixth days, such dangling tasks cause the batch zone to remain at full power for the entire batch interval. Fixing this requires improving both the algorithm for calculating the number of tasks for each job and the ratio of map-to-reduce slots.

5.3 Task Slots Per Job

The evaluation thus far considered only the default algorithm for computing the number of tasks per job, as specified by `taskcalc`. Recall that we consider two other algorithms: *Actual* assigns the same number of map and reduce tasks as given in the trace and corresponds to settings at Facebook. *Latency-bound* assigns a number of tasks such that no task will run for more than 1 hour. Figure 10 compares the default versus actual and latency-bound algorithms. The actual

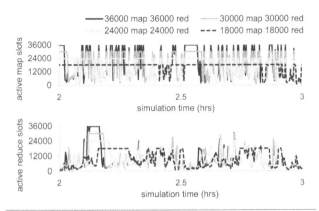

Figure 7. The number of concurrently active tasks for clusters of different sizes (in terms of total task slots, `totalsize`).

Figure 8. Energy savings for different batch interval lengths as given by `batchlen`. Energy savings are non-negligible for large batch intervals only. Note that `taskcalc` is set to default, `mapreduceratio` is set to 1:1, `totalsize` is set to 72000 slots, and `interruptible` is set to 24 hours.

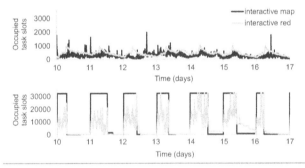

Figure 9. Active slots for a `batchlen` of 24 hours. Showing slot occupancy in the interactive zone (top) and in the batch zone (bottom). Showing one week's behavior. Note that `taskcalc` is set to default, `mapreduceratio` is set to 1:1, `totalsize` is set to 72000 slots, and `interruptible` is set to 24 hours.

policy does the worst, unsurprising because the task assignment algorithm at Facebook is not yet optimized for energy efficiency. The latency-bound policy does the best; this indicates that good task execution time prediction can improve task assignment and achieve greater energy savings.

Observing task slot occupancy over time provides insight into the effects of `taskcalc`. Using the actual algorithm (Figure 11(a)), slots in the interactive zone reach capacity more frequently, suggesting that the Facebook algorithm seeks to increase parallelism to decrease the amount of computation per task and lower the completion latency of interactive jobs. In contrast, tasks in the batch zone behave similarly under the default and Facebook algorithm for

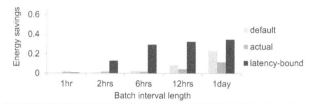

Figure 10. Energy savings for different `taskcalc` algorithms. Note that `mapreduceratio` is set to 1:1, and `interruptible` is set to 24 hours. The *actual* (Facebook) algorithm does worst and the *latency-bound* algorithm does best.

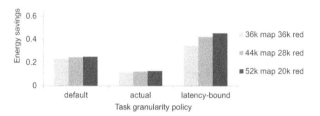

Figure 12. Energy savings for different values of `mapreduceratio`. Increasing the number of map slots increases energy savings for all `taskcalc` algorithms, with the improvement for *latency-bound* being the greatest. Note that `totalsize` is set to 72000 slots, `batchlen` is set to 24 hours, and `interruptible` is set to 24 hours.

the week shown in Figure 11(a). Aggregated over the entire trace, the actual policy turns out to have more dangling tasks overall, diminishing energy savings.

In contrast, task slot occupancy over time for the latency-bound policy eliminates all dangling tasks of long durations (Figure 11(b)). This results in high cluster utilization during batches, as well as clean batch completion, allowing the cluster to be transitioned into a low-power state at the end of a batch. There is still room for improvement in Figure 11(b): the active reduce slots are still far from reaching maximum task slot capacity. This suggests that even if we keep the total number of task slots constant, we can harness more energy savings by changing some reduce slots to map slots.

5.4 Map to Reduce Slot Ratio

The evaluation thus far illustrates that reduce slots are utilized less than map slots. Changing `mapreduceratio` (i.e., increasing the number of map slots and decreasing the number of reduce slots while keeping cluster size constant) should allow map tasks in each batch to complete faster without affecting reduce tasks completion rates. Figure 12 shows that doing so leads to energy efficiency improvements, especially for the latency-bound algorithm.

Viewing the task slot occupancy over time reveals that this intuition about the map-to-reduce-slot ratio is correct. Figure 13(a) compares batch zone slot occupancy for two different ratios using the default algorithm. With a larger number of map slots, the periods of maximum map slot occupancy are shorter, but there are still dangling reduce tasks. The same ratio using the latency-bound algorithm

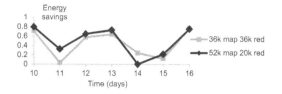

Figure 14. Energy savings per day for the latency-bound policy comparison in Figure 13(b). Daily energy savings range from 0 to 80%. Neither static policy achieves best energy savings for all days.

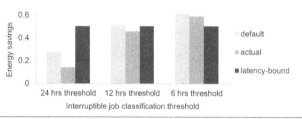

Figure 15. Energy savings for different values of `interruptible`. Lowering the threshold leads to increased energy savings for actual and default algorithms. Note that `mapreduceratio` is set to 13:5 and `batchlen` is set to 24 hours. Note that for actual and default algorithms, having a low `interruptible` causes the queue for waiting interrupted jobs to grow without limit; the latency-bound policy is preferred despite seemingly lower energy savings (Section 5.5).

avoids these dangling reduce tasks, as shown in Figure 13(b), achieving higher energy savings.

Nevertheless, the latency-bound algorithm still has room for improvement. During the fifth and sixth days in Figure 13(b), the batches are in fact limited by available reduce slots. Figure 14 shows that neither static policy for map versus task ratios achieve the best savings for all days. A dynamically adjustable ratio of map and reduce slots is best. A dynamic ratio can ensure that every batch is optimally executed, bottlenecked on neither map slots nor reduce slots.

5.5 Interruptible Threshold

The last dimension to evaluate is `interruptible`, the task duration threshold that determines when a job is classified as interruptible. In the evaluation so far, `interruptible` has been set to 24 hours. Decreasing this threshold should cause more jobs to be classified as interruptible, and fewer jobs as batch. A lower interruptible threshold allows faster batch completions and potentially more capacity for the interactive zone, at the cost of higher average job latency, as more jobs are spread over multiple batches.

Figure 15 shows the energy saving improvements from lowering `interruptible`. (The latency-bound algorithm, by design, does not result in any interruptible jobs, unless the `interruptible` is set to less than an hour, so the energy savings for the latency-bound algorithm are unaffected.) Actual and default algorithms show considerable energy savings improvements, at the cost of longer latency for some jobs. It would be interesting to see how many cluster users and administrators are willing to make such trades.

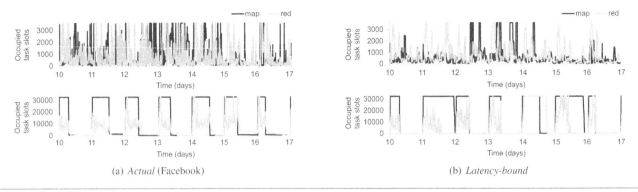

(a) *Actual* (Facebook)   (b) *Latency-bound*

Figure 11. Slot occupancy over time in the interactive zone (top graph) and batch zone (bottom graph). Showing one week's behavior. Note that `batchlen` is set to 24 hours, `mapreduceratio` is set to 1:1, and `interruptible` is set to 24 hours.

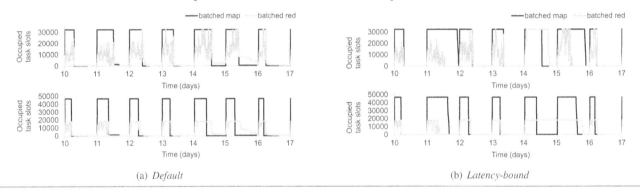

(a) *Default*   (b) *Latency-bound*

Figure 13. Batch zone slot occupancy over time using a `mapreduceratio` of 1:1 for the top graph, and a `mapreduceratio` of 13:5 for the bottom graph. Showing one week's behavior. Note that `batchlen` is set to 24 hours and `interruptible` is set to 24 hours.

Lowering `interruptible` too much would cause the queue of waiting interruptible jobs to build without bound. Consider the ideal-case upper bound on possible energy savings. The Facebook workload has a historical average of 21029 active map tasks and 7745 active reduce tasks. A cluster of 72000 task slots can service 72000 concurrent tasks at maximum. Thus, the best case energy savings is $1 - (21029 + 7745)/72000 = 0.60$. As we lower `interruptible`, any energy "savings" above this ideal actually represents the wait queue building up.

The best policy combination we examined achieves energy savings of 0.55 fraction of the baseline, as shown Figure 15, with `taskcalc` set to default and `interruptible` set to 6 hours. This corresponds to 92% of this ideal case.

5.6 Overhead

The energy savings come at the cost of increased job latency. Figure 16 quantifies the latency increase by looking at normalized job durations for each job type. BEEMR achieves minimal latency overhead for interactive jobs, and some overhead for other job types. This delayed execution overhead buys us energy savings for non-interactive jobs.

For interactive jobs, more than 60% of jobs have ratio of 1.0, approximately 40% of jobs have ratio less than 1.0, and a few outliers have ratio slightly above 1.0. This indicates that a dedicated interactive zone can lead to either unaffected job latency, or even improved job latency from having dedicated

resources. The small number of jobs with ratio above 1.0 is caused by peaks in interactive job arrivals. This suggests that it would be desirable to increase the capacity of the interactive zone during workload peaks.

For batched jobs, the overhead spans a large range. This is caused by the long batch interval, and is acceptable as a matter of policy. A job that arrives just after the beginning of one batch would have delay of at least one batch interval, leading to large latency. Conversely, a job that arrives just before a batch starts will have almost no delay. This is the same delayed execution behavior as policies in which users specify, say, a daily deadline.

For interruptible jobs, the overhead is also small for most jobs. This is surprising because interruptible jobs can potentially execute over multiple batches. The result indicates that interruptible jobs are truly long running jobs. Executing them over multiple batches imposes a modest overhead.

5.7 Sensitivity

The evaluation thus far has set a `totalsize` of 72000 task slots and discovered the best parameter values based on this setting. A cluster size of 72000 forms a conservative baseline for energy consumption. Using BEEMR on larger clusters yields more energy savings, as shown in Figure 17.

BEEMR extracts most, but not all, of the ideal energy savings. The discrepancy arises from long tasks that hold up batch completion (Section 5.2) and transient imbalance be-

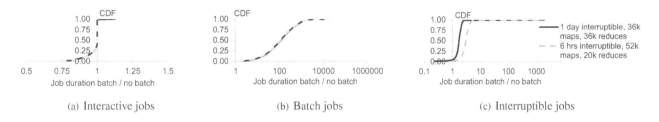

(a) Interactive jobs   (b) Batch jobs   (c) Interruptible jobs

Figure 16. Latency ratio by job type between BEEMR with `totalsize` set to 72000, `taskcalc` set to default, and (1) `batchlen` set to 24 hours, `mapreduceratio` set to 1:1, or (2) `batchlen` set to 6 hours, `mapreduceratio` set to 13:5; versus the baseline with no batching. A ratio of 1.0 indicates no overhead. Some interactive jobs see improved performance (ratio < 1) due to dedicated resources. Some batch jobs have very long delays, the same behavior as delayed execution under deadline-based policies. Interruptible jobs have less overhead than batch jobs, indicating that those are truly long running jobs. The delayed execution in non-interactive jobs buys us energy savings.

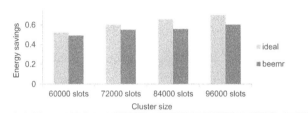

Figure 17. Ideal and observed energy savings for different cluster sizes. Both increase as cluster size increases. Note that `batchlen` is set to 24 hours, `taskcalc` is set to default, `mapreduceratio` is set to 13:5, and `interruptible` is set to 6 hours.

Figure 18. Simulator validation for stand-alone jobs. Showing the ratio between simulated job duration and average job duration from 20 repeated measurements on a real cluster. The ratio is bounded for both large and small jobs and is very close to 1.0 for sort jobs of size 100s of MB to 10s of GB.

tween map and reduce slots (Section 5.4). If the fraction of time that each batch runs at maximum slot occupancy is already small, then the effects of long tasks and map/reduce slot imbalance are amplified. Thus, as cluster size increases, the gap between BEEMR energy savings and the ideal also increases. One way to narrow the gap would be to extend the batch interval length, thus amortizing the overhead of long tasks holding up batch completion and transient map/reduce slot imbalance. In the extreme case, BEEMR can achieve arbitrarily close to ideal energy savings by running the historical workload in one single batch.

5.8 Validation

Empirical validation of the simulator provides guidance on how simulation results translate to real clusters. The BEEMR simulator explicitly trades simulation scale and speed for accuracy, making it even more important to quantify the simulation error.

We validate the BEEMR simulator using an Amazon EC2 cluster of 200 "m1.large" instances [1]. We ran three experiments: (1) a series of stand-alone sort jobs, (2) replay several day-long Facebook workloads using the methodology in [12], which reproduces arrival patterns and data sizes using synthetic MapReduce jobs running on synthetic data, (3) replay the same workloads in day-long batches. For Experiments 1 and 2, we compare the job durations from these experiments to those obtained by a simulator configured with the same number of task slots and the same policies regarding task granularity. For Experiment 3, we compare the en-

ergy savings predicted by the simulator to that from the EC2 cluster. These experiments represent an essential validation step before deployment on the actual front-line Facebook cluster running live data and production code.

Figure 18 shows the results from stand-alone sort jobs. This ratio is bounded on both ends and is very close to 1.0 for sort jobs of size 100s of MB to 10s of GB. The simulator underestimates the run time (the ratio is less than 1.0) for small sort sizes. There, the overhead of starting and terminating a job dominates; this overhead is ignored by the simulator. The simulator overestimates the run time (the ratio is greater than 1.0) for large sort sizes. For those jobs, there is non-negligible overlap between map and reduce tasks; this overlap is not simulated. The simulation error is bounded for both very large and very small jobs.

Also, there is low variance between different runs of the same job, with 95% confidence intervals from 20 repeated measurements being barely visible in Figure 18. Thus, pathologically long caused by task failures or speculative/abandoned executions are infrequent; not simulating these events causes little error.

Figure 19 shows the results of replaying one day's worth of jobs, using three different day-long workloads. The ratio is again bounded, and close to 0.75 for the majority of jobs. This is because most jobs in the workload have data sizes in the MB to GB range (Figure 1). As explained previously,

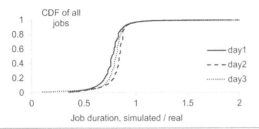

Figure 19. Simulator validation for three day-long workloads, without batching. Showing the ratio between simulated and real job duration. This ratio is bounded on both ends and is very close to 0.75 for the vast majority of jobs.

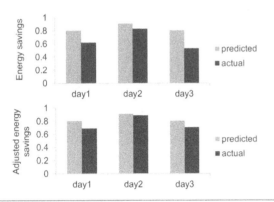

Figure 20. Simulator validation for three different day-long workloads, with `batchlen` set to 24 hours. Showing the predicted versus actual energy savings (top graph, average 22% simulation error), and the predicted versus actual energy savings after adjusting for the slot occupancy capacity on the real-life cluster (bottom graph, average 13% simulation error).

job startup and termination overhead lead to the simulator to underestimate the duration of these jobs.

Figure 20 shows the validation results from batching the three day-long workloads. The simulation error varies greatly between three different days. The average error is 22% of the simulated energy savings (top graph in Figure 20). We identify two additional sources of simulator error: (1) The BEEMR simulator assumes that all available task slots are occupied during the batches. However, on the EC2 cluster, the task slot occupancy averages from 50% to 75% of capacity, a discrepancy again due to task start and termination overhead — the scheduler simply cannot keep all task slots occupied. Adjusting the simulator by using a lower cluster size than the real cluster yields the bottom graph in Figure 20, with the error decreased to 13% of the simulated energy savings. (2) The BEEMR simulator assumes that task times remain the same regardless of whether the workload is executed as jobs arrive, or executed in batch. Observations from the EC2 cluster reveals that during batches, the higher real-life cluster utilization leads to complex interference between jobs, with contention for disk, network, and other resources. This leads to longer task times when a workload executes in batch, and forms another kind of simulation error that is very hard to model.

Overall, these validation results mean that the simulated energy savings of 50-60% (Section 5.5) would likely translate to 40-50% on a real cluster.

6. Discussion

The results in Section 5 raise many interesting questions. Some additional issues await further discussion below.

6.1 Power Cycles versus Reliability

Transitioning machines to low-power states is one way to achieve power proportionality for MIA workloads while more power proportional hardware is being developed. Large scale adoption of this technique has been limited by worries that power cycling increases failure rates.

There have been few published, large-scale studies that attribute increased failure rates to power cycling. The authors in [41] observed a correlation between the two, but point out that correlation could come simply from failed systems needing more reboots to restore. To identify a causal relationship would require a more rigorous methodology, comparing mirror systems servicing the same workload, with the only difference being the frequency of power cycles.

One such comparison experiment ran for 18 months on 100s of machines, and found that power cycling has no effect on failure rates [39]. Larger scale comparisons have been stymied by the small amount of predicted energy savings, and uncertainty about how those energy savings translate to real systems. BEEMR gives empirically validated energy savings of 40-50%. This represents more rigorous data to justify further exploring the thus far unverified relationship between power cycles and failure rates.

6.2 MIA Generality Beyond Facebook

MIA workloads beyond Facebook lend themselves to a BEEMR-like approach. We analyzed four additional Hadoop workloads from e-commerce, telecommunications, media, and retail companies. These traces come from production clusters of up to 700 machines, and cover 4 cluster-months of behavior. The following gives a glimpse of the data. We are seeking approval to release these additional workloads.

One observation that motivated BEEMR is that most jobs access small files that make up a small fraction of stored bytes (Figure 4). This access pattern allows a small interactive zone to service its many jobs. Figure 21 shows that such access patterns exist for all workloads. For FB-2010, input paths of < 10GB account for 88% of jobs and 1% of stored bytes. For workloads A and D, the same threshold respectively accounts for 87% and 87% of jobs, and 4% and 2% of stored bytes. For workloads B and C, input paths of < 1TB accounts for 86% and 91% of jobs, as well as 12% and 17% of stored bytes.

Another source of energy savings comes from the high peak-to-average ratio in workload arrival patterns (Figure 2). The cluster has to be provisioned for the peak, which makes

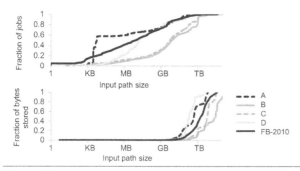

Figure 21. Access patterns vs. input path size. Showing cummulative fraction of jobs with input paths of a certain size (top) and cummulative fraction of all stored bytes from input paths of a certain size (bottom). Contains data from Figure 4 for the FB-2010 workload, and four additional workloads from e-commerce, telecommunications, media, and retail companies.

it important to achieve energy proportionality either in hardware or by workload managers such as BEEMR. For the five workloads (Facebook and workloads A through D), the peak-to-average ratios are: 8.9, 30.5, 23.9, 14.5, and 5.9. BEEMR potentially extracts higher energy savings from workloads with higher peak-to-average arrival ratios, though the exact energy savings and the tradeoff between policy parameters is workload specific. These additional workloads give us confidence that the BEEMR architecture can generalize beyond the Facebook workload.

6.3 Methodology Reflections

Evaluating the energy efficiency of large scale distributed systems presents significant methodological challenges. This paper strikes a balance between scale and accuracy. Future work could improve on our techniques.

Simulation vs. replay. The inherent difference between MIA and other workloads suggest that the best energy efficiency mechanisms would be highly workload dependent. Even for MIA workloads, the behavior varies between use cases and over time (Figures 14 and 21). Thus, only evaluation over long durations can reveal the true historical savings (Figure 14). Days or even weeks-long experiments are unrealistic, especially to explore multiple design options at large scale. Hence, we are compelled to use simulations.

Choice of simulator. We considered using Mumak [37] and MRPerf [53]. Mumak requires logs generated by the Rumen tracing tool [44], which is not yet in universal use and not used at Facebook. MRPerf generates a simulation event per control message and per packet, which limits simulation scale and speed. Neither simulator has been verified at the multi-job workload level. Thus, we developed the BEEMR simulator, which intentionally trades simulation detail and accuracy to gain scale and speed. We also verify the simulator at the workload level (Section 5.8).

Choice of power model. One accurate way to measure system power is by a power meter attached at the machine wall socket [11]. This method does not scale to clusters of 1000s

of machines. The alternative is to use empirically verified power models, which are yet to be satisfactorily developed for MapReduce. The translation between SPECpower [49] measurements and MapReduce remains unknown, as it is between MapReduce workload semantics and detailed CPU, memory, disk, and network activity. We chose an on-off power model, i.e., machines have "max" power when on and "zero" power when off. This simple model allow us to scale the experiments in size and in time.

Towards improved methodology. The deliberate tradeoffs we had to make reflect the nascent performance understanding and modeling of large scale systems such as MapReduce. We encourage the research community to seek to overcome the methodology limitations of this study.

6.4 Future Work for MapReduce in General

Designing and evaluating BEEMR has revealed several opportunities for future improvements to MapReduce.

1. The BEEMR policy space is large. It would be desirable to automatically detect good values for the policy parameters in Table 3.

2. The ability to interrupt and resume jobs is desirable. This feature is proposed under Next Generation Hadoop for fast resume from failures [38]. Energy efficiency would be another motivation for this feature.

3. A well-tuned `taskcalc` algorithm can significantly affect various performance metrics (Section 5.3). However, choosing the correct number of tasks to assign to a job remains an unexplored area. Given recent advances in predicting MapReduce execution time [20, 36], we expect a dedicated effort would discover many improvements.

4. The chatty HDFS/Hadoop messaging protocols limits the dynamic power of machines to a narrow range. There is an opportunity to re-think such protocols for distributed systems to improve power proportionality.

5. The disjoint interactive and batch zones can be further segregated into disjoint interactive and batch clusters. Segregated versus combined cluster operations need to balance a variety of policy, logistical, economic, and engineering concerns. More systematic understanding of energy costs helps inform the discussion.

6. The gap between ideal and BEEMR energy savings increases with cluster size (Section 5.7). It is worth exploring whether more fine-grained power management schemes would close the gap and allow operators to provision for peak while conserving energy costs.

7. Closing Thoughts

BEEMR is able to cut the energy consumption of a cluster almost *in half* (after adjusting for empirically quantified simulation error) without harming the response time of latency-sensitive jobs or relying on storage replication, while allowing jobs to retain the full storage capacity and compute bandwidth of the cluster. BEEMR achieves such results because its design was guided by a thorough analysis of a real-world, large-scale instance of the targeted workload. We dubbed this widespread yet under-studied workload MIA. The key insight from our analysis of MIA workloads is that although MIA clusters host huge volumes of data, the interactive jobs operate on just a small fraction of the data, and thus can be served by a small pool of dedicated machines; the less time-sensitive jobs can run in a batch fashion on the rest of the cluster. We are making available the sanitized Facebook MIA workload traces (`https://github.com/SWIMProjectUCB/SWIM/wiki`) to ensure that ongoing efforts to design large scale MapReduce systems can build on the insights derived in this paper.

References

[1] Amazon Web Services. Amazon Elastic Computing Cloud. http://aws.amazon.com/ec2/.

[2] G. Ananthanarayanan et al. Scarlett: coping with skewed content popularity in mapreduce clusters. In *Eurosys 2011*.

[3] R. H. Arpaci et al. The interaction of parallel and sequential workloads on a network of workstations. In *SIGMETRICS 1995*.

[4] I. Ashok and J. Zahorjan. Scheduling a mixed interactive and batch workload on a parallel, shared memory supercomputer. In *Supercomputing 1992*.

[5] L. A. Barroso. Warehouse-scale computing: Entering the teenage decade. In *ISCA 2011*.

[6] C. Belady. In the data center, power and cooling costs more than the IT equipment it supports. *Electronics Cooling Magazine*, Feb. 2007.

[7] R. Bianchini and R. Rajamony. Power and energy management for server systems. *Computer*, Nov. 2004.

[8] D. Borthakur. Facebook has the world's largest Hadoop cluster! http://hadoopblog.blogspot.com/2010/05/facebook-has-worlds-largest-hadoop.html.

[9] D. Borthakur et al. Apache Hadoop goes realtime at Facebook. In *SIGMOD 2011*.

[10] L. Breslau et al. Web Caching and Zipf-like Distributions: Evidence and Implications. In *INFOCOM 1999*.

[11] Y. Chen, L. Keys, and R. H. Katz. Towards Energy Efficient MapReduce. Technical Report UCB/EECS-2009-109, EECS Department, University of California, Berkeley, Aug 2009.

[12] Y. Chen et al. The Case for Evaluating MapReduce Performance Using Workload Suites. In *MASCOTS 2011*.

[13] Y. Chen et al. Statistical Workloads for Energy Efficient MapReduce. Technical Report UCB/EECS-2010-6, EECS Department, University of California, Berkeley, Jan 2010.

[14] J. Corbet. LWN.net 2009 Kernel Summit coverage: How Google uses Linux. 2009.

[15] J. Dean and S. Ghemawat. MapReduce: Simplified Data Processing on Large Clusters. *Comm. of the ACM*, 51(1):107–113, January 2008.

[16] Q. Deng et al. Memscale: active low-power modes for main memory. In *ASPLOS 2011*.

[17] EMC and IDC iView. Digital Universe. http://www.emc.com/leadership/programs/digital-universe.htm.

[18] S. Eyerman and L. Eeckhout. System-level performance metrics for multiprogram workloads. *Micro, IEEE*, 28(3):42–53, May-June 2008.

[19] X. Fan, W.-D. Weber, and L. A. Barroso. Power provisioning for a warehouse-sized computer. In *ISCA 2007*.

[20] A. Ganapathi et al. Statistics-driven workload modeling for the cloud. In *ICDEW 2010*.

[21] J. Gray et al. Quickly generating billion-record synthetic databases. In *SIGMOD 1994*.

[22] Gridmix. HADOOP-HOME/mapred/src/benchmarks/gridmix2 in Hadoop 0.20.2 onwards.

[23] Hadoop World 2011. Hadoop World 2011 Speakers. http://www.hadoopworld.com/speakers/.

[24] J. Hamilton. Overall Data Center Costs. http://perspectives.mvdirona.com/2010/09/18/OverallDataCenterCosts.aspx, 2010.

[25] Hewlett-Packard Corp., Intel Corp., Microsoft Corp., Phoenix Technologies Ltd., Toshiba Corp. Advanced Configuration and Power Interface 5.0. http://www.acpi.info/.

[26] M. Isard et al. Quincy: fair scheduling for distributed computing clusters. In *SOSP 2009*.

[27] R. T. Kaushik et al. Evaluation and Analysis of GreenHDFS: A Self-Adaptive, Energy-Conserving Variant of the Hadoop Distributed File System. In *IEEE CloudCom 2010*.

[28] W. Lang and J. Patel. Energy management for mapreduce clusters. In *VLDB 2010*.

[29] J. Leverich and C. Kozyrakis. On the Energy (In)efficiency of Hadoop Clusters. In *HotPower 2009*.

[30] P. Lieberman. White paper: Wake on lan technology, June 2006.

[31] B. Liu et al. A study of networks simulation efficiency: Fluid simulation vs. packet-level simulation. In *Infocom 2001*.

[32] D. Meisner et al. Power management of online data-intensive services. In *ISCA 2011*.

[33] D. Meisner et al. Powernap: eliminating server idle power. In *ASPLOS 2009*.

[34] S. Melnik et al. Dremel: interactive analysis of web-scale datasets. In *VLDB 2010*.

[35] A. K. Mishra et al. Towards characterizing cloud backend workloads: insights from Google compute clusters. *SIGMETRICS Perform. Eval. Rev.*, 37:34–41, March 2010.

[36] K. Morton et al. ParaTimer: a progress indicator for MapReduce DAGs. In *SIGMOD 2010*.

[37] Mumak. Mumak: Map-Reduce Simulator. https://issues.apache.org/jira/browse/MAPREDUCE-728.

[38] A. Murthy. Next Generation Hadoop Map-Reduce. Apache Hadoop Summit 2011.

[39] D. Patterson. Energy-Efficient Computing: the State of the Art. Microsoft Research Faculty Summit 2009.

[40] Personal email. Communication regarding release of Google production cluster data.

[41] E. Pinheiro et al. Failure trends in a large disk drive population. In *FAST 2007*.

[42] G. F. Riley, T. M. Jaafar, and R. M. Fujimoto. Integrated fluid and packet network simulations. In *MASCOTS 2002*.

[43] S. Rivoire et al. Joulesort: a balanced energy-efficiency benchmark. In *SIGMOD 2007*.

[44] Rumen: a tool to extract job characterization data from job tracker logs. https://issues.apache.org/jira/browse/MAPREDUCE-751.

[45] A. Ryan. Next-Generation Hadoop Operations. Bay Area Hadoop User Group, February 2010.

[46] J. H. Saltzer. A simple linear model of demand paging performance. *Commun. ACM*, 17:181–186, April 1974.

[47] K. Shvachko. HDFS Scalability: the limits to growth. *Login*, 35(2):6–16, April 2010.

[48] D. C. Snowdon et al. Accurate on-line prediction of processor and memory energy usage under voltage scaling. In *EMSOFT 2007*.

[49] SPEC. SPECpower 2008. http://www.spec.org/power_ssj2008/.

[50] The Green Grid. The Green Grid Data Center Power Efficiency Metrics: PUE and DCiE, 2007.

[51] A. Thusoo et al. Data warehousing and analytics infrastructure at Facebook. In *SIGMOD 2010*.

[52] U.S. Environmental Protection Agency. Report to Congress on Server and Data Center Energy Efficiency, Public Law 109-431, 2007.

[53] G. Wang et al. A simulation approach to evaluating design decisions in MapReduce setups. In *MASCOTS 2009*.

[54] M. Zaharia et al. Delay scheduling: a simple technique for achieving locality and fairness in cluster scheduling. In *EuroSys 2010*.

GreenHadoop: Leveraging Green Energy in Data-Processing Frameworks

Íñigo Goiri

Dept. of Computer Science
Rutgers University
goiri@cs.rutgers.edu

Kien Le

Dept. of Computer Science
Rutgers University
lekien@cs.rutgers.edu

Thu D. Nguyen

Dept. of Computer Science
Rutgers University
tdnguyen@cs.rutgers.edu

Jordi Guitart

Universitat Politècnica de Catalunya
Barcelona Supercomputing Center
jguitart@ac.upc.edu

Jordi Torres

Universitat Politècnica de Catalunya
Barcelona Supercomputing Center
torres@ac.upc.edu

Ricardo Bianchini

Dept. of Computer Science
Rutgers University
ricardob@cs.rutgers.edu

Abstract

Interest has been growing in powering datacenters (at least partially) with renewable or "green" sources of energy, such as solar or wind. However, it is challenging to use these sources because, unlike the "brown" (carbon-intensive) energy drawn from the electrical grid, they are not always available. This means that energy demand and supply must be matched, if we are to take full advantage of the green energy to minimize brown energy consumption. In this paper, we investigate how to manage a datacenter's computational workload to match the green energy supply. In particular, we consider data-processing frameworks, in which many background computations can be delayed by a bounded amount of time. We propose GreenHadoop, a MapReduce framework for a datacenter powered by a photovoltaic solar array and the electrical grid (as a backup). GreenHadoop predicts the amount of solar energy that will be available in the near future, and schedules the MapReduce jobs to maximize the green energy consumption within the jobs' time bounds. If brown energy must be used to avoid time bound violations, GreenHadoop selects times when brown energy is cheap, while also managing the cost of peak brown power consumption. Our experimental results demonstrate that Green-Hadoop can significantly increase green energy consumption and decrease electricity cost, compared to Hadoop.

Categories and Subject Descriptors   D.4.1 [*Operating Systems*]: Process Management—Scheduling

Keywords   Green energy; renewable energy; MapReduce; energy-aware scheduling; cost-aware scheduling

1. Introduction

It is well-known that datacenters consume an enormous amount of power [31], representing a financial burden for their operating organizations, an infrastructure burden on power utilities, and an environmental burden on society. Large Internet companies (e.g., Google and Microsoft) have significantly improved the energy efficiency of their multi-megawatt datacenters. However, the majority of the energy consumed by datacenters is actually due to countless small and medium-sized ones [31], which are much less efficient. These facilities range from a few dozen servers housed in a machine room to several hundreds of servers housed in a larger enterprise installation.

These cost, infrastructure, and environmental concerns have prompted some datacenter operators to either generate their own solar/wind energy or draw power directly from a nearby solar/wind farm. Many small and medium datacenters (partially or completely) powered by solar and/or wind energy are being built all over the world (see *http://www.eco-businesslinks.com/green_web_hosting.htm* for a partial list). This trend will likely continue, as these technologies' capital costs continue to decrease (e.g., the cost of solar energy has decreased by 7-fold in the last two decades [29]) and governments continue to provide incentives for green power generation and use (e.g., federal and state incentives in New Jersey can reduce capital costs by 60% [7]).

For the scenarios in which green datacenters are appropriate, we argue that they should connect to both the solar/wind energy source and the electrical grid, which acts as a backup when green energy is unavailable. The major challenge with solar or wind energy is that, unlike brown energy drawn from the grid, it is not always available. For example, photovoltaic (PV) solar energy is only available during the day and the amount produced depends on the weather and the season.

To mitigate this variability, datacenters could "bank" green energy in batteries or on the grid itself (called net metering). However, these approaches have many problems: (1) batteries incur energy losses due to internal resistance and self-discharge; (2) battery-related costs can dominate in solar-powered systems [11]; (3) batteries use chemicals that are harmful to the environment; (4) net metering incurs losses due to the voltage transformation involved in feeding the green energy into the grid; (5) net metering is unavailable in many parts of the world; and (6) where net metering is available, the power company may pay less than the retail electricity price for the green energy. Given these problems, the best way to take full advantage of the available green energy is to match the energy demand to the energy supply.

Thus, in this paper, we investigate how to manage the computational workload to match the green energy supply in small/medium datacenters running data-processing frameworks. In particular, we consider the MapReduce framework [6] and its Hadoop implementation [4]. Data-processing frameworks are an interesting target for our research, as they are popular and often run many low-priority batch processing jobs, such as background log analysis, that do not have strict completion time requirements; they can be delayed by a bounded amount of time. However, scheduling the energy consumption of MapReduce jobs is challenging, because they do not specify the number of servers to use, their run times, or their energy needs. Moreover, power-managing servers in these frameworks requires guaranteeing that the data to be accessed by the jobs remains available.

With these observations in mind, we propose Green-Hadoop, a MapReduce framework for datacenters powered by PV solar arrays and the electrical grid (as a backup). GreenHadoop seeks to maximize the green energy consumption of the MapReduce workload, or equivalently to minimize its brown energy consumption. GreenHadoop predicts the amount of solar energy that will likely be available in the future, using historical data and weather forecasts. It also estimates the approximate energy needs of jobs using historical data. Using these predictions, GreenHadoop may then decide to delay some (low-priority) jobs to wait for available green energy, but always within their time bounds. If brown energy must be used to avoid bound violations, it schedules the jobs at times when brown energy is cheap, while also managing the cost of peak brown power consumption. GreenHadoop controls energy usage by using its predictions and knowledge of the data required by the scheduled jobs. With this information, it defines how many and which servers to use; it transitions other servers to low-power states to the extent possible.

We evaluate GreenHadoop using two realistic workloads running on a 16-server cluster. We model the datacenter's solar array as a scaled-down version of an existing Rutgers solar farm. The brown energy prices and peak brown power charges are from a power company in New Jersey. We compare GreenHadoop's green energy consumption and brown electricity cost to those of standard Hadoop and of an energy-aware version of Hadoop that we developed. Our results demonstrate that GreenHadoop can increase green energy consumption by up to 31% and decrease brown electricity cost by up to 39%, compared to Hadoop. In addition, our results show that GreenHadoop is robust to workload variability and effective for a range of time bounds.

GreenHadoop is most closely related to our own Green-Slot [9], a green energy-aware scheduler for scientific computing jobs. However, GreenSlot relies on extensive user-provided information about job behavior, assumes that persistent data is always available to jobs regardless of the servers' power states, and does not manage the cost of peak brown power consumption. In contrast, GreenHadoop requires no job behavior information, and explicitly manages data availability and peak brown power costs.

We conclude that green datacenters and software that is aware of the characteristics of both green and brown electricities can have a key role in building a more sustainable and cost-effective Information Technology (IT) ecosystem.

In summary, we make the following contributions:

- We introduce GreenHadoop, a MapReduce framework for datacenters partly powered by solar energy;

- We introduce MapReduce job scheduling and data management techniques that are aware of green energy, brown energy prices, and peak brown power charges;

- We demonstrate that it is possible to manage green energy use and brown electricity cost when the jobs' run times and energy demands are not specified; and

- We present extensive results isolating the impact of different aspects of the implementation.

2. Background

Use of solar energy in datacenters. Solar and wind are two of the most promising green energy technologies, as they do not cause the environmental disruption of hydroelectric energy and do not have the waste storage problem of nuclear energy. Solar/wind equipment produces Direct Current (DC) electricity, which is typically converted to Alternating Current (AC) by DC/AC inverters.

In this paper, we assume that the datacenter generates its own PV solar energy. (Except for our solar energy predictions, our work is directly applicable to wind energy as well.) Self-generation is attractive for multiple reasons, including (1) the fact that energy losses with power transformation and transmission can exceed 40%; (2) the ability to survive grid outages, which are common in some developing countries;

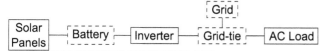

Figure 1. Components of a (partially) solar-powered computer system. Dashed boxes represent optional components.

(3) the fact that PV power scales poorly, as the cost/W does not decrease beyond 800KW (the maximum inverter size today [28]); and (4) the ability to eventually lower costs. In fact, based on the results from Section 5 and the governmental incentives in New Jersey, the current capital cost of installing solar panels for the datacenter we model can be amortized by savings in brown energy cost in 10.6 years of operation. This amortization period is substantially shorter than the typical 20-30 years lifetime of the panels. The period will be even shorter in the future, as solar costs continue to decrease at a rapid pace [29]. The increasing popularity of distributed generation and microgrids suggests that many people find self-generation attractive.

There are multiple ways to connect solar panels to a datacenter. Figure 1 shows a general setup. The solar panels can be connected to batteries for storing excess energy during periods of sunlight and discharging it during other periods. The datacenter must also be connected to the electrical grid via a grid-tie device if it must be operational even when solar energy is not available. Where net metering is available, it is possible to feed excess solar energy into the grid for a reduction in brown energy costs.

The design we study does not include batteries or net metering for the reasons mentioned in the Introduction. Thus, any green energy not immediately used is wasted. Fortunately, GreenHadoop is very successful at limiting waste.

Brown energy prices and peak brown power charges. Datacenters often contract with their power companies to pay variable brown energy prices, i.e. different dollar amounts per kWh of consumed brown energy. The most common arrangement is for the datacenter to pay less for brown energy consumed during an off-peak period (e.g., at night) than during an on-peak period (e.g., daytime). Thus, it would be profitable for the datacenter to schedule part of its workload during the off-peak periods if possible.

However, high brown energy costs are not the only concern. Often, datacenters also have to pay for their peak brown power consumption, i.e. a dollar amount per kW of brown power at the highest period of brown power usage. Even though these charges have almost always been overlooked in the literature, the peak brown power charge can be significant, especially during the summer. Govindan *et al.* estimate that this component can represent up to 40% of the overall electricity cost of a datacenter [10].

To compute the peak charges, utilities typically monitor the average brown power consumption within 15-minute windows during each month. They define the maximum of these averages as the peak brown power for the month.

MapReduce and Hadoop. MapReduce is a framework for processing large data sets on server clusters [6]. Each MapReduce program defines two functions: map and reduce. The framework divides the input data into a set of blocks, and runs a *map task* for each block that invokes the map function on each key/value pair in the block. The framework groups together all intermediate values produced by the map tasks with the same intermediate key. It then runs the *reduce tasks*, each of which invokes the reduce function on each intermediate key and its associated values from a distinct subset of generated intermediate keys. The reduce tasks generate the final result.

Hadoop is the best-known, publicly available implementation of MapReduce [4]. Hadoop comprises two main parts: the Hadoop Distributed File System (HDFS) and the Hadoop MapReduce framework. Data to be processed by a MapReduce program is stored in HDFS. HDFS splits files across the servers' local disks. A cluster-wide NameNode process maintains information about where to find each data block.

Users submit *jobs* to the framework using a client interface. This interface uses each job's configuration parameters to split the input data and set the number of tasks. Jobs must identify all input data at submission time. The interface submits each job to the JobTracker, a cluster-wide process that manages job execution. Each server runs a configurable number of map and reduce tasks concurrently in compute "slots". The JobTracker communicates with the NameNode to determine the location of each job's data. It then selects servers to execute the jobs, preferably ones that store the needed data if they have slots available. Hadoop's default scheduling policy is FIFO.

3. MapReduce in Green Datacenters

We propose GreenHadoop, a data-processing framework for datacenters powered by PV solar panels and the electricity grid. GreenHadoop relies on predictions of the availability of solar energy, and a scheduling and data availability algorithm that is aware of green energy, brown energy prices, and peak brown power charges. We refer to the overall brown energy and power costs as the brown electricity cost.

To achieve its goals of maximizing green energy usage and minimizing brown electricity cost, GreenHadoop may delay the execution of some jobs. To avoid excessive delays, GreenHadoop attempts to complete all jobs within a bounded amount of time from their submissions. GreenHadoop is beneficial because datacenters are often underutilized and many jobs have loose performance requirements (e.g., data and log analysis, long simulations, jobs submitted on Friday whose output is not needed until Monday).

Figure 2 illustrates the behavior of GreenHadoop (bottom), in comparison to conventional Hadoop (top) and an energy-aware version of Hadoop (middle) for three MapReduce jobs. Hadoop executes the jobs immediately when they arrive, using all servers to complete the jobs as quickly as

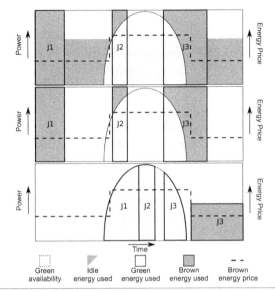

Figure 2. Scheduling 3 MapReduce jobs (J1-J3) with Hadoop (top), energy-aware Hadoop (middle), and GreenHadoop (bottom).

possible. Hadoop keeps all servers active even if they are idle. As a result, Hadoop wastes substantial green and brown energy, and incurs unnecessary energy costs. In contrast, the energy-aware Hadoop that we implemented reduces waste by transitioning idle servers to a low-power state.

GreenHadoop behaves differently. It uses as many servers as green energy can sustain when it is available, fewer servers (if possible) when brown energy is cheap, and even fewer (if at all necessary) when brown energy is expensive. Figure 2(bottom) shows that GreenHadoop delayed jobs J1 and J2 to maximize the green energy consumption. More interestingly, GreenHadoop executed part of J3 with green energy, and delayed the other part until the brown energy became cheaper. Moreover, GreenHadoop did not use all servers to run J3 with brown energy to limit the peak brown power costs. When certain servers need not be fully active, GreenHadoop transitions them to lower power states.

Essentially, GreenHadoop determines how many and which servers to use at each point in time, and schedules the jobs on those servers. The other servers can be deactivated to conserve energy.

We designed GreenHadoop as a wrapper around a modified version of Hadoop. The wrapper implements the scheduling, data management, and prediction of solar energy availability described in the remainder of the section. We also briefly discuss our modest changes to Hadoop.

3.1 Scheduling and Data Availability

3.1.1 Overview

At submission time, users can specify the priority for their jobs. Like standard Hadoop, GreenHadoop has five priority classes: very high, high, normal, low, and very low. Green-Hadoop executes very high and high priority jobs as soon as possible, giving them all the servers they can use. In contrast,

GreenHadoop may delay some of the normal, low, and very low priority jobs by a bounded amount of time (by default, at most one day in our experiments). These behaviors reflect our performance goals: high-priority jobs should complete as quickly as in standard Hadoop, whereas low-priority ones must complete within their time bounds.

GreenHadoop divides time into fixed-size "epochs" (four minutes in our experiments). At the beginning of each epoch, GreenHadoop determines whether the number of active servers should be changed and whether all the data needed by the scheduled jobs is available. Specifically, servers can be in one of three states in GreenHadoop: Active, Decommissioned, or Down (ACPI's S3 state). In the Decommissioned state, no new tasks are started on the server, but previously running tasks run to completion. Moreover, no new blocks are stored at a decommissioned server, but it still serves accesses to the blocks it currently stores. Whenever servers are not needed for computation, GreenHadoop first transitions them to the Decommissioned state, and then later sends them to the Down state. To prevent data unavailability, it replicates any data needed by scheduled jobs from the decommissioned servers before sending them down. Every so often, GreenHadoop reduces the amount of replication.

Estimating the jobs' energy and time requirements is challenging. Unlike traditional batch job schedulers, e.g. [8, 32], GreenHadoop does not have information about the jobs' desired number of servers or expected running times, from which we could estimate their energy needs. Instead, GreenHadoop computes average running times and energy consumptions based on prior history, relying on aggregate statistics of the datacenter's workload, rather than information about specific jobs or applications. These averages are then used to estimate the resource requirements of groups of jobs, not each individual job, during the "scheduling horizon" (one day ahead in our experiments).

GreenHadoop is electricity-cost-aware in that it favors scheduling jobs in epochs when energy is cheap. To prioritize green energy, it is assumed to have zero cost. When the price of brown energy is not fixed and brown energy must be used, GreenHadoop favors the cheaper epochs. In addition, GreenHadoop manages the peak brown power usage by limiting the number of active servers, if that can be done without violating any time bounds.

3.1.2 Algorithm Details

Figure 3 shows the pseudo-code of the GreenHadoop algorithm. As line 1 suggests, GreenHadoop maintains two job queues: Run and Wait. The Run queue is implemented by Hadoop, whereas we implement the Wait queue entirely in the wrapper. Jobs submitted with very high or high priority are sent straight to the Hadoop queue in FIFO order, whereas others initially go to the Wait queue also in FIFO order.

Assigning deadlines. Lines 2-26 describe the system's behavior at the beginning of each epoch. First (line 3), it as-

```
0.  At job submission time:
1.      Very high and high priority jobs go straight to the Run queue; other jobs go to the Wait queue

2.  At the beginning of each epoch:
3.      Assign internal latest-start deadlines to all waiting jobs that arrived in the previous epoch
4.      Calculate the number of active servers to use during the scheduling horizon (defined in lines 11-18)
5.      Select waiting jobs to move to the Run queue (in line 10):
6.          If a job is about to violate its latest-start deadline, select the job
7.          If a job has all the data it needs available, select the job
8.          If the active servers are not fully utilized, select the jobs that require data access to the fewest servers
9.      Manage the servers' states and data availability (defined in lines 19-26)
10.     When the data required by the selected jobs is available, move them to the Run queue

11. Calculate the number of active servers to use:
12.     Calculate the dynamic energy required by all running and waiting jobs
13.     Compute/predict the energy available for each type of energy during the scheduling horizon
14.     Subtract the static energy of the entire system from the energy available
15.     Subtract the dynamic energy required by any very high or high priority jobs from the energy available
16.     Assign the remaining green energy to waiting jobs
17.     Assign the remaining brown energy and power to waiting jobs, considering brown energy prices and peak brown power charges
18.     If some waiting jobs have not been assigned energy, reject new jobs that arrive in the next epoch

19. Manage the servers' states and data availability:
20.     Ensure that all the data required by the selected jobs is available in active or decommissioned servers
21.     If some data is not available, turn into Decommissioned state the min set of down servers containing the data
22.     If current number of active servers is smaller than desired number, transition servers from Decommissioned to Active state
23.         If we still need more active servers, transition them from Down state to Active state
24.     If current number of active servers is larger than desired number, transition active servers to Decommissioned state
25.     Replicate the data from servers in Decommissioned state, if necessary
26.     Check if servers that are in Decommissioned state can be sent to Down state
```

Figure 3. GreenHadoop algorithm for scheduling and data availability.

signs internal "latest-start deadlines" to any waiting jobs that were queued in the previous epoch. The latest-start deadline specifies the latest epoch in which the job needs to start, so that it is expected to complete within the system's desired completion time bound. GreenHadoop computes the latest-start deadline for each job based on its arrival epoch, the expected duration of the group of jobs after (and including) it in the Wait queue, and the completion time bound.

Calculating the number of active servers. Second (lines 4, 11-18), GreenHadoop calculates the number of active servers to use in each epoch during the scheduling horizon. This calculation involves computing the dynamic energy required by the jobs currently in the system. GreenHadoop computes this energy by multiplying the average dynamic energy per job by the number of waiting jobs and adding the leftover dynamic energy required by the running jobs. GreenHadoop estimates the average dynamic energy per job using an exponentially weighted moving average of the dynamic energy consumed during the last ten epochs divided by the number of jobs executed in this period.

After computing the dynamic energy required by the jobs, GreenHadoop assigns the available green, cheap brown, and expensive brown energies to them (lines 13-17). GreenHadoop predicts the green energy that will be available (see Section 3.2). It computes the brown energy available assuming that all servers could be active during the (pre-defined) periods of cheap and expensive brown energy. From these three types of energy, GreenHadoop subtracts the static energy (corresponding to the energy consumed by all servers in Down state, the switch, and an always-on server) to be consumed. In addition, it subtracts the dynamic energy needed by any very high or high priority jobs in the Run queue.

In assigning the remaining energy to jobs, GreenHadoop first assigns the green energy, then the cheap brown energy, and finally the expensive brown energy. In the absence of peak brown power charges, it uses all the servers to consume the brown energies. Otherwise, it records the peak brown power that has been reached so far this month. We refer to this quantity as "past-peak-brown-power". It then finds the best brown power at which to limit consumption between past-peak-brown-power and the maximum achievable power (i.e., all machines activated). Increasing the peak brown power increases peak charges, but those charges may be offset by reduced runtime in periods of expensive brown energy. The best peak brown power is the one that provides enough energy to complete the schedule and leads to the minimum electricity cost.

The number of active servers during each epoch within the horizon derives from the amount of dynamic energy assigned to the epoch. Since we know the length of the epoch, the dynamic energy can be transformed into an average dynamic power, which in turn can be transformed into a number of active servers. For example, suppose that the average available dynamic power in an epoch is 1000W. Suppose also that we currently have 3 active servers running jobs and serving data, and 3 decommissioned servers just serving data; the other servers are down and, thus, consume no dynamic power. In our experiments, active servers and decommissioned servers consume at most roughly 136W and 66W of dynamic power, respectively. Thus, the current total dynamic power consumption is $606W = 3 \times 136W + 3 \times 66W$, leaving 394W available. In response, GreenHadoop would activate the 3 decommissioned servers and 1 down server for a total of $952W = 606W + 3 \times (136W - 66W) + 136W$;

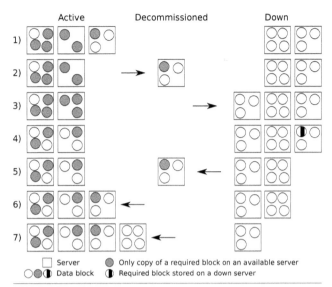

Figure 4. Server power state and data management sequence. 1) Initial configuration; 2) GreenHadoop does not need one of the active servers and sends the active server with the fewest data blocks required by the jobs in the Run queue to the Decommissioned state; 3) GreenHadoop replicates the required block from the decommissioned server to an active server, and then transitions the decommissioned server to the Down state; 4) A new job is moved to the Run queue, requiring data stored only on a down server; 5) GreenHadoop transitions the down server to Decommissioned to provide the needed data; 6) GreenHadoop needs one more active server, transitioning the decommissioned server to the Active state; 7) GreenHadoop still needs another server, and so it activates the down server with the most data.

the remaining 48W would not be usable. If some waiting jobs cannot be assigned energy within the scheduling horizon (line 18), the system is overcommitted, so GreenHadoop rejects the jobs arriving in the next epoch.

Selecting waiting jobs to move to the Run queue. Third (lines 5-8), GreenHadoop selects some waiting jobs that will soon be moved to the Run queue. GreenHadoop considers each waiting job in order and selects the job if (1) it is about to violate its latest-start deadline, (2) all the data it needs is on active or decommissioned servers, or (3) an active server is under-utilized (i.e., not all of its compute slots are being used) and the job requires the fewest down servers to be brought up for its data. GreenHadoop moves the selected jobs to the Run queue when the data they require becomes available (line 10). Jobs selected due to their latest-start deadlines are sent to the Run queue with very high priority.

Managing server power states and data availability. Finally, GreenHadoop manages the servers' states and the data availability (lines 9, 19-26). If not all data required by the selected jobs is currently available in active or decommissioned servers, GreenHadoop transitions the needed servers from the Down state to the Decommissioned state (lines 20 and 21). It then adjusts the number of active servers based on the target number computed earlier (lines 22-26).

Figure 4 illustrates an example of GreenHadoop managing its servers' power states and data availability. When it reduces the number of active servers (step 2), GreenHadoop splits them into two groups: (a) those that have executed tasks of still-running jobs, and (b) those that have not. Then, it sorts each group in ascending order of the amount of data stored at the server that is required by jobs in the Run queue. Finally, it starts sending servers in group (b) to the Decommissioned state, and then moves to group (a), stopping when the target reduction has been reached.

After adjusting the number of active servers, GreenHadoop considers sending decommissioned servers to the Down state (step 3). A decommissioned server cannot go down if it has executed a task of still-running jobs. Moreover, before the server can go down, GreenHadoop must copy (replicate) any data that is required by a job in the Run queue but that is not currently available on the active servers.

In the opposite direction, when servers need to be transitioned from Decommissioned to Active (step 6), GreenHadoop divides the decommissioned servers into the same two groups as above. Then, it sorts each group in decreasing order of the amount of data stored at the server that is required by the jobs in the Run queue. It starts activating the decommissioned servers in group (a) and then moves to group (b), stopping if the target number is reached. If more active servers are needed (i.e., the decommissioned servers are not enough to reach the target), GreenHadoop activates the servers in Down state that store the most data required by jobs in the run queue (step 7).

3.1.3 Power State and Data Management Rationale

GreenHadoop relies on dynamic replication of data blocks to guarantee data availability when servers are turned off. However, it is possible to manage power states and data availability without dynamic replication, as in the covering subset approach [20]. This approach ensures that at least one copy of every data block stored in a Hadoop cluster is kept on a designated subset of servers (the covering subset); keeping these servers in either the Active or Decommissioned state would statically guarantee the availability of all data.

Unfortunately, using the covering subset approach would limit GreenHadoop's ability to send servers to the Down state. For example, if each data block is replicated 3 times—a typical replication level—then to keep storage balanced across the cluster, roughly 1/3 of the servers would have to be in the covering subset. The servers in the covering subset cannot be sent to the Down state, even if they are not needed for running computations.

In contrast, GreenHadoop guarantees availability only for data required by jobs in the Run queue. When the load is low, e.g. only one job is running, the required data is typically a small subset of all data stored in the cluster, enabling GreenHadoop to send all but one server to the Down state. Thus, our approach trades off the energy required to replicate (and later dereplicate) data against the energy savings from transitioning servers to the Down state when they are not needed for computation. This tradeoff is advantageous since (1) current servers are not power-proportional, so a server that is mostly idle only servicing data requests requires a large fraction of its peak power; (2) transitions to and from the S3 state take on the order of only several seconds; (3) GreenHadoop transitions servers to S3 in an order that tries to maximize energy savings; (4) replicating a data block is typically a cheap operation compared to the duration and power consumption of the compute task that operates on it; and (5) dereplication is nearly free of cost. We evaluate GreenHadoop's data management approach in Section 5.

3.2 Predicting the Availability of Solar Energy

GreenHadoop can easily use any model that predicts the availability of green energy. In fact, it would even adapt to wind energy predictions without modification. Our current implementation uses the model introduced by Sharma *et al.* [26] to predict solar energy. This model is based on the simple premise that energy generation is inversely related to the amount of cloud coverage, and is expressed as: $E_p(t) = B(t)(1 - CloudCover)$, where $E_p(t)$ is the amount of solar energy predicted for time t, $B(t)$ is the amount of solar energy expected under ideal sunny conditions, and *CloudCover* is the forecasted percentage cloud cover (given as a fraction between 0 and 1).[1]

We implement solar energy prediction using the above model at the granularity of an hour. We use weather forecasts from Intellicast.com, which provides hourly predictions that include cloud coverage for up to 48 hours into the future. We use historical data to instantiate $B(t)$. We compute a distinct $B(t)$ for each month of the year to account for seasonal effects. For each month, we set $B(t)$ to the actual energy generated by the day with the highest energy generation from the same month of the previous year. (For new installations, it is also possible to use data from the previous month.)

Unfortunately, weather forecasts can be wrong. For example, we have observed that predictions of thunderstorms are frequently inaccurate and can remain inaccurate throughout a day. Furthermore, weather is not the only factor that affects energy generation. For example, after a snow storm, little energy will be generated while the solar panels remain covered by snow even if the weather is sunny.

To increase accuracy in these hard-to-predict scenarios, we use an alternate method of instantiating *CloudCover* proposed by Goiri *et al.* [9]. Specifically, we assume that the recent past can predict the near future [26], and compute *CloudCover* using the observed energy generated in the previous hour. When invoked, our prediction module compares the accuracy of the two prediction methods for the last hour and chooses the more accurate method to instantiate *Cloud-*

Cover for the remainder of the current day. Beyond the current day, we instantiate *CloudCover* using weather forecasts.

3.3 Modified Hadoop

As already mentioned, most of GreenHadoop is implemented in a wrapper external to Hadoop. However, we also extended Hadoop itself with power management functionality. Our main changes include (1) the introduction of the Decommissioned and Down states for servers, which involved changes to the JobTracker and NameNode processes; (2) enabling the NameNode process to know what data is present in down servers, so that they can be activated when their data is not replicated elsewhere; and (3) improvements to the block replication and replica removal functionality already present in Hadoop.

4. Evaluation Methodology

Hardware and software. We evaluate GreenHadoop using a 16-server cluster, where each server is a 4-core Xeon machine with 8GB RAM and a 7200-rpm SATA disk with 64GB of free space for data. The servers are inter-connected by a Gigabit Ethernet switch.

GreenHadoop extends Hadoop version 0.21 for Linux with roughly 5000 uncommented lines of Python wrapper code, and adds around 100 lines to Hadoop itself. We study 3 versions of GreenHadoop: "GreenOnly", which makes decisions based on knowledge about green energy availability; "GreenVarPrices", which considers both green energy and variable brown energy prices, and "GreenVarPricesPeak" which considers green energy, variable brown energy prices, and peak brown power charges. The GreenVarPricesPeak version is the full-blown GreenHadoop.

For comparison, we also study "Hadoop", the regular Hadoop FIFO scheduler; and "Energy-Aware Hadoop" ("EAHadoop"), our own extension of Hadoop that manages data availability and transitions servers to lower power states when they are not required. EAHadoop is simply a version of GreenHadoop that disregards green energy, brown energy prices, and peak brown power charges. In fact, EAHadoop's pseudo-code is that in Figure 3 minus lines 13, and 15-17.

Workloads. We study two widely differing workloads: (1) a synthetic workload, called "Facebook-Derived" or simply "FaceD", that models Facebook's multi-user production workload [33]; and (2) the Web indexing part of the Nutch Web-search system [5], called "Nutch Indexing" or simply "NutchI". FaceD contains jobs with widely varying execution time and data set sizes, representing a scenario where the cluster is used to run many different types of applications. NutchI jobs are relatively homogeneous, representing a scenario where the cluster is used to run a continuous production batch workload. By default, we submit all jobs of these workloads with normal priority to provide the maximum flexibility to GreenHadoop. We study the impact of different mixes of priorities in Section 5.

---

[1] Factors other than cloud cover, such as temperature, can affect the amount of solar energy produced. However, Section 5 shows that ignoring these factors still leads to sufficient accuracy for our purposes.

Cat.	% Jobs	# Maps	# Reds	In (GB)	Out (GB)
0	59.0%	4	1	0.25	0.01
1	9.8%	10	1-2	0.63	0.03
2	8.7%	20	1-5	1.25	0.06
3	8.5%	40	2-10	2.50	0.13
4	5.7%	80	4-20	5.00	0.25
5	4.4%	150	8-38	9.38	0.48
6	2.5%	300	15-75	18.75	0.95
7	1.3%	600	30-150	37.50	1.90

Table 1. FaceD workload characteristics.

FaceD is a scaled-down version of the workload studied in [33] because our cluster is significantly smaller. As in that paper, we do not run the Facebook code itself; rather, we mimic the characteristics of its jobs using "loadgen." Loadgen is a configurable MapReduce job from the Gridmix benchmark included in the Hadoop distribution. We scale the workload down in two ways: we reduce the number of maps by a factor of 4, and eliminate the largest 1.7% of jobs.

Table 1 summarizes FaceD, which comprises 8 categories of jobs (leftmost column). The 2nd column lists the fraction of the jobs that corresponds to each category. The 3rd and 4th columns list the number of maps and reduces in each job. The length of each map task is uniformly distributed between 9s and 60s. Each reduce task takes between 2s and 12s per map in the job. The 5th and 6th columns list the amount of input and output data that each job handles. Each map task operates on a data block of 64MB (the default Hadoop block size), and each reduce task outputs roughly 13MB. On average, each job touches 2.5GB of data with a minimum of 250MB and a maximum of 37.5GB. Jobs arrive at the cluster continuously according to a Poisson distribution with mean inter-arrival time of 30s. These parameters lead to a cluster utilization of 56% in Hadoop, which is substantially higher than those typically seen in the small and medium-sized datacenters that we target [25]. We investigate the impact of utilization in Section 5.

NutchI consists of jobs that index groups of pages previously fetched from our Web domain. Each job runs 42 map tasks and 1 reduce task. Each map task takes either 4s or 12s, whereas the reduce tasks take 50s. On average, each job touches 85MB of data. Jobs arrive according to a Poisson distribution with mean inter-arrival time of 20s. These characteristics lead to a cluster utilization of 35%.

Power consumption and solar panel array. We measured the power consumption of a server running Hadoop jobs using a Yokogawa multimeter. A Down server consumes 9W of static power, whereas a Decommissioned server consumes 75W (9W static + 66W dynamic). A server executing 1 to 4 tasks consumes 100W, 115W, 130W, and 145W, respectively. Together with the 55W consumed by the switch, the common-case peak power consumption of our system for our workloads is $2375W = 16 \times 145W + 55W$. Transitioning into and out of Down state takes 9 seconds.

We model the solar panel array as a scaled-down version of the Rutgers solar farm, which can produce 1.4MW of power. Specifically, we estimate the production of the smaller installation by scaling the farm's actual energy production over time compared its maximum capacity. We scale the farm's production down to 14 solar panels capable of producing 3220W. We select this scaled size because, after derating, it produces roughly the common-case peak power consumption of our system.

We considered more than one year worth of solar energy production by the farm starting on March 8, 2010. From this set, we picked 5 pairs of consecutive days to study in detail. Each pair represents a different pattern of solar energy production for the 1st and 2nd days, and was chosen randomly from the set of consecutive days with similar patterns. For example, days 05/09/11 and 05/10/11 represent two consecutive days with high solar energy production. We refer to this pair as "High-High" and use it as our default. For the "High-Low", "Low-High", "Low-Low", and "Very Low-Very Low" scenarios, we use the pairs of days starting on 05/12, 06/14, 06/16, and 05/15 in 2011, with 43.2, 29.8, 32.4, 25.9, and 8.4 kWh of generated solar energy, respectively. We study these pairs of days because they correspond to different weather patterns that affect both the amount of energy produced and the accuracy of our energy production predictor. In particular, predictions are typically very accurate for sunny days with "High" energy production, somewhat less accurate for cloudy days with "Very Low" energy production, and possibly much less accurate for partially cloudy days with "Low" energy production (see Section 5).

Brown electricity pricing. We assume on-peak/off-peak pricing, the most common type of variable brown energy pricing. In this scheme, energy costs less during off-peak times (11pm to 9am) and more during on-peak times (9am to 11pm). The difference in prices is largest in the summer (June-September). We assume the energy prices charged by PSEG in New Jersey: $0.13/kWh and $0.08/kWh (summer) and $0.12/kWh and $0.08/kWh (rest of year). We also assume the peak brown power charges from PSEG: $13.61/kW (summer) and $5.59/kW (rest of year). Winter pricing applies to the High-High and High-Low days.

Accelerating the experiments. To fully observe the behavior of GreenHadoop and its versions in real time, we would have to execute each of our experiments for at least one entire day. This would allow us to exactly reproduce the periods of solar energy production (~10 hours), on-peak/off-peak energy prices (14 and 10 hours, respectively), and peak power accounting (15 minutes). However, it would also entail 62 days of non-stop experiments, which would be infeasible. Thus, to speed up our study while demonstrating GreenHadoop's full functionality, we run the unchanged FaceD and NutchI workloads, while shortening the above three periods, GreenHadoop's epoch, and GreenHadoop's

	Prediction Error (%)					
	1	**3**	**6**	**12**	**24**	**48**
Average	12.6	17.6	21.6	21.4	21.2	20.6
Median	11.0	16.4	20.4	20.4	20.3	17.5
90th percentile	22.2	28.9	34.0	37.4	37.9	37.8

Table 2. Error when predicting 1, 3, 6, 12, 24, and 48 hours ahead.

horizon by a factor of 24. This shortening factor means that each of our 2-day experiments executes in just 2 hours.

GreenHadoop's scheduling and data availability algorithm itself cannot be accelerated. For FaceD, it takes a maximum of 0.4 seconds (without any optimizations) to prepare a schedule on one of our servers. This maximum occurs when the largest number of jobs (40) is in the Wait queue. Data replication and de-replication also cannot be accelerated. This presents the worse-case scenario for Green-Hadoop because the energy consumption of these activities are amortized across a much shorter period.

5. Evaluation Results

This section presents our experimental results. First, we evaluate the accuracy of our solar energy predictions. Second, we compare GreenOnly, GreenVarPrices, and Green-VarPricesPeak in turn with Hadoop and EAHadoop to isolate the benefits of being aware of green energy, being aware of brown energy prices, and being aware of peak brown power charges. Third, we consider the impact of various parameters, including the amount of green energy available, datacenter utilization, fraction of high priority jobs, and shorter time bounds. Fourth, we study the accuracy of GreenVarPricesPeak's energy estimates. Finally, we compare the GreenVarPricesPeak results for FaceD and NutchI.

Throughout these experiments, none of the systems we study violates any job time bounds except when we explore time bounds of 12 hours or less.

Predicting solar energy. Table 2 shows the percentage prediction error for daily energy production when predicting 1 to 48 hours ahead for the two months that include the 10 days used in our evaluation. We compute this error as the sum of the absolute difference between the predicted value and actual energy production for each hour in a day, divided by the ideal daily production (i.e., $\sum_{t=0}^{23} B(t)$).

These results show that the predictions are reasonably accurate, achieving median and 90th percentile errors of 11.0% and 22.2%, respectively, when predicting energy production for the next hour. The predictions tend to be less accurate for Low energy days because predicted cloud cover levels are more inaccurate when the weather is partly cloudy. The predictions become more accurate when the weather is mostly cloudy, as in the Very Low-Very Low days. Interestingly, while prediction accuracy drops as the prediction horizon stretches from 1 to 6 hours, beyond 6 hours accuracy sometimes improves. The reason is that the accuracy of the cloud

cover information tends to vary widely with time. Of the 5 pairs of days we consider, predictions are most accurate for the High-High pair, with an average 1-hour ahead prediction error of 6.1%, and worst for the Low-Low pair, with an average 1-hour ahead prediction error of 23.8%.

To understand the impact of these mispredictions, we compare GreenVarPricesPeak when using our prediction vs. when using (idealized) perfect future knowledge of energy production. This comparison shows that the difference in green energy consumption, and total brown electricity cost per job between the two versions is always under 16.4%. The maximum difference occurs on the "Low-Low" days. This suggests that GreenHadoop could benefit somewhat from greater green energy prediction accuracy.

Scheduling for solar energy. Figures 5 and 6 show the behavior of Hadoop and EAHadoop, respectively, for the FaceD workload and the High-High days. The X-axis represents time, whereas the Y-axis represents cluster-wide power consumption (left) and brown energy prices (right). The figures depict the green and brown energy consumptions using areas colored light gray and dark gray, respectively. The two line curves represent the green energy available (labeled "Green actual") and the brown energy price ("Brown price").

These figures show that EAHadoop successfully reduces the overall energy consumption of the workload. This effect is most obvious around noon on Tuesday. However, both Hadoop versions waste a large amount of green energy (31% for both), which could be used instead of brown energy.

In contrast, Figure 7 depicts the behavior of GreenOnly under the same conditions. In this figure, we plot the amount of green energy that GreenHadoop predicted to be available an hour earlier (labeled "Green predicted"). The green prediction line does not exactly demarcate the light gray area, because our predictions are sometimes inaccurate.

A comparison between the three figures clearly illustrates how GreenOnly is capable of using substantially more green energy and less brown energy than Hadoop and EAHadoop, while meeting all job time bounds. GreenOnly spreads out job execution, always seeking to reduce the consumption of brown energy within resource and time constraints. Overall, GreenOnly consumes 30% more green energy than Hadoop and EAHadoop, respectively, in this experiment. Although GreenOnly does not consider brown energy prices, its brown electricity cost savings reach 30% and 29% compared to Hadoop and EAHadoop, respectively. (Note that these cost calculations do not consider peak brown power charges.)

Compared to Hadoop, the above gains come from: (1) batching of delayed jobs, which increases server energy efficiency and reduces overall energy consumption; (2) reducing idle energy by transitioning servers to low-power states; and (3) replacing some of the remaining brown energy with green energy. Compared to EAHadoop, the gains come from sources (1) and (3), as well as the fact that batching reduces the number of state transitions incurred by servers.

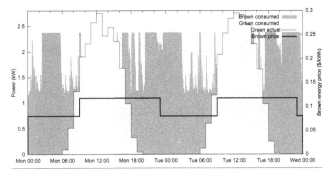

Figure 5. Hadoop for FaceD workload and High-High days.

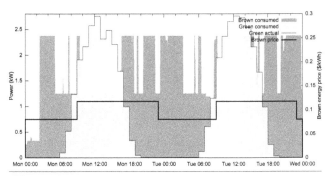

Figure 6. EAHadoop for FaceD workload and High-High days.

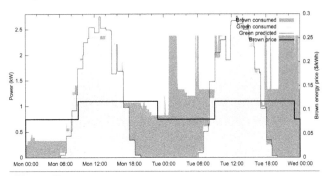

Figure 7. GreenOnly for FaceD workload and High-High days.

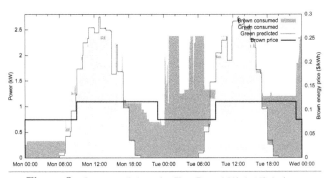

Figure 8. GreenVarPrices for FaceD and High-High days.

Scheduling for variable brown energy prices. Green-Hadoop can reduce costs further when brown energy prices vary and brown energy must be used to avoid time bound violations. To quantify these additional savings, we now study GreenVarPrices in the absence of peak brown power charges.

Figure 8 shows the behavior of GreenVarPrices for FaceD and the High-High days. Comparing this figure against Figure 7, one can see that GreenVarPrices moves many jobs that must consume brown energy to periods with cheap brown energy. For example, GreenOnly runs many jobs on Tuesday night that consume expensive brown energy. Those jobs get scheduled during periods of cheap energy (starting at 11pm on Tuesday and lasting beyond the 2-day window depicted in the figure) under GreenVarPrices. As a result, GreenVarPrices exhibits higher brown electricity cost savings of 41% compared to Hadoop for the same days.

Scheduling for peak brown power charges. So far, we considered scenarios in which there are no peak brown power charges. However, datacenters are often subject to them [10]. Thus, we next study GreenVarPricesPeak and compare it to the other versions of GreenHadoop, Hadoop, and EAHadoop in the presence of those charges.

Figure 9 shows the behavior of GreenVarPricesPeak for FaceD and the High-High pair of days. Comparing this figure against Figure 8, one can see that GreenVarPricesPeak limits the peak brown power consumption as much as possible, while avoiding time bound violations. In this experiment, GreenVarPricesPeak reaches 1.47kW of peak brown power, whereas GreenVarPrices reaches 2.38kW. This lower peak translates into brown electricity cost savings of 39%

and 37% compared to Hadoop and EAHadoop, both of which also reach 2.38kW.

To illustrate these behaviors further, Figure 10 shows the servers' states over time under GreenVarPricesPeak. The figure shows the number of servers that are in Decommissioned and Active states, as well as those active servers that are actually running jobs. The remaining servers are in Down state. The figure shows that GreenVarPricesPeak keeps the vast majority of the servers in Decommissioned or Down state, whenever green energy is unavailable. When it is available, GreenVarPricesPeak matches its availability by activating many servers to execute the load.

Figures 11 and 12 summarize our metrics of interest (with respect to the Hadoop results) in the absence and presence of peak brown power charges, respectively. Note that the cost savings bars represent the percent decrease in electricity cost per job executed. Considering the EAHadoop results, these figures demonstrate that it is not enough to consume less energy than Hadoop to increase the green energy consumption. To do so, it is also necessary to move the load around as in GreenHadoop. Considering GreenHadoop, Figure 11 clearly shows that its benefits are significant in terms of both green energy and brown electricity costs in the absence of peak brown power charges. When these charges are in effect (Figure 12), GreenOnly and GreenVarPrices achieve lower (but still important) savings in brown electricity costs, as they do not consider the charges in their scheduling. Both Green-Only and GreenVarPrices reach the maximum peak brown power, so they incur the same peak brown power costs of Hadoop and EAHadoop. Overall, GreenVarPricesPeak is the

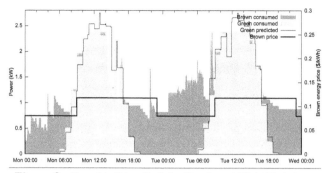

Figure 9. GreenVarPricesPeak for FaceD and High-High days.

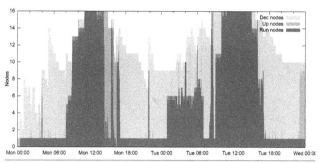

Figure 10. Server states under GreenVarPricesPeak. "Run servers" are active and running jobs. Down servers are not shown.

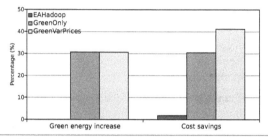

Figure 11. Summary in the absence of peak brown power charges.

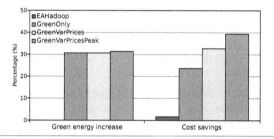

Figure 12. Summary with peak brown power charges.

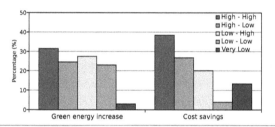

Figure 13. Impact of green energy availability on GreenVar-PricesPeak. Results are normalized to EAHadoop.

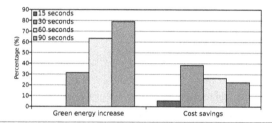

Figure 14. Impact of mean job inter-arrival time on GreenVar-PricesPeak. Results are normalized to EAHadoop.

best version, as it explicitly and effectively manages the high costs of peak brown power consumption when those charges are in effect. When they are not, GreenVarPricesPeak reverts to GreenVarPrices.

Impact of the amount of green energy. Here we evaluate the behavior of GreenVarPricesPeak across the pairs of days we consider. Figure 13 summarizes the results with each bar in a group representing one pair of days. Since EAHadoop achieves roughly the same results as Hadoop but with a lower energy usage, we normalize against EAHadoop.

As one would expect, the figure shows that GreenHadoop increases green energy consumption by a smaller percentage when there is less green energy. However, its brown electricity cost savings remain high ($> 13\%$), except when there is almost no green energy *and* the prediction is inaccurate.

Impact of datacenter utilization. Another important factor that affects GreenHadoop is datacenter utilization. Under very high utilization, GreenHadoop may be unable to avoid using expensive brown electricity, may be forced to violate time bounds, and/or even reject newly submitted jobs.

To investigate these effects, we perform experiments with EAHadoop and GreenVarPricesPeak for three additional datacenter utilizations. Specifically, we vary the mean inter-arrival time from 15s (giving 92% utilization in EAHadoop) up to 90s (13% utilization). Recall that our default results assume a 30s mean inter-arrival time (49% utilization in EAHadoop). Figure 14 illustrates these results.

The figure shows that the environmental benefits of GreenHadoop tend to increase as utilization decreases. At 13% utilization, a common utilization in existing datacenters [25], GreenVarPricesPeak increases green energy use by 79%, and reduces brown electricity cost by 22%. At the uncommonly high utilization of 92%, there is little or no opportunity for GreenVarPricesPeak to increase green energy use. Utilization is so high that there is no need to move load around. However, GreenVarPricesPeak is still able to decrease brown electricity cost by 5% (by lowering the brown energy cost), while not violating any time bounds.

Impact of fraction of high-priority jobs. So far, we have assumed that all jobs in the workload are submitted with normal priority. Here, we investigate the impact of having dif-

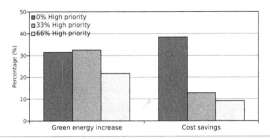

Figure 15. Impact of fraction of high-priority jobs on green energy and brown electricity cost. Normalized to EAHadoop.

ferent percentages of high-priority jobs. We selected jobs to be assigned high priority randomly, according to the desired percentage. Recall that GreenHadoop does not delay high- or very-high priority jobs.

Figure 15 shows the results for three percentages of high-priority jobs: 0% (our default), 33%, and 66%. As one would expect, larger fractions of high-priority jobs make it harder for GreenHadoop to increase green energy consumption and reduce brown electricity cost. Nevertheless, its benefits are still significant even at 66% high-priority jobs. Further, GreenHadoop achieves these benefits without degrading the performance of high-priority jobs noticeably.

Impact of shorter time bounds. The experiments so far use time bounds of one day. In those experiments, GreenHadoop never causes a time bound violation, nor does it need to take any action to prevent a time bound violation. We now explore GreenHadoop's ability to meet tighter time bounds of 6 and 12 hours. Our results show that GreenHadoop delays 19% of the jobs past their 6 hour time bounds (only 3% of the jobs are delayed by more than 20%), and 3% past their 12-hour time bounds. Note that some of the jobs in the FaceD workload take longer than 5 hours, making the 6-hour time bound tight. Further, most of the violations occur on the second day, after GreenHadoop has delayed many jobs to use green energy. At that point, an additional heavy load arrives, including two very large jobs, which prevents the system from meeting all bounds.

Impact of data availability approach. We compare Green-Hadoop's data management against the covering subset approach [20]. Specifically, we run FaceD at different datacenter utilizations (from 13% to 92%) for the High-High days. The results show that, for low utilizations, GreenHadoop reduces brown electricity cost by more than 23% compared to the covering subset approach. GreenHadoop achieves this reduction by deactivating all but one server (when possible), whereas the covering subset approach requires at least four servers to be active at all times (see Section 3.1.2). Under high utilizations, the two approaches perform similarly because there are fewer opportunities to deactivate servers.

One potential drawback of our data management approach is that data may not be immediately available for arriving high-priority jobs. We run FaceD with 66% of high-priority jobs to assess this delay. The results show that all jobs start less than 6 seconds after submission; this delay can include the time to wake up to 15 servers.

Impact of workload (NutchI). Thus far, we have focused exclusively on FaceD. We have also studied NutchI to investigate whether GreenHadoop's benefits extrapolate to a substantially different workload. The results from these experiments support our most important observations with FaceD: (1) EAHadoop provides little benefit on its own; (2) Green-VarPricesPeak is able to conserve a significant amount of brown energy by batching load, transitioning servers to low-power states, and leveraging green energy; and (3) it increases the green energy consumption and reduces brown electricity cost significantly. For example, GreenHadoop increases green energy use by 23% and reduces brown electricity cost by 64% compared to Hadoop for the High-High days. These results show that GreenHadoop is robust to different workload characteristics.

Impact of energy estimation. Finally, an important component of GreenHadoop is its estimate of the average energy required per job in a batch of jobs. To study the accuracy of this estimation, we collected the estimates and actual averages over time for the experiment with GreenVarPricesPeak, FaceD, and High-High days. Note that jobs in FaceD are highly heterogeneous and so present a challenging scenario for our prediction. Approximately 75% of the predictions are within 20% of the observed average energy consumption. This shows that the estimate is reasonably accurate in most cases, but it can also be substantially inaccurate.

Our results above already provide strong evidence that GreenHadoop is robust to prediction inaccuracies. To further confirm this robustness, we evaluate how GreenHadoop reacts to a large, sudden change in the workload. Specifically, using the High-High days, we run FaceD during the first day and then abruptly switch to running NutchI on the second day. Right after this switch, GreenHadoop's energy usage prediction per job becomes off by approximately 50%. However, GreenHadoop is able to adjust its energy estimation to less than 15% error within two hours, and, at the end of the two days, uses 21% more green energy than EAHadoop, reducing the cost of brown energy by 57%.

GreenHadoop is robust to inaccurate energy usage predictions because of two reasons. First, the effect of inaccurate predictions is partly compensated by the much more numerous accurate ones. Second and most important, Green-Hadoop re-evaluates and reacts to the system state every epoch. If it is over-estimating the average energy usage, it may be forced to use (more expensive) brown energy when not necessary. However, scheduled jobs will finish faster than expected, causing GreenHadoop to adjust by scheduling more jobs from the Wait queue. If it is under-estimating, in the worst case, it may end up causing jobs to miss their time bounds. However, pressure on the Wait queue will force GreenHadoop to schedule jobs faster, even if it has to start using (more expensive) brown energy.

Summary. The results above demonstrate that GreenHadoop provides consistent increases in green energy consumption (i.e., decreases in brown energy consumption) and reductions in brown electricity cost, compared to Hadoop and EAHadoop. The benefits are highest when most jobs are given low priority, green energy is abundant, and datacenter utilizations are low or moderate.

GreenHadoop may violate the time bound in some scenarios, including (1) the submission of very large jobs that are poorly described by the measured average energy used per job, (2) the arrival of a large burst of jobs after many previous jobs have been delayed to better use green energy, and/or (3) a very high datacenter utilization. However, our results show that GreenHadoop does not violate the time bound or does so only rarely with reasonable slack and datacenter utilization. For example, FaceD contains jobs that are up to 150 times longer than the common-case job. Yet, GreenHadoop never violates a 24-hour time bound and only rarely misses a 12-hour bound (3%).

6. Related Work

Exploiting green energy in datacenters. GreenHadoop lowers brown energy/power consumption, monetary costs, and environmental impact. Previous works have addressed some of these issues [17, 19, 22, 30]. Stewart and Shen discuss how to maximize green energy use in datacenters [30]. However, their main focus was on request distribution in multi-datacenter interactive services. Similarly, [17, 19, 22] focused on these services. Akoush et al. [1] considered workload distribution in virtualized systems. Our work differs in many ways. Specifically, only [22] considered green energy predictions, and only [17, 19, 22] considered variable brown electricity prices. None of these papers considered peak power or MapReduce job scheduling. MapReduce jobs typically run longer than interactive service requests and often have loose completion time requirements, thereby increasing the opportunity to exploit green energy.

Goiri et al. [9] and Krioukov et al. [14, 15] have proposed green energy-aware batch job schedulers for a single datacenter. Unlike GreenHadoop, however, these works require extensive user-provided information (numbers of required servers, run times, and completion time deadlines) for each job. Moreover, these schedulers do not manage data availability, assuming that the entire dataset of all jobs is either network-attached or replicated at every server. GreenHadoop is substantially more challenging, since it does not leverage any user-provided information about job behavior, and explicitly manages data availability.

Aksanli et al. [2] used green energy to process Hadoop jobs that share the same datacenter with an interactive service. However, they did not consider high-priority jobs, data management, brown energy prices, or peak power charges.

Willow [12] assumes that decreases in green energy supply affect the servers differently, and migrates load away from energy deficient servers within a datacenter. In contrast, Blink [27] considered managing server power states when the amount of green energy varies but the datacenter is *not* connected to the electrical grid. We argue that it is not realistic for datacenters to depend completely on green energy, since this may cause unbounded performance degradation. Our approach for managing green energy consumption is through scheduling, rather than load migration or server power state management.

At a much lower level, SolarCore [21] is a multi-core power management scheme designed to exploit PV solar energy. SolarCore focuses on a single server, so it is closer to the works that leverage green energy in embedded systems.

Managing brown energy prices and peak brown power charges. Most works that have considered variable energy prices have targeted request distribution across multiple datacenters in interactive Internet services [17, 19, 22, 24]. The exception is [18], which considers variable energy prices and peak power charges in multi-datacenter high-performance computing clouds. Our work differs in that it seeks to maximize green energy use, predict green energy availability, and schedule MapReduce jobs within a single datacenter.

Also within a single datacenter, Goiri et al. [9] scheduled scientific batch jobs taking into account brown energy prices, but not peak brown power charges. Govindan et al. [10] studied how energy stored in the UPS batteries of conventional datacenters can be used to manage peak power and its costs. GreenHadoop targets a different type of clustered system and relies solely on software to manage peak costs.

Traditional job schedulers. Traditional batch job schedulers for clusters, e.g. [8, 32], seek to minimize waiting times, makespan, and/or bounded slowdown; unlike GreenHadoop, they never consider green energy, brown energy prices, or peak brown power charges. In addition, similarly to real-time scheduling [23], GreenHadoop recognizes that many jobs have loose performance requirements (i.e., can be delayed within a bound) and exploits this in favor of higher green energy consumption and lower brown electricity cost.

MapReduce and Hadoop. Several efforts have sought to reduce the energy consumption of Hadoop clusters, e.g. [13, 20]. The main issue that these efforts address is how to place data replicas in HDFS, so that servers can be turned off without affecting data availability. Amur et al. addresses a similar issue in a power-proportional distributed file system, called Rabbit [3], based on HDFS. These data placement efforts could be combined with GreenHadoop to reduce the need for it to replicate data to turn servers off.

In contrast, Lang and Patel propose an approach called the All-In Strategy (AIS) [16]. Instead of turning some servers off when utilization is low, AIS either turns the entire cluster on or off. In essence, AIS attempts to concentrate load, possibly by delaying job execution, to have high utilization during on periods and zero energy consumption during off periods. AIS's delay of load to increase efficiency is similar to our approach. However, AIS neither considers green energy availability nor brown energy and power costs.

7. Conclusions

In this paper, we proposed GreenHadoop, a MapReduce framework for a datacenter powered by solar energy and the electrical grid. GreenHadoop seeks to maximize the green energy consumption within the jobs' time bounds. If brown energy must be used, GreenHadoop selects times when brown energy is cheap, while also managing the cost of peak brown power consumption. Our results demonstrate that GreenHadoop can increase green energy consumption by up to 31% and decrease electricity cost by up to 39%, compared to Hadoop. Based on these positive results, we conclude that green datacenters and software that is aware of the key characteristics of both green and brown electricities can have an important role in building a more sustainable and cost-effective IT ecosystem.

To demonstrate this in practice, we are building a prototype micro-datacenter powered by a solar array and the electrical grid (http://parasol.cs.rutgers.edu). The micro-datacenter will use free cooling almost year-round and will be placed on the roof of our building.

Acknowledgements

We would like to thank Kevin Elphinstone and the anonymous reviewers for their help in improving our paper. We are also grateful to our sponsors: Spain's Ministry of Science and Technology and the European Union under contract TIN2007-60625, COST Action IC0804 and grant AP2008-0264, the Generalitat de Catalunya grants 2009-SGR-980 2010-PIV-155, NSF grant CSR-1117368, and the Rutgers Green Computing Initiative.

References

[1] S. Akoush et al. Free Lunch: Exploiting Renewable Energy for Computing. In *HotOS*, 2011.

[2] B. Aksanli et al. Utilizing Green Energy Prediction to Schedule Mixed Batch and Service Jobs in Data Centers. In *HotPower*, 2011.

[3] H. Amur et al. Robust and Flexible Power-Proportional Storage. In *SOCC*, June 2010.

[4] Apache. Apache Hadoop. http://hadoop.apache.org/, .

[5] Apache. Apache Nutch, . http://nutch.apache.org/.

[6] J. Dean and S. Ghemawat. MapReduce: Simplified Data Processing on Large Clusters. In *OSDI*, December 2004.

[7] DSIRE. Database of State Incentives for Renewables and Efficiency. http://www.dsireusa.org/.

[8] D. Feitelson et al. Parallel Job Scheduling – A Status Report. In *JSSPP*, June 2004.

[9] I. Goiri et al. GreenSlot: Scheduling Energy Consumption in Green Datacenters. In *Supercomputing*, November 2011.

[10] S. Govindan et al. Benefits and Limitations of Tapping into Stored Energy for Datacenters. In *ISCA*, June 2011.

[11] A. Jossen et al. Operation conditions of batteries in PV applications. *Solar Energy*, 76(6), 2004.

[12] K. Kant et al. Willow: A Control System for Energy and Thermal Adaptive Computing. In *IPDPS*, May 2011.

[13] R. T. Kaushik et al. Evaluation and Analysis of GreenHDFS: A Self-Adaptive, Energy-Conserving Variant of the Hadoop Distributed File System. In *CloudCom*, December 2010.

[14] A. Krioukov et al. Integrating Renewable Energy Using Data Analytics Systems: Challenges and Opportunities. *Bulletin of the IEEE Computer Society Technical Committee*, March 2011.

[15] A. Krioukov et al. Design and Evaluation of an Energy Agile Computing Cluster. Technical Report EECS-2012-13, University of California at Berkeley, January 2012.

[16] W. Lang and J. Patel. Energy Management for MapReduce Clusters. In *VLDB*, September 2010.

[17] K. Le et al. Cost- And Energy-Aware Load Distribution Across Data Centers. In *HotPower*, October 2009.

[18] K. Le et al. Reducing Electricity Cost Through Virtual Machine Placement in High Performance Computing Clouds. In *Supercomputing*, November 2011.

[19] K. Le et al. Capping the Brown Energy Consumption of Internet Services at Low Cost. In *IGCC*, August 2010.

[20] J. Leverich and C. Kozyrakis. On the Energy (In)efficiency of Hadoop Clusters. In *HotPower*, October 2009.

[21] C. Li et al. SolarCore: Solar Energy Driven Multi-core Architecture Power Management. In *HPCA*, February 2011.

[22] Z. Liu et al. Greening Geographical Load Balancing. In *SIGMETRICS*, June 2011.

[23] S. Oikawa and R. Rajkumar. Linux/RK: A Portable Resource Kernel in Linux. In *RTAS*, May 1998.

[24] A. Qureshi et al. Cutting the Electric Bill for Internet-Scale Systems. In *SIGCOMM*, August 2009.

[25] P. Ranganathan et al. Ensemble-level Power Management for Dense Blade Servers. In *ISCA*, June 2006.

[26] N. Sharma et al. Cloudy Computing: Leveraging Weather Forecasts in Energy Harvesting Sensor Systems. In *SECON*, June 2010.

[27] N. Sharma et al. Blink: Managing Server Clusters on Intermittent Power. In *ASPLOS*, March 2011.

[28] SMA. Sunny Central 800CP, 2012.

[29] SolarBuzz. Marketbuzz, 2011.

[30] C. Stewart and K. Shen. Some Joules Are More Precious Than Others: Managing Renewable Energy in the Datacenter. In *HotPower*, October 2009.

[31] US Environmental Protection Agency. Report to Congress on Server and Data Center Energy Efficiency, August 2007.

[32] A. Yoo et al. SLURM: Simple Linux Utility for Resource Management. In *JSPP*, June 2003.

[33] M. Zaharia et al. Job Scheduling for Multi-User MapReduce Clusters. In *TR UCB/EECS-2009-55, Berkeley*, August 2009.

Frugal Storage for Cloud File Systems

Krishna P. N. Puttaswamy, Thyaga Nandagopal *, Murali Kodialam

Bell Labs, Alcatel-Lucent, Murray Hill, NJ

Abstract

Enterprises are moving their IT infrastructure to cloud service providers with the goal of saving costs and simplifying management overhead. One of the critical services for any enterprise is its file system, where users require real-time access to files. Cloud service providers provide several building blocks such as Amazon EBS, or Azure Cache, each with very different pricing structures that differ on the basis of storage, access and bandwidth costs. Moving an entire file system to the cloud using such services is not cost-optimal if we rely on only one of these services. In this paper, we propose FCFS, a storage solution that drastically reduces the cost of operating a file system in the cloud. Our solution integrates multiple storage services and dynamically adapts the storage volume sizes of each service to provide a cost-efficient solution with provable performance bounds. Using real-world large scale data sets spanning a variety of work loads from an enterprise data center, we show that FCFS can reduce file storage and access costs in current cloud services by a factor of two or more, while allowing users to utilize the benefits of the various cloud storage services.

Categories and Subject Descriptors D.4.2 [*Storage Management*]: Storage hierarchies

General Terms Algorithms, Design, Experimentation

Keywords Cloud computing, Storage, Storage cost, Caching

1. Introduction

Data center based cloud services have become the choice of enterprises and businesses to host their data, including mission-critical services such as application data and file systems. Enterprises are moving their internal IT services to the cloud, in order to reduce their IT capital expenses as well as reduce network management overhead. While enterprise data can be stored in several forms, it is typically in the form of a large collection of files in a file system.

Cost is the primary driver behind the migration to the cloud. Storage services in the cloud allow users to expand/contract their storage outlay on a dynamic basis at the granularity of several megabytes to gigabytes for very short time scales (hours). However, with the different array of pricing options for the variety of storage services, it is often unclear which type of storage model is the right choice for a specific type of service. In Table 1 we summarize the pricing options for popular storage services based on storage and I/O accesses. For e.g., Amazon S3 provides low cost storage[1], but charges more for accesses, while Amazon EBS provides low-cost access to files, but at a higher storage cost. Services such as Amazon ElastiCache and AzureCache[2] provide a low-latency high cost memory. Complicating this matter is the multi-tier pricing adopted within each storage model by the different providers. For example, the per-GB costs within S3 and ElastiCache differ by a factor of 3 between the low and high cost tiers, based on the size of the storage volume.

	S3	EBS	ElastiCache
Storage pricing (per GB-month)	0.08	$0.10	$40
Request pricing (per 1 million I/O requests)			
PUT requests	$10.00	$0.10	0
GET requests	$1.00		0
Data transfer pricing			
per GB incoming	$0.00	$0.00	0
per GB outgoing	$0.12	$0.05	0

Table 1. Cloud Storage Pricing as of October 1, 2011 [2–4].

The choice of what combination of storage options to use in order to minimize the operational costs depends on the memory and access costs for the different storage options as well as the working set for the different data sets. Depending on the nature of the application workload at any given

---

* This work was done while at Bell Labs, Alcatel-Lucent. The author is currently affiliated with the National Science Foundation.

---

[1] Storage pricing shown for S3 assumes a petabyte-scale file system.

[2] The AzureCache [5] has a different pricing model: Each GB of storage costs $110 per month, and buying this storage provides certain number of PUT/GET requests and a pre-determined amount of bandwidth for free. Higher usage migrates the user to the next storage tier pricing.

time, different storage services might be the optimal choice for hosting data. An I/O intensive workload might prefer EBS while a workload that does not have much I/O accesses might prefer S3. Within a single file system, the pattern of workload might require these different characteristics at various points over a large period of time. It is clearly evident that a single storage system may not be a cost-optimal solution for an application at any time. Our goal in this paper is to *minimize the total cost of storing and accessing data in the cloud by effectively utilizing and integrating the various choices of cloud storage services.*

1.1 Related Work

The problem is related to cache eviction problems and hierarchical storage management (HSM) [15], where data moves automatically between high-cost and low-cost storage media. The wide body of research on cache eviction policies such as Least Recently Used (LRU) or Adaptive Replacement Cache (ARC) [10] assume that there is a fixed cache size and focus on how to move data blocks in and out of the cache in order to minimize overall cache miss rate. Our problem generalizes this to the case where the cache sizes themselves can change in response to demand patterns and focuses on minimizing the cost.

HSM systems are utilized to reduce data storage costs for enterprises, with the low-cost storage typically being tape-drives and optical disks, while the high-cost storage involves hard-disks and flash drives. Thus, the high-cost storage media act as a cache for the slower low-cost media. The decision to move a file between these storage media is made based on how long a file has been inactive, typically of the order of months. There are three-stage HSMs involving Fiber Channel SANs, SATA HDD arrays, and tape drives, or using a combination of flash drives, SATA HDD and tape.

Conventional HSM models assume that a strict hierarchy of storage options are given and the sizes of the high-cost (and high-performance) tiers are fixed. Therefore, given a specific workload, the goal is minimize overall file access latency. This is the common model, whether it is used for a content-agnostic RAID cluster [16], content-specific file system [6], or for relational databases [7].

The problem addressed in this paper differs from the general problems addressed in the HSM literature in two important aspects:

- Unlike a standard hierarchical storage system, we do not assume that the amount of memory at different levels of the hierarchy is fixed. We assume that the amount of memory at different levels can be expanded and contracted based on current needs. Our model fits a cloud storage service quite well since elasticity of storage is a key selling point of the cloud storage services.

- In a traditional HSM, memory is a sunk cost. Therefore cost optimization is not the focus in HSM literature. Since memory can be added and deleted in very short

time scales in a cloud storage system, it is possible to tailor the mix of memory based on the current working set requirements of the file systems. Our objective is to determine the mix of memory that minimizes the operational cost.

1.2 Contributions

These differences lead to a richer and more complex problem that deals with how files can be stored in order to minimize the overall cost. In this paper, we consider this problem of constructing a cost-effective file storage solution using the array of cloud storage services available. Our contributions in this paper are as follows.

1. We present a dynamic storage framework for cost-efficient file system storage in the cloud.

2. We present two schemes to determine how files can be moved between different storage systems dynamically, and derive tight performance bounds for the cost incurred in these schemes while accounting for the storage, I/O access and bandwidth costs. Both these schemes automatically adapt to the current file system requirements, but independent of the access patterns, in order to determine the most cost effective way of serving the demands.

3. Using simulations based on real-life disk traces representative of a medium-size data center, we demonstrate that our algorithms can reduce overall costs by a factor of two or more, and are within 85% of the optimal costs.

We motivate our dynamic storage framework in Section 2. We describe the Frugal Cloud File System in Section 3, and present our algorithms in Section 4. In Section 5 we describe our experimental setup and describe the real-life traces used in our evaluation. Experimental evaluation results are shown in Section 6. We conclude in Section 7 with a discussion on our observations.

2. Dynamic Storage Management

In the cloud, storage resources can purchased and discarded on fine-grained time-scales, of the order of hours. Moreover, there is no strict hierarchy of storage tiers as in a traditional HSM model. From Table 1, we can see that depending on the access patterns of the resource, the high-cost tier itself can vary. For example, for an I/O intensive workload, Amazon EBS will be cost-optimal and hence will be the highest tier, while for a sparse I/O workload, Amazon S3 might be cost-optimal. Thus, unlike a conventional HSM model, the preference among storage tiers may not be global and will be workload dependent.

Let us consider, for example, Amazon S3 and Amazon EBS. The access costs in EBS are far lower than in S3, which leads one to think that from a cost perspective, we could cache the working set of files in EBS and store all data in S3. In models currently provided by Amazon [2], the entire file system is hosted on EBS with periodic incremental

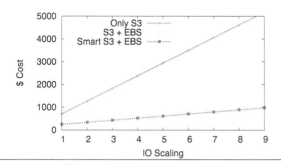

Figure 1. Cost with variable I/O.

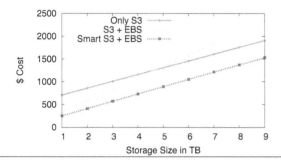

Figure 2. Cost with variable storage.

snapshots maintained in S3. The other alternative is to host the entire file system on S3 and serve all accesses from there.

We tested three schemes: (a) *Only S3*: where the file system is in S3 and data is accessed directly from there, (b) *S3 + EBS*: the way file systems are mounted today, and (c) *Smart S3 + EBS*: using S3 for keeping all the data and retrieving only working set files into a fixed-size EBS volume (instead of the whole image), updating them, and flushing the files to S3 when we are done.

For the Smart S3 + EBS scheme (referred henceforth as the Smart scheme), the EBS volume size is kept fixed, as it is in current caching models. If the working set size exceeds the size of the allocated EBS volume, then, as in a cache, we use LRU as the block replacement policy.

Using the CIFS stats from Leung et.al. [9], we measured the monetary cost of running such a file system in the three schemes. There were 352 million I/Os, out of which 6% was writes (hence accounted under the PUT costs in S3) and the rest were accounted under the GET costs in S3. The CPU cost and bandwidth transfer costs between the S3/EBS and the compute instance hosting the file server are the same in all the schemes, and hence are not shown in the plots.

The first set of tests was with respect to the number of I/Os. We used the number of I/Os in the above traces as a baseline, and scaled it up by up to a factor of 10, using the baseline access distribution. We set the EBS volume size for the Smart scheme to 10% of the file system size, and measured the total costs for all three schemes. The result is shown in Figure 1. When the workload is completely I/O dependent, S3 + EBS and the Smart scheme perform very

well. But, Smart is the winner overall since it keeps only a limited set of files inside EBS.

Next, we varied the amount of storage required by the file system from the baseline of 1TB to 10TB, with the same number of I/Os, thereby modifying the ratio of storage to I/O. The cumulative costs are shown in Figure 2. For high storage-to-I/O ratios, the Smart scheme works remarkably well, as expected. Interestingly, at some point, S3 beats S3+EBS (at around 5 TB), and is also eventually better than the Smart scheme at around 70 TB. This suggests that when storage-to-I/O ratio is really high, it is better to run from S3 directly. This behavior is entirely expected, and suggests that the storage-to-I/O ratio is an important metric to consider while optimizing costs.

We finally varied the working set size that is allocated in EBS for handling files that are accessed frequently in our Smart scheme, while keeping the storage at 1TB and using the same I/O as in the traces. The results are shown in Figure 3. One can see that the size of the working set directly correlates to the overall cost, and it is in our best interests to keep the working set in EBS as low as possible.

The above tests point out the benefits of a tiered storage framework in the cloud. However, different file systems have varying amounts of working sets that depend on the workload and the time-of-day [12]. Reserving a fixed size such as the 10% share of the file system size, as we did above for our example using EBS, is not truly cost-effective, because the working set might be much higher or lower than this fixed threshold during any given time window.

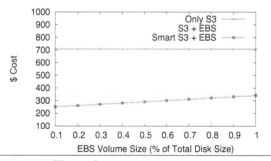

Figure 3. Cost vs. working set size.

2.1 Cost Tradeoff with Working Set Size

In order to see how the optimal working set threshold might vary for different file systems, we ran various file system workloads from Narayanan et.al. [11, 12], and compared the total cost as a function of the size of the EBS volume in the Smart scheme, using the same experimental setup as before. Figure 4 shows the variation of the aggregate normalized costs versus the EBS volume size expressed as a percentage of the total file system size. The y-axis is normalized based on the least value of the cost during the run for that particular trace. From the figure, we can clearly see how the costs vary with different working set sizes.

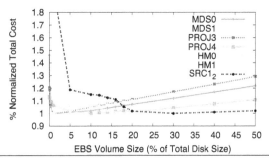

Figure 4. Cost for file systems with different EBS volume sizes.

In Table 2, we specify the values of the EBS volume size for each trace that minimizes overall costs. We also show the corresponding costs on a unit storage cost basis, since each of the traces have different file system sizes. Notice that the min cost point is different for different traces. The minimum cost is achieved when the EBS volume size is near 30% of the total file system size for some traces, while for others it is as small as 0.25%. Another key observation from this table is that the minimum costs shown here (on a per TB basis) do not have a linear relationship with the size of the EBS volume. In other words, a quadrupling of the ideal EBS size across traces does not lead to a quadrupling of operations cost. In fact, there is no clear relationship between the two, apart from a general increasing trend.

Trace Name	Ideal EBS Volume Size (in %)	Operations Cost ($/TB)
MDS1	0.25	42.94
HM1	0.5	43.63
MDS0	1	47.46
PROJ3	1	38.47
PROJ4	10	68.39
HM0	18	113.34
SRC12	30	223.75

Table 2. Ideal EBS volume size and the corresponding cost.

Note that even this variation does not account for dynamic patterns of access within a single workload over time. Accounting for those patterns can lead to even substantial savings in costs. This insight leads us to design a dynamic storage framework for file systems in the cloud.

2.2 Storage performance versus cost

In this paper, we mainly focus on optimizing the operational cost of a cloud-based file system. Typically the cost of a storage service also reflects its performance, i.e., latency[3]. For instance, Amazon-ElastiCache offers better latency than Amazon-EBS, which in turn offers better latency than S3. At the same time, storage costs decrease as we move from ElastiCache towards S3, with I/O costs moving in the opposite direction. We notice two general trends here: (a) storage costs are inversely proportional to I/O access costs, given a choice of multiple storage systems, and (b) a storage system with lower I/O access cost also provides very low access latency.

Therefore, these trends suggest that, for any workload, regardless of the access patterns, we should automatically move data blocks to the appropriate storage layer that optimizes costs (as a function of access), and doing so will in some sense also optimize performance. A highly accessed data block should move to a layer with lower I/O access cost, while a data block that is never accessed should be stored in a layer with the lowest storage cost.

This dependency between costs and performance will be broken only when this pricing model is violated, i.e., there exists one storage layer with lowest I/O cost but very high I/O latency. We have also not come across such a storage model in existing cloud storage services. If one were to be offered in the future, we could impose performance (latency) constraints on the cost optimization framework presented here to create a low cost storage system that meets certain performance criteria.

In the subsequent sections, we outline our design and present algorithms that minimize costs using dynamic storage.

3. A Frugal Cloud File System

Our design is motivated by two factors: (a) in the cloud, storage resources can be purchased on fine time-scales, and (b) the working set of a file system can change drastically over short time-periods.

Storage resources in the cloud can be purchased on a very granular basis, e.g., GB per hour on Amazon S3 or EBS. These resources can be purchased as often as needed for a single compute instance, e.g., up to a max of 16 distinct volumes in EBS.

This granular purchase feature is very useful, especially since modern file systems show remarkable variation in the size of the file system accessed over a fixed time-window of the order of minutes or hours. Our study of the data used in Narayanan et.al. [11, 12] also confirms this variation in nearly all traces.

Hence, our goal is to *design a cloud storage system that can span multiple cloud storage services, and adaptively grow/shrink in response to the file system workload with the aim of reducing cumulative storage and access costs.*

3.1 Components

We present our *Frugal Cloud File System*, or FCFS, in Figure 5. FCFS consists of three components: (a) Cost Optimizer, (b) Workload Analyzer, and (c) Disk Volume Resize Engine. We explain the functions of each of these components below.

---

[3] We do not consider storage throughput as a performance criteria at this time, though the discussion presented here equally applies to it as well.

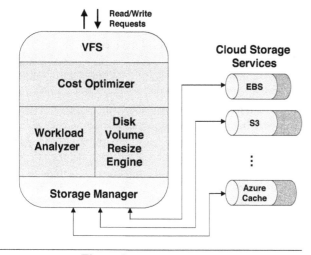

Figure 5. FCFS Structure.

Cost Optimizer:
Given storage systems with varying storage, I/O and bandwidth costs for storing and accessing data, the Cost Optimizer computes the optimal location for each file, and the duration for which the file should stay in this location. The details of this module are presented in Section 4.1.

Workload Analyzer:
The Workload Analyzer looks at the file system working set over time and moves files between the different storage volumes as dictated by their deadlines as decided by the Cost Optimizer. It also determines if some files should be moved ahead of their deadline, using some form of cache replacement policies, such as LRU or ARC [10]. The working of this module is explained in Sections 4.2 and 4.3.

Disk Volume Resize Engine:
Using inputs from the Workload Analyzer and the Cost Optimizer, this module adjusts the sizes of the different storage volumes at different time instants in a way that minimizes overall cost of operation of the file system in the cloud. The design and implementation details of this component are described in Section 5.1.

3.2 Illustrative Example

A simple high-level example here can illustrate the above functions. Consider a data block of size 4MB that is stored in the Amazon S3. Using the data from Table 1, the cost of fetching this block from S3 (GET request) once is the same as the cost of storing it in ElastiCache for 4.5 hours. We show in the next section that this information is all that the Cost Optimizer needs to determine the duration for which the file is stored in the ElastiCache.

If the block is not accessed for this duration in Elasti-Cache, one could move it to S3 and relinquish the corresponding space in ElastiCache. Similarly, if the block stored in S3 is being accessed, then we have to decide if we want

to either bring this into ElastiCache by either replacing an existing block in the ElastiCache volume or add additional space to bring it into the ElastiCache volume. This is the job of the Workload Analyzer. If we decide to replace an existing block, then we use LRU to find this replacement block.

The Disk Volume Resize Engine will decide how often to increase/decrease the size of the ElastiCache volume and by how much. For example, say the increases in ElastiCache are performed once every 4 minutes. During any such 4 minute period, let the existing size of the ElastiCache volume be 2GB, and the total number of blocks displaced by the Workload Analyzer in the past 4 minutes add up to 1 GB. Thus, the Resize Engine can decide to increase the ElastiCache volume by 1 GB for the next four minutes. Conversely, if there are data items that have been removed on account of exceeding their duration, or if there has been no block displacement for the past 4 minutes, then the Resize Engine can reduce the ElastiCache volume to keep only those items that are still within the cost-optimal time window.

In the next section, we present algorithms that dictate the behavior of these three modules.

4. Cost Optimization Algorithms

For ease of understanding, we explain our proposed Frugal Cloud File System (FCFS) using a dual storage system model: one composed of a low-latency system such as Amazon ElastiCache or EBS, while the other is composed of a (relatively) high-latency system such as Amazon S3. We call these two tiers *Cache* and *Disk* respectively.

The main expense of running a file system are the access and storage costs. The cost of fetching data from the disk consists of two components: (a) a per-block I/O access cost that is independent of the size of the block, and (b) bandwidth cost of transferring the block, which depends on the size of the block[4]. The storage cost is expressed in units of dollars per block per hour, the per-I/O access cost of moving data is in dollars per access per block, and the bandwidth cost is expressed in dollars per block. We can combine the bandwidth cost and the per-I/O cost into one fetch-cost parameter. Clearly, these parameters will change when the block size changes. Our goal is to optimize the overall costs involved for storing and accessing X bytes of data in the file system with these dual storage systems.

Let the cost of storing data and fetching data from the Disk (Cache) be m_d (m_c) and f_d (f_c) respectively. This is illustrated in Figure 6.

There are three questions that need to be answered to address this problem:
(a) where should data reside by default,
(b) when should data move from Disk to Cache and vice versa, and

---

[4] In AWS, bandwidth cost of transfer between S3 and EBS/ElastiCache instances in the same data center is zero.

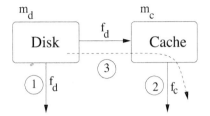

Figure 6. Dual Storage Systems and the Data Read Paths

(c) when should the size of the Cache be increased or decreased?

In current cloud storage services, services that serve data from main memory instances are more expensive than the services that serve data from permanent stores (such as hard disk). For instance, the per-MB storage costs of Amazon ElastiCache [3] and Azure AppFabric Cache [5] are three and two orders of magnitude more expensive than Amazon S3 and EBS storage services respectively. One of the key reasons, among others, seems to be that serving data from main memory also requires a CPU instance (either rented directly by the customers as in ElastiCache or hidden behind the service cost as in Azure Cache), where as disk-based services (running on NAS and SAN) do not.

It is simple to see that all data must by default reside in the Disk, which has the lowest cost of storage among the two tiers (i.e., $m_d < m_c$). This is because data has to be stored in one of these two systems by default, and clearly the low storage cost location, i.e., Disk, minimizes this default storage cost.

From the Disk, data can be accessed in one of three ways, shown in Figure 6. First, it can be fetched straight from the Disk, while in the second method, it can be fetched from the Cache if it exists there. The third way is the conventional caching model, where data is fetched from the Disk and stored in the Cache, from where it is served henceforth until it is removed from the Cache. Note that in this method, the data could also be removed from Disk once it is cached, thus storing it in only one location. Given the very small size of the cache compared to the Disk, doing so has very low impact on cost. However, removing data from Disk has substantial implications on the resiliency of the data in a cloud storage system, and therefore we do not consider this method further. We simply assume that the a version of the data resides in Disk as well even after it is moved to Cache.

If $f_d \leq f_c$, then it makes no sense to keep any data in the cache, since the total costs are lowered by always accessing data from the disk. However, this is not common in practice, since $f_c \ll f_d$ in cloud storage systems. Given that $f_d > f_c$, and that future arrivals are not known, one should consider keeping data in the cache for some amount of time, whenever it is retrieved from the disk to serve an access.

Hence, we consider the third method more carefully. When a block is requested, it is read from the disk to the cache and is then read from the cache to the VM. This incurs a cost of $f_d + f_c$. At this point the block is in both the disk and the cache. The system now has the option of keeping this block in the cache for additional time. During this time when the block is in the cache, if there is a request for the block, then it can be read from the cache at a cost of f_c. Note however, that during the time the block is in the cache, the storage cost rate is $m_c + m_d$. At any point in time, a block can be evicted from the cache. If this is done, then the block is only in the disk and the memory cost rate will be m_d. Our objective is to devise an eviction policy from the cache that minimizes the overall operational cost.

In developing the cache replacement algorithms we do not make any assumptions about future arrival patterns. Instead, we develop online algorithms that have a cumulative cost that is provably within a constant factor of the optimal cost. In determining the optimal cost, we assume that all access times to the blocks are known ahead of time. We show that even when compared to the scenario where all accesses are known ahead of time, our algorithm performs remarkably well. The algorithm as well as the analysis can be viewed as generalizations of the classical ski-rental problem [8].

4.1 Determining the Optimal Cost

We first determine the optimal cumulative storage and access cost when the access times for the block are known ahead of time. Henceforth, the term *cost*, when used alone, refers to this cumulative storage and access cost, unless explicitly specified otherwise. When the block is accessed, it is read from the disk onto the cache. Assume that we know that the next access to the block is after ℓ time units. If after the current retrieval the block is stored in the cache for the next ℓ time units, then the cost will be $(m_c + m_d)\ell + f_c$. If we do not store the current access in the cache and instead leave it in the disk, then the cost for the next access will be $m_d\ell + f_c + f_d$. The optimal policy will depend on when the next access will occur. It is better to keep the block in the cache and retrieve it from the cache, if

$$(m_c + m_d)\ell + f_c \leq m_d\ell + f_c + f_d \Rightarrow \ell \leq \frac{f_d}{m_c}$$

If $\ell > \frac{f_d}{m_c}$, then it is more cost effective to discard the block from the cache and retrieve it from the disk. We use

$$T = \frac{f_d}{m_c}$$

to denote this crossover time.

We denote by $OPT(\ell)$ the optimum cost if the next access occurs after ℓ time units. Therefore, from the above discussion,

$$OPT(\ell) = \begin{cases} (m_c + m_d)\ell + f_c & \text{if } \ell \leq T \\ m_d\ell + f_c + f_d & \text{if } \ell > T \end{cases}$$

4.2 Deterministic Online Scheme

In an online algorithm, we assume that we do not have any knowledge of when the next access will occur. We describe here a deterministic online scheme.

DET: When a block is accessed (either from the disk or the cache)

- It is stored in the cache for T more time units from the current time.

- It is evicted from the cache after T time units.

If the next access occurs before T time units, then the block is retrieved from the cache, and is kept for a further T time units. If the access occurs after T time units, it is retrieved from the disk, at which time it is brought back to the cache, and the cycle starts over again.

Let $\mathrm{DET}(\ell)$ represent the cost of the deterministic online scheme when the next access occurs after ℓ time units. We want to show that the ratio of $\mathrm{DET}(\ell)$ to $\mathrm{OPT}(\ell)$ is bounded for all values of ℓ.

4.2.1 Cost Analysis of DET

We do the analysis in two parts:
(a) **Next Access Before** T: If $\ell \leq T$, then the cost of the online algorithm as well as the optimal algorithm is $(m_c + m_d)\ell + f_c$, and the ratio of the costs is one.

$$\frac{\mathrm{DET}(\ell)}{\mathrm{OPT}(\ell)} = 1, \quad \forall \ell \leq T.$$

(b) **Next Access After** T: If the next access occurs at time $\ell > T$, then the cost for the online algorithm is $(m_c + m_d)T + m_d(\ell - T) + f_c + f_d$. The first term is the memory cost of keeping the block in the cache and the disk for T time units. The block is discarded from the cache at time period T. For the remaining $(\ell - T)$ time units, the memory cost is $m_d(\ell - T)$. The last two terms are the retrieval cost of the block from the disk. The optimum cost is $m_d\ell + f_c + f_d$. Therefore

$$\begin{aligned} \frac{\mathrm{DET}(\ell)}{\mathrm{OPT}(\ell)} &= \frac{(m_c + m_d)T + m_d(\ell - T) + f_c + f_d}{m_d\ell + f_c + f_d} \\ &= 1 + \frac{m_cT}{m_d\ell + f_c + f_d} \\ &= 1 + \frac{f_d}{m_d\ell + f_c + f_d} < 2 \end{aligned}$$

where we used the fact that $T = \frac{f_d}{m_c}$ in the penultimate step. It is possible to show that no deterministic algorithm can perform better than the ratio of 2, using an adversarial workload. Next we outline a probabilistic online algorithm that gives a better expected performance ratio.

4.3 Probabilistic Online Scheme

The deterministic scheme holds a block for T time units in the cache from the last access and then discards it. A natural question to ask is whether the expected cost can be reduced by probabilistically evicting blocks from the cache even before time T. Indeed this can be done if the eviction probabilities are chosen carefully.

PROB: When a block is accessed (either from the disk or the cache)

- We compute a block eviction time based on a probability density function $p(t)$ that describes the probability of discarding a block from the cache at time $t \in [0, T]$ from the last access time of the block.

- The block is evicted after this time has elapsed with no subsequent access to this block.

In this scheme, the block is definitely discarded from the cache by time T from its last access time, implying that $\int_0^T p(t)dt = 1$. Let $E[\mathrm{PROB}(\ell)]$ denote the expected cost of the probabilistic eviction scheme when the next access is after ℓ time units. Note that the expectation is due to the uncertainty in when the block will be discarded. We do not make any probabilistic assumptions about when the next access will occur. We now want to pick $p(t)$ in order to ensure that the expected competitive ratio

$$\alpha = \max_\ell \frac{E[\mathrm{PROB}](\ell)}{\mathrm{OPT}(\ell)}$$

is as small as possible.

4.3.1 Cost Analysis of PROB

Assume that we have an access at time ℓ, while the block is discarded from the cache at time t. The expected cost of the probabilistic online algorithm $E[\mathrm{PROB}(\ell)]$ is

$$\int_0^\ell [(m_d + m_c)t + f_c + f_d + m_d(\ell - t)]\, p(t)dt$$

$$+ \int_\ell^t [(m_d + m_c)\ell + f_c]\, p(t)dt$$

The first integral represents the expected cost if the block is discarded at some time t before the retrieval time ℓ. There is a disk and cache cost of $(m_c + m_d)t$ and a disk cost of $m_d(\ell - t)$ from the discard time t until access time ℓ. In addition, there is the reading cost of $f_c + f_d$ from the disk since the block has been discarded from the cache before the access time ℓ. The second integral represents the cost when the access time ℓ is before the discard time t. In this case, there is a memory cost of $(m_d + m_c)\ell$ and the read cost from the cache. Each of these costs are weighted with the probability of discarding the block from the cache at time t.

Our objective is to solve the following optimization problem.

$$\min \quad \alpha \tag{1}$$

$$E[\text{PROB}(\ell)] \leq \alpha \ \text{OPT}(\ell), \ \forall \ell \tag{2}$$

$$\int_0^T p(t)dt = 1 \tag{3}$$

Differentiating Equation (2) with respect to ℓ and simplifying, we get

$$m_d \int_0^\ell p(t)dt + f_d p(\ell) + (m_d + m_c)\int_\ell^T p(t)dt \leq \frac{d\text{OPT}(\ell)}{d\ell}$$

Differentiating again with respect to x, we get

$$f_d p'(\ell) - m_c p(\ell) \leq \frac{d^2\text{OPT}(\ell)}{d\ell^2}$$

Note that from the definition of $\text{OPT}(\ell)$, $\frac{d^2\text{OPT}(\ell)}{d\ell^2} = 0$. Moreover, at the optimal point, this constraint is tight, and hence the inequality can be replaced by an equality sign. Recall that $T = \frac{f_d}{m_c}$ and the above differential equation can be rewritten as

$$p'(t) - \frac{1}{T}p(t) = 0.$$

We can now solve for $p(t)$ to obtain $p(t) = Ke^{t/T}$. Using Equation (3), we can solve for K to get $K = \frac{1}{T(e-1)}$. Therefore the optimal probability distribution is

$$p(t) = \frac{1}{T(e-1)}e^{t/T}$$

Substituting this in Equation (2) and solving for α gives the optimum value of

$$\alpha = 1 + \frac{1}{e-1}\left(\frac{f_d}{m_d + f_d + f_c}\right) \leq 1 + \frac{1}{e-1} < 1.582.$$

Therefore, PROB has an expected competitive ratio of 1.582. Note that this ratio is much better than the competitive ratio of 2 obtained for DET. We now outline how the eviction time is generated in the PROB scheme.

4.3.2 Generating Block Eviction Time

Whenever a block enters the cache or is accessed while in the cache, an eviction time for the block is computed as follows:

- Compute $T = \frac{f_d}{m_c}$ for the block.
- Generate U which is a uniformly distributed random variable in the range $[0:1]$.
- Generate the block eviction time from the current time as $T\log[(e-1)U + 1]$.

In cases where the cache is examined only periodically, the eviction time is rounded to the closest time at which the cache is examined. This rounding can affect the performance ratio if the rounding intervals are very long, but our results show that this effect is negligible.

5. Implementation and Trace Details

We implemented a dual storage system simulator to evaluate our algorithms. We implemented the simulator in C++ with about 6.5K lines of code. This simulator is highly configurable, which enabled us to experiment with different storage services with different pricing options. We simulated three types of storage services: S3, EBS, and CloudCache – a version of storage that has similar pricing and properties as that of ElastiCache [3] and Azure Cache [5]. We set the storage prices of CloudCache to $100 per GB per month. We used the current pricing values for the rest of the services in our simulator and used the most common values for other parameters. For e.g., we set the block size in EBS to 4KB (which is the size used by most file systems). Below, we describe important implementation decisions pertinent to FCFS.

5.1 Volume Resizing

The ideal cache size should be the minimum cache needed to host the working set of data from the file system. Ideally, no blocks should be evicted from the cache because there was no space (via LRU) in the cache volume, but only due to cost constraints. As the working set changes, the cache size should also change accordingly. Let the resizing happen at periodic intervals, and let the size of the cache at the moment of a re-sizing be S GB. Between two re-sizing events, we keep track of how many blocks are replaced in S before their eviction time due to LRU. Let this add up to B_{LRU} GB. This describes the level of inadequacy of the current cache size. In the same interval, let the number of blocks that have been evicted by FCFS add up to B_{evict} GB. This indicates the size of the cache that is no longer needed to hold the blocks. Therefore, at the next re-sizing event, we set the new cache volume size to be $S + B_{LRU} - B_{evict}$.

The analysis in the previous section assumed that the cache can be expanded and contracted at any time instant. In practice there are restrictions on how often and by how much the cache volume can be resized. We describe these in detail next.

Resizing Intervals. We set volume resizing interval values as follows: every 4 minutes we attempt to increase the cache size, but the cache size decrease is attempted only at the end of every hour. The reasoning behind this is as follows. Amazon EBS, for instance, allows a maximum of 16 volumes to be attached to a VM at any point in time. But once a volume is allocated, it is paid for the next hour, and hence it would be a waste of resource to deallocate it before the end of an hour. Moreover, allocating or deallocating a volume involves moving blocks around, which can cause a lot of overhead if done frequently. As a result, we set the interval time for incrementing the size to 4 mins and the interval for decrementing to one hour. We noticed that having a larger time period for decreasing the size avoids frequent fluctuations in the size, thus making the cache volume size more stable.

Resizing Granularity.   There are practical restrictions on the granularity of increasing or decreasing the storage volume size, as well, in the cloud. For e.g., in Amazon, the minimum increment/decrement size for the cache in 1GB. In the description in Pseudocode 1, we use G to represent the granularity of resizing the volume. For instance $G = 1$GB in Amazon. If $B_{LRU} \geq B_{evict}$ then $B_{LRU} - B_{evict}$ represents the amount by which the cache size has to be increased. If $B_{LRU} < B_{evict}$ then $B_{LRU} - B_{evict}$ represents the amount by which the cache size has to be decreased. Due to the granularity restrictions, we round the increase or decrease to the nearest multiple of G. This is shown in Line 26 in Pseudocode 1.

5.2 Separate Read and Write Volumes

Second, we allocate a separate read and write cache in EBS and CloudCache. If the cloud storage service charges differently for writes and reads, as is the case for Amazon S3, then the replacement thresholds for a file opened for a read or a write should intuitively be different. Based on the expression for the replacement threshold in the previous section, and from the differential pricing in Table 1 for PUTs and GETs in the S3 service, a file opened for write has a replacement threshold that is 10 times longer than that of a file that has been opened for a read.

5.3 Block Sizes

We set the block size of data in S3 to 4MB; S3's pricing does not require a specific block size – the prices are based on the number of operations with a limit of 1GB per operation. But choosing a block size has to navigate a tradeoff: large blocks reduce the I/O cost due to coalescing of writes but increases the storage cost in EBS/Cache, and vice versa. Some of the prior systems operating on S3 have found the block size in the order of MBs to provide good tradeoff [14], and even Amazon uses 4MB for snapshotting [1]. We deal with the discrepancy in the block size between S3 and EBS/Cache as follows: Whenever a S3 read is issued by EBS, we use range read to read only the relevant blocks (of 4KB). But whenever a dirty block is evicted from EBS/Cache, we write back all the 4KB blocks that are dirty in the evicted block's 4MB S3 block. EBS and CloudCache block sizes, however, are set to 4KB, as mentioned before.

5.4 FCFS Pseudocode

The pseudocode for the FCFS algorithm is shown below in Pseudocode 1. This Pseudocode is for block reads. The code for block writes is the same, with additional code to track dirty blocks, write back dirty blocks upon eviction, and periodic checkpointing of dirty blocks. Pseudocode 1 presents four functions. Initialize is called at the start of the system, Access_Block is called to answer every read request

---

Pseudocode 1 FCFS_Read(Disk, Cache)

```
 1: function Initialize()
 2:   Cache size, S = 1 GB; B_LRU = B_evict = 0; T ← f_d/m_c
 3:
 4: function Access_Block(Block A) {// Every block read}
 5:   t ← current time
 6:   if A ∈ Cache then
 7:     Serve_Access_Request (A)
 8:   else { A ∉ Cache}
 9:     fetch A from Disk
10:     if Cache is full then
11:       R ← FindReplacementBlock(LRU)
12:       evict R from Cache
13:       if evictionTime(R) > t then
14:         B_LRU = B_LRU + block size
15:       end if
16:     end if
17:     Load A into Cache
18:   end if
19:   evictionTime(A) ← t + Compute_Eviction_Time()
20:
21: function Volume_Resize(Cache) {// Periodic}
22:   t ← current time
23:   I ← All blocks in Cache with evictionTime ≤ t
24:   evict all blocks in I
25:   B_evict = B_evict + |I| * block size
26:   S = S + ⌊(B_LRU − B_evict)/G⌋ * G
27:   B_LRU = B_evict = 0
28:
29: function Compute_Eviction_Time()
30:   if Eviction Method is Deterministic then
31:     return T
32:   else {Probabilistic eviction method}
33:     r ← Random[0 : 1]
34:     return T log[(e − 1)r + 1]
35:   end if
```

---

from the application, Volume_Resize is called periodically to resize the Cache, and finally, Compute_Eviction_Time is called to decide the eviction time of a block upon access.

5.5 Traces Used for Evaluation

We used the traces from a prior file system study [12]. The authors graciously made the traces public [11], which we use for our work. The original paper [12] has all the details of the trace, we only present some basic information here.

The trace dataset has block-level read and write requests captured below the file system cache for 36 disk volumes from a medium-sized enterprise data center. These disks belong to a wide range of services, ranging from web server, source code control system, user home directories, to print servers. This dataset was captured for a period of 168 hours starting from February 22nd 2007 5PM GMT [12]. Each entry in each of these trace files is of the format: <**Timestamp, Hostname, DiskNumber, Type, Offset, Size, ResponseTime**>. We only use the timestamp (when the request arrives), type (read or write), offset (where the read/write starts in the disk), and size (the amount of data to be read/written) for our work. This trace does not have details about the size of each disk. As a result, we conservatively estimate the size of the disk to be the same as that of the highest offset value found in the entire trace. Finally, even though this dataset had traces of 36 different file systems, due to memory limitations in our experimental setup, we could only run experiments on 33 of these file system traces.

5.6 Storage Strategies for Evaluation

We implemented four different storage strategies for evaluation. They are as follows.

- Average working set size strategy (AVG). In this strategy, we set the size of the cache storage layer to be the size of the average per-day working set of a file system averaged over a period of one week.

- FCFS with deterministic kickoff time (DET). In this strategy we set the time to remove a block from the cache layer to be the ratio of the disk volume I/O cost to the cache volume storage cost.

- FCFS with probabilistic kickoff time (PROB). In this strategy the blocks are probabilistically kicked out at the end of every one hour.

- Optimal strategy based on trace analysis (OPT). This strategy allocates the cache sizes optimally for each trace at every point in time. Here we pre-process the trace to learn the complete knowledge of the future arrivals of requests to each file system block and use it to decide if the block should be stored in the cache upon access or should be thrown out immediately after access.

Note that the AVG strategy is not implemented in the cloud storage systems of today, but it is an intuitive scheme that can be expected to do very well to reduce cumulative storage and access costs.

6. Trace-Driven Experimental Results

In this section, we present the results from our trace-driven experiments to understand the improvements from dynamic storage tiers. The main question we seek to answer is: *What are the cost and storage savings due to our algorithms if we use different cloud storage services as our choices for the cache and disk volumes?* We answer this question with experiments on four different combination of storage services.
1) We look at the S3-EBS combination just the way it's used today on Amazon AWS.
2) We look at the S3-CloudCache combination, where we use CloudCache instead of EBS. In both these cases, the minimum granularity by which the the cache storage can be resized is set to 1GB.

3) We explore the savings that we can get if the cloud storage providers were to offer a finer resizing granularity of 64MB, much along the lines of the offering in Windows Azure Caching service (granularity = 128MB).
4) Finally, we compare the cost of S3-EBS and S3-CloudCache combinations with a setting where only S3 is used to offer a file system service.

6.1 Savings in S3-EBS

A file system running on S3-EBS today [13] stores the entire file system image in both S3 and EBS. We used this setting (called FULL from here onwards) in our simulator, and then used DET (where only the relevant blocks are stored in EBS). We then compared FULL with DET, by normalizing the DET costs by that of FULL.

The ratio of I/O in S3 to the storage in EBS for a 4KB block is 1800 hours for reads and 18000 hours for writes. Unfortunately, the traces we have are only 168 hours long. As a result, DET, PROB or OPT strategies do not really get a chance to shrink the EBS volume size, which does not help us understand how these strategies perform. So we only compare FULL with DET in S3-EBS setting where the EBS volume size keeps increasing for the entire 168 hours.

Figure 7 shows the savings in the total cost and Figure 8 shows the savings in the EBS storage size due to DET. As shows in Figure 7, average savings in total cost is about 22%. The average storage savings, however, is 84% compared to S3-EBS. This high storage savings does not lead to high cost savings due to two reasons: a) In many file system traces the contribution of EBS storage costs to the total cost is quite small, as majority of the contributions come from the I/O costs to EBS and S3. This is the most common reason for the discrepancy in savings. b) In some rare cases, the increase in the I/O cost to S3 (due to reduction in the EBS volume size) is more than the savings due to the decrease in the EBS storage cost. This is mainly due to sudden and high peaks in some traces that increase the required memory size faster than the increase in the EBS memory size during DET (1GB every 4 mins). In this case, many requests will not be cached in EBS forcing them to be fetched from S3 again later. SRC1_1 is an example for this case, which shows a negative cost savings of 5% as this slow increase misses to cache data from two peaks in the incoming requests. By making the EBS increase more aggressive, however, this second problem can be avoided.

A more interesting result from the above two graphs is the significant savings in the storage size, *despite* the fact that EBS volume kept growing throughout the week (as the code to shrink will only be triggered after 18K hours). This is due to the fact that the working set of a file system is generally much less than the total file system. The average working set in a week was about 16% across all of our traces.

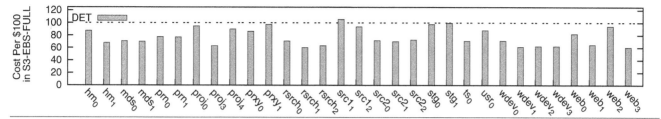

Figure 7. A plot of the % savings in the total cost while using DET over today's S3-EBS-based file systems for 33 different file system traces. The average cost savings is about 22%.

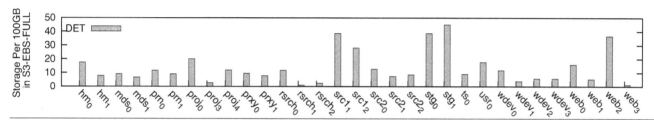

Figure 8. A plot of the % savings in the EBS storage size while using DET over today's S3-EBS-based file systems for 33 different file system traces. The average storage savings is about 84%.

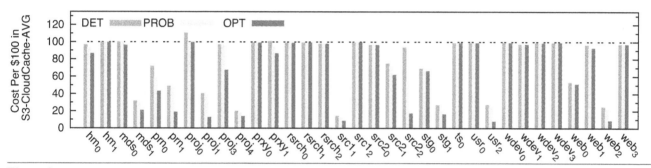

Figure 9. A plot of the % savings in the total cost while using S3-CloudCache with 1GB CloudCache granularity. The results are normalized by the AVG strategy – for every $100 spent by AVG, the amount spent by the other three strategies are shown.

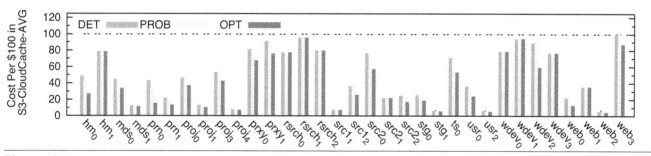

Figure 10. A plot of the % savings in the total cost while using S3-CloudCache with 64MB CloudCache granularity. The results are normalized by the AVG strategy – for every $100 spent by AVG, the amount spent by the other strategies are shown.

6.2 Savings in S3-CloudCache

CloudCache storage cost ($100 per GB per month) is 1000 times more expensive than EBS, while the other costs are the same as in the previous experiment. This increase in the storage cost, however, changes the time to cache for reads to 1.8 hours and time to cache of writes to 18 hours. This increase in the storage cost also means that almost all of the contributions to the total file system cost is due to savings in the CloudCache storage. As a result, we only show the graphs for total cost savings (as it is almost identical to the storage savings graph).

Due to the shorter time scales for eviction times in the volume with the one week trace, we were able to run all the four different strategies outlined before. We present the results from these in Figure 9, where we show the results normalized by the values of the AVG strategy. The Figure shows the details about the savings in S3-CloudCache for 33 different traces. On an average, in these traces, there is a savings of about 20 to 25% in the total cost. Specifically, for every $100 spent by AVG, the amount spent by DET, PROB, OPT are $79, $76, and $69 respectively. The competitive ratio (CR) for PROB and DET are 1.36, and 1.49 respectively.

The main reason the savings is so low is because in many of the traces, the performance of all four strategies are identical. We found out that this is due to the fact that the minimum granularity of allocation or deallocation is set to 1GB in our implementation. This is akin to the setting in Amazon AWS, but the problem is that many traces have their average per-day working set size smaller than a GB (working set is computed separately for reads and writes). And all these traces get a minimum of 1GB. This is much more than the necessary size and does not shrink any further. This makes the cost of all the strategies identical. In almost all the traces, however, we see the trend we expect: AVG costs more than DET, which costs more than PROB, and OPT is the cheapest. In some rare cases, when the working set size of AVG is very close to 1 GB, DET temporarily increases the size of the cache volume and hence incurs a slightly higher cost than AVG (as in Proj_0, Prxy_1, and Mds_0).

6.3 S3-CloudCache with Smaller Storage Granularity

As described in the previous section, the larger granularity of allocation and deallocation in a storage service does not allow our algorithms to extract higher cost savings. So here we explore the impact of finer granularity on our algorithms. Specifically, we set the granularity of allocation to 64MB, and re-run the experiments from the previous section.

Figure 10 shows the savings for the 33 different traces. Clearly, the number of traces where AVG performs as good as the OPT has now gone down. The average savings in the cost has also gone up significantly. For every $100 spent by AVG, the amount spent by DET, PROB and OPT are $54, $52, and $46 respectively. This is about 30% more than the savings with 1GB granularity. Along similar lines, the competitive ratio (CR) from the experiments for DET and PROB have gone down to 1.25, and 1.18 respectively.

We then re-ran the experiments with 4MB granularity to understand the benefits of very fine granularity. In this case, for every $100 spent by AVG, $53, $46, and $43 were spent respectively by DET, PROB, and OPT strategies. And the CR for DET and PROB were respectively 1.18 and 1.07. Clearly, there is diminishing returns in reducing the granularity size beyond 64MB. In addition, the cost of our system with 64MB granularity is only 5 to 10% worse than the cost with very fine granularity of 4MB.

Table 3 presents a summary of the key results. It shows the savings we have observed in different storage service combinations for the three strategies we evaluate in this paper.

	S3EBS-FULL	S3CloudCache-AVG		
Granularity	1GB	1GB	64MB	4MB
DET	22%	21%	46%	47%
PROB	-	24%	48%	54%
OPT	-	31%	54%	57%

Table 3. Summary of the average cost savings of DET, PROB, and OPT schemes under different storage combinations. The 90th percentile of the cost savings across all traces is generally within 2% of the average values shown here.

6.4 Comparing Only-S3 with Other Combinations

Finally, we compare the cost of running the different file systems only on S3 with the cost of running them on S3-EBS and S3-CloudCache (64MB) combinations using DET. Running directly on S3 saves us the EBS and CloudCache storage costs, but the I/O costs increase due to higher I/O cost of S3. We want to know if running on S3 directly outperforms running a file system on higher cost storage services such as CloudCache.

In Figure 11 we plot the ratio of the cost of DET running on S3-EBS to Only S3 along with the ratio of DET on S3-CloudCache with 64MB granularity to Only S3. The average ratio of the two comparisons across the 33 traces is 0.69 for S3-EBS-DET and 0.9 for S3-CloudCache-DET. The ratio of S3-EBS to only S3 is less than 1 in 22 out of the 33 traces. In the other traces, the number of I/O operations are quite low, causing the ratio to go above 1. A more interesting result is that the average ratio of S3-CloudCache to only S3 is also less than 1, even though CloudCache is 1000 times more expensive than EBS. CloudCache comes with a huge performance (latency) boost to the file systems at generally a very high storage cost, and yet we can get all the benefits of hosting the file system on CloudCache using our proposed FCFS system, at a cost that is even lower than that of the cheapest disk-based storage service based on S3.

6.5 Performance of FCFS

We now quantify the performance of FCFS by comparing it against a file system that has the entire image in the cache (like the file system run on S3-EBS combination today). We measure the performance in terms of the hit fraction, which is the fraction of the total number of requests that were served from the cache. In S3-EBS-FULL, all the requests would be served form the cache, and hence all requests incur the cache read/write delay. We show the hit ratio in Figure 12 for the DET, PROB, and OPT schemes, when the cache increments are in steps of 1GB. Ideally, we would like to see very high hit ratios indicating overall low latency of access. The general observation from the figure is that

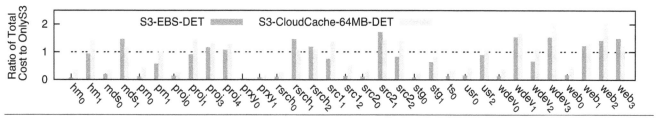

Figure 11. A plot of the ratios of the total cost of DET on S3-EBS to only S3, and DET on S3-CloudCache to only S3.

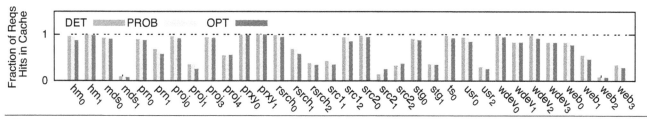

Figure 12. A plot of the fraction of the requests that were hit from the cache for various file system traces in our S3-CloudCache setup.

FCFS does indeed perform well and provides low latency in a majority of the file system traces in S3-CloudCache setup. In fact, nearly half of the traces have a hit ratio over 0.9. The average hit fraction is 0.7 and less than one-third of the traces have a hit ratio below 0.5. Remarkably, both DET and PROB perform well and are within a small fraction away from the OPT scheme (DET is usually better, as expected). For those set of traces with very low hit-ratios across all three schemes, we observe that much of the data is accessed exactly in one narrow time interval and never accessed again, thereby leading to cache misses in a vast majority of accesses in such traces.

The OPT scheme will intuitively have a slightly lower hit ratio than the DET and PROB schemes. The reasoning behind this is as follows. Since OPT proactively knows if a block will be accessed within the cost-optimal time threshold following its last access, and if not, that block will be kicked out right away from the cache. This leads to a smaller active cache size than DET or PROB schemes. Therefore, the decrease portion of our FCFS algorithm will aggressively reduce the cache size of OPT in the initial stages. However, this process will stabilize with time, wherein all three schemes will have similar hit ratios from the cache. This is the reason why the DET and PROB schemes are very close to the OPT scheme as well.

As a part of our future work, we are looking into ways of providing performance SLAs while also optimizing the cost of the Cloud storage services.

7. Conclusion

There are a wide variety of storage options in the cloud and an enterprise is faced with the problem of deciding what combination of storage services to use in order to build a cost effective cloud file system. Using actual pricing

data, we have shown that for a typical enterprise, no single storage option provides a cost effective file system solution. The appropriate combination of storage options depends on the working set dynamics of the file system. The correct combination to use can vary over time. In this paper we have:

- Presented the Frugal Cloud File System (FCFS) that provides a dynamic framework for cost effective file storage in the cloud.

- Developed and analyzed two cache resizing schemes that significantly reduce the cost of storing files in the cloud. Theoretical analysis show that the resizing algorithms provide constant factor performance guarantees. These guarantees are independent of the access patterns.

- Experimented using several real-world file system traces and have shown that FCFS reduces the cost of running the file system significantly.

In summary, FCFS integrates multiple storage services and dynamically adapts the storage volume sizes of each service to provide a cost-efficient cloud file system with provable performance bounds. As a part of our future work, we are looking into extending the benefits of FCFS from two-layered storage hierarchy to a generic multi-tier storage framework that provides cost optimality within the required performance bounds.

Acknowledgments

We thank Eric Jul for his thoughful comments on the earlier versions of this paper.

References

[1] Amazon. EBS to S3 Snapshot Block Size, . https://forums.aws.amazon.com/message.jspa?messageID =142082.

[2] Amazon. Elastic block store, . http://aws.amazon.com/ebs/.

[3] Amazon. Elasticache, . http://aws.amazon.com/elasticache/.

[4] Amazon. Simple storage service faqs, . http://aws.amazon.com/s3/faqs/.

[5] Azure. Caching service. http://msdn.microsoft.com/en-us/library/windowsazure/gg278356.aspx.

[6] S.-H. Gary Chan and F. A. Tobagi. Modeling and dimensioning hierarchical storage systems for low-delay video services. *IEEE Transactions on Computers*, 52, July 2003.

[7] D. Isaac. Hierarchical storage management for relational databases. In *Symposium on Mass Storage Systems*, 1993.

[8] A. Karlin, M. Manasse, L. McGeoch, and S. Owicki. Competitive randomized algorithms for non-uniform problems. In *Proc. of ACM-SIAM Symposium on Discrete Algorithms (SODA)*, 1990.

[9] A. W. Leung, S. Pasupathy, G. Goodson, and E. L. Miller. Measurement and analysis of large-scale network file system workloads. In *Proc. of the USENIX (ATC) Annual Technical Conference*, 2008.

[10] N. Megiddo and D. Modha. Arc: A self-tuning,. low overhead replacement cache. In *Proceedings of the USENIX Conference on (FAST) File and Storage Technologies*, 2003.

[11] D. Narayanan, A. Donnelly, and A. Rowstron. MSR Cambridge Traces. http://iotta.snia.org/traces/388.

[12] D. Narayanan, A. Donnelly, and A. Rowstron. Write off-loading: practical power management for enterprise storage. In *Proceedings of the USENIX Conference on (FAST) File and Storage Technologies*, 2008.

[13] S3-EBS. Amazon's Elastic Block Store explained. http://blog.rightscale.com/2008/08/20/amazon-ebs-explained/.

[14] S3Backer. FUSE-based single file backing store via Amazon S3. http://code.google.com/p/s3backer/wiki/ChoosingBlockSize.

[15] Wikipedia. Hierarchical storage management. http://en.wikipedia.org/wiki/Hierarchical_storage_management.

[16] J. Wilkes, R. Golding, C. Staelin, and T. Sullivan. The hp autoraid hierarchical storage system. *ACM Transactions on Computer Systems*, 14, Feb 1996.

Kineograph: Taking the Pulse of a Fast-Changing and Connected World

Raymond Cheng[*†]   Ji Hong[*‡]   Aapo Kyrola[*◇]   Youshan Miao[*§]   Xuetian Weng[*♮]
Ming Wu[*]   Fan Yang[*]   Lidong Zhou[*]   Feng Zhao[*]   Enhong Chen[§]

[*]Microsoft Research Asia   [†]University of Washington   [‡]Fudan University   [◇]Carnegie Mellon University
[§]University of Science and Technology of China   [♮]Peking University

ryscheng@cs.washington.edu   ji_hong@fudan.edu.cn   akyrola@cs.cmu.edu   youshan.miao@gmail.com
{v-xuweng,miw,fanyang,lidongz,zhao}@microsoft.com   cheneh@ustc.edu.cn

Abstract

Kineograph is a distributed system that takes a stream of incoming data to construct a continuously changing graph, which captures the relationships that exist in the data feed. As a computing platform, Kineograph further supports graph-mining algorithms to extract timely insights from the fast-changing graph structure. To accommodate graph-mining algorithms that assume a static underlying graph, Kineograph creates a series of consistent snapshots, using a novel and efficient *epoch commit* protocol. To keep up with continuous updates on the graph, Kineograph includes an incremental graph-computation engine. We have developed three applications on top of Kineograph to analyze Twitter data: user ranking, approximate shortest paths, and controversial topic detection. For these applications, Kineograph takes a live Twitter data feed and maintains a graph of edges between all users and hashtags. Our evaluation shows that with 40 machines processing 100K tweets per second, Kineograph is able to continuously compute global properties, such as user ranks, with less than 2.5-minute timeliness guarantees. This rate of traffic is more than 10 times the reported peak rate of Twitter as of October 2011.

Categories and Subject Descriptors   D.4.7 [*Operating Systems*]: Organization and Design; D.1.3 [*Programming Techniques*]: Concurrent Programming

General Terms   Design, Performance

Keywords   Graph processing, Distributed storage

1. Introduction

Increasingly popular services such as Twitter, Facebook, and Foursquare represent a significant departure from web-search and web-mining applications that have been driving much of the distributed systems research in the last decade. Information available on those emerging services has two defining characteristics. First, new information (e.g., tweets) is continuously generated and is far more time-sensitive than mostly-static web pages. Breaking news appears and propagates quickly, with new popular activities and trending topics arising constantly from real-time events in the physical world. Second, while each piece of information may be small and contains limited textual content, rich connections between entities such as users, topics, and tweets can be powerful in revealing important social phenomena. Information search and retrieval on micro-blogs has started to receive a lot of attention [27].

Kineograph is a distributed system designed for the need to extract *timely* insights from such a *continuous* influx of information with *rich* structure and connections. Kineograph has to address a set of new challenges. First, Kineograph must handle continuous updates, and its computation must produce timely results. Ideally, new updates should be reflected in the computed results within a short budget of 1-2 minutes. The widely adopted batch-processing paradigm (e.g., MapReduce [9]) optimizes for throughput and cannot provide the needed timeliness guarantees. Second, Kineograph must maintain a graph structure that captures the relationships among various entities. This is particularly challenging because the graph is often large and must be maintained *consistently* while being stored in a distributed fashion. Third, Kineograph must support graph-mining algorithms that extract insights from the graph structure. A continuously changing graph poses a challenge for many graph-mining algorithms. For example, most of the graph-mining algorithms assume a static underlying graph and their results may no longer offer the same expected meaning when operating on a constantly changing graph.

Kineograph addresses those challenges by designing a distributed in-memory graph storage system, along with a graph engine that supports incremental iterative propagation-based graph mining. The distributed graph store produces reliable and consistent snapshots periodically, so that existing graph-mining algorithms can be applied on a static snapshot. This design also decouples graph mining from graph updates to avoid any unnecessary interference, as graph mining works on existing snapshots while new updates are used to create new ones. Leveraging the nature of graph updates, a simple and novel *epoch commit* protocol with quorum-based replication is used to handle graph updates to achieve consistency and reliability efficiently, without global locking or significant cross-server coordination. With reliable consistent snapshots, computation does not need to be made deterministic or replicated. Kineograph resorts to re-execution in face of failures during graph mining. The final computation results can be replicated using traditional primary-backup schemes.

We have designed Kineograph to be a flexible platform, upon which developers can build scalable graph applications using Kineograph's APIs. We have developed three representative applications on Kineograph with real Twitter feeds for experimentation: TunkRank [31] for user ranking, SP [28] for approximate shortest path, and K-exposure [27] for controversial topic detection. We have conducted experiments on a real Twitter data set that generated a graph with more than 8 million vertices and 29 million edges, at a rate of more than 100,000 tweets per second. Our results show that Kineograph produces timely mining results, such that on average the computed results reflected all tweets updated within 2.5 minutes.

The rest of the paper is organized as follows. Section 2 presents an overview of Kineograph, with details described in the following sections. Section 3 explains how Kineograph maintains and creates distributed consistent graph snapshots. Section 4 introduces Kineograph's graph-computation model. Section 5 illustrates how to build applications in Kineograph, along with the description of three representative applications we built. Section 6 describes Kineograph's support of fault tolerance, incremental expansion, and decaying. Evaluations of the representative applications are reported in Section 7, followed by discussions of related work in Section 8. We conclude in Section 9.

2. Overview

Figure 1 shows an overview of Kineograph. Raw data feeds (e.g., tweets) come into Kineograph through a set of *ingest nodes* (step 1). An ingest node analyzes each incoming record (e.g., a tweet and its associated context), creates a "transaction" of graph-update operations, assigns a sequence number to the transaction, and distributes operations with the sequence number to *graph nodes* (step 2). Graph nodes essentially form a reliable distributed in-memory key/value

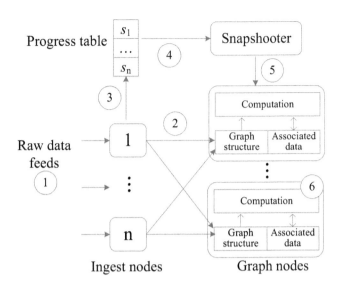

Figure 1. System overview.

store, with enhanced graph support. Rather than an opaque value field, the storage engine on each graph node maintains with each vertex, an adjacency list as its *graph structure metadata* and stores separately each application's associated data. In addition, the storage engine supports snapshots. Graph nodes first store the graph updates from ingest nodes. Afterwards, each ingest node reports the graph update progress in a global *progress table* maintained by a central service (step 3). Periodically, a *snapshooter* instructs all graph nodes to take a *snapshot* based on the current vector of sequence numbers in the progress table (step 4). This vector is used as a global logical clock to define the end of an *epoch*. Graph nodes are then instructed to execute and commit all stored local graph updates in this epoch following a pre-determined order. The end result of this *epoch commit* produces a graph-structure snapshot (step 5). Updates in the graph structure due to epoch commit further trigger incremental graph computation on the new snapshot to update associated values of interest (step 6).

A key decision that differentiates Kineograph from existing systems is the *separation* of graph updates and graph computation. This key insight leads to a simple, yet effective system architecture. To enable the separation, Kineograph stores the graph-structure metadata separately from the application data associated with the graph. Graph updates modify only the metadata that defines the graph structure and are therefore simple (e.g., adding a vertex and adding an edge). The separation also gives rise to the epoch commit protocol where graph nodes first store updates and then execute them in an epoch-granularity in order to create globally consistent snapshots on graph structures without global locks. Kineograph further uses the snapshots to decouple graph computation from graph updates in a staged manner: graph computation is performed on static snapshots, greatly simplifying the graph algorithm design. Finally, the separation of graph updates and computation enables the development of separate and simple fault tolerance mechanisms in different components of Kineograph (as will be described in Section 6.1).

3. Creating Consistent Distributed Snapshots

Graph nodes in Kineograph consist of two layers: a *storage layer* that is responsible for maintaining graph data and a *computation layer* that is responsible for graph computation. We describe the storage layer in this section and leave the computation layer to the next.

The storage layer of graph nodes implements a distributed key/value store, enhanced with primitive graph features. A graph is split into a fixed number (say 512) of logical partitions, which are further assigned to physical machines. Currently, graph partitioning is based on the hashing of vertex ids, without any locality considerations. This scheme is simple and generally good for load balance. Each logical partition consists of a set of vertices, each with a set of directed weighted edges stored in a sorted list. Edges are considered part of the graph structure, and are added and modified by the snapshot mechanism in the storage layer. Each vertex also has a set of named *vertex-fields* that store the *associated data* for each configured graph mining algorithm. The type of values stored in vertex-fields is arbitrary, as long as it can be serialized.

A key function provided by the storage layer is to provide consistent snapshots of graph structures. The snapshot mechanism is implemented through cooperation among ingest nodes, graph nodes, and a global progress table. The ingest nodes in Kineograph do not just serve as simple frontends, but play an important role in the system. An ingest node is responsible for turning each incoming record into a transaction consisting of a set of graph-update operations that might span multiple partitions (e.g., creating vertex v_2, adding an outgoing edge to vertex v_1, and adding an incoming edge to vertex v_2). Each of those operations can be executed entirely on the data structure associated with a vertex. In addition, each ingest node creates a sequence of transactions, each with a continuously increasing sequence number. Those sequence numbers are used to construct a *global logical timestamp* to decide which transactions should be included in a snapshot and also used as the identifier for that snapshot.

Kineograph's snapshot mechanism implements an *epoch commit* protocol that defers applying updates until an epoch is defined, as in the following process. An ingest node sends graph update operations to graph nodes, along with the sequence number of the transaction they belong to. A global progress table keeps track of the progress made by each ingest node by recording a sequence number for each ingest node. An ingest node i updates its entry to sequence number s_i if it has received acknowledgments from all relevant graph nodes that graph-update operations for all transactions up to s_i have been received and stored. Periodically (say every 10

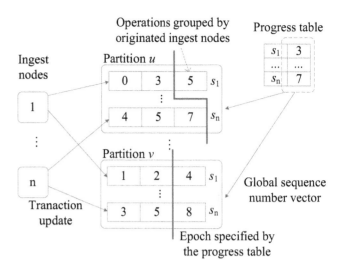

Figure 2. An example of creating a consistent snapshot across partition u and v.

seconds), the *snapshooter* takes the vector of sequence numbers from the current global progress table, $\langle s_1, s_2, \ldots, s_n \rangle$, where s_i is the sequence number associated with ingest node i, and uses it as a global logical timestamp to define the end of the current epoch. The decision is broadcasted to all graph nodes, where all graph updates belonging to this epoch are processed in the same deterministic, but artificial, order in all logical partitions. A graph-update from ingest node i with sequence number s is included in epoch $\langle s_1, s_2, \ldots, s_n \rangle$ if and only if $s \leq s_i$ holds. Even when operations on a logical partition are processed in serial, there are usually enough logical partitions on each graph node, leading to sufficient concurrency at the server level. Figure 2 shows an example where partition u and v are instructed to create a consistent snapshot by a global logical timestamp from the progress table.

The process of creating a snapshot does not stop incoming updates. Ingest nodes continuously send new graph updates into the system with higher sequence numbers. The process of (ingest nodes) dispatching and (graph nodes) storing graph-update operations overlaps with the process of creating snapshots by applying those updates. This property ensures that the deferred execution does not affect throughput over a sufficiently long period of time, even though it might introduce extra latency. Kineograph effectively batches operations in a small epoch window to strike a balance between reasonable timeliness and being able to handle high incoming rate of updates. At a higher rate, batching becomes more effective.

Consistency. The epoch commit protocol provides a nontraditional concurrency control solution that avoids blocking among the ingest nodes. The protocol does not require global serialization when ingest nodes are sending transactional operations, due to the simplicity of graph updates. Global serialization is deferred and implicitly achieved by the snapshooter that retrieves global logical timestamps (a form of vector clock) from the progress table, keeping it off the system's critical path. This process is fundamentally different from existing schemes such as two-phase locking or timestamp ordering [30].

Kineograph guarantees atomicity in that either all operations in a transaction are included in a snapshot or none of them are. This ensures that we cannot have a snapshot that includes one vertex with an outgoing edge, but with no matching incoming edge to the destination vertex. Kineograph further ensures that all transactions from the same ingest node are processed in the same sequence number order. It is worth pointing out that due to the separation of graph updates and graph computation, Kineograph has to deal with only simple graph updates when creating consistent snapshots and leverages the fact that each transaction consists of a set of graph-structure updates that can each be applied on a single vertex structure. Only in the computation phase (for graph mining) have we seen cases where updates depend on the states of other vertices.

In essence, the snapshot mechanism in Kineograph ensures consensus on the set of transactions to be included in a snapshot and can even impose an artificial order within that set, so that all the transactions are processed in the same order. However, the order is artificial. For example, graph nodes can be instructed to process all updates from the first ingest node before processing those from the second, and so on. This externally imposed order does not take into account any causal relationship. It reflects neither the physical-time order nor any causal order. We find it sufficient in our case, partly because Kineograph separates graph updates from graph mining—graph updates are usually simple and straightforward. In most cases, order does not matter at all. Even if updates were applied in a different order, the resulting graphs would stay the same, provided the same order on all graph nodes. One important property Kineograph ensures is deterministic vertex creation. For example, if there is a vertex created for each Twitter user ID, that vertex has an internal ID that depends on that Twitter user ID deterministically. This way, we can create an edge from or to that vertex even before that vertex is created, thereby eliminating cross-operation dependencies.

4. Supporting Incremental Graph-Mining Computation

The computation layer of graph nodes in Kineograph is responsible for executing incremental graph-mining. Computation results are updated based on recent changes in the graph, reflected in new snapshots. Graph-mining algorithms operate on a set of user-defined vertex-fields that store the associated data for those algorithms.

Kineograph adopts a vertex-based computation model [17, 18]. In this model, the data of interest is stored along

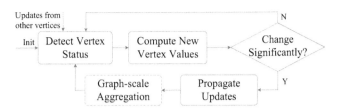

Figure 3. Computation overview.

with vertices, and computation proceeds by processing across vertices.

4.1 Overview

Figure 3 illustrates the overall graph mining process from a vertex's point of view. Initially, Kineograph uses user-defined rules to check the vertex status compared to the previous snapshot. If the vertex has been modified (e.g., edges added, values changed), Kineograph invokes user-specified function(s) to compute the new values associated with the vertex. If the value changes significantly, Kineograph will propagate the changes to a user-defined set of vertices (usually in the neighborhood). There is an optional aggregation phase in the computation within which a vertex might be involved in graph-scale reductions to compute global values. These can be arbitrary complex values, such as top X influential users, or the number of vertices of a certain type. The next iteration of the computation on a vertex is also driven by the status change, but this time it is triggered by the propagation received from other vertices. During a typical computation process, changes in user-defined vertex-fields propagate in a sub-graph, sparked by some change in the structure of the graph (such as adding an edge). The propagation proceeds until no status changes happen across all vertices in the graph, which designates the termination of the computation.

To better support various graph mining algorithms that might require different inter-vertex communication patterns, Kineograph support the *push* and the *pull* models in the computation [17, 26]. To check the status of a vertex and perform computation, the push model allows other vertices to push updates to a specific vertex and a vertex in the pull model proactively pulls data from neighboring vertices. Kineograph further enhances the two models to support incremental computation and efficient distributed execution.

The following subsections elaborate the details of the computation.

4.2 Push model

In the push model, each vertex can send a partial update to another vertex's user-defined vertex-field. For example, the PageRank [22] of a vertex is a weighted sum of the PageRanks of its neighboring vertices. In the push-model, each vertex sends its PageRank to its out-neighbors and the system adds them together to form the total pagerank. In *incremental* algorithms, each vertex sends its incremental change. In the PageRank example, each vertex only needs to send the difference of its current and previous PageRank.

One key feature of the push-model is the ability to perform sender-side aggregation. For each vertex-field, programmers can define a local aggregation function that combines updates sent by several vertices to one single update (see `accumulator` in Section 5). In our implementation, we observe that sender-side aggregation could reduce more than 90% of the total RPC calls during the computation, which shortens the overall computation time significantly.

To further support incremental computation, Kineograph keeps track of *dirty* (i.e., modified) vertices for a new snapshot and during computation (see `trigger` in Section 5). When a field is declared dirty, its *update function* is invoked. The role of an update function is to calculate and *push* the difference of a new value and its previous value to other vertices (see `updateFunction` in Section 5). Kineograph keeps track of the value that is sent to each of the neighboring vertices and performs incremental computation.

4.3 Pull model

A typical vertex update function in a pull model reads the values of its neighbor-vertices and produces a new value for itself. If it determines the change was significant, the function will ask the system to notify its neighbors, and the computation propagates in the graph dynamically.

In Kineograph, to reduce the communication cost an update function could read values from a specified subset of neighboring vertices. For example, some application only needs neighbors of a certain type or an individual vertex (such as a newly created vertex). Likewise, the requested data can be specified as a subset of the data associated with the vertices. In addition, different update functions might need different types of data: perhaps most functions require only the value in a particular vertex-field of a neighboring vertex, but some functions require more data, e.g., a list of edges of a neighbor.

Kineograph schedules updates to vertices in a way that minimizes network communications. In particular, it combines requests to the same vertices (if several update functions request for the same vertex) and executes the updates only when all requested data is available. This is in contrast to the synchronous model where the program issues synchronous calls to vertices while it is being executed. Requests are aggressively batched so there are more chances to merge requests and to reduce the number of RPC-calls.

Kineograph pull-model supports incremental computation by starting the computation from only the changed part of the graph, i.e., new or updated vertices/edges.

4.4 Initializations

Users can define functions that are invoked when there exist new vertices or new in/out-edges in a snapshot (see `initialize` in Section 5). Those are used to initialize the incremental graph computation. In the push model, it is typ-ical to set the corresponding vertex-field to dirty, which will subsequently lead to invoking the update function on the vertex. Likewise, in the pull model, an initialization phase involves asking the system to prepare the data needed to execute an update function.

4.5 Global aggregates

In addition to vertex-based computation, Kineograph provides a mechanism to compute global values using an *aggregator* functions that perform a distributed reduction over all vertices. This mechanism is identical to the Aggregators in Pregel [18] or Sync-mechanism of GraphLab [17], and we do not discuss it in details in this paper.

4.6 Execution schedule

Kineograph is designed for frequent incremental computation steps. It adopts a scheduling mechanism similar to the *partitioned scheduler* introduced in GraphLab [17]. Computation proceeds by executing consecutive *super-steps* on which scheduled vertices are executed across partitions.

The execution model of Kineograph can be seen as a hybrid of the BSP used in Pregel and the dynamic scheduling championed by GraphLab. Unlike GraphLab, Kineograph does not enforce computational consistency: neighboring vertices can be updated in parallel. However, as Kineograph does not allow direct writes to neighbors, write-write races are not possible. In our experiments, we did not notice the need for a stronger consistency guarantee (sequential consistency) for the computation.

Kineograph executes a defined maximum number of super-steps at each snapshot unless the task-queues are empty and there are no vertices to compute, which usually implies the computation has converged. Global aggregators are updated after each super-step.

5. Building Applications on Kineograph

Kineograph is designed to be a platform, where applications can be built on top by having a set of functions instantiated and customized appropriately. First, each ingest node can be instantiated with a function that parses a record in an input stream and produces a transaction consisting of a set of graph-update operations. This function defines the graph structure for an application. In addition to platform-supported graph operations like add edge/vertex, it is possible for an application to define a customized graph-update operation (e.g., increasing the weight of an edge by 10%): the application simply provides a callback function to be invoked when that operation is applied on a graph node in generating a snapshot. An application can further control the configuration of Kineograph in terms of the mapping of vertex IDs to logical partitions, as well as the assignment of logical partitions and their replicas to servers.

Second, an application can define a list of vertex-fields as associated values for a vertex. An application can further define a set of functions to implement a graph-mining algorithm. For the push model, an application defines vertex-fields that can be pushed to as push-fields. They have the following attributes:

- τ defines the type of the field.
- $value_0$ is the initial value of the field.
- `initialize` marks the changed vertices to initiate pushes.
- `updateFunction(vertex)`: the function that will be invoked by the `trigger` function.
- `trigger(oldval : τ, newval :τ) : boolean`: the function that detects whether the field has changed enough (dirty) to trigger an `updateFunction`.
- `accumulator(accumValue : τ, update : τ) : τ` accumulates two push updates into one.

For the pull model, an application defines two functions.

- `initialize` provides an update function to process changed vertices and generates a list of `vertex-request` for other vertices (i.e., pull). The `vertex-request` specifies the data fields required from a vertex.
- `updateFunction(vertex,List[readonly-vertex])` modifies the data field of a `vertex`. It is passed a list of *read-only* vertices that correspond to the list of `vertex-request` generated in the `initialize` function. The type is *read-only*, because Kineograph does not allow update functions to directly modify other vertices. These vertices only contain the data fields that were specified in the `initialize` function.

We have implemented three applications on Kineograph. We describe them in the rest of this section.

5.1 TunkRank: computing user influences

One of the most common applications for social network analysis is to estimate the influence of certain users. For our experiments, we use the TunkRank algorithm [31], which is similar to PageRank [22]. In this model, influence of a user X is defined as:

$$\text{Influence(X)} = \sum_{Y \in \text{Followers}(X)} \frac{1 + p * \text{Influence(Y)}}{|\text{Following(Y)}|},$$

where p is a constant retweet probability.

In our experiments, instead of measuring the influence based on "followers", we use a stronger connection between users based on who mentions who. In Twitter, if a tweet contains "@username", it means that the submitter of the micro-blog mentions user *username* (i.e., pays attention to *username*). According to [27], the resulting attention-graph is a more reliable metric of the actual influence than the follower-graph.

To compute the TunkRank, we use the push model as follows:

```
ProcessTweet(tweet) {
  foreach(word in tweet.text) {
    if (word starts "@") {
      mentionedUser = word[1:]
      EmitOperations(createEdge,
        from: tweet.user, to: mentionedUser)
    }
  }
}
```

Figure 4. Pseudo-code of the function for each ingest node that is used to create the attention graph.

```
UpdateTunkRank(v) {
  val newRankToPush =
    (1+p*v["tunkrank"])  /v.numOutEdges()

  foreach(e in vertex.outEdges()) {
    val prevSent = v.("tunkrank", e.target)
    val delta = newRankToPush - prevSent
    if (|delta| > threshold)
      v.pushDeltaTo("tunkrank", e.target,
                delta)
  }
}
```

Figure 5. Pseudo-code for the update-function for TunkRank algorithm.

- `graph`: a graph of user-vertices with edges connecting users who have mentioned each other. Figure 4 shows the function that ingest nodes use to construct the graph. Each `EmitOperations` emits two `createEdge` operations: one for the source to add an outgoing edge and the other for the destination to add an incoming edge.
- `initialize`: for new out-edges, mark the vertex.
- `updateFunction(vertex)`: sends the difference of the new and the previous weighted TunkRank to its neighbors. Its pseudo-code is shown in Figure 5.
- `accumulator`: sum-operation.
- `trigger(oldval,newval)`: `abs(oldval-newval)>ε`.

By adjusting the ϵ in the `trigger`, we can adjust the accuracy/computation time trade-off. In addition, we use an global aggregator object to maintain a list of K most influential users. In the experiment, we set ϵ to 0.001, a value sufficient to find top influential users.

5.2 SP: approximating shortest paths

Computing shortest paths between two vertices in a graph is a classic problem that is interesting in the context of social-network graphs and so on. We implement a landmark-based algorithm introduced by [28]. The algorithm uses a set S of vertices as landmarks (*seeds*). For each vertex, we maintain the shortest-path information from and to S. The shortest path between two arbitrary vertices v_1 and v_2 can then be approximated by the concatenation of shortest paths between v_1 to s and between s and v_2 for some $s \in S$. It has been shown that this approximation is satisfactory with a reasonable set of landmarks. In our experiment, we use the results of TunkRank and selects the top-ranked users as landmarks.

To maintain the shortest-path information from v to a landmark s, we use a *relaxation*-based algorithm derived from Bellman Ford algorithm [8]. The algorithm involves iteratively performing the following operations until no changes occur: for any vertex v, for each of its *inNeighbor* u, check whether u can get a shorter path toward s with v as its first step (i.e., checking whether $dist(v) + 1 < dist(u)$). If so, reset the distance of u as the smaller value and then schedule a same procedure from u later. We implement this algorithm in the push model.

- graph: same mention-graph as in TunkRank.
- initialize: for new in-edges, mark the vertex.
- updateFunction(vertex): sends its own length of shortest path plus one as candidates to its in-neighbors.
- accumulator: minimize-operation.
- trigger(oldval,newval): oldval.length > newval.length.

5.3 K-exposure: detecting controversial topics

Our third algorithm was recently proposed in [27] as a way of identifying hashtags ("#tag") that are *controversial*. [27] discovered in particular that political hashtags of controversial subjects had a clearly different spreading pattern than light topics such as celebrity-related hashtags. To study these patterns, an *exposure histogram* is computed for each hashtag. Exposure is computed as follows: let S be a micro-blog post by user U that contains hashtag H at time t. Then $k(S)$ is defined as follows:

$$k(S) = |\{\text{neighbors of U}\} \cap \\ \{ \text{users who posted a message with } H \text{ at time } < t\}|.$$

Note that t is defined by the timestamp information attached to every tweet.

By computing $k(\cdot)$ for posts that contain H, we can compute the *k-exposure histogram* for each hashtag. Our implementation of this algorithm uses the pull model, is incremental, and does not propagate.

- graph: for each unique hashtag and user we create a vertex and assign an edge from the hashtag to the user. In addition, we utilize the same mention-graph created for TunkRank.

- initialize: for each out-edge added to a hashtag, schedule the update function and request all edges of the corresponding user (target vertex of the edge).
- updateFunction(hashtagVertex, [userVertex]): compute the intersection of the out-edges of userVertex and hashtagVertex and update the k-exposure value of hashtagVertex.

6. Fault Tolerance, Incremental Expansion, and Decaying

As a distributed system, Kineograph must tolerate failures and allow incremental expansion to cope with increasing update rates and computation needs. Unique to Kineograph, because of the time-sensitive nature of the applications it targets, Kineograph should ideally support decaying, so that newer information has a higher weight in the results we produce. The design of Kineograph makes it easy to support fault tolerance, incremental expansion, and decaying, as we describe in detail here.

6.1 Fault tolerance

Kineograph has servers taking different roles in the system; each of them needs to be designed to cope with failures. A Paxos-based [15] solution (e.g., Chubby [4] or ZooKeeper [12]) can be used to implement Kineograph's centralized functionalities, such as maintaining the global progress table, coordinating graph-mining computation, monitoring machines, and tracking replicas. As the mechanism is well-explained in existing literature under similar settings, we do not describe it in detail here. Our current implementation uses a single server.

Ingest nodes. Because ingest nodes in Kineograph are more than just stateless front-ends, care must be taken in handling their failures. Kineograph's epoch commit protocol assumes that each ingest node produces monotonically increasing sequence numbers for transactions of graph-structure updates. This property must be preserved despite machine failures. Note that it is possible for an ingest node to fail in the middle of sending updates to multiple graph nodes.

Kineograph introduces *incarnation numbers* and leverages the global progress table to address this problem. Each ingest node has an incarnation number. We replace sequence numbers with pairs $\langle c, s \rangle$, where c is an incarnation number and s is a sequence number. They are used in graph-structure updates sent to graph nodes and recorded in the global progress table. When an ingest node fails and recovers, or when a new machine takes the role of a failed ingest node, that resurrected ingest node i consults the global progress table for the pair $\langle c_i, s_i \rangle$ associated with ingest node i. It seals c_i at s_i and uses $c_i + 1$ as the new incarnation number. It can reset the sequence number to 0 or continue at $s_i + 1$.

By sealing c_i at s_i, all requests with $\langle c_i, s \rangle$ where $s > s_i$ are considered invalid and discarded. To avoid any loss of transactions, all incoming data feeds must be stored reliably and can only be garbage collected after they have been reflected in the progress table. Here, we are taking advantage of epoch commit to "undo" operations for free.

Replication at the storage layer. The separation of graph updates and graph computation is crucial in simplifying fault tolerance in Kineograph, as Kineograph uses two different mechanisms to handle failures at the storage layer and at the computation layer.

At the storage layer, graph-update operations and the resulting graph data need to be stored reliably on graph nodes. We leverage ingest nodes and use a simple quorum-based replication mechanism: each logical partition is replicated on k (say 3) different machines and can tolerate f (say 1) failure, where $k \geq 2f + 1$ holds. Graph-update operations are then sent to all replicas and an ingest node considers the operation reliably stored as long as $f + 1$ replicas have responded.

Some replicas might miss some operations for its logical partition. An ingest node keeps a counter for the number of operations for each logical partition and attaches the counter with each operation. A replica can use the counter to identify holes and ask the missing information from other replicas. (Note that some transactions might not touch certain logical partitions. Therefore, we cannot use sequence numbers to identify missing operations.) All replicas will create the same snapshots as they apply the same set of operations in the same order. We rely on the fact that graph update operations are deterministic.

A replica G loses all the in-memory data in case of machine failures. Kineograph will replace G with a new node G'. In order to retrieve the lost data and catch up with the other replicas in the same replica group R, G' first asks each ingest node s to send all future operations hosted on R to G' starting from sequence number t_i $(1 \leq i \leq n)$. Once G' learns from the snapshooter that a snapshot P with a vector clock $\langle s_1, s_2, \ldots, s_n \rangle$ satisfying $s_i \geq t_i$ for each $1 \leq i \leq n$ is created, G' retrieves snapshot P from other replicas in R and hence has all the information needed to take over G. During the recovery process, other replicas in R continue to serve graph updates and produce snapshots, hence the service will not be interrupted.

Replication at the computation layer. Kineograph triggers incremental graph-mining computation on consistent snapshots. Each invocation of computation takes a relatively small amount of time (up to the order of minutes in our experiments). Because snapshots are reliably stored with replication at the storage layer, Kineograph simply rolls back and re-executes if it encounters any failures in a computation phase. The result of a computation can be replicated to tolerate failures. We do not perform replicated graph-mining computation on replicas since certain graph computation is non-deterministic. Instead, we use a simple primary/backup replication scheme, where the primary does the computation and copies the results to the secondaries.

6.2 Incremental expansion

The scale of Kineograph depends on many factors, including the rate of incoming data feeds, the size of the resulting graphs, and the complexity of graph-mining computation. There are cases where Kineograph needs to recruit more machines into the system in order to handle higher load, larger amount of data, and/or heavier computation. In our experiments, we have seen continuously increasing memory footprint as the system takes in more and more data, partly because we have not implemented any decaying mechanism. It would be ideal to be able to spread the graphs onto a larger set of machines when needed.

In our design, we create a large number of logical partitions up front. Incremental expansion can then be achieved by moving certain logical partitions to new machines, rather than splitting logical partitions, although technically splitting logical partitions can easily be achieved as well.

Live migration of a partition can be challenging in general, but is made much easier thanks to our snapshot mechanism. For simplicity, we ignore replication in the description, as adding replication into the protocol is straightforward. The overall procedure is similar to the failure recovery mechanism at the Kineograph storage layer. Suppose Kineograph wants to migrate a logical partition from S to T. It communicates with each ingest node s about the migration and a promise to send all future operations on that logical partition to both S and T starting from sequence number t_i. Once a snapshot with a logical clock $\langle s_1, s_2, \ldots, s_n \rangle$ satisfying $s_i \geq t_i$ for each $1 \leq i \leq n$ is created, Kineograph instructs a copy of that snapshot from S to T. Once T receives the snapshot, it has all the information needed to take over the logical partition from S. Because computation overlaps with incoming updates, T can usually catch up with S quickly without causing any performance degradation. We have not implemented incremental expansion at the time of this writing.

6.3 Decaying

In our experiments, we have seen a continuous increase in the graph size as Kineograph contunuously takes in more data. In practice, the value of information decays over time and outdated information should gradually have decreasing impact on results. Although we have not implemented this mechanism, we outline here how Kineograph could support decaying by leveraging global logical clocks based on sequence numbers.

Suppose we care only about the information in the last n days and that the information within those n days has a different weight depending on which day it is. Kineograph can essentially create $n + 1$ parallel graphs to track the last n days and plus the current day. The window slides as a day

Kineograph	LoC	Applications	LoC
Storage	6180	TunkRank	310
Computation	6714	K-Exposure	137
RpcLib	1177	SP	487
Log	2123	GraphUpdate	527
Total: 17655			

Table 1. Line of code count breakdown.

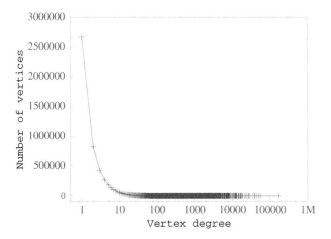

Figure 6. In-edge degree distribution across vertices.

passes. Instead of using real time, which could lead to inconsistencies in a graph due to different interpretations of real time on different servers, Kineograph align those decaying time boundaries with the epochs defined by logical clocks of sequence numbers. When a day passes in the real time, Kineograph can look at the current epoch number and use this as the boundary. The real graph used for computation can be constructed by taking a weighted average of those parallel graphs.

7. Evaluation

We have implemented Kineograph using C# with more than 17,000 lines of code, excluding test code. Table 1 summarizes the lines of code for different components in the Kineograph system and its applications. Note that we have developed our own RPC library that allows optimized data marshalling.

We evaluated Kineograph on a cluster with up to 51 machines, each connected with Gigabit Ethernet. 25 of the machines contained an Intel Xeon X3360 CPU (quad-core, 2.83GHz) and 8GB memory. The remaining had an Intel Xeon X5550 CPU (quad-core, 2.67GHz) and 12GB memory. All the machines ran the 64-bit version of Windows Server 2008R2 with .NET framework 4.0.

In our experiments, we simulated a live Twitter stream by feeding our system from a bank of 100 million archived tweets. This data set forms a graph of over 8 million vertices (users and hashtags) and 29 million edges. Figure 6 shows the edge distribution in the graph Kineograph constructs. The distribution exhibits *power law*, where very few vertices

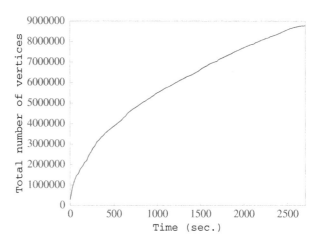

Figure 7. Number of vertices increases over time with 2 ingest nodes and 32 graph nodes.

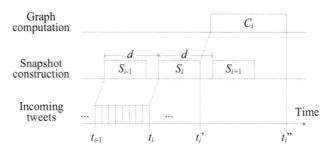

Figure 8. A streamlined view of graph updates and graph computation.

have extremely high degrees (more than 200k). Figure 7 shows how the graph size changes when we feed the data into the system with two ingest nodes.

To understand the end-to-end performance of the system, we ran evaluations across the three applications described in Section 5 on top of Kineograph.

Kineograph is designed to capture and mine a changing data set (graph) in a timely manner. There are two key system properties that are of interest to potential Kineograph users. i) *Update throughput*: whether Kineograph is able to support high update rates to the graph. ii) *Data timeliness*: whether Kineograph can help applications compute timely results out of the changing graph. We will report the experimental results and our findings in the rest of this section.

7.1 Graph update throughput

Kineograph should be able to support high update throughput that matches existing popular on-line services like Twitter. As of October 2011, the peak amount of Twitter traffic was 8.9K tweets per second [29]. Ideally, the system should further take the future growth of the Twitter service into account.

In Kineograph, throughput is measured by counting the number of tweets that have been processed after Kineograph finishes constructing a snapshot for each epoch. As illustrated in Figure 8, snapshot construction is performed at a

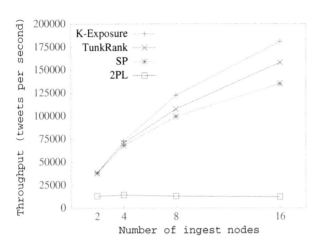

Figure 9. Graph-update throughput on 32 graph nodes with varying numbers of ingest nodes and with different applications. Snapshot interval is set to 10 seconds.

Snapshot Interval(s)	SCT Max/Avg	Avg SCT(s)	Throughput(t/s)
10	3.1	1.9	137.6k
30	2.2	4.4	143.0k
60	1.9	8.4	150.8k

Table 2. The impact of transient imbalance on throughput under K-Exposure, with 8 ingest nodes, 32 graph nodes. SCT Max/Avg: The ratio of maximum over average Snapshot Construction Time.

regular interval d. Snapshot S_{i-1} is constructed out of the tweets accumulated before time t_{i-1}. Snapshot S_i is constructed with those tweets logged between time t_{i-1} and t_i (denoted as $N[t_{i-1}, t_i]$). Therefore, the average throughput is calculated by $N[t_{i-1}, t_i]/d$.

To evaluate the peak graph-update throughput, we use a preprocessor to parse the retrieved tweets and keep only the information of interest to the applications (e.g., tweet text, user name, and time stamp). The pre-processing reduces the data-processing burden on an ingest node so that we can generate more loads with a small number of ingest nodes to the system for higher update throughput. By default, Kineograph enables batch update (batch size set to 512) to improve communication efficiency.

In our first experiment, we use different numbers of ingest nodes to inject input streams at different rates and measure the average graph-update throughput of Kineograph. All experiments use 32 graph nodes with the snapshot interval set to 10 seconds. The results are shown in Figure 9: the update throughput increases with the number of ingest nodes. With 16 ingest nodes, the sustained average update throughput can be more than 180k tweets per second, 20 times more than the recorded Twitter traffic peak as of Oct. 2011 [29].

Figure 9 also shows that the update throughput varies under different applications. This is because the update procedure competes for computation resources (e.g., CPU cycles and network bandwidth) with applications running on top of Kineograph. Since different applications consume different amounts of computation power, update throughputs suffer from different levels of interference. For example, SP and TunkRank require more computation power than K-Exposure. Thus the update throughput under K-Exposure is higher than those under the other two applications.

To understand further the benefit of the epoch commit protocol for graph updates, we implement a simplified two-

phase locking (2PL) scheme [30], where ingest nodes obtain locks from graph nodes in a fixed-order (to avoid deadlocks) and release locks when all locks are obtained. We omit the actual execution of the operations and enable batching (with a batch size of 512) to improve throughput. Batching reduces the number of round-trips, but at the risk of introducing more contention due to coarse granularity. Our experiments do show better throughput at that batch size. Figure 9 shows that the throughput of a 2PL-based scheme does not increase with the number of ingest nodes. A closer look reveals significant contention in the system, mostly due to well-connected vertices in the graph. Due to the power-law distribution shown in Figure 6, most concurrent updates compete for the access to very few vertices, which results in significant lock contention.

Figure 9 also shows that the update throughput increases sub-linearly with the number of ingest nodes. Our investigation attributes this to *transient load imbalance* during updates. In particular, we find that some graph nodes take more time to construct a snapshot locally than others. Table 2 shows an example in which the graph node with the maximum snapshot construction time (SCT) can spend 3 times as much as the average time of snapshot construction (denoted as SCT Max/Avg ratio).

We further observe that the imbalance is *transient*. Smaller snapshot windows, translates to more severe imbalances, and correspondingly, lower aggregated throughput. For example, if we increase the snapshot interval from 10 to 60, the SCT Max/Avg ratio decreases from 3.0 to 1.9. Consequently, the total update throughput increases by 10%. (Note that larger interval also makes batching more effective.) A larger snapshot interval improves throughput, at the expense of timeliness.

In summary, Kineograph can support the current peak throughput and leaves plenty of capacity for future growth of online services.

7.2 Data timeliness

The next set of experiments focus on data timeliness. As shown in Figure 8, the computation for snapshot S_i completes at time t_i''. The computation result C_i reflects the input data between t_{i-1} and t_i. We define timeliness for the input window $[t_{i-1}, t_i]$ to be between $t_i'' - t_i$ and $t_i'' - t_{i-1}$.

As shown in Figure 8, data timeliness depends on snapshot interval d, snapshot construction time (SCT) for snap-

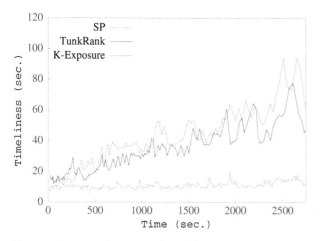

Figure 10. Data timeliness for different applications with 2 ingest nodes and 32 graph nodes.

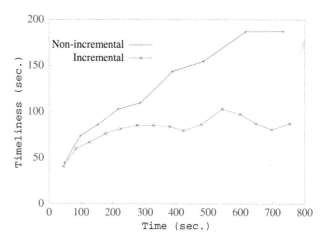

Figure 11. Timeliness changes over time for incremental and non-incremental graph computation with TunkRank, 4 ingest nodes, and 32 graph nodes.

shot S_i, and computation time for the corresponding result C_i. Since computation complexity of different applications varies, the actual data timeliness differs on different applications, even when Kineograph has stable system behavior.

Figure 10 shows data timeliness of different applications and confirms the impact of application complexity. Compared to K-Exposure, the TunkRank and SP algorithms are more complex, require multiple rounds, and suffers from worse data timeliness.

Figure 10 also shows that data timeliness becomes worse over time. A closer look shows that this property is mainly due to increases of the graph size over time, as shown in Figure 7. We did not use decaying in our experiments.

The overall data timeliness is within minutes. In the case of TunkRank, Figures 9 and 14 show that Kineograph is able to provide data timeliness of less than 3 minutes, with the update throughput more than 100k tweets per second, more than 10 times the peak throughput of Twitter (as of Oct. 2011). Two factors contribute to such good timeliness results: support of incremental graph computation and the use of a distributed system. We evaluate the effect of these two factors in our subsequent experiments.

Figure 11 shows the benefit of incremental TunkRank computation over the non-incremental version. Because the incremental version reuses the previous results as the starting points, we actually see that the benefit grows over time. As the graph size grows, the non-incremental version has to compute TunkRank from scratch at an increasing cost. Figure 12 shows similar benefits of incremental computation for all three applications.

Figure 13 demonstrates the scalability of TunkRank running on Kineograph. With more graph nodes involved in the computation, the data timeliness becomes better, an indication of reduced computation time. This data shows that Kineograph scales well with the increase of graph nodes, for this particular application. The 32-node case has 84% better timeliness than the 8-node case. Note that the 32-node case

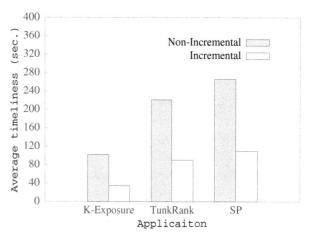

Figure 12. Average timeliness improvement of incremental applications under 4 ingest nodes and 32 graph nodes.

has more than 4 times speedup over the 8-node case, mainly due to the extra memory management cost (e.g., garbage collection) in the 8-node case.

Another factor that affects timeliness is the incoming data rate on the system. Figure 14 shows that with added ingest nodes and increased incoming data rate, the data timeliness becomes worse. The results arise from three factors. First, for the given input stream at the same time instance, the graph size becomes larger at a higher rate; computation over a larger graph is expected to take more time. Second, at a higher rate, the *change* of the graph between two snapshots becomes larger. Consequently, it takes more time to finish the computation, even with incremental computation. Finally, a higher incoming rate leads to higher throughput and more resource consumption, taking resources away from computation and causing it to slow down.

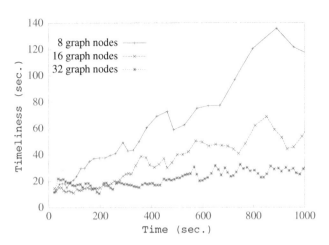

Figure 13. Scalability of TunkRank with different numbers of graph nodes and 2 ingest nodes.

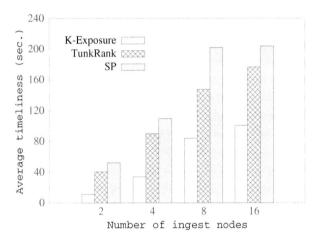

Figure 14. Average data timeliness with different number of ingest nodes and 32 graph nodes.

7.3 Fault tolerance

We demonstrate the system behavior under machine failure using 2 ingest nodes and 48 graph nodes, running TunkRank. The graph nodes host 16 graph partitions in total, i.e., every partition has three replicas. To fully utilize computation resources, for every graph partition, each of the three replicas is responsible for the computation of 1/3 of the graph partition.

Figure 15 shows how the system performance changes over time when we kill one graph node during the experiment. At the time around 324 seconds (t_0) after the experiment begins (after the construction of snapshot 31), we terminate one graph node. The system detects the failure and initiates the failure recovery process for the graph node as described in Section 6.1.

As shown in Figure 15, since the storage layer of Kineograph uses a quorum-based replication scheme, the graph update throughput does not suffer from the machine failure. The computation layer, however, is more vulnerable to fail-

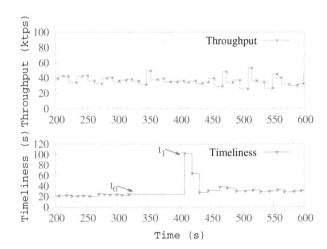

Figure 15. TunkRank data timeliness (s) and graph update throughput (1k tweet/s) with 2 ingest nodes and 48 graph nodes under 1 graph node failure.

ures since Kineograph does not replicate computation. The TunkRank computation stops right after the failure occurs. Therefore we observe no timeliness data during the failure time (between t_0 and t_1). The computation restarts after the resurrected graph node catches up with other replicas at snapshot 35 (around 360 seconds). As expected, the data timeliness right after the recovery increases greatly because the graph data has been accumulated over 30 seconds and the benefit of incremental computation decreases due to larger graph changes. Actually, Kineograph produces the first computation result at t_1, more than 40 seconds after the completion of the failure recovery procedure. The data timeliness becomes normal after several rounds of computation since the TunkRank incremental computation gradually catches up with the changes in the graph.

In summary, the failure behavior of Kineograph matches our design goal well.

8. Related Work

Kineograph builds on a large body of existing literature in distributed systems and database systems. We focus on three most related areas: distributed in-memory storage (key/value) systems, incremental data processing, and graph computation.

Distributed in-memory storage systems. Distributed in-memory key/value stores have received a lot of attention, both in the research community and in the industry [13, 19, 21]. Kineograph leverages this technology, adds basic graph support, and more importantly supports snapshots.

Incremental data processing. Recently, many research efforts have focused on improving computation efficiency through augmenting existing scalable batch-processing engines with incremental computation capability. Systems like

Incoop [2], Haloop [3], DryadInc [25], Yahoo continuous bulk processing (CBP) [16], Comet [11], and Nectar [10] achieve this by allowing their applications to reuse existing computation results. However, those systems are not designed for scenarios with fast continuous data updates and timely computation results. Most of the work focuses on variations of relational or MapReduce models, rather than a graph model.

Google Percolator [24] provides a trigger-based event-driven programming model for incremental web index construction. It provides a lock-based mechanism to support update transactions with snapshot isolation. Their design targets the scenarios where the conflict rate of transactions is low. This is unfortunately not the case in highly-connected graph structures. Instead of using locking, Kineograph uses epoch commit to construct consistent snapshots.

There are also extensive works in the database community on incremental computation [5–7]. Stream processing databases continuously accept new incoming updates, incrementally maintain database view, and adopt window-based relational operators to process the incoming data and generate results in real-time. Kineograph differentiates itself from them on the following aspects. First, rather than incremental computation only on a window of incoming updates, Kineograph supports computation on a new global snapshot and needs to merge efficiently new updates with the existing snapshot to construct a new one. Secondly, Kineograph targets graph computations, which might not be well supported in a relational data model [1, 20].

Graph computation. In recent years there has been a lot of interest in the research and industry towards graph computation, which has been driven by the rapid growth of graph data, such as social networks and the web. In addition, the scientific computation community has been studying planar and grid-graphs for decades. Recent influential works on *vertex-based* computation include Google's Pregel [18] and GraphLab [17]. Pearce et al [23] propose an asynchronous graph computation model for multi-core that is based on an extended version of the graph visitor pattern. To process graphs that do not fit in memory, [23] employs efficient mechanisms to store part of the graph in flash-memory, while we provide a distributed computation model. Pegasus [14] is a collection of highly scalable batch graph-mining algorithms written for Hadoop. Unlike the existing offline graph engines that perform graph computation on static graph structures, Kineograph extends them with snapshot-awareness on a fast and continuously changing graph structure, and provides the ability to perform incremental graph-mining to produce timely computation results.

9. Concluding Remarks

Kineograph reflects our belief that there is a potential paradigm shift in distributed-system research. It departs from the now "traditional" areas of high-throughput and scalable batch systems, as represented by systems such as GFS and MapReduce. The new paradigm is inspired by increasingly popular social networking, micro-blogging, and mobile Internet applications. These services are more centered around graph-based storage and computation, while striking a different and delicate balance among timeliness, consistency, and throughput. While this paper focuses on an overall architectural design with novel constructs, we expect to see new abstractions and building blocks emerging in the near future.

Acknowledgments

We are in debt to Emre Kiciman, Sean McDirmid, and Vijayan Prabhakaran for the discussions and feedback on Kineograph. We would also like to thank the reviewers and our shepherd Niels Provos for their valuable comments and suggestions.

References

[1] R. Angles and C. Gutierrez. Survey of graph database models. *ACM Computing Surveys (CSUR)*, 40(1):1–39, 2008.

[2] P. Bhatotia, A. Wieder, R. Rodrigues, U. Acar, and R. Pasquini. Incoop: MapReduce for incremental computations. In *ACM SoCC*, 2011.

[3] Y. Bu, B. Howe, M. Balazinska, and M. Ernst. HaLoop: Efficient iterative data processing on large clusters. In *VLDB*, 2010.

[4] M. Burrows. The Chubby lock service for loosely-coupled distributed systems. In *OSDI*, 2006.

[5] D. Carney, U. Cetintemel, M. Cherniack, C. Convey, S. Lee, G. Seidman, M. Stonebraker, N. Tatbul, and S. Zdonik. Monitoring streams – a new class of data management applications. In *VLDB*, 2002.

[6] S. Chandrasekaran, O. Cooper, A. Deshpande, M. Franklin, J. Hellerstein, W. Hong, S. Krishnamurthy, S. Madden, V. Raman, F. Reiss, and M. Shah. TelegraphCQ: Continuous dataflow processing for an uncertain world. In *CIDR*, 2003.

[7] J. Chen, D. J. Dewitt, F. Tian, and Y. Wang. NiagaraCQ: A scalable continuous query system for internet databases. In *SIGMOD*, 2000.

[8] T. Cormen, C. Leiserson, R. Rivest, and C. Stein. *Introduction to Algorithms*. MIT Press and McGraw-Hill, 2nd. edition, 2001.

[9] J. Dean and S. Ghemawat. MapReduce: Simplified data processing on large clusters. *Communications of the ACM*, 51(1): 107–113, 2008.

[10] P. Gunda, L. Ravindranath, C. Thekkath, Y. Yu, and L. Zhuang. Nectar: Automatic management of data and computation in datacenters. In *OSDI*, 2010.

[11] B. He, M. Yang, Z. Guo, R. Chen, B. Su, W. Lin, and L. Zhou. Comet: Batched stream processing in data intensive distributed computing. In *ACM SoCC*, 2010.

[12] P. Hunt, M. Konar, F. P. Junqueira, and B. Reed. ZooKeeper: Wait-free coordination for internet-scale systems. In *USENIX ATC*, 2010.

[13] R. Kallman, H. Kimura, J. Natkins, A. Pavlo, A. Rasin, S. Zdonik, E. P. C. Jones, S. Madden, M. Stonebraker, Y. Zhang, J. Hugg, and D. J. Abadi. H-Store: A high-performance, distributed main memory transaction processing system. In *VLDB*, 2008.

[14] U. Kang, C. E. Tsourakakis, and C. Faloutsos. Pegasus: A peta-scale graph mining system. In *IEEE International Conference on Data Mining*, 2009.

[15] L. Lamport. The part-time parliament. *ACM Trans. Comput. Syst.*, 16(2):133–169, 1998.

[16] D. Logothetis, C. Olston, B. Reed, K. Webb, and K. Yocum. Stateful bulk processing for incremental analytics. In *ACM SoCC*, 2010.

[17] Y. Low, J. Gonzalez, A. Kyrola, D. Bickson, C. Guestrin, and J. Hellerstein. GraphLab: A new parallel framework for machine learning. In *Conference on Uncertainty in Artificial Intelligence(UAI)*, 2010.

[18] G. Malewicz, M. Austern, A. Bik, J. Dehnert, I. Horn, N. Leiser, and G. Czajkowski. Pregel: A system for large-scale graph processing. In *SIGMOD*, 2010.

[19] memcached. Memcached: A distributed memory object caching system, 2011. http://memcached.org.

[20] Neo4j. Neo4j: The graph database, 2011. http://neo4j.org. Accessed October, 2011.

[21] D. Ongaro, S. M. Rumble, R. Stutsman, J. Ousterhout, and M. Rosenblum. Fast crash recovery in ramcloud. In *SOSP*, 2011.

[22] L. Page, S. Brin, R. Motwani, and T. Winograd. The pagerank citation ranking: Bringing order to the web. *Stanford Technical Report*, 1999.

[23] R. Pearce, M. Gokhale, and N. Amato. Multithreaded asynchronous graph traversal for in-memory and semi-external memory. In *ACM/IEEE International Conference for High Performance Computing, Networking, Storage and Analysis (SC)*, 2010.

[24] D. Peng and F. Dabek. Large-scale incremental processing using distributed transactions and notifications. In *OSDI*, 2010.

[25] L. Popa, M. Budiu, Y. Yu, and M. Isard. Dryadinc: Reusing work in large-scale computations. In *HotCloud*, 2009.

[26] R. Power and J. Li. Piccolo: Building fast, distributed programs with partitioned tables. In *OSDI*, 2010.

[27] D. Romero, B. Meeder, and J. Kleinberg. Differences in the mechanics of information diffusion across topics: Idioms, political hashtags, and complex contagion on twitter. In *WWW*, 2011.

[28] A. Sarma, S. Gollapudi, M. Najork, and R. Panigrahy. A sketch-based distance oracle for web-scale graphs. In *WSDM*, 2010.

[29] D. Sullivan. Tweets about steve jobs spike but don't break twitter peak record, 2011. http://searchengineland.com/tweets-about-steve-jobs-spike-but-dont-break-twitter-record-96048.

[30] A. Tanenbaum. *Distributed Operating Systems*. Prentice Hall, 1995.

[31] D. Tunkelang. A twitter analog to pagerank. *Retrieved from http://thenoisychannel. com/2009/01/13/a-twitter-analog-to-pagerank*, 2009.

Jockey: Guaranteed Job Latency in Data Parallel Clusters

Andrew D. Ferguson
Brown University
adf@cs.brown.edu

Peter Bodik
Microsoft Research
peterb@microsoft.com

Srikanth Kandula
Microsoft Research
srikanth@microsoft.com

Eric Boutin
Microsoft Bing
eric.boutin@microsoft.com

Rodrigo Fonseca
Brown University
rfonseca@cs.brown.edu

Abstract

Data processing frameworks such as MapReduce [8] and Dryad [11] are used today in business environments where customers expect guaranteed performance. To date, however, these systems are not capable of providing guarantees on job latency because scheduling policies are based on fair-sharing, and operators seek high cluster use through statistical multiplexing and over-subscription. With Jockey, we provide latency SLOs for data parallel jobs written in SCOPE. Jockey precomputes statistics using a simulator that captures the job's complex internal dependencies, accurately and efficiently predicting the remaining run time at different resource allocations and in different stages of the job. Our control policy monitors a job's performance, and dynamically adjusts resource allocation in the shared cluster in order to maximize the job's economic utility while minimizing its impact on the rest of the cluster. In our experiments in Microsoft's production Cosmos clusters, Jockey meets the specified job latency SLOs and responds to changes in cluster conditions.

Categories and Subject Descriptors D.4.1 [*Operating Systems*]: Process Management—Scheduling

General Terms Algorithms, Performance

Keywords deadline, scheduling, SLO, data parallel, dynamic adaptation, Dryad, MapReduce

1. Introduction

Batch processing frameworks for data parallel clusters such as MapReduce [8] and SCOPE [6] on Dryad [11] are see-ing increasing use in business environments as part of near-real time production systems at Facebook [5] and Microsoft. These frameworks now run recurring, business-critical jobs, and organizations require strict service-level objectives (SLOs) on latency, such as finishing in less than one hour. Missing a deadline often has significant consequences for the business (e.g., delays in updating website content), and can result in financial penalties to third parties. The outputs of many jobs feed into other data pipelines throughout the company; long job delays can thus affect other teams unable to fix the input jobs. Operators who monitor these critical jobs are alerted when they fall behind, and have to manually resolve problems by restarting jobs, or adjusting resource allocations. A framework which automatically provided latency SLOs would eliminate such manual repairs.

The ability to meet an SLO in data parallel frameworks is challenging for several reasons. First, unlike interactive web requests [23], data parallel jobs have complex internal structure with operations (e.g., map, reduce, join, etc.) which feed data from one to the other [6, 7]. Barriers, such as aggregation operations, require the synchronization of all nodes before progress can continue. Failures, be they at task, server or network granularity, cause unpredictable variation, and particularly delay progress when they occur before a barrier.

Secondly, statistical multiplexing and over-subscription ensure high utilization of such clusters. This creates variability in response times due to work performed by other jobs. Finally, work-conserving allocation policies add variation by providing jobs with spare resources [12, 27]. Under these policies, each admitted job is guaranteed some task slots; slots that go unused are distributed to other jobs that have pending tasks. While this improves cluster efficiency, job latency varies with the availability of spare capacity in the cluster.

We provide latency guarantees for data parallel jobs in shared clusters with Jockey, which combines a detailed per-job resource model with a robust control policy. Given a previous execution of the job[1] and a utility function, Jockey models the relationship between resource allocation and expected job utility. During job runtime, the control policy computes the progress of the job and estimates the resource allocation that maximizes job utility and minimizes cluster impact by considering the task dependency structure, individual task latencies, and failure probabilities and effects.

While the resource allocator in Jockey operates on individual jobs, we can use admission control to ensure that sufficient guaranteed capacity is available to all admitted SLO jobs. Jockey's job model can be used to check whether a newly submitted job would "fit" in the cluster – that is, that all previously accepted SLO jobs would still be able to meet their deadlines – before permitting it to run. If a submitted SLO job does not fit in the cluster, the cluster scheduler would need to arbitrate between the jobs to determine an allocation which maximizes the global utility at the risk of missing some SLO deadlines. We leave the development of such a global arbiter as future work.

Prior approaches to providing guaranteed performance fall into one of three classes. The first class partitions clusters into disjoint subsets and is used at companies such as Facebook [10]. Jobs which require guaranteed performance are run in a dedicated cluster, and admission control prevents contention between jobs. This class achieves guarantees by sacrificing efficiency because the dedicated cluster must be mostly idle to meet SLOs. A second class of solutions shares the cluster, but provides priority access to SLO-bound jobs – tasks from such jobs run when ready and with optimal network placement. This shields SLO-bound jobs from variance due to other jobs. However, the impact on non-SLO jobs is significant: their partially complete tasks may have to vacate resources or lose locality when a higher-priority task arrives. In addition, this approach can only support a limited number of SLO-bound jobs to prevent negative interference between them. A final class of solutions, common across many domains, models the workload and selects a static resource allocation that ensures the deadline is met. We find that simple models for more general data parallel pipelines are imprecise, and dynamic adaptation is necessary to cope with runtime changes in the cluster and job structure.

Our core contribution is an approach that combines a detailed job model with dynamic control. Experiments on large-scale production clusters indicate that Jockey is remarkably effective at guaranteeing job latency – in 94 experiments it missed only a single deadline, by only 3% – and that neither the model nor control is effective without the other. Jockey is successful because it (a) minimizes the impact of SLO-bound jobs on the cluster while still providing guarantees, (b) pessimistically over-allocates resources at the start to compensate for potential future failures, and (c) can meet latency SLOs without requiring guaranteed performance from individual resources such as the cluster network and disks.

2. Experiences from production clusters

To motivate our method for guaranteeing job latency in a production data-parallel cluster, we first describe the architecture of the cluster and the importance of latency SLOs. We then show that SLOs are difficult to meet due to high variance in job latency, and illustrate the causes of such variance.

2.1 Cluster Background

To gain insight into the problem, we examine a single cluster in Cosmos, the data parallel clusters that back Bing and other Microsoft online properties. Example applications running on this cluster include generating web indices, processing end-user clickstreams, and determining advertising selections. Jobs are written in SCOPE [6], a mash-up language with both declarative and imperative elements similar to Pig [17] or HIVE [22]. A compiler translates the job into an *execution plan graph* wherein nodes represent *stages* such as map, reduce or join, and edges represent dataflow [7, 9, 12]. Each stage consists of one or more parallel *tasks*. For stages that are connected by an edge, communication between their tasks ranges from one-to-one to all-to-all. A *barrier* occurs when tasks in a dependent stage cannot begin until every task in the input stage finishes. Barriers are often due to operations that are neither associative nor commutative. Job data files reside in a distributed file system which is implemented using the same servers that run tasks, similar to Hadoop's HDFS or the Google File System [9]. The cluster is shared across many business groups; at any time, there are many jobs running in the cluster and several tasks running on each server.

Similar to other cluster schedulers [27], our cluster employs a form of fair sharing across business groups and their jobs. Each job is guaranteed a number of *tokens*, as dictated by cluster policy, and each running task uses one token, which is released upon task completion. For efficiency, spare tokens are allocated to jobs that have pending tasks. Jobs are admitted to the cluster such that the total tokens guaranteed to admitted jobs remains bounded. While a token guarantees a task's share of CPU and memory, other resources such as network bandwidth and disk queue priority are left to their default sharing mechanisms, which are either per-flow or per-request based.

2.2 SLOs in Data Parallel Clusters

Setting an SLO deadline depends on a number of factors, most of which relate to the job's purpose. At a minimum, the deadline must be feasible: it cannot be shorter than the amount of time required to finish the job given an infinite amount of resources (*i.e.*, the length of the critical path). Feasibility can be checked with trial job executions, or estimated using a simulator such as the one in Jockey (see Section 4.1).

Deadlines for some jobs are derived from contractual agreements with external (non-Microsoft) customers, such

---

[1] Recurring jobs, which include most SLO-bound jobs, account for over 40% of runs in our cluster, providing ready historical data for our models.

as advertisers or business partners, while others are set to ensure customer-facing online content is kept fresh and up-to-date. In each case, missing a deadline can be financially detrimental to the business, either because of a contractually-specified penalty or the associated loss of revenue. Because final outputs are often the product of a pipeline of jobs, a deadline on the final output leads to individual deadlines for many different jobs running in Cosmos.

Finally, many internal deadlines are "soft" – that is, finishing after four hours instead of three is undesirable, but does not trigger a financial penalty. However, a single cluster runs a large number of concurrent jobs, some of which have no deadlines, some have soft deadlines, and some have very strict deadlines. With standard weighted fair sharing, it is difficult to map latency objectives for each of type of deadline onto an appropriate weight. Directly specifying a utility function to indicate a job's deadline and importance alleviates this problem for our users.

In our experiments (Section 5), we set the target deadline based on the length of the critical path, and for seven of the jobs, we test with two different deadlines.

2.3 Variance in Job Latency

We quantify variance in the cluster by comparing completion times across runs of recurring jobs, such as the many production jobs which repeatedly execute on newly arrived data. By being mostly similar, recurring jobs provide a ready yet real source for cross-job comparison. The executions we examine consist of production-cluster jobs that repeated at least ten times each during September 2011.

Across the runs of each recurring job, we compute the completion time's coefficient of variation (CoV), i.e., $\frac{stdev}{mean}$. Table 1 shows that the median recurring job has a CoV of 0.28, and 10% of all jobs have a CoV over 0.59. While a CoV value less than 1 is considered to be low variance, these results imply that for half (or 10%) of recurring jobs the latency of a sixth of their runs is > 28% (or > 59%) larger than the mean.

We find that the size of the input data to be processed varies across runs of recurring jobs. To discount the impact of input size on job latency, we further group runs of the same job into clusters containing runs with input size differing by at most 10%. Table 1 shows that much of the variation still persists even within these clusters.

2.4 Causes of Variance

A potential cause of job latency variance is the use of spare tokens. Recall that our cluster re-allocates tokens which are unused by the jobs to which they were guaranteed. To explore this hypothesis, we compared runs of seven jobs described in Section 5.2 with experimental runs that were restricted to using guaranteed capacity only – the CoV dropped by up to five times. While these jobs are smaller than the median job in our cluster, and thus the specific decrease may not be representative, we believe it confirms our hypothesis that spare tokens add variance to job latency.

Statistic	Percentiles			
	10th	50th	90th	99th
CoV across recurring jobs	.15	.28	.59	1.55
CoV across runs with inputs differing by at most 10%	.13	.20	.37	.85

Table 1. The coefficient of variation (CoV) of completion time across runs of recurring jobs. Variation persists across runs with similar input sizes.

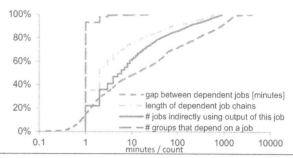

Figure 1. Dependence between jobs: 20% of jobs have more than 20 other jobs depending on their output. Over half of the directly dependent jobs start within 10 minutes of the earlier job and are hence likely to stall if the earlier job is delayed. Long chains of dependent jobs are common, and many chains span business groups.

The use of spare capacity creates variance in a job's run time for two reasons. First, the availability of spare tokens fluctuates because it depends on the nature of other jobs running in the cluster – if other jobs have more barriers or more outliers due to data skew, more tokens will be spare. In the above experiments, the fraction of the job's vertices that executed using the spare capacity varied between 5% and 80%. Second, tasks using spare tokens run at a lower priority than those using guaranteed tokens, and thus can be evicted or pushed into the background during periods of contention.

Task runtimes also vary due to hardware and software failures, and contention for network bandwidth and server resources. In public infrastructures, such as EC2 and Azure, such contention is even higher than in our cluster [13, 25].

2.5 Impact on Job Pipelines

Because many business processes consist of pipelines of multiple jobs, variance in the completion time of a single job can have a wide impact. To quantify this impact, we examined all jobs in our cluster over a period of three days. When a job's input contains data blocks written by an earlier job, we infer a dependence. We did not track dependences due to changes to the filesystem (e.g., copying or renaming blocks) and use of data outside the cluster (e.g., downloading a job's output to train a classifier which is then used by other jobs).

For the 10.2% of jobs with at least one dependency, which includes most SLO-bound jobs, Fig. 1 quantifies those dependences. The violet (solid) line shows that the median job's output is used by over ten other jobs – for the top 10% of jobs, there are over a hundred dependent jobs. The blue (small dashes) line shows that many directly dependent jobs start soon after the completion of a job – the median gap is ten minutes. This means that delays in the job will delay the start of these subsequent jobs. The green (dash-dot line) shows that the chains of dependent jobs can be quite long and span different business groups (red or big dash line). At business group or company boundaries, these delays can cause financial penalties and require manual intervention.

2.6 Lessons for Jockey

Jockey uses the number of guaranteed tokens as the mechanism to adjust a job's performance because it directly addresses one source of variance in our cluster. Because our tokens are analogous to tickets in a lottery scheduler or the weights in a weighted fair queuing regime, Jockey's methodology is directly applicable to other systems which use a weighted fair approach to resource allocation.

Jockey uses readily available prior executions to build a model of a recurring job's execution. Such a model is essential to translating resource allocation into expected completion time. We will show later how Jockey makes use of prior executions despite possible variations in input size.

3. Solutions for Providing SLOs

We consider three solutions to our goal of providing SLO-like guarantees of job completion times in Cosmos. The first is to introduce an additional priority class in the cluster-wide scheduler, and map different SLOs onto each class. The second is to manually determine resource quotas for each job. Finally, we develop a novel method to dynamically adjust resources based on the job's current performance and historical data.

3.1 Additional priority classes

The first potential solution is to implement a third class of tokens with a new, higher priority. Jobs with the strictest SLOs can be allocated and guaranteed these "SuperHigh" tokens. Through the combination of strict admission control, repeated job profiling to determine the necessary allocation, and a paucity of SuperHigh tokens at the cluster-scale, it is possible to meet SLOs with this design.

However, there are numerous downsides to this approach. When a job runs with SuperHigh tokens it increases contention for local resources. This has a negative impact on regular jobs, which can be slowed or potentially lose locality – the beneficial co-location of storage and computational resources. Secondly, the cluster scheduler must be overly pessimistic about the number of SuperHigh-priority jobs which can execute simultaneously. If too many such jobs are admitted to the cluster, the jobs will thrash and cluster goodput will fall. Finally, the heart of this solution is to introduce ordinal priority classes into the system, which are known to have weak expressive power and can lead to poor scheduling decisions when the system is overloaded [4]. We did not further evaluate this solution because its use would impact actual SLO-bound jobs in our production cluster.

3.2 Quotas for each job

A second potential solution for meeting SLO-bound jobs is to introduce strict, static quotas with the appropriate number of guaranteed tokens for each job. This solution is evaluated in Section 5.2 as *Jockey w/o adaptation*, and we find it to be unsatisfactory for three reasons. First, as cluster conditions change due to node failures and other events detailed later, the number of tokens required to meet the SLO also changes. Therefore, it would be necessary to regularly rebalance the quotas for all such SLO jobs.

Second, we have observed that determining weights and quotas is difficult for many users of large clusters. To reduce the chance of missing an SLO, some users request too many resources, which makes useful admission control challenging. Others request too few because they have relied on overly-optimistic trial runs, or a tenuous bounty of spare capacity tokens in the past. To explore the ability of users to correctly size their resource requests, we examined the guaranteed allocations and the maximum achieved parallelism of production jobs during a one-month period. We found that the maximum parallelism of one-third of the jobs was less than the guaranteed allocation. Futhermore, the maximum parallelism of one-quarter of the jobs reached more than ten times the guaranteed allocation thanks to the spare capacity.

Finally, it is clear that when multiple SLO-bound jobs exist in the system, the cluster's goodput can be improved by dynamically re-allocating resources from jobs with slack SLOs to those with tight SLOs.[2] This motivates the design of our solution, along with additional requirements described next.

3.3 Dynamic resource management

In order to meet the desired SLOs in Cosmos, we developed a dynamic resource management system, Jockey, which we describe in detail in Section 4. Our design was guided by the limitations of the two solutions above, the variability of job performance described in Section 2.3, and the structure of SCOPE programs. We also faced additional constraints such as the need to adapt to changes in cluster availability, delays in job submission, and changes in the SLO after job initialization.

The variability of job performance implies that the scheduler needs to react to changing cluster conditions, periodically re-allocating resources at a fine timescale during job execution. We discuss the sensitivity of the scheduler to this timescale in Section 5.5. Because resource allocations are recalculated during the job's execution, it is necessary to have an accurate indicator of the job's current progress, in addition to a model of the job's end-to-end latency.

The DAG structure of jobs in Cosmos creates two challenges. A first is that Jockey must make decisions which respect dependencies between tasks. A second is the wide variation in a job's degree of parallelism during execution. Some stages may be split into hundreds of tasks, while others, such

---

[2] A few Cosmos users even tried to do this by hand in the past!

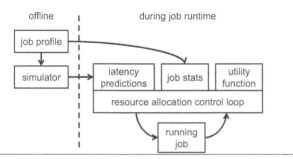

Figure 2. Architecture diagram: in the offline phase, we use a profile of a previous run to estimate job statistics and use the simulator to estimate completion times. During runtime, the control loop monitors the job and uses job statistics, latency predictions and the utility function to propose the minimum resource allocation that maximizes the utility of the job.

as an aggregation stage, are split into few tasks. The scheduler must allocate enough resources early in the job so that it does not attempt in vain to speed-up execution by increasing the resources for a later stage beyond the available parallelism. Jockey must also be aware of the probability and effect of failures at different stages in the job so there is an appropriate amount of time remaining to recover before the deadline.

4. Jockey

Jockey is composed of three components: a *job simulator*, which is used offline to estimate the job completion time given the current job progress and token allocation, a *job progress indicator*, which is used at runtime to characterize the progress of the job, and a *resource allocation control loop*, which uses the job progress indicator and estimates of completion times from the simulator to allocate tokens such that the job's expected utility is maximized and its impact on the cluster is minimized (see the architecture diagram in Fig. 2). We describe these components in more detail in the following three sections, and address limitations of our approach in Section 4.4.

4.1 Job Completion Time Prediction

In order to allocate the appropriate number of tokens to meet an SLO, Jockey must be able to predict the job's completion time under different token allocations given the current progress. This is challenging because the system has to consider all remaining work in the job and the dependencies between stages. We consider two methods for this prediction: an event-based simulator, and an analytical model inspired by Amdahl's Law. Based on our evaluation in Section 5.3, we use the simulator approach in the current version of Jockey.

Job simulator and the offline estimation

The job simulator produces an estimate of the job completion time given a particular allocation of resources and job progress. These estimates are based on one or more previous runs of the job, from which we extract performance statistics such as the per-stage distributions of task runtimes and initialization latencies, and the probabilities of single and multi-

ple task failures. The job simulator takes as input these statistics, along with the job's algebra (list of stages, tasks and their dependencies), and simulates events in the execution of the job. Events include allocating tasks to machines, restarting failed tasks and scheduling tasks as their inputs become available. This simulator captures important features of the job's performance such as outliers (tasks with unusually high latency) and barriers (stages which start only when all tasks in dependent stages have finished), but does not simulate all aspects of the system, such as input size variation and the scheduling of duplicate tasks. We discuss the accuracy of the simulator in Section 5.3.

A basic implementation of the resource allocation control loop could invoke the simulator during each iteration by marking the completed tasks and simulating forward. Then, for each resource allocation under consideration, multiple simulations could be used to estimate the distribution of completion times and thus the expected utility given that allocation. However, depending on the number of allocations considered and the size of the job, these simulations could take a long time and add a significant delay to the control loop. Therefore, we develop a method that only uses the simulator offline, precomputing all information necessary to accurately and quickly allocate resources.

For each SLO job, we estimate $C(p, a)$ – a random variable denoting the remaining time to complete the job when the job has made progress p and is allocated a tokens. In the control loop, we use these precomputed values to select an appropriate allocation. We present an approach to compute the job progress p in Section 4.2.

We estimate the distribution of $C(p, a)$ by repeatedly simulating the job at different allocations. From each simulation, say at allocation a that finishes in time T, we compute for all discrete $t \in [0, T]$ the progress of the job p_t at time t and the remaining time to completion $t_c = T - t$. Clearly, $t_c = C(p_t, a)$, i.e., the value t_c is one sample from the distribution of $C(p_t, a)$. Iterating over all t in a run and simulating the job many times with different values of a provides many more samples, allowing us to estimate the distribution well. Because the logic in the simulator is close to that of the real system, these estimates approximate real run times well.

Amdahl's Law

Rather than using the simulator above, we can use a modified version of Amdahl's Law [1] to estimate the job's completion time given a particular allocation. Amdahl's Law states that if the serial part of a program takes time S to execute on a single processor, and the parallel part takes time P, then running the program with N processors takes $S + P/N$ time. In our case, we let S be the length of the critical path of the job and P be the aggregate CPU time spent executing the job, minus the time on the critical path. To estimate the remaining completion time of a job when allocated a tokens, we evaluate the above formula with $N = a$.

To use Amdahl's Law in our resource allocation loop, we need to estimate the total work remaining in the job, P_t, and the length of the remaining critical path, S_t, while the job is running. For each stage s, let f_s be the fraction of tasks that finished in stage s, l_s be the execution time of the longest task in stage s, L_s be the longest path from stage s to the end of the job and T_s be the total CPU time to execute all tasks in stage s. Note that the last three parameters can be estimated from prior runs before the job starts, and f_s can easily be maintained by the job manager at run time. Now, $S_t = \max_{\text{stage } s: f_s < 1} (1 - f_s) l_s + L_s$ and $P_t = \sum_{\text{stage } s: f_s < 1} (1 - f_s) T_s$. In words, across stages with unfinished tasks $f_s < 1$, we estimate the total CPU time that remains to be P_t and the longest critical path starting from any of those stages to be S_t.

4.2 Job Progress Estimation

As introduced above, we use a progress indicator to capture the state of the job and to index into $C(p, a)$, the remaining time distributions that were pre-computed from the simulator. The progress indicator should faithfully reflect the work that has happened and the work that remains. In particular, it should account for parallel stages whose tasks can finish in any order, tasks that differ widely in completion time, and stages that differ in their numbers of tasks. Furthermore, tasks sometimes fail, requiring previous output to be recomputed, and the indicator should reflect such events as well.

A job progress indicator can integrate several characteristics of a running job. Examples include the fraction of completed tasks in each stage, the aggregate CPU time spent executing, the relative time when a particular stage is started or completed, and the length of the remaining critical path. We built six progress indicators that use different subsets of these aspects. Here we describe the progress indicator that worked best in our experiments. See Section 5.4 for description and evaluation of the remaining indicators.

The *totalworkWithQ* indicator estimates job progress to be the total time that completed tasks spent enqueued or executing. Based on past run(s) of the job, we compute for each stage s, the total time tasks spend executing T_s and enqueued Q_s. At runtime, given f_s, the fraction of tasks in stage s that are complete, the progress estimate is $\sum_{\text{stage } s} f_s (Q_s + T_s)$.

This indicator is simple. In particular, it assumes that tasks in the same stage have similar queuing and running times and ignores potentially useful information such as the intra-task progress, dependencies between future stages, barriers, and the length of remaining critical path. However, our goal is to design an indicator that is an effective index into the $C(p, a)$ distributions computed in Section 4.1. Our experience (see Sections 5.2 and 5.4) shows that this indicator performs better in Jockey than more complex indicators across a wide range of conditions.

4.3 Resource Allocation Control Loop

The goal of the resource allocation control loop is to implement a policy which maximizes the job's utility and mini-

mizes its impact on the cluster by adjusting the job's resource allocation. There are four inputs to the control loop:

1. f_s, the fraction of completed tasks in stage s
2. t_r, the time the job has spent running
3. $U(t)$, the utility of the job completing at time t. A typical utility function used in our environment would be nearly flat until the job deadline, drop to zero some time after the deadline and, in some cases, keep dropping well below zero to penalize late finishes.
4. Either the precomputed $C(p, a)$ distributions, Q_s and T_s, for each stage s (when using the simulator-based approach), or the precomputed l_s, L_s, and T_s for each stage s (when using the Amdahl's Law-based approach).

The policy's output is the resource allocation for the job.

The basic policy logic periodically observes the job's progress and adapts the allocated resources to ensure it finishes with high utility. First, it computes the progress p using a job progress indicator. Next, the expected utility from allocating a tokens is computed as follows: given progress p and the time the job has been running t_r, the expected utility is $U_a = U(t_r + C(p, a))$. Finally, the minimum allocation that maximizes utility is $A^r = \arg\min_a \{a : U_a = \max_b U_b\}$.

Inaccuracies in predicting job latencies and the non-deterministic performance of the cluster can cause the raw allocation A^r to under- or over-provision resources, or oscillate with changes. To moderate these scenarios, Jockey integrates three standard control-theory mechanisms:

1. **Slack**: To compensate for inaccuracy in the job latency estimate (by the simulator or Amdahl's Law), we multiply the predictions from $C(p, a)$ by a constant factor $\mathcal{S}$. For example, with slack $\mathcal{S} = 1.2$, we would add an additional 20% to the predictions.
2. **Hysteresis**: To smooth oscillations in the raw allocation, we use hysteresis parametrized by α. In particular, we adapt A_t^s – the smoothed allocation at time t – as follows: $A_t^s = A_{t-1}^s + \alpha(A^r - A_{t-1}^s)$. Whereas a value of $\alpha = 1$ implies that the allocation immediately jumps to the desired value, for $\alpha \in (0, 1)$ the gap between the allocation and the desired value reduces exponentially with time.
3. **Dead zone**: To dampen noise in the job progress indicator, we add a dead zone of length D, i.e., shift the utility function leftwards by D and change allocations only if the job is at least D behind schedule. For example, with $D = 3$ minutes, a deadline of 60 minutes is treated as a deadline of 57 minutes, and the policy won't act unless the job is at least 3 minutes delayed.

Our results in Section 5 show the need for dynamic adaptation. We also report on the incremental contributions due to each of the above techniques. In Section 5.5 we perform a sensitivity analysis of parameter choices, and find that the slack, hysteresis, and dead zone parameters have wide operating regimes. Values for these parameters can be set in advance with the aid of Jockey's simulator: slack can be set based on simulator's margin of error when compared with actual job executions, values for hysteresis and dead zone can be determined experimentally with a simulated control loop. While the simulator does not perfectly reproduce the actual dynamics of the cluster and jobs, it provides guidance when adjusting these settings.

4.4 Limitations and Future Work

As described here, Jockey makes local decisions to ensure each job finishes within the SLO while using as few resources as necessary. We plan to extend Jockey to reach globally optimal allocations when managing multiple SLO-bound jobs. Doing so requires an additional inter-job arbiter that dynamically shifts resources from jobs with low expected marginal utility to those with high expected marginal utility.

At this time, Jockey is only capable of meeting SLOs for jobs it has seen before. We consider this a reasonable limitation since most of the business-critical jobs are recurring. For non-recurring jobs, a single profile run is enough to generate accurate job completion estimates, as demonstrated in Section 5.2. Extending Jockey to support novel jobs, either through sampling or other methods, is left for future work.

Jockey is agnostic to small changes in the input size of the job and in the execution plans. Large changes to either are visible to Jockey and can be treated as new jobs; i.e., train new completion time distributions based on the changed runs. In practice, we build Jockey's offline distributions using the largest observed input because Jockey automatically adapts the allocation based on the actual resource needs during the lifetime of the job.

We acknowledge that Jockey cannot recover from serious failures or degenerate user code. For example, if running the job on the entire cluster would not meet the SLO, Jockey is of little use. However, such cases are rare, and for common failures Jockey can meet deadlines by running the job at appropriately higher parallelism. In either case, Jockey will attempt to meet the SLO by continuously increasing the amount of resources guaranteed to the job until the model indicates that the deadline will be met, the job completes, or a hard limit is reached.

A few enhancements to the current design are also under consideration. Additional input signals to the control loop, such as the size of the input data, progress within running tasks, and cluster-wide performance metrics, could improve adaptivity. Additional control knobs such as the aggressiveness of mitigating stragglers [2], the OS priority of tasks, and the bandwidth shares of network transfers, could broaden what Jockey can do to meet SLOs. Finally, rather than use progress indicators, efficient ways to integrate the simulator with the online phase, perhaps as a less frequent control loop, could provide more precise control over job progress.

5. Evaluation

In this section, we first evaluate the ability of Jockey to meet job latency SLOs in various scenarios: different deadlines, changes in cluster conditions, and changes in deadlines during job runtime. Then, we evaluate Jockey's three components: the latency prediction, the progress indicators, and the sensitivity of the control loop to changes in its parameters in Sections 5.3, 5.4, and 5.5.

5.1 Methodology

We evaluate Jockey on 21 production jobs; these were all the recurring jobs of a business group in Microsoft that were neither too short to use in our evaluation, nor too big for the guaranteed cluster slice available to our experiments. We use a single production run of these jobs as input to the simulator (Section 4.1) to pre-compute the completion time distribution ($C(p, a)$) and other statistics (l_s, L_s, T_s, and Q_s). Experimental runs were performed using a modified job manager that implements progress indicators and adapts allocations dynamically (Sections 4.2 and 4.3). We perform more detailed analysis for a subset of these jobs; their characteristics are in Table 2 and stage dependency structure is illustrated in Fig. 3.

The analysis and experiments were performed on a large-scale cluster running production workloads with an average utilization of 80% and a number of compute nodes in the high thousands. Each node is a commodity, multi-core machine with tens of GBs of RAM. There are approximately 40 machines per rack, connected by a network oversubscribed by a small factor.

For most jobs, we evaluate Jockey's ability to meet a deadline of 60 minutes. For the detailed subset, we used two different deadlines – the longer always twice the shorter. A deadline of d minutes translates to a piecewise-linear utility function going through these points: $(0, 1)$, $(d, 1)$, $(d + 10, -1)$, $(d + 1000, -1000)$. This means that the utility drops significantly after the deadline. We ran at least three experiments for each combination of job, deadline and policy. In total, we report results from more than 800 experiments.

Our evaluation metrics are as follows: 1) did the job complete before the specified deadline?, 2) how much earlier or later did the job finish compared to the deadline?, and 3) what was the impact on the rest of the cluster for jobs that met the deadline? We measure the job's impact using the notion of *oracle allocation*. For a deadline of d minutes and a job that requires aggregate CPU time of T minutes, the oracle allocation is $O(T, d) = \lceil T/d \rceil$ tokens. This is the minimum allocation required in theory to finish the job in d minutes. This estimate is optimistic since it assumes the total work is known in advance, and the job can continuously run at a parallelism of $O(T, d)$ (that is, it is agnostic to the job's structure). However, it is a good baseline for comparing different resource allocation approaches. The job's impact on the cluster is measured as the fraction of job allocation requested by the policy that

stat	A	B	C	D	E	F	G
vertex runtime median [sec]	16.3	4.0	2.6	6.1	8.0	3.6	3.0
vertex runtime 90th percentile [sec]	61.5	54.1	5.7	25.1	130.0	17.4	7.7
vertex runtime 90th percentile [sec] (fastest stage)	4.0	3.3	1.7	1.4	3.9	3.3	1.6
vertex runtime 90th percentile [sec] (slowest stage)	126.3	116.7	21.9	72.6	320.6	110.4	68.3
total data read [GB]	222.5	114.3	151.1	268.7	195.7	285.6	155.3
number of stages	23	14	16	24	11	26	110
number of barrier stages	6	0	3	3	1	1	15
number of vertices	681	1605	5751	3897	2033	6139	8496

Table 2. Statistics of seven jobs used in evaluation.

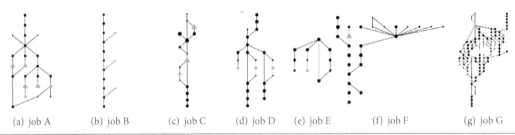

| (a) job A | (b) job B | (c) job C | (d) job D | (e) job E | (f) job F | (g) job G |

Figure 3. Stage dependencies of seven jobs used in evaluation. Each node represents a stage in a job; blue, triangular nodes are stages with full shuffle. Sizes of the nodes are proportional to the number of vertices in the stage, and edges represent stage dependencies (top to bottom). In this visualization, a typical MapReduce job would be represented by a black circle connected to a blue triangle.

is *above the oracle allocation*. See Fig. 6 for examples of the oracle allocation.

In our experiments, we re-run the resource allocation control loop (Section 4.3) each minute and use the totalworkWithQ progress indicator. We use a slack of 1.2 to accommodate the inaccuracy of job latency prediction, hysteresis parameter of 0.2 to smooth the requested resource allocation, and a dead zone of 3 minutes. We discuss Jockey's sensitivity to these values in Section 5.5, and compare progress indicators in Section 5.4.

We compare Jockey – based on predictions from the job simulator and adapting allocations at runtime – with three other policies. *Jockey w/o adaptation* uses the job simulator to find an *a priori* resource allocation that maximizes job utility, but does not adapt allocations during job runtime. *Jockey w/o simulator* does adapt but uses the simpler Amdahl's Lawbased model of the job. Finally, we compare against the *max allocation* policy which guarantees all the resources available (in these experiments, 100 tokens) to finish the SLObound job as quickly as possible.

While the max allocation policy is able to meet all of the SLO deadlines, as shown below, it is not a practical policy to use. Because it guarantees all allocated resources to each job, it is not possible to run more than one job at a time using the max allocation policy. Because the maximum parallelism of Dryad jobs varies, running one job at a time would create "valleys" before the barrier stages, during which the resources would be underutilized (indeed, this problem would be worse for those jobs which cannot make use of all allocated resources at any point). Filling those valleys with additional

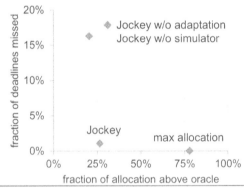

Figure 4. Comparison of average allocation above the oracle allocation and fraction of missed deadlines for each policy.

jobs naturally requires a dynamic allocation policy, as we develop with Jockey.

5.2 SLO-based Resource Allocation

Fig. 4 summarizes our experiments; there are more than 80 runs per policy. The x-axis shows the fraction of job allocation above the oracle allocation; the y-axis shows the fraction of experiments that missed deadlines. In both cases, lower values are better. Jockey misses the deadline in one experiment (see below for an explanation), and has a low impact on the rest of the cluster. Jockey w/o adaptation has a slightly higher impact on the cluster, but misses many more deadlines because of its inability to adapt to cluster changes. Jockey w/o simulator, which uses Amdahl's Law to estimate job completion times, achieves the lowest impact on the cluster, but misses many deadlines. This is because the simple analytic model of the job leads to imprecise predictions of the com

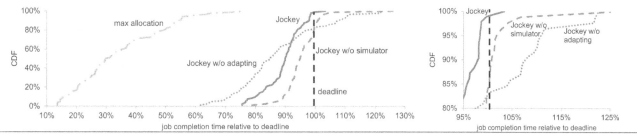

Figure 5. Left, CDFs of job completion times relative to the specified deadline for different policies. Right, detail of the upper-right corner.

pletion time. Finally, the max allocation policy meets every deadline by significantly over-provisioning the job – potentially starving other jobs in the cluster. Further, when multiple SLO-bound jobs must run simultaneously, this policy provides no benefits.

Fig. 5 presents the experimental results in more detail. The x-axis on the graph represents the job completion time relative to the specified deadline; values below 100% represent experiments that met the SLO, values above 100% (right of the dashed black line) are experiments that did not. Notice that jobs using the max allocation policy finish significantly before the deadline – the median such job finishes approximately 70% early – which translates to a large impact on the rest of the cluster; jobs under the other three policies finish much closer to the deadline. Finally, notice that using dynamic resource allocation in Jockey (solid line) further reduces the variance in latency compared to Jockey w/o adaptation (dotted line), which uses a fixed allocation of tokens.

On the right in Fig. 5, we see that while both Jockey w/o simulator and Jockey w/o adaptation miss the same fraction of deadlines, the late jobs using Jockey w/o simulator finish much earlier post-deadline. The median *late* job of Jockey w/o simulator finishes only 1% late, while the median late job of Jockey w/o adaptation finishes 10% late. This shows that even though Amdahl's Law provides less accurate latency predictions than the simulator, dynamic allocation causes jobs to finish close to the deadline. See Fig. 6 for detailed examples of experiments using our simulation-based policy.

Adapting to changes in cluster conditions

Because Jockey is dynamic, it is robust to inaccurate latency predictions and can respond to changes in cluster conditions. For example, a fixed allocation calculated using a model of job performance (such as a simulator), can be too low to meet the deadline, as demonstrated above. In our experiments, the Jockey w/o adaptation policy misses the SLO deadline in 18% of experiments, even though this policy uses the same slack factor of 1.2 as our dynamic policy experiments.

One reason such off-line predictions are inaccurate is that cluster conditions change. Because access is shared and other jobs run concurrently, use of network and CPU resources varies over time. Further detail from the experiment in which Jockey misses the SLO illustrates these variations.

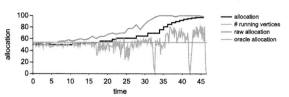

(a) job F, 45-minute deadline: as described in the text, the actual job took twice as much time to execute due to an overloaded cluster. Our policy realized the slower progress and started adding resource early. In the end, the job finished only 3% late.

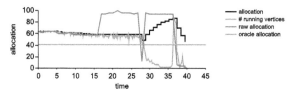

(b) job E, 45-minute deadline: policy started adding resources after it noticed a particular stage was taking longer to complete.

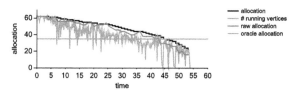

(c) job G, 60-minute deadline: policy over-provisioned the job at the beginning and released resources as the deadline approached.

Figure 6. Three examples of dynamic resource allocation policy experiments. The blue line is the raw allocation based on the job's utility and current progress, the black line is the allocation set by the policy, the red line is the number of vertices running, and the green line is the oracle allocation.

statistic	training	job 1	job 2
total work [hours]	12.7	23.5	18.5
queueing median [sec]	5.8	6.8	6.9
queueing 90th perc. [sec]	8.4	11.6	11.4
latency median [sec]	3.6	5.8	5.2
latency 90th perc. [sec]	17.4	36.6	27.1

Table 3. For job F, comparing the metrics of the training job used to create the $C(p, a)$ distributions in the simulator with two actual runs, jobs 1 and 2. Both the runs require more work; job 1 needs almost twice as much work to complete. Jockey notices the slow-down and allocates extra resources at runtime to finish job 2 on time and job 1 finishes only 90s late.

We compare the training execution that was used to compute the completion distributions, $C(p, a)$, with two actual runs of the same job when controlled by Jockey. In Table 3, *job 1* is the run that missed the deadline, whereas *job 2* met the deadline. Fig. 6(a) plots the timelapse of how Jockey adapted during job 1. Notice that the total amount of work required to finish both jobs is higher than their training runs, with job 1 needing almost twice the total work. The median and 90th percentile of vertex queueing and execution latencies are also higher. In spite of this, Jockey added enough resources to finish job 2 on time. From Fig. 6(a), we see that Jockey noticed job 1 to be slower and added resources (blue line on top), missing the deadline by only 90 seconds. Figures 6(b) and (c) show other types of adaptations. In the former, Jockey identifies a stage taking more time than usual and increases the allocation. In the latter, the job finishes faster than usual, and Jockey frees resources to be used by other jobs.

Adapting to changes in deadlines

An important feature of dynamic resource allocation is that it can adapt to changing job deadlines by adding more resources to meet a stricter deadline, or vice versa. This is crucial when multiple SLO-bound jobs must be run since we might need to slow a job to ensure a more important job finishes on time. While arbitrating among multiple SLO-bound jobs is not Jockey's focus, we view changes in deadlines as a mechanism to ensure the on-time completion of individual jobs as used by a future multi-job scheduler. The success of a such a scheduler thus depends on Jockey's ability to successfully adapt to changing deadlines. Finally, although extending a deadline does not require any change in resources in order to meet the new, longer deadline, by decreasing the amount of guaranteed resources, Jockey can make more guaranteed resources available for future SLO-bound jobs.

For each of the seven jobs, we performed three separate experiments in which, ten minutes after start of the job, we cut the deadline in half, doubled the deadline or tripled the deadline, respectively. In each run, Jockey met the new deadline. In the runs where we lowered the deadline by half, the policy had to increase resource allocation by 148% on average. In the runs where we doubled or tripled the deadline, the policy released 63% or 83% (respectively) of the allocated resources on average. See two example runs in Fig. 7.

5.3 Job Latency Prediction Accuracy

While our policy can adapt to small errors in latency estimates, larger errors can lead to significant over-provisioning or under-provisioning of resources. To evaluate the accuracy of the end-to-end latency predictions made by the simulator and Amdahl's Law, we executed each of the seven jobs three times at eight different allocations. We initialized the variables for both our predictors, the simulator and modified Amdahl's Law, based on jobs at one allocation and estimated their accuracy at predicting latency for other allocations. In practice, we care about the worst-case completion time, so we

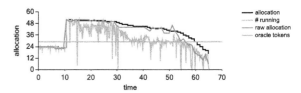

(a) Deadline changed from 140 to 70 minutes. The policy adjusted the resource allocation (black line) to meet the new deadline.

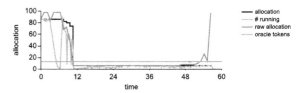

(b) Deadline increased from 20 to 60 minutes. The policy released more than 90% of the resources and still met the new deadline.

Figure 7. Examples of two experiments with changing deadlines.

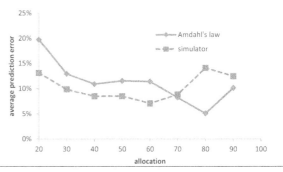

Figure 8. Average simulator and Amdahl's Law prediction error. The x-axis indicates allocations at which the job's latency was predicted.

compare the largest prediction from either predictor to the slowest run at each allocation. Across jobs and allocations, the average errors of the simulator and Amdahl's Law were 9.8% and 11.8%, respectively; see details in Fig. 8. Amdahl's Law has high error at low allocations, but performs much better at higher allocations, where the job's runtime is closer to the length of the critical path.

While the average error of Amdahl's Law is only slightly higher than the simulator's, Jockey w/o simulator missed 16% of the deadlines. The explanation of most of these SLO violations is that the policy using Amdahl's Law initially allocated too few tokens and was unable to catch-up during job run time. Also, the job simulator captures the variance of the end-to-end job latency due to outliers and failures, and therefore creates a safety buffer to make sure SLOs can be met despite this variance.

5.4 Job Progress Indicators

When dynamically allocating resources to a job, having an accurate prediction of end-to-end job latency is not enough; the control policy also needs an accurate estimate of job's progress in order to index into the remaining time distributions. Jockey uses *totalworkWithQ*, which uses the total queueing and execution time of completed vertices, to estimate job progress (Section 4.2).

Here, we describe a few other progress indicators we considered: *totalwork* computes progress as the fraction of the total execution time of completed vertices; *vertexfrac* uses the total fraction of vertices that completed; *cp* uses the fraction of the job's remaining critical path; the *minstage* and *minstage-inf* indicators use the typical start and end times of the individual stages relative to the job. If t_s^b and t_s^e are the relative start and end times of stage s, minstage infers these values from the previous run of the job while minstage-inf uses a simulation of the job with no constraint on resources and hence focusses on the critical path. Both estimate job progress as the stage furthest from when it typically completes, i.e., $\min_{\text{stage } s: f_s < 1}\{t_s^b + f_s(t_s^e - t_s^b)\}$, where f_s is the fraction of vertices completed in stage s.

To evaluate these indicators, we measure how accurately they predict the end-to-end job latency during the runtime of a job. When Jockey calls the control loop at time t after the start of the job, the progress indicator estimates progress to be p_t, which is indexed into the remaining time distribution and a completion time estimate is calculated as $T_t = t + C(p_t, a)$. We compare the T_t obtained from different indicators with the actual time at which the job finishes.

The values of the progress indicator (normalized to range from 0 to 100) and the estimated completion times T_t for two of the progress indicators are shown in Fig. 9. An undesirable characteristic of a progress indicator is getting stuck (ie., reporting constant values) even when the job is making progress. We see that the CP indicator is stuck from t=20min to t=40min causing T_t to increase during this period. Such behavior confuses the control policy into assuming that the job is not making progress and increases the job's resource allocation even though the job may finish on time with the existing allocation. An ideal indicator would generate $T_t = D$ when enough resources are available, where D is the job duration, for all times t; the more T_t diverges from D, the more the control policy has to unnecessarily adjust the resource allocation of the job.

We compare these indicators using two metrics; the *longest constant interval*, i.e., the longest period, relative to the duration of the job, when the progress indicator was constant and the *average* $\triangle T$, which measures the oscillations in the T_t estimates and is computed as the average of $|T_t - T_{t+1}|$ relative to the duration of the job. The larger the value of either metric, the greater opportunity for needless oscillations in allocations. See the comparison in Table 10.

The totalworkWithQ indicator, which incorporates the duration and queueing time of vertices in each stage, performs best. The minstage, minstage-inf and CP indicators, which consider the structure of the job, perform significantly worse because their progress estimates are based on the stage which has made the least progress, and do not reflect progress

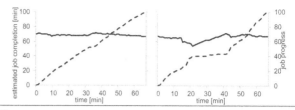

Figure 9. The totalworkWithQ (left) and CP (right) progress indicators for job G. The solid lines (left axes) show the estimated worst-case job completion times T_t, the dashed lines (right axes) correspond to the values of the progress indicator.

indicator	$\triangle T$	longest constant interval
totalworkWithQ	2.0%	8.5%
totalwork	2.3%	9.3%
vertexfrac	2.2%	10.1%
CP	3.0%	15.2%
minstage	3.3%	19.9%
minstage-inf	3.9%	26.7%

Figure 10. Comparison of progress indicators.

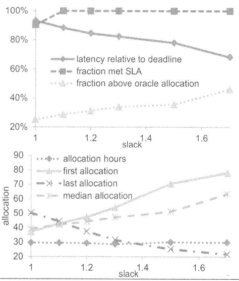

Figure 12. Sensitivity of the slack parameter. Top, the fraction of jobs that met the SLO and the fraction of job allocation above the oracle allocation. Bottom, average of first, last and median allocations during each experiment, and average of total machine hours allocated by the policy.

in other stages. TotalworkWithQ considers progress in all running stages, and thus increments more smoothly.

5.5 Sensitivity Analysis

To evaluate the control loop's sensitivity, we adjusted its parameters and ran each of the seven jobs three times with a single deadline after each adjustment. The baseline here is Jockey with default parameter values. The results are summarized in Fig. 11. Running our policy with no hysteresis and no dead zone, results in meeting only 57% of the SLOs, while using the hysteresis with no dead zone, meets 90% of the SLOs. Using hysteresis is clearly crucial; without it, the allocation fluctuates too much in each direction. When it drops too much

experiment	met SLA	latency vs. deadline	allocation above oracle	median allocation
baseline	95%	-14%	35%	52.9
no hysteresis, no deadzone	57%	-2%	25%	49.7
no deadzone	90%	-9%	30%	50.3
no slack, less hysteresis	76%	-5%	27%	44.9
5-min period	95%	-22%	35%	45.7
minstage progress	100%	-16%	34%	48.2
CP progress	95%	-16%	31%	44.9

Figure 11. Results of sensitivity analysis. The baseline results are a subset of results reported in Section 5.2.

because of this oscillation, Jockey cannot catch-up later. We tried running with no slack, but instead use an increased value of the hysteresis parameter to let Jockey adapt more quickly when jobs fall behind. Here, on average, Jockey allocated too few tokens at the start of the job and missed 24% of the deadlines. Next, changing the period at which adaptation happens from one to five minutes still met 95% of the deadlines. But, for jobs that were over-provisioned, Jockey did not quickly reduce the allocation, resulting in jobs finishing 22% before the deadlines (compared to 14% in our baseline). We also ran Jockey using the minstage and CP indicators, which met 100% and 95% of the deadlines (respectively), and had a similar impact on the cluster as the baseline. As shown in Section 5.4, these indicators have some undesirable properties as inputs to a control loop, but these experiments suggest that with hysteresis, they can still perform well in practice.

Results for different slack values are presented in Fig. 12, based on 21 runs for each value. The only SLO violations occurred in experiments without slack; adding even 10% slack was enough to meet the SLOs. Adding more slack led to jobs finishing well before the deadline and having a larger impact on the rest of the cluster because it directly causes overallocation of resources. This can be seen in the increasing initial and median job allocations as slack is increased.

Results for different values of the hysteresis parameter are presented in Fig. 13. For each value of the parameter and each of the seven jobs, we ran three experiments. Only three experiments did not meet the SLO; two at the lower extreme value – 0.05, high smoothing – and one at the upper extreme – 1.0, no smoothing. Overall, experiments with higher values of the hysteresis parameter finished closer to the deadline and had slightly less impact on the rest of the cluster, but the maximum allocation requested by the policy was much higher than with greater smoothing.

5.6 Summary

Our evaluation on a large-scale production cluster shows that Jockey can reliably meet job latency SLOs; in 94 experiments that ran Jockey missed one deadline by 3% due to much higher load on the cluster at that time. Without the simulator, or without dynamic resource adaptation, Jockey performed significantly worse. While the max-allocation policy met all SLOs, Jockey had 3× less impact on the rest of the cluster, which allows more SLO-bound jobs to be run simultaneously. We also demonstrated that Jockey can dynamically adapt to

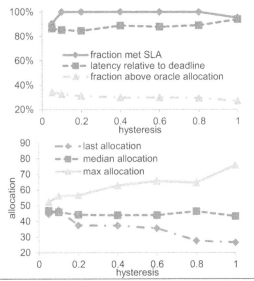

Figure 13. Sensitivity of the hysteresis parameter. Top, fraction of jobs that met the SLO, fraction of allocations above the oracle, and job latencies relative to deadlines. Bottom, average of median, max and last allocations during each run, and average of total machine hours Jockey allocated.

changing job deadlines, which allows us to trade resources between multiple jobs based on their utilities.

Jockey's success chiefly derives from an accurate model of the job, one that captures the remaining execution time as a function of resource allocation and job progress. However, when the model is not 100% accurate, standard techniques from control theory (such as hysteresis and adding slack) can partially compensate for the inaccuracy. We show in our sensitivity analysis that, without these techniques, Jockey's approach performs much worse.

Nonetheless, in certain cases, the job execution can significantly diverge from the model and the control loop could either overprovision the job (taking resources from other jobs) or underprovision it (allocating too few resources and missing the SLO). This could happen if the inputs of the job change substantially – resulting in a more expensive execution – or if the whole cluster is experiencing performance issues, such as an overloaded network. In these cases, we could quickly update the model by running the simulator at runtime, or simply fall back on weighted fair-sharing once the control loop detects large errors in model predictions.

6. Related Work

Job scheduling and resource management are not new problems, and there has been much related work in these areas. Jockey builds upon recent work on performance indicators and improvements in MapReduce-like clusters, as well as previous work in grid computing and real-time systems.

6.1 Performance in data parallel clusters

Jockey is most closely related to the Automatic Resource Inference and Allocation for MapReduce Environments project (ARIA), which also proposes a method to allocate resources in a large-scale computational framework for meeting soft deadlines [24]. Both the ARIA work and our own feature a control loop which estimates the job's progress, uses past execution profiles to predict the completion time, and adjusts the resources assigned to the task to meet the target deadline.

However, Jockey differs from ARIA in several important ways. First, the ARIA project was developed for map-reduce frameworks which feature only three computational phases: a Map phase, a Shuffle phase, and a Reduce phase; the framework used here supports directed acyclic graphs (DAGs) of arbitrarily long pipelines of independent and dependent stages. Second, the ARIA authors develop analytic equations which estimate each stage's completion time, similar to the Amdahl's Law-based approach we consider. But, as noted above, we found simulations to be more accurate for predicting future progress in DAGs because they incorporate the effects of vertex outliers, failures and barriers. Third, the approach described here is robust to changes in the cluster conditions or the deadlines or the amount of job's input. Our experiments show that slack, hysteresis and a dead zone are necessary for meeting SLOs in a production setting. Finally, the experiments here are more realistic. They are performed on a large shared production cluster with all the allied noise and a wide variety of bottlenecks. ARIA used a dedicated cluster of 66 nodes without any network bottleneck. Hence, we believe Jockey is a better match for production DAG-like frameworks such as Hive [22], Pig [17], and Ciel [16]

To predict the completion time of a running job, Jockey must estimate the job's current progress. Our approach is informed by the ParaTimer progress indicator [15], which is most similar to the vertexfrac function which we first consider. As discussed above, the vertexfrac design was not the best method for Jockey because it incorrectly indicates a lack of progress during long-running stages with a low degree of parallelism, and because it can be overly optimistic about failures and data skew [15]. When developing Jockey, we found it to be more effective to slow a job running ahead of deadline due to prior pessimism about failures, rather than attempt to speed-up a job which is running behind.

As a side-effect of predictably meeting SLOs, Jockey decreases the variance in job completion latencies. This goal is shared with work on reducing such variance directly, such as Mantri [2] and Scarlett [3]. The approach taken by Jockey, to automatically adjust resource allocations in response to predicted fluctuations in latency, is complementary to this earlier work. While we have not yet studied the effect of combining these approaches, we believe that such a combination will further improve Jockey's ability to meet SLOs.

6.2 Deadlines in grid and HPC workloads

The Amdahl's Law-like approach described in Section 4.1 is inspired by the value-maximizing, deadline-aware scheduler for animation rendering tasks by Anderson *et al.* [4], which they term the *disconnected staged scheduling problem* (DSSP). The approach developed estimates the amount of resources required to complete the task using two quantities: the aggregate CPU time (the time to complete the job on a single processor), and the length of the critical path (the time to complete the job on an infinite number of processors).

Finally, Sandholm and Lai have explored the relationship between a job's weight in a fair-sharing scheduler and the chance of meeting a given deadline in both grid-computing environments [19, 20] and MapReduce-like contexts [21]. Jockey automatically makes these weight decisions based on the utility curve submitted by the user, whereas Sandholm and Lai's methods price the system's resources based on aggregate demand and permit users to allocate resources based on their own budgets and deadlines.

6.3 Deadlines in real-time workloads

Previous work on real-time systems has advocated dynamic resource management to perform admission control [26], meet deadlines [18] and maximize aggregate utility [14], as Jockey does for data parallel clusters. Jockey differs by operating at a significantly larger scale, managing larger computational jobs with longer deadlines, and adjusting the resource allocation during a job's execution, rather than only between repeated executions of the same job. Jockey also uses a simulator to estimate a distribution of job completion times for a given allocation of resources, rather than rely upon an analytic model of the critical path.

7. Conclusion

In today's frameworks, providing guaranteed performance for pipelines of data parallel jobs is not possible on shared clusters. Jockey bridges this divide. To do so, it must combat varying availability and responsiveness of resources, two problems which are compounded by the dependency structure of data parallel jobs. By combining detailed job models with robust dynamic adaptation, Jockey guarantees job latencies without over-provisioning resources. Such "right-sizing" of allocations lets Jockey successfully run SLO-bound jobs – it met 99% of the SLOs in our experiments – in a cluster simultaneously running many other jobs – Jockey only needed 25% more resources than the theoretical minimum.

When a shared environment is underloaded, guaranteed performance brings predictability to the user experience;

when it is overloaded, utility-based resource allocation ensures jobs are completed according to importance. Jockey brings these benefits to data parallel processing in large-scale shared clusters.

Acknowledgments

The authors wish to thank Sameer Agarwal, Jonathan Perry, Moises Goldszmidt, and our shepherd Karsten Schwan for helpful comments and advice during the development of this project and while preparing our paper, as well as the many members of the Cosmos development team, particularly Jay Finger, Astha Gupta, Solom Heddaya, Pat Helland, Bikas Saha, Shoaib Sehgal, and Jingren Zhou.

References

[1] G. M. Amdahl. Validity of the single processor approach to achieving large scale computing capabilities. In *Proc. AFIPS '67 (Spring)*, pages 483–485, New York, NY, USA, 1967.

[2] G. Ananthanarayanan, S. Kandula, A. Greenberg, I. Stoica, Y. Lu, B. Saha, and E. Harris. Reining in the Outliers in MapReduce Clusters using Mantri. In *Proc. OSDI '10*, Vancouver, Canada, 2010.

[3] G. Ananthanarayanan, S. Agarwal, S. Kandula, A. Greenberg, I. Stoica, D. Harlan, and E. Harris. Scarlett: Coping with Skewed Content Popularity in MapReduce Clusters. In *Proc. EuroSys '11*, Salzburg, Austria, 2011.

[4] E. Anderson, D. Beyer, K. Chaudhuri, T. Kelly, N. Salazar, C. Santos, R. Swaminathan, R. Tarjan, J. Wiener, and Y. Zhou. Value-maximizing deadline scheduling and its application to animation rendering. In *Proc. SPAA '05*, Las Vegas, Nevada, USA, 2005.

[5] D. Borthakur, J. Gray, J. S. Sarma, K. Muthukkaruppan, N. Spiegelberg, H. Kuang, K. Ranganathan, D. Molkov, A. Menon, S. Rash, R. Schmidt, and A. Aiyer. Apache Hadoop goes Realtime at Facebook. In *Proc. SIGMOD '11*, Athens, Greece, 2011.

[6] R. Chaiken, B. Jenkins, P. Larson, B. Ramsey, D. Shakib, S. Weaver, and J. Zhou. SCOPE: Easy and Efficient Parallel Processing of Massive Data Sets. *Proc. VLDB*, 1(2):1265–1276, 2008.

[7] C. Chambers, A. Raniwala, F. Perry, S. Adams, R. R. Henry, R. Bradshaw, and N. Weizenbaum. FlumeJava: Easy, efficient data-parallel pipelines. In *Proc. PLDI '10*, Toronto, Ontario, Canada, 2010.

[8] J. Dean and S. Ghemawat. MapReduce: Simplified data processing on large clusters. *Commun. ACM*, 51(1):107–113, 2008.

[9] S. Ghemawat, H. Gobioff, and S.-T. Leung. The Google file system. *SIGOPS Oper. Syst. Rev.*, 37(5):29–43, 2003.

[10] H. Herodotou, F. Dong, and S. Babu. No One (Cluster) Size Fits All: Automatic Cluster Sizing for Data-intensive Analytics. In *Proc. SoCC '11*, Cascais, Portugal, 2011.

[11] M. Isard, M. Budiu, Y. Yu, A. Birrell, and D. Fetterly. Dryad: Distributed Data-parallel Programs from Sequential Building Blocks. In *Proc. EuroSys '07*, Lisbon, Portugal, 2007.

[12] M. Isard, V. Prabhakaran, J. Currey, U. Wieder, K. Talwar, and A. Goldberg. Quincy: Fair Scheduling for Distributed Computing Clusters. In *Proc. SOSP '09*, Big Sky, Montana, USA, 2009.

[13] A. Li, X. Yang, S. Kandula, and M. Zhang. CloudCmp: Comparing public cloud providers. In *Proc. IMC '10*, Melbourne, Australia, 2010.

[14] C. Lumezanu, S. Bhola, and M. Astley. Online optimization for latency assignment in distributed real-time systems. In *Proc. ICDCS '08*, June 2008.

[15] K. Morton, M. Balazinska, and D. Grossman. ParaTimer: a progress indicator for MapReduce DAGs. In *Proc. SIGMOD '10*, Indianapolis, IN, USA, 2010.

[16] D. G. Murray, M. Schwarzkopf, C. Smowton, S. Smith, A. Madhavapeddy, and S. Hand. CIEL: a universal execution engine for distributed data-flow computing. In *Proc. NSDI'11*, Boston, MA, 2011.

[17] C. Olston, B. Reed, U. Srivastava, R. Kumar, and A. Tomkins. Pig latin: a not-so-foreign language for data processing. In *Proc. SIGMOD '08*, Vancouver, Canada, 2008.

[18] B. Ravindran, P. Kachroo, and T. Hegazy. Adaptive resource management in asynchronous real-time distributed systems using feedback control functions. In *Proc. of 5th Symposium on Autonomous Decentralized Systems*, 2001.

[19] T. Sandholm and K. Lai. Prediction-based enforcement of performance contracts. In *Proc. GECON'07*, Rennes, France, 2007.

[20] T. Sandholm and K. Lai. A statistical approach to risk mitigation in computational markets. In *Proc. HPDC '07*, Monterey, CA, USA, 2007.

[21] T. Sandholm and K. Lai. MapReduce optimization using regulated dynamic prioritization. In *Proc. SIGMETRICS '09*, Seattle, WA, USA, 2009.

[22] A. Thusoo, J. S. Sarma, N. Jain, Z. Shao, P. Chakka, S. Anthony, H. Liu, P. Wyckoff, and R. Murthy. Hive: a warehousing solution over a map-reduce framework. *Proc. VLDB Endow.*, 2: 1626–1629, August 2009.

[23] B. Urgaonkar, P. Shenoy, A. Ch, and P. Goyal. Dynamic provisioning of multi-tier internet applications. In *Proc. ICAC '05*, 2005.

[24] A. Verma, L. Cherkasova, and R. H. Campbell. SLO-Driven Right-Sizing and Resource Provisioning of MapReduce Jobs. In *Proc. LADIS '11*, 2011.

[25] G. Wang and T. Ng. The Impact of Virtualization on Network Performance of Amazon EC2 Data Center. In *Proc. IEEE INFOCOM '10*, March 2010.

[26] D. Xuan, R. Bettati, J. Chen, W. Zhao, and C. Li. Utilization-Based Admission Control for Real-Time Applications. In *Proc. ICPP '10*, Washington, DC, USA, 2000.

[27] M. Zaharia, D. Borthakur, J. Sen Sarma, K. Elmeleegy, S. Shenker, and I. Stoica. Delay Scheduling: A Simple Technique for Achieving Locality and Fairness in Cluster Scheduling. In *Proc. EuroSys '10*, Paris, France, 2010.

The Xen-Blanket: Virtualize Once, Run Everywhere

Dan Williams[†‡]
djwill@cs.cornell.edu

Hani Jamjoom[‡]
jamjoom@us.ibm.com

Hakim Weatherspoon[†]
hweather@cs.cornell.edu

[†] Cornell University, Ithaca, NY
[‡] IBM T. J. Watson Research Center, Hawthorne, NY

Abstract

Current Infrastructure as a Service (IaaS) clouds operate in isolation from each other. Slight variations in the virtual machine (VM) abstractions or underlying hypervisor services prevent unified access and control across clouds. While standardization efforts aim to address these issues, they will take years to be agreed upon and adopted, if ever. Instead of standardization, which is by definition provider-centric, we advocate a *user-centric* approach that gives users an unprecedented level of control over the virtualization layer. We introduce the *Xen-Blanket*, a thin, immediately deployable virtualization layer that can homogenize today's diverse cloud infrastructures. We have deployed the Xen-Blanket across Amazon's EC2, an enterprise cloud, and a private setup at Cornell University. We show that a user-centric approach to homogenize clouds can achieve similar performance to a paravirtualized environment while enabling previously impossible tasks like cross-provider live migration. The Xen-Blanket also allows users to exploit resource management opportunities like oversubscription, and ultimately can reduce costs for users.

Categories and Subject Descriptors   D.4 [*OPERATING SYSTEMS*]: Organization and Design

General Terms   Design, Experimentation, Performance

Keywords   Nested Virtualization, Cloud Computing, Xen

1. Introduction

Current Infrastructure as a Service (IaaS) clouds—both public and private—are not interoperable. As a result, cloud users find themselves locked into a single provider, which may or may not suit their needs. Evidenced by the Amazon Elastic Compute Cloud (EC2) downtime in April 2011, outages can affect even large, mature and popular public

clouds. A multi-cloud deployment, on the other hand, facilitates fault tolerance strategies that can withstand the failure of an entire provider. Furthermore, multi-cloud deployments can offer new resource management and economic alternatives to would-be cloud users that are already managing their own elaborate private cloud infrastructures. If well-integrated with private clouds, public clouds can provide an outlet for excess load or growth.

Fundamentally, today's clouds lack the homogeneity necessary for cost-effective multi-cloud deployments. That is, a single VM image cannot be deployed—unmodified—on any IaaS cloud. Even worse, there is no consistent set of hypervisor-level services across providers. While some progress towards multi-cloud homogeneity is expected through standardization efforts such as the Open Virtualization Format [11], these *provider-centric* approaches will likely be limited to simple cloud attributes—like image format—and take years to be universally adopted.

We propose a different way of implementing multi-cloud homogeneity. Instead of relying on cloud providers to change their environments, we advocate a *user-centric* view of homogenization, where users are able to run their unmodified VMs on any cloud without any special provider support. As such, users can implement or deploy hypervisor services or management tools on clouds that do not supply them. Towards this goal, we present the Xen-Blanket, a system that transforms existing heterogeneous clouds into a uniform user-centric homogeneous offering. The Xen-Blanket consists of a second-layer hypervisor that runs as a guest inside a VM instance on a variety of public or private clouds, forming a *Blanket layer*. The Blanket layer exposes a homogeneous interface to second-layer guest VMs, called *Blanket guests*, but is completely user-centric and customizable. With the Xen-Blanket, hypervisor-level techniques and management tools, like VM migration, page sharing, and oversubscription, can all be implemented inside the Blanket layer. Meanwhile, the Blanket layer contains *Blanket drivers* that allow it to run on heterogeneous clouds while hiding interface details of the underlying clouds from guests.

Existing nested virtualization techniques (like the Turtles project [2]), focus on an efficient use of hardware virtualization primitives by both layers of virtualization. This re-

EuroSys'12,   April 10–13, 2012, Bern, Switzerland.
Copyright © 2012 ACM 978-1-4503-1223-3/12/04…$10.00

quires the underlying hypervisor—controlled by the cloud provider—to expose hardware primitives. None of today's clouds currently offer such primitives. In contrast, the Xen-Blanket can be deployed on third-party clouds today, requiring no special support. Thus, the contributions of the Xen-blanket are fundamentally different: the Xen-blanket enables competition and innovation for products that span multiple clouds, whether support is offered from cloud providers or not. Further, the Xen-blanket enables the use of unsupported features such as oversubscription, CPU bursting, VM migration, and many others.

The Xen-Blanket is deployed today on both Xen-based and KVM-based hypervisors, on public and private infrastructures within Amazon EC2, an enterprise cloud, and Cornell University. The Xen-Blanket has successfully homogenized these diverse environments. For example, we have migrated VMs to and from Amazon EC2 with no modifications to the VMs. Furthermore, the user-centric design of the Xen-Blanket affords users the flexibility to oversubscribe resources such as network, memory, and disk. As a direct result, a Xen-Blanket image on EC2 can host 40 CPU-intensive VMs for 47% of the price per hour of 40 small instances with matching performance. Blanket drivers achieve good performance: network drivers can receive packets at line speed on a 1 Gbps link, while disk I/O throughput is within 12% of single level paravirtualized disk performance. Despite overheads of up to 68% for some benchmarks, Web server macrobenchmarks can match the performance of single level virtualization (i.e., both are able to serve an excess of 1000 simultaneous clients) while increasing CPU utilization by only 1%.

In this paper, we make four main contributions:

- We describe how user-centric homogeneity can be achieved at the hypervisor level to enable multi-cloud deployments, even without any provider support.

- We enumerate key extensions to Xen, including a set of *Blanket drivers* and hypervisor optimizations, that transform Xen into an efficient, homogenizing Blanket layer on top of existing clouds, such as Amazon EC2.

- We demonstrate how the Xen-Blanket can provide an opportunity for substantial cost savings by enabling users to oversubscribe their leased resources.

- We discuss our experience using hypervisor-level operations that were previously impossible to implement in public clouds, including live VM migration between an enterprise cloud and Amazon EC2.

The paper is organized as follows. Section 2 further motivates the need for user-centric homogenization to be deployed on today's clouds. Section 3 introduces the concept of a Blanket layer, and describes how the Xen-Blanket provides a user-centric homogenized layer, with the implementation details of the enabling Blanket drivers in Section 4. Some overheads and advantages of the Xen-Blanket are

quantified in Section 5, while qualitative practical experience is described in Section 6. Finally, Section 7 identifies future directions, Section 8 surveys related work, and Section 9 concludes.

2. My Cloud, My Way

A cloud user would achieve several benefits from a homogeneous interface to a cloud that encompasses many different cloud providers. If a single VM image can be deployed on every cloud, image management, even upgrading and patching, is simplified. If any service offered by one cloud was available in any other cloud, users would not feel locked-in to a particular vendor. Hypervisor-level resource management techniques and cloud software stacks would emerge that truly span providers, offering users the control to utilize and manage cloud resources to their full potential.

Today's clouds lack homogeneity in three ways. First, VM images—the building blocks of cloud applications—cannot be easily instantiated on different clouds. Second, clouds are becoming diverse in terms of the services they provide to VMs. For example, Amazon EC2 provides tools such as CloudWatch (integrated monitoring), AutoScaling, and Elastic Load Balancing, whereas Rackspace contains support for VM migration to combat server host degradation and CPU bursting to borrow cycles from other instances. Third, a class of resource management opportunities that exist in a private cloud setting—in particular, tools that operate at the hypervisor level—are not consistently available between providers. For example, there is no unified set of tools with which users can specify VM co-location on physical machines [29], page sharing between VMs [16, 23], or resource oversubscription [28].

The desire for a homogeneous interface across cloud providers is *not* a call for standardization. We distinguish between *provider-centric* and *user-centric* homogenization. Standardization is an example of provider-centric homogenization, in which every cloud provider must agree on an image format, services, and management interfaces to expose to users. Standards are emerging; for example, Open Virtualization Format (OVF) [11] describes how to package VM images and `virtio` defines paravirtualized device interfaces. However, until *all* clouds (e.g., Amazon EC2, Rackspace, etc.) adopt these standards, VM configurations will continue to vary depending on the cloud they run on. Even worse, it is unlikely—and infeasible—that the vast array of current and future services available to VMs become standardized across all clouds. Attempts at standardization often lead to a set of functionality that represents the "least common denominator" across all participating providers. Many users will still demand services that are not in the standard set and cloud providers will continue to offer services that differentiate their offering. As a result, standardization, or provider-centric homogenization, is not sufficient.

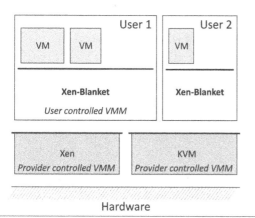

Figure 1. The Xen-Blanket, completely controlled by the user, provides a homogenization layer across heterogeneous cloud providers without requiring any additional support from the providers.

User-centric homogenization, in contrast, enables cloud users to homogenize the cloud and customize it to match their needs. It allows users to select their own VM image format and services, then transform every cloud to support it. The user is not tied into a "least common denominator" of functionality, but quite the opposite: even completely customized services and image formats can be deployed. The user can then develop management tools that work for *their* VMs across *their* (now homogenized) cloud. For example, a user can experiment with new features like Remus [10] across clouds and perhaps achieve high availability even in the case of an entire provider failing.

Finally, any system that implements user-centric homogenization must be immediately and universally deployable. A system that enables user-centric homogenization cannot be dependent on emerging features that are not standard across clouds, such as the low overhead nested virtualization solution proposed in the Turtles Project [2].

3. The Xen-Blanket

The Xen-Blanket leverages nested virtualization to form a *Blanket layer*, or a second layer of virtualization software that provides a user-centric homogeneous cloud interface, as depicted in Figure 1. A Blanket layer embodies three important concepts. First, the *bottom half* of the Blanket layer communicates with a variety of underlying hypervisor interfaces. No modifications are expected or required to the underlying hypervisor. Second, the *top half* of the Blanket layer exposes a single VM interface to Blanket (second-layer) guests such that a single guest image can run on any cloud without modifications. Third, the Blanket layer is completely under the control of the user, so functionality typically implemented by providers in the hypervisor, such as live VM migration, can be implemented in the Blanket layer.

The bottom half of the Xen-Blanket ensures that the Xen-Blanket can run across a number of different clouds without requiring changes to the underlying cloud system or hypervisor. The bottom half is trivial if the following two assumptions hold on all underlying clouds. First, if device I/O is emulated, then the Blanket hypervisor does not need to be aware of the underlying hypervisor's paravirtualized I/O interfaces. Second, if hardware-assisted full virtualization for x86 (called HVM in Xen terminology) is available, then the Blanket hypervisor can run unmodified. However, these assumptions limit the number of clouds that the Blanket layer can cover; for example, we are not aware of any public cloud that satisfies both assumptions.

The Xen-Blanket relaxes the emulated device assumption by interfacing with a variety of underlying cloud paravirtualized device I/O implementations. Paravirtualized device I/O has proved essential for performance and is required by some clouds, such as Amazon EC2. However, there is currently no standard paravirtualized device I/O interface. For example, older Xen-based clouds, including Amazon EC2, require device drivers to communicate with Xen-specific subsystems, such as the XenBus and XenStore, whereas KVM-based systems expect device drivers to interact with the hypervisor through `virtio` interfaces. The Xen-Blanket supports such non-standard interfaces by modifying the bottom half to contain cloud-specific *Blanket drivers*.

On the other hand, the Xen-Blanket does rely on support for hardware-assisted full virtualization for x86 on all clouds. Currently, this assumption somewhat limits deployment opportunities. For example, a large fraction of both Amazon EC2 and Rackspace instances expose paravirtualized, not HVM interfaces, with Amazon EC2 only offering an HVM interface to Linux guests in 4XL-sized cluster instances. EC2 does, however, expose an HVM interface to other sized instances running Windows, which we believe can also be converted to deploy the Xen-Blanket. Further efforts to relax the HVM assumption are discussed as future work in Section 7.

The top half of the Blanket layer exposes a consistent VM interface to (Blanket) guests. Guest VMs therefore do not need any modifications in order to run on a number of different clouds. In order to maximize the number of clouds that the Xen-Blanket can run on, the top half of the Xen-Blanket does not depend on state of the art nested virtualization interfaces (e.g., the Turtles Project [2]). The Xen-Blanket instead relies on other x86 virtualization techniques, such as paravirtualization or binary translation. For our prototype Blanket layer implementation we chose to adopt the popular open-source Xen hypervisor, which uses paravirtualization techniques when virtualization hardware is not available. The Xen-Blanket subsequently inherits the limitations of paravirtualization, most notably the inability to run unmodified

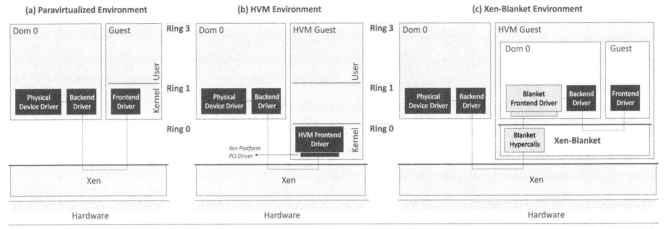

Figure 2. Guests using paravirtualized devices implement a front-end driver that communicates with a back-end driver (a). In HVM environments, a Xen Platform PCI driver is required to set up communication with the back-end (b). The Xen-Blanket modifies the HVM front-end driver to become a *Blanket driver*, which, with support of *Blanket hypercalls*, runs in hardware protection ring 1, instead of ring 0 (c).

operating systems, such as Microsoft Windows.[1] However, this limitation is not fundamental. A Blanket layer can be constructed using binary translation (e.g., a VMWare [21]-Blanket), upon which unmodified operating systems would be able to run. Blanket layers can also be created with other interfaces, such as Denali [25], alternate branches of Xen, or even customized hypervisors developed from scratch.

The Xen-Blanket inherits services that are traditionally located in the hypervisor or privileged management domains and allows the user to run or modify them. For instance, users can issue xm commands from the Xen-Blanket. Users can co-locate VMs [29] on a single Xen-Blanket instance, share memory pages between co-located VMs [16, 23], and oversubscribe resources [28]. If Xen-Blanket instances on different clouds can communicate with each other, live VM migration or high availability [10] across clouds become possible.

4. Blanket Drivers

The Xen-Blanket contains Blanket drivers for each of the heterogeneous interfaces exposed by today's clouds. In practice, the drivers that must be implemented are limited to dealing with paravirtualized device interfaces for network and disk I/O. As described in Section 3, Blanket drivers reside in the bottom half of the Xen-Blanket and are treated by the rest of the Xen-Blanket as drivers interacting with physical hardware devices. These "devices" are subsequently exposed to guests through a consistent paravirtualized device interface, regardless of which set of Blanket drivers was instantiated.

This section is organized as follows: we present background on how paravirtualized devices work on existing clouds. Then, we describe the detailed design and implementation of Blanket drivers. Finally, we conclude with a discussion of hypervisor optimizations for the Xen-Blanket and a discussion of the implications of evolving virtualization support in hardware and software.

4.1 Background

To understand Blanket drivers, we first give some background as to how paravirtualized device drivers work in Xen-based systems.[2] First, we describe device drivers in a fully paravirtualized Xen, depicted in Figure 2(a). The Xen-Blanket uses paravirtualization techniques in the Blanket hypervisor to provide guests with a homogeneous interface to devices. Then, we describe paravirtualized device drivers for hardware assisted Xen (depicted in Figure 2(b)), an underlying hypervisor upon which the Xen-Blanket successfully runs.

Xen does not contain any physical device drivers itself; instead, it relies on device drivers in the operating system of a privileged guest VM, called Domain 0, to communicate with the physical devices. The operating system in Domain 0 multiplexes devices, and offers a paravirtualized device interface to guest VMs. The paravirtualized device interface follows a *split driver* architecture, where the guest runs a *front-end* driver that is paired with a *back-end* driver in Domain 0. Communication between the front-end and back-end driver is accomplished through shared memory ring buffers and an event mechanism provided by Xen. Both the guest and Domain 0 communicate with Xen to set up these communication channels.

In hardware assisted Xen, or HVM Xen, paravirtualized device drivers are called PV-on-HVM drivers. Unlike paravirtualized Xen, guests on HVM Xen can run unmodified,

---

[1] Despite the limitations of paravirtualization and the increasingly superior performance of hardware assisted virtualization, paravirtualization remains popular. Many cloud providers, including Amazon EC2 and Rackspace, continue to offer paravirtualized Linux instances.

[2] A discussion of the paravirtualized drivers on KVM, which are similar, is postponed to the end of Section 4.2.

so by default, communication channels with Xen are not initialized. HVM Xen exposes a *Xen platform PCI device*, which acts as a familiar environment wherein shared memory pages are used to communicate with Xen and an IRQ line is used to deliver events from Xen. So, in addition to a front-end driver for each type of device (e.g. network, disk), an HVM Xen guest also contains a Xen platform PCI device driver. The front-end drivers and the Xen platform PCI driver are the only Xen-aware modules in the HVM guest.

4.2 Design & Implementation

The Xen-Blanket consists of a paravirtualized Xen inside of either a HVM Xen or KVM guest. We will center the discussion around Blanket drivers for Xen, and discuss the conceptually similar Blanket drivers for KVM at the end of this subsection. Figure 2(c) shows components of Blanket drivers. The Blanket layer contains both a Xen hypervisor as well as a privileged *Blanket Domain 0*. Guest VMs are run on top of the Blanket layer, each containing standard paravirtualized front-end device drivers. The Blanket Domain 0 runs the corresponding standard back-end device drivers. The back-end drivers are multiplexed into the Blanket drivers, which act as set of front-end drivers for the underlying hypervisors.

There are two key implementation issues that prohibit standard PV-on-HVM front-end drivers from acting as Blanket drivers.[3] First, the Xen hypercalls required to bootstrap a PV-on-HVM PCI platform device cannot be performed from the Blanket Domain 0 hosting the Blanket drivers because the Blanket Domain 0 does not run with the expected privilege level of an HVM guest OS. Second, the notion of a physical address in the Blanket Domain 0 is not the same as the notion of a physical address in a native HVM guest OS.

Performing Hypercalls

Typically, the Xen hypervisor proper runs in hardware protection ring 0, while Domain 0 and other paravirtualized guests run their OS in ring 1 with user spaces in ring 3. HVM guests, on the other hand, are designed to run unmodified, and can use non-root mode from the hardware virtualization extensions to run the guest OS in ring 0 and user space in ring 3. In the Xen-Blanket, in non-root mode, the Blanket Xen hypervisor proper runs in ring 0, while the Blanket Domain 0 runs in ring 1, and user space runs in ring 3 (Figure 2(c)).

In normal PV-on-HVM drivers, hypercalls, in particular `vmcall` instructions, are issued from the OS in ring 0. In the Xen-Blanket, however, Blanket drivers run in the OS of the Blanket Domain 0 in ring 1. The `vmcall` instruction must be issued from ring 0. We overcome this by augmenting the second-layer Xen to contain *Blanket hypercalls* that issue their own hypercalls to the underlying Xen on behalf of the Blanket Domain 0.

[3] Our implementation also required renaming of some global variables and functions to avoid namespace collisions with the second-layer Xen when trying to communicate with the bottom-layer Xen.

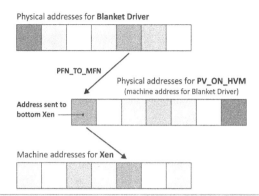

Figure 3. The PV-on-HVM drivers can send physical addresses to the underlying Xen, whereas the Blanket drivers must first convert physical addresses to machine addresses.

Physical Address Translation

Guest OSs running on top of paravirtualized Xen, including Domain 0, have a notion of physical frame numbers (PFNs). The PFNs may or may not match the actual physical frame numbers of the machine, called machine frame numbers (MFNs). The relationship between these addresses is shown in Figure 3. However, the guest can access the mapping between PFNs and MFNs, in case it is necessary to use a real MFN, for example, to utilize DMA from a device. HVM guests are not aware of PFNs vs. MFNs. Instead, they only use physical frame numbers and any translation necessary is done by the underlying hypervisor.

For this reason, PV-on-HVM device drivers pass physical addresses to the underlying hypervisor to share memory pages with the back-end drivers. In the Xen-Blanket, however, the MFN from the Blanket Domain 0's perspective, and thus the Blanket drivers', matches the PFN that the underlying hypervisor expects. Therefore, Blanket drivers must perform a PFN-to-MFN translation before passing any addresses to the underlying hypervisor, either through hypercalls or PCI operations.

Blanket Drivers for KVM

The implementation of Blanket drivers for KVM is very similar. Paravirtualized device drivers in KVM use the `virtio` framework, in which a PCI device is exposed to guests, similar to the Xen platform PCI device. Unlike the Xen platform PCI device, all communication with the underlying KVM hypervisor can be accomplished as if communicating with a physical PCI device. In particular, no direct hypercalls are necessary, simplifying the implementation of Blanket drivers. The only modifications required to run `virtio` drivers in the Xen-Blanket are the addition of PFN-to-MFN translations.

4.3 Hypervisor Optimizations

The Xen-Blanket runs in non-root mode in an HVM guest container. As virtualization support improves, the performance of software running in non-root mode becomes close to running on bare metal. For example, whereas page table manipulations would cause a vmexit, or trap, on early versions of Intel VT-x processors, a hardware feature called extended page tables (EPT) has largely eliminated such traps. However, some operations continue to generate traps, so designing the Blanket layer to avoid such operations can often provide a performance advantage.

For example, instead of flushing kernel pages from the TLB on every context switch, the x86 contains a bit in the cr4 control register called the "Page Global Enable" (PGE). Page Global Enable allows certain pages to be mapped as "global" so that they do not get flushed automatically. Xen enables then disables the PGE bit in order to flush the global TLB entries before doing a domain switch between guests. Unfortunately, these cr4 operations each cause vmexits to happen, generating high overhead for running Xen in an HVM guest. By not using PGE and instead flushing all pages from the TLB on a context switch, vmexits are avoided, because of the EPT processor feature in non-root mode.

4.4 Implications of Future Hardware and Software

As discussed above the virtualization features of the hardware, such as EPT, can have a profound effect on the performance of the Xen-Blanket. Further improvements to the HVM container, such as the interrupt path, may eventually replace hypervisor optimizations and workarounds or enable even better performing Blanket layers.

Other hardware considerations include thinking about non-root mode as a place for virtualization. For example, features that aided virtualization before hardware extensions became prevalent, such as memory segmentation, should not die out. Memory segmentation is a feature in 32 bit x86 processors that paravirtualized Xen leverages to protect Xen, the guest OS, and the guest user space in the same address space to minimize context switches during system calls. The 64 bit x86_64 architecture has dropped support for segmentation except when running in 32 bit compatibility mode. Without segmentation, two address spaces are needed to protect the three contexts from each other, and two context switches are required on each system call, resulting in performance loss.

On the software side, support for nested virtualization of unmodified guests [2] may begin to be adopted by cloud providers. While this development could eventually lead to fully virtualized Blankets such as a KVM-Blanket, relying on providers to deploy such a system is provider-centric: every cloud must incorporate such technology before a KVM-Blanket becomes feasible across many clouds. It may be possible, however, for exposed hardware virtualization extensions to be leveraged as performance accelerators for a system like the Xen-Blanket.

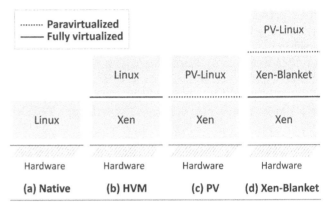

Figure 4. We run benchmarks on four different system configurations in order to examine the overhead caused by the Xen-Blanket. *Native* represents an unmodified CentOS 5.4 Linux. *HVM* represents a standard single-layer Xen-based virtualization solutions using full, hardware-assisted virtualization. *PV* represents a standard single-layer Xen-based virtualization solutions using paravirtualization. *Xen-Blanket* consists of a paravirtualized setup inside of our Xen-Blanket HVM guest.

5. Evaluation

We have built Blanket drivers and deployed the Xen-Blanket on two underlying hypervisors, across three resource providers. In this section, we first examine the overhead incurred by the Xen-Blanket. Then, we describe how increased flexibility resulting from a user-centric homogenization layer can result in significant cost savings—47% of the cost per hour—on today's clouds, despite overheads.

5.1 Overhead

Intuitively, we expect some amount of degraded performance from the Xen-Blanket due to the overheads of running a second-layer of virtualization. We compare four different scenarios, denoted by *Native*, *HVM*, *PV*, and *Xen-Blanket* (Figure 4). The Native setup ran an unmodified CentOS 5.4 Linux. The next two are standard single-layer Xen-based virtualization solutions using full, hardware-assisted virtualization (HVM, for short) or paravirtualization (PV, for short), respectively. The fourth setup (Xen-Blanket) consists of a paravirtualized setup inside an HVM guest.[4] All experiments in this subsection were performed on a pair of machines connected by a 1 Gbps network, each with two six-core 2.93 GHz Intel Xeon X5670 processors,[5] 24 GB of memory, and four 1 TB disks. Importantly, the virtualization capabilities of the Xeon X5670 include extended page table support (EPT), enabling a guest OS to modify page tables without generating vmexit traps. With the latest hardware virtualization support, HVM is expected to outperform

---

[4] We have also run experiments on KVM with comparable results, but focus on a single underlying hypervisor for a consistent evaluation.

[5] Hyperthreading causes the OS to perceive 24 processors on the system.

	Native	HVM	PV	Xen-Blanket
Processes (μs)				
null call	0.19	0.21	0.36	0.36
null I/O	0.23	0.26	0.41	0.41
stat	0.85	1.01	1.19	1.18
open/close	1.33	1.43	1.84	1.86
slct TCP	2.43	2.79	2.80	2.86
sig inst	0.25	0.39	0.54	0.53
sig hndl	0.90	0.79	0.94	0.94
fork proc	67	86	220	258
exec proc	217	260	517	633
sh proc	831	1046	1507	1749
Context Switching (μs)				
2p/0K	0.40	0.55	2.85	3.07
2p/16K	0.44	0.57	3.03	3.46
2p/64K	0.45	0.66	3.18	3.46
8p/16K	0.74	0.85	3.60	4.00
8p/64K	1.37	1.18	4.14	4.53
16p/16K	1.05	1.10	3.80	4.14
16p/64K	1.40	1.22	4.08	4.47
File & Virtual Memory (μs)				
0K file create	4.61	4.56	4.99	4.97
0K file delete	3.03	3.18	3.19	3.14
10K file create	14.4	18.1	19.9	28.8
10K file delete	6.17	6.02	6.01	6.08
mmap latency	425.0	820.0	1692.0	1729.0
prot fault	0.30	0.28	0.38	0.40
page fault	0.56	0.99	2.00	2.10

Table 1. The Xen-Blanket achieves performance within 3% of PV for simple `lmbench` operations, but incurs overhead up to 30% for file creation microbenchmarks.

PV, because of reduced hypervisor involvement. Therefore, since the Xen-Blanket setup contains a PV setup, PV can be roughly viewed as a best case for the Xen-Blanket.

System Microbenchmarks

To examine the performance of individual operations, such as null system calls, we ran `lmbench` in all setups. In order to distinguish the second-layer virtualization overhead from CPU contention, we ensure that one CPU is dedicated to the guest running the benchmark. To clarify, one VCPU backed by one physical CPU is exposed to the guest during single-layer virtualization experiments, whereas the Xen-Blanket system receives two VCPUs backed by two physical CPUs: one is reserved for the second-layer Domain 0 (see Figure 2(c)), and the other one for the second-layer guest.

Table 1 shows the results from running `lmbench` in each of the setups. For simple operations like a null syscall, the performance of the Xen-Blanket is within 3% of PV, but even PV is slower than native or HVM. This is because a syscall in any paravirtualized system first switches into (the top-most) Xen before being bounced into the guest OS. We stress that, for these operations, nesting Xen does not introduce additional overhead over standard paravirtualization. All context switch benchmarks are within 12.5% of PV,

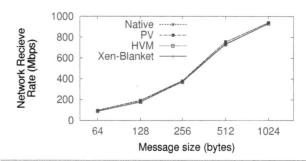

Figure 5. Network I/O performance on the Xen-Blanket is comparable to a single layer of virtualization.

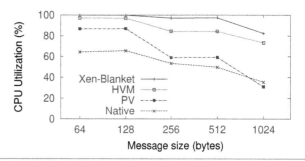

Figure 6. CPU utilization while receiving network I/O on the Xen-Blanket is within 15% of a single layer of virtualization.

with most around 8% of PV. Eliminating `vmexits` caused by the second-layer Xen is essential to achieve good performance. For example, if the second-layer Xen uses the `cr4` register on every context switch, overheads increase to 70%. Worse, on processors without EPT, which issue `vmexits` much more often, we measured overheads of up to 20×.

Blanket Drivers

Device I/O is often a performance bottleneck even for single-layer virtualized systems. Paravirtualization is essential for performance, even in fully-virtualized environments. To examine the network and disk performance of the Xen-Blanket, we assign each of the configurations one VCPU (we disable all CPUs except for one in the native case). Figure 5 and Figure 6 show the UDP receive throughput and the corresponding CPU utilization[6] under various packet sizes. We use `netperf` for the throughput measurement and `xentop` in the underlying Domain 0 to measure the CPU utilization of the guest (or Xen-Blanket and guest). The CPU utilization of the native configuration is determined using `top`. Despite the two layers of paravirtualized device interfaces, guests running on the Xen-Blanket can still match the network throughput of all other configurations for all packet sizes, and receive network traffic at full capacity over a 1 Gbps

---

[6] Errorbars are omitted for clarity: all CPU utilization measurements were within 1.7% of the mean.

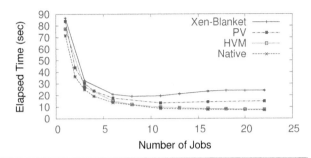

Figure 7. The Xen-Blanket can incur up to 68% overhead over PV when completing a `kernbench` benchmark.

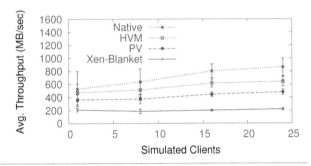

Figure 8. The Xen-Blanket can incur up to 55% overhead over PV when performing the `dbench` filesystem benchmark.

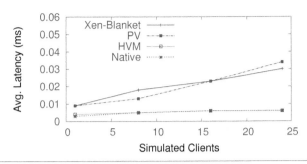

Figure 9. The average latency for ReadX operations during the `dbench` benchmark for Xen-Blanket remains comparable to PV.

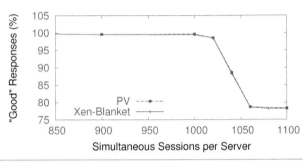

Figure 10. The Xen-Blanket performs just as well as PV for the SPECweb2009 macrobenchmark.

link. The Xen-Blanket does incur more CPU overhead because of the extra copy of packets in the Blanket layer. We also ran `dd` to get a throughput measure of disk I/O. System caches at all layers were flushed before reading 2GB of data from the root filesystem. Native achieved read throughput of 124.6 MB/s, HVM achieved 86.3 MB/s, PV achieved 76.6 MB/s, and the Xen-Blanket incurred an extra overhead of 12% over PV, with disk read throughput of 67.6 MB/s.

Macrobenchmarks

Macrobenchmarks are useful for demonstrating the overhead of the system under more realistic workloads. For these experiments, we dedicate 2 CPUs and 8 GB of memory to the lowest layer Domain 0. The remaining 16 GB of memory and 22 CPUs are allocated to single layer guests. In the case of the Xen-Blanket, we allocate 14 GB of memory and 20 CPUs to the Blanket guest, dedicating the remainder to the Blanket Domain 0. Unlike the microbenchmarks, resource contention does contribute to the performance measured in these experiments.

`kernbench`[7] is a CPU throughput benchmark that consists of compiling the Linux kernel using a configurable number of concurrent jobs. Figure 7 shows the elapsed time for the kernel compile. With a single job, the Xen-Blanket stays within 5% of PV, however, performance falls to about

68% worse than PV for high concurrency. The performance loss here can be attributed to a high number of `vmexits` due to APIC (Advanced Programmable Interrupt Controller) operations to send inter-processor-interrupts (IPIs) between VCPUs. Despite this overhead, the flexibility of the Xen-Blanket enables reductions in cost, as described in Section 5.2.

`dbench`[8] is a filesystem benchmark that generates load on a filesystem based on the standard `NetBench` benchmark. Figure 8 show the average throughput during load imposed by various numbers of simulated clients. Figure 9 shows the average latency for ReadX operations, where ReadX is the most common operation during the benchmark. PV and the Xen-Blanket both experience significantly higher latency than HVM. The advantage of HVM can be attributed to the advantages of hardware memory management because of extended page tables (EPT). The Xen-Blanket incurs up to 55% overhead over PV in terms of throughput, but the latency is comparable.

Finally, we ran the banking workload of SPECweb2009 for a web server macrobenchmark. For each experiment, a client workload generator VM running on another machine connected by a 1 Gbps link drives load for a server that runs PHP scripts. As SPECweb2009 is a Web server benchmark, the back-end database is simulated. A valid SPECweb2009

---

[7] version 0.50

[8] version 4.0

Type	CPU (ECUs)	Memory (GB)	Disk (GB)	Price ($/hr)
Small	1	1.7	160	0.085
Cluster 4XL	33.5	23	1690	1.60
Factor	33.5×	13.5×	10×	18.8×

Table 2. The resources on Amazon EC2 instance types do not scale up uniformly with price. The user-centric design of Xen-Blanket allows users to exploit this fact.

run involves 95% of the page requests to compete under a "good" time threshold (2s) and 99% of the requests to be under a "tolerable" time threshold (4s). Figure 10 shows the number of "good" transactions for various numbers of simultaneous sessions. VMs running in both PV and Xen-Blanket scenarios can support an identical number of simultaneous sessions.[9] This is because the benchmark is I/O bound, and the Blanket drivers ensure efficient I/O for the Xen-Blanket. The SPECweb2009 instance running in the Xen-Blanket does utilize more CPU to achieve the same throughput, however: average CPU utilization rises from 4.3% to 5.1% under 1000 simultaneous client sessions.

5.2 User-defined Oversubscription

Even though running VMs in the Xen-Blanket does incur overhead, its user-centric design gives a cloud user the flexibility to utilize cloud resources substantially more efficiently than possible on today's clouds. Efficient utilization of cloud resources translates directly into monetary savings. In this subsection, we evaluate oversubscription on the Xen-Blanket instantiated within Amazon EC2 and find CPU-intensive VMs can be deployed for 47% of the cost of small instances.

Table 2 shows the pricing per hour on Amazon EC2 to rent a small instance or a quadruple extra large cluster compute instance (cluster 4XL). Importantly, while the cluster 4XL instance is almost a factor of 19 times more expensive than a small instance, some resources are greater than 19 times more abundant (e.g. 33.5 times more for CPU) while other resources are less than 19 times more abundant (e.g 10 times more for disk). This suggests that if a cloud user has a number CPU intensive VMs normally serviced as small instances, it may be more cost efficient to rent a cluster 4XL instance and oversubscribe the memory and disk. This is not an option provided by Amazon; however, the Xen-Blanket is user-centric and therefore gives the user the necessary control to implement such a configuration. A number of would-be small instances can be run on the Xen-Blanket within a cluster 4XL instance, using oversubscription to reduce the price per VM.

To illustrate this point, we ran a CPU-intensive macrobenchmark, `kernbench`, simultaneously in a various num-

---

[9] PV and Xen-Blanket run the same VM and thus the same configuration of this complex benchmark. We omit a comparison with native and HVM to avoid presenting misleading results due to slight configuration variation.

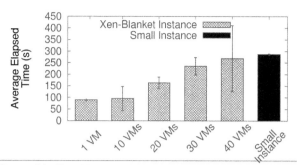

Figure 11. The Xen-Blanket gives the flexibility to oversubscribe such that each of 40 VMs on a single 4XL instance can simultaneously complete compilation tasks in the same amount of time as a small instance.

bers of VMs running inside a single cluster 4XL instance with the Xen-Blanket. We also ran the benchmark inside a small EC2 instance for a comparison point. The benchmark was run without concurrency in all instances for consistency, because a small instance on Amazon only has one VCPU. Figure 11 shows the elapsed time to run the benchmark in each of these scenarios. Each number of VMs on the Xen-Blanket corresponds to a different monetary cost. For example, to run a single VM, the cost is $1.60 per hour. 10 VMs reduce the cost per VM to $0.16 per hour, 20 VMs to $0.08 per VM per hour, 30 VMs to $0.06 per VM per hour, and 40 VMs to $0.04 per VM per hour. Running a single VM, the benchmark completes in 89 seconds on the Xen-Blanket, compared to 286 seconds for a small instance. This is expected, because the cluster 4XL instance is significantly more powerful than a small instance. Furthermore, the average benchmark completion time for even 40 VMs remains 33 seconds faster than for a small instance. Since a small instance costs $.085 per VM per hour, this translates to 47% of the price per VM per hour. It should be noted, however, that the variance of the benchmark performance significantly increases for large numbers of VMs on the same instance.

In some sense, the cost benefit of running CPU intensive instances inside the Xen-Blanket instead of inside small instances simply exploits an artifact of Amazon's pricing scheme. However, other benefits from oversubscription are possible, especially when considering VMs that have uncorrelated variation in their resource demands. Every time one VM experiences a burst of resource usage, others are likely quiescent. If VMs are not co-located, each instance must operate with some resources reserved for bursts. If VMs are co-located, on the other hand, a relatively small amount of resources can be shared to be used for bursting behavior, resulting in less wasted resources.

Co-location of VMs also affect the performance of enterprise applications, made up of a number of VMs that may heavily communicate with one another [20]. To demonstrate the difference that VM placement can make to network performance, we ran the `netperf` TCP benchmark between

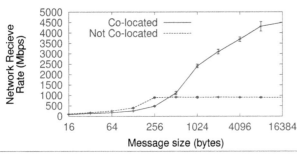

Figure 12. Co-location of VMs to improve network bandwidth is another simple optimization made possible by the user-centric approach of the Xen-Blanket.

two VMs. In the first setup, the VMs were placed on two different physical servers on the same rack, connected by a 1 Gbps link. In the second, the VMs were co-located on the same physical server. Figure 12 shows the network throughput. The co-located servers are not limited by the network hardware connecting the physical machines. By enabling co-location, the Xen-Blanket can increase inter-VM throughput by a factor of 4.5. This dramatic result is without any modification to the VMs. The user-centric design of the Xen-Blanket enables other optimization opportunities, including CPU bursting, page sharing and resource oversubscription, that can offset the inherent overhead of the approach.

6. Experience with Multi-Cloud Migration

The Xen-Blanket homogenizes and simplifies the process of migrating a VM between two clouds managed by two different providers. While it is possible to migrate VMs between multiple clouds today, the process is cloud-specific and fundamentally limited. For example, it is currently impossible to live migrate [8, 18] a VM between cloud providers. We give a qualitative comparison to illustrate the difficulty faced in migrating a Xen VM from our private Xen environment to Amazon EC2 with and without the Xen-Blanket. We also show how one can reintroduce live migration across multi-clouds using the Xen-Blanket. In our experiment, we use a VM housing a typical legacy LAMP-based[10] application that contained non-trivial customizations and approximately 20 GB of user data.

6.1 Non-Live Multi-Cloud Migration

Figure 13 summarizes the four steps involved in a migration: *modifying* the VM's disk image to be compatible with EC2, *bundling* or compressing the image to be sent to EC2, *uploading* the bundled image, and *launching* the image at the new location. In both scenarios, bundling, uploading and launching took one person about 3 hrs. However, the modify step caused the scenario without the Xen-Blanket to be much more time consuming: 24 hrs additional work as compared to no additional work with the Xen-Blanket.

---
[10] Linux, Apache, MySQL, and PHP

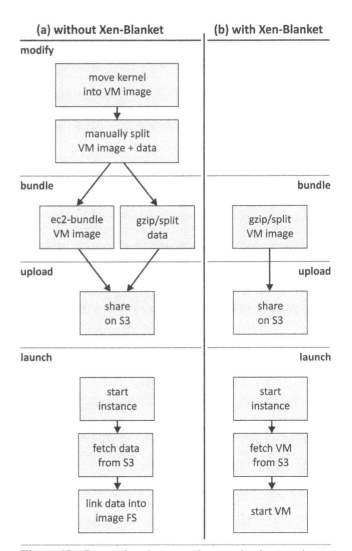

Figure 13. Comparison between the steps it takes to migrate (offline) an image into Amazon's EC2 with and without the Xen-Blanket

Migrating a VM image from our private setup to Amazon EC2 is relatively straightforward given the Xen-Blanket. No image modifications are required, so the process begins with bundling, or preparing the image to upload for use in EC2. The image was compressed with `gzip`, split into 5 GB chunks for Amazon's Simple Storage Service (S3), and uploaded. Then, we started an EC2 instance running the Xen-Blanket, retrieved the disk image from S3, concatenated the pieces of the file, and unzipped the image. The VM itself was created using standard Xen tools, such as `xm create`.

Without the Xen-Blanket, there currently exists a EC2-specific process to create an Amazon Machine Image (AMI) from an existing Xen disk image, roughly matching the bundle, upload, and launch steps. Before that, two modifications were required to our VM image. First, we had to modify the image to contain the kernel because no compatible kernel was offered by EC2.[11] This task was complicated by the fact that our private Xen setup did not have the correct tools to boot the kernel within the image. Second, we had to shrink our 40 GB disk image to fit within the 10 GB image limit on EC2. This involved manually examining the disk image in order to locate, copy, and remove a large portion of the application data, then resizing the VM's filesystem and image. After the modifications were complete, we used an AMI tool called `ec2-bundle-image` to split the VM image into pieces and then compressed, split and uploaded the relocated data to S3. We then started an EC2 instance with our new AMI, configured it to mount a disk, and reintegrated the user data from S3 into the filesystem.

It should be noted that subsequent launches of the migrated VMs do not require all of the steps outlined above. However, if a modified or updated version of the VM is released, the entire process must be redone. Even worse, we expect migrating to other clouds to be similarly arduous and provider-specific, if possible at all. In contrast, using the Xen-Blanket, the migration process will always be the same, and can be reduced to a simple remote copy operation.

6.2 Live Multi-Cloud Migration

Live migration typically relies on memory tracing: a hypervisor-level technique. Such techniques are not available across clouds.[12] The Xen-Blanket enables immediate implementation of live migration across cloud providers. We have experimented with live migration between an enterprise cloud and Amazon EC2. We note that since live migration between two clouds is not currently possible without provider support or the Xen-Blanket, we do not have a comparison point to present.

Beyond the ability to implement hypervisor-level features like memory tracing, there are two key challenges to implement live multi-cloud migration on the Xen-Blanket. First, Xen-Blanket instances in different clouds are in different IP subnets, causing communication issues before and after Blanket guest migrations. Second, Xen-Blanket instances in different clouds do not share network attached storage, which is often assumed for live VM migration.

To address the networking issues, each Xen-Blanket instance runs a virtual switch in Domain 0 to which the virtual network interfaces belonging to Blanket guest VMs are attached. A layer-2 tunnel connects the virtual switches across the Internet. The result is that VMs on either of the two Xen-Blanket instances appear to be sharing a private LAN. A few basic network services are useful to introduce onto the virtual network. A gateway server VM can be run with two virtual network interfaces: one attached to the virtual

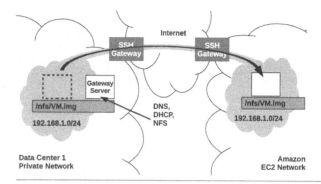

Figure 14. Xen-Blanket instances are connected with a layer-2 tunnel, while a gateway server VM provides DNS, DHCP and NFS to the virtual network, eliminating the communication and storage barriers to multi-cloud live migration.

switch and the virtual network; the other attached to the externally visible interface of the Xen-Blanket instance. The gateway server VM, shown in Figure 14, runs `dnsmasq` as a lightweight DHCP and DNS server.

Once VMs on the Xen-Blanket can communicate, the storage issues can be addressed with a network file system, such as NFS. NFS is useful for live VM migration because it avoids the need to transfer the entire disk image of the VM at once during migration. In our setup, the gateway server VM also runs an NFS server. The NFS server exports files onto the virtual network and is mounted by the Domain 0 of each Xen-Blanket instance. Both Xen-Blanket instances mount the NFS share at the same location. Therefore, during VM migration, the VM root filesystem image can always be located at the same filesystem location, regardless of the physical machine.

With Xen-Blanket VMs able to communicate, maintain their network addresses, and access storage within either cloud, live VM migration proceeds by following the typical procedure in the Blanket hypervisor. However, while we have successfully live-migrated a VM from an enterprise cloud to Amazon EC2 and back, this is simply a proof-of-concept. It is clearly inefficient to rely on a NFS disk image potentially residing on another cloud instead of a local disk. Moreover, the layer-2 tunnel only connects two machines. More sophisticated wide-area live migration techniques exist [5], that can, as future work, be implemented and evaluated on the Xen-Blanket.

7. Future Work

Two limitations of the current Xen-Blanket are the inability to support unmodified guest OSs (such as Microsoft Windows) and the reliance on fully virtualized (HVM) containers. To address the first limitation, as discussed earlier, unmodified guests can be supported with binary translation, for example a VMWare-Blanket. The performance implications of such a system is a subject of future research. The second

---

[11] Until recently, Amazon EC2 only allowed a limited selection of a few standard kernels and initial ramdisks for use outside the image. Luckily, in July 2010, Amazon EC2 began to support kernels stored within the image.

[12] While some providers expose an interface for users to use live migration within their own cloud, as with other provider-centric approaches, standardization may take years.

limitation can be addressed by allowing a version of the Xen-Blanket to run on a paravirtualized interface, while continuing to export a homogeneous interface to guests. Paravirtualizing the Blanket layer is technically feasible, but may encounter performance issues in the memory subsystem where hardware features such as Extended Page Tables (EPT) cannot be used and is another subject of future research.

More broadly, a user-centric, homogeneous Blanket layer enables future projects to examine features such as cross-provider live migration (see Section 6.2), high availability [10], and security [12] on one or more existing clouds. It also offers researchers an environment within which novel systems and hypervisor level experimentation can be performed. We also plan to research issues in running entire cloud stacks, such as Eucalyptus [14] or OpenStack [1], in nested environments and across multiple clouds.

8. Related Work

There are several techniques that exist today to deploy applications on multiple clouds, but none afford the user the flexibility or level of control of the Xen-Blanket. Conversely, there are also a number of existing systems that offer a user similar levels of control as the Xen-Blanket. However, none of these systems are able to be deployed on today's public clouds.

Nested virtualization is leveraged by the Xen-Blanket in order to allow a user to implement its own version of homogeneity, including hypervisor-level services. Graf and Roedel [15] and the Turtles Project [2] are pioneers of enabling nested virtualization with one or more levels of full virtualization, on AMD and Intel hardware, respectively. Berghmans [3] describes the performance of several nested virtualization environments. CloudVisor [30] explores nested virtualization in a cloud context, but for security, where the provider controls both layers. The Xen-Blanket sacrifices full nested virtualization for immediate deployment on existing clouds.

8.1 Multi-Cloud Deployments

Using tools from Rightscale [9], a user can create ServerTemplates, which can be deployed on a variety of clouds and utilize unique features of clouds without sacrificing portability. However, users are unable to homogenize the underlying clouds, particularly hypervisor-level services.

Middleware, such as IBM's Altocumulus [17] system homogenizes both IaaS clouds like Amazon EC2 and Platform as a Service (PaaS) clouds like Google App Engine into a PaaS abstraction across multiple clouds. However, without control at the IaaS (hypervisor) level, the amount of customization possible by the cloud user is fundamentally limited.

fos [24], deployed on EC2 today and potentially deployable across a wide variety of heterogeneous clouds, exposes a single system image instead of a VM interface. However, users must learn to program their applications for fos; the familiar VM interface and legacy applications contained within must be abandoned.

Eucalyptus [14] and AppScale [7] are open-source cloud computing systems that can enable private infrastructures to share an API with Amazon EC2 and Google App Engine respectively. However, the user cannot implement their own multi-cloud hypervisor-level feature. OpenStack [1] is another open-source implementation of an IaaS cloud, with the same limitation.

The RESERVOIR project [19] is a multi-cloud agenda in which two or more independent cloud providers create a *federated cloud*. A provider-centric approach is assumed; standardization is necessary before federation can extend beyond the testbed. With the Xen-Blanket, such an agenda could be applied across today's public clouds.

8.2 User-Centric Design and Control

OpenCirrus [6] is an initiative that aims to enable cloud targeted system level research—deploying a user-centric cloud—by allowing access to bare hardware, as in Emulab [26], in a number of dedicated data centers. However, OpenCirrus is not aimed at applying this ability to existing cloud infrastructures.

Cloud operating systems such as VMWare's vSphere [22] allow the administrator of a private cloud to utilize a pool of physical resources, while providing features like automatic resource allocation, automated failover, or zero-downtime maintenance. These features, which are examples of hypervisor-level services, cannot easily be integrated with current public cloud offerings.

Finally, the Xen-Blanket is an instantiation of our extensible cloud, or xCloud, proposal [27], which is influenced by work on extensible operating systems. For example, SPIN [4] allows extensions to be downloaded into the kernel safely using language features, while Exokernels [13] advocate hardware to be exposed to a library OS controlled by the user. However, these extensibility strategies are provider-centric, and unlikely to be incorporated in today's clouds. The combination of deployment focus and user-level control sets the Xen-Blanket apart from existing work.

9. Conclusion

Current IaaS clouds lack the homogeneity required for users to easily deploy services across multiple providers. We have advocated that instead of standardization, or provider-centric homogenization, cloud users must have the ability to homogenize the cloud themselves. We presented the Xen-Blanket, a system that enables user-centric homogenization of existing cloud infrastructures.

The Xen-Blanket leverages a second-layer Xen hypervisor—completely controlled by the user—that utilizes a set of provider-specific Blanket drivers to execute on top of existing clouds without requiring any modifications to the provider. Blanket drivers have been developed for both Xen and KVM based systems, and achieve high performance: network and disk throughput remain within 12% of paravirtualized drivers in a single-level paravirtualized guest. The Xen-Blanket is currently running on Amazon EC2, an enterprise cloud, and private servers at Cornell University. We have migrated VM images between the three different sites with no modifications to the images and performed live migration to and from Amazon EC2. We have exploited the user-centric nature of the Xen-Blanket to oversubscribe resources and save money on EC2, achieving a cost of 47% of the price per hour of small instances for 40 CPU-intensive VMs, despite the inherent overheads of nested virtualization.

We have only scratched the surface in terms of the applications and functionality made possible by user-centric homogenization, and the Xen-Blanket in particular. The Xen-Blanket project website is located at `http://xcloud.cs.cornell.edu/`, and the code for the Xen-Blanket is publicly available at `http://code.google.com/p/xen-blanket/`. We hope other projects adopt the Xen-Blanket and look forward to expanding the Xen-Blanket to cover even more underlying cloud providers.

Acknowledgments

This work was partially funded and supported by an IBM Faculty Award received by Hakim Weatherspoon, DARPA, NSF TRUST and NSF FIA. Also, this work was performed while Dan Williams was an intern at the IBM T. J. Watson Research Center in Hawthorne, NY. We would like to thank our shepherd, Andreas Haeberlen, and the anonymous reviewers for their comments.

References

[1] OpenStack. `http://www.openstack.org/`, Oct. 2010.

[2] M. Ben-Yehuda, M. D. Day, Z. Dubitzky, M. Factor, N. Har'El, A. Gordon, A. Liguori, O. Wasserman, and B.-A. Yassour. The turtles project: Design and implementation of nested virtualization. In *Proc. of USENIX OSDI*, Vancouver, BC, Canada, Oct. 2010.

[3] O. Berghmans. Nesting virtual machines in virtualization test frameworks. *Masters thesis, University of Antwerp*, May 2010.

[4] B. N. Bershad, S. Savage, P. Pardyak, E. G. Sirer, M. E. Fiuczynski, D. Becker, C. Chambers, and S. Eggers. Extensibility, safety and performance in the SPIN operating system. In *Proc. of ACM SOSP*, Copper Mountain, CO, Dec. 1995.

[5] R. Bradford, E. Kotsovinos, A. Feldmann, and H. Schiöberg. Live wide-area migration of virtual machines including local persistent state. In *Proc. of ACM VEE*, San Diego, CA, June 2007.

[6] R. Campbell, I. Gupta, M. Heath, S. Y. Ko, M. Kozuch, M. Kunze, T. Kwan, K. Lai, H. Y. Lee, M. Lyons, D. Miloji-

cic, D. O'Hallaron, and Y. C. Soh. Open cirrus^{TM} cloud computing testbed: federated data centers for open source systems and services research. In *Proc. of USENIX HotCloud*, San Diego, CA, June 2009.

[7] N. Chohan, C. Bunch, S. Pang, C. Krintz, N. Mostafa, S. Soman, and R. Wolski. Appscale: Scalable and open appengine application development and deployment. In *Proc. of ICST CLOUDCOMP*, Munich, Germany, Oct. 2009.

[8] C. Clark, K. Fraser, S. Hand, J. G. Hansen, E. Jul, C. Limpach, I. Pratt, and A. Warfield. Live migration of virtual machines. In *Proc. of USENIX NSDI*, Boston, MA, May 2005.

[9] T. Clark. Rightscale. http://www.rightscale.com, 2010.

[10] B. Cully, G. Lefebvre, D. Meyer, M. Feeley, N. Hutchinson, and A. Warfield. Remus: high availability via asynchronous virtual machine replication. In *Proc. of USENIX NSDI*, San Francisco, CA, Apr. 2008.

[11] Distributed Management Task Force, Inc. (DMTF). Open virtualization format white paper version 1.00. `http://http://www.dmtf.org/sites/default/files/standards/documents/DSP2017_1.0.0.pdf`, Feb. 2009.

[12] G. W. Dunlap, S. T. King, S. Cinar, M. A. Basrai, and P. M. Chen. ReVirt: Enabling intrusion analysis through virtual-machine logging and replay. In *Proc. of USENIX OSDI*, Boston, MA, Dec. 2002.

[13] D. R. Engler, M. F. Kaashoek, and J. W. O'Toole. Exokernel: An operating system architecture for application-level resource management. In *Proc. of ACM SOSP*, Copper Mountain, CO, Dec. 1995.

[14] Eucalyptus Systems, Inc. Eucalyptus open-source cloud computing infrastructure - an overview. `http://www.eucalyptus.com/pdf/whitepapers/Eucalyptus_Overview.pdf`, Aug. 2009.

[15] A. Graf and J. Roedel. Nesting the virtualized world. In *Linux Plumbers Conference*, Portland, OR, Sept. 2009.

[16] D. Gupta, S. Lee, M. Vrable, S. Savage, A. C. Snoeren, G. Varghese, G. M. Voelker, and A. Vahdat. Difference engine: Harnessing memory redundancy in virtual machines. In *Proc. of USENIX OSDI*, San Diego, CA, Dec. 2008.

[17] E. M. Maximilien, A. Ranabahu, R. Engehausen, and L. C. Anderson. IBM altocumulus: a cross-cloud middleware and platform. In *Proc. of ACM OOPSLA Conf.*, Orlando, FL, Oct. 2009.

[18] M. Nelson, B.-H. Lim, and G. Hutchins. Fast transparent migration for virtual machines. In *Proc. of USENIX Annual Technical Conf.*, Anaheim, CA, Apr. 2005.

[19] B. Rochwerger, D. Breitgand, A. Epstein, D. Hadas, I. Loy, K. Nagin, J. Tordsson, C. Ragusa, M. Villari, S. Clayman, E. Levy, A. Maraschini, P. Massonet, H. Muñoz, and G. Tofetti. Reservoir - when one cloud is not enough. *IEEE Computer*, 44(3):44–51, 2011.

[20] V. Shrivastava, P. Zerfos, K. won Lee, H. Jamjoom, Y.-H. Liu, and S. Banerjee. Application-aware virtual machine migration in data centers. In *Proc. of IEEE INFOCOM Mini-conference*, Shanghai, China, Apr. 2011.

[21] J. Sugerman, G. Venkitachalam, and B.-H. Lim. Virtualizing I/O devices on VMware workstation's hosted virtual machine monitor. In *Proc. of USENIX Annual Technical Conf.*, Boston, MA, June 2001.

[22] VMware. "VMware vsphere, the first cloud operating system, provides an evolutionary, non-disruptive path to cloud computing". `http://www.vmware.com/files/pdf/cloud/VMW_09Q2_WP_Cloud_OS_P8_R1.pdf`, 2009.

[23] C. A. Waldspurger. Memory resource management in VMware ESX server. In *Proc. of USENIX OSDI*, Boston, MA, Dec. 2002.

[24] D. Wentzlaff, C. Gruenwald, III, N. Beckmann, K. Modzelewski, A. Belay, L. Youseff, J. Miller, and A. Agarwal. An operating system for multicore and clouds: mechanisms and implementation. In *Proc. of ACM SoCC*, Indianapolis, IN, June 2010.

[25] A. Whitaker, M. Shaw, and S. D. Gribble. Scale and performance in the Denali isolation kernel. In *Proc. of USENIX OSDI*, Boston, MA, Dec. 2002.

[26] B. White, J. Lepreau, L. Stoller, R. Ricci, S. Guruprasad, M. Newbold, M. Hibler, C. Barb, and A. Joglekar. An integrated experimental environment for distributed systems and networks. In *Proc. of USENIX OSDI*, Boston, MA, Dec. 2002.

[27] D. Williams, E. Elnikety, M. Eldehiry, H. Jamjoom, H. Huang, and H. Weatherspoon. Unshackle the cloud! In *Proc. of USENIX HotCloud*, Portland, OR, June 2011.

[28] D. Williams, H. Jamjoom, Y.-H. Liu, and H. Weatherspoon. Overdriver: Handling memory overload in an oversubscribed cloud. In *Proc. of ACM VEE*, Newport Beach, CA, Mar. 2011.

[29] T. Wood, G. Tarasuk-Levin, P. Shenoy, P. Desnoyers, E. Cecchet, and M. D. Corner. Memory buddies: Exploiting page sharing for smart colocation in virtualized data centers. In *Proc. of ACM VEE*, Washington, DC, Mar. 2009.

[30] F. Zhang, J. Chen, H. Chen, and B. Zang. CloudVisor: Retrofitting protection of virtual machines in multi-tenant cloud with nested virtualization. In *Proc. of ACM SOSP*, Cascais, Portugal, Oct. 2011.

Isolating Commodity Hosted Hypervisors with HyperLock

Zhi Wang   Chiachih Wu   Michael Grace   Xuxian Jiang

Department of Computer Science
North Carolina State University
{zhi_wang, cwu10, mcgrace}@ncsu.edu   jiang@cs.ncsu.edu

Abstract

Hosted hypervisors (e.g., KVM) are being widely deployed. One key reason is that they can effectively take advantage of the mature features and broad user bases of commodity operating systems. However, they are not immune to exploitable software bugs. Particularly, due to the close integration with the host and the unique presence underneath guest virtual machines, a hosted hypervisor – if compromised – can also jeopardize the host system and completely take over all guests in the same physical machine.

In this paper, we present HyperLock, a systematic approach to strictly isolate privileged, but potentially vulnerable, hosted hypervisors from compromising the host OSs. Specifically, we provide a secure *hypervisor isolation runtime* with its own separated address space and a restricted instruction set for safe execution. In addition, we propose another technique, i.e., *hypervisor shadowing*, to efficiently create a separate shadow hypervisor and pair it with each guest so that a compromised hypervisor can affect *only* the paired guest, not others. We have built a proof-of-concept HyperLock prototype to confine the popular KVM hypervisor on Linux. Our results show that HyperLock has a much smaller (12%) trusted computing base (TCB) than the original KVM. Moreover, our system completely removes QEMU, the companion user program of KVM (with > 531K SLOC), from the TCB. The security experiments and performance measurements also demonstrated the practicality and effectiveness of our approach.

Categories and Subject Descriptors   D.4.6 [*Operating Systems*]: Security and Protection—Security kernels

General Terms   Design, Security

Keywords   Virtualization, Hypervisor, KVM, Isolation

EuroSys'12,   April 10–13, 2012, Bern, Switzerland.
Copyright © 2012 ACM 978-1-4503-1223-3/12/04. . . $10.00

1. Introduction

Recent years have witnessed the accelerated adoption of hosted or Type-II hypervisors (e.g., KVM [19]). Compared to bare-metal or Type-I hypervisors (e.g., Xen [5]) that run directly on the hardware, hosted hypervisors typically run within a conventional operating system (OS) and rely on this "host" OS to manage most system resources. By doing so, hosted hypervisors can immediately benefit from various key features of the host OS that are mature and stable, including abundant and timely hardware support, advanced memory management, efficient process scheduling, and so forth. Moreover, a hosted hypervisor extends the host OS non-intrusively as a loadable kernel module, which is arguably much easier to install and maintain than a bare-metal hypervisor. Due to these unique benefits, hosted hypervisors are increasingly being adopted in today's virtualization systems [28].

From another perspective, despite recent advances in hardware virtualization (such as Intel VT [18]), virtualizing a computer system is still a complex task. For example, a commodity hosted hypervisor, such as KVM, typically involves a convoluted shadow paging mechanism to virtualize the guest memory (including emulating five different modes of operation in x86: paging disabled, paging with 2, 3, or 4 levels of page tables, and hardware assisted memory virtualization, including EPT/NPT [18]). For performance reasons, many hypervisors also support an "*out-of-sync*" (OOS) shadow paging scheme that synchronizes the shadow page table with the guest only when absolutely necessary. In addition, hosted hypervisors still suffer from a large attack surface, because they take many untrusted guest virtual machine (VM) states as input. For example, shadow paging needs to read guest page tables for synchronization, while instruction emulation – another complicated component of a hypervisor – involves fetching guest instructions for interpretation and execution.

Due to inherent high complexity and broad attack surface, contemporary hosted hypervisors are not immune to serious security vulnerabilities. A recent study of the National Vulnerability Database (NVD) [25] indicates that there were 24 security vulnerabilities found in KVM and 49 in VMware Workstation over the last three years. These vulnerabilities can be potentially exploited to execute arbitrary code with the highest privilege, putting the whole host system at risk. In fact, successful attacks against both KVM [12] and VMware Workstation [21] have been publicly demonstrated to escape from a guest VM and directly attack the host OS. Worse, a compromised hypervisor can also easily take over all the other guests, leading to disruption of hosted services or stealing of sensitive information. This can have a devastating effect in the scenario where a single physical machine may host multiple VMs from different organizations (e.g., in a cloud setting). In light of the above threats, there is a pressing need to secure these hosted hypervisors and protect the host system – as well as the other guest VMs – from a compromised hypervisor.

To address the need, researchers have explored a number of approaches. For example, seL4 [20] takes a formal approach to verify that a small micro-kernel (~8.7K source lines of code or SLOC) is secure including the absence of certain software vulnerabilities (e.g., buffer overruns and NULL pointer references). However, it is not scalable or still incomplete in accommodating commodity hypervisors (e.g., KVM) that have a much larger code base and support various complex x86 CPU/chipset features [30]. HyperSafe [39] enables self-protection for bare-metal hypervisors to enforce their control flow integrity. Unfortunately, as admitted in [39], the proposed approach cannot be applied for hosted hypervisors due to different design choices in the commodity host OS (e.g. frequent page table updates) from bare-metal hypervisors. Other approaches [32, 42] take a layer-below method to isolate untrusted device drivers, which is also not applicable because hosted hypervisors already run at the lowest level on the system.

In this paper, we present HyperLock, a system that is able to establish a tight security boundary to isolate hosted hypervisors. Specifically, we encapsulate the execution of a hosted hypervisor with a secure *hypervisor isolation runtime*, which has its own separate address space and a reduced instruction set for safe execution. By doing so, the host system is not accessible to the hypervisor. Instead, it must go through a well-defined interface, which is mediated and sufficiently narrowed-down by HyperLock to block any unexpected side-effects. Moreover, we further propose a *hypervisor shadowing* technique, which can efficiently create a separate shadow hypervisor for (and pair it with) each guest so that a compromised hypervisor can affect *only* the paired guest, not others. By exploiting recent memory de-duplication techniques, these shadow hypervisors can be created without incurring additional resource overhead.

We have implemented a proof-of-concept HyperLock prototype for the popular KVM hypervisor (version kvm-2.6.36.1 and qemu-0.14.0). Our experience shows that HyperLock can be implemented with a small code base (~4K SLOC). We demonstrate its effectiveness and practicality by performing additional security analysis and performance measurement. To summarize, this paper makes the following contributions:

- To address the imperative need to confine commodity hosted hypervisors, we propose a secure *hypervisor isolation runtime* with a dedicated address space and a reduced instruction set to strictly confine their execution. To the best of our knowledge, the proposed hypervisor isolation runtime is among the first to isolate hosted hypervisors and protect the host OSs from being jeopardized by them.

- To effectively prevent a compromised hosted hypervisor from taking over all guests in the same physical machine, we propose another key technique, i.e., *hypervisor shadowing*, to create a guest-specific shadow hypervisor without additional resource overhead. By doing so, we ensure that a compromised hypervisor will only affect the corresponding guest, *not* others.

- We have developed a HyperLock prototype and used it to protect the popular KVM hypervisor. Our prototype introduces a very small TCB (~4K SLOC) to the current OS kernel while completely removing the original KVM code (~33.6K SLOC) as well as the companion QEMU program (~531K SLOC) from the TCB of the host OS. The security analysis and evaluation with standard benchmark programs shows that our prototype is not only effective, but also lightweight (< 5% performance slowdown).

The rest of the paper is structured as follows: we first present the design of HyperLock with a focus on the KVM hypervisor in Section 2. After that, we discuss the implementation and evaluation of HyperLock in Sections 3, and 4, respectively. Issues and possible improvements are discussed in Section 5. Finally, we describe related work in Section 6 and conclude the paper in Section 7.

2. Design

Before presenting our system design, we first briefly review the basic architecture of existing hosted hypervisors and the associated threat model. For simplicity, we use KVM as the representative example throughout the paper. As a popular, open-source hypervisor, KVM is incredibly simple to deploy and run. It can be dynamically loaded as a kernel module on Linux and once loaded, it instantly extends the host OS with virtualization support (based on hardware virtualization extensions such as Intel VT [18]). KVM uses a companion user program, i.e., a QEMU variant, to cooperatively emulate hardware devices for a guest (e.g., hard disks). In Figure 1(a), we show the main execution flow of a KVM-powered guest, which involves close interaction between KVM and QEMU. For example, when QEMU issues an `ioctl` command (e.g. KVM_RUN – arrow 1) to KVM, KVM proceeds by switching into the guest mode for the VM execution (arrow 2), which means the guest code

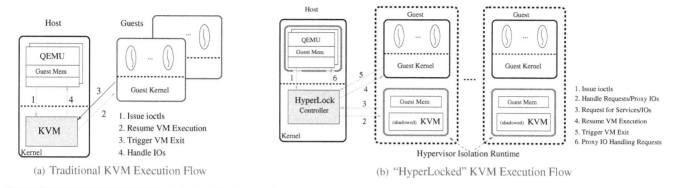

(a) Traditional KVM Execution Flow

Figure 1. Traditional KVM Execution vs. "HyperLocked" KVM Execution

can run natively on the CPU. The guest mode continues until certain events (e.g., an I/O port access – arrow 3) happen to cause a *VM exit* back to KVM. Based on the VM exit reason, KVM may directly resolve it or delegate it to QEMU (arrow 4). After the VM exit is resolved, the guest can now enter the guest mode again for native VM execution (arrow 2).

In this work, we assume an adversary model where an attacker can successfully subvert the underlying hosted hypervisor from a malicious guest. To do that, the attacker can choose to exploit vulnerabilities either in the hypervisor itself (e.g., memory corruption in KVM) or in its companion user-level program (e.g., vulnerabilities in device emulation). As part of the exploitation process, the attacker may attempt to execute arbitrary malicious code in the compromised hypervisor or the user-level program [8]. In other words, by assuming the presence of exploitable software vulnerabilities in hosted hypervisors, we aim to deal with the threats from an untrusted guest so that the hosted hypervisor, even compromised, cannot take over the host and other guests.

Figure 1(b) illustrates the high-level architecture of HyperLock. To isolate hosted hypervisors, it has two key components, i.e., a *hypervisor isolation runtime* and a *hyperlock controller*. With these two components, unlike the traditional case of directly running KVM in the host OS (Figure 1(a)), HyperLock confines the KVM execution in a secure hypervisor isolation runtime with its own separate address space, where only unambiguous instructions from a reduced instruction set will be allowed to execute. Further, one isolation runtime is bound to one particular guest. That is, every guest logically has its own separate copy of the hypervisor code and data. Therefore, guests are completely isolated from each other. To confine KVM's user-level companion program, i.e., QEMU, HyperLock limits its system call interface and available resources with system call interposition. By doing so, HyperLock can mediate the runtime interaction between QEMU and KVM by acting as a proxy to forward commands from QEMU to KVM or relay requests from KVM on the opposite direction. The controller

is also designed to provide runtime services to KVM as some tasks cannot be entrusted or delegated to KVM.

2.1 Hypervisor Isolation Runtime

Our first component – the hypervisor isolation runtime – is designed to safely isolate or confine the privileged hosted hypervisor so that even it is compromised, our host can still be protected. Isolation is achieved through two main mechanisms: *memory access control* and *instruction access control*. In the following, we describe each mechanism in detail.

2.1.1 Memory Access Control

To confine the privileged KVM module, we create a separate address space based on the CPU paging mechanism. Before permitting KVM to run, HyperLock switches to the KVM-specific address space by loading the CR3 register with the corresponding page table base address. The KVM-specific page table is maintained by HyperLock and cannot be changed by KVM because we map it read-only inside the KVM address space to facilitate the guest page table update (Section 3.3). We stress that it is critical to make the KVM page table unmodifiable to KVM. Otherwise, a compromised KVM can take advantage of it to access or modify the host OS memory and corrupt the whole system. In our design, we further enforce W⊕X [2] in the KVM address space. That is, there is no memory page in the isolated KVM address space that is simultaneously executable and writable. Also, as there is no legitimate need for KVM to execute any of the guest code, the whole guest memory is marked as non-executable in the KVM address space. In fact, within this address space, only the KVM module contains the executable code (one exception is the trampoline code we introduced to switch the address space from KVM back to the host – Section 2.1.2). By doing so, HyperLock guarantees that *no code inside the isolation runtime can alter its memory layout or change the memory protection settings*.

Within the isolation runtime, KVM can directly read from or write to the guest memory as usual. For performance reasons, it is important to allow KVM access to the guest memory. Specifically, if an I/O instruction executed by the guest is trapped and emulated by KVM, it requires several guest memory accesses for I/O emulation: It has to first traverse the guest page table to convert the guest virtual address to its corresponding guest physical address (which can further be converted to a host address usable by KVM); After that, KVM can then read or write the guest memory again to actually emulate the I/O operation. Because physical memory for the guest is linearly mapped inside the isolation runtime (starting at address zero), guest physical addresses can be directly used by KVM to access guest memory without further conversion.

There also exists a trampoline code inside the isolation runtime to switch the context back to the host, which will be discussed in the second isolation mechanism (Section 2.1.2).

2.1.2 Instruction Access Control

In addition to a separate address space for the hosted KVM hypervisor, we further restrict the instructions that will be allowed to execute within it. This is possible because KVM does not contain any dynamic code, and our memory access control removes the possibility of introducing any new additional code in the isolation runtime. However, challenges arise from the need of executing privileged instructions (of hardware virtualization extension) in the KVM module. For example, KVM needs to execute VMWRITE, a privileged instruction that updates the VM control structure (or VMCS [18]). Though we could potentially replace these VMWRITE instructions with functions to enlist help from HyperLock, the performance overhand could be prohibitively high due to context switching between the isolation runtime and the host kernel.

Existing hardware does not allow granting privileges to individual instructions. Therefore, while still running the KVM code at the highest privilege, there is a need to prevent this privilege from being misused. Specifically, our instruction access control scheme guarantees that *no privileged instructions other than explicitly-allowed ones can be executed within the isolation runtime*. In our prototype, we permit only two privileged instructions, i.e., VMREAD and VMWRITE, for direct execution while re-writing other privileged instructions to rely on the trusted supporting routines in HyperLock (Section 3.3). Note that these two permitted privileged instructions could be executed frequently (e.g., tens of times per VM exit) and it is thus critical to execute them directly to avoid unnecessary context-switching overhead. Moreover, to avoid the highest privilege from being abused, we need to prune the KVM instructions to remove any other "unexpected" privileged ones. Specifically, due to x86's variable length instruction set, it is still possible to uncover "new" or unintended instructions, including privileged ones (e.g., by fetching or interpreting the same memory stream from different offsets [8]). To remove these unintended instructions, we enforce the same instruction

Figure 2. Trampoline Code Layout: Each code fragment starts with a one-byte INT3 and ends with a short JMP, which skips over the next INT3 of the following code fragment. The starting address of the trampoline code is loaded into an IDT entry as the interrupt handler.

alignment rules as in PittSFIeld [23] and Native Client (NaCl) [43] to allow for unambiguous, reliable disassembly of KVM instructions. Specifically, in our prototype, the KVM code is organized and instrumented into equal-length fragments (32 bytes). As a result, no instruction can overlap the fragment boundary. Also, computed (or indirect) control transfers are instrumented so that they can only transfer to fragment boundaries. These two properties ensure that all the instructions that are executable inside the isolation runtime are known at compile time [43]. With that, we can then scan the instrumented code to verify that KVM can only contain the two explicitly-allowed privileged instructions, and not any other privileged ones.

In addition to effectively restricting the instructions allowed to execute within the isolation runtime, our scheme also provides a way to safely return back to the host kernel. This is needed as KVM is now strictly confined in its own address space and will enlist HyperLock for the tasks that cannot be delegated to itself. To achieve that, we design a trampoline that will safely load the CR3 register with the host kernel page table base address. For isolation purposes, the trampoline code also needs to switch a number of critical machine registers, including x86 segment descriptor table (GDT/LDT), interrupt descriptor table (IDT), and task state segment (TSS) [18], which means that a number of critical state registers need to be accessible to KVM. Fortunately, from the trampoline's perspective, these registers are static across the context switches. Therefore, we simply collect them in a separate memory page, mark it read-only to KVM, and make it available to the trampoline code. In other words, as long as we stay inside the isolation runtime, this critical state becomes write-protected.

Because critical hardware state is updated by the trampoline code, we take a step further by ensuring the atomicity of its execution, thus preventing the partial loading of hardware state. Specifically, we ensure that the trampoline code can be entered only from a single entry point inside the isolation runtime, and its execution cannot be interrupted. In our prototype, KVM has to issue a software interrupt (using the INT instruction) to execute the trampoline code and exit the isolation runtime. Hardware interrupts are automatically disabled by the hardware to run the interrupt handler (i.e., the trampoline code) and will not be enabled until it has returned to the host. The handler for this software interrupt is the entry point to the trampoline code. To further make sure it is the only entry point, we need to foil any attempts that jump to the middle of the trampoline code. In our design, we arrange the trampoline akin to the service runtime call in NaCl for this purpose (Figure 2). Specifically, we put a single byte INT3 instruction at the beginning of each code fragment in the trampoline. If executed, this INT3 instruction will immediately cause a debug exception. As mentioned earlier, HyperLock enforces instruction alignment rules for any code running inside KVM. This guarantees that indirect control flow transfers (that may be controlled by the attacker) can only jump to code fragment boundaries. By putting an INT3 instruction at these locations, HyperLock can immediately catch any attempts to subvert the trampoline code (since there is no legitimate code in the original KVM to call the trampoline). On the other hand, legitimate invocation of the trampoline code will not be interrupted by INT3 because a short jump is placed at the end of each code fragment to skip over them. As such, we can effectively ensure a single entry to the trampoline code and the atomicity of its execution.

2.2 HyperLock Controller

Our second component is designed to accomplish three tasks complementary to the first one. Specifically, the first task is to achieve complete guest isolation by duplicating a KVM hypervisor (running inside an isolation runtime) for each guest. Traditionally, a compromised KVM hypervisor immediately brings down all the running guests. By duplicating the hypervisor for each guest and blocking inter-hypervisor communication, we can ensure that a compromised KVM can only take over one guest, not all of them. However, instead of simply duplicating all the hypervisor code and data, which unnecessarily increases memory footprint of our system, we propose a hypervisor shadowing technique by assigning each guest a shadow copy. The shadow copy is virtually duplicated to segregate the hypervisor instances; there is only a single physical copy. This is possible because all the shadow copies share identical (static) hypervisor code, which means we can apply classic copy-on-write or recent memory de-duplication techniques [1] to maintain a single physical copy, thus avoiding additional memory consumption overhead. Each shadow copy still runs within a hypervisor isolation runtime and can legitimately access the memory space of one and only one guest within its own address space.

The second task is to act as a proxy connecting QEMU and the isolated KVM. On one hand (arrow 2 in Figure 1(b)), it accepts ioctl commands from QEMU (e.g. CREATE_VM, CREATE_VCPU, and KVM_RUN) and passes them to KVM via remote procedure calls (RPCs). Our system maintains the same ioctl interface and thus supports the same companion QEMU program without any modification. On the other hand (arrow 3 in Figure 1(b)), HyperLock provides runtime services for tasks that either require interaction with the host OS (e.g. to allocate memory for the guest), or that cannot be safely entrusted to KVM (e.g. to update shadow page tables). Because HyperLock relies on the host OS to implement these runtime services, it is critical to understand the possible impact should KVM be compromised or these services be misused. To proactively mitigate these consequences, our prototype defines a narrow interface that exposes only five well-defined services, which are sufficient to support commodity OSs (including both Linux and Windows XP) as VMs. These five services include (1) map_gfn_to_pfn to convert a guest physical page number (gfn) to the physical page number (pfn) of its backing memory, (2) update_spt/npt to batch-update the shadow page table (spt) or the nested page table (npt), (3) read_msr to read x86 machine-specific registers (MSRs), (4) write_msr to write MSRs, and (5) enter_guest to switch the guest execution into guest mode. In our prototype, we scrutinize possible arguments to these services and block any unexpected values. Furthermore, resources allocated by HyperLock on behalf of each guest will be accounted to that guest to foil any attempts to deplete or misuse resources.

The third task is to reduce the exposed system call interface to the user-level companion program, i.e., QEMU. Specifically, we manually obtain the list of system calls that will be used in QEMU and then define a stand-alone system call table for it. This system call table is populated with only those allowed entries to prevent QEMU from being abused. In addition, we also limit the allowed parameters for each system call and deny anomalous ones. As this technique has been well studied [16, 27], we omit the details here.

3. Implementation

We have implemented a HyperLock prototype to isolate the KVM hypervisor (version 2.6.36.1 with $\sim 33.6K$ SLOC) and QEMU (version 0.14.0 with $> 531K$ SLOC). Our prototype runs on Linux/x86 and has $\sim 4.1K$ SLOC. Specifically, our prototype contains 862 lines of C code for the hypervisor isolation runtime and 270 lines of assembly code for the trampoline that manages the context switches between the host and KVM. The five runtime services take 569 SLOC. The remaining code ($\sim 2.3K$ SLOC) is primarily helper routines to manage the host state, confine QEMU, and support its interaction with KVM. Our current prototype is implemented and evaluated based on a Dell machine (with an Intel Core i7 920 CPU and 3GB memory) running Ubuntu 10.04 LTS and a Linux 2.6.32.31 kernel. In the rest of this section, we present details about our prototype based on the Intel VT [18] hardware virtualization extension. Note that our prototype is implemented on the 32-bit x86 architecture. As we will explain in the paper, new features of the 64-bit x86 architecture (e.g., the interrupt stack table) actually make the implementation less challenging than on the 32-bit architecture.

3.1 Memory Access Control

HyperLock confines the KVM memory access by creating a separate paging-based address space. Within this address space, there are three components: KVM itself, guest memory, and the trampoline code for host and KVM context switches. Among these three components, the memory layout for KVM and our trampoline code do not change after initialization, while the page table entries (PTEs) for guest memory have to be updated on demand (because the guest memory layout and mapping might be changed frequently when the guest is running). To set up these PTEs, KVM needs to notify HyperLock (via the map_gfn_to_pfn service), which then checks whether a page of memory can be successfully allocated for the guest. If it can, HyperLock fills in the corresponding PTE. Otherwise, it returns failure back to KVM. Notice that from the host OS's perspective, the guest is just a normal process, i.e., the QEMU process. Therefore, the guest memory may be swapped out or in by the host OS when under certain memory pressure. To accommodate that, HyperLock needs to synchronize the KVM page table when such events happen. In our prototype, we register an MMU notifier [11] with the host kernel in order to receive notifications of these events. Upon every notification, our prototype will update the affected page table entries in the notification handler and further forward these events to KVM so that KVM can synchronize the SPT/NPT for the guest.

HyperLock's paging based memory access control is relatively straightforward to implement. However, there is one subtlety related to TLB (translation lookaside buffer) in the x86 paging mechanism. To illustrate, TLB is known as a fast cache of virtual to physical address mapping; if a mapping is already cached in TLB, CPU directly returns the mapping without bothering to traverse page tables again to translate it. Also, reloading the CR3 register flushes all TLB entries *except* those for global pages [18], which are being used by Linux to retain TLB entries for kernel memory during the task switching. However, global pages could lead to serious security vulnerabilities in HyperLock. More specifically, because of these global pages, memory mappings for the host kernel will remain in the TLB cache even after switching to the isolation runtime for KVM, which means KVM can exploit the stale cache to access the mapped host OS kernel memory or instructions. As such, the host kernel's memory would be exposed to the untrusted KVM code. In our prototype, we had to disable the global page support in CPU by clearing the PGE bit in the CR4 register before entering the isolation runtime for KVM execution. By doing so, we can ensure that CPU flushes all TLB entries when switching to the KVM address space, thus making host kernel pages inaccessible to KVM. Although disabling the global page support leads to more frequent TLB reloading for kernel memory, the Linux kernel's use of large pages ($2MB$) for kernel memory relieves some

performance overhead. In our prototype, we also considered using the VPID (virtual-processor identifier) feature [18] of Intel-VT. However, we found that the feature cannot be used to avoid disabling global page support, because it is always set to zero in the non-guest mode.

3.2 Instruction Access Control

In addition to memory access control, HyperLock also confines the available instructions inside the isolation runtime. Specifically, we first enforce instruction alignment [23, 43] on the KVM and our trampoline code by compiling them through the Native Client (NaCl) compiler, a customized gcc compiler developed by Google. With the help of instruction alignment, we can then reliably disassemble available code inside the isolation runtime with the assurance of no unintended instructions. As mentioned earlier, our prototype blocks all privileged instructions that can be executed inside the isolation runtime, except VMREAD and VMWRITE for performance reasons. To remove disallowed instructions, we further create a small script to scan the (reliably-disassembled) instructions of KVM and replace every privileged instruction (except VMREAD and VMWRITE) with a call to the corresponding runtime service.

Based on Intel VT, each guest is associated with a VMCS memory page that contains 148 fields to control the behavior of both the host and the guest. These fields can be roughly divided into four categories: *host state*, *VM execution control*, *guest state*, and *VM exit info*. Generally speaking, the first two categories need to be handled by trusted code because they can critically affect the host behavior. For example, HOST_RIP specifies the instruction CPU will return to after a VM exit; and EPT_POINTER stores the address of EPT/NPT table for the guest. In our prototype, we directly handle them outside the isolation runtime. Our development experience indicates that KVM handles these VMCS fields in a rather simple way: Most of these fields involve just loading the host state directly into its corresponding VMCS field, and will never change after the initial setup. Fields belong to the latter two categories can be safely delegated to untrusted KVM since they reflect the guest VM's state. For example, VM_EXIT_REASON gives the reason that caused the VM exit; and GUEST_CS_SELECTOR contains the current CS segment selector for the guest. Unlike host state and VM execution control fields, these fields are frequently retrieved and updated by KVM during each VM exit. For performance reasons, we would like to grant KVM direct access to guest state and VM exit information while preventing it from touching any other fields relating to host state or VM execution control. That is also the reason why our prototype makes an exception for the VMREAD and VMWRITE instructions.

To avoid these two instructions from being misused, our prototype takes the following precautions: First, we prevent KVM from directly accessing VMCS memory. Specifically, Intel VT requires that *physical address* of VMCS must

```
movl     $0xc00195d7,      %eax
movl     $GUEST_EIP,       %edx
vmwrite  %eax,             %edx
```

Figure 3. A VMWRITE macro-instruction that writes 0xc00195d7 into the GUEST_EIP VMCS field.

be loaded to CPU before software can access its fields with VMREAD and VMWRITE. However, nothing prevents attackers from directly overwriting its fields if the VMCS is virtually mapped in the KVM address space. As such, HyperLock allocates VMCS for the guest outside of the isolation runtime, and loads its physical address to CPU before entering the KVM. The VMCS structure itself is not mapped inside the KVM address space, therefore attackers cannot manipulate its fields by directly changing the VMCS. Meanwhile, the CPU has no problem executing the VMREAD and VMWRITE instructions because it uses a *physical address* to access the VMCS. Second, both the VMREAD and VMWRITE instructions take a VMCS field index as a parameter. Our prototype ensures that only fields belonging to guest state and VM exit information can be passed to them. More specifically, we define two macro-instructions (similar to nacljmp in NaCl [43]) for VMREAD and VMWRITE as shown in Figure 3. Each macro-instruction first fetches the hard-coded field index from KVM's code section (which is read-only, because it is protected by $W \oplus X$) into a register, then passes the register directly to VMREAD or VMWRITE. Further, we verify that the macro-instructions (each 17 bytes long) cannot overlap a fragment boundary (32 bytes) to block attackers from jumping into the middle of macro-instructions. There is a subtlety here: if an attacker is able to interrupt the CPU right before a VMWRITE, he might maliciously modify the register content saved by the interrupt handler. When the interrupt handler returns, registers are restored and the malicious field index gets used by VMWRITE. HyperLock avoids this problem because the trampoline handles the interrupt context, so it is not accessible to KVM. Finally, our script to scan KVM's assembly code also makes sure that only fields pertaining to guest state and VM exit information can be passed to these two macro-instructions.

The trampoline code for host and KVM context switches is also worth mentioning. To prevent KVM from monopolizing the CPU and to ensure a timely response to hardware interrupts, we need to enable interrupt delivery while KVM is running. Specifically, the trampoline code contains a handler for each exception or interrupt. The handler for a hardware interrupt first switches to the host OS and redirects control to the host OS's corresponding interrupt handler (defined in the host IDT table). Execution of the KVM will resume after host interrupt handler returns. The handler for an exception, which is caused by error conditions in the KVM, instead switches to the host OS and then immediately terminates the VM after dumping the KVM's state for

auditing and debugging purposes. Under normal conditions, KVM should never cause exceptions, in particular, page faults: updates to the guest memory mapping by the host OS (e.g., paging out a block of memory) are synchronized to KVM through an MMU notifier [11]. When the need arises for KVM to access guest memory, it proactively calls the map_gfn_to_pfn service to read in the page, thus avoiding page faults.

At first glance, enabling interrupt delivery while KVM runs may only require setting up the IDT (Interrupt Descriptor Table). However, one quirk of the x86 architecture makes this more complicated than it should be: when an interrupt happens, the CPU will save the current state (such as EIP, ESP, and EFLAGS) to the stack so that it can resume the execution of the interrupted task. Because the sandbox is running at the highest privilege (ring 0), this state is saved to the current stack, which could then be manipulated by the attacker to launch a denial of service attack on the *32-bit* x86 platform. For example, a double fault will be triggered if the attacker manages to set the stack pointer ESP to an invalid (unmapped or write-protected) memory address and then write to the stack. The first write to the stack will cause a page fault. To handle the page fault, CPU tries to push more content to the *invalid* stack, which will lead to a second page fault. This time, CPU throws a double fault instead of more page faults. However, the stack pointer remains invalid for the double fault handler. Eventually, the CPU can only be recovered by power-cycling the machine. An astute reader may point out that we can switch to an interrupt task (thus a known-good stack) through task gate for an interrupt handler, and it has been used by Linux to handle double faults. Unfortunately, task gate cannot be securely deployed inside the isolation runtime where untrusted code runs. Specifically, to switch to an interrupt task, CPU uses a data structure called the TSS (task state segment) descriptor that specifies where to load CPU state information from, including CR3, EIP and ESP. Therefore, it is critical to write-protect the TSS descriptor. However, this structure cannot be write-protected in this case because CPU needs to change the descriptor's B (busy) bit *from zero to one* before switching to the interrupt task. Write-protecting the TSS descriptor will lead to another undesirable situation where the CPU can only be recovered by a hardware reset.

To accommodate that in 32-bit x86 architecture, our system always keeps a valid ESP to foil such attacks. Specifically, we allocate three continuous memory pages ($12KB$ total) at a *fixed* location in the KVM address space: the middle page is used for the stack itself (the same size as the stack in recent Linux kernels), while the top and bottom pages are used as overflow space. At the compiling time, we instrument the instructions that change ESP to maintain the stack location invariant by replacing the page number part (top 20 bits) of ESP to that of the pre-allocated stack (the middle page). This can be implemented with an AND

Runtime Service	SLOC
`map_gfn_to_pfn`	84
`update_spt/npt`	251
`read_msr, write_msr`	156
`enter_guest`	78

Table 1. The breakdown of HyperLock's runtime service implementation. `read_msr` and `write_msr` are implemented together. `enter_guest` includes 53 lines of inline assembly code and 25 lines of C code.

instruction (6 bytes) and an OR instruction (6 bytes). Both of them take a 4-byte constant and ESP as operands. As such, no scratch registers are required for this instrumentation. Moreover, to prevent the check from being circumvented, the check and its related instruction are kept in the same fragment (A similar inline software guard to prevent stack overflow was also explored in XFI [13].) HyperLock support for 64-bit x86 architecture will not suffer from the same issue because the CPU can be programmed to always switch to a known-good stack for interrupt handling with the help of a new feature called IST (interrupt stack table) [18].

3.3 Others

To properly isolate the KVM hypervisor, HyperLock also exposes a narrow interface to five well-defined runtime services to KVM. All these five services were implemented in a small number of lines of source code (Table 1). Among them, `update_spt/npt` is the most involved as it is directly related to the memory virtualization in KVM. For a concrete example, we use hardware assisted memory virtualization (NPT) to describe how `update_spt/npt` is implemented.

With NPT support, the CPU uses two page tables to translate a guest virtual address to the corresponding physical address: a guest page table (GPT) to convert a guest virtual address to a guest physical address, and a nested page table (NPT) to further convert a guest physical address to the (actual) physical address. The guest kernel has full control over GPT, while KVM is responsible for maintaining the NPT. Since NPT maps physical memory into the guest, only the trusted NPT should be loaded to CPU for guest address translation. In HyperLock, KVM still maintains its own NPT for the guest. However, this NPT is not used for address translation. Instead, HyperLock creates a mirror of the NPT outside the hypervisor isolation runtime to translate guest addresses. The NPT table and its mirror are synchronized via `update_npt` calls. In `update_npt`, HyperLock ensures that *only physical pages belonging to this guest will be mapped to the guest*. Noticing that the guest memory is mapped in the hypervisor isolation runtime with the (HyperLock-maintained) KVM page table, this guarantee can be efficiently achieved using the KVM page table. More specifically, KVM provides a guest physical page number and its memory protection attributes as parameters to `update_npt`. In this function, HyperLock traverses the

KVM page table to find the physical page for this guest physical page and combine it with the memory protection attributes to update the corresponding page table entry in the NPT mirror. Moreover, the KVM page table is made available to KVM (by mapping it read-only in the KVM address space) so that KVM can use it to maintain its own NPT in the same way.

Overall, to isolate KVM with the proposed hypervisor isolation runtime, our prototype re-organizes KVM in a slightly different way. However, our modification to KVM is minor and focuses on three areas. First, the original `ioctl` based communication interface between KVM and QEMU is replaced by our RPC calls through HyperLock, which results in changing six `ioctl` functions in KVM (e.g., `kvm_dev_ioctl`, `kvm_vm_ioctl`, etc.). Second, we replace certain dangerous KVM calls with RPCs to runtime services, which results in changing eight functions in KVM. As an example, the original KVM's function (`__set_spte`) that writes directly to shadow page table entries is replaced by the `update_spt` service. Third, we also need to reduce one file, i.e., `vmx.c`, to avoid changing host state and VM execution control fields of VMCS in KVM. Instead, functions that access these two categories are moved to HyperLock while the rest stays the same. Our experience shows these changes (1) are mainly one-time effort as they essentially abstract the underlying interaction with hardware, which remains stable over the time, and (2) do not involve the bulk KVM code, which could undergo significant changes in future releases.

4. Evaluation

In this section, we present our evaluation results by first analyzing the security guarantees provided by HyperLock. After that, we report the performance overhead with several standard benchmarks.

4.1 Security Analysis

Based on our threat model (Section 2), an attacker starts from a compromised guest and aims to escape from HyperLock's isolation and further take over the host OS or control other guests (by exploiting vulnerabilities in KVM or QEMU). In HyperLock, we create a separate system call table for the QEMU process to constrain system calls available to it and validate their parameters. The security guarantee provided by such a system call interposition mechanism has been well studied [16, 27, 40]. In the following, we focus our analysis on the threats from a (compromised) KVM hypervisor when it aims to break out of HyperLock confinement.

Breaking Memory Access Control The first set of attacks aims to subvert memory protection in the isolation runtime to inject malicious code or modify important data structures, especially (read-only) control data in the trampoline. Since $W \oplus X$ is enforced in the isolation runtime, any attempt to directly overwrite their memory will immediately trigger a page fault and further cause the guest to be terminated by HyperLock. Having failed direct memory manipulation, the attacker may try to disable $W \oplus X$ protection by altering the KVM page table. Since the KVM page table is not directly changeable in the isolation runtime, the attacker has to leverage the trusted HyperLock code to manipulate the KVM page table. Fortunately, HyperLock will never change memory attributes for the (static) trampoline and KVM after initial setup, and the whole guest memory is marked as non-executable. Another possibility is for the attacker to trick HyperLock to map the host or HyperLock memory (e.g. host page table) into the isolation runtime or a malicious guest as (writable) guest memory. Sanity checks in the map_gfn_to_pfn and update_spt/npt service would prevent this from happening.

Subverting Instruction Access Control   Since the hypervisor isolation runtime has the highest privilege, it is critical to prevent attackers from executing arbitrary privileged instructions. With the protection of $W \oplus X$ and instruction alignment, the attackers cannot inject code or uncover "new" instructions based on legitimate ones. Instead, they would have to target existing legitimate privileged instructions in the isolation runtime, for example, to maliciously modify host state or VM execution control fields in the VMCS by exploiting the field index parameter of the VMWRITE instruction (Figure 3). Notice that hard coding the field index (GUEST_EIP in Figure 3) and instruction alignment alone can *not* prevent misuse of the VMWRITE instruction. This is because that the second (fetching the field index into a register) and third instructions (executing VMWRITE) can be separated by an instruction fragment boundary. In other words, VMWRITE is the first instruction in an instruction fragment. With the capability to jump to any instruction fragment boundary under the instruction alignment rule, the attacker can directly jump to the VMWRITE instruction after loading the edx register with a malicious field index. This attack is prevented in HyperLock by ensuring that the three-instruction sequence (17 bytes) in Figure 3 cannot overlap any fragment boundary, thus ensuring VMWRITE and VMREAD always receive the fixed known-good field index parameters.

Another source of legitimate privileged instruction is the trampoline code (to load CR3 etc). Similar to the VMWRITE instruction, it is necessary for HyperLock to prevent the attacker from jumping to the middle of the trampoline code. Unfortunately, the trampoline code (about $4K$ bytes) cannot fit in a single instruction fragment. In HyperLock, we set up a one-byte INT3 instruction at each fragment boundary of the trampoline code to capture direct jumps to the middle of the trampoline. Moreover, the execution of the trampoline cannot be disrupted by KVM because interrupts are disabled by the hardware and will not be enabled until the trampoline has safely returned to the host.

The attacker may also try to perform a denial of service attack by corrupting the interrupt stack (Section 3.2). Such

Name	Version	Configuration
Bonnie++	1.03*e*	`bonnie++ -f`
Kernel (61MB) build	2.6.32.39	`make defconfig;make`
SPEC CPU 2006	1.0.1	`reportable int`
Ubuntu desktop	10.04.2 LTS	Linux-2.6.32.31
Ubuntu server	10.04.2 LTS	Linux-2.6.32.28

Table 2. Software Packages used in Our Evaluation

attempts will be foiled by the runtime check before the ESP-changing instructions. Similar to the VMWRITE instruction, the runtime check and its following instruction that modifies ESP cannot overlap the fragment boundary. Therefore, the runtime check cannot be bypassed by the attacker.

Misusing HyperLock Services   Another set of targets for the attacker is the five services provided to KVM by HyperLock. Since they can directly access the host OS, we have sanity checks in place to prevent these services from being misused. For example, we validate that only guest memory can be mapped by the update_spt/npt services, and map_gfn_to_pfn can never allocate more memory than that specified by the user when starting the VM. Moreover, as shown in Table 1, these services have a small code base (569 SLOC) and therefore can be thoroughly reviewed and verified to remove vulnerabilities.

Case Studies   To better understand the protection provided by HyperLock, we examine several real-world vulnerabilities from NVD [25] and show how HyperLock could mitigate these threats. The first vulnerability we examined is CVE-2010-3881, a kernel-level bug in KVM in which data structures are copied to user space with padding and reserved fields uninitialized. This bug could potentially lead to leaking of sensitive content on the kernel stack. Under HyperLock, the host OS is not directly accessible to KVM and each guest is paired with its own KVM instance. Therefore, only data related to the guest itself could be leaked to it. The second vulnerability we examined is CVE-2010-0435, in which a malicious guest can crash the host by causing a NULL pointer dereference in KVM's x86 emulator. Under HyperLock, this vulnerability could be similarly exploited by the guest and trigger an exception. However, instead of crashing the host, HyperLock would terminate only the KVM instance paired with this guest (Section 3.2). The last vulnerability we examined is CVE-2011-4127, a bug related to device emulation in QEMU in which a guest can gain access to the data of other guests that reside on the same physical device due to insufficient checks of the SCSI ioctl commands. Under HyperLock, this vulnerability could be mitigated by system call introspection on QEMU.

4.2   Performance Evaluation

To evaluate the performance overhead caused by Hyper-Lock, we test the guest performance with several standard benchmarks, including SPEC CPU 2006 [33], Bonnie++ (a

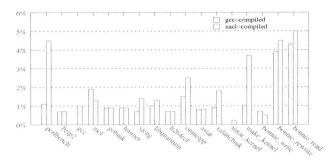

Figure 4. Normalized Overhead of HyperLock

file system performance benchmark) [9], and two application benchmarks (Linux kernel decompression and compilation). Our test platform is based on the Dell XPS studio desktop with a 2.67GHz Intel Core™ i7 CPU and 3GB memory. The host runs a default installation of Ubuntu 10.04 LTS desktop with the 2.6.32.31 kernel. The guest is based on the standard Ubuntu 10.04 LTS server edition. Table 2 lists the software packages and configurations used in our experiments. Among these benchmarks, SPEC CPU 2006, kernel decompression are CPU intensive tasks, while the other two tests (kernel compilation and Bonnie++) are more intensive in I/O accesses. For the kernel decompression and compilation test, we run the tests in the guest with the `time` command, and reported the sum of system and user time. As a result, these two experiments are based on the virtual time and due to the difficulty of keeping exact time in the guest OS [37], they could be less accurate. However, we did not observe clock drift during our experiments.

In our evaluation, we repeated the experiments with three different KVM configurations: the vanilla KVM, the gcc-compiled KVM under HyperLock, and the NaCl-compiled KVM under HyperLock. Comparing the performance of gcc- and NaCl-compiled KVM allows us to separate the effects of memory access control (switching between address spaces) and instruction access control (instruction alignment). As shown in Figure 4, the overall performance overhead introduced by HyperLock is less than 5%. Moreover, the gcc-compiled system has better performance than the NaCl-compiled system in most tests except mcf and Bonnie++ write. Generally speaking, instruction alignment will increase the binary size and reduce the performance because of additional code (mostly NOPs) inserted to align instructions. For example, the NaCl-compiled KVM in HyperLock contains 99, 695 instructions, 265% more than the gcc-compiled version's 37, 553 instructions. Also, 91.2% (56, 713 out of 62, 142) of the added instructions are NOPs. Meanwhile, due to complex interaction of instruction alignment, instruction cache and TLB, the NaCl-compiled system may actually perform better than the gcc-compiled system [43].

To better understand the performance of HyperLock, we measured the latency of context switching between the host

OS and hypervisor isolation runtime in HyperLock. Specifically, we created a null RPC in the isolation runtime that did nothing but returned directly back to the host, then called this function 1, 000, 000 times from the host OS and calculated the average latency of round trip to the isolation runtime. Our results show that each round trip to the isolation runtime costs about 953 ns, or 45% of that to the guest mode (2, 115 ns). The performance overhead of HyperLock is directly related to the frequency of context switches to the isolation runtime, which is further determined by the frequency of VM exits as illustrated by Figure 1 (at runtime, arrows 3, 4, 5, and 2 form the most active execution path). Advances in both hardware virtualization support (e.g., EPT [18]) and hypervisor software (e.g., para-virtualized devices [29]) have significantly reduced the number of necessary VM exits. For example, the average number of VM exits for the kernel compilation benchmark is 4, 913 per second. Also, the latency of address space switch in 64-bit x86 architecture could be significantly reduced by using a new CPU feature called process-context identifier (PCID) [18]. When PCID is enabled, the CPU tags each TLB entry with the current process-context id, thus rendering it unnecessary to flush all the TLB entries during an address space switch. However, we must still disable global page support (Section 3.1) because TLB entries for global pages are shared by all the address spaces even though PCID is enabled.

5. Discussion

In this section, we re-visit our system design and explore possible alternatives for either enhancement or justification. First, HyperLock confines KVM with its own paging-based memory space, *not* segmentation. Though segmentation could potentially provide another viable choice (especially in 32-bit x86 architecture), in HyperLock, we are in favor of paging for two reasons. (1) The 64-bit x86 architecture does not fully support segmentation [18]. Using paging can make HyperLock compatible with both the 32-bit and 64-bit x86 architectures. (2) Paging provides more flexible control over the layout and protection (e.g., *readable*, *writable*, or *executable*) of our isolation runtime. For example, our system maps the guest physical memory starting at address zero, which allows a guest physical address to be directly used by KVM to access guest memory without further address translation. While segmentation may limit memory access to a continuous range, unnecessary components (e.g., system libraries) could be loaded in the middle of this range and cannot be excluded from the segment.

Second, for performance reasons, HyperLock allows KVM to retain and execute two privileged instructions, i.e., `VMREAD` and `VMWRITE`. This design choice significantly affects the design of hypervisor isolation runtime for KVM confinement. Particularly, because KVM is still privileged, it is critical to prevent it from executing any unwanted privileged instructions, either intended or unintended [8].

Also, certain x86 architecture peculiarities complicate the design for safe context switches between the host and KVM, which will be invoked by the unsafe KVM. If it runs non-privileged, the design would be much simpler and straightforward. On the other hand, we may choose to run KVM at ring-3 by further replacing these two privileged instructions with runtime services. The use of runtime services is necessary because Intel VT mandates accessing the VMCS with the `VMREAD` and `VMWRITE` instructions as the format of the VMCS is not architecturally defined [18]. Thus, it is not feasible to simply map the VMCS in the KVM address space and use memory move instructions to access it. The overhead of frequent VMCS access through runtime services could potentially be reduced though pre-fetching VMCS reads and batch-processing VMCS writes. As such, this design and HyperLock offer different design trade-offs. We leave further consideration of the implications of this choice to future work.

Third, HyperLock enforces instruction alignment [23, 43] to prevent unintended instructions from being generated out of legitimate ones. Alternatively, we can enforce control-flow integrity (CFI) [3, 39] on KVM inside the isolation runtime to provide a stronger security guarantee, especially in eliminating recent return-oriented programming (ROP)-based code-reuse attacks [8]. However, one challenge behind CFI enforcement is the lack of an accurate and complete points-to analysis tool that could be readily applied to KVM. From another perspective, the lack of CFI does not weaken our security guarantee because by design the isolation runtime is not trusted and has been strictly confined within its own address space. In HyperLock, for ease of implementation, we choose to enforce the instruction alignment and combine it with other instruction/memory access control mechanisms to meet our design goal of isolating hosted hypervisors.

Finally, our current prototype defines a narrow interface that exposes five runtime services to support guests with virtual devices. A few more runtime services could be added to incorporate new functionality. For example, our current prototype does not support multi-core VMs, which could be accommodated by adding a new service to handle Inter-Processor Interrupts (IPIs). For the current lack of hardware pass-through support, we can develop a new service to request and release a PCI device on demand and accordingly manage `IOMMUs` [18] to enforce hardware isolation (e.g., to block DMA-based attacks). Further, a service to release guest memory back to the host OS might also be needed to support a balloon driver for cooperative memory management. However, as mentioned earlier, the number of added services should be kept to a minimum and scrutinized to avoid being abused (as they will be considered as part of the HyperLock TCB). Furthermore, our prototype implements `update_spt/npt` by mirroring the corresponding KVM data structure. This makes the

prototype relatively simpler to implement by trading off extra memory. This additional memory could be reclaimed in future enhancements to the prototype by sharing the SPT/NPT between HyperLock (readable and writable) and KVM (read-only).

6. Related Work

Hypervisor Integrity   The first area of related work is recent efforts in enforcing or measuring the hypervisor integrity. By applying formal verification, seL4 provides strong security guarantees that certain types of vulnerabilities can never exist in a micro-kernel. However, its application to protect commodity hypervisors that run on complex x86 hardware still remains to be demonstrated [30]. HyperSafe [39] enables the self-protection of bare-metal hypervisors by enforcing CFI. However, certain design choices in the host OS make it difficult to be applied to hosted hypervisors. For example, HyperSafe implicitly assumes infrequent updates to page tables in the supported bare-metal hypervisors, which is not the case in commodity OSs (and hosted hypervisors). Moreover, it is important for HyperLock to isolate memory writes from untrusted hypervisors, which cannot be achieved by CFI alone because CFI can only regulate the *control data* access. NoHype [36] removes the (type-I) hypervisor layer by leveraging the virtualization extension to processors and I/O devices. Due to tight coupling between the host OS and the (hosted) hypervisor, NoHype cannot be directly applied to protect hosted hypervisors. The Turtles project [6] and Graf et al. [17] implement nested virtualization support for KVM. However, in these systems, KVM, particularly the (lowest-level) L0 hypervisor, is still tightly integrated with the host (including the sharing of the same address space). As such, HyperLock can be used in these systems to better achieve the isolation of the lowest-level L0 hypervisor. From another perspective, HyperSentry [4] measures the hypervisor for integrity violations using the system management mode (SMM), which has a different goal from HyperLock.

There also exist related efforts in reducing the hypervisor TCB, often adopting the micro-kernel principles. For example, NOVA [34] applies the micro-kernel approach to build a bare-metal hypervisor. Xoar [10] also applies the approach to partition the control domain (of type-I hypervisors) into single-purpose components. Xen disaggregation [24] shrinks the TCB for Xen by moving the privileged domain builder to a minimal trusted component. KVM-L4 [26] extends a micro-kernel with CPU and memory virtualization to efficiently support virtual machines. Compared to these systems, HyperLock focuses on the isolation of *hosted* hypervisors by replacing the hypervisor's TCB in the host kernel with the smaller (12%) and simpler HyperLock code.

Device Driver Isolation   The second area of related work includes systems that isolate faults or malicious behaviors in device drivers. For example, Nooks [35] improves OS reliability by isolating device drivers in the light-weight kernel protection domain. Nooks assumes the drivers to be faulty but not malicious. Accordingly, the Nooks sandbox by design lacks instruction access control and malicious drivers cannot be completely isolated by Nooks. A closely related system is SUD [7] that can securely confine malicious device drivers in the user space. SUD relies on IOMMU, transaction filtering in PCI express bridges, and IO permission bits in TSS to securely grant user space device drivers direct access to hardware. However, SUD cannot be applied to the hosted hypervisors such as KVM simply because that hardware virtualization extension (e.g., Intel VT) is not constrained by the IOMMU or other hardware mechanisms that SUD relies on. Microdrivers [15] reduces device driver's TCB in the kernel by slicing the driver into a privileged performance-critical kernel part and the remaining unprivileged user part. RVM [41] executes device drivers in the user space and uses a reference monitor to validate interactions between a driver and its corresponding device. In HyperLock, we securely confine the privileged KVM code in the hypervisor isolation runtime. Gateway [32], HUKO [42], and SIM [31] are systems that use a hypervisor (e.g., KVM) to isolate kernel device drivers or security monitors. We did not take this approach because otherwise we will face the recursive question of how to isolate the hypervisor that runs at the lowest level.

Software Fault Isolation The third area of related work is a series of prior efforts [3, 13, 14, 23, 38, 43] in implementing SFI to confine untrusted code in a host application. For example, PittSFIeld [23] and Native Client [43] both apply instruction alignment to enable the reliable disassembly of untrusted code. CFI [3] constrains runtime control flow to a statically determined control flow graph. Among them, Native Client is closely related but with a different application domain in leveraging user-level SFI to web plugins. As a kernel-level isolation environment, HyperLock needs to address challenges that arise from the needs of enforcing access control of privileged instructions and supporting x86 hardware architecture peculiarities (Section 3). XFI [13] and LXFI [22] are two closely related works. Based on CFI and data sandboxing, XFI combines inline software guards and a two-stack execution model to isolate system software. LXFI ensures API integrity and establishes module principals to partition and isolate device drivers. In comparison, HyperLock focuses on the secure isolation of hosted hypervisors and needs to address additional challenges that are unique to virtualization, such as how to prevent VMWRITE from being misused or how to securely support memory virtualization. To the best of our knowledge, HyperLock is the first system that has been designed and implemented to confine hosted hypervisors so that the host OS and other guests can be protected.

7. Conclusion

We have presented the design, implementation and evaluation of HyperLock, a system that establishes secure isolation of hosted hypervisors. Specifically, we confine the hypervisor execution in the isolation runtime with a separated address space and a constrained instruction set. Moreover, we create a logically separated hypervisor for each guest, thus ensuring a compromised hypervisor can only affect its own guest. We have implemented a prototype of HyperLock for the popular open source KVM hypervisor. The prototype is only 12% of KVM's code size, and further completely removes QEMU from the TCB (of the host and other guests). Security analysis and performance benchmarks show that HyperLock can efficiently provide the intended isolation.

Acknowledgments

We would like to deeply thank our shepherd, Hermann Härtig, and the anonymous reviewers for their numerous, insightful comments that greatly helped improve the presentation of this paper. This work was supported in part by the US Army Research Office (ARO) under grant W911NF-08-1-0105 managed by NCSU Secure Open Systems Initiative (SOSI) and the US National Science Foundation (NSF) under Grants 0855297, 0855036, 0910767, and 0952640. Any opinions, findings, and conclusions or recommendations expressed in this material are those of the authors and do not necessarily reflect the views of the ARO and the NSF.

References

[1] Kernel Samepage Merging. http://lwn.net/Articles/330589/.

[2] W∧X. http://en.wikipedia.org/wiki/W∧X.

[3] ABADI, M., BUDIU, M., ERLINGSSON, U., AND LIGATTI, J. Control-Flow Integrity: Principles, Implementations, and Applications. In *Proceedings of the 12th ACM Conference on Computer and Communications Security* (November 2005).

[4] AZAB, A. M., NING, P., WANG, Z., JIANG, X., ZHANG, X., AND SKALSKY, N. C. HyperSentry: Enabling Stealthy In-context Measurement of Hypervisor Integrity. In *Proceedings of the 17th ACM Conference on Computer and Communications Security* (October 2010).

[5] BARHAM, P., DRAGOVIC, B., FRASER, K., HAND, S., HARRIS, T. L., HO, A., NEUGEBAUER, R., PRATT, I., AND WARFIELD, A. Xen and the Art of Virtualization. In *Proceedings of the 19th ACM Symposium on Operating Systems Principles* (October 2003).

[6] BEN-YEHUDA, M., DAY, M. D., DUBITZKY, Z., FACTOR, M., HAREL, N., GORDON, A., LIGUORI, A., WASSERMAN, O., AND YASSOUR, B.-A. The Turtles Project: Design and Implementation of Nested Virtualization. In *Proceedings of the 9th USENIX Symposium on Operating Systems Design and Implementation* (October 2010).

[7] BOYD-WICKIZER, S., AND ZELDOVICH, N. Tolerating Malicious Device Drivers in Linux. In *Proceedings of the*

2010 USENIX Annual Technical Conference (June 2010).

[8] BUCHANAN, E., ROEMER, R., SHACHAM, H., AND SAVAGE, S. When Good Instructions Go Bad: Generalizing Return-Oriented Programming to RISC. In *Proceedings of the 15th ACM Conference on Computer and Communications Security* (October 2008).

[9] COKER, R. Bonnie++. `http://www.coker.com.au/bonnie++/`.

[10] COLP, P., NANAVATI, M., ZHU, J., AIELLO, W., COKER, G., DEEGAN, T., LOSCOCCO, P., AND WARFIELD, A. Breaking Up is Hard to Do: Security and Functionality in a Commodity Hypervisor. In *Proceedings of the 23rd ACM Symposium on Operating Systems Principles* (October 2011).

[11] CORBET, J. Memory Management Notifiers. http://lwn.net/Articles/266320/.

[12] ELHAGE, N. Virtualization Under Attack: Breaking out of KVM. `http://www.blackhat.com/html/bh-us-11/bh-us-11-briefings.html`.

[13] ERLINGSSON, U., VALLEY, S., ABADI, M., VRABLE, M., BUDIU, M., AND NECULA, G. C. XFI: Software Guards for System Address Spaces. In *Proceedings of the 7th USENIX Symposium on Operating Systems Design and Implementation* (November 2006).

[14] FORD, B., AND COX, R. Vx32: Lightweight User-level Sandboxing on the x86. In *Proceedings of 2008 USENIX Annual Technical Conference* (June 2008).

[15] GANAPATHY, V., RENZELMANN, M. J., BALAKRISHNAN, A., SWIFT, M. M., AND JHA, S. The Design and Implementation of Microdrivers. In *Proceedings of the 13th International Conference on Architectural Support for Programming Languages and Operating Systems* (March 2008).

[16] GARFINKEL, T. Traps and Pitfalls: Practical Problems in System Call Interposition Based Security Tools. In *Proceedings of the 20th Annual Network and Distributed Systems Security Symposium* (February 2003).

[17] GRAF, A., AND ROEDEL, J. Nesting the Virtualized World. Linux Plumbers Conference, September 2009.

[18] INTEL. *Intel 64 and IA-32 Architectures Software Developer's Manual Volume 3: System Programming Guide, Part 1 and Part 2*, 2010.

[19] KIVITY, A., KAMAY, Y., LAOR, D., LUBLIN, U., AND LIGUORI, A. kvm: the Linux Virtual Machine Monitor. In *Proceedings of the 2007 Ottawa Linux Symposium* (June 2007).

[20] KLEIN, G., ELPHINSTONE, K., HEISER, G., ANDRONICK, J., COCK, D., DERRIN, P., ELKADUWE, D., ENGELHARDT, K., KOLANSKI, R., NORRISH, M., SEWELL, T., TUCH, H., AND WINWOOD, S. seL4: Formal Verification of an OS Kernel. In *Proceedings of the 22nd ACM Symposium on Operating Systems Principles* (October 2009).

[21] KORTCHINSKY, K. CLOUDBURST: A VMware Guest to Host Escape Story. `http://www.blackhat.com/presentations/bh-usa-09/KORTCHINSKY/BHUSA09-Kortchinsky-Cloudburst-SLIDES.pdf`.

[22] MAO, Y., CHEN, H., ZHOU, D., , WANG, X., ZELDOVICH, N., AND KAASHOEK, M. F. Software Fault Isolation with API Integrity and Multi-principal Modules. In *Proceedings of the 23rd ACM Symposium on Operating Systems Principles* (October 2011).

[23] MCCAMANT, S., AND MORRISETT, G. Evaluating SFI for a CISC architecture. In *Proceedings of the 15th conference on USENIX Security Symposium* (July 2006).

[24] MURRAY, D. G., MILOS, G., AND HAND, S. Improving Xen Security through Disaggregation. In *Proceedings of the 4th ACM SIGPLAN/SIGOPS International Conference on Virtual Execution Environments* (March 2008).

[25] National Vulnerability Database. http://nvd.nist.gov/.

[26] PETER, M., SCHILD, H., LACKORZYNSKI, A., AND WARG, A. Virtual Machines Jailed: Virtualization in Systems with Small Trusted Computing Bases. In *Proceedings of the 1st EuroSys Workshop on Virtualization Technology for Dependable Systems* (March 2009).

[27] PROVOS, N. Improving Host Security with System Call Policies. In *Proceedings of the 12th Usenix Security Symposium* (August 2002).

[28] RED HAT. KVM: Kernel-based Virtual Machine. www.redhat.com/f/pdf/rhev/DOC-KVM.pdf.

[29] RUSSELL, R. Virtio: Towards a De-facto Standard for Virtual I/O Devices. *ACM SIGOPS Operating Systems Review 42*, 5 (2008).

[30] RUTKOWSKA, J. On Formally Verified Microkernels (and on attacking them). `http://theinvisiblethings.blogspot.com/2010/05/on-formally-verified-microkernels-and.html`.

[31] SHARIF, M., LEE, W., CUI, W., AND LANZI, A. Secure In-VM Monitoring Using Hardware Virtualization. In *Proceedings of the 16th ACM Conference on Computer and Communications Security* (November 2009).

[32] SRIVASTAVA, A., AND GIFFIN, J. Efficient Monitoring of Untrusted Kernel-Mode Execution. In *Proceedings of the 18th Annual Network and Distributed System Security Symposium* (February 2011).

[33] STANDARD PERFORMANCE EVALUATION CORPORATION. SPEC CPU2006. `http://www.spec.org/cpu2006`.

[34] STEINBERG, U., AND KAUER, B. NOVA: a Microhypervisor-based Secure Virtualization Architecture. In *Proceedings of the 5th European Conference on Computer Systems* (April 2010).

[35] SWIFT, M. M., BERSHAD, B. N., AND LEVY, H. M. Improving the Reliability of Commodity Operating Systems. In *Proceedings of the 19th ACM symposium on Operating Systems Principles* (October 2003).

[36] SZEFER, J., KELLER, E., LEE, R. B., AND REXFORD, J. Eliminating the Hypervisor Attack Surface for a More Secure Cloud. In *Proceedings of the 18th ACM Conference on Computer and Communications Security* (October 2011).

[37] VMWARE. Timekeeping in VMware Virtual Machines. `http://www.vmware.com/files/pdf/Timekeeping-In-VirtualMachines.pdf`.

[38] WAHBE, R., LUCCO, S., ANDERSON, T. E., AND GRAHAM, S. L. Efficient Software-based Fault Isolation. In *Proceedings of the 14th ACM Symposium On Operating System Principles* (December 1993).

[39] WANG, Z., AND JIANG, X. HyperSafe: A Lightweight Approach to Provide Lifetime Hypervisor Contr ol-Flow Integrity. In *Proceedings of the 31st IEEE Symposium on Security and Privacy* (May 2010).

[40] WATSON, R. N. M., ANDERSON, J., LAURIE, B., AND KENNAWAY, K. Capsicum: Practical Capabilities for UNIX. In *Proceedings of the 19th USENIX Security Symposium* (August 2010).

[41] WILLIAMS, D., REYNOLDS, P., WALSH, K., SIRER, E. G., AND SCHNEIDER, F. B. Device Driver Safety through a Reference Validation Mechanism. In *Proceedings of the 8th USENIX Conference on Operating Systems Design and Implementation* (December 2008).

[42] XIONG, X., TIAN, D., AND LIU, P. Practical Protection of Kernel Integrity for Commodity OS from Untrusted Extensions. In *Proceedings of the 18th Annual Network and Distributed System Security Symposium* (February 2011).

[43] YEE, B., SEHR, D., DARDYK, G., CHEN, J. B., MUTH, R., ORM, T., OKASAKA, S., NARULA, N., FULLAGAR, N., AND INC, G. Native Client: A Sandbox for Portable, Untrusted x86 Native Code. In *Proceedings of the 30th IEEE Symposium on Security and Privacy* (May 2009).

Delusional Boot: Securing Cloud Hypervisors without Massive Re-engineering

Anh Nguyen[†], Himanshu Raj[*], Shravan Rayanchu[‡], Stefan Saroiu[*], and Alec Wolman[*]

[†]UIUC, [‡]University of Wisconsin, and [*]Microsoft Research

Abstract: The set of virtual devices offered by a hypervisor to its guest VMs is a virtualization component ripe with security exploits – more than half of all vulnerabilities of today's hypervisors are found in this codebase. This paper presents Min-V, a hypervisor that disables all virtual devices not critical to running VMs in the cloud. Of the remaining devices, Min-V takes a step further and eliminates all remaining functionality not needed for the cloud.

To implement Min-V, we had to overcome an obstacle: the boot process of many commodity OSes depends on legacy virtual devices absent from our hypervisor. Min-V introduces delusional boot, *a mechanism that allows guest VMs running commodity OSes to boot successfully without developers having to re-engineer the initialization code of these commodity OSes, as well as the BIOS and pre-OS (e.g., bootloader) code. We evaluate Min-V and demonstrate that our security improvements incur no performance overhead except for a small delay during reboot of a guest VM. Our reliability tests show that Min-V is able to run unmodified Linux and Windows OSes on top of this minimal virtualization interface.*

Categories and Subject Descriptors D.4.6 [*Security and Protection*]: Security kernels

1. Introduction

Cloud providers rely on commodity virtualization systems to enforce isolation among their customers' guest VMs. Any vulnerability that could be exploited by a guest VM has serious consequences for the cloud because it can lead to corrupting the entire cloud node or to launching DoS attacks on other guest VMs. We manually examined all such vulnerabilities found in a few online security databases [25, 27, 34, 40] and we discovered 74 such vulnerabilities in Xen,

	Xen	VMWare ESX	VMWare ESXi	Total
# of security vulnerabilities in entire codebase	31	23	20	74
# of security vulnerabilities in virtual devices codebase	20	17	15	52
# of security vulnerabilities found in devices Min-V removes	**16**	**15**	**13**	**44**

Table 1. Security Vulnerabilities in Commodity Virtualization Systems. *These vulnerabilities were collected from four online databases [25, 27, 34, 40].*

VMWare ESX, and VMWare ESXi, combined. Over 70% of them (52 security vulnerabilities) were present in these systems' virtualization stacks, that is in the code implementing the virtualized I/O offered to each guest VM. Table 1 presents a breakdown of these findings.

These statistics suggest that minimizing the codebase implementing the virtualization stacks of these systems can go a long way towards preventing attacks from rogue VMs. We argue that the nature of cloud computing lends itself to making these virtualization stacks much smaller and thus more safe. First, cloud computing VMs have fewer I/O device requirements than general-purpose VMs. For example, Hyper-V offers up to 39 virtual devices to service its guests; these include a graphics card, a serial port, a DVD/CD-ROM, a mouse, a keyboard, and many other such devices that cloud VMs make no use of. In our experience, most cloud VMs only require processing, disk storage, and networking functionality from the underlying virtualization stack. Second, much of a virtual device's codebase is not required for handling the common cases of device use. For example, large swaths of code handle device initialization and power management, operations that are not critical to cloud guest VMs. In contrast, the code handling common device operations (e.g., reads and writes in case of a disk) is only a small piece of the overall virtual device's codebase. Finally, eliminating those virtual devices that emulate legacy hardware though low-level interfaces reduces complexity.

We present the design and implementation of Min-V, a cloud virtualization system based on Microsoft's Hyper-V. Min-V disables all virtual devices not critical to running VMs in the cloud and offers just nine virtual devices out of a set of 39. For the remaining devices, Min-V takes a step further and virtualizes only their common functionality without handling device initialization or power management. To implement Min-V, we had to overcome a significant challenge: many commodity operating systems, such as generic configurations of Linux and Windows, fail to boot on our hypervisor. This occurs for two reasons: (1) the BIOS or the operating systems themselves check for the presence of several legacy devices at boot time, devices that are not critical to cloud VMs; and (2) they perform device initialization and power management, functionalities deliberately disabled in Min-V. One possibility is to rewrite commodity BIOSes and OSes. However, such an approach is challenging because it requires a significant amount of effort (numerous man-years of engineering) in a challenging development environment (low-level, pre-OS boot). Even worse, for cloud providers such an alternative may not be viable because they may lack source code access to the specific commodity OS a customer wants to boot in their environment.

As an alternative, Min-V sidesteps these engineering challenges with *delusional boot*. Delusional boot provides a full set of devices with complete functionality to the OS only during the boot process. Later on, it disables the non-critical devices and it replaces the critical ones with a set of barebones virtual devices that only offer common case functionality. With delusional boot, the guest VM is first booted using a normal configuration of Hyper-V with many of the virtual devices enabled, on a special node isolated from the rest of the datacenter. After the guest OS has finished booting, Min-V takes a VM snapshot, migrates it to a node in the datacenter, and restores the guest VM on the Min-V hypervisor that supports only the set of barebones virtual devices. Min-V uses a new TPM-based software attestation protocol that allows us to implement delusional boot using off-the-shelf servers and switches.

While delusional boot allows Min-V to successfully boot commodity OSes, guest OSes might still attempt to invoke functions via one of the removed devices. Min-V handles such accesses safely by returning a legitimate hypervisor error code (0xFF in Hyper-V). This simple error handling is sufficient to avoid crashing any of the commodity OSes (Windows 7, Windows XP, and Ubuntu) we tested. While these OSes panic during boot if they detect missing or faulty hardware, once running these OSes are often hardened against hardware errors that manifest gracefully through an error code. The graphics card best illustrates this behavior – although several commodity OSes refuse to boot if they lack a graphics card, they do not crash when the virtualized graphics hardware starts returning 0xFF at runtime. We used several workloads and a commercial reliability benchmark to investigate the robustness of delusional boot, and all three OSes tested remained stable throughout our experiments.

Of the 52 vulnerabilities described earlier, we estimate that removing virtual devices not needed in the cloud would eliminate at least 44 of them. Our estimate is conservative;

for some of these vulnerabilities, it was not specified what device they belong to or whether they appear in the emulated portion of a device (such portions are removed by Min-V). Since Min-V also minimizes the functionality of the remaining devices, it is possible that even more vulnerabilities are eliminated; however, quantifying this effect on the data is much harder.

Our evaluation shows that Min-V reduces virtual device interfaces by 60% based on counting the number of lines source code in Hyper-V. This reduction in the attack surface is done with no performance penalty during the VM runtime. Min-V's sole performance overhead occurs when the guest VM needs to reboot, a relatively infrequent operation. In the case of Ubuntu, rebooting a guest VM in Min-V has an overhead of less than a minute in addition to the two minutes spent to boot the OS alone. We also evaluate Min-V's reliability using an industrial reliability benchmark and we found that all tested OSes remain stable.

2. Design Alternatives for Secure Cloud Virtualization

The need for secure virtualization for the cloud is greater than ever. Cases of cloud customers' software turning rogue have already been documented. For example, Amazon's EC2 machines have been used to send spam [21] and to launch denial-of-service attacks on other Amazon customers [3]. These examples demonstrate how cloud customers (knowingly or unknowingly) have started to abuse the cloud infrastructure for illegitimate activities. Compromised guest VMs can become launching pads for much more serious attacks on the cloud infrastructure or on other customers' VMs.

The security of cloud-based architectures rests on the virtualization stack and the hypervisor remaining uncompromised and enforcing isolation between guest VMs that may exhibit malicious behavior. One alternative is to start with a fresh design of a virtualization stack that uses small and well-defined paravirtualized channels for I/O communication. While such a clean-slate approach can offer strong security, it would also restrict the choice of the guest VM operating system to those that support this "special" virtual stack. Also, commodity OSes were designed to rely on a rich set of devices, and changing such an assumption requires serious re-engineering. Section 9 will present a more in-depth analysis of the requirements of porting a commodity OS to a minimal virtualization stack, and will describe why such an alternative is expensive. Instead, here we focus on design alternatives that continue to offer full virtualization stacks to guest VMs. Such approaches to secure cloud virtualization can be classified in three categories.

1. Commodity Hypervisors. Commodity hypervisors, such as Xen, VMware, and Hyper-V, can run commodity OSes with high performance. These systems can accommodate many guest VMs running simultaneously with adequate performance. Their codebases are continuously upgraded to

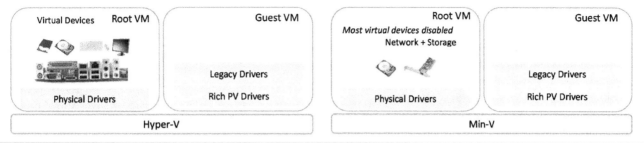

Figure 1. Hyper-V and Min-V Architectures: *In Hyper-V (on the left), the root VM offers a full set of virtual devices to the guest VMs. The guest VMs use legacy (hardware-emulation) drivers and rich paravirtualized drivers to interact with all virtual devices. In Min-V (on the right), the root VM disables most virtual devices. The only devices are left to support networking and storage. The guest VMs' drivers receive error codes if they try access non-existing devices.*

offer more functionality and higher performance. Unfortunately, these improvements come with a cost: the TCBs of these systems continue to grow. As the TCB grows, so does the potential for security vulnerabilities.

2. "Tiny" Hypervisors. Research projects have begun to investigate ways of offering virtualization without including a full-fledged operating system in their TCB [13, 22, 35]. For example, one recent project demonstrated a hypervisor with a very small codebase, only 7889 lines of C code [22], that is capable of running a commodity operating system. With such a small codebase, it may be possible to use verification to demonstrate that the system's implementation adheres to its specification [20]. However, to stay small, the hypervisor compromises on functionality and performance: while it is capable of virtualizing one commodity OS, it cannot run multiple guest VMs at the same time. Running multiple VMs simultaneously requires implementing multiplexing and demultiplexing functionality for I/O devices, which in turn requires much more code. For example, implementing a fast networking I/O path among co-located guest VMs requires code that implements the functionality of a network switch; in fact, Xen uses Linux's iptables and ebtables packages to implement switching. Such codebases tend to be large and complex.

3. Disaggregated Hypervisors. Another approach is to compartmentalize the virtualization stack in multiple isolated containers [8, 10, 24, 37, 42]. In some cases, the design of the disaggregation support is primarily driven by the reliability needs of the virtualization stack because each isolated container can be restarted upon a crash without needing a full system reboot [42]. Nevertheless, such isolation improves the overall system's security because an exploit within one container only compromises the data exposed within that container, rather than leading to a system-wide compromise [8, 37]. However, disaggregation only limits the impact of security vulnerabilities, it does not reduce the size of the TCB nor the number of vulnerabilities. Furthermore, delusional boot can be applied to disaggregated hypervisors as well. When such hypervisors need to boot a commodity

OS that expects a full virtualization stack, delusional boot can simplify booting these OSes in a secure manner.

3. Threat Model

Cloud computing raises many different security threats and Min-V only addresses a portion of them. Our threat model assumes that attackers can run arbitrary code inside a guest VM with root privileges, and they have full access to the interfaces provided by the hypervisor. We make no assumptions about the configuration of the customer's VMs, because cloud providers prefer to impose minimal requirements on their customers. These OSes can be corrupt, they might not be upgraded or patched, and they may run rootkits and Trojans.

Min-V improves security on behalf of both cloud providers and cloud customers. Because cloud nodes often use the homogeneous software configurations, one exploit may compromise a large number of cloud nodes. Min-V protects cloud customers because, if an attacker compromises a cloud node's root VM, the attacker can further compromise other customers' VMs.

Cloud computing raises additional threats that are beyond the scope of our work. For example, a malicious administrator in a datacenter could try to compromise customers' guest VMs or steal physical disks loaded with customers' data. Alternatively, an administrator could be negligent in how they handle both software and hardware, which could lead to accidental data loss. Customers' data could also be subject to subpoenas [4], and data disclosures may not even be revealed to the customers [12]. Finally, software developers may introduce backdoors into the code which could be later exploited to gain access to guest VMs code and data.

4. Design Goals and Design Principles

This section provides a brief overview of the Min-V architecture, its design goals, and its design principles. Figure 1 shows an architecture diagram of our system and contrasts it with the original Hyper-V system.

4.1 Design Goals

1. Minimize the interface between the TCB and the guest VMs. To meet this goal, Min-V disables most virtual devices because they comprise most of the interface complexity between the TCB and the guest VMs.

2. Support legacy OSes in guest VMs. Min-V allows customers to run any legacy OS configurations and applications inside their guest VMs. In our experiments, we used three commodity OSes (Windows 7, Windows XP, and Ubuntu 9.10) which are representative of typical cloud environments. To narrow the virtual devices, Min-V replaces all remaining devices with a set of barebones virtual devices. This is done by installing a set of drivers in each OS. In addition of being smaller, these paravirtualized drivers offer fast performance.

3. Minimize the performance overhead. Performance is critical in cloud environments. Our goal is to meet the cloud provider's security needs without significantly impacting guest VM performance. To meet this goal, Min-V does not add any performance overhead to running VMs. As we will describe later, Min-V does increase the time it takes to reboot guest VMs.

4.2 Design Principles

In the context of the above design goals, four key principles guide our design:

1. Economy of interfaces. Any interface between the TCB of the virtualization system and the guest VMs that is not necessary for cloud computing should be eliminated.

2. Use high-level device interfaces rather than low-level ones. It is easier to secure high-level paravirtualized interfaces than to secure low-level legacy device interfaces.

3. Isolate a cloud node from the network whenever it executes potentially insecure operations. Whenever a guest OS must run with a full, commodity virtualization stack, it must be disconnected from the network to prevent compromises from spreading within the datacenter. The node must attest that it runs a minimal virtualization stack before being allowed to reconnect to the network.

4. Use little customization. Our solution should not require massive re-engineering of the OSes or special-purpose hardware, such as switches that incorporate trusted computing primitives into their logic. Such solutions are often expensive and they are hard to deploy in practice.

5. Disabling Virtual Devices

A virtualized cloud computing environment, such as Min-V, differs from a general purpose virtualization platform in that customers access guest VMs entirely via the network. As a result, many standard physical devices on cloud servers need not be exposed to the guest VM. For example, physical devices such as the keyboard, mouse, USB ports, and DVD drive serve little purpose for a cloud customer. In fact, many of these devices have virtual equivalents that are provided by remote desktop protocols such as RDP or VNC. For example, a customer running Windows in a guest VM can use RDP to redirect many devices over the network, such as the keyboard, mouse, graphics card, printer, and even USB storage.

In the rest of this section, we describe the types of devices that Hyper-V provides by default to guest VMs, and how they are powered-up and initialized. We then discuss the device requirements of operating systems that run in the guest VMs, and we describe the steps we took to actually remove devices from the virtualization stack.

5.1 Hyper-V Devices

Most *virtual devices* provided by Hyper-V to guest VMs correspond to real physical devices, such as the NIC, the IDE storage controller, or the keyboard controller. There are three common approaches to implementing a virtual device: 1) multiplexing the virtual device over the corresponding real physical device provided by the operating system running in the root VM; 2) emulating the hardware device entirely in software to provide the desired functionality; and 3) providing virtualization services through a device interface. As examples of the latter category, Hyper-V provides the *VMBus* device that provides a fast, shared-memory based communication channel between the root VM and a guest VM and a *heartbeat* integration component that provides a way to keep track of the guest VM's health status.

In its default configuration, Hyper-V offers 39 virtual devices to each guest VM. This large number of devices is not unique to Hyper-V; Xen offers a comparable number of devices to guest VMs. For each VM, Hyper-V creates and maintains a *virtual motherboard* device, which acts as a container for the set of internal devices available to that VM. Each virtual motherboard has a *virtual device manifest*, which is just a table that enumerates all devices found on the virtual motherboard. When a VM is initialized, each device listed in the manifest is instantiated and attached to the virtual motherboard. Once initialization completes, the motherboard and its devices are all powered on. At this point, virtual devices register their handlers with the hypervisor, so that guest VM accesses to certain I/O ports and MMIO addresses are dispatched to the appropriate virtual device.

Virtual devices often have dependencies on one another. For example, all enlightened devices depend on the VMBus device because the VMBus implements the shared memory bus between the root and a guest VM. Another example is the emulated NIC which depends on the emulated PCI bus to function properly. Figure 2 depicts the 39 devices found in Hyper-V as nodes which are connected by directed edges that represent dependencies. Because of these dependencies, the order in which devices are initialized is important. For example, the VMBus is the first device initialized by Hyper-V's virtual motherboard. Similarly, the emulated PCI bus is initialized before the emulated NIC. For Min-V, determining these device dependencies is important because *disabling a*

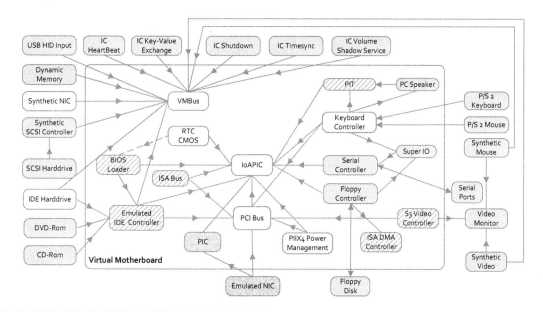

Figure 2. Virtual stack dependencies. *Devices that we simply removed from Min-V have a dark background. The stripe background represents devices that Windows 7 or the virtual BIOS check for at boot time, and we successfully "removed" them with delusional boot. Devices with a white background are those remaining in our system. Arrowed lines show virtual device dependencies, and the dashed line represents a dependency we manually removed.*

virtual device cannot be done unless all its dependent devices are also disabled. Next, we describe how we determined device dependencies.

5.2 Determining Device Dependencies

We use three heuristics to determine device dependencies in Hyper-V. Each heuristic allows us to test for the presence or absence of a dependency between two devices. While each heuristic has different shortcomings (e.g., some cannot find all dependencies, while others do not scale), their combination allows us to find all dependencies shown in Figure 2. Our heuristics cannot guarantee that *all* dependencies are discovered. However, any missed dependency represents a missed opportunity for further codebase reduction without affecting the performance or correctness of our current implementation.

1. Using object file references. We classify the object files created at compile time to determine which ones contain the functionality of a single device alone. Although in some cases an object file can include more than one device (e.g., the floppy disk and the floppy controller end up in the same object file after compilation), in most cases there was a one-to-one mapping between devices and object files. For such object files, we examine their symbol tables searching for external references to symbols defined in other object files. Whenever we find such a reference, we note a dependency between these two devices.

This heuristic is not guaranteed to find all dependencies because certain invocations may be performed as indirect calls though function pointers. It is challenging to use static

analysis to identity such runtime dependencies, because you would need to locate each indirect jump instruction and then understand which instructions were used to calculate the jump target.

2. Disabling device instantiation. Another heuristic we use is to comment out devices in the virtual motherboard's manifest, one device at a time, and test whether a guest VM fails to boot. Such a failure indicates the presence of another device that depends on the removed device. We then automate the search for that other device by disabling different candidates until the OS boots successfully. This indicates a device dependency.

3. Code inspection. In some cases, we resort to code inspection to find additional dependencies. For example, we discovered a dependency between the emulated IDE controller and the VMBus which does not lead to OS instability. The IDE controller is a hybrid device that checks whether the VMBus is instantiated to take advantage of it for faster I/O. If the VMBus is not present, the IDE controller continues to function properly by falling back to emulation-only mode. While rigorous code inspection will find all dependencies between devices, this is challenging because of the codebase size and the error-prone nature of the process. Instead of relying only on code inspection, we use the first two heuristics to quickly discover many device dependencies, and we only use code inspection to supplement their shortcomings.

Based on the combination of these heuristics, we discovered 68 device dependencies. Figure 2 uses arrows to illustrate all dependencies except for those involving the virtual motherboard. There are 17 devices dependent on the virtual motherboard and they are all shown within a bounding box representing the virtual motherboard. Heuristic #1 discovered 55 device dependencies including all the 17 dependencies involving the virtual motherboard. Heuristic #2 discovered 11 device dependencies, and the remaining two dependencies were discovered using the last heuristic.

5.3 Removing Devices

Because Min-V targets cloud virtualization environments, our goal is to provide the minimum set of devices needed for guest VMs running in the cloud: a CPU, a clock, an interrupt controller, a disk, and a NIC. After discovering device dependencies, we naively thought that we could disable all devices except for the virtual motherboard, the RTC CMOS, the IoAPIC, the enlightened NIC, the IDE harddrive, and their dependency, which is the VMBus. However, we quickly ran into three obstacles.

First, the Hyper-V boot model requires the presence of the IDE harddrive device and its dependencies (the emulated IDE controller, and the PCI Bus). Hyper-V uses a boot model for guest VMs that mirrors the way in which physical machines boot. In particular, Hyper-V provides a virtual BIOS that expects the OS to boot from a legacy virtual IDE. To overcome this obstacle, the BIOS must be paravirtualized in a way that allows the guest OS to boot over the VMBus.

Second, the Hyper-V BIOS requires the presence of five devices. They are the BIOS loader, the RTC CMOS, and the keyboard, video, and ISA DMA controllers. Unfortunately changing the BIOS to eliminate these dependencies was impossible because we did not have the source code of the BIOS. Even with access to the BIOS source code, we expect modifying it to be a challenging task because of the low-level, pre-OS nature of the environment.

Third, commodity operating systems often check for the presence of certain devices at boot time in order to initialize them. For example, Windows 7 and Ubuntu 9.10 check for the presence of a video card and panic if they do not find one. To identify which devices are expected at boot time, we ran a series of experiments where we would disable one device at a time, attempt to boot an operating system, and check if the OS would panic. To perform these experiments, we began by disabling the devices which had no dependencies, and we made sure never to disable a device where any its dependencies were not already disabled. We used three different OSes; the results are presented in Table 2.

In summary, one way to overcome these three obstacles is to add the VMBus driver support to the BIOS, rewrite the BIOS to remove its dependencies on devices which are not needed for the cloud, and paravirtualize all the guest OSes to no longer attempt to initialize devices at boot time other than the synthetic NIC and disk. However, such a plan requires a drastic amount of effort, comparable to implementing and testing a new release of a commodity operating system.

Min-V overcomes these challenges in two steps.

Virtualized BIOS	BIOS loader, Keyboard controller, Video, ISA DMA Controller, RTC CMOS
Windows 7	PIT, ISA Bus, Video, RTC CMOS, Power management
Windows XP	PIT, ISA Bus, Keyboard controller, RTC CMOS, Power management
Ubuntu 9.10	PIT, Video, RTC CMOS, Power management

Table 2. Devices Needed at Boot Time.

5.3.1 Step #1: Removing extraneous devices

The first step is removing extraneous devices – devices whose removal does not raise any of the challenges shown above. For this, we modify the virtual device manifest to remove all the extraneous devices at the time a guest VM is created. These devices will neither be initialized nor powered on by Hyper-V.

5.3.2 Step #2: Using delusional boot

In step # 2, Min-V uses a technique called *delusional boot*: the guest VM is first booted, using a normal configuration of Hyper-V with many virtual devices enabled, on a special node that is isolated from the rest of the datacenter. After the guest OS finishes booting, Min-V takes a snapshot by pausing the VM and saving its state. Min-V then migrates the VM snapshot to the datacenter production environment, and restores the guest VM using a version of Hyper-V that only offers a barebones set of virtual devices. Section 6 will provide an in-depth discussion of the delusional boot technique. Figure 3 illustrates the devices left in the Min-V virtualization stack after removing 24 devices in step #1 and removing an additional six virtual devices in step #2. Both steps are critical to reducing the virtualization stack's codebase; we leave an in-depth examination of how much code each step eliminated to the evaluation section.

One challenge that arises with delusional boot is *safety*: what happens if the guest OS attempts to access one of the devices that was removed after boot? If such accesses are not handled or prevented, they could potentially lead to guest OS instabilities. Min-V uses two techniques to address this challenge. First, some devices can be safely removed before booting the OS. These devices include certain Hyper-V services, such as the VM heartbeat device, plug-and-play devices, and also physical devices often missing from many PC configurations, such as a floppy drive. By disabling these devices, the commodity OS never learns about their existence. Second, Min-V uses remote desktop protocols (e.g., RDP and VNC) that virtualize several missing devices, such as the keyboard, mouse, and display. All I/O to and from these devices is redirected over the network interface, an interface still available in Min-V. To increase confidence in our examination, we performed a series of reliability experiments whose results are described in our evaluation section.

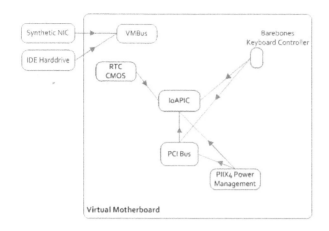

```
PowerOn //Before delusional boot

- get reference to SuperIO device
- get reference to PCIBus device
- get reference to IOApic device
- get reference to PIT device
- get reference to Speaker device

//setup PS/2, A20, speaker, CPU reset
- setup IO emulation for port 0x60
- setup IO emulation for port 0x61
- setup IO emulation for port 0x62
- setup IO emulation for port 0x63
- setup IO emulation for port 0x64

- initialize PS2 keyboard
- initialize PS2 mouse
```

```
PowerOn //After delusional boot

- get reference to PCIBus device
- get reference to IOApic device

//setup CPU reset only
- setup IO emulation for port 0x64
```

Figure 3. The virtual devices left in Min-V's virtualization stack. *Nine devices are left in Min-V, out of which three are paravirtualized and five are emulated. While the set of paravirtualized devices and the set of emulated devices appear disconnected in the illustration, both sets are instantiated through the virtual motherboard device.*

Figure 4. Re-implementing the keyboard controller. *After the delusional boot, we can switch to a barebones keyboard controller device.*

5.3.3 Implementation Details

We modified the Hyper-V virtual motherboard initialization code to skip all devices not needed at boot time. These devices will not register their handlers with the hypervisor, and guest accesses to their I/O address spaces fall back to the *null* device model: all writes are discarded, and all reads returns a default error value (for Hyper-V, this value is 0xFF). We also eliminated a dependency between the clock (RTC CMOS) and the BIOS loader. At boot time, the RTC code initializes itself by calling into the BIOS to retrieve the clock. Since this code is never executed after the OS has booted, we simply rewrote the RTC CMOS device in Min-V to eliminate this dependency.

To implement a working CPU, a NIC, a disk, an interrupt controller, and a clock, Min-V must offer six devices: the virtual motherboard, the VMBus, the synthetic NIC, the synthetic IDE harddrive, the RTC CMOS, and the IoAPIC (which the clock depends on). However, our current implementation ends up offering three additional devices: the PIIX4 power management device, the PCI bus, and the keyboard controller. Hyper-V uses PIIX4 to save/restore VMs, a functionality Min-V also requires for delusional boot. The PIIX4's role is to dispatch hibernate commands to the guest OS so that the OS can save its state appropriately before shutting down. Because the PIIX4 device uses the PCI bus, Min-V also has to offer the PCI bus device. Finally, Min-V needs the keyboard controller (not to be confused with the keyboard device) because guest VMs use it to reset their CPUs.

We took additional steps to further minimize the codebase of the remaining devices. For example, the keyboard controller device offers four pieces of functionality out of which only one is needed by Min-V. These are: (1) control-

ling and receiving inputs from the PS/2 keyboard and mouse; (2) controlling the A20 line [36] to enable protected mode; (3) controlling the PC speaker; and (4) controlling the guest VMs' CPU reset. We rewrote the keyboard controller device to remove the first three pieces of functionality which are not needed by Min-V. Figure 4 illustrates the pseudo-code of the original device (on the left) and the newer, barebones, keyboard controller used by Min-V (on the right). Although we only re-implemented the keyboard controller, reducing all remaining virtual devices to barebones devices is left as future work.

6. Delusional Boot

At a high-level, there are three steps to delusional boot: 1. copying the customer's VM image to an isolated boot server, 2. booting the VM on the isolated server and 3. copying the VM image back to the production environment.

1. Copying the VM Image to the Boot Server. Min-V detects that a guest VM is ready to be rebooted by interposing on the keyboard controller port 0x64. This port links to the CPU reset pin in the original x86 PC architecture and tells the hypervisor that the guest OS has finished shutting down and the VMM stack should be rebooted. At this point, Min-V saves the guest VM to a file and requests service from an available boot server.

2. Isolated Boot. Delusional boot relies on an *isolated* boot server located in an environment separate from the rest of the production nodes (e.g., a *quarantined* environment). This boot server runs the *Min-V boot stack*, a different version of the virtualization stack than the *Min-V production stack* that runs in production. First, the isolated boot server copies the guest VM disk image and VM configuration from the production server, disconnects from the network, and then reboots into a configuration that offers a full virtualized stack. At this point, the server boots up the VM. After the guest OS finishes booting on the boot server, the role of the full virtualization stack is now complete. The boot server then *snapshots* the VM state (including the virtual device state) to a file, and then reboots and reconnects to the network.

3. Copying the VM image back to Production. The VM snapshot is migrated back to a production server, and the Min-V virtualization stack on this server replaces all the disabled virtual devices with a *null device* virtualization model. This model treats all accesses to these devices as no-ops. In particular, all memory-mapped and port-mapped device reads return the value 0xFF, and all writes are discarded. Together, these steps complete the delusional boot and achieve the end goal of running a guest VM on the production server with enhanced isolation properties.

6.1 Threat Model of Delusional Boot

We designed delusional boot to handle the following three classes of attacks:

1. Vulnerabilities that persist across reboots. Such an attack could be launched by booting a malicious VM which would then install a rootkit (e.g., through a firmware exploit) on the boot server. If left unhandled, an installed rootkit can compromise all future guest VMs booting on the server. To stop such attacks, our implementation of delusional boot uses a TPM to measure all firmware and the entire OS image booting on the server. If any modifications are detected in this software, the boot process stops because new injected code has been discovered on the server's boot path. While such an approach stops injected code from surviving reboots, it does not eliminate the vulnerability. Fixing such a vulnerability requires an OS or firmware update.

2. Exploiting a bug in the VM migration protocol. Numerous optimizations are possible to perform fast VM migration (e.g., compression, deduplication), and many such optimizations are implemented in commodity virtualization solutions. However, such optimizations require running a larger or more complex software stack on the boot server. To reduce the possibility of an exploit in the VM migration protocol, our implementation of delusional boot is deliberately kept simple – it is just a networking transfer of the VM image.

3. The VM of one customer infecting the VM of another. The boot server offers a full virtualization stack to a guest VM for rebooting purposes. A guest VM can exploit a vulnerability and compromise a co-located VM. To eliminate this possibility, we require the boot server to run co-located VMs only when they belong to the same customer.

6.2 Securing Delusional Boot

A guest VM may try to compromise the boot server's virtualization stack because it exposes a large interface consisting of a full set of virtual devices. However, our design relies on two properties to ensure such compromises do not lead to

security breaches. First, the boot server's network connection is disabled unless it is able to attest (using a TPM) to running a pre-established, sanitized software configuration; such a configuration *never* runs third-party guest VMs. Second, only guest VM snapshots are loaded back from the boot server into production, and they are subjected to the same security protocol used when importing any untrusted customer VM image. This ensures any compromises remain isolated inside the guest VM.

6.2.1 Modes for the Isolated Boot Server

The isolated boot server offers two modes of operation: 1) a *clean mode* only used when importing and exporting customer VM images in and out of the isolated boot environment; and 2) a *dirty mode* used for actually booting the customer-provided VMs. The network switch connecting the isolated boot server moved is configured to only offer network connectivity when the boot server is in clean mode.

Initially, we planned to use a TPM-based attestation protocol [32] to detect the boot server's configuration (clean vs. dirty). The boot server would produce a TPM-signed software attestation which would be transmitted to the switch. The switch would verify the attestation before enabling access to the network. There is already an open protocol designed to solve this exact problem, namely TCG's Trusted Network Connect (TNC). Although switch manufacturers are starting to adopt TNC, we could not find an inexpensive, commodity switch that supports TNC. We overcame this temporary obstacle by designing a new software attestation protocol that works with commodity switches. We only require the switch to support IP and MAC address filtering for access control, which is widely available today. In addition to IP and MAC filtering, our software verification protocol uses the boot server's TPM chip and Microsoft's BitLocker.

6.2.2 Min-V Software Attestation Protocol

We start by configuring the switch with a whitelist of MAC and private IP addresses; the switch enables network connectivity whenever a boot server's NIC presents one of the whitelisted addresses. For any other addresses, the switch denies network connectivity. The software attestation protocol ensures that a boot server can configure the NIC with valid IP and MAC addresses only when booted in clean mode. If the boot server is booted in dirty mode, our protocol ensures that the server cannot configure valid IP and MAC addresses.

To explain how our protocol works, we start with a quick overview of BitLocker, a disk volume encryption feature of Windows that uses the TPM to protect its volume encryption keys. BitLocker can only retrieve the encryption key if the following two conditions hold. First, decryption must be done on the same machine that encrypted the volume. Second, the machine's boot configuration, as recorded by the TPM, must match the configuration that saved the volume

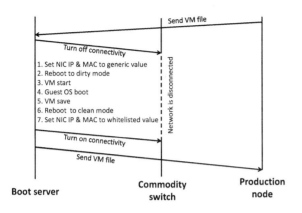

Figure 5. The software attestation protocol in Min-V.

encryption key. To provide these two guarantees, BitLocker *seals* the the encryption key to the chain of trust rooted in the physical TPM and recorded in the TPM's Platform Configuration Registers (PCRs). The PCR values consist of hashes of the BIOS, the I/O devices' firmware, the Master Boot Record (MBR), the Windows Boot Manager (BootMgr), and the boot configuration data. The key can only be *unsealed* by the boot manager *before* the OS is launched while the PCR registers are set to the appropriate values. The key remains safe because an attacker cannot modify the boot manager or else the PCR values will not match and the unseal operation will fail.

Min-V uses a modified version of BitLocker that protects the boot server's whitelisted IP and MAC addresses in the same way that BitLocker protects its volume encryption keys. The valid addresses are unsealed successfully only if the boot server has booted in clean mode. Any other configuration (i.e., dirty mode) cannot unseal the valid addresses, and without these addresses the network traffic will be blocked by the switch. Guessing the "correct" MAC and IP addresses is hard; the search space is 72 bits long. Also, the network switch is configured to isolate each boot server from any other device to prevent network sniffing attacks. Figure 5 shows the Min-V software attestation protocol.

6.3 Security Discussion

If a boot server becomes compromised, it might try to: 1) attack other nodes in the cloud infrastructure; 2) compromise the clean mode execution environment on the boot server; or 3) launch a DoS attack by refusing to restart the boot server in clean mode. We consider each of these attacks in turn.

To prevent the first class of attacks, Min-V ensures that network connectivity to the production nodes is disabled in all configurations other than the clean one. The network switch will not re-enable the network port unless the boot server can configure its NIC with the valid IP and MAC addresses. The boot server cannot retrieve these addresses hidden in the encrypted volume unless it is booted in a clean configuration. Any other configuration wanting to decrypt

the partition storing these addresses would need to modify the boot manager to unseal the key protected by BitLocker. Modifying the boot manager leads to a mismatch in the PCR values, which prevents the unseal operation from revealing the key.

To prevent the second attack, the trusted clean execution environment is also stored on a TPM-sealed partition. This prevents a malicious boot server from modifying the encrypted partition where the trusted execution environment is stored. While the boot server could potentially delete the entire encrypted partition and put a new malicious version in its place, this would simply delete the whitelisted addresses, and prevent the boot server from successfully attesting to the network switch. When the boot server runs in clean mode, the customer's VM image is only stored as a file and is never activated.

Finally, Min-V does not currently prevent the third class of attack. When booted in dirty mode, a compromised boot server might refuse to reboot back into clean mode, effectively mounting a DoS attack. Another way to mount a DoS attack would be for the compromised boot server to modify or delete the clean configuration. For example, it could delete the encrypted volume or manipulate the boot manager's configuration parameters for booting in clean mode. This would cause clean mode to no longer boot successfully since the TPM unseal operation would fail. In the future, Min-V could mitigate certain DoS attacks by using an out-of-band control mechanism, such as Intel's management processor [15], which can force a boot server to reboot into clean mode.

6.4 Performance Discussion

Two performance concerns with delusional boot are that (1) it introduces additional latency overhead to guest VM rebooting and (2) the boot server can become a bottleneck if multiple VMs need to reboot simultaneously. As Section 7 will show guest VM reboots are already relatively slow spanning multiple minutes and the additional overhead due to delusional boot is small. To alleviate the second performance concern, Min-V can rely on a small cluster of boot servers rather than just on a single machine. Such a design should easily scale because there is no state sharing across these boot servers. We also examined a trace of server reboots collected across 130 production nodes over the course of one month. Server reboots in the cloud were relatively rare (only 10 servers rebooted) and there were only two occurrences of simultaneous reboots. In both cases, two servers rebooted simultaneously. Finally, it is possible for a single boot server to reboot multiple guest VMs *as long as* they belong to the same customer since Min-V does not need to isolate guest VMs belonging to the same customer. While such a design extension is possible, we leave it as future work.

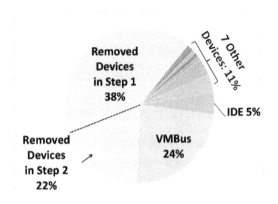

Figure 6. Percentage of lines of virtual devices code removed by Min-V.

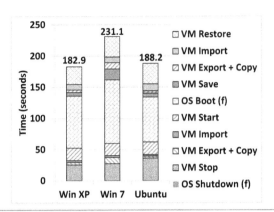

Figure 7. Performance of Delusional Boot. *The overhead of delusional boot is broken down for each of the steps taken by the protocol. There is a total of ten steps. Only two steps (OS Shutdown and OS Boot) appear in a regular boot, and thus we marked them with "(f)" (standing for "fixed cost"). The remaining eight steps are all overhead due to delusional boot.*

7. Evaluation

This section presents a three-pronged evaluation of Min-V. First, we measure how much smaller the virtual device interface is for Min-V. Second, we evaluate the performance of delusional boot by measuring its operational latency. Finally, we evaluate the stability of guest OSes in Min-V.

Methodology In our experiments with Min-V we used Intel Core 2 Duo machines, each equipped with a E6600 2.4GHz CPU and 3GB of RAM. These machines were linked via 1Gbps dedicated network. We experimented with three commodity operating systems: Windows XP Professional, Windows 7 Ultimate, and Ubuntu Linux version 9.10 (kernel ver. 2.6.28-16 SMP x86_64). Each commodity system ran inside of a guest VM that was allocated 1GB of RAM and a dynamically-sized virtual disk set to a maximum of 120GB. The performance experiments were obtained by repeating each experiment three times and reporting the average results. There is very little variance across the different runs of our experiments.

In our delusional boot experiments, we used the Hyper-V's differential VHDs mechanism to minimize the amount of data shipped between the production nodes and the boot server. To implement this, we assumed the boot server already has saved the original "golden image" of the VHDs for each commodity OS.

In our evaluation of boot server throughput, we used a trace of node reboots in the cloud. Our trace comes from a live cluster of 130 servers as part of *anonymized* application running in a large datacenter; the trace spans 1.5 months from mid January 2009 to early March 2009.

7.1 Reducing the Attack Surface

We use the number of lines of source code to evaluate our reduction in the virtual device interface. While the relationship between code size and number of vulnerabilities is not precisely known, software engineers estimate that the density of bugs in production quality source code is about one

to ten bugs in 1000 lines of code [14]. The codebase implementing the virtual device interface in Hyper-V is on the order of a few hundred thousand lines of code. Figure 6 shows the percentage of the lines of code that Min-V eliminates from the interface to the TCB by removing virtual devices. To reduce the clutter in the graph, we collapsed the names of seven devices we remove into one label: "7 Other Devices". These seven devices constitute 11% of the codebase and they are: the NIC (4%), virtual motherboard (4%), and the PIIX4 power management, the PCI bus, the keyboard controller, the I/O APIC, and the RTC CMOS, each with 1% or less.

Both device removal steps are effective in reducing our codebase size. Removing extraneous devices (step #1) provides a 38% codebase reduction, whereas delusional boot (step #2) gives an additional 22% reduction in the codebase. The VMBus constitutes the bulk of the remaining codebase. This is encouraging because the interfaces exposed by the VMBus are based on high-level message passing rather than the memory-mapped IO of legacy devices. Our experience with devices tells us that new, paravirtualized devices are much more secure (because of their style of interfaces) than legacy ones. Furthermore, we have started to build *VMBus light*, a smaller version of the VMBus that removes some of the functionality unnecessary in the cloud, such as power management and initialization.

7.2 Delusional Boot Latency

We instrumented our implementation of delusional boot to record time spent in each of its steps required to reboot a customer's guest VM.

Figure 7 shows the performance of delusional boot for the three commodity OSes we used. The OS shutdown and boot steps are the only two steps present in a regular boot, whereas the rest of the steps is the overhead introduced by delusional boot. The end-to-end cost of booting an OS in Min-V is 3.05 minutes to complete for Windows XP Professional, 3.85 minutes for Windows 7 Ultimate, and 3.14 minutes for Ubuntu. In contrast, the cost of regular reboot in Hyper-V is 2.16 minutes for Windows XP, 2.83 minutes for Windows 7, and 2.2 minutes for Ubuntu. The difference in the performance of Windows 7 on one side and Windows XP and Ubuntu on the other is due to the different image sizes of these OSes. The size of a fresh Windows 7 install is 8.5GB as opposed to 3.4GB for Windows XP and 3GB for Ubuntu. A larger image size increases three steps in the delusional boot process: the VM export + copy, the OS boot, and the VM save.

7.3 Reliability

With Min-V, guest OSes operate in an environment where many virtual devices are either missing or not properly emulated. This could introduce reliability issues if the OS would want to access a virtual device and this access wouldn't be properly handled by Min-V. To evaluate whether Min-V remains reliable, we used an industrial reliability benchmark called PassMark BurnIn Test. This benchmark tests the I/O subsystems of a traditional PC for reliability and stability; one common use of this benchmark is to test whether PCs remain stable when their CPUs are overclocked. This experiment's goal is to detect whether the OS would crash given the large load of I/O calls made to the virtualization stack. A run of the benchmark completed in about 15 minutes on the machines used in our evaluation. Figure 8 shows a summary of the test results from running PassMark on Windows 7 in Min-V.

The main finding of our experiment is that all three OSes remained stable even when booted with delusional boot. We closely inspected the logs and compared them to the logs obtained when running the benchmark on an OS that booted normally. We found the logs to be similar overall: many tests passed on both normally booted and delusional booted OSes while some tests failed. Most of the failed tests showed identical errors. However, this was not always the case. For example, one test checked whether the graphics card supports hardware-only DirectDraw object creation operations. This test succeeded when we booted the OS normally because the virtual device is able to relay DirectDraw commands. Min-V uses RDP and the RDP graphics driver does not support DirectDraw. This check however made the benchmark conduct an additional series of tests for DirectDraw on the normally booted OS, and many of these tests failed. In fact this causes the error count to be higher for the normally booted OS than the delusional booted one.

To increase our confidence in the reliability of our guest VMs, we also installed and ran four common applications: a browser, a Web server, an FTP server, and an SSH server. We used these applications ourselves over the course of two days (48 hours), and we experienced no instabilities. In all

Test Name	Cycles	Operations	Result	Errors
CPU	165	78.231 Billion	PASS	0
Memory (RAM)	3	4.044 Billion	PASS	0
Printer	1	5714	PASS	0
Network	16	135600	PASS	0
Video (RDP)	12	376	PASS	0
Disk (C:)	2	7.024 Billion	PASS	0
2D (Graphics)	0	0	FAIL	85
3D (Graphics)	0	0	FAIL	5
Sound	4	7.96 Million	FAIL	260
Parallel Port	0	0	FAIL	85
Tape	0	0	FAIL	57
USB Plug 1	0	0	FAIL	1
USB Plug 2	0	0	FAIL	1
Serial Port 1	0	0	FAIL	78
Serial Port 2	57	0	FAIL	58
Disk (A:)	0	0	FAIL	3

Figure 8. Summary of results from running PassMark on Windows 7 in Min-V.

our reliability tests whether done through the benchmark or whether by running common applications, access to removed devices were handled safely, and all three OSes remained stable.

8. Related Work

The most common approach to improving the security of hypervisor-based systems is to reduce the size of the TCB [13, 19, 22, 26, 35]. For example, SecVisor [35] provides kernel code integrity using a very small hypervisor combined with hardware support for memory protection. TrustVisor [22] enables efficient data protection and execution integrity using a small special-purpose hypervisor, yet it only supports one guest VM, and therefore is not suitable for cloud computing environments. NoHype [19] goes one step further to entirely remove the virtualization layer, yet it requires additional hardware support and it only provides static partitioning to allocate machine resources. NOVA [37] relocates non-critical components into user mode to reduce its TCB, but device drivers need to be rewritten from scratch. In contrast, Min-V's goal is not to reduce the TCB's size, but rather the size of the interface between the TCB and the guest VMs. Min-V assumes as little as possible regarding the guest OS.

Min-V is not the first system to investigate narrowing the interfaces to make virtualized systems more secure. Bunker [23] uses a crippled OS with restricted I/O drivers to implement secure network trace analysis code, and Terra [11] uses tamper-resistant hardware to offer a closed-box abstraction on commodity hardware. Min-V differs from these systems primarily in the target application: virtualized cloud computing imposes different device requirements and requires support for commodity OSes.

Another approach to improving the security of virtualized systems consists of disaggregating the TCB by partitioning it into isolated components [8, 9, 10, 24, 37]. This approach does not eliminate vulnerabilities from the TCB, but instead it limits their impact. This isolation improves security because an exploit in one container only compromises the data exposed to that container. A recent project [8] takes a step further and uses microreboots to restart some of the hypervisor's components in an effort to reduce their temporal attack surface. Such techniques are different than Min-V's delusional boot whose goal is to support booting commodity OSes without re-engineering the startup code.

Cloud security is becoming a significant concern, and several research efforts have proposed solutions to address: storing data in the cloud [1, 5], nested virtualization [2, 18], side-channel attacks in cloud infrastructure [28], preventing information leakage for map-reduce applications [29], information flow-control between VMs [31], and enabling confidentiality and integrity of customer computations in the cloud [16, 33, 43]. Unlike Min-V, none of these efforts focus on reducing the impact of security vulnerabilities in the virtualized systems' TCB.

Device drivers are a well-known source of reliability and security issues for OSes [7, 38]. Much of the research effort in this area has focused on minimizing the impact of driver bugs [17, 30, 39] to make operating systems more reliable. However, one recent effort [6, 41] moves device drivers out of the TCB by running them in user-space. This approach requires significant modifications to device drivers and conflicts with our design principle of using little customization.

9. Discussion

9.1 Porting Commodity OSes to a Minimal Virtualization Stack

One alternative to delusional boot is a clean-slate approach – porting all OSes to eliminate their dependencies on legacy virtual devices. Such an approach could start by defining a new set of interfaces between the hypervisor and the guest environments. Such interfaces do not need to emulate legacy hardware. Thus, they can be much simpler and offer narrow APIs than today's interfaces based on hardware emulation. Such a clean-slate approach is attractive because it can potentially offer security and robustness guarantees beyond those of Min-V. However, such a porting effort needs to overcome two challenges.

The first challenge is maintaining backward compatibility. Even today, several Linux configurations and Windows Embedded can run "headless" and have fewer device dependencies than those of commodity Linux and Windows versions. However, such configurations often offer more limited functionality (e.g., fewer libraries, less flexibility) than their commodity counterparts. We believe cloud providers strongly desire running commodity OSes in their datacenters, ideally with no change from their non-virtualized counterparts. Such backward compatibility would allow customers to image their physical machines in order to migrate them to the cloud. An effort-less cloud migration story would make the cloud computing vision very compelling.

Second, porting the OS is insufficient. Today, all configurations of VMware and Hyper-V, and most configurations of Xen boot guest VMs using a legacy BIOS interface. Only after boot, the OS kernel can switch to a paravirtualized interface. Even an OS designed to run on a minimal paravirtualized interface will continue to use legacy devices at boot time. Delusional boot could offer an inexpensive way of bypassing the legacy BIOS dependencies and not include them in the TCB.

9.2 Evaluating the Complexity of the Virtualization Stack

Min-V's goal is to make the virtualization stack "simpler" in order to reduce the hypervisor's attack surface. However, it is unclear what the "right" design is to build a "simpler" interface. Our evaluation section used lines of code as a metric, but such a metrics is far from perfect. In our experience, it is very easy to introduce bugs when writing devices that emulate hardware because hardware APIs are arcane and complex.

For example, the codebase of a keyboard controller device is relatively small. Yet, the code implementing such a device in software is quite minute and elaborate. A keyboard controller offers a register-based interface. Often, the bits of these registers have different meanings depending on the device's manufacturer or the context in which the device is used. The code needs to handle all these special cases correctly, making heavy use of pointers, shifts, and XORs. We found it quite easy to make mistakes when writing such low-level code.

10. Conclusions

This paper presents Min-V, a system that improves the security of commodity virtualization systems. By disabling all virtual devices not critical to running customer VMs in the cloud, Min-V minimizes the codebase of the virtualization stack. To accomplish this without significant re-engineering of the guest operating system, we introduce delusional boot. Delusional boot ensures that commodity OSes can boot in the absence of many legacy devices that Min-V eliminates. Our evaluation shows that Min-V's security improvements incur only a small performance overhead during boot time. Our reliability tests show that Min-V is able to run unmodified Windows and Linux OSes on top of this minimal virtualization interface.

Acknowledgments

This paper benefited from comments and insights provided by Timothy Roscoe (our shepherd), Paul England, Brandon

Baker, Andy Warfield, Sam King, Krishna Gummadi, and the anonymous reviewers. We are grateful for their help.

References

[1] G. Ateniese, S. Kamara, and J. Katz. Proofs of Storage from Homomorphic Identification Protocols. In *Proc. of the 15th International Conference on the Theory and Application of Cryptology and Information Security (ASIACRYPT)*, 2009.

[2] M. Ben-Yehuda, M. D. Day, Z. Dubitzky, M. Factor, N. Har'El, A. Gordon, A. Liguori, O. Wasserman, and B.-A. Yassour. The turtles project: Design and implementation of nested virtualization. In *Proc. of the 9th Symposium on Operating Systems Design and Implementation (OSDI)*, 2010.

[3] BitBucket. On our extended downtime, Amazon and whats coming, 2009. http://blog.bitbucket.org/2009/10/04/on-our-extended-downtime-amazon\discretionary{-}{}{}and-whats-coming/.

[4] Boston Globe. Google subpoena roils the web, January, 2006. http://boston.com/news/nation/articles/2006/01/21/google_subpoen\a_roils_the_web/.

[5] K. D. Bowers, A. Juels, and A. Oprea. HAIL: a high-availability and integrity layer for cloud storage. In *Proc. of the 16th ACM Conference on Computer and Communications Security (CCS)*, 2009.

[6] S. Boyd-Wickizer and N. Zeldovich. Tolerating malicious device drivers in linux. In *Proc. of the 2010 USENIX conference (ATC)*, 2010.

[7] A. Chou, J. Yang, B. Chelf, S. Hallem, and D. Engler. An empirical study of operating systems errors. In *Proc. of the 18th ACM Symposium on Operating Systems Principles (SOSP)*, 2001.

[8] P. Colp, M. Nanavati, J. Zhu, W. Aiello, G. Cooker, T. Deegan, P. Loscocco, and A. Warfield. Breaking Up is Hard to Do: Security and Funtionality in a Commodity Hypervisor. In *Proceedings of the 23rd ACM Symposium on Operating Systems Principles (SOSP)*, Cascais, Portugal, 2011.

[9] K. Fraser, S. Hand, R. Neugebauer, I. Pratt, A. Warfield, and M. Williamson. Reconstructing I/O. Technical Report UCAM-CL-TR-596, University of Cambridge, Computer Laboratory, 2004.

[10] K. Fraser, S. Hand, R. Neugebauer, I. Pratt, A. Warfield, and M. Williamson. Safe Hardware Access with the Xen Virtual Machine Monitor. In *Proc. of the 1st Workshop On Operating System and Architectural Support for the on demand IT Infrastructure (OASIS)*, Boston, MA, October 2004.

[11] T. Garfinkel, B. Pfaff, J. Chow, M. Rosenblum, and D. Boneh. Terra: a virtual machine-based platform for trusted computing. In *Proc. of the 19th ACM Symposium on Operating Systems Principles (SOSP)*, Bolton Landing, NY, October 2003.

[12] R. Gellman. Privacy in the Clouds: Risks ot Privacy and Confidentiality from Cloud Computing, 2009. http://www.worldprivacyforum.org/pdf/WPF_Cloud_Privacy_Report.pdf.

[13] M. Hohmuth, M. Peter, H. Hartig, and J. S. Shapiro. Reducing TCB size by using untrusted components - small kernels versus virtual-machine monitors. In *Proc. of 11th ACM SIGOPS European Workshop*, Leuven, Belgium, September 2004.

[14] G. J. Holzmann. The logic of bugs. In *Proc. of Foundations of Software Engineering (FSE)*, Charleston, SC, 2002.

[15] Intel. Intel Active Management Technology. http://www.intel.com/technology/platform-technology/intel-amt/.

[16] M. Jensen, J. Schwenk, N. Gruschka, and L. L. Iacono. On technical security issues in cloud computing. In *Proc. of the IEEE International Conference on Cloud Computing (CLOUD-II)*, Bangalore, India, 2009.

[17] A. Kadav, M. J. Renzelmann, and M. M. Swift. Tolerating hardware device failures in software. In *Proc. of the 22nd Symposium on Operating Systems Principles (SOSP)*, Big Sky, MT, October 2009.

[18] B. Kauer, P. Verissimo, and A. Bessani. Recursive virtual machines for advanced security mechanisms. In *Proc. of the 1st International Workshop on Dependability of Clouds, Data Centers and Virtual Computing Environments (DCDV)*, 2011.

[19] E. Keller, J. Szefer, J. Rexford, and R. B. Lee. NoHype: Virtualized Cloud Infrastructure without the Virtualization. In *Proc. of 37th International Symposium on Computer Architecture (ISCA)*, Saint-Malo, France, 2010.

[20] G. Klein, K. Elphinstone, G. Heiser, J. Andronick, D. Cock, P. Derrin, D. Elkaduwe, K. Engelhardt, M. Norrish, R. Kolanski, T. Sewell, H. Tuch, and S. Winwood. seL4: Formal Verification of an OS Kernel. In *Proc. of the 22nd Symposium on Operating Systems Principles (SOSP)*, Big Sky, MT, October 2009.

[21] B. Krebs. Amazon: Hey Spammers, Get Off My Cloud. Washington Post, July 1 2008.

[22] J. M. McCune, Y. Li, N. Qu, Z. Zhou, A. Datta, V. Gligor, and A. Perrig. TrustVisor: Efficient TCB Reduction and Attestation. In *Proc. of IEEE Symposium on Security and Privacy*, Oakland, CA, May 2010.

[23] A. G. Miklas, S. Saroiu, A. Wolman, and A. D. Brown. Bunker: A Privacy-Oriented Platform for Network Tracing. In *Proc. of the 6th USENIX Symposium on Networked Systems Design and Implementation (NSDI)*, Boston, MA, April 2009.

[24] D. Murray, G. Miob, and S. Hand. Improving Xen Security Through Disaggregation. In *Proc. of the 4th ACM International Conference on Virtual Execution Environments (VEE)*, Seattle, WA, March 2008.

[25] National Institute of Standards and Techonology. National Vulnerability Database. http://nvd.nist.gov/home.cfm.

[26] A. M. Nguyen, N. Schear, H. Jung, A. Godiyal, S. T. King, and H. D. Nguyen. MAVMM: Lightweight and Purpose Built VMM for Malware Analysis. In *Proc. of the 2009 Annual Computer Security Applications Conference (ACSAC)*, Honolulu, HI, 2009.

[27] S. Özkan. CVE Details: The ultimate security vulnerability datasource. http://www.cvedetails.com/index.php.

[28] T. Ristenpart, E. Tromer, H. Shacham, and S. Savage. Hey, You, Get Off of My Cloud: Exploring Information Leakage in Third-Party Compute Clouds. In *Proc. of 16th ACM Conference on Computer and Communications Security (CCS)*, Chicago, IL, November 2009.

[29] I. Roy, H. E. Ramadan, S. T. V. Setty, A. Kilzer, V. Shmatikov, and E. Witchel. Airavat: Security and Privacy for MapReduce. In *Proc. of the 7th USENIX Symposium on Networked Systems Design and Implementation (NSDI)*, San Jose, CA, 2010.

[30] L. Ryzhyk, P. Chubb, I. Kuz, and G. Heiser. Dingo: Taming device drivers. In *Proc. of the 4th ACM European Conference on Computer Systems (Eurosys)*, Nuremberg, Germany, 2009.

[31] R. Sailer, E. Valdez, T. Jaeger, R. Perez, L. van Doorn, J. L. Griffin, and S. Berger. sHype: Secure Hypervisor Approach to Trusted Virtualized Systems. Technical Report RC 23511, IBM Research, 2005.

[32] R. Sailer, X. Zhang, T. Jaeger, and L. van Doorn. Design and Implementation of a TCG-based Integrity Measurement Architecture. In *Proc. of the 13th USENIX Security Symposium*, San Diego, CA, 2004.

[33] N. Santos, K. P. Gummadi, and R. Rodrigues. Towards Trusted Cloud Computing. In *Proc. of the Workshop on Hot Topics in Cloud Computing (HotCloud)*, San Diego, CA, June 2009.

[34] Secunia. Secunia Advisories. http://secunia.com/advisories/.

[35] A. Seshadri, M. Luk, N. Qu, and A. Perrig. SecVisor: A Tiny Hypervisor to Provide Lifetime Kernel Code Integrity for Commodity OSes. In *Proc. of the ACM Symposium on Operating Systems Principles (SOSP)*, Stevenson, WA, October 2007.

[36] T. Shanley. *Protected mode software architecture*. Taylor & Francis, 1996.

[37] U. Steinberg and B. Kauer. NOVA: A Microhypervisor-Based Secure Virtualization Architecture. In *Proc. of the ACM European Conference on Computer Systems (EuroSys)*, Paris, France, April 2010.

[38] M. M. Swift, M. Annamalai, B. N. Bershad, and H. M. Levy. Recovering Device Drivers. In *Proc. of the 6th Symposium on Operating Systems Design and Implementation (OSDI)*, San Francisco, CA, 2004.

[39] M. M. Swift, B. N. Bershad, and H. M. Levy. Improving the Reliability of Commodity Operating Systems. In *Proc. of the 19th Symposium on Operating Systems Principles (SOSP)*, Bolton Landing, NY, 2003.

[40] VMware. Security Advisories & Certifications. `http://www.vmware.com/security/advisories/`.

[41] D. Williams, P. Reynolds, K. Walsh, E. G. Sirer, and F. B. Schneider. Device Driver Safety Through a Reference Validation Mechanism. In *Proc. of the 8th Symposium on Operating Systems Design and Implementation (OSDI)*, San Diego, CA, 2008.

[42] Xen. Xen User Manual v3.3. `http://bits.xensource.com/Xen/docs/user.pdf`.

[43] F. Zhang, J. Chen, H. Chen, and B. Zang. CloudVisor: Retrofitting Protection of Virtual Machines in Multi-tenant Cloud with Nested Virtualization. In *Proceedings of the 23rd ACM Symposium on Operating Systems Principles (SOSP)*, Cascais, Portugal, 2011.

A Critique of Snapshot Isolation

Daniel Gómez Ferro   Maysam Yabandeh *

Yahoo! Research
Barcelona, Spain
{danielgf,maysam}@yahoo-inc.com

Abstract

The support for transactions is an essential part of a database management system (DBMS). Without this support, the developers are burdened with ensuring atomic execution of a transaction despite failures as well as concurrent accesses to the database by other transactions. Ideally, a transactional system provides serializability, which means that the outcome of concurrent transactions is equivalent to a serial execution of them. Based on experiences on lock-based implementations, nevertheless, serializability is known as an expensive feature that comes with high overhead and low concurrency. Commercial systems, hence, compromise serializability by implementing weaker guarantees such as *snapshot isolation*. The developers, therefore, are still burdened with the anomalies that could arise due to the lack of serializability.

There have been recent attempts to enrich large-scale data stores, such as HBase and BigTable, with transactional support. Not surprisingly, inspired by traditional database management systems, serializability is usually compromised for the benefit of efficiency. For example, Google Percolator, implements lock-based snapshot isolation on top of BigTable. We show in this paper that this compromise is not necessary in lock-free implementations of transactional support. We introduce *write-snapshot isolation*, a novel isolation level that has a performance comparable with that of snapshot isolation, and yet provides serializability. The main insight in write-snapshot isolation is to prevent read-write conflicts in contrast to write-write conflicts that are prevented by snapshot isolation.

Categories and Subject Descriptors H.2.4 [*Database Management*]: Systems–concurrency, transaction processing

---

* The authors are listed in alphabetical order.

General Terms Design, Theory, Performance

Keywords Read-write conflict, write-write conflict, serializability, snapshot isolation, distributed data stores, HBase, transactions, key-value stores, lock-free transactional support

1. Introduction

A transaction is an atomic unit of execution and may contain multiple read and write operations to a given database. A reliable transactional system provides ACID properties: atomicity, consistency, isolation, and durability. *Isolation* defines the system behavior in presence of concurrent transactions. Ideally, the isolation level guarantees serializability, which means that the behavior of the system is equivalent to a system that serially runs the transactions (with no concurrency). Serializability, however, is known to be expensive because of (i) the high implementation overhead, (ii) the lower level of concurrency.

Commercial data storage systems [23, 24], such as Google Percolator [23, 24], hence, often implement a weaker guarantee, *snapshot isolation* [5], since it allows for high concurrency between transactions. In snapshot isolation, the snapshot from which a transaction reads is not affected by the concurrent transactions. To provide read snapshots, the database maintains multiple versions of the data [6] and the transactions observe different versions of the data depending on their start time. Two concurrent transactions still conflict if they write into the same data element, which is known as *write-write* conflict.

One advantage of snapshot isolation is that it checks only for write-write conflicts, which its lock-based implementation [24] is very straightforward: a transaction locks a data item before modifying it and aborts if it is already locked (or waits for the lock to be released). Furthermore, the read-only transactions, which comprise the majority of the transactional traffic, could run without any extra locking overhead since snapshot isolation does not require maintaining locks for reads. The drawback is that serializability, which sometimes requires detecting *read-write* conflicts, is not provided by snapshot isolation. (See Section 7 for the list of approaches for adding serializability to snapshot isolation.)

Adding read-write conflict detection to a lock-based transactional system, however, comes with a non-negligible overhead. This is because the read operations, which are the majority in a typical workload, have to maintain the locks as well. Moreover, in a naive implementation of read-write conflict detection, read-only transactions could be aborted, which would greatly reduce the level of concurrency that the system could provide.

In lock-free implementations of snapshot isolation [20], which is suitable for OLTP traffic, the list of identifiers of modified rows is submitted to a centralized status oracle, where they are checked for write-write conflicts. To check for read-write conflicts instead, the transactions could also submit the identifiers of read rows to the status oracle, to be checked against the modified rows of committed transactions. Therefore, restricting the prevented conflicts to only write-write no longer offers a benefit in terms of implementation overhead. It is time, thus, to revisit the core ideas behind write-write and read-write conflict detections and analyze the guarantees as well as the level of concurrency that they provide.

In this paper, we analyze write-write and read-write conflicts. We show that write-write conflict detection that is provided by snapshot isolation is not necessary for providing serializability. In other words, a system could be serializable and still allow for write-write conflicts. More importantly, we prove that read-write conflict detection is sufficient for providing serializability. Based on this analysis, we see that serializability could be brought into large-scale data stores with an overhead comparable to that of snapshot isolation. We present *write-snapshot isolation*, a new isolation level that prevents read-write conflicts instead of write-write conflicts. Each transaction running under write-snapshot isolation writes into a separate snapshot of the database specified by the transaction commit timestamp. Although a transaction reads from a snapshot specified by its start timestamp, it aborts if the read rows are modified by a concurrent, committed transaction.

We expect the level of concurrency offered by write-snapshot isolation to be comparable with that of snapshot isolation. First, as we show in Section 4, neither write-snapshot isolation nor snapshot isolation aborts read-only transactions, which comprise the majority of transactional traffic [10, 12]. Second, two concurrent (write) transactions that have write-write or read-write conflict could still be serializable, and preventing either one could unnecessarily abort some transactions. Consequently, neither of snapshot isolation and write-snapshot isolation have a clear advantage over the other in terms of the offered level of concurrency, which highly depends on the data access pattern in each application. We therefore leave it to the experimental results to show which isolation level overall offers a higher concurrency.

We have implemented both write-snapshot isolation and snapshot isolation on top of HBase [1], a widely used distributed data store. The experimental results show that the level of concurrency offered by write-snapshot isolation is comparable with that offered by snapshot isolation. Serializability, therefore, could be brought to lock-free transactional systems without, however, hurting the performance.

Main Contributions Here we list the main contributions of this paper:

1. We present an analysis of the core ideas behind snapshot isolation and serializability.
2. We introduce a new isolation level, write-snapshot isolation, that checks for read-write conflicts instead of write-write conflicts.
3. We prove that write-snapshot isolation provides serializability.
4. We present a lock-free implementation of write-snapshot isolation on top of HBase, and show that although write-snapshot isolation provides the precious feature of serializability, it is comparable with snapshot isolation in terms of both the implementation overhead and the offered level of concurrency.

Roadmap The remainder of this paper is organized as follows. Section 2 explains snapshot isolation and overviews both its lock-based and lock-free implementations. Serializability is defined in Section 3, which also analyzes the executions that are allowed under snapshot isolation. Write-snapshot isolation is introduced in Section 4, which is followed by its lock-free implementation presented in Section 5. After evaluating our lock-free implementation of write-snapshot isolation on top of HBase in Section 6, we review the related work in Section 7. This section also gives an overview of the related work in making snapshot isolation serializable [1, 2, 8, 16, 19]. We finish the paper with some concluding remarks in Section 8.

2. Snapshot Isolation

Here, we give an overview on both lock-based and lock-free implementations of snapshot isolation. This overview is also presented in our previous work on lock-free implementation of snapshot isolation [20].

Snapshot isolation guarantees that the snapshot from which a transaction reads is not affected by the concurrent transactions. To implement snapshot isolation, the database maintains multiple versions of the data in some *data servers*, and transactions, run by *clients*, observe different versions of the data depending on their start time. Implementations of snapshot isolation have the advantage that writes of a transaction do not block the reads of others. Two concurrent transactions still conflict if they write into the same data

---

[1] http://hbase.apache.org

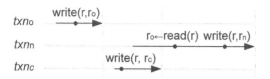

Figure 1. An example run under snapshot isolation guarantee. $write(r, v)$ writes value v into data item r, and $read(r)$ returns the value in data item r. Transaction txn_n observes the commits of transaction txn_o since txn_o commits before txn_n starts. It, however, does not read the writes of transaction txn_c, as it is not committed at the time txn_n start timestamp is assigned. Transactions txn_n and txn_c have both spatial and temporal overlap and at least one of them must abort.

item, say a database row. [2] The conflict must be detected by the snapshot isolation implementation, and at least one of the transactions must abort.

To implement snapshot isolation, each transaction receives two timestamps: one before reading and one before committing the modified data. In both lock-based and lock-free approaches, timestamps are assigned by a centralized server, the *timestamp oracle*, and hence provide a commit order between transactions. Transaction txn_i with assigned start timestamp $T_s(txn_i)$ and commit timestamp $T_c(txn_i)$ (denoted $[T_s(txn_i), T_c(txn_i)]$) reads the latest version of data with commit timestamp $\delta < T_s(txn_i)$. In other words, the transaction observes all its own changes as well as the modifications of transactions that have committed before txn_i starts. In the example of Figure 1, transaction txn_n reads the modifications by the committed transaction txn_o, but not the ones made by the concurrent transaction txn_c.

If txn_i does not have any write-write conflict with another concurrent transaction, it commits its modifications with a commit timestamp. Two transactions txn_i and txn_j conflict if the following holds:

1. **Spatial overlap**: both write into row r;

2. **Temporal overlap**:
   $T_s(txn_i) < T_c(txn_j)$ and $T_s(txn_j) < T_c(txn_i)$.

In the example of Figure 1, both transactions txn_n and txn_c write into the same row r and therefore conflict (spatial overlap). Since they also have temporal overlap, the snapshot isolation implementation must abort at least one of them.

2.1 Lock-based Implementation of Snapshot Isolation

Percolator [24] is a state-of-the-art implementation of this approach on top of a distributed data store. The uncommitted data are written directly into the main database with a version equals to the transaction start timestamp. Percolator [24] adds two extra columns to each column family: *lock* and *write*. The write column maintains the commit times-

---

[2] Here, we use the row-level granularity to detect the write-write conflicts. It is possible to consider finer degrees of granularity, but investigating it further is out of the scope of this work.

tamp. The client runs a 2PC algorithm to update this column on all modified data items. The lock columns provide low granularity locks to be used by the 2PC algorithm. In the first phase of 2PC, the client writes the data and acquires the corresponding locks. Depending on the implementation, if a transaction tries to write into a locked data, it could (i) wait on the lock, (ii) abort, or (iii) force the abort of the transaction that is holding the lock. In the second phase of 2PC, the client updates the data with the commit timestamp and removes the locks. Although using locks simplifies the write-write conflict detection, the locks a failed or slow transaction holds prevent the others from making progress during recovery.

2.2 Lock-free Implementation of Snapshot Isolation

In the lock-free implementation of snapshot isolation, a single server, *i.e.*, the status oracle, receives the commit requests accompanied by the set of the identifiers of modified rows, R. Since status oracle has observed the modified rows by the previous commit requests, it could maintain the commit data and therefore has enough information to check the temporal overlap condition for each modified row. Efficient implementations of this approach could service up to 50K TPS [20] (where each transaction modifies 10 rows on average), which shows that the status oracle is not a bottleneck for scalability of the system. Appendix A explains how the related work [20] addresses the challenges in implementing the status oracle in an efficient and reliable manner. Appendix A presents a brief overview of the techniques presented in our previous work [20] to address the challenges in implementing the status oracle in an efficient and reliable manner.

Algorithm 1 describes the procedure to process a commit request for a transaction txn_i. In the algorithm, R is the list of all the modified rows, T_c is the state of status oracle containing the commit timestamp of transactions, and *lastCommit* is the state of status oracle containing the last commit timestamp of the modified rows.

Algorithm 1 Commit request $(T_s(txn_i), R)$: {commit, abort}

1: **for** each row $r \in R$ **do**
2:     **if** $lastCommit(r) > T_s(txn_i)$ **then**
3:         **return** abort;
4:     **end if**
5: **end for**
                                  ▷ Commit txn_i
6: $T_c(txn_i) \leftarrow$ TimestampOracle.next();
7: **for** each row $r \in R$ **do**
8:     $lastCommit(r) \leftarrow T_c(txn_i)$;
9: **end for**
10: **return** commit;

To check for write-write conflicts, Algorithm 1 checks temporal overlap for all the already committed transactions. In other words, in the case of a write-write conflict, the algorithm commits the transaction for which the commit request is received sooner. Temporal overlap condition must be checked on every row r modified by transaction txn_i against all the committed transactions that have modified the row. Line 2 performs this check, but only for the latest committed transaction txn_l that has modified row r. We can show by induction that this check guarantees that temporal overlap condition is respected by all the committed transactions that have modified row r. Also, notice that Line 2 verifies only the first part of temporal overlap property. This is sufficient in the status oracle because the commit timestamps are obtained by status oracle in contrast to the general case in which commit timestamp could be obtained by clients [24]. Line 6 maintains the mapping between the transaction start and commit timestamps. This data could be used later to process queries about the transaction statuses [20].

To obtain the read snapshot of a transaction, the transaction compares its start timestamp with the commit timestamp of the written values. The reading transaction txn_r skips a particular version, if the transaction txn_w that has written it is (i) not committed yet, (ii) aborted, or (iii) committed with a commit timestamp larger than the start timestamp of txn_r. The commit timestamps could in general be obtained form the status oracle server. Alternatively, to avoid additional calls into the status oracle server, depending on the implementation, they could be written back into the database [20] or be replicated on the clients [17]. The experiments in this paper is performed on an implementation based on the latter approach.

3. Serializability

A *history* represents the interleaved execution of transactions as a linear ordering of their operations [5]. To show the histories, we use the notation presented in [5]: "w1[x]" and "r1[x]" denotes a write and a read by transaction txn_1 on data item x, respectively. Commits and aborts of txn_1 are shown by "c1" and "a1", respectively. A history is *serial* if its transactions are not concurrent. Two histories are equivalent if they include the same transactions and produce the same output.

3.1 Is Write-write Conflict Avoidance *Sufficient* for Serializability?

Snapshot isolation is not serializable [5], which means that it allows histories that do not have serial equivalence. For example, if transaction txn_1 reads x and writes y and transaction txn_2 reads y and writes x, then the following history is possible under snapshot isolation:

H 1. *r1[x] r2[y] w1[y] w2[x] c1 c2*

The snapshot isolation implementation does not prevent History 1 since the transactions write into different data items, i.e., do not have spatial overlap. This could lead to a well-known anomaly called *write skew* [5]. The practical problem that write skew could arise is that the write set of the interleaving transactions could be related by a *constraint*

in the database. Even if each transaction validates the constraint before its commit, two concurrent transactions could still violate the constraint. For example, assume the constraint of $x + y > 0$ and initial values of $x = y = 1$. Further assume that transaction txn_1 reads x and y, and decreases x by one if the constraint condition is still valid. Transaction txn_2 does the same but decreases from y. Snapshot isolation allows the following history:

H 2. *r1[x] r1[y] r2[x] r2[y] w1[x] w2[y] c1 c2*

History 2 is not serializable and transforms the database into the state of $x = y = 0$, which violates the constraint.

3.2 Is Write-write Conflict Avoidance *Necessary* for Serializability?

Although snapshot isolation is not serializable, it prevents many anomalies in data, including the ones listed in the ANSI SQL Standard [3]: (i) *dirty read*: reading an uncommitted value, (ii) *fuzzy read*: having an already read value deleted by a concurrent transaction, and (iii) *phantom*: the set of items that satisfy a search condition vary due to modifications made by concurrent transactions. Snapshot isolation does not have this problem since it reads from a snapshot of the database that is not affected by concurrent transactions. Note that this is independent of the particular conflict detection mechanism, which is write-write conflict detection here, and these anomalies do not manifest even if we do not prevent any kind of conflicts. Besides the ANSI-listed anomalies, it prevents the *Lost Update* anomaly [5], in which the updates of a committed transaction are lost after the commit of a concurrent transaction. For example, in the following unserializable history the updated value x by transaction txn_1 is lost after commit of transaction txn_2.

H 3. *r1[x] r2[x] w2[x] w1[x] c1 c2*

Snapshot isolation prevents History 3 because both transactions write to x and therefore have write-write conflict. Note that in History 3 if transaction txn_2 does not read x (i.e., blind write to x), such as in History 4, the lost update anomaly does not manifest.

H 4. *r1[x] w2[x] w1[x] c1 c2*

This is because the history is equivalent to the following serial history:

H 5. *r1[x] w1[x] c1 w2[x] c2*

After the execution of both histories, x is updated by the write of txn_2, i.e., w2[x]. The modifications made by transaction txn_1 are updated by txn_2, but they are certainly *not lost*. They are visible by any transaction txn_k with a start timestamp between the two commits: $T_c(txn_1) < T_s(txn_k) < T_c(txn_2)$. The lost update anomaly was vaguely explained in [5] (by mentioning the read of transaction txn_2 in parenthesis), which could give the wrong impression that avoiding write-write conflicts is always necessary. Quite the contrary, avoiding write-write conflicts could unnecessarily prevents some serializable histories such as History 4. In other words, write-write conflict avoidance of snapshot isolation, besides allowing some histories that are not serializable, unnecessarily lowers the concurrency of transactions by preventing some valid, serializable histories.

4. Read-Write vs. Write-Write

Multi-version databases [6] (MVCC) maintain multiple versions for the data and add the new data as a new version instead of rewriting the old data. This enables the transactions to read from an arbitrary snapshot of the database (usually specified by the transaction start timestamp) and write to an arbitrary snapshot (specified by the transaction commit timestamp). To implement optimistic concurrency control [21] on top of a multi-version database, further checks must be performed at the commit time.

Snapshot isolation adds write-write conflict detection to MVCC. In fact, snapshot isolation could be termed *read-snapshot isolation* since the read phase of a transaction is never interrupted by concurrent transactions, i.e., the *read* snapshot is isolated. Instead of write-write conflict detection, *write-snapshot isolation* adds read-write conflict detection to MVCC, which means that a transaction does not commit if its read set is modified by a concurrent transaction. However, in contrast with read-snapshot isolation, the write phase of a transaction running under write-snapshot isolation is never interrupted by concurrent transactions, i.e., the *write* snapshot is isolated. We showed in Section 3 that (read-) snapshot isolation prevents some histories that are serializable (e.g., History 4) and allows some that are not (e.g., History 2). In this section, we formally define write-snapshot isolation and the guarantees it provides.

4.1 Write-Snapshot Isolation

As we explained, multi-version databases enable the transactions to operate on separate snapshots, where snapshots are composed of different versions of data. The precise definition of the snapshot from which a transaction txn_i reads depends on the implementation of the isolation level. Similarly to snapshot isolation, write-snapshot isolation assigns unique start and commit timestamps to transactions and ensures that txn_i reads the latest version of data with commit timestamp $\delta < T_s(txn_i)$. In other words, the transaction observes all its own changes as well as the modifications of transactions that have committed before txn_i starts. The difference between write-snapshot isolation and snapshot isolation is, however, in the way the conflict between two transactions is defined.

Formally speaking, two transactions txn_i and txn_j conflict under write-snapshot isolation if the following holds:

1. **RW-spatial overlap**: txn_j writes into row r and txn_i reads from row r;

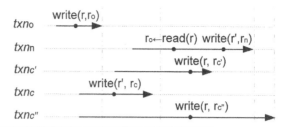

Figure 2. An example run under write-snapshot isolation guarantee. $write(r, v)$ writes value v into data item r, and $read(r)$ returns the value in data item r. Transaction txn_n observes the commits of transaction txn_o since txn_o commits before txn_n starts. It, however, does not read the writes of transaction $txn_{c'}$ as it is not committed at the time txn_n start timestamp is assigned. Transactions txn_n and $txn_{c'}$ have both rw-spatial and rw-temporal overlap and at least one of them must abort. Although transactions txn_n and txn_c have rw-temporal overlap, they do not have read-write conflict since txn_c does not write into row r that is in the read set of txn_n. Similarly, txn_n and $txn_{c''}$ do not have conflict because they do not have rw-temporal overlap.

2. **RW-temporal overlap**:
   $$T_s(txn_i) < T_c(txn_j) < T_c(txn_i).$$

In other words, transactions that commit during the lifetime of transaction txn_i should not modify its read data.

Note: The definition of rw-temporal overlap is different from the temporal overlap explained in Section 2. For example, although transactions txn_n and $txn_{c''}$ in Figure 2 have temporal overlap under snapshot isolation, they do not have rw-temporal overall under write-snapshot isolation. This is because $txn_{c''}$ that modifies the read data of txn_n does not commit during the lifetime of transaction txn_n. Since transaction txn_n does not modify the read data of transaction $txn_{c''}$ (which is empty here), its commit time being during the lifetime of transaction $txn_{c''}$ does not cause an rw-temporal overlap.

In the example of Figure 2, transaction $txn_{c'}$ writes into the same row from which txn_n has read (rw-spatial overlap). Since they also have rw-temporal overlap, the write-snapshot isolation implementation must abort at least one of them. However, although transactions txn_n and txn_c write into the same row r', they do not have rw-spatial overlap under write-snapshot isolation since transaction txn_c does not modify the read data of transaction txn_n, i.e., row r. Two concurrent transactions txn_n and $txn_{c''}$ do not have rw-temporal overlap (because $T_c(txn_{c''}) > T_c(txn_n)$) and therefore are allowed under write-snapshot isolation.

Read-only transactions We use the term "*write transaction*" to refer to a transaction in which the write set is not empty. A transactions is *read-only* if its write set is empty. These transactions are important since they constitute a large part of transactional traffic. For example, in TPC-E [12] benchmark around 77% of transactions are read-only [10], and efficient support for them have a huge impact on the overall performance. Moreover, Google Megastore [4], which services 23 billion transactions daily on top of a key-value store [3], reports more than 86% share for read-only transactions. It is, therefore, very important to ensure that (i) the overhead of running read-only transactions under write-snapshot isolation is close to a minimum, and (ii) the read-only transactions never abort under write-snapshot isolation. We will show in Section 5.1 that the sole overhead of write-snapshot isolation for read-only transactions is obtaining the start timestamp, the same overhead as in snapshot isolation. Here, we show how to avoid abort of read-only transactions in write-snapshot isolation.

Plainly, since a read-only transaction does not perform any writes, it does not affect the values read by other transactions, and therefore does not affect the concurrent transactions as well. Because the reads in both snapshot isolation and write-snapshot isolation are performed on a fixed snapshot of the database that is determined by the transaction start timestamp, the return value of a read operation is always the same, independent of the real time that the read is executed. Hence, a read-only transaction is not affected by concurrent transactions and intuitively does not have to be aborted. As depicted in Figure 3, a read transaction $[T_s(txn_r), T_c(txn_r)]$ is equivalent to transaction $[T_s(txn_r), T_c']$, where $T_s(txn_r) \leq T_c'$. We, therefore, optimize the definition of read-write conflict in write-snapshot isolation by adding the following condition:

3. **Not read-only**: none of transactions txn_i and txn_j is read-only.

In other words, the read-only transactions are not checked for conflicts and hence never abort.

4.2 Is Read-write Conflict Avoidance *Sufficient* for Serializability?

Here we prove that write-snapshot isolation is serializable. To this aim, we need to show that each history, h, run under write-snapshot isolation is *equivalent* to a *serial* history $serial(h)$ [5]. To keep two histories *equivalent*, we keep the same order for (i) operations inside a transaction and (ii) transaction commits. In this way, if a transaction in the new history reads from the same snapshot as in the original history, it commits the same values as well. One way to achieve that is to keep the same order for transaction starts as well. In this way, a transaction observes the same history of commits and, therefore, reads from the same snapshot as in the original history. However, to have the new history *serial*, we must avoid overlapping between transactions. We do that by shifting operations of write (resp. read-only)

[3] Megastore achieves this performance by sacrificing serializability. It partitions the data store, and provides limited consistency guarantees across partitions. See Section 7 for further details.

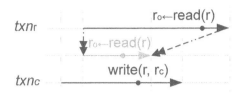

Figure 3. Each read-only transaction run under write-snapshot isolation is equivalent to a shorter transaction with the same start timestamp. This is because the read operations are serviced from a snapshot of the database, and the real time of performing the read does not affect the return value.

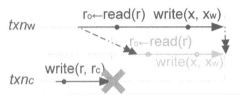

Figure 4. Each write transaction run under write-snapshot isolation is equivalent to a shorter transaction with the same commit timestamp. This is because the read set of a write transaction is not modified by any transaction with rw-temporal overlap.

transactions to the commit (resp. start) point. Intuitively, because write-snapshot isolation prevents read-write conflicts between write transactions, the shifting does not affect the observed commits by transactions.

Putting it together, we construct history $serial(h)$ by:

1. Using the same commit order of history h for write transactions;

2. Maintaining the order of operations inside each transaction;

3. Moving all the operations of a read-only transaction to right after its start.

4. Moving all the operations of a write transaction to right before its commit.

The aborted transactions could be excluded since, similarly to snapshot isolation, their modifications are not read by other transactions.

Lemma 1. *History $serial(h)$ is serial.*

Proof. Since all operations of each transaction are either right before its commit or right after its start, and the assigned timestamps are unique, there are no concurrent transactions in $serial(h)$, and it is, therefore, serial. $\square$

Lemma 2. *History $serial(h)$ is equivalent to history h.*

Proof. As we explained before, the values read by a read-only transaction change by neither the real time of the read operations nor the commit time. Since the commit times-tamp of write transactions is preserved, by using the same start timestamp a read-only transaction observes the same commits in its read snapshot, and hence read the same values. The output of a history is determined by the commit of write transactions. Since the commit order of write transactions is preserved in history $serial(h)$, the output is the same as that of history h, as long as the read values by each write transaction is the same. As depicted in Figure 4, this is the case since read-write conflicts do not manifest in a write-snapshot isolation history. In other words, a write transaction $[T_s(txn_i), T_c(txn_i)]$ is equivalent to transaction $[T_s', T_c(txn_i)]$, where $T_s(txn_i) \leq T_s' \leq T_c(txn_i)$. This is because the read set of write transaction txn_i is not modified by any transaction that is committed during the lifetime of txn_i. $\qquad\square$

Theory 1. *write-snapshot isolation is serializable.*

Proof. Based on Lemmas 1 and 2, for each history h run under write-snapshot isolation, we can construct a serial history $serial(h)$, which is equivalent to history h. $\qquad\square$

We showed that for each write-snapshot isolation history, we can obtain a serial-equivalent history in which the transactions are ordered according to their commit timestamp. Since write-snapshot isolation is serializable, it does not allow the anomalies specified by the ANSI SQL Standard [3] (which are avoided by snapshot isolation) as well as the anomalies that could manifest under snapshot isolation. For example, in History 1 txn_1 (i) commits during the lifetime of txn_2, and (ii) writes into y from which txn_2 has read, and one of them, therefore, must abort. Also, in History 2, which is an example of write skew, txn_1 that commits sooner, writes into x from which txn_2 reads and they, hence, conflict. Moreover, the lost update anomaly that is prevented by snapshot isolation is also prevented by write-snapshot isolation. For example, in History 3 txn_1 (i) writes into x from which txn_2 has read, and (ii) commits during the lifetime of txn_2, and therefore has read-write conflict with txn_2.

4.3 Is Read-write Conflict Avoidance *Necessary* for Serializability?

One advantage of write-snapshot isolation over snapshot isolation is that the concurrent transactions that are unnecessarily aborted due to a write-write conflict in snapshot isolation are allowed in write-snapshot isolation. For example, write-snapshot isolation allows serializable History 4 because (i) $T_c(txn_1) < T_c(txn_2)$, and (ii) txn_1 does not write into the read set of txn_2 (which is empty). Nevertheless, some other serializable histories are unnecessarily prevented by write-snapshot isolation as well. For example, consider the following history:

H 6. *r1[x] r2[z] w2[x] w1[y] c2 c1*

In this history, after commit c2 the new value of x is updated based on the value of z, and after commit c1 the value of y is updated based on the old value of x that was read before commit c2. Write-snapshot isolation prevents History 6 because transaction txn_2 that commits during lifetime of transaction txn_1 writes into x from which txn_1 has read. However, the history is serializable as shown in the following history:

H 7. *r1[x] w1[y] c1 r2[z] w2[x] c2*

After running serial History 7, the value of y is updated based on the old value of x, and the new value of x is updated based on the value of z, which is the same output as History 6.

Write-snapshot isolation has the advantage of offering serializability, the precious feature that snapshot isolation is missing. Both snapshot isolation and write-snapshot isolation unnecessarily abort some serializable transactions. The rate of unnecessary aborts highly depends on the particular workload under which the system runs. We, therefore, leave it to the experimental results to show that overall which isolation level offers a higher concurrency.

5. Lock-free Implementation of Write-snapshot Isolation

Here, we present a lock-free implementation of write-snapshot isolation and show that in the lock-free scheme, the overhead of snapshot isolation and write-snapshot isolation are comparable.

Similar to the lock-free implementation of snapshot isolation presented in Section 2, we use the status oracle server to commit the transaction. The status oracle maintains the list of identifiers of modified rows by committed transactions. Each commit request comprises two sets: the set of identifiers of modified rows, R_w, and the set of identifiers of read rows, R_r. The read set is checked against the modified rows of concurrent committed transactions. If there is no read-write conflict, the status oracle commits the transaction and uses the write set to update the list of modified rows in the status oracle. Note that the set of identifiers of the read rows that is submitted to the status oracle is computed based on the rows that are actually read by the transaction, whether these rows were originally specified by their primary keys or by a search condition.

Algorithm 2 describes the procedure to process a commit request for a transaction txn_i. In the algorithm, R_w is the list of all the modified rows, R_r is the list of all the read rows, T_c is the state of status oracle containing the commit timestamp of transactions, and *lastCommit* is the state of status oracle containing the last commit timestamp of the modified rows.

Similar to Algorithm 1, Line 2 performs the rw-spatial check only for the latest committed transaction txn_l that has modified row $r \in R_r$. Notice that here we check for the read rows R_r in contrast with the write rows in Algorithm 1. Af-

Algorithm 2 Commit request $(T_s(txn_i), R_w, R_r) : \{$commit, abort$\}$

1: **for** each row $r \in R_r$ **do**
2:    **if** $lastCommit(r) > T_s(txn_i)$ **then**
3:       **return** abort;
4:    **end if**
5: **end for**
                                         ▷ Commit txn_i
6: $T_c(txn_i) \leftarrow$ TimestampOracle.next();
7: **for** each row $r \in R_w$ **do**
8:    $lastCommit(r) \leftarrow T_c(txn_i)$;
9: **end for**
10: **return** commit;

---

ter committing the transaction, Line 8 updates the *lastCommit* state by the write set R_w. As we can see, the changes into the implementation of snapshot isolation presented in Section 2 are a few and the overhead of lock-free implementations of snapshot isolation and write-snapshot isolation are comparable. The commit request is a little bigger in write-snapshot isolation since it also includes set R_r. However, since status oracle is a CPU-bound service [17, 20], the network interface bandwidth of the status oracle server is greatly under-utilized and slightly larger packet sizes do not affect its performance.

5.1 Read-only Transactions

We showed in Section 4 that neither of write-snapshot isolation and snapshot isolation aborts the read-only transactions. Here we show that the centralized implementations of write-snapshot isolation and snapshot isolation impose the same overhead for read-only transactions.

Since a read-only transaction always commits in both write-snapshot isolation and snapshot isolation, the client does not have to submit any value with the commit request and the status oracle server does not pay the cost of processing the commit request. This is naturally followed in snapshot isolation since a read-only transaction in snapshot isolation submits an empty list of written rows with its commit request [4]. Therefore, according to Algorithm 1 the transaction always commits since there is no write-write conflict with other transactions. To implement this feature in write-snapshot isolation, the client submits an empty read set to the status oracle if its write set is empty (i.e., is read-only). According to Algorithm 2, therefore, since both read and write sets are empty, the status oracle commits without performing any computation for the transaction.

5.2 Analytical Traffic

The lock-free implementation using a centralized status oracle [20] is designed for online transaction processing (OLTP), which is typically composed of small, short trans-

actions. Analytical traffic, which could include transactions with a very large read set, is out of the scope of this paper. For example, a transaction could scan the entire database and compute some statistics over a field. To illustrate the possible future work, here we mention the two main challenges in extending this implementation for efficient support of occasional analytical traffic. First, the read set could become very large and submitting that to the status oracle could be expensive. Second, the larger the read set, the higher is the probability of a read-write conflict and thus the higher is the abort rate. To address the former, analytical transactions could submit to the status oracle a compact, over-approximated representation of the read set, e.g., table name and row ranges. The latter challenge, which is more fundamental, could be addressed by treating the analytical transactions differently. For example, if a mechanism could ensure that the computed statistics by the analytical traffic are not used by OLTP transactions, which is normally the case, their commit will not affect the OLTP traffic and could be entirely skipped.

6. Evaluation

Here we compare the concurrency level offered by a centralized, lock-free implementation of write-snapshot isolation with that of snapshot isolation presented in [20]. We have implemented two prototypes that integrate write-snapshot isolation (WSI) and snapshot isolation (SI) with HBase, a clone of Bigtable [9] that is widely used in production applications. HBase provides a scalable key-value store, which supports multiple versions of data. It splits groups of consecutive rows of a table into multiple regions, and each region is maintained by a single data server (RegionServer in HBase terminology). A transaction client has to read/write cell data from/to multiple regions in different data servers when executing a transaction. To read and write versions of cells, clients submit get/put requests to data servers. The versions of cells in a table row are determined by timestamps [20].

We used 34 machines with 2.13 GHz Dual-Core Intel(R) Xeon(R) processor, 2 MB cache, and 4 GB memory: 1 for the ZooKeeper coordination service [18], 2 for Book-Keeper [5], 1 for status oracle, 25 for data servers, and 5 for hosting clients. BookKeeper is a system to perform write-ahead logging efficiently and reliably: every change into the memory of the status oracle that is related to a transaction commit/abort is persisted in multiple remote storages via BookKeeper. ZooKeeper is a coordination service that is used by both HBase and BookKeeper. HBase is initially loaded with a table of size 100 GB comprising 100M rows. Since the allocated memory to each HBase process is 3 GB, this table size ensures that the data does not fit into the memory of data servers, representing a system operating on very large-scale data. A random read, therefore, causes an IO

---

[4] In general, it is possible to completely drop the commit request of a read-only transaction, but it will incur some recovery cost on the status oracle since it suspects the failure of the client [20].

[5] http://zookeeper.apache.org/bookkeeper

operation from either a local or remote hard disk. The evaluations aim to answer the following questions:

1. What is the overhead of checking for read-write conflicts in write-snapshot isolation compared to checking for write-write conflicts in snapshot isolation?

2. What is the level of concurrency offered by write-snapshot isolation compared to that of snapshot isolation?

6.1 Benchmark

Ideally, the centralized implementation of write-snapshot isolation and snapshot isolation should be benchmarked with a standard application, generating a typical workload representing the behavior of practical systems. However, transactional support is a new feature to large data stores [20, 24] and the applications that are adapted to use transactions are being developed. Well-established benchmarks such as TPC-E [12], also, have the problem of being designed for SQL databases rather than key-value stores, for which centralized, lock-free implementations of snapshot isolation are developed [20]. We, therefore, use the Yahoo! Cloud Serving Benchmark, YCSB [11], which is a framework for benchmarking large key-value stores. The vanilla implementation operates on single rows and thus does not support transactions. We modified YCSB to add support for transactions, which touch multiple rows. We defined two types of transactions:

1. *Read-only*: where all operations are only read.

2. *Complex*: consists of 50% read and 50% write operations.

Each transaction operates on n rows, where n is a uniform random number between 0 and 20. Based on these types of transactions, we define a *complex* workload, consisting of only complex operations, and a *mixed* workload consisting of 50% read-only and 50% complex transactions.

6.2 Microbenchmarks

Here we run the system with one client and break down the latency of different operations involved in a transaction: (i) start timestamp request, (ii) read, (iii) write, and (iv) commit request. The commit latency is measured from the moment that the commit request is sent to status oracle until when its response is received. The average commit latency is 4.1 ms, which is mainly contributed by persistent storage of the commit data into the WAL via BookKeeper. The average latency of start timestamp request is 0.17 ms. Although the assigned start timestamps must also be persisted, the timestamp oracle could reserve thousands of timestamps per each write into the write-ahead log, and therefore on average servicing timestamps does not inflict a persistence cost.

Each random read and write into HBase takes 38.8 ms and 1.13 ms on average, respectively. The writes are in general less expensive since they usually include only writing into memory and appending into a write-ahead log. Random reads, on the other hand, might inflict the cost of loading an

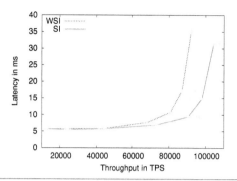

Figure 5. Overhead on the status oracle.

entire block from HDFS (the distributed file system used by HBase), and therefore have higher delays.

6.3 Overhead on the status oracle

The complexity of the commit algorithm in the status oracle is very similar in both snapshot isolation and write-snapshot isolation and we do not expect a big difference in the performance that the status oracle delivers. To measure the relative overhead of snapshot isolation and write-snapshot isolation on the status oracle, here we evaluate both snapshot isolation and write-snapshot isolation on a recent implementation of the status oracle [17]. To stress the status oracle, we need to generate a large volume of traffic, which requires thousands of HBase servers. We therefore evaluate the status oracle in isolation from HBase, and leave measuring the overhead on HBase for the next experiment. This allows the clients to emulate thousands of transactions and stress the status oracle under a high load. Each client allows for 100 outstanding transactions with the execution time of zero, which means that the clients keep the pipe on the status oracle full. We exponentially increase the number of clients from 1 to 2^6 and plot the average latency vs. the average throughput in Figure 5. The read-only transactions do not cause to the status oracle the cost of checking for conflicts as well as the cost of persisting data into the WAL. To evaluate the write-snapshot isolation performance under a high load, we, therefore, use a *complex* workload where rows are randomly selected out of 20M rows. [6]

As Figure 5 depicts, by increasing the load on the status oracle, the throughput with write-snapshot isolation increases up to 80K TPS with average latency of 10.7 ms. After this point, with increasing the load the latency increases (mostly due to the buffering delay at the status oracle) with only marginal improvement in throughput (92K TPS). Although the difference between the performance of status oracle with snapshot isolation and write-snapshot isolation is

---

[6] Note that the complex workload is different from the write-only workload, for which we reported the throughput of 50K TPS in our previous work [20]. Moreover, the reported performance is for one status oracle implemented on a simple dual-core machine. To get a higher throughput, one could partition the database and use a status oracle for each partition.

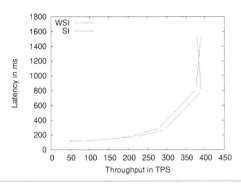

Figure 6. Performance with normal distribution.

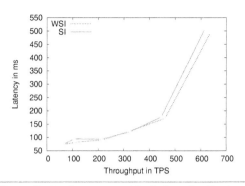

Figure 7. Performance with zipfian distribution.

negligible when status oracle is not overloaded, status oracle eventually saturates sooner with write-snapshot isolation than with snapshot isolation (104K TPS). The reason is that for the sake of simplicity, the current implementation of status oracle executes the conflict detection algorithm in a critical section. The running time of the critical section is slightly higher with write-snapshot isolation since it requires loading as twice memory items as with snapshot isolation. While write-snapshot isolation loads some memory items to check against the read set and after commit loads some others to update with the write set, snapshot isolation updates the same memory items that are already loaded into the processor cache for write-write conflict detection. Although, this does not cause a tangible increase in processing the individual commit requests, under a heavy load it makes the system be saturated sooner. For future work, we are considering using smaller critical sections to alleviate this issue both for snapshot isolation and write-snapshot isolation. Note that it is not advisable to use a system in its saturation point, and therefore the difference between snapshot isolation and write-snapshot isolation remains negligible under a normal load.

6.4 Overhead on HBase

To compare the overhead of supporting snapshot isolation and write-snapshot isolation, we increase the number of clients from 5 to 10, 20, 40, 80, 160, 320, 640, and plot the average latency vs. the average throughput in Figure 6. The throughput indicates the concurrency level and the difference between the latencies of the two isolation levels compares their relative overhead. The client runs one transaction at a time, where each transaction updates n rows, randomly selected with a uniform distribution on 20M rows. The uniform distribution of rows evenly distributes the load on all the data servers. Therefore, the probability of accessing the same row by two transactions is low and the abort rate will be close to zero. Since almost no transaction is aborted by either write-snapshot isolation or snapshot isolation, the results of this experiments emphasis the overhead of checking the conflicts in write-snapshot isolation and snapshot isolation, excluding the level of concurrency that they could offer.

As we expected from the analysis in Section 5, the overhead of supporting two isolation levels is almost the same and both write-snapshot isolation and snapshot isolation have almost the same performance. After 320 clients, the HBase servers saturate with 391 TPS in write-snapshot isolation. At this point adding more clients does not improve the throughput and increases only the latency due to queuing delays.

6.5 Concurrency

To assess the offered concurrency, we repeat the same experiments but with *zipfian* and *zipfianLatest* distributions for selecting the rows. Zipfian distribution models the use cases in which some items are extremely popular [11]. The popular items in zipfianLatest distribution are among the recently inserted data. The high frequent access to popular items increases the probability of conflict between two transactions, and therefore challenges the concurrency level offered by the isolation levels.

Figure 7 depicts the performance under zipfian distribution. Because with this distribution most of the traffic operates on a small proportion of data, random reads are most likely to be serviced from the data already loaded into data servers. Therefore, we see a better throughput and lower latency compared to experiments with a uniform distribution. After 160 clients, however, the cost of processing messages saturates the data servers and adding more clients largely increases the latency, with only marginal improvement on throughput. At this point, the throughput of write-snapshot isolation is 461 TPS and the latency is 172 ms. Overall, the performance of write-snapshot isolation is comparable to that of snapshot isolation.

Figure 8 plots the average abort rate vs. the average throughput for zipfian distribution. The abort rate linearly increases with the increase of throughput, up to 20% in write-snapshot isolation. Although the abort rate in write-snapshot isolation is slightly higher than in snapshot isolation, the difference is negligible. This shows that both snapshot isolation

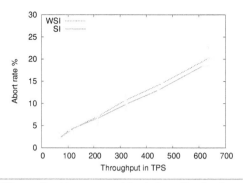

Figure 8. Abort rate with zipfian distribution.

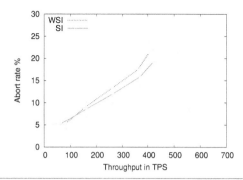

Figure 10. Abort rate with zipfianLatest distribution.

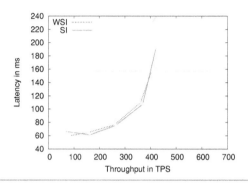

Figure 9. Performance with zipfianLatest distribution.

and write-snapshot isolation offer the same level of concurrency for the mixed workload with zipfian distribution.

Figure 9 depicts the performance under zipfianLatest distribution. The performance in this distribution is in general less than in zipfian distribution. Both write-snapshot isolation and snapshot isolation saturate at 40 clients, where the throughput of write-snapshot isolation is 361 TPS and the latency is 110 ms. Nevertheless, the two systems offer a very similar performance. Figure 10 illustrates the abort rate with this distribution. The abort rate with zipfianLatest increases more quickly compared to zipfian. Although the abort rates are similar in write-snapshot isolation and snapshot isolation, it is slightly larger in write-snapshot isolation: with throughput of 361 TPS the abort rate under write-snapshot isolation is 21%, which is 2% larger than that under snapshot isolation. This is because in zipfianLatest the read set is selected mostly from the recent written data, which increases the chance of a read-write conflict in write-snapshot isolation. This slight overhead is the cost that we pay to benefit from the serializability feature offered by write-snapshot isolation.

7. Related Work

Here we review the related work in literature. First, we contrast our work with related research in isolation levels. Then, we review the recent implementations of snapshot isolation in large-scale data stores. Finally, we list the large-scale data stores that provide some level of serializability.

7.1 Isolation Level

Some previous works [7, 15, 21], check for both read-write and write-write conflicts to provide serializability. Optimistic Concurrent Control (OCC) suggests optimistically running the transactions and postponing the check for conflicts to the commit time [21]. To provide serializability, Kung and Robinson [21] present two lock-based algorithms: one inefficient algorithm with serial validation that hold a write-lock on the whole database (which essentially avoids write-write conflicts), and one efficient algorithm with parallel validation that checks for both read-write and write-write conflicts. Write-snapshot isolation is an implementation of optimistic concurrency control, but further assumes an underlying multi-version database and provides serializability by performing only read-write checks. Moreover, the definition of a read-write conflict (presented in Section 4) is different from that presented in [21].

In the field of transactional memory, TL2 [15] is a lock-based algorithm that checks for both read-write and write-write conflicts. Holding locks on write elements performs the latter: a transaction aborts if it cannot acquire all the locks on the write set. A more recent work that provides one-copy serializability for a replicated database system [7] uses a centralized certifier, which is similar to the status oracle presented in this paper, to check for both read-write and write-write conflicts. One main contribution of this paper is to show that read-write conflict detection is sufficient for serializability, which could be efficiently implemented in lock-free approaches.

There have been several attempts to serialize snapshot isolation. Some are based on a static analysis on the application source code to detect potential conflicting transactions under snapshot isolation [16, 19] and to suggest changes in the application to avoid those conflicts [16]. The modifications proposed by [16] essentially translate the potential conflicts into some write-write conflicts, which are detectable by snapshot isolation. These approaches cannot apply to dynamically generated transactions and require the developer's knowledge on the semantics of snapshot isolation. Our approach is serializable and does not demand any expert knowledge of the developers. Moreover, our approach detects the conflict at the database level and hence does not depend on the application source code. One advantage of write-snapshot isolation over the above, complicated approaches is its simplicity: by slight modifications into the snapshot isolation implementation, write-snapshot isolation adds serializability into the transactional system.

In theory, the anomalies of any isolation level, including snapshot isolation, could be dynamically detected at runtime by verifying the dependency graph [1, 2]. However, these approaches are very expensive for practical implementations. Cahill et. al [8] identify some low-granularity patterns that manifest in non-serializable executions of snapshot isolation. The verification of the patterns has, therefore, lower overhead compared to that of dependency graph. It, however, allows for false positives, which further lowers the concurrency level due to unnecessary aborts. Our lock-free implementation of write-snapshot isolation has the same overhead as lock-free implementation of snapshot isolation.

All the above approaches that try to serialize snapshot isolation inherit the unnecessary abort problem of write-write conflict avoidance. Write-snapshot isolation also unnecessarily aborts some transactions in read-write conflict avoidance. This is up to experimental results to show that which approach offers a higher level of concurrency. Our experiments in Section 6 show that the concurrency level offered by write-snapshot isolation under the mixed workload is comparable to that of snapshot isolation.

In an effort to generalize the ANSI isolation levels [3], Adya et. al. [1, 2] define anti-dependency for a transaction that writes a newer version of a value read by another transaction. The different isolation levels are, then, defined by avoiding certain cycles on the dependency graph. Although anti-dependency is not equivalent to read-write conflict defined in this paper, it was meant to capture the read-write conflicts in the dependency graph [1]. We define a read-write conflict only when they have rw-temporal overlap, while anti-dependency definition does not restrict the start and end of transactions. Moreover, anti-dependency makes sense when it is used to detect cycles on the dependency graph, where we have a perfect but expensive serializability without any false positive. In contrast, read-write conflict detection of this paper is a practical approach that is used without the global dependency graph of transactions and could, therefore, unnecessarily abort some transactions, similarly to the write-write conflict detection of snapshot isolation.

7.2 Implementations of Snapshot Isolation in Large-scale Data Stores

Percolator [24] takes a lock-based, distributed approach to implement snapshot isolation on top of BigTable. Percolator adds two extra columns to each column family: lock and write. Each transaction performs its writes directly into the main table. The write column is used to store commit timestamps. The lock columns simplify the write-write conflict detection since the two-phase commit algorithm run for each transaction avoids writing into a locked column. If a reading transaction finds the column locked, it has to check the status of the transaction that has locked the column. For this purpose, Percolator uses the state of a predefined modified entry by the transaction. The reading transaction, therefore, has to send a query to the server that maintains that particular entry.

Although using locks simplifies the write-write conflict detection, the locks held by a failed or slow transaction prevent the others from making progress until the full recovery from the failure. Moreover, maintaining the lock column as well as responding the queries about a transaction status coming from reading transactions puts extra load on data servers. To alleviate this extra load, Percolator [24] was forced to use heavy batching of messages sent to data servers, which inflicted a nontrivial, multi-second delay on transaction processing. We presented a lock-free implementation of write-snapshot isolation that does not suffer from the problems of using locks, and further provides serializability, the feature that snapshot isolation is missing.

Similar to Percolator, Zhang and Sterck [26] use the HBase data servers to store transactional data for snapshot isolation. However, the transactional data are stored on some separate tables. Even the timestamp oracle is a table that stores the latest timestamp. The benefit is that the system can run on bare-bone HBase. The disadvantage, however, is the low performance due to the many more accesses to the data servers to maintain the transactional data. Our approach provides serializability with a negligible overhead on data servers. ecStore [25] also provides snapshot isolation. To detect write-write conflicts, it runs a two-phase commit algorithm among all participant nodes, which has a scalability problem for general workloads.

7.3 Implementations of Serializability in Large-scale Data Stores

To achieve scalability, MegaStore [4], ElasTras [13], and G-Store [14] rely on partitioning the data store, and provide ACID semantics within partitions. The partitions could be created statically, such as in MegaStore and ElasTras, or dynamically, such as in G-Store. However, ElasTras and G-Store have no notion of consistency across partitions and MegaStore [4] provides only limited consistency guarantees across them. ElasTras [13] partitions the data among some transaction managers (OTM) and each OTM is responsible for providing consistency for its assigned partition. There is no notion of global serializability. In G-Store [14], the partitions are created dynamically by a *Key Group* algorithm, which essentially labels the individual rows on the database with the group identifier.

MegaStore [4] uses a write-ahead log to synchronize the writes within a partition. Each participant writes to the main database only after it successfully writes into the write-ahead log. Paxos is run between the participants to resolve the contention between multiple writes into the write-ahead log. Although transactions across multiple partitions are supported with an implementation of the two-phase commit algorithm, the applications are discouraged from using that due to performance issues.

Similar to Percolator, Deuteronomy [22] uses a lock-based approach to provide ACID. In contrast to Percolator where the locks are stored in the same data tables, Deuteronomy uses a centralized lock manager (TC). Furthermore, TC is the portal to the database and all the operations must go through it, making it the bottleneck for scalability. This leads to a low throughput offered by TC [22]. On the contrary, our approach is lock-free and can scale up to 50K TPS (500K write operations per second). Moreover, the data is accessed directly through HBase servers and in contrary to Deuteronomy do not go through the status oracle.

8. Concluding Remarks

In this paper, we contrasted read-write conflict with write-write conflict that is targeted by snapshot isolation. We proved that read-write conflict detection has the advantage of being serializable, the precious feature that snapshot isolation is missing. We showed that, similarly to snapshot isolation, write-snapshot isolation does not abort read-only transactions, which comprise the majority of transactional traffic. We then presented a new isolation level, write-snapshot isolation, which checks for read-write conflicts instead of write-write conflicts. Perhaps, the most important advantage of write-snapshot isolation is its simplicity for it efficiently adds serializability to a lock-free implementation of snapshot isolation by the slightest changes.

We showed that in a centralized, lock-free scheme of transactional support, which is suitable for large-scale data stores, the overhead of implementing both snapshot isolation and write-snapshot isolation is comparable. The offered level of concurrency highly depends on the particular workload that the application generates. The experimental results showed that snapshot isolation and write-snapshot isolation offer a comparable level of concurrency under a mixed, synthetic workload. The open source release of our implementation, Omid, is available to public [7], and can be tried out on future real-world transactional applications that will operate on top of distributed data stores.

A. Implementation Details

Here, we briefly present our implementation of the status oracle that is covered in our previous works [17, 20]. The timestamps are obtained from a timestamp oracle integrated into the status oracle. The two main concerns related to the centralized scheme of status oracle are (i) *efficiency*, as the status oracle could potentially be a performance bottleneck,

[7] https://github.com/yahoo/omid

and (ii) *reliability*, as the status oracle could be a single point of failure.

Our implementation of the status oracle deployed on a simple dual core machine scales up to 50K TPS (where each transaction modifies 10 rows in average). To achieve this scale, the status oracle services requests from memory: it does not require a read from a hard disk to commit a transaction. However, to detect conflicts Line 2 of Algorithm 3 requires the commit timestamp of all the rows in the database, which does not fit in memory. To address this issue, the status oracle keeps only the state of the last NR committed rows that fit into the main memory, but it also maintains $T_{\max}$, the maximum timestamp of all the removed entries from memory. Algorithm 3 shows the status oracle procedure to process commit requests.

Algorithm 3 Commit request: {commit, abort}

1: **for** each row $r \in R$ **do**
2:    **if** $lastCommit(r) \neq$ null **then**
3:       **if** $lastCommit(r) > T_s(txn_i)$ **then**
4:          **return** abort;
5:       **end if**
6:    **else**
7:       **if** $T_{\max} > T_s(txn_i)$ **then**
8:          **return** abort;
9:       **end if**
10:   **end if**
11: **end for**
                    ▷ Commit txn_i
12: **for** each row $r \in R$ **do**
13:    $committed(r)T_s(txn_i) \leftarrow T_c(txn_i)$
14: **end for**
15: **return** commit

Line 8 pessimistically aborts the transaction, which means that some transaction could unnecessarily abort. It is not a problem if $T_{\max} - T_s(txn_i) \gg MaxCommitTime$. Assuming 8 bytes for unique identifiers, we estimate the required space to keep a row data, including row identifier, start timestamp, and commit timestamp, at 32 bytes. Assuming 1 GB of memory, we can fit data of 32M rows in memory. If each transaction modifies 8 rows on average, then the rows for the last 4M transactions are in memory. Assuming a maximum workload of 80K TPS, the row data for the last 50 seconds are in memory, which is far more than the average commit time, *i.e.*, hundreds of milliseconds.

To check if a read version in the read snapshot of a transaction, we need access to the commit timestamp of the transaction that has written the version. The algorithm for performing this check is also changed to take into account the value of $T_{\max}$. We refer the readers to our previous work [20] for more details. To reduce the load of performing this check on the status oracle, a read-only copy of the commit timestamps could be maintained in (i) data servers, beside the actual data [20], or (ii) the clients [17]. The results reported in this paper are produced using the latter approach.

To provide reliability for the in-memory data, the status oracle persists commit data into a write-ahead log. In this way, if the status oracle server fails, the same status oracle after recovery, or another fresh instance of the status oracle could still recreate the memory state from the write-ahead log and continue servicing the commit requests. The write-ahead log is also replicated across multiple remote storage devices to prevent loss of data after a storage failure. Writing into multiple remote machines could be very expensive and it is important to prevent it from becoming a bottleneck. We use Bookkeeper for this purpose, which could efficiently perform up to 20,000 writes of size 1028 bytes per second into a write-ahead log. Since status oracle requires frequent writes into the write-ahead log, multiple writes could be batched with no perceptible increase in processing time. With a batching factor of 10, BookKeeper is able to persist data of 200K TPS. The write of the batch to BookKeeper is triggered either by batch size, after 1 KB of data is accumulated, or by time, after 5 ms since the last trigger.

Acknowledgments

We thank Russell Sears, the anonymous reviewers, and our shepherd, Maurice Herlihy, for the useful comments. This work has been partially supported by the Cumulo Nimbo project (ICT-257993), funded by the European Community.

References

[1] A. Adya. *Weak consistency: a generalized theory and optimistic implementations for distributed transactions.* PhD thesis, Citeseer, 1999.

[2] A. Adya, B. Liskov, and P. O'Neil. Generalized isolation level definitions. In *Data Engineering, 2000. Proceedings. 16th International Conference on*, pages 67–78. IEEE, 2000.

[3] A. Ansi. x3. 135-1992, american national standard for information systems-database language-sql, 1992.

[4] J. Baker, C. Bondç, J. C. Corbett, J. J. Furman, A. Khorlin, J. Larson, J. M. Leon, Y. Li, A. Lloyd, and V. Yushprakh. Megastore: Providing Scalable, Highly Available Storage for Interactive Services. In *CIDR*, 2011.

[5] H. Berenson, P. Bernstein, J. Gray, J. Melton, E. O'Neil, and P. O'Neil. A critique of ansi sql isolation levels. *SIGMOD Rec.*, 1995.

[6] P. Bernstein, V. Hadzilacos, and N. Goodman. *Concurrency control and recovery in database systems*, volume 5. Addison-wesley New York, 1987.

[7] M. Bornea, O. Hodson, S. Elnikety, and A. Fekete. One-copy serializability with snapshot isolation under the hood. In *Data Engineering (ICDE), 2011 IEEE 27th International Conference on*, pages 625–636. IEEE, 2011.

[8] M. Cahill, U. Röhm, and A. Fekete. Serializable isolation for snapshot databases. *ACM Transactions on Database Systems (TODS)*, 34(4):20, 2009.

[9] F. Chang, J. Dean, S. Ghemawat, W. C. Hsieh, D. A. Wallach, M. Burrows, T. Chandra, A. Fikes, and R. E. Gruber. Bigtable: A distributed storage system for structured data. *TOCS*, 2008.

[10] S. Chen, A. Ailamaki, M. Athanassoulis, P. Gibbons, R. Johnson, I. Pandis, and R. Stoica. Tpc-e vs. tpc-c: characterizing the new tpc-e benchmark via an i/o comparison study. *ACM SIGMOD Record*, 39(3):5–10, 2011.

[11] B. F. Cooper, A. Silberstein, E. Tam, R. Ramakrishnan, and R. Sears. Benchmarking cloud serving systems with ycsb. In *SoCC'10*, 2010.

[12] T. P. P. Council. Tpc benchmark e standard specification version 1.12.0, September 2010.

[13] S. Das, D. Agrawal, and A. El Abbadi. Elastras: an elastic transactional data store in the cloud. In *HotCloud'09*, 2009.

[14] S. Das, D. Agrawal, and A. El Abbadi. G-store: a scalable data store for transactional multi key access in the cloud. In *SoCC'10*, 2010.

[15] D. Dice, O. Shalev, and N. Shavit. Transactional locking ii. *Distributed Computing*, pages 194–208, 2006.

[16] A. Fekete, D. Liarokapis, E. O'Neil, P. O'Neil, and D. Shasha. Making snapshot isolation serializable. *ACM Transactions on Database Systems (TODS)*, 30(2):492–528, 2005.

[17] D. G. Ferro, F. Junqueira, B. Reed, and M. Yabandeh. Lock-free Transactional Support for Distributed Data Stores. In *SOSP Poster Session*, 2011.

[18] P. Hunt, M. Konar, F. Junqueira, and B. Reed. Zookeeper: wait-free coordination for internet-scale systems. In *Proceedings of the 2010 USENIX conference on USENIX annual technical conference*, pages 11–11. USENIX Association, 2010.

[19] S. Jorwekar, A. Fekete, K. Ramamritham, and S. Sudarshan. Automating the detection of snapshot isolation anomalies. In *Proceedings of the 33rd international conference on Very large data bases*, pages 1263–1274. VLDB Endowment, 2007.

[20] F. Junqueira, B. Reed, and M. Yabandeh. Lock-free Transactional Support for Large-scale Storage Systems. In *HotDep*, 2011.

[21] H. Kung and J. Robinson. On optimistic methods for concurrency control. *ACM Transactions on Database Systems (TODS)*, 6(2):213–226, 1981.

[22] J. J. Levandoski, D. Lome, M. F. Mokbel, and K. K. Zhao. Deuteronomy: Transaction Support for Cloud Data. In *CIDR*, 2011.

[23] Y. Lin, K. Bettina, R. Jiménez-Peris, M. Patiño Martínez, and J. E. Armendáriz-Iñigo. Snapshot isolation and integrity constraints in replicated databases. *ACM Trans. Database Syst.*, 2009.

[24] D. Peng and F. Dabek. Large-scale incremental processing using distributed transactions and notifications. In *OSDI*, 2010.

[25] H. Vo, C. Chen, and B. Ooi. Towards elastic transactional cloud storage with range query support. *Proceedings of the VLDB Endowment*, 3(1-2):506–514, 2010.

[26] C. Zhang and H. De Sterck. Supporting multi-row distributed transactions with global snapshot isolation using bare-bones hbase. *Proc. of Grid2010*, 2010.

LazyBase: Trading Freshness for Performance in a Scalable Database

James Cipar, Greg Ganger

Carnegie Mellon University

Kimberly Keeton, Charles B. Morrey III
Craig A. N. Soules, Alistair Veitch

HP Labs, Palo Alto

Abstract

The LazyBase scalable database system is specialized for the growing class of data analysis applications that extract knowledge from large, rapidly changing data sets. It provides the scalability of popular NoSQL systems without the query-time complexity associated with their eventual consistency models, offering a clear consistency model and explicit per-query control over the trade-off between latency and result freshness. With an architecture designed around batching and pipelining of updates, LazyBase simultaneously ingests atomic batches of updates at a very high throughput and offers quick read queries to a stale-but-consistent version of the data. Although slightly stale results are sufficient for many analysis queries, fully up-to-date results can be obtained when necessary by also scanning updates still in the pipeline. Compared to the Cassandra NoSQL system, LazyBase provides 4X–5X faster update throughput and 4X faster read query throughput for range queries while remaining competitive for point queries. We demonstrate LazyBase's tradeoff between query latency and result freshness as well as the benefits of its consistency model. We also demonstrate specific cases where Cassandra's consistency model is weaker than LazyBase's.

Categories and Subject Descriptors H.2.4 *Database Management Systems, Parallel Databases, Distributed Databases*

General Terms *Design, Experimentation, Measurement, Performance*

Keywords *Consistency, Freshness, Pipeline*

1. Introduction

Data analytics activities have become major components of enterprise computing. Increasingly, time-critical business decisions are driven by analyses of large data sets that grow and change at high rates, such as purchase transactions, news updates, click streams, hardware monitoring events, tweets and other social media, and so on. They rely on accurate and nearly up-to-date results from sequences of read queries against these data sets, which also need to simultaneously accommodate the high rate of updates.

Unfortunately, current systems fall far short on one or more dimensions. The traditional approach to decision support couples an OLTP system, used for maintaining the primary copy of a database on which update transactions are performed, with a distinct data warehouse system. The latter stores a copy of the data in a format that allows efficient read-only queries, re-populated infrequently (typically daily) from the primary database by a process known as extract, transform, and load (ETL) [19]. For decision support activities that can rely on stale versions of OLTP data, this model is ideal. However, for many modern data analytics activities, which depend upon very high update rates and a greater degree of *freshness* (i.e., up-to-date-ness), it is not.

So-called "NoSQL" database systems, such as Cassandra [1], HBase [2], CouchDB [3] and MongoDB [4], have emerged as an alternate solution. Generally speaking, these systems support arbitrarily high ingest and query rates, scaling effectively by relaxing consistency requirements to eliminate most of the locking and transactional overheads that limit traditional OLTP systems. Most NoSQL systems adopt an *eventual consistency* model, which simplifies the design of the system but complicates its use for correctness-critical data analytics. Programmers of analytics applications often struggle with reasoning about consistency when using such systems, particularly when results depend on data from recent updates. For example, when a client updates a value in the Cassandra database, not all servers receive the new value immediately. Subsequent reads may return either the old value or the new one, depending on which server answers them. Confusingly, a client may see the new value for one read operation, but the old value for a subsequent read if it is serviced by a different server.

LazyBase provides a new point in the solution space, offering a unique blend of properties that matches modern data analytics well. Specifically, it provides scalable high-throughput ingest together with a clear, strong consistency model that allows for a per-read-query tradeoff between latency and result freshness. Exploiting the insight that many queries can be satisfied with slightly out-of-date data, LazyBase batches together seconds' worth of incoming data into sizable atomic transactional units to achieve high throughput updates with strong semantics. LazyBase's batching approach is akin to that of incremental ETL systems, but avoids their freshness delays by using a pipelined architecture that allows different stages of the pipeline to be queried independently. Queries that can use slightly out-of-date data (e.g., a few minutes old) use only the final output of the pipeline, which corresponds to the fully ingested and indexed data. In this case, updates are effectively processed in the background and do not interfere with the foreground query workload, thus resulting in query latencies and throughputs achievable with read-only database systems. Queries that require even fresher results can access data at any stage in the pipeline, at progressively higher processing costs as the freshness increases. This approach provides applications with control over and understanding of the freshness of query results.

LazyBase's architecture also enhances its throughput and scalability. Of course, batching is a well-known approach to improving throughput. In addition, the stages of LazyBase's pipeline can be independently parallelized, permitting flexible allocation of resources (including machines) to ingest stages to accommodate workload variability and overload.

We evaluate LazyBase's performance by comparing to Cassandra both for update performance as well as point and range query performance at various scalability levels. Because of its pipelined architecture and batching of updates, LazyBase maintains 4X–5X higher update throughput than Cassandra at all scalability levels. LazyBase achieves only 45–55% of Cassandra's point query throughput, however, due to the relative efficiency of Cassandra's single row lookups. Conversely, because LazyBase stores data sorted sequentially in the keyspace of the query being performed, LazyBase achieves 4X the range query throughput of Cassandra. LazyBase achieves this performance while maintaining consistent point-in-time views of the data, whereas Cassandra does not.

This paper makes several contributions. Most notably, it describes a novel system (LazyBase) that can provide the scalability of NoSQL database systems while providing strongly consistent query results. LazyBase also demonstrates the ability to explicitly trade off freshness and read-query latency, providing a range of options within which costs are only paid when necessary. It shows how combining batching and pipelining allows for the three key features: scalable ingest, strong consistency, and explicit control of the freshness vs. latency tradeoff.

2. Background and motivation

This section discusses data analytics applications, features desired of a database used to support them, and major short-comings of the primary current solutions. Related work is discussed in more detail in Section 6.

Data analytics applications. Insights and predictions extracted from large, ever-growing data corpuses have become a crucial aspect of modern computing. Enterprises and service providers often use observational and transactional data to drive various decision support applications, such as sales or advertisement analytics. Generally speaking, the data generation is continuous, requiring the decision support database system to support high update rates. The system must also simultaneously support queries that mine the data to accurately produce the desired insights and predictions. Often, though, query results on a slightly out-of-date version of the data, as long as it is self-consistent, are fine. Table 1 lists various example applications across a number of domains and with varied freshness requirements.

As one example, major retailers now rely heavily on data analytics to enhance sales and inventory efficiency, far beyond traditional nightly report generation [28]. For example, in order to reduce shipping costs, many retailers are shifting to just-in-time inventory delivery at their stores, requiring hour-by-hour inventory information in order to manage transportation of goods [15]. In addition to transaction records from physical point-of-sale systems, modern retailers exploit data like clickstreams, searches, and purchases from their websites to drive additional sales. For example, when a customer accesses a store website, recent activity by the same and other customers can be used to provide on-the-spot discounts, suggestions, advertisements, and assistance.

Social networking is another domain where vast quantities of information are used to enhance user experiences and create revenue opportunities. Most social networking systems rely on graphs of interconnected users that correspond to publish-subscribe communication channels. For example, in Twitter and Facebook, users follow the messages/posts of other users and are notified when new ones are available from the users they follow. Queries of various sorts allow users to examine subsets of interest, such as the most recent messages, the last N messages from a given user, or messages that mention a particular "hashtag" or user's name. A growing number of applications and services also rely on broader analysis of both the graphs themselves and topic popularity within and among the user communities they represent. In addition to targeted advertisements and suggestions of additional social graph connections, social media information can rapidly expose hot-topic current events [10], flu/cold epidemics [22], and even provide an early warning system for earthquakes and other events [5].

Desired properties. Data analytics applications of the types discussed above are demanding and different from more traditional OLTP activities and report generation. Supporting them well requires an interesting system design point with respect to data ingest, consistency, and result freshness.

Application domain	Desired freshness		
	seconds	minutes	hours+
Retail	real-time coupons, targeted ads and suggestions	just-in-time inventory management	product search, trending, earnings reports
Social networking	message list updates, friend/follower list changes	wall posts, photo sharing, news updates and trending	social graph analytics
Transportation	emergency response, air traffic control	real-time traffic maps, bus/plane arrival prediction	traffic engineering, bus route planning
Investment	real-time micro-trades, stock tickers	web-delivered graphs	trend analyses, growth reports
Enterprise information management	infected machine identification	email, file-based policy violations	enterprise search results, e-discovery requests
Data center and network monitoring	automated problem detection and diagnosis	human-driven diagnosis, online performance charting	capacity planning, availability analyses, workload characterization

Table 1. Freshness requirements for application families from a variety of domains.

Data ingest: Such applications rely on large data corpuses that are updated rapidly, such as clickstreams, Twitter tweets, location updates, or sales records. Any system used to support such analytics must be able to ingest and organize (e.g., index) the data fast enough to keep up with the data updates. At the same time it sustains these high data ingestion rates, the system must also be able to answer the read-only queries it receives. Fortunately though, high-throughput ingest analytics data tends to be observational or declarative data, such that the updates and the queries are independent. That is, the updates add, replace or delete data but do not require read-modify-write transactions on the data corpus. So, a decision support system can handle updates separately from read-only analytic queries. As discussed further below, it is important that the system support atomic updates to a set of related data items, so that consistent query results can be obtained.

Consistency: To simplify the programming of decision support applications, query results typically must have a consistency model that analysts and application writers can understand and reason about. Weak forms of consistency, such as eventual consistency, where the storage system guarantees that if no new updates are made to the object, eventually all accesses will return the last updated value [42], are difficult to reason about. As a result, application developers generally seek stronger properties [40, 42], such as a consistent prefix, monotonic reads, "read my writes," causal consistency, or self-consistency. By requesting a consistent prefix, a reader will observe an ordered sequence of writes starting with the first write to a data object. With monotonic read consistency, if a reader has seen a particular value for an object, any subsequent accesses in that session will never return any previous values; as such, it is often called a "session guarantee." The read my writes property guarantees that the effects of all writes performed by a client are visible to the client's subsequent reads. Causal consistency is a generalization of read my writes, where any process with a causal relationship to a process that has updated an object will see the updated value. Self-consistency refers to the property that the data set has been updated in its entirety, in the face of

multi-row (or even multi-table) update transactions. Without such stronger consistency properties, application writers struggle to produce accurate insights and predictions. For example, for just-in-time inventory management, not having a consistent view of the data can lead to over- or underestimating delivery needs, either wasting effort or missing sales opportunities due to product unavailability. As another example, a user notified of a new tweet could, upon trying to retrieve it, be told that it does not exist. Even disaster recovery for such systems becomes more difficult without the ability to access self-consistent states of the data; simple solutions, such as regular backups, require consistent point-in-time snapshots of the data.

Freshness: For clarity, we decouple the concepts of data consistency (discussed above) and data *freshness*. Freshness (also known as bounded staleness [40]) describes the delay between when updates are ingested into the system, and when they are available for query – the "eventual" of eventual consistency. Of course, completely-up-to-date freshness would be ideal, but the scalability and performance costs of such freshness has led almost all analytics applications to accept less. For most modern analytics, bounded staleness (e.g., within seconds or minutes) is good enough. We believe that it would be best for freshness (or the lack thereof) to be explicit and, even better, application-controlled. Application programmers should be able to specify freshness goals in an easy-to-reason-about manner that puts a bound on how out-of-date results are (e.g., "all results as of 5 minutes ago"), with a system supplying results that meet this bound but not doing extra work to be more fresh. The system may provide even fresher results, but only if it can do so without degrading performance. Such an approach matches well with the differences in freshness needs among applications from the various domains listed in Table 1.

In the next section, we describe LazyBase, which provides a new point in the solution space to satisfy the needs of modern data analytics applications. In particular, it combines scalable and high-throughput data ingest, a clear consistency model, and explicit per-read-query control over the tradeoff between latency and result freshness.

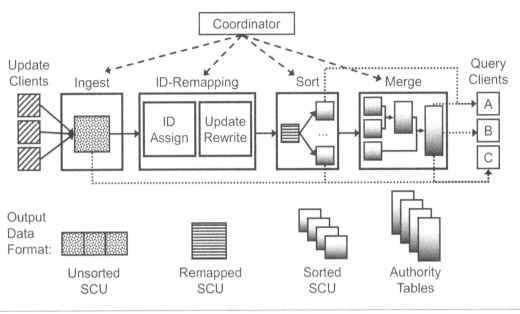

Figure 1. LazyBase pipeline.

3. Design and implementation

LazyBase is a distributed database that focuses on high-throughput updates and high query rates using batching. Unlike most batching systems, LazyBase can dynamically trade data freshness for query latency at query time. It achieves this goal using a pipelined architecture that provides access to update batches at various points throughout their processing. By explicitly accessing internal results from the pipeline stages, applications can trade some query performance to achieve the specific data freshness they require.

This section outlines LazyBase's design and implementation, covering the application service model, how data is organized in the system, its pipelined architecture, work scheduling, scaling, fault tolerance, query model, and on-disk data format.

3.1 Service model

LazyBase provides a *batched update/read query* service model, which decouples update processing from read-only queries. Unlike an OLTP database, LazyBase cannot simultaneously read and write data values in a single operation. Queries can only read data, while updates (e.g., adds, modifies, deletes) are *observational*, meaning that a new/updated value must always be given; this value will overwrite (or delete) existing data, and cannot be based on any data currently stored. For example, there is no way to specify that a value should be incremented, or be assigned the results of subtracting one current value from another, as might happen in a conventional database. This restriction is due to the complexity of maintaining read my writes consistency in a distributed batch-processing system. Methods for providing this functionality are an area of future work, although we have not found it to be a limitation in any of our applications to date.

Clients upload a set of updates that are batched into a single *self-consistent update* or SCU. An SCU is the granularity of work performed at each pipeline stage, and LazyBase's ACID semantics are on the granularity of an SCU. The set of changes contained within an SCU is applied *atomically* to the tables stored in the database, using the mechanisms described in Section 3.2. An SCU is applied *consistently*, in that all underlying tables in the system must be consistent after the updates are applied. SCUs are stored *durably* on disk when they are first uploaded, and the application of an SCU is *isolated* from other SCUs. In particular, LazyBase provides *snapshot isolation*, where all reads made in a query will see a consistent snapshot of the database; in practice, this is the last SCU that was applied at the time the query started. This design means that LazyBase provides readers self-consistency, monotonic reads, and a consistent prefix with bounded staleness.

Updates are specified as a set of Thrift [6] RPC calls, to provide the data values for each row update. For efficiency, queries are specified programmatically. Like MapReduce [21], each query maps to a restricted dataflow pattern, which includes five phases: filter, uniquify, group_by, aggregate, and post_filter. These phases and their implementation are described in more detail in Section 3.7.

3.2 Data model

Similar to conventional RDBMS/SQL systems, LazyBase organizes data into tables with an arbitrary number of named and typed columns. Each table is stored using a *primary view* that contains all of the data columns and is sorted on a *primary key*: an ordered subset of the columns in the table. For example, a table might contain three columns $\langle A, B, C \rangle$ and its primary view key could be $\langle A, B \rangle$, meaning it's sorted first by A and then by B for equal values of A. The remaining columns are referred to as the *data columns*. Tables may also have any number of materialized *secondary views* which contain a subset of the columns in the table and are sorted on a different *secondary key*. The secondary key columns must be a superset of the primary key columns to enforce uniqueness, but can specify any column order for sorting. LazyBase has no concept of non-materialized views.

Because these tables describe both *authority* data that has been fully processed by the pipeline as well as *update* data that is in-flight, they also contain additional hidden fields. Each row is assigned a timestamp indicating the time at which it should be applied as well as a delete marker indicating if the specified primary key should be removed (as opposed to inserted or modified). Each data column is also assigned an additional timestamp indicating at what time that column was last updated. These timestamps can vary in the case of partial row updates.

Like many other databases, LazyBase supports the concept of an auto-increment column (also known as a database surrogate key), by which a given key (potentially multi-column) can be assigned a single unique incrementing value in the system, allowing users of the system to improve query and join times and reducing storage requirements for large keys. For instance, two strings specifying the hostname and path of a file could be remapped to a single integer value, which is then used in other tables to store observational data about that file. We refer to these auto-increment columns as *ID-key* columns.

3.3 Pipelined design

The design of the LazyBase pipeline is motivated by the goal of ingesting and applying updates as efficiently as possible while allowing queries to access these intermediate stages if needed to achieve their freshness goals. Figure 1 illustrates the pipeline stages of LazyBase: ingest, id-remapping, sort, and merge. In addition to these stages, a coordinator is responsible for tracking and scheduling work in the system.

The *ingest* stage batches updates and makes them durable. Updates are read from clients and written into the current SCU as rows into an unsorted primary view for the appropriate table type. Rows are assigned timestamps based on their ingestion time. ID-keys in the updates are assigned temporary IDs, local to the SCU, and the mapping from key to temporary ID is stored in the SCU (allowing queries to use this mapping if needed). LazyBase marks an SCU as complete once either sufficient time has passed (based on a timeout) or sufficient data has been collected (based on a watermark). At this point, new clients' updates are directed to the next SCU and any remaining previously connected clients complete their updates to the original SCU. Once complete, the ingest stage notifies the coordinator, which as-

signs it a globally unique SCU number and schedules the SCU to be processed by the rest of the pipeline.

The *id-remapping* stage converts SCUs from using their internal temporary IDs to using the global IDs common across the system. Internally, the stage operates in two phases, id-assignment and update-rewrite, that are also pipelined and distributed. In id-assignment, LazyBase does a bulk lookup on the keys in the SCU to identify existing keys and then assigns new global IDs to any unknown keys, generating a temporary ID:global ID mapping for this update. Because id-assignment does a lookup on a global key-space, it can only be parallelized through the use of *key-space partitioning*, as discussed below. In update-rewrite, LazyBase rewrites the SCU's tables with the correct global IDs and drops the temporary mappings.

The *sort* stage sorts each of the SCU's tables for each of its views based on the view's key. Sorting operates by reading the table data to be sorted into memory and then looping through each view for that table, sorting the data by the view's key. The resulting sorted data sets form the sorted SCU. If the available memory is smaller than the size of the table, sorting will break a table into multiple memory-sized chunks and sort each chunk into a separate output file to be merged in the merge stage. While writing out the sorted data, LazyBase also creates an index of the data that can be used when querying.

The *merge* stage combines multiple sorted SCUs into a single sorted SCU. By merging SCUs together, we reduce the query cost of retrieving fresher results by reducing the number of SCUs that must be examined by the query. LazyBase utilizes a tree-based merging based on the SCU's global number. SCUs are placed into a tree as leaf nodes and once a sufficient span of SCUs is available (or sufficient time has passed), they are merged together. This merging applies the most recent updates to a given row based on its data column timestamps, resulting in a single row for each primary key in the table. Eventually, all of the updates in the system are merged together into a single SCU, referred to as the *authority*. The authority is the minimal amount of data that must be queried to retrieve a result from LazyBase. Just as in the sort stage, LazyBase creates an index of the merged data while it is being written that can be used when querying.

When each stage completes processing, it sends a message to the *coordinator*. The coordinator tracks which nodes in the system hold which SCUs and what stages of processing they have completed, allowing it to schedule each SCU to be processed by the next stage. The coordinator also tracks how long an SCU has existed within the system, allowing it to determine which SCUs must be queried to achieve a desired level of freshness. Finally, the coordinator is responsible for tracking the liveness of nodes in the system and initiating recovery in the case of a failure, as described in Section 3.6.

3.4 Scheduling

LazyBase's centralized coordinator is responsible for scheduling all work in the system. Nodes, also called *workers*, are part of a pool, and the coordinator dynamically schedules tasks on the next available worker. In this manner, a worker may perform tasks for whatever stage is required by the workload. For example, if there is a sudden burst of updates, workers can perform ingest tasks, followed by sorting tasks, followed by merging tasks, based on the SCU's position in the pipeline. Currently workers are assigned tasks without regard for preserving data locality; such optimizations are the subject of future work.

3.5 Scaling

Each of the pipeline stages exhibit different scaling properties, as described above. Ingest, sort, and the update-rewrite sub-phase of id-remapping maintain no global state, and can each be parallelized across any number of individual SCUs.[1] Merge is log-n parallelizable, where n is the fan-out of the merge tree. With many SCUs available, the separate merges can be parallelized; however, as merges work their way toward the authority, eventually only a single merge to the authority can occur. Sort and merge can also be parallelized across the different table types, with different tables being sorted and merged in parallel on separate nodes. Finally, all of the stages could be parallelized through key-space partitioning, in which the primary keys for tables are hashed across a set of nodes with each node handling the updates for that set of keys. This mechanism is commonly employed by many "cloud" systems [1].

Automatically tuning the system parameters and run-time configuration to the available hardware and existing workload is an area of ongoing research. Currently, LazyBase implements the SCU-based parallelism inherent in ingest, sort, update-rewrite, and merge.

3.6 Fault tolerance

Rather than explicitly replicating data at each stage, Lazy-Base uses its pipelined design to survive node failures: if a processing node fails, it recreates the data on that node by reprocessing the data from an earlier stage in the pipeline. For example, if a merge node fails, losing data for a processed SCU, the coordinator can re-schedule the SCU to be processed through the pipeline again from any earlier stage that still contains the SCU. The obvious exception is the ingest stage, where data must be replicated to ensure availability.

Similarly, if a node storing a particular SCU representation fails, queries must deal with the fact that the data they desire is unavailable, by either looking at an earlier representation (albeit at slower performance) or waiting for the desired representation to be recomputed (perhaps on another,

available node). Once SCUs have reached the authority, it may be replicated both for availability and query load balancing. LazyBase can then garbage collect older representations from the previous stages.

LazyBase detects worker and coordinator failures using a standard heartbeat mechanism. If the coordinator fails, it is restarted and then requests the current state of the pipeline by retrieving SCU information from all live workers. If a worker fails, it is restarted and then performs a local integrity check followed by reintegration with the coordinator. The coordinator can determine what SCU data on the worker is still relevant based on pipeline progress at reintegration time. If a worker is unavailable for an extended period of time, the coordinator may choose to re-process SCU data held on that worker from an earlier stage to keep the pipeline busy.

3.7 Queries

Queries can operate on the SCUs produced by any of Lazy-Base's stages. In the common case, queries that have best-effort freshness requirements will request results only from the authority SCU. To improve freshness, queries can contact the coordinator, requesting the set of SCUs that must be queried to achieve a given freshness. They then retrieve each SCU depending on the stage at which it has been processed and join the results from each SCU based on the result timestamps to form the final query results. For sorted or merged SCUs, the query uses the index of the appropriate table to do the appropriate lookup. For unsorted SCUs, the query does a scan of the table data to find all of the associated rows. If joins against ID-key columns are required, the unsorted data's internal temporary ID-key mappings must also be consulted.

Queries follow a five-phase dataflow: filter, uniquify, group_by, aggregate and post_filter. Filtering is performed in parallel on the nodes that contain the SCU data being queried, to eliminate rows that do not match the query. For example, a query that requires data from two merged SCUs and a sorted SCU will run the queries against those SCUs in parallel (in this case three-way parallelization). The results are collected and joined by the caller in the uniquify phase. The goal of this phase is to eliminate the duplicates that may exist because multiple SCUs can contain updates to a single row. This phase effectively applies the updates to the row. The group_by and aggregate phases gather data that belongs in matching groups, and compute aggregate functions, such as sum, count, and max, over the data. To access row data directly, we also include a trivial first aggregate that simply returns the first value it sees from each group. Finally, the post_filter phase allows the query to filter rows by the results of the aggregates.

3.8 Data storage

Our implementation makes heavy use of DataSeries [12], an open-source compressed table-based storage layer designed for streaming throughput. DataSeries stores sets of

---

[1] Because the mapping from temporary ID to global ID is unique to the SCU being converted, any number of update-rewrites can be performed in parallel on separate SCUs.

rows into *extents*, which can be dynamically sized and are individually compressed. Extents are the basic unit of access, caching, and indexing within LazyBase. LazyBase currently uses a 64KB extent size for all files. DataSeries files are self-describing, in that they contain one or more XML-specified extent types that describe the schema of the extents. Different extent types are used to implement different table views. DataSeries provides an internal index in each file that can return extents of a particular type.

LazyBase stores an SCU in DataSeries files differently for each stage. In the ingest stage an SCU is stored in a single DataSeries file with each table's primary view schema being used to hold the unsorted data for each table. In the id-remapping stage, the ID-key mappings are written out as sorted DataSeries files, two for each ID-key mapping (one in id order, the other in key order). In the sort and merge stages, the SCU is stored as a separate sorted DataSeries file for each view in each table.

LazyBase also uses external extent-based indexes for all of its sorted files. These index files store the minimum and maximum values of the view's sort key for each extent in a file. Unlike a traditional B+tree index, this *extent-based* index is very small (two keys and an offset for each extent), and with 64KB extents can index a 4 TB table with a 64-bit key in as little as 250 MB, which can easily fit into the main memory of modern machine. Although the range-based nature of the index may result in false positives, reducing any lookup to a single disk access still dramatically improves query performance for very large tables.

In addition to its focus on improved disk performance, DataSeries uses type-specific code to improve its performance over many other table-based storage layers. LazyBase automatically generates code for ingestion, sorting, merging, and basic querying of indexes from XML-based schema definitions.

4. Evaluation

The goal of LazyBase is to provide a high-throughput, scalable update system that can trade between query freshness and query latency while providing an understandable consistency model. We evaluate LazyBase's pipeline and query performance against Cassandra [1], a popular scalable NoSQL database that is considered to be "write-optimized" in its design [20]. In addition, we demonstrate the effect of LazyBase's batching on update performance, and Lazy-Base's unique freshness-queries, demonstrating the user-tunable trade-off between latency and freshness. Finally, we compare the consistency models of LazyBase and Cassandra.

4.1 Experimental setup

All nodes in our experiments were Linux Kernel-based Virtual Machines (KVM's) with 6 CPU cores, 12 GB of RAM, and 300 GB of local disk allocated through the Linux logical volume manager (LVM), running Linux 2.6.32 as the guest OS. Each KVM was run on a separate physical host, with 2-way SMP quad-core 2.66 GHz Intel Xeon E5430 processors, 16GB of RAM and an internal 7200 RPM 1 TB Seagate SA-TAII Enterprise disk drive. A second internal 400 GB disk stored the OS, 64-bit Debian "squeeze." Nodes were connected via switched Gigabit Ethernet using a Force10 S50 switch. These physical nodes were part of the OpenCirrus cloud computing research testbed [17].

Unless otherwise stated, experiments were run using 10 database nodes and 20 upload nodes. In LazyBase, the 10 database nodes were split between a single node running the id-assignment sub-stage and the coordinator and the other nine worker nodes running an ingest stage as well as a second dynamically assigned stage (e.g., id-update-rewrite, sort or merge). Cassandra was configured with nine nodes, equivalent to the nine workers in LazyBase. We use a default unsorted SCU size of 1.95M rows and in the merge stage we merge at most eight SCUs together at a time.

Our experimental data set is a set of 38.4 million tweets collected from Twitter's streaming API between January and February 2010 as part of a study on spam detection in Twitter [25]. Each observation contains the tweet's ID, text, source, and creation time, as well as information about the user (e.g., id, name, description, location, follower count, and friends count). The table's primary view is sorted on tweet id. The total data set is 50GB uncompressed, the average row size (a single tweet) is slightly over 1KB. While the Twitter data is a realistic example of an application that requires high-throughput update, it uses a simple schema with only one sort order and no ID-keys. In addition to the Twitter data we used an artificial data generator that can create arbitrarily large data sets that exercise the indexing and sorting mechanisms of LazyBase. Section 4.5 describes this data set in more detail.

4.2 Update

LazyBase strives for a high-performance pipeline in two respects: efficiency and scalability. This section evaluates LazyBase's choices for batching to achieve high efficiency and explores LazyBase's scalability and how it compares with the scalability of Cassandra.

4.2.1 Efficiency

LazyBase batches together updates into sizable SCUs to achieve high-throughput ingest with stronger semantics than eventually consistent systems. Figure 2 illustrates the sensitivity of LazyBase's update throughput to SCU size. As expected, as the SCUs get larger, update throughput increases. However, the per-pipeline stage latency also increases, leading to a greater freshness spectrum for LazyBase queries. To maximize throughput, we choose a default SCU size of 1.95M rows for use in subsequent experiments.

Table 2 lists the average latency and throughput of each pipeline stage for our workload. Because the merge stage

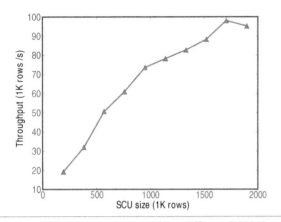

Figure 2. Inserts per second for different SCU sizes

Stage	Latency (s)	Rows/s
Ingest	49.7	39,000
ID Remap	5.5	327,000
Sort	12.0	158,000
Merge	31.0+	120,000

Table 2. Performance of individual pipeline stages. Note that this workload does not contain ID-keys, making the ID Remap phase very fast.

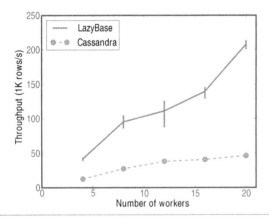

Figure 3. Inserts processed per second. Error bars represent the min and max of three runs, while the line plots the mean.

latency is highly dependent upon the total size of the SCUs being merged, the reported latency is for the smallest 8-SCU merge. We observe that stages run at varying speeds, indicating that the ability to parallelize individual stages is important to prevent bottlenecks and improve overall system throughput.

4.2.2 Update scalability

To demonstrate LazyBase's update scalability, we compared equally sized LazyBase and Cassandra clusters. Figure 3 il-

lustrates this comparison from four worker nodes up through 20 worker nodes. In the LazyBase configuration, one additional node ran the id-assignment and coordinator stages and the remaining nodes ran one ingest worker and one dynamically assigned worker (e.g., id-update-rewrite, sort or merge). In the Cassandra configuration, each node ran one Cassandra process using a write-one policy (no replication). For each cluster size, we measured the time to ingest the entire Twitter data set into each system.

We observe that both systems scale with the number of workers, but LazyBase outperforms Cassandra by a factor of 4X to 5X, due to the architectural differences between the systems. Updates in Cassandra are hashed by key to separate nodes. Each Cassandra node utilizes a combination of a commit log for durability and an indexed in-memory structure in which it keeps updates until memory pressure flushes them to disk. Cassandra also performs background compaction of on-disk data similar to LazyBase's merge stage. Unlike LazyBase, Cassandra shows little improvement with increased batch sizes, and very large batches cause errors during the upload process. Conversely, LazyBase dedicates all of the resources of a node to processing a large batch of updates. In turn, this reduction in contention allows LazyBase to take better advantage of system resources, improving its performance. LazyBase's use of compression improves disk throughput, while its use of schemas improves individual stage processing performance, giving it additional performance advantages over Cassandra.

4.3 Query

We evaluate LazyBase's query performance on two metrics. First, we compare it to Cassandra for both point and range queries, showing query throughput for increasing numbers of query clients. Second, we demonstrate LazyBase's unique ability to provide user-specified query freshness, showing the effects of query freshness on query latency.

To provide an equitable query comparison to Cassandra, we added a distribution step at the end of LazyBase's pipeline to stripe authority data across all of the worker nodes in batches of 64K rows. Because this distribution is not required for low-latency authority queries, we did not include its overhead in the ingestion results; for our workload the worst-case measured cost of this distribution for the final authority is 314 seconds (a rate of 120K rows/s). We further discuss how such striping could be tightly integrated into LazyBase's design in Section 5.

To support range queries in Cassandra, we added a set of *index rows* that store contiguous ranges of keys. Similar to the striped authority file in LazyBase, each index row is keyed by the high-order 48 bits of the 64 bit primary table key (i.e., each index row represents a 64K range of keys). We add a column to the index row for every key that is stored in that range, allowing Cassandra to quickly find the keys of all rows within a range using a small number of point queries. In our tests, the range queries only retrieve the

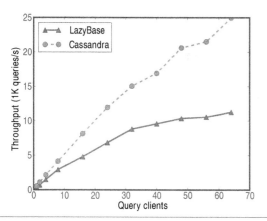

Figure 4. Random single row queries for LazyBase and Cassandra. Measured as queries per second with increasing numbers of query clients running 1000 queries per client.

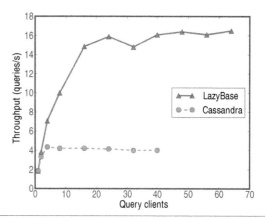

Figure 5. Random range queries for LazyBase and Cassandra with 0.1% selectivity. Measured as queries per second with increasing numbers of query clients running 10 queries per client.

existing keys in the range, and no data columns, allowing Cassandra to answer the query by reading only the index rows. Having Cassandra also perform the point lookups to retrieve the data columns made individual 0.1% selectivity queries in Cassandra take over 30 minutes.

We also ran all experiments on a workload that would fit into the memory of the Cassandra nodes, since Cassandra's performance out-of-core was more than 10 times slower than LazyBase. We believe this to be due to Cassandra's background compaction approach, in which all uncompacted tables must be examined in reverse-time order when querying until the key is found. To mitigate this effect, we issued each query twice: once to warm up the cache, and a second time to measure the performance.

Figure 4 illustrates single-row query performance of both LazyBase and Cassandra. We exercise the query throughput of the two systems using increasing numbers of query clients, each issuing 1000 random point queries. We see that Cassandra's throughput is approximately twice that of Lazy-Base, due primarily to the underlying design of the two systems. Cassandra distributes rows across nodes using consistent hashing and maintains an in-memory hash table to provide extremely fast individual row lookups. LazyBase keeps a small in-memory index of extents, but must decompress and scan a full extent in order to retrieve an individual row. The result is that LazyBase has a high query latency, which results in slower absolute throughput for the fixed workload.

Figure 5 illustrates range query performance of both LazyBase and Cassandra. These queries simply return the set of valid tweet IDs within the range, allowing Cassandra to service the query from the index rows without using a set query to access the data belonging to those tweets. We exercise the query throughput of the two systems using increasing numbers of query clients, each issuing 10 random queries retrieving a range over 0.1% of the key-space. With a low number of query clients, LazyBase and Cassandra have

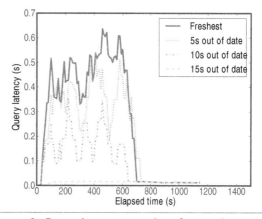

Figure 6. Query latency over time for steady-state workload. Sampled every 15s, and smoothed with a sliding window average over the past minute.

similar performance; however, LazyBase continues to scale up to 24 clients, while Cassandra tops out at four. Lazy-Base's sorted on-disk data format allows it to serve range queries as streaming disk I/O, while Cassandra must read many tables to retrieve a range.

Figure 6 illustrates the query latency when run with concurrent updates in LazyBase for four different point query freshnesses, 15 seconds, 10 seconds, 5 seconds, and 0 seconds. In this experiment, we ran an ingest workload of 59K inserts per second for a period of 650 seconds. Pipeline processing continued until 1133 seconds at which point the merged SCUs were fully up-to-date.

Figure 7 illustrates a 200-second window of this ingest workload, measuring the effective staleness of the sorted SCUs in the system. When a sort process completes, the staleness drops to zero, however, as the next sort process

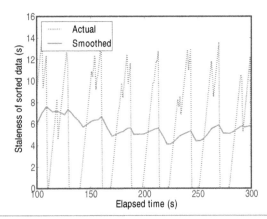

Figure 7. The staleness of the sorted data over a 200-second window of the steady-state workload. That is, at any point in time, the freshness limit that would have to be set to avoid expensive queries to unsorted data. The smoothed line is over a 60-second sliding window.

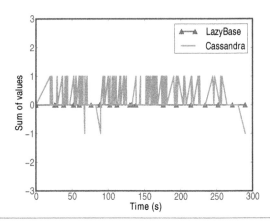

Figure 8. The sum of the values of two rows updated within a single client session. Non-zero values indicate an inconsistency in the view of the two rows.

continues, the staleness continues to increase until the next SCU is available at that stage. The result is that although the average staleness is around 6 seconds, the instantaneous staleness varies between 0 and 14 seconds.

Taken together, Figures 6 and 7 effectively demonstrate the cost of query freshness in a live system. In the case of the 15-second query, we see that query latency remained stable throughout the run. Because newly ingested data was always processed through the sort stage before the 15 second deadline, the 15-second query always ran against sorted SCUs, with its latency increasing only slightly as the index size for these files increased. In the case of a 0-second query, the query results occasionally fall into the window where sorted SCUs are completely fresh, but usually included unsorted SCUs that required linear scans, increasing query latency. Because the results in Figure 6 are smoothed over a 60-second window, points where only sorted data was examined show up as dips rather than dropping to the lowest latency. The 10-second query was able to satisfy its freshness constraint using only sorted SCUs much more frequently, causing its instantaneous query latency to occasionally dip to that of the 15-second query. As a result, its average query latency falls between the freshest and least fresh queries. At 650 seconds ingest stops and shortly thereafter all SCUs have been sorted. This results in all query freshnesses achieving the same latency past 662 seconds.

4.4 Consistency

To compare the consistency properties of LazyBase and Cassandra, we performed an experiment involving a single-integer-column table with two rows. Our LazyBase client connected to the database, issued two row updates incrementing the value of the first row and decrementing the value of the second row, and then issued a commit. Our Cassandra

client performed the same updates as part of a "batch update" call and used the `quorum` consistency model, in which updates are sent to a majority of nodes before returning from an update call. Conceptually, from a programmer's perspective, this would be equivalent to doing a transactional update of two rows, to try to ensure that the sum of the two rows' values is zero. We also maintained a background workload to keep the databases moderately busy, as they might be in a production system. During the experiment we ran a query client that continuously queried the two rows of the table and recorded their values. In the case of Cassandra, our query client again used the `quorum` consistency model, in which queries do not return until they receive results from a majority of the nodes.

Figure 8 graphs the sum of the values of the two rows over the lifetime of the experiment. In the case of LazyBase, we see that the sum is always zero, illustrating its consistency model: all updates within a single SCU are applied together atomically. In the case of Cassandra, we see that the sum of the values varies between -1, 0, and 1, illustrating that Cassandra does not provide self-consistency to its users.

Figure 9 further illustrates the difficulty placed on users of systems like Cassandra, showing the effective timestamps of the retrieved rows for each query over a 100-second period of the experiment.[2] In the case of LazyBase, we see that its batch consistency model results in a step function, in which new values are seen once a batch of updates has been processed. Under this model, the two rows always remain consistent. In the case of Cassandra, not only do the two rows differ in timestamp, but often the returned result of a given value is older than the previously returned result, illustrated by a dip in the effective time for that row. This

---

[2] Note that we show both rows for Cassandra, but only a single row for LazyBase, as LazyBase's consistency model ensures that both rows always have the same timestamp.

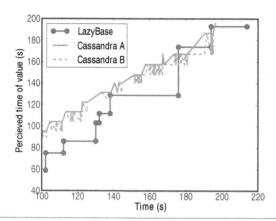

Figure 9. The effective timestamp of the returned rows at query time. Differences between Cassandra row A and Cassandra row B indicate inconsistencies between the rows at query time. Dips in the timestamps of a single row indicate violations in monotonic read consistency.

violation of monotonic read consistency adds a second layer of complexity for users of the system.

We also see that LazyBase generally provides less fresh results than Cassandra, as is expected in a batch processing system. However, because LazyBase is able to process updates more effectively, it less frequently goes into overload. Thus, in some cases of higher load, it is actually able to provide fresher results than Cassandra, as demonstrated in the period from 180 to 185 seconds in the experiment.

4.5 Complex schema

Although the Twitter data set used in the previous examples represents an interesting real-world application, it has a fairly simple schema and indexing structure. We also evaluate the performance of LazyBase with a more complex artificial data set. This data set consists of three tables, TestID, TestOne and TestTwo. TestID contains a 64-bit integer ID-key, which is used in the primary key for TestOne and TestTwo. For each ID-key, TestOne contains a string, stringData, and a 32-bit integer intData. TestTwo contains a one-to-many mapping from each ID-key to attribute-value pairs, both 32-bit integers. In addition to the primary view, each table also has a secondary view, sorted on a secondary key. TestOne's secondary view is sorted by the stringData field, while TestTwo's is sorted by the value field.

When uploading this data set to Cassandra, both primary and secondary views are stored using the technique described above for range queries: a separate "index table" stores one row for each value (e.g., the sort key for the view) and a column for every primary key that has that value. For example, the secondary index table for TestTwo contains one row for each value and a column for every primary key that has that value in an attribute.

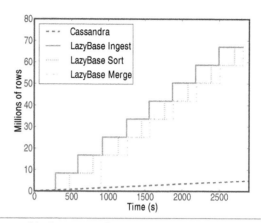

Figure 10. Ingest performance for the complex schema workload. The x-axis represents the elapsed time, and the y-axis represents the number of rows that are available in the database. For LazyBase each line represents the number of rows available at a particular stage of the pipeline.

Stage	Latency (s)	Rows/s
Ingest	311	27,000
ID Remap	61	138,000
Sort	206	41,000
Merge	115	73,000

Table 3. Performance of individual pipeline stages on the complex workload.

Figure 10 shows the performance of ingesting the complex data set to a cluster of nine servers for both LazyBase and Cassandra. For LazyBase the graph shows the number of rows available at each stage of the pipeline. The batch size for Cassandra was set to 1K rows, while the batch size for LazyBase was set to 8M rows. Cassandra's batch size is limited because batching must be done by the client, and each batch must be transmitted in a single RPC. Even within the hard limits imposed by Cassandra, larger batch sizes produce performance problems: we found that Cassandra's write performance for batches of 10K rows was worse than with smaller batches. LazyBase, which is designed with batching in mind, performs batching on the ingest server and stores batches on disk, allowing them to be arbitrarily large. Because of the large batch sizes, the number of rows available at any stage of LazyBase is a step function. The same is true for Cassandra, but because the batch sizes are much smaller, the steps are not visible in the graph.

We also computed the average per-stage latency, similar to Table 2. These results are shown in Table 3. Compared to Table 2, all stages of the pipeline are slowed down in this test, due to two factors: the complexity of the schema and the lack of parallelism in ingest. Compared to the first schema, which required no remapping and produced only a single sort order, this schema must remap the two tables' primary keys, and produce and merge two sort orders for each table. Furthermore, the previous experiment was able to take advantage of parallelism during the ingest stage: multiple data streams were uploaded simultaneously and merged into a single SCU, increasing the throughput of the ingest stage. In this experiment a single client is performing all uploads, so there is no ingest stage parallelism.

4.6 Summary

The results of our evaluation of LazyBase illustrate its many benefits. By trading off query freshness for batching, Lazy-Base's pipelined architecture can process updates at rates 4X to 5X faster than the popular Cassandra NoSQL database. Although Cassandra's in-memory hash-table has twice the point query throughput as LazyBase, LazyBase's sorted on-disk format gives 4X the range query throughput. When performing out-of-core queries, LazyBase exceeds Cassandra's query latency by more than 10 times. We also illustrate how users of LazyBase, unlike other systems, can dynamically choose to trade query latency for query freshness at query time.

LazyBase exhibits these properties while also providing a clear consistency model that we believe fits a broader range of applications. Our evaluation of Cassandra's consistency illustrated violations of both self-consistency, where we observed inconsistencies in multi-row queries, and monotonic read consistency, where we observed clients seeing an older version of a row up to 5 seconds after seeing the newest version of that row. These types of inconsistencies are not possible in LazyBase by design, and our experimental results showed that they do no occur in practice.

5. Discussion

We have developed LazyBase to perform well under a particular set of use cases. In this section, we describe modifications to LazyBase's design that could broaden its applicability or make it more suitable to a different set of use cases.

Data distribution: LazyBase's pipelined design offers several trade-offs in how data is distributed amongst nodes for the purposes of query scalability. Our experiments were run using an authority file striping approach; however, it may be advantageous to perform this striping during the sort stage of the pipeline to provide the same kind of query scalability to freshness queries. This approach would require a more robust striping strategy, perhaps using consistent hashing of key ranges to ensure even distribution of work. Furthermore, the choice of stripe size has an effect on both range query performance and workload distribution.

Alternate freshness models: LazyBase's freshness model currently describes requirements by putting a bound on how out-of-date results are (e.g., "all results as of an hour ago"). Other freshness models may also be desirable, such as only the most recent updates (e.g., "all results that were received in the last hour") or a past point in time (e.g., "all results as of three weeks ago"). Given LazyBase's pipelined design, one could easily add analysis stages after ingest to provide stream query analysis of incoming updates. Because LazyBase doesn't overwrite data in-place, by not deleting data, LazyBase could generate consistent point-in-time snapshots of the system that could be tracked by the coordinator to provide historical queries.

Scheduling for different freshnesses: LazyBase's scheduler provides the same priority for processing of all tables in the system. However, some applications may desire that queries to particular tables (e.g., a table of security settings) are always fresher. To better support those applications, LazyBase could adjust its scheduling to prioritize work based on desired freshness for those tables.

Integration with other big-data analysis: In some cases, it may be desirable to integrate the resulting data tables of LazyBase with other big-data analysis techniques such as those offered by the Hadoop project. LazyBase could easily integrate with such frameworks, potentially even treating the analysis as an additional pipeline stage and scheduling it with the coordinator on the same nodes used to run the rest of LazyBase.

6. Related work

The traditional approach to decision support loads data generated by operational OLTP databases, via an ETL process, into a system optimized for efficient data analytics and read-only queries. Recent "big data" systems such as Hadoop [26] and Dremel [31] allow large-scale analysis of data across hundreds of machines, but also tend to work on read-only data sets.

Several research efforts (e.g. [33, 36]) have examined efficient means to support both data models from the same database and storage engine using specialized in-memory layouts. RiTE [41] caches updates in-memory, and batches updates to the underlying data store to achieve batch update speeds with insert-like freshness. Similarly, Vertica's hybrid storage model caches updates in a write-optimized memory format and uses a background process to transform updates into the read-optimized on-disk format [7]. Both of these techniques provide up-to-date freshness, but require sufficient memory to cache the update stream. LazyBase separates the capture of the update stream from the transform step, reducing freshness but improving resource utilization and responsiveness to burst traffic.

FAS [34] maintains a set of databases at different freshness levels, achieving a similar effect to LazyBase, but requiring significant data replication, reducing their scalability and increasing cost. Other groups have examined techniques for incrementally updating materialized views, but rely on the standard mechanisms to ingest data to the base table, leaving the problem described here mostly unsolved [11, 35]. Further, researchers have examined data structures to provide a spectrum between update and query performance [23, 24]. These structures provide a flexible tradeoff similar to that of LazyBase, and we believe that LazyBase could benefit by employing some of these techniques in the future.

LazyBase's use of update tables is similar to ideas used in other communities. Update files are commonly used for search applications in information retrieval [16, 30]. Consulting differential files to provide up-to-date query results is a long-standing database technique, but has been restricted to large databases with read-mostly access patterns [37]. More recent work for write-optimized databases limits queries to the base table, which is lazily updated [29]. Google's BigTable [18] provides a large-scale distributed database that uses similar update and merge techniques, but its focus on OLTP-style updates requires large write-caches and cannot take advantage of the trade-off between freshness and performance inherent in LazyBase's design.

BigTable is also one of a class of systems, including Dynamo [27], SimpleDB [8], SCADS [13], Cassandra [1], Greenplum [9] and HBase [2] in which application developers have built their own data stores with a focus on high availability in the face of component failures in highly distributed systems. These systems provide performance scalability with a relaxed, eventual consistency model, but do not allow the application to specify desired query freshness. Unlike LazyBase, the possibility of inconsistent query results limits application scope, and can make application development more challenging.

SCADS [13] describes a scalable, adjustable-consistency key-value store for interactive Web 2.0 application queries. SCADS also trades off performance and freshness, but does so in a greedy manner, relaxing goals as much as possible to save resources for additional queries.

Incremental data processing systems, such as Percolator [32], incrementally update an index or query result as new values are ingested. These systems focus on continuous queries whose results are updated over time, rather than sequences of queries to the overall corpus. They do not address the same application needs (e.g., freshness vs. query speed) as LazyBase, but their techniques could be used in a LazyBase-like system to maintain internal indices.

Sumbaly et al. [39] extend the Voldemort key-value store to provide efficient bulk loading of large, immutable data sets. Like LazyBase, the system uses a pipelined approach to compute the next authority version of the data set, in this case using Hadoop to compute indices offline. Unlike LazyBase, it does not permit queries to access the intermediate data for fresher results.

Some distributed "continuous query" systems, such as Flux [38] and River [14], used a similar event-based parallel processing model to achieve scalability when scheduling a set of independent operations (e.g., analysis of time series data) across a set of nodes. However, they have no concept of

coordinating a set of operations, as is required for providing self-consistency. Additionally, they are not designed to provide access to the results of intermediate steps, as required for the freshness/performance trade-off in LazyBase.

7. Conclusions

We propose a new data storage system, LazyBase, that lets applications specify their *result freshness* requirements, allowing a dynamic tradeoff between freshness and query performance. LazyBase optimizes updates through bulk processing and background execution of SCUs, which allows consistent query access to data at each stage of the pipeline.

Our experiments demonstrate that LazyBase's pipelined architecture and batched updates provide update throughput that is 4X to 5X higher than Cassandra's at all scalability levels. Although Cassandra's point queries outperform LazyBase's, LazyBase's range query throughput is 4X higher than Cassandra's. We also show that LazyBase's pipelined design provides a range of options on the read-query freshness-latency spectrum and that LazyBase's consistency model provides clear benefits over other "eventually" consistent models such as Cassandra's.

8. Acknowledgments

We wish to thank our shepherd, Guillaume Pierre; the anonymous reviewers; and Ilari Shafer for their suggestions for improvements to the paper. We thank Eric Anderson for his assistance with DataSeries. We thank the members and companies of the PDL Consortium (including APC, EMC, Emulex, Facebook, Google, Hewlett-Packard, Hitachi, IBM, Intel, LSI, Microsoft, NEC, NetApp, Oracle, Riverbed, Samsung, Seagate, STEC, Symantec, and VMWare) for their interest, insights, feedback, and support. This research was sponsored in part by an HP Labs Innovation Research Program award and Intel, via the Intel Science and Technology Center for Cloud Computing (ISTC-CC). This research was enabled by hardware donations from Intel and NetApp.

References

[1] Apache Cassandra, http://cassandra.apache.org/.

[2] Apache HBase, http://hbase.apache.org/.

[3] CouchDB, http://couchdb.apacheorg/.

[4] MongoDB, http://www.mongodb.org/.

[5] Twitter Earthquake Detector, http://recovery.doi.gov/press/us-geological-survey-twitter-earthquake-detector-ted/.

[6] Apache Thrift, http://thrift.apache.org/.

[7] HP Vertica, http://www.vertica.com/.

[8] Amazon SimpleDB, http://aws.amazon.com/simpledb/.

[9] EMC Greenplum, http://www.greenplum.com/.

[10] A look at Twitter in Iran http://blog.sysomos.com/2009/06/21/a-look-at-twitter-in-iran/.

[11] B. Adelberg, H. Garcia-Molina, and B. Kao. Applying update streams in a soft real-time database system. In *Proc. SIGMOD*, 1995.

[12] E. Anderson, M. Arlitt, C. B. Morrey III, and A. Veitch. DataSeries: An efficient, flexible data format for structured serial data. *ACM SIGOPS Operating Systems Review*, 43(1):70–75, January 2009.

[13] M. Armbrust, A. Fox, D. A. Patterson, N. Lanham, B. Trushkowsky, J. Trutna, and H. Oh. SCADS: Scale-independent storage for social computing applications. In *Proc. CIDR*, January 2009.

[14] R. H. Arpaci-Dusseau, E. Anderson, N. Treuhaft, D. E. Culler, J. M. Hellerstein, D. Patterson, and K. Yelick. Cluster I/O with River: Making the fast case common. In *Proc. Workshop on Input/Output in Parallel and Distributed Systems (IOPADS '99)*, May 1999.

[15] C. Babcock. Data, data, everywhere. *Information Week*, January 2006.

[16] S. Buttcher and C. L. A. Clarke. Indexing time vs. query time: trade-offs in dynamic information retrieval systems. *Proc. 14th ACM Intl. Conf. on Information and Knowledge Management (CIKM)*, pages 317–318, 2005.

[17] R. Campbell, I. Gupta, M. Heath, S. Ko, M. Kozuch, M. Kunze, T. Kwan, K. Lai, H. Lee, M. Lyons, D. Milojicic, D. O'Hallaron, and Y. Soh. Open cirrus cloud computing testbed: Federated data centers for open source systems and services research. In *Proc. of USENIX HotCloud*, June 2009.

[18] F. Chang, J. Dean, S. Ghemawat, W. C. Hsieh, D. A. Wallach, M. Burrows, T. Chandra, A. Fikes, and R. E. Gruber. BigTable: A distributed storage system for structured data. In *Proc. OSDI*, November 2006.

[19] S. Chaudri, U. Dayal, and V. Ganti. Database technology for decision support systems. *Computer*, 34(12):48–55, December 2001.

[20] B. Cooper, A. Silberstein, E. Tam, R. Ramakrishnan, and R. Sears. Benchmarking cloud serving systems with YCSB. In *Proc. of Symposium on Cloud Computing (SOCC)*, June 2010.

[21] J. Dean and S. Ghemawat. MapReduce: Simplified data processing on large clusters. In *Proc. OSDI*, pages 137–150, 2004.

[22] J. Ginsberg, M. H. Mohebbi, R. S. Patel, L. Brammer, M. S. Smolinski, and L. Brilliant. Detecting influenza epidemics using search engine query data. *Nature*, pages 1012–1014, February 2009.

[23] G. Graefe. Write-optimized B-trees. In *Proc. VLDB*, pages 672–683, 2004.

[24] G. Graefe. B-tree indexes for high update rates. *ACM SIGMOD Record*, 35(1):39–44, March 2006.

[25] C. Grier, K. Thomas, V. Paxson, and M. Zhang. @spam: The underground on 140 characters or less. In *Proc. of ACM Conf. on Computer and Communications Security*, October 2010.

[26] Hadoop. http:// hadoop.apache.org/.

[27] D. Hastorun, M. Jampani, G. Kakulapati, A. Pilchin, S. Sivasubramanian, P. Voshall, and W. Vogels. Dynamo: Amazon's highly available key-value store. In *Proc. SOSP*, pages 205–220, 2007.

[28] D. Henschen. 3 big data challenges: Expert advice. *Information Week*, October 2011.

[29] S. Hildenbrand. Performance tradeoffs in write-optimized databases. Technical report, Eidgenossiche Technische Hochschule Zurich (ETHZ), 2008.

[30] N. Lester, J. Zobel, and H. E. Williams. In-place versus rebuild versus re-merge: index maintenance strategies for text retrieval systems. *Proc. 27th Australian Conf. on Computer Science (ACSC)*, 2004.

[31] S. Melnik, A. Gubarev, J. J. Long, G. Romer, S. Shivakumar, M. Tolton, and T. Vassilakis. Dremel: Interactive analysis of web-scale datasets. *Proc. VLDB*, pages 330–339, September 2010.

[32] D. Peng and F. Dabek. Large-scale incremental processing using distributed transactions and notifications. In *Proc. OSDI*, pages 1–15, 2010.

[33] H. Plattner. A common database approach for OLTP and OLAP using an in-memory column database. In *Proc. SIGMOD*, July 2009.

[34] U. Röhm, K. Böhm, H.-J. Schek, and H. Schuldt. FAS - a freshness-sensitive coordination middleware for a cluster of OLAP components. In *Proc. VLDB*, pages 754–765, 2002.

[35] K. Salem, K. Beyer, and B. Lindsay. How to roll a join: Asynchronous incremental view maintenance. In *Proc. SIGMOD*, 2000.

[36] J. Schaffner, A. Bog, J. Kruger, and A. Zeier. A hybrid row-column OLTP database architecture for operational reporting. In *Proc. Intl. Conf. on Business Intelligence for the Real-Time Enterprise*, 2008.

[37] D. G. Severance and G. M. Lohman. Differential files: their application to the maintenance of large databases. *ACM Trans. on Database Systems*, 1(3):256–267, 1976.

[38] M. A. Shah, J. M. Hellerstein, S. Chandrasekaran, and M. J. Franklin. Flux: An adaptive partitioning operator for continuous query systems. *Proc. ICDE*, pages 25–36, 2003.

[39] R. Sumbaly, J. Kreps, L. Gao, A. Feinberg, C. Soman, and S. Shah. Serving large-scale batch computed data with project voldemort. In *Proc. 10th USENIX Conf. on File and Storage Technologies (FAST)*, 2012.

[40] D. Terry. Replicated data consistency explained through baseball. Technical Report MSR-TR-2011-137, Microsoft Research, October 2011.

[41] C. Thomsen, T. B. Pedersen, and W. Lehner. RiTE: Providing on-demand data for right-time data warehousing. In *Proc. ICDE*, 2008.

[42] W. Vogels. Eventually consistent. *Commun. ACM*, 52:40–44, January 2009.

Cache Craftiness for Fast Multicore Key-Value Storage

Yandong Mao, Eddie Kohler[†], Robert Morris

MIT CSAIL, †Harvard University

Abstract

We present Masstree, a fast key-value database designed for SMP machines. Masstree keeps all data in memory. Its main data structure is a trie-like concatenation of B^+-trees, each of which handles a fixed-length slice of a variable-length key. This structure effectively handles arbitrary-length possibly-binary keys, including keys with long shared prefixes. B^+-tree fanout was chosen to minimize total DRAM delay when descending the tree and prefetching each tree node. Lookups use optimistic concurrency control, a read-copy-update-like technique, and do not write shared data structures; updates lock only affected nodes. Logging and checkpointing provide consistency and durability. Though some of these ideas appear elsewhere, Masstree is the first to combine them. We discuss design variants and their consequences.

On a 16-core machine, with logging enabled and queries arriving over a network, Masstree executes more than six million simple queries per second. This performance is comparable to that of memcached, a non-persistent hash table server, and higher (often much higher) than that of VoltDB, MongoDB, and Redis.

Categories and Subject Descriptors H.2.4 [*Information Systems*]: DATABASE MANAGEMENT – Concurrency

Keywords multicore; in-memory; key-value; persistent

1. Introduction

Storage server performance matters. In many systems that use a single storage server, that server is often the performance bottleneck [1, 18], so improvements directly improve system capacity. Although large deployments typically spread load over multiple storage servers, single-server performance still matters: faster servers may reduce costs, and may also reduce load imbalance caused by partitioning data among servers. Intermediate-sized deployments may be able to avoid the complexity of multiple servers by using

EuroSys'12, April 10–13, 2012, Bern, Switzerland.

sufficiently fast single servers. A common route to high performance is to use different specialized storage systems for different workloads [4].

This paper presents Masstree, a storage system specialized for key-value data in which all data fits in memory, but must persist across server restarts. Within these constraints, Masstree aims to provide a flexible storage model. It supports arbitrary, variable-length keys. It allows *range queries* over those keys: clients can traverse subsets of the database, or the whole database, in sorted order by key. It performs well on workloads with many keys that share long prefixes. (For example, consider Bigtable [12], which stores information about Web pages under permuted URL keys like "edu.harvard.seas.www/news-events". Such keys group together information about a domain's sites, allowing more interesting range queries, but many URLs will have long shared prefixes.) Finally, though efficient with large values, it is also efficient when values are small enough that disk and network throughput don't limit performance. The combination of these properties could free performance-sensitive users to use richer data models than is common for stores like memcached today.

Masstree uses a combination of old and new techniques to achieve high performance [8, 11, 13, 20, 27–29]. It achieves fast concurrent operation using a scheme inspired by OLFIT [11], Bronson *et al.* [9], and read-copy update [28]. Lookups use no locks or interlocked instructions, and thus operate without invalidating shared cache lines and in parallel with most inserts and updates. Updates acquire only local locks on the tree nodes involved, allowing modifications to different parts of the tree to proceed in parallel. Masstree shares a single tree among all cores to avoid load imbalances that can occur in partitioned designs. The tree is a trie-like concatenation of B^+-trees, and provides high performance even for long common key prefixes, an area in which other tree designs have trouble. Query time is dominated by the total DRAM fetch time of successive nodes during tree descent; to reduce this cost, Masstree uses a wide-fanout tree to reduce the tree depth, prefetches nodes from DRAM to overlap fetch latencies, and carefully lays out data in cache lines to reduce the amount of data needed per node. Operations are logged in batches for crash recovery and the tree is periodically checkpointed.

We evaluate Masstree on a 16-core machine with simple benchmarks and a version of the Yahoo! Cloud Serving Benchmark (YCSB) [16] modified to use small keys and values. Masstree achieves six to ten million operations per second on parts A–C of the benchmark, more than 30× as fast as VoltDB [5] or MongoDB [2].

The contributions of this paper are as follows. First, an in-memory concurrent tree that supports keys with shared prefixes efficiently. Second, a set of techniques for laying out the data of each tree node, and accessing it, that reduces the time spent waiting for DRAM while descending the tree. Third, a demonstration that a single tree shared among multiple cores can provide higher performance than a partitioned design for some workloads. Fourth, a complete design that addresses all bottlenecks in the way of million-query-per-second performance.

2. Related work

Masstree builds on many previous systems. OLFIT [11] is a B^{link}-tree [27] with optimistic concurrency control. Each update to a node changes the node's version number. Lookups check a node's version number before and after observing its contents, and retry if the version number changes (which indicates that the lookup may have observed an inconsistent state). Masstree uses this idea, but, like Bronson *et al.* [9], it splits the version number into two parts; this, and other improvements, lead to less frequent retries during lookup.

PALM [34] is a lock-free concurrent B^+-tree with twice the throughput of OLFIT. PALM uses SIMD instructions to take advantage of parallelism *within* each core. Lookups for an entire batch of queries are sorted, partitioned across cores, and processed simultaneously, a clever way to optimize cache usage. PALM requires fixed-length keys and its query batching results in higher query latency than OLFIT and Masstree. Many of its techniques are complementary to our work.

Bohannon *et al.* [8] store parts of keys directly in tree nodes, resulting in fewer DRAM fetches than storing keys indirectly. AlphaSort [29] explores several ideas to minimize cache misses by storing partial keys. Masstree uses a trie [20] like data structure to achieve the same goal.

Rao *et al.* [30] propose storing each node's children in contiguous memory to make better use of cache. Fewer node pointers are required, and prefetching is simplified, but some memory is wasted on nonexistent nodes. Cha *et al.* report that a fast B^+-tree outperforms a CSB^+-tree [10]; Masstree improves cache efficiency using more local techniques.

Data-cache stalls are a major bottleneck for database systems, and many techniques have been used to improve caching [14, 15, 21, 31]. Chen *et al.* [13] prefetch tree nodes; Masstree adopts this idea.

H-Store [25, 35] and VoltDB, its commercial version, are in-memory relational databases designed to be orders of magnitude faster than previous systems. VoltDB partitions

data among multiple cores to avoid concurrency, and thus avoids data structure locking costs. In contrast, Masstree shares data among all cores to avoid load imbalances that can occur with partitioned data, and achieves good scaling with lock-free lookups and locally locked inserts.

Shore-MT [24] identifies lock contention as a major bottleneck for multicore databases, and improves performance by removing locks incrementally. Masstree provides high concurrency from the start.

Recent key-value stores [2, 3, 12, 17, 26] provide high performance partially by offering a simpler query and data model than relational databases, and partially by partitioning data over a cluster of servers. Masstree adopts the first idea. Its design focuses on multicore performance rather than clustering, though in principle one could operate a cluster of Masstree servers.

3. System interface

Masstree is implemented as a network key-value storage server. Its requests query and change the mapping of keys to values. Values can be further divided into columns, each of which is an uninterpreted byte string.

Masstree supports four operations: $get_c(k)$, $put_c(k,v)$, *remove*(k), and $getrange_c(k,n)$. The c parameter is an optional list of column numbers that allows clients to get or set subsets of a key's full value. The *getrange* operation, also called "scan," implements a form of range query. It returns up to n key-value pairs, starting with the next key at or after k and proceeding in lexicographic order by key. *Getrange* is not atomic with respect to inserts and updates. A single client message can include many queries.

4. Masstree

Our key data structure is Masstree, a shared-memory, concurrent-access data structure combining aspects of B^+-trees [6] and tries [20]. Masstree offers fast random access and stores keys in sorted order to support range queries. The design was shaped by three challenges. First, Masstree must efficiently support many key distributions, including variable-length binary keys where many keys might have long common prefixes. Second, for high performance and scalability, Masstree must allow fine-grained concurrent access, and its get operations must never dirty shared cache lines by writing shared data structures. Third, Masstree's layout must support prefetching and collocate important information on small numbers of cache lines. The second and third properties together constitute cache craftiness.

4.1 Overview

A Masstree is a trie with fanout 2^{64} where each trie node is a B^+-tree. The trie structure efficiently supports long keys with shared prefixes; the B^+-tree structures efficiently support short keys and fine-grained concurrency, and their medium fanout uses cache lines effectively.

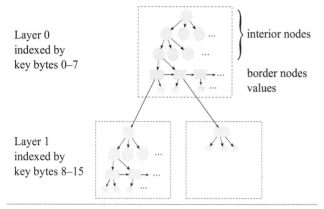

Layer 0
indexed by
key bytes 0–7

interior nodes

border nodes
values

Layer 1
indexed by
key bytes 8–15

Figure 1. Masstree structure: layers of B$^+$-trees form a trie.

---

struct **interior_node**:
  uint32_t *version*;
  uint8_t *nkeys*;
  uint64_t *keyslice*[15];
  node* *child*[16];
  interior_node* *parent*;

union **link_or_value**:
  node* *next_layer*;
  [opaque] *value*;

struct **border_node**:
  uint32_t *version*;
  uint8_t *nremoved*;
  uint8_t *keylen*[15];
  uint64_t *permutation*;
  uint64_t *keyslice*[15];
  link_or_value *lv*[15];
  border_node* *next*;
  border_node* *prev*;
  interior_node* *parent*;
  keysuffix_t *keysuffixes*;

Figure 2. Masstree node structures.

Put another way, a Masstree comprises one or more *layers* of B$^+$-trees, where each layer is indexed by a different 8-byte *slice* of key. Figure 1 shows an example. The trie's single root tree, layer 0, is indexed by the slice comprising key bytes 0–7, and holds all keys up to 8 bytes long. Trees in layer 1, the next deeper layer, are indexed by bytes 8–15; trees in layer 2 by bytes 16–23; and so forth.

Each tree contains at least one *border* node and zero or more *interior* nodes. Border nodes resemble leaf nodes in conventional B$^+$-trees, but where leaf nodes store only keys and values, Masstree border nodes can also store pointers to deeper trie layers.

Keys are generally stored as close to the root as possible, subject to three invariants. (1) Keys shorter than $8h + 8$ bytes are stored at layer $\leq h$. (2) Any keys stored in the same layer-h tree have the same $8h$-byte prefix. (3) When two keys share a prefix, they are stored at least as deep as the shared prefix. That is, if two keys longer than $8h$ bytes have the same $8h$-byte prefix, then they are stored at layer $\geq h$.

Masstree creates layers as needed (as is usual for tries). Key insertion prefers to use existing trees; new trees are created only when insertion would otherwise violate an invariant. Key removal deletes completely empty trees but does not otherwise rearrange keys. For example, if t begins as an empty Masstree:

1. t.*put*("01234567AB") stores key "01234567AB" in the root layer. The relevant key slice, "01234567", is stored separately from the 2-byte suffix "AB". A *get* for this key first searches for the slice, then compares the suffix.

2. t.*put*("01234567XY"): Since this key shares an 8-byte prefix with an existing key, Masstree must create a new layer. The values for "01234567AB" and "01234567XY" are stored, under slices "AB" and "XY", in a freshly allocated B$^+$-tree border node. This node then replaces the "01234567AB" entry in the root layer. Concurrent gets observe either the old state (with "01234567AB") or the new layer, so the "01234567AB" key remains visible throughout the operation.

3. t.*remove*("01234567XY") traverses through the root layer to the layer-1 B$^+$-tree, where it deletes key "XY". The "AB" key remains in the layer-1 B$^+$-tree.

Balance A Masstree's shape depends on its key distribution. For example, 1000 keys that share a 64-byte prefix generate at least 8 layers; without the prefix they would fit comfortably in one layer. Despite this, Masstrees have the same query complexity as B-trees. Given n keys of maximum length ℓ, query operations on a B-tree examine $O(\log n)$ nodes and make $O(\log n)$ key comparisons; but since each key has length $O(\ell)$, the total comparison cost is $O(\ell \log n)$. A Masstree will make $O(\log n)$ comparisons in each of $O(\ell)$ layers, but each comparison considers *fixed-size* key slices, for the same total cost of $O(\ell \log n)$. When keys have long common prefixes, Masstree outperforms conventional balanced trees, performing $O(\ell + \log n)$ comparisons per query (ℓ for the prefix plus $\log n$ for the suffix). However, Masstree's range queries have higher worst-case complexity than in a B$^+$-tree, since they must traverse multiple layers of tree.

Partial-key B-trees [8] can avoid some key comparisons while preserving true balance. However, unlike these trees, Masstree bounds the number of non-node memory references required to find a key to at most one per lookup. Masstree lookups, which focus on 8-byte key slice comparisons, are also easy to code efficiently. Though Masstree can use more memory on some key distributions, since its nodes are relatively wide, it outperformed our pkB-tree implementation on several benchmarks by 20% or more.

4.2 Layout

Figure 2 defines Masstree's node structures. At heart, Masstree's interior and border nodes are internal and leaf nodes of a B$^+$-tree with width 15. Border nodes are linked to facilitate *remove* and *getrange*. The *version*, *nremoved*, and *permutation* fields are used during concurrent updates and described below; we now briefly mention other features.

The *keyslice* variables store 8-byte key slices as 64-bit integers, byte-swapped if necessary so that native less-than comparisons provide the same results as lexicographic string comparison. This was the most valuable of our coding tricks, improving performance by 13–19%. Short key slices are padded with 0 bytes.

Border nodes store key slices, lengths, and suffixes. Lengths, which distinguish different keys with the same slice, are a consequence of our decision to allow binary strings as keys. Since null characters are valid within key strings, Masstree must for example distinguish the 8-byte key "ABCDEFG\0" from the 7-byte key "ABCDEFG", which have the same slice representation.

A single tree can store at most 10 keys with the same slice, namely keys with lengths 0 through 8 plus either one key with length > 8 or a link to a deeper trie layer.[1] We ensure that all keys with the same slice are stored in the same border node. This simplifies and slims down interior nodes, which need not contain key lengths, and simplifies the maintenance of other invariants important for concurrent operation, at the cost of some checking when nodes are split. (Masstree is in this sense a restricted type of prefix B-tree [7].)

Border nodes store the suffixes of their keys in *keysuffixes* data structures. These are located either inline or in separate memory blocks; Masstree adaptively decides how much per-node memory to allocate for suffixes and whether to place that memory inline or externally. Compared to a simpler technique (namely, allocating fixed space for up to 15 suffixes per node), this approach reduces memory usage by up to 16% for workloads with short keys and improves performance by 3%.

Values are stored in link_or_value unions, which contain either values or pointers to next-layer trees. These cases are distinguished by the *keylen* field. Users have full control over the bits stored in *value* slots.

Masstree's performance is dominated by the latency of fetching tree nodes from DRAM. Many such fetches are required for a single *put* or *get*. Masstree prefetches all of a tree node's cache lines in parallel before using the node, so the entire node can be used after a single DRAM latency. Up to a point, this allows larger tree nodes to be fetched in the same amount of time as smaller ones; larger nodes have wider fanout and thus reduce tree height. On our hardware, tree nodes of four cache lines (256 bytes, which allows a fanout of 15) provide the highest total performance.

4.3 Nonconcurrent modification

Masstree's tree modification algorithms are based on sequential algorithms for B$^+$-tree modification. We describe them as a starting point.

Inserting a key into a full border node causes a *split*. A new border node is allocated, and the old keys (plus the inserted key) are distributed among the old and new nodes. The new node is then inserted into the old node's parent

interior node; if full, this interior node must itself be split (updating its children's *parent* pointers). The split process terminates either at a node with insertion room or at the root, where a new interior node is created and installed. Removing a key simply deletes it from the relevant border node. Empty border nodes are then freed and deleted from their parent interior nodes. This process, like split, continues up the tree as necessary. Though remove in classical B$^+$-trees can redistribute keys among nodes to preserve balance, removal without rebalancing has theoretical and practical advantages [33].

Insert and remove maintain a per-tree doubly linked list among border nodes. This list speeds up range queries in either direction. If only forward range queries were required, a singly linked list could suffice, but the backlinks are required anyway for our implementation of concurrent remove.

We apply common case optimizations. For example, sequential insertions are easy to detect (the item is inserted at the end of a node with no *next* sibling). If a sequential insert requires a split, the old node's keys remain in place and Masstree inserts the new item into an empty node. This improves memory utilization and performance for sequential workloads. (Berkeley DB and others also implement this optimization.)

4.4 Concurrency overview

Masstree achieves high performance on multicore hardware using fine-grained locking and optimistic concurrency control. Fine-grained locking means writer operations in different parts of the tree can execute in parallel: an update requires only local locks.[2] Optimistic concurrency control means reader operations, such as *get*, acquire no locks whatsoever, and in fact *never write to globally-accessible shared memory*. Writes to shared memory can limit performance by causing contention—for example, contention among readers for a node's read lock—or by wasting DRAM bandwidth on writebacks. But since readers don't lock out concurrent writers, readers might observe intermediate states created by writers, such as partially-inserted keys. Masstree readers and writers must cooperate to avoid confusion. The key communication channel between them is a per-node *version* counter that writers mark as "dirty" before creating intermediate states, and then increment when done. Readers snapshot a node's *version* before accessing the node, then compare this snapshot to the *version* afterwards. If the versions differ or are dirty, the reader may have observed an inconsistent intermediate state and must retry.

Our optimistic concurrency control design was inspired by read-copy update [28], and borrows from OLFIT [11] and Bronson *et al.*'s concurrent AVL trees [9].

Masstree's correctness condition can be summarized as *no lost keys*: A *get(k)* operation must return a correct value

---

[1] At most one key can have length > 8 because of the invariants above: the second such key will create the deeper trie layer. Not all key slices can support 10 keys—any slice whose byte 7 is not null occurs at most twice.

[2] These data structure locks are often called "latches," with the word "lock" reserved for transaction locks. We do not discuss transactions or their locks.

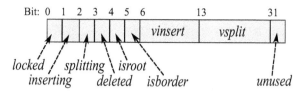

Figure 3. Version number layout. The *locked* bit is claimed by update or insert. *inserting* and *splitting* are "dirty" bits set during inserts and splits, respectively. *vinsert* and *vsplit* are counters incremented after each insert or split. *isroot* tells whether the node is the root of some B$^+$-tree. *isborder* tells whether the node is interior or border. *unused* allows more efficient operations on the version number.

for k, regardless of concurrent writers. (When *get(k)* and *put(k, v)* run concurrently, the *get* can return either the old or the new value.) The biggest challenge in preserving correctness is concurrent splits and removes, which can shift responsibility for a key away from a subtree even as a reader traverses that subtree.

4.5 Writer–writer coordination

Masstree writers coordinate using per-node spinlocks. A node's lock is stored in a single bit in its *version* counter. (Figure 3 shows the version counter's layout.)

Any modification to a node's keys or values requires holding the node's lock. Some data is protected by other nodes' locks, however. A node's *parent* pointer is protected by its parent's lock, and a border node's *prev* pointer is protected by its previous sibling's lock. This minimizes the simultaneous locks required by split operations; when an interior node splits, for example, it can assign its children's *parent* pointers without obtaining their locks.

Splits and node deletions require a writer to hold several locks simultaneously. When node n splits, for example, the writer must simultaneously hold n's lock, n's new sibling's lock, and n's parent's lock. (The simultaneous locking prevents a concurrent split from moving n, and therefore its sibling, to a different parent before the new sibling is inserted.) As with B^{link}-trees [27], lock ordering prevents deadlock: locks are always acquired up the tree.

We evaluated several writer–writer coordination protocols on different tree variants, including lock-free algorithms relying on compare-and-swap operations. The current locking protocol performs as well or better. On current cache-coherent shared-memory multicore machines, the major cost of locking, namely the cache coherence protocol, is also incurred by lock-free operations like compare-and-swap, and Masstree never holds a lock for very long.

4.6 Writer–reader coordination

We now turn to writer–reader coordination, which uses optimistic concurrency control. Note that even an all-put workload involves some writer–reader coordination, since the ini-

```
stableversion(node n):
        v ← n.version
        while v.inserting or v.splitting:
            v ← n.version
        return v

lock(node n):
        while n ≠ NIL and swap(n.version.locked, 1) = 1:
            // retry

unlock(node n):                    // implemented with one memory write
        if n.version.inserting:
            + + n.version.vinsert
        else if n.version.splitting:
            + + n.version.vsplit
        n.version.{locked, inserting, splitting} ← 0

lockedparent(node n):
retry:    p ← n.parent; lock(p)
        if p ≠ n.parent:                    // parent changed underneath us
            unlock(p); goto retry
        return p
```

Figure 4. Helper functions.

tial *put* phase that reaches the node responsible for a key is logically a reader and takes no locks.

It's simple to design a correct, though inefficient, optimistic writer–reader coordination algorithm using *version* fields.

1. Before making any change to a node n, a writer operation must mark *n.version* as "dirty." After making its change, it clears this mark and increments the *n.version* counter.

2. Every reader operation first snapshots *every* node's *version*. It then computes, keeping track of the nodes it examines. After finishing its computation (but before returning the result), it checks whether any examined node's *version* was dirty or has changed from the snapshot; if so, the reader must retry with a fresh snapshot.

Universal before-and-after version checking would clearly ensure that readers detect any concurrent split (assuming version numbers didn't wrap mid-computation[3]). It would equally clearly perform terribly. Efficiency is recovered by eliminating unnecessary version changes, by restricting the version snapshots readers must track, and by limiting the scope over which readers must retry. The rest of this section describes different aspects of coordination by increasing complexity.

4.6.1 Updates

Update operations, which change values associated with existing keys, must prevent concurrent readers from observing intermediate results. This is achieved by atomically updat-

---

[3] Our current counter could wrap if a reader blocked mid-computation for 2^{22} inserts. A 64-bit version counter would never overflow in practice.

```
split(node n, key k):                          // precondition: n locked
        n' ← new border node
        n.version.splitting ← 1
        n'.version ← n.version                  // n' is initially locked
        split keys among n and n', inserting k
ascend:  p ← lockedparent(n)                    // hand-over-hand locking
        if p = NIL:                             // n was old root
            create a new interior node p with children n, n'
            unlock(n); unlock(n'); return
        else if p is not full:
            p.version.inserting ← 1
            insert n' into p
            unlock(n); unlock(n'); unlock(p); return
        else:
            p.version.splitting ← 1
            unlock(n)
            p' ← new interior node
            p'.version ← p.version
            split keys among p and p', inserting n'
            unlock(n'); n ← p; n' ← p'; goto ascend
```

Figure 5. Split a border node and insert a key.

```
findborder(node root, key k):
retry:    n ← root; v ← stableversion(n)
          if v.isroot is false:
              root ← root.parent; goto retry
descend: if n is a border node:
              return ⟨n, v⟩
          n' ← child of n containing k
          v' ← stableversion(n')
          if n.version ⊕ v ≤ "locked":  // hand-over-hand validation
              n ← n'; v ← v'; goto descend
          v'' ← stableversion(n)
          if v''.vsplit ≠ v.vsplit:
              goto retry                  // if split, retry from root
          v ← v''; goto descend           // otherwise, retry from n
```

Figure 6. Find the border node containing a key.

ing values using aligned write instructions. On modern machines, such writes have atomic effect: any concurrent reader will see either the old value or the new value, not some unholy mixture. Updates therefore don't need to increment the border node's version number, and don't force readers to retry.

However, writers must not delete old values until all concurrent readers are done examining them. We solve this garbage collection problem with read-copy update techniques, namely a form of epoch-based reclamation [19]. All data accessible to readers is freed using similar techniques.

4.6.2 Border inserts

Insertion in a conventional B-tree leaf rearranges keys into sorted order, which creates invalid intermediate states. One solution is forcing readers to retry, but Masstree's border-node *permutation* field makes each insert visible in one atomic step instead. This solves the problem by eliminating invalid intermediate states. The *permutation* field compactly represents the correct key order plus the current number of keys, so writers expose a new sort order *and* a new key with a single aligned write. Readers see either the old order, without the new key, or the new order, with the new key in its proper place. No key rearrangement, and therefore no version increment, is required.

The 64-bit *permutation* is divided into 16 four-bit subfields. The lowest 4 bits, *nkeys*, holds the number of keys in the node (0–15). The remaining bits constitute a fifteen-element array, *keyindex*[15], containing a permutation of the numbers 0 through 15. Elements *keyindex*[0] through *keyindex*[*nkeys* − 1] store the indexes of the border node's live keys, in increasing order by key. The other elements list currently-unused slots. To insert a key, a writer locks

the node; loads the permutation; rearranges the permutation to shift an unused slot to the correct insertion position and increment *nkeys*; writes the new key and value to the previously-unused slot; and finally writes back the new permutation and unlocks the node. The new key becomes visible to readers only at this last step.

A compiler fence, and on some architectures a machine fence instruction, is required between the writes of the key and value and the write of the permutation. Our implementation includes fences whenever required, such as in *version* checks.

4.6.3 New layers

Masstree creates a new layer when inserting a key k_1 into a border node that contains a conflicting key k_2. It allocates a new empty border node n', inserts k_2's current value into it under the appropriate key slice, and then replaces k_2's value in n with the *next_layer* pointer n'. Finally, it unlocks n and continues the attempt to insert k_1, now using the newly created layer n'.

Since this process only affects a single key, there is no need to update n's *version* or *permutation*. However, readers must reliably distinguish true values from *next_layer* pointers. Since the pointer and the layer marker are stored separately, this requires a sequence of writes. First, the writer marks the key as UNSTABLE; readers seeing this marker will retry. It then writes the *next_layer* pointer, and finally marks the key as a LAYER.

4.6.4 Splits

Splits, unlike non-split inserts, remove active keys from a visible node and insert them in another. Without care, a *get* concurrent with the split might mistakenly report these shifting keys as lost. Writers must therefore update *version* fields to signal splits to readers. The challenge is to update these fields in writers, and check them in readers, in such a way that no change is lost.

Figures 5 and 6 present pseudocode for splitting a border node and for traversing down a B$^+$-tree to the border node responsible for a key. (Figure 4 presents some helper functions.) The split code uses hand-over-hand locking and marking [9]: lower levels of the tree are locked and marked as "splitting" (a type of dirty marking) before higher levels. Conversely, the traversal code checks versions hand-over-hand in the opposite direction: higher levels' versions are verified before the traversal shifts to lower levels.

To see why this is correct, consider an interior node B that splits to create a new node B$'$:

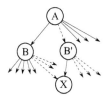

(Dashed lines from B indicate child pointers that were shifted to B$'$.) The split procedure changes versions and shifts keys in the following steps.

1. B and B$'$ are marked *splitting*.

2. Children, including X, are shifted from B to B$'$.

3. A (B's parent) is locked and marked *inserting*.

4. The new node, B$'$, is inserted into A.

5. A, B, and B$'$ are unlocked, which increments the A *vinsert* counter and the B and B$'$ *vsplit* counters.

Now consider a concurrent findborder(X) operation that starts at node A. We show that this operation either finds X or eventually retries. First, if findborder(X) traverses to node B$'$, then it will find X, which moved to B$'$ (in step 2) before the pointer to B$'$ was published (in step 4). Instead, assume findborder(X) traverses to B. Since the findborder operation retries on any version difference, and since findborder loads the child's version before double-checking the parent's ("hand-over-hand validation" in Figure 6), we know that findborder loaded B's version before A was marked as *inserting* (step 3). This in turn means that the load of B's version happened before step 1. (That step marks B as *splitting*, which would have caused stableversion to retry.) Then there are two possibilities. If findborder completes before the split operation's step 1, it will clearly locate node X. On the other hand, if findborder is delayed past step 1, it will always detect a split and retry from the root. The B.*version* $\oplus$ *v* check will fail because of B's *splitting* flag; the following stableversion(B) will delay until that flag is cleared, which happens when the split executes step 5; and at that point, B's *vsplit* counter has changed.

Masstree readers treat splits and inserts differently. Inserts retry locally, while splits require retrying from the root. Wide B-tree fanout and fast code mean concurrent splits are rarely observed: in an insert test with 8 threads, less than 1

```
get(node root, key k):
retry:     ⟨n,v⟩ ← findborder(root,k)
forward:  if v.deleted:
               goto retry
          ⟨t,lv⟩ ← extract link_or_value for k in n
          if n.version ⊕ v > "locked":
               v ← stableversion(n);  next ← n.next
               while !v.deleted and next ≠ NIL and k ≥ lowkey(next):
                    n ← next;  v ← stableversion(n);  next ← n.next
               goto forward
          else if t = NOTFOUND:
               return NOTFOUND
          else if t = VALUE:
               return lv.value
          else if t = LAYER:
               root ← lv.next_layer;  advance k to next slice
               goto retry
          else: // t = UNSTABLE
               goto forward
```

Figure 7. Find the value for a key.

insert in 10^6 had to retry from the root due to a concurrent split. Other algorithms, such as backing up the tree step by step, were more complex to code but performed no better. However, concurrent inserts are (as one might expect) observed 15× more frequently than splits. It is simple to handle them locally, so Masstree maintains separate split and insert counters to distinguish the cases.

Figure 7 shows full code for Masstree's *get* operation. (Puts are similar, but since they obtain locks, the retry logic is simpler.) Again, the node's contents are extracted between checks of its *version*, and *version* changes cause retries.

Border nodes, unlike interior nodes, can handle splits using their links.[4] The key invariant is that nodes split "to the right": when a border node *n* splits, its *higher* keys are shifted to its new sibling. Specifically, Masstree maintains the following invariants:

- The initial node in a B$^+$-tree is a border node. This node is not deleted until the B$^+$-tree itself is completely empty, and always remains the leftmost node in the tree.

- Every border node *n* is responsible for a range of keys [lowkey(n),highkey(n)). (The leftmost and rightmost nodes have lowkey(n) = $-\infty$ and highkey(n) = ∞, respectively.) Splits and deletes can modify highkey(n), but lowkey(n) remains constant over n's lifetime.

Thus, *get* can reliably find the relevant border node by comparing the current key and the next border node's lowkey.

The first lines of findborder (Figure 6) handle stale roots caused by concurrent splits, which can occur at any layer. When the layer-0 global root splits, we update it immediately, but other roots, which are stored in border nodes'

---

[4] B^{link}-trees [27] and OLFIT [11] also link interior nodes, but our "B$^-$ tree" implementation of remove [33] breaks the invariants that make this possible.

next_layer pointers, are updated lazily during later operations.

4.6.5 Removes

Masstree, unlike some prior work [11, 27], includes a full implementation of concurrent remove. Space constraints preclude a full discussion, but we mention several interesting features.

First, *remove* operations, when combined with inserts, must sometimes cause readers to retry! Consider the following threads running in parallel on a one-node tree:

$get(n, k_1)$:
   locate k_1 at n position i

                     $remove(n, k_1)$:
                         remove k_1 from n position i
                     $put(n, k_2, v_2)$:
                         insert k_2, v_2 at n position j

$lv \leftarrow n.lv[i]$; check *n.version*;
return *lv.value*

The *get* operation may return k_1's (removed) value, since the operations overlapped. *Remove* thus must not clear the memory corresponding to the key or its value: it just changes the *permutation*. But then if the *put* operation happened to pick $j = i$, the *get* operation might return v_2, which isn't a valid value for k_1. Masstree must therefore update the *version* counter's *vinsert* field when removed slots are reused.

When a border node becomes empty, Masstree removes it and any resulting empty ancestors. This requires the border-node list be doubly-, not singly-, linked. A naive implementation could break the list under concurrent splits and removes; compare-and-swap operations (some including flag bits) are required for both split and remove, which slightly slows down split. As with any state observable by concurrent readers, removed nodes must not be freed immediately. Instead, we mark them as *deleted* and reclaim them later. Any operation that encounters a *deleted* node retries from the root. *Remove*'s code for manipulating interior nodes resembles that for split; hand-over-hand locking is used to find the right key to remove. Once that key is found, the *deleted* node becomes completely unreferenced and future readers will not encounter it.

Removes can delete entire layer-h trees for $h \geq 1$. These are not cleaned up right away: normal operations lock at most one layer at a time, and removing a full tree requires locking both the empty layer-h tree and the layer-$(h-1)$ border node that points to it. Epoch-based reclamation tasks are scheduled as needed to clean up empty and pathologically-shaped layer-h trees.

4.7 Values

The Masstree system stores values consisting of a version number and an array of variable-length strings called *columns*. Gets can retrieve multiple columns (identified by integer indexes) and puts can modify multiple columns.

Multi-column puts are atomic: a concurrent *get* will see either all or none of a *put*'s column modifications.

Masstree includes several value implementations; we evaluate one most appropriate for small values. Each value is allocated as a single memory block. Modifications don't act in place, since this could expose intermediate states to concurrent readers. Instead, put creates a new value object, copying unmodified columns from the old value object as appropriate. This design uses cache effectively for small values, but would cause excessive data copying for large values; for those, Masstree offers a design that stores each column in a separately-allocated block.

4.8 Discussion

More than 30% of the cost of a Masstree lookup is in computation (as opposed to DRAM waits), mostly due to key search within tree nodes. Linear search has higher complexity than binary search, but exhibits better locality. For Masstree, the performance difference of the two search schemes is architecture dependent. On an Intel processor, linear search can be up to 5% faster than binary search. On an AMD processor, both perform the same.

One important PALM optimization is parallel lookup [34]. This effectively overlaps the DRAM fetches for many operations by looking up the keys for a batch of requests in parallel. Our implementation of this technique did not improve performance on our 48-core AMD machine, but on a 24-core Intel machine, throughput rose by up to 34%. We plan to change Masstree's network stack to apply this technique.

5. Networking and persistence

Masstree uses network interfaces that support per-core receive and transmit queues, which reduce contention when short query packets arrive from many clients. To support short connections efficiently, Masstree can configure per-core UDP ports that are each associated with a single core's receive queue. Our benchmarks, however, use long-lived TCP query connections from few clients (or client aggregators), a common operating mode that is equally effective at avoiding network overhead.

Masstree logs updates to persistent storage to achieve persistence and crash recovery. Each server query thread (core) maintains its own log file and in-memory log buffer. A corresponding logging thread, running on the same core as the query thread, writes out the log buffer in the background. Logging thus proceeds in parallel on each core.

A put operation appends to the query thread's log buffer and responds to the client without forcing that buffer to storage. Logging threads batch updates to take advantage of higher bulk sequential throughput, but force logs to storage at least every 200 ms for safety. Different logs may be on different disks or SSDs for higher total log throughput.

Value version numbers and log record timestamps aid the process of log recovery. Sequential updates to a value obtain distinct, and increasing, version numbers. Update version numbers are written into the log along with the operation, and each log record is timestamped. When restoring a database from logs, Masstree sorts logs by timestamp. It first calculates the recovery cutoff point, which is the minimum of the logs' last timestamps, $\tau = \min_{\ell \in L} \max_{u \in \ell} u.timestamp$, where L is the set of available logs and u denotes a single logged update. Masstree plays back the logged updates in parallel, taking care to apply a value's updates in increasing order by version, except that updates with $u.timestamp \geq \tau$ are dropped.

Masstree periodically writes out a checkpoint containing all keys and values. This speeds recovery and allows log space to be reclaimed. Recovery loads the latest valid checkpoint that completed before τ, the log recovery time, and then replays logs starting from the timestamp at which the checkpoint began.

Our checkpoint facility is independent of the Masstree design; we include it to show that persistence need not limit system performance, but do not evaluate it in depth. It takes Masstree 58 seconds to create a checkpoint of 140 million key-value pairs (9.1 GB of data in total), and 38 seconds to recover from that checkpoint. The main bottleneck for both is imbalance in the parallelization among cores. Checkpoints run in parallel with request processing. When run concurrently with a checkpoint, a put-only workload achieves 72% of its ordinary throughput due to disk contention.

6. Tree evaluation

We evaluate Masstree in two parts. In this section, we focus on Masstree's central data structure, the trie of B^+-trees. We show the cumulative impact on performance of various tree design choices and optimizations. We show that Masstree scales effectively and that its single shared tree can outperform separate per-core trees when the workload is skewed. We also quantify the costs of Masstree's flexibility. While variable-length key support comes for free, range query support does not: a near-best-case hash table (which lacks range query support) can provide 2.5× the throughput of Masstree.

The next section evaluates Masstree as a system. There, we describe the performance impact of checkpoint and recovery, and compare the whole Masstree system against other high performance storage systems: MongoDB, VoltDB, Redis, and memcached. Masstree performs very well, achieving 26–1000× the throughput of the other tree-based (range-query-supporting) stores. Redis and memcached are based on hash tables; this gives them $O(1)$ average-case lookup in exchange for not supporting range queries. memcached can exceed Masstree's throughput on uniform workloads; on other workloads, Masstree provides up to 3.7× the throughput of these systems.

6.1 Setup

The experiments use a 48-core server (eight 2.4 GHz six-core AMD Opteron 8431 chips) running Linux 3.1.5. Each core has private 64 KB instruction and data caches and a 512 KB private L2 cache. The six cores in each chip share a 6 MB L3 cache. Cache lines are 64 bytes. Each of the chips has 8 GB of DRAM attached to it. The tests use up to 16 cores on up to three chips, and use DRAM attached to only those three chips; the extra cores are disabled. The goal is to mimic the configuration of a machine more like those easily purchasable today. The machine has four SSDs, each with a measured sequential write speed of 90 to 160 MB/sec. Masstree uses all four SSDs to store logs and checkpoints. The server has a 10 Gb Ethernet card (NIC) connected to a switch. Also on that switch are 25 client machines that send requests over TCP. The server's NIC distributes interrupts over all cores. Results are averaged over three runs.

All experiments in this section use small keys and values. Most keys are no more than 10 bytes long; values are always 1–10 bytes long. Keys are distributed uniformly at random over some range (the range changes by experiment). The key space is not partitioned: a border node generally contains keys created by different clients, and sometimes one client will overwrite a key originally inserted by another. One common key distribution is "1-to-10-byte decimal," which comprises the decimal string representations of random numbers between 0 and 2^{31}. This exercises Masstree's variable-length key support, and 80% of the keys are 9 or 10 bytes long, causing Masstree to create layer-1 trees.

We run separate experiments for gets and puts. Get experiments start with a full store (80–140 million keys) and run for 20 seconds. Put experiments start with an empty store and run for 140 million total puts. Most puts are inserts, but about 10% are updates since multiple clients occasionally put the same key. Puts generally run 30% slower than gets.

6.2 Factor analysis

We analyze Masstree's performance by breaking down the performance gap between a binary tree and Masstree. We evaluate several configurations on 140M-key 1-to-10-byte-decimal get and put workloads with 16 cores. Each server thread generates its own workload: these numbers do not include the overhead of network and logging. Figure 8 shows the results.

Binary We first evaluate a fast, concurrent, lock-free binary tree. Each 40-byte tree node here contains a full key, a value pointer, and two child pointers. The fast jemalloc memory allocator is used.

+Flow, +Superpage, +IntCmp Memory allocation often bottlenecks multicore performance. We switch to Flow, our implementation of the Streamflow [32] allocator ("+Flow"). Flow supports 2 MB x86 superpages, which, when introduced ("+Superpage"), improve throughput by 27–37% due

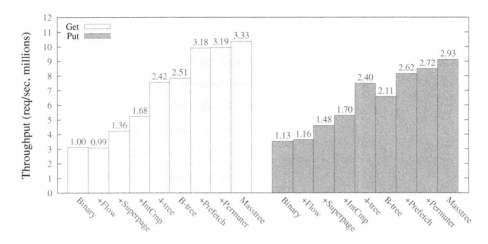

Figure 8. Contributions of design features to Masstree's performance (§6.2). Design features are cumulative. Measurements use 16 cores and each server thread generates its own load (no clients or network traffic). Bar numbers give throughput relative to the binary tree running the get workload.

to fewer TLB misses and lower kernel overhead for allocation. Integer key comparison (§4.2, "+IntCmp") further improves throughput by 15–24%.

4-tree A balanced binary tree has $\log_2 n$ depth, imposing an average of $\log_2 n - 1$ serial DRAM latencies per lookup. We aim to reduce and overlap those latencies and to pack more useful information into cache lines that must be fetched. "4-tree," a tree with fanout 4, uses both these techniques. Its wider fanout nearly halves average depth relative to the binary tree. Each 4-tree node comprises two cache lines, but usually only the first must be fetched from DRAM. This line contains all data important for traversal—the node's four child pointers and the first 8 bytes of each of its keys. (The binary tree also fetches only one cache line per node, but most of it is not useful for traversal.) All internal nodes are full. Reads are lockless and need never retry; inserts are lock-free but use compare-and-swap. "4-tree" improves throughput by 41–44% over "+IntCmp".

B-tree, +Prefetch, +Permuter 4-tree yields good performance, but would be difficult to balance. B-trees have even wider fanout and stay balanced, at the cost of somewhat less efficient memory usage (nodes average 75% full). "B-tree" is a concurrent B^+-tree with fanout 15 that implements our concurrency control scheme from §4. Each node has space for up to the first 16 bytes of each key. Unfortunately this tree *reduces* put throughput by 12% over 4-tree, and does not improve get throughput much. Conventional B-tree inserts must rearrange a node's keys—4-tree never rearranges keys—and B-tree nodes spend 5 cache lines to achieve average fanout 11, a worse cache-line-to-fanout ratio than 4-tree's. However, wide B-tree nodes are easily prefetched to overlap these DRAM latencies. When prefetching is added, B-tree improves throughput by 9–31%

over 4-tree ("+Prefetch"). Leaf-node permutations (§4.6.2, "+Permuter") further improve put throughput by 4%.

Masstree Finally, Masstree itself improves throughput by 4–8% over "+Permuter" in these experiments. This surprised us. 1-to-10-byte decimal keys can share an 8-byte prefix, forcing Masstree to create layer-1 trie-nodes, but in these experiments such nodes are quite empty. A 140M-key put workload, for example, creates a tree with 33% of its keys in layer-1 trie-nodes, but the average number of keys per layer-1 trie-node is just 2.3. One might expect this to perform worse than a true B-tree, which has better node utilization. Masstree's design, thanks to features such as storing 8 bytes per key per interior node rather than 16, appears efficient enough to overcome this effect.

6.3 System relevance of tree design

Cache-crafty design matters not just in isolation, but also in the context of a full system. We turn on logging, generate load using network clients, and compare "+IntCmp," the fastest binary tree from the previous section, with Masstree. On 140M-key 1-to-10-byte-decimal workloads with 16 cores, Masstree provides 1.90× and 1.53× the throughput of the binary tree for gets and puts, respectively.[5] Thus, if logging and networking infrastructure are reasonably well implemented, tree design can improve system performance.

6.4 Flexibility

Masstree supports several features that not all key-value applications require, including range queries, variable-length keys, and concurrency. We now evaluate how much these features cost by evaluating tree variants that do not support them. We include network and logging.

---

[5] Absolute Masstree throughput is 8.03 Mreq/sec for gets (77% of the Figure 8 value) and 5.78 Mreq/sec for puts (63% of the Figure 8 value).

Variable-length keys We compare Masstree with a concurrent B-tree supporting only fixed-size 8-byte keys (a version of "+Permuter"). When run on a 16-core get workload with 80M 8-byte decimal keys, Masstree supports 9.84 Mreq/sec and the fixed-size B-tree 9.93 Mreq/sec, just 0.8% more. The difference is so small likely because the trie-of-trees design effectively has fixed-size keys in most tree nodes.

Keys with common prefixes Masstree is intended to preserve good cache performance when keys share common prefixes. However, unlike some designs, such as partial-key B-trees, Masstree can become superficially unbalanced. Figure 9 provides support for Masstree's choice. The workloads use 16 cores and 80M decimal keys. The X axis gives each test's key length in bytes, but only the final 8 bytes vary uniformly. A 0-to-40-byte prefix is the same for every key. Despite the resulting imbalance, Masstree has $3.4\times$ the throughput of "+Permuter" for relatively long keys. This is because "+Permuter" incurs a cache miss for the suffix of every key it compares. However, Masstree has $1.4\times$ the throughput of "+Permuter" even for 16-byte keys, which "+Permuter" stores entirely inline. Here Masstree's performance comes from avoiding repeated comparisons: it examines the key's first 8 bytes once, rather than $O(\log_2 n)$ times.

Concurrency Masstree uses interlocked instructions, such as compare-and-swap, that would be unnecessary for a single-core store. We implemented a single-core version of Masstree by removing locking, node versions, and interlocked instructions. When evaluated on one core using a 140M-key, 1-to-10-byte-decimal put workload, single-core Masstree beats concurrent Masstree by just 13%.

Range queries Masstree uses a tree to support range queries. If they were not needed, a hash table might be preferable, since hash tables have $O(1)$ lookup cost while a tree has $O(\log n)$. To measure this factor, we implemented a concurrent hash table in the Masstree framework and measured a 16-core, 80M-key workload with 8-byte random alphabetical keys.[6] Our hash table has $2.5\times$ higher total throughput than Masstree. Thus, of these features, only range queries appear inherently expensive.

6.5 Scalability

This section investigates how Masstree's performance scales with the number of cores. Figure 10 shows the results for 16-core get and put workloads using 140M 1-to-10-byte decimal keys. The Y axis shows per-core throughput; ideal scalability would appear as a horizontal line. At 16 cores, Masstree scales to $12.7\times$ and $12.5\times$ its one-core performance for gets and puts respectively.

The limiting factor for the get workload is high and increasing DRAM fetch cost. Each operation consumes about

---

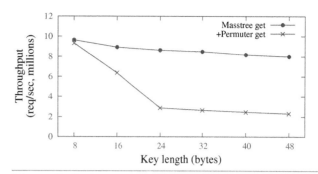

Figure 9. Performance effect of varying key length on Masstree and "+Permuter." For each key length, keys differ only in the last 8 bytes. 16-core get workload.

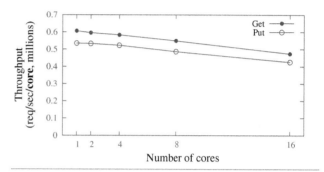

Figure 10. Masstree scalability.

1000 cycles of CPU time in computation independent of the number of cores, but average per-operation DRAM stall time varies from 2050 cycles with one core to 2800 cycles with 16 cores. This increase roughly matches the decrease in performance from one to 16 cores in Figure 10, and is consistent with the cores contending for some limited resource having to do with memory fetches, such as DRAM or interconnect bandwidth.

6.6 Partitioning and skew

Some key-value stores partition data among cores in order to avoid contention. We show here that, while partitioning works well for some workloads, sharing data among all cores works better for others. We compare Masstree with 16 separate instances of the single-core Masstree variant described above, each serving a partition of the overall data. The partitioning is static, and each instance holds the same number of keys. Each instance allocates memory from its local DRAM node. Clients send each query to the instance appropriate for the query's key. We refer this configuration as "hard-partitioned" Masstree.

Tests use 140M-key, 1-to-10-byte decimal get workloads with various partition skewness. Following Hua *et al.* [22], we model skewness with a single parameter δ. For skewness δ, 15 partitions receive the same number of requests, while the last one receives $\delta\times$ more than the others. For example,

---

[6] Digit-only keys caused collisions and we wanted the test to favor the hash table. The hash table is open-coded and allocated using superpages, and has 30% occupancy. Each hash lookup inspects 1.1 entries on average.

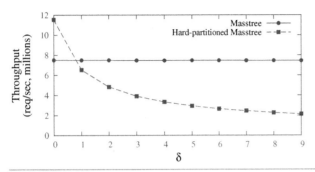

Figure 11. Throughput of Masstree and hard-partitioned Masstree with various skewness (16-core get workload).

Server	C/C++ client library	Batched query	Range query
MongoDB-2.0	2.0	No	Yes
VoltDB-2.0	1.3.6.1	Yes	Yes
memcached-1.4.8	1.0.3	Yes for get	No
Redis-2.4.5	latest hiredis	Yes	No

Figure 12. Versions of tested servers and client libraries.

at $\delta = 9$, one partition handles 40% of the requests and each other partition handles 4%.

Figure 11 shows that the throughput of hard-partitioned Masstree decreases with skewness. The core serving the hot partition is saturated for $\delta \geq 1$. This throttles the entire system, since other partitions' clients must wait for the slow partition in order to preserve skewness, leaving the other cores partially idle. At $\delta = 9$, 80% of total CPU time is idle. Masstree throughput is constant; at $\delta = 9$ it provides $3.5\times$ the throughput of hard-partitioned. However, for a uniform workload ($\delta = 0$), hard-partitioned Masstree has $1.5\times$ the throughput of Masstree, mostly because it avoids remote DRAM access (and interlocked instructions). Thus Masstree's shared data is an advantage with skewed workloads, but can be slower than hard-partitioning for uniform ones. This problem may diminish on single-chip machines, where all DRAM is local.

7. System evaluation

This section compares the performance of Masstree with that of MongoDB, VoltDB, memcached, and Redis, all systems that have reputations for high performance. Many of these systems support features that Masstree does not, some of which may bottleneck their performance. We disable other systems' expensive features when possible. Nevertheless, the comparisons in this section are not entirely fair. We provide them to put Masstree's throughput in the context of other systems used in practice for key-value workloads.

Figure 12 summarizes the software versions we tested. The client libraries vary in their support for batched or pipelined queries, which reduce networking overheads. The memcached client library does not support batched puts.

Except for Masstree, these systems' storage data structures are not designed to scale well when shared among multiple cores. They are intended to be used with multiple instances on multicore machines, each with a partition of the data. For each system, we use the configuration on 16 cores that yields the highest performance: eight MongoDB processes and one configuration server; four VoltDB processes,

each with four sites; 16 Redis processes; and 16 memcached processes. Masstree uses 16 threads.

VoltDB is an in-memory RDBMS. It achieves robustness through replication rather than persistent storage. We turn VoltDB's replication off. VoltDB supports transactions and a richer data and query model than Masstree.

MongoDB is a key-value store. It stores data primarily on disk, and supports named columns and auxiliary indices. We set the MongoDB chunk size to 300MB, run it on an in-memory file system to eliminate storage I/O, and use the "_id" column as the key, indexed by a B-tree.

Redis is an in-memory key-value store. Like Masstree, it logs to disk for crash recovery. We give each Redis process a separate log, using all four SSDs, and disable checkpointing and log rewriting (log rewriting degrades throughput by more than 50%). Redis uses a hash table internally and thus does not support range queries. To implement columns, we used Redis's support for reading and writing specific byte ranges of a value.

memcached is an in-memory key-value store usually used for caching non-persistent data. Like Redis, memcached uses a hash table internally and does not support range queries. The memcached client library supports batched gets but not batched puts, which limits its performance on workloads involving many puts.

Our benchmarks run against databases initialized with 20M key-value pairs. We use two distinct sets of workloads. The first set's benchmarks resemble those in the previous section: get and put workloads with uniformly-distributed 1-to-10-byte decimal keys and 8-byte values. These benchmarks are run for 60 seconds. The second set uses workloads based on the YCSB cloud serving benchmark [16]. We use a Zipfian distribution for key popularity and set the number of columns to 10 and size of each column to 4 bytes. The small column size ensures that no workload is bottlenecked by network or SSD bandwidth. YCSB includes a benchmark, YCSB-E, dependent on range queries. We modify this benchmark to return one column per key, rather than all 10, again to prevent the benchmark from being limited by the network. Initial tests were client limited, so we run multiple client processes. Finally, some systems (Masstree) do not yet support named columns, and on others (Redis) named column support proved expensive; for these systems we modified YCSB to identify columns by number rather than name. We call the result MYCSB.

Workload	Throughput (req/sec, millions, and as % of Masstree)									
	Masstree	MongoDB		VoltDB		Redis		Memcached	
Uniform key popularity, 1-to-10-byte decimal keys, one 8-byte column									
get	9.10	0.04	0.5%	0.22	2.4%	5.97	65.6%	**9.78**	107.4%
put	**5.84**	0.04	0.7%	0.22	3.7%	2.97	50.9%	1.21	20.7%
1-core get	**0.91**	0.01	1.1%	0.02	2.6%	0.54	59.4%	0.77	84.3%
1-core put	**0.60**	0.04	6.8%	0.02	3.6%	0.28	47.2%	0.11	17.7%
Zipfian key popularity, 5-to-24-byte keys, ten 4-byte columns for get, one 4-byte column for update & getrange									
MYCSB-A (50% get, 50% put)	**6.05**	0.05	0.9%	0.20	3.4%	2.13	35.2%	N/A	
MYCSB-B (95% get, 5% put)	**8.90**	0.04	0.5%	0.20	2.3%	2.69	30.2%	N/A	
MYCSB-C (all get)	**9.86**	0.05	0.5%	0.21	2.1%	2.70	27.4%	5.28	53.6%
MYCSB-E (95% getrange, 5% put)	**0.91**	0.00	0.1%	0.00	0.1%	N/A		N/A	

Figure 13. System comparison results. All benchmarks run against a database initialized with 20M key-value pairs and use 16 cores unless otherwise noted. Getrange operations retrieve one column for n adjacent keys, where n is uniformly distributed between 1 and 100.

Puts in this section's benchmarks modify existing keys' values, rather than inserting new keys. This made it easier to preserve MYCSB's key popularity distribution with multiple client processes.

We do not run systems on benchmarks they don't support. The hash table stores can't run MYCSB-E, which requires range queries, and memcached can't run MYCSB-A and -B, which require individual-column update. In all cases Masstree includes logging and network I/O.

Figure 13 shows the results. Masstree outperforms the other systems on almost all workloads, usually by a substantial margin. The exception is that on a get workload with uniformly distributed keys and 16 cores, memcached has 7.4% better throughput than Masstree. This is because memcached, being partitioned, avoids remote DRAM access (see §6.6). When run on a single core, Masstree slightly exceeds the performance of this version of memcached (though as we showed above, a hash table could exceed Masstree's performance by 2.5×).

We believe these numbers fairly represent the systems' absolute performance. For example, VoltDB's performance on uniform key distribution workloads is consistent with that reported by the VoltDB developers for a similar benchmark, volt2 [23].[7]

Several conclusions can be drawn from the data. Masstree has good efficiency even for challenging (non-network-limited) workloads. Batched query support is vital on these benchmarks: memcached's update performance is significantly worse than its get performance, for example. VoltDB's range query support lags behind its support for pure gets. As we would expect given the results in §6.6, partitioned stores perform better on uniform workloads than skewed workloads: compare Redis and memcached on the uniform get workload with the Zipfian MYCSB-C workload.

8. Conclusions

Masstree is a persistent in-memory key-value database. Its design pays particular attention to concurrency and to efficiency for short and simple queries. Masstree keeps all data in memory in a tree, with fanout chosen to minimize total DRAM delay when descending the tree with prefetching. The tree is shared among all cores to preserve load balance when key popularities are skewed. It maintains high concurrency using optimistic concurrency control for lookup and local locking for updates. For good performance for keys with long shared prefixes, a Masstree consists of a trie-like concatenation of B^+-trees, each of the latter supporting only fixed-length keys for efficiency. Logging and checkpointing provide consistency and durability.

On a 16-core machine, with logging enabled and queries arriving over a network, Masstree executes more than six million simple queries per second. This performance is comparable to that of memcached, a non-persistent hash table server, and higher (often much higher) than that of VoltDB, MongoDB, and Redis.

Acknowledgments

We thank the Eurosys reviewers and our shepherd, Eric Van Hensbergen, for many helpful comments. This work was partially supported by the National Science Foundation (awards 0834415 and 0915164) and by Quanta Computer. Eddie Kohler's work was partially supported by a Sloan Research Fellowship and a Microsoft Research New Faculty Fellowship.

References

[1] Sharding for startups. `http://www.startuplessonslearned.com/2009/01/sharding-for-startups.html`.

[2] MongoDB. `http://mongodb.com`.

[3] Redis. `http://redis.io`.

---

[7] We also implemented volt2; it gave similar results.

[4] Cassandra @ Twitter: An interview with Ryan King. http://nosql.mypopescu.com/post/407159447/cassandra-twitter-an-interview-with-ryan-king.

[5] VoltDB, the NewSQL database for high velocity applications. http://voltdb.com.

[6] R. Bayer and E. McCreight. Organization and maintenance of large ordered indices. In *Proc. 1970 ACM SIGFIDET (now SIGMOD) Workshop on Data Description, Access and Control*, SIGFIDET '70, pages 107–141.

[7] R. Bayer and K. Unterauer. Prefix B-Trees. *ACM Transactions on Database Systems*, 2(1):11–26, Mar. 1977.

[8] P. Bohannon, P. McIlroy, and R. Rastogi. Main-memory index structures with fixed-size partial keys. *SIGMOD Record*, 30:163–174, May 2001.

[9] N. G. Bronson, J. Casper, H. Chafi, and K. Olukotun. A practical concurrent binary search tree. In *Proc. 15th ACM PPoPP Symposium*, Bangalore, India, 2010.

[10] S. K. Cha and C. Song. P*TIME: Highly scalable OLTP DBMS for managing update-intensive stream workload. In *Proc. 30th VLDB Conference*, pages 1033–1044, 2004.

[11] S. K. Cha, S. Hwang, K. Kim, and K. Kwon. Cache-conscious concurrency control of main-memory indexes on shared-memory multiprocessor systems. In *Proc. 27th VLDB Conference*, 2001.

[12] F. Chang, J. Dean, S. Ghemawat, W. C. Hsieh, D. A. Wallach, M. Burrows, T. Chandra, A. Fikes, and R. E. Gruber. Bigtable: A distributed storage system for structured data. *ACM Transactions on Computer Systems*, 26:4:1–4:26, June 2008.

[13] S. Chen, P. B. Gibbons, and T. C. Mowry. Improving index performance through prefetching. In *Proc. 2001 SIGMOD Conference*, pages 235–246.

[14] J. Cieslewicz and K. A. Ross. Data partitioning on chip multiprocessors. In *Proc. 4th International Workshop on Data Management on New Hardware*, DaMoN '08, pages 25–34, New York, NY, USA, 2008.

[15] J. Cieslewicz, K. A. Ross, K. Satsumi, and Y. Ye. Automatic contention detection and amelioration for data-intensive operations. In *Proc. 2010 SIGMOD Conference*, pages 483–494.

[16] B. F. Cooper, A. Silberstein, E. Tam, R. Ramakrishnan, and R. Sears. Benchmarking cloud serving systems with YCSB. In *Proc. 1st ACM Symposium on Cloud Computing*, SoCC '10, pages 143–154, New York, NY, USA, 2010.

[17] G. DeCandia, D. Hastorun, M. Jampani, G. Kakulapati, A. Lakshman, A. Pilchin, S. Sivasubramanian, P. Vosshall, and W. Vogels. Dynamo: Amazon's highly available key-value store. In *Proc. 21st ACM SOSP*, pages 205–220, 2007.

[18] B. Fitzpatrick. LiveJournal's backend—a history of scaling. http://www.danga.com/words/2005_oscon/oscon-2005.pdf.

[19] K. Fraser. Practical lock-freedom. Technical Report UCAM-CL-TR-579, University of Cambridge Computer Laboratory, 2004.

[20] E. Fredkin. Trie memory. *Communications of the ACM*, 3:490–499, September 1960.

[21] N. Hardavellas, I. Pandis, R. Johnson, N. G. Mancheril, A. Ailamaki, and B. Falsafi. Database servers on chip multiprocessors: Limitations and opportunities. In *3rd Biennial Conference on Innovative Data Systems Research (CIDR)*, Asilomar, Califormnia, USA, January 2007.

[22] K. A. Hua and C. Lee. Handling data skew in multiprocessor database computers using partition tuning. In *Proc. 17th VLDB Conference*, pages 525–535, 1991.

[23] J. Hugg. Key-value benchmarking. http://voltdb.com/company/blog/key-value-benchmarking.

[24] R. Johnson, I. Pandis, N. Hardavellas, A. Ailamaki, and B. Falsafi. Shore-MT: A scalable storage manager for the multicore era. In *Proc. 12th International Conference on Extending Database Technology: Advances in Database Technology*, pages 24–35, New York, NY, USA, 2009.

[25] R. Kallman, H. Kimura, J. Natkins, A. Pavlo, A. Rasin, S. Zdonik, E. P. C. Jones, S. Madden, M. Stonebraker, Y. Zhang, J. Hugg, and D. J. Abadi. H-Store: A high-performance, distributed main memory transaction processing system. *Proc. VLDB Endowment*, 1:1496–1499, August 2008.

[26] A. Lakshman and P. Malik. Cassandra: A decentralized structured storage system. *ACM SIGOPS Operating System Review*, 44:35–40, April 2010.

[27] P. L. Lehman and S. B. Yao. Efficient locking for concurrent operations on B-trees. *ACM Transactions on Database Systems*, 6(4):650–670, 1981.

[28] P. E. McKenney, D. Sarma, A. Arcangeli, A. Kleen, O. Krieger, and R. Russell. Read-copy update. In *Proc. 2002 Ottawa Linux Symposium*, pages 338–367, 2002.

[29] C. Nyberg, T. Barclay, Z. Cvetanovic, J. Gray, and D. Lomet. AlphaSort: A cache-sensitive parallel external sort. *The VLDB Journal*, 4(4):603–627, 1995.

[30] J. Rao and K. A. Ross. Making B+-trees cache conscious in main memory. *SIGMOD Record*, 29:475–486, May 2000.

[31] K. A. Ross. Optimizing read convoys in main-memory query processing. In *Proc. 6th International Workshop on Data Management on New Hardware*, DaMoN '10, pages 27–33, New York, NY, USA, 2010. ACM.

[32] S. Schneider, C. D. Antonopoulos, and D. S. Nikolopoulos. Scalable locality-conscious multithreaded memory allocation. In *Proc. 5th International Symposium on Memory Management*, ISMM '06, pages 84–94. ACM, 2006.

[33] S. Sen and R. E. Tarjan. Deletion without rebalancing in balanced binary trees. In *Proc. 21st SODA*, pages 1490–1499, 2010.

[34] J. Sewall, J. Chhugani, C. Kim, N. Satish, and P. Dubey. PALM: Parallel architecture-friendly latch-free modifications to B+ trees on many-core processors. *Proc. VLDB Endowment*, 4(11):795–806, August 2011.

[35] M. Stonebraker, S. Madden, J. D. Abadi, S. Harizopoulos, N. Hachem, and P. Helland. The end of an architectural era: (it's time for a complete rewrite). In *Proc. 33rd VLDB Conference*, pages 1150–1160, 2007.

MadLINQ: Large-Scale Distributed Matrix Computation for the Cloud

Zhengping Qian[†]   Xiuwei Chen[†]   Nanxi Kang[♮]   Mingcheng Chen[♮]   Yuan Yu[‡]

Thomas Moscibroda[†]   Zheng Zhang[†]

[†] Microsoft Research Asia, [♮] Shanghai Jiaotong University, [‡] Microsoft Research Silicon Valley

Abstract

The computation core of many data-intensive applications can be best expressed as matrix computations. The MadLINQ project addresses the following two important research problems: the need for a highly scalable, efficient and fault-tolerant matrix computation system that is also easy to program, and the seamless integration of such specialized execution engines in a general purpose data-parallel computing system.

MadLINQ exposes a unified programming model to both matrix algorithm and application developers. Matrix algorithms are expressed as sequential programs operating on tiles (i.e., sub-matrices). For application developers, MadLINQ provides a distributed matrix computation library for .NET languages. Via the LINQ technology, MadLINQ also seamlessly integrates with DryadLINQ, a data-parallel computing system focusing on relational algebra.

The system automatically handles the parallelization and distributed execution of programs on a large cluster. It outperforms current state-of-the-art systems by employing two key techniques, both of which are enabled by the matrix abstraction: exploiting extra parallelism using fine-grained pipelining and efficient on-demand failure recovery using a distributed fault-tolerant execution engine. We describe the design and implementation of MadLINQ and evaluate system performance using several real-world applications.

Categories and Subject Descriptors   D.1.3 [*PROGRAMMING TECHNIQUES*]: Concurrent Programming—*Distributed programming*

General Terms   Design, Performance, Reliability

Keywords   Matrix Computation, Distributed Systems, Cluster Computing, Pipelining, Fault-tolerance, Dataflow

1. Introduction

Distributed execution engines (MapReduce [19], Hadoop [2], or Dryad [23]) and high-level language support (Pig [30], HIVE [3], and DryadLINQ [36]) have been widely adopted with great success in the development of large-scale, distributed data-intensive applications. Two factors largely account for the success of these systems. First, they provide programmers with easy access to a core subset of relational algebra operators, such as filtering, projection, aggregation, sorting and joins, and allow further extensions via arbitrary user-defined functions. This pragmatic strategy addresses the critical need to deal with the large corpus of Web data. Second, they adopt the direct-acyclic-graph (DAG) execution model, which is both more scalable and failure-resilient compared to alternative parallel-computing paradigms, such as SPMD (Single Process, Multiple Data).

On the other hand, the relational algebra semantics supported by these Web-scale distributed systems is ill-suited to efficiently solve a large class of important problems which require a deeper analysis or manipulation of the data at hand. In such cases, analysis tools involving linear algebra and matrix computations are often called for instead. Machine learning applications, for example, routinely require matrix computations such as multiplication, Cholesky factorization, singular value decomposition (SVD) or LU factorization [21]. The same is true for sophisticated ranking or classification algorithms. And many algorithms commonly used in, say, social web mining or information retrieval on microblogs boil down to traversal-based graph algorithms (e.g., Betweeness Centrality (BC) [20], PageRank, Breadth-First Search (BFS)) that are also essentially sparse matrix computations.

Given the importance of matrix computation, it is therefore logical to design a scalable engine for linear algebra (which could naturally accommodate many important graph algorithms as well). Ideally, such an engine would achieve the following properties: it should allow developers to easily program matrix algorithms and naturally exploit matrix specific optimization, while at the same time maintaining the system scalability and robustness of a DAG execution

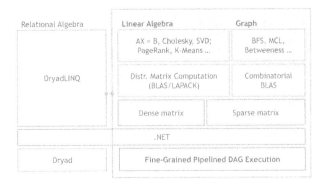

Figure 1. The MadLINQ system stack, and how it interacts with DryadLINQ.

model. Furthermore, it should unify with other, existing engines to deliver a holistic and seamless development experience, ideally in a modern programming language.

Unfortunately, existing solutions fall short in achieving these properties. On the one hand, efficient matrix computation has traditionally been the realm of High-Performance Computing (HPC), with well-known solutions such as ScaLA-PACK [17]. These systems require deep understanding of low level primitives such as MPI abstraction to develop new algorithms. The execution model is SPMD, with coarse-grained bulk synchronizations (i.e., barriers). Furthermore, the entire problem must be brought into and efficiently maintained in memory. These constraints severely affect programmability, scalability and robustness and as a result, HPC solutions are rarely considered in Web-scale big data analysis. On the other hand, there have been attempts to implement matrix operations on top of the MapReduce framework (e.g., HAMA [32]). While this removes the constraint of problem size (often referred to as *out-of-core* computing), the MapReduce interface is fundamentally restrictive, making it difficult to program efficient real-world linear algebra algorithms that are structurally far more complex than typical MapReduce jobs. While the execution model is dataflow, MapReduce is implicitly globally synchronized (i.e., no reducers can proceed unless all mappers complete). Further, as we will show later, it fails to take advantage of the well-defined semantics of matrix operations to implement sophisticated optimizations such as pipelining.

These observations motivated us to develop MadLINQ, a system that achieves all the aforementioned desirable properties. Fig. 1 gives the conceptual overview of the MadLINQ system stack. At the bottom is its fine-grained pipelining protocol that exploits the specific structure of matrices, and serves as the fabric to compose the DAG execution on a cluster of machines. Machine-level computation is carried out by industrial-strength multi-core-ready matrix libraries. This execution layer handles both dense and sparse matrix data models, adaptively choosing the appropriate library. Further up the stack, we have developed a large fraction of the traditional linear algebra routines.

In summary, we make the following contributions:

- We introduce a simple programming model for describing matrix computations, based on the familiar tile abstraction in linear algebra. The model supports both dense and sparse matrix data schema, and can easily be used to implement complex matrix algorithms. This flexibility allows us to rapidly develop highly compact programs, covering not only linear algebra routines and graph algorithms, but also new domain-specific algorithms.

- We develop a new *fine-grained pipelining* (FGP) execution model. Unlike existing DAG engines such as Dryad, FGP exchanges data among computing nodes in a pipelined fashion to aggressively overlap computation of depending vertices. As a result, MadLINQ's performance is competitive and often better than mature, highly-customized MPI-based products. For instance, MadLINQ outperforms ScaLAPACK on a 128-node (512-core) cluster, for the standard benchmark of Cholesky by as much as 31.6%.

- We design and implement a lightweight fault-tolerance protocol for FGP, which reduces redundant computation in case of failure to the theoretical minimum. We then show how matrix computation can exploit this to be highly performant and failure resilient. In our test, the system sustains massive failure of machines and arbitrary additions and/or removals of machines, whereas ScaLAPACK cannot withstand any single failure. [1]

- We adopt the language integration approach advocated by LINQ to integrate the domain-specific runtime into a general purpose high-level programming model. This approach allows us to seamlessly combine MadLINQ with other data processing systems such as DryadLINQ, and thus provide the functionality of relational algebra, linear algebra and graph algorithms in one unified platform.

The rest of the paper is organized as follows. Section 2 gives background of matrix algorithms and their building blocks. Section 3 describes MadLINQ's programming model. Section 4 details our design, including DAG generation, execution, and failure handling. We present evaluation results in Section 5 and discuss related work in Section 6. We conclude with a discussion of lessons learned and future work in Section 7.

2. Background & Preliminaries

As mentioned in the introduction, existing large-scale distributed computing engines are typically tailored to solve problems that require relational operators. On the other hand, matrix operations used in many modern data mining or inferencing algorithms are typically hard to capture using such operators.

---

[1] ScaLAPACK can be made fault-tolerant by invoking global checkpointing only at the cost of a large performance hit; MadLINQ outperforms ScaLA-PACK while at the same time being fault-tolerant.

In fact, systems research work that deals with scalable and fault-tolerant matrix computation has often downplayed the complexity and challenge of this problem. To give just one example, an algorithm such as PageRank, which is often used for evaluating such systems, is already quite hard to implement efficiently on MapReduce. But, real-world matrix algorithms are often even much more complicated in their structure, often containing multiple iterations chained together, each of which possibly being multi-level nested; and engaging multiple operators (e.g., addition, multiplication, factorization, etc.). As a result, while PageRank may be harder to efficiently implement in MapReduce than Word-Count or other typical MapReduce jobs, implementing complex data mining algorithms in the MapReduce framework becomes exceedingly hard.

Cholesky Factorization: To illustrate these points, consider a matrix operations such as *Cholesky factorization* [21]. Cholesky factorization is a highly efficient way of solving linear equations, and it is one of the most useful and well-studied linear algebra kernels, with a wide range of important applications, including the solving of partial differential equations, Monte Carlo simulation, non-linear optimization and Kalman filters. As an additional example, the Cholesky factorization is also used in one of the real-world applications that had originally inspired this work, and which we use in the evaluation: the computation of topic models of Web documents (RLSI, see Section 3). Technically, if A is a symmetric and positive definite matrix, then the equation $A \times x = b$ can be solved by first computing the Cholesky factorization $A = L \times L^T$, then solving $L \times y = b$ for y, and finally solving $L^T \times x = y$ for x. As we show in Section 3, the Cholesky factorization kernel highlights some of the key characteristics and typical behaviors of the type of operations used by many experimental matrix algorithms. It has become a de facto benchmark in the HPC community (e.g., [9]), and we will also use it to illustrate the key features of our system design.

Tile Algorithms: As with most matrix algorithms, advanced implementations of Cholesky use the concept of *tiles*. A tile is a square sub-matrix, and the entire matrix is divided into a grid of tiles and indexed appropriately. When extending to cover sparse matrices, tiles of rectangular shape may be used for load-balancing purposes. The concept of tiling (or blocking) has a long history, adopted widely in multi-core-ready math libraries such as Intel's MKL[1]. The idea is to leverage the structured access pattern of matrix computation to maximize cache locality. MadLINQ makes use of this structural characteristic of matrix algorithms and explicitly supports tile algorithms in an efficient way.

Fig. 2 (a), (b), and (c) show the tile algorithms of Page-Rank (for one iteration), matrix multiplication and Cholesky, respectively. Our aim in showing these algorithms in tile form is to give the reader a feel for the relative structural complexity of the kind of matrix operations commonly

```
for (int i = 0; i < n; i++)     // R: n-tile long column vector of ranks
  R[i] = 0;                       // P: n x n-tile (adjacent) matrix of page links
  for (int j = 0; j < n; j++)
    R[i] += (P[i, j] * R[j]);
           (a) PageRank as matrix-vector multiplication

for (int i = 0; i < m; i++)
  for (int j = 0; j < k; j++)  // A: m x n-tile, B: n x k-tile matrix
    C[i, j] = 0;               // C: m x k-tile result matrix
    for (int l = 0; l < n; l++)
      C[i, j] += (A[i, l] * B[l, j]);
           (b) Matrix-matrix multiplication

for (int k = 0; k < n; k++)
  A[k, k] = DPOTRF(A[k, k]);              // A: n x n-tile symmetric positive
  for (int l = k + 1; l < n; l++)        //     definite (input) matrix
    A[l, k] = DTRSM(A[k, k], A[l, k]);
  for (int m = k+1; m < n; m++)
    A[m, m] = DSYRK(A[m, k], A[m, m]);
    for (int l = m+1; l < n; l++)
      A[l, m] = DGEMM(A[l, k], A[m, k], A[l, m])
           (c) Cholesky factorization
```

Figure 2. Tile algorithm for PageRank (one iteration), multiplication and Cholesky factorization. DPOTRF, DTRSM, DSYRK and DGEMM are standard tile operators, respectively.

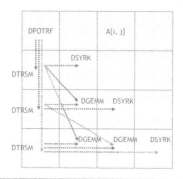

Figure 3. One iteration of tiled Cholesky factorization.

found in modern machine learning algorithms. The pseudo-code illustrates that a matrix operation like Cholesky has significantly higher structural complexity compared to Page-Rank. The operations DPOTRF, DTRSM, DSYRK and DGEMM used by Cholesky are standard math operations, and are implemented in all of the well-known matrix libraries (e.g., BLAS [25], LAPACK [7]).

Specifically, a run of Cholesky factorization on a matrix divided into a grid of n^2 tiles involves the following steps. In the k-th iteration, the algorithm first performs Cholesky factorization on the k-th diagonal tile (routine DPOTRF), and then the $n - k$ column tiles below (DTRSM), with a parallelism of $O(1)$ and $O(n)$, respectively (see Fig. 3). This is then followed by the updating of the trailing tiles to the right (DSYRK and DGEMM), with a parallelism of $O(n^2)$. This discussion highlights another common feature of complex matrix operations: the non-trivial interplay of phases of high parallelism and low parallelism. Thus, in Cholesky, the diagonal and panel tile updates have low parallelism, and the same is true in later iterations. MadLINQ is efficient in utilizing the available opportunities for parallelization by using pipelining.

3. Programming Model

MadLINQ embeds a set of domain-specific language constructs into a general-purpose programming language (C#), similar to the approach taken by DryadLINQ and Flume-Java [15] for data-parallel programming. This embedding allows us to expose a unified programming model for developing both matrix algorithms and applications. In particular, it allows us to integrate MadLINQ with DryadLINQ, making it easily accessible to a general purpose data-intensive computing system. In this section, we provide a high-level view of the programming model, using real-world applications as examples to highlight its key aspects. We will evaluate the performance of MadLINQ using these examples in Section 5, and contrast our experience programming using the popular MapReduce paradigm.

3.1 Programming Language

The new domain-specific language constructs are designed to express matrix algorithms efficiently with familiar notations. The key data abstraction is `Matrix`, which, simply defined as a C# class, encapsulates the tile representation of a matrix. Matrix computations are then expressed as a sequence of operations on tiles. For example, the following is the MadLINQ code for the tile-based matrix multiplication algorithm:

```
MadLINQ.For(0, m, 1, i =>
{
  MadLINQ.For(0, p, 1, j =>
  {
    c[i, j] = 0;
    MadLINQ.For(0, n, 1, k =>
      c[i, j] += a[i, k] * b[k, j]);
  });
});
```

The language allows even complex algorithms to be expressed naturally. For example, the MadLINQ implementation of Cholesky is almost a line-by-line translation of its tile algorithm [9] given in Fig. 3 and discussed in Section 2. Note that `DPOTRF` is a LAPACK's name for Cholesky, and it is applied to the diagonal tile in the beginning of each outer iteration.

```
MadLINQ.For(0, n, 1, k =>
{
  L[k, k] = A[k, k].DPOTRF();
  MadLINQ.For(k + 1, n, 1, l =>
    L[l, k] = Tile.DTRSM(L[k, k], A[l, k]));
  MadLINQ.For(k + 1, n, 1, m =>
  {
    A[m, m] = Tile.DSYRK(A[m, k], A[m, m]);
    MadLINQ.For(m + 1, n, 1, l =>
      A[l, m] = Tile.DGEMM(A[l, k], A[m, k], A[l, m]));
  });
});
```

The example shows that programming a tile algorithm in MadLINQ is straightforward, literally a direct translation of the algorithm into a sequential program. That is, the code looks simple even though (as discussed in the previous section) the computational structure of Cholesky is complex. We have also implemented singular value decomposition (SVD), which involves three nested iterations, with the innermost body itself containing two back-to-back loops. It would be challenging to program such algorithms in a MapReduce-style programming environment.

3.2 Programming Applications in MadLINQ

We have developed a library including the core set of linear algebra routines; the library is a set of C# methods and can be easily extended. To check the usefulness of the MadLINQ programming model, we implemented several real-world applications, three of which we will describe in detail here as they form the basis of our evaluation.

Collaborative Filtering (CF): We implement the baseline algorithm of collaborative filtering [11] and evaluate it using the data set from the Netflix challenge [8] in Section 5. In that data set, the matrix R records users' rating on movies, with $R[i, j]$ being user j's rating on movie i. So $R \times R^T$ gives us the similarity between the movies, and multiplying the result with R again yields the predicted ratings of all movies for each user. Matrix R is sparse while matrix *score* is dense. A final normalization step normalizes the scores.

```
Matrix similarity = R.Multiply(R.Transpose());
Matrix scores = similarity.Multiply(R).Normalize();
```

To illustrate the difference in programming style and effort between implementing CF in MadLINQ and MapReduce, we provide a discussion in Section 3.4.

Markov Clustering: MadLINQ supports both dense and sparse matrices. Since a graph can be represented as an adjacency matrix, we can naturally implement many graph algorithms, including Breadth-First Search, PageRank and Approximate Betweeness Centrality [10, 20] and Markov Clustering (MCL) [34] which we discuss below.

```
MadLINQ.For(0, DEPTH, 1, i =>
{
  // Expansion
  G = G.Multiply(G);

  // Inflate: element-wise x^2 and row-based normalization
  G = G.EWiseMult(G).Normalize().Prune();
});
```

Unlike clustering such as K-means that requires the number of clusters as a parameter, the clusters are derived from the underlying graph structure. The algorithm operates over a single adjacency matrix A, with non-zeros in the i-th column identifying the set of nodes connected to node i. There are two phases in each iteration. The expansion phase performs an in-place update to A with $A \times A$. The net effect is that the updated $A[i, j]$ has greater value if j can reach i through more paths. This is then followed by an inflation phase, which raises the power of each column, normalizes it, and finally prunes the smaller entries. Therefore, strongly connected nodes gradually cluster together.

Notice that in addition to multiplication, our MCL implementation demonstrates the use of two APIs from the Combinatorial BLAS [12] library, whose basic data structures are sparse matrices: element-wise multiplication to raise the power (`EWiseMult`) and pruning (`Prune`) to cut low-strength edges.

Algorithm 1 Regularized Latent Semantic Indexing

Require: $\mathbf{D} \in \mathbb{R}^{M \times N}$
1: $\mathbf{V}^{(0)} \in \mathbb{R}^{K \times N} \leftarrow$ random matrix
2: **for** $t = 1 : T$ **do**
3:     $\mathbf{U}^{(t)} \leftarrow \text{UpdateU}(\mathbf{D}, \mathbf{V}^{(t-1)})$
4:     $\mathbf{V}^{(t)} \leftarrow \text{UpdateV}(\mathbf{D}, \mathbf{U}^{(t)})$
5: **end for**
6: **return** $\mathbf{U}^{(T)}, \mathbf{V}^{(T)}$

Algorithm 3 UpdateV

Require: $\mathbf{D} \in \mathbb{R}^{M \times N}, \mathbf{U} \in \mathbb{R}^{M \times K}$
1: $\mathbf{\Sigma} \leftarrow \left(\mathbf{U}^T \mathbf{U} + \lambda_2 \mathbf{I}\right)^{-1}$
2: $\mathbf{\Phi} \leftarrow \mathbf{U}^T \mathbf{D}$
3: **for** $n = 1 : N$ **do**
4:     $v_n \leftarrow \mathbf{\Sigma}\phi_n$, where ϕ_n is the nth column of $\mathbf{\Phi}$
5: **end for**
6: **return** $\mathbf{V}$

Figure 4. Kernel routines of Regularized Latent Semantic Index algorithm.

Regularized Latent Semantic Index (RLSI): Our last example is RLSI [35], a new Web-mining algorithm. The goal of the algorithm is to derive an approximate topic model for Web documents. Unlike the more expensive SVD-based topic model and assuming that the topics are sparse, RLSI relies on a series of cheaper operations to factorize the matrix. The algorithm operates over a giant sparse matrix (D) and a (skinnier but also giant) dense matrix (V). D is a doc-to-term matrix, whereas V records the mapping of doc-to-topic. The structure of the algorithm is similar to non-negative matrix factorization (NMF) [26], kernel routines of which are outlined in Fig. 4. Note that the algorithm calls Cholesky factorization as a subroutine when updating V. Interestingly, while the MadLINQ code is about 10 LoC, an implementation in SCOPE [13] requires 1100+ LoC, which is to a large extent due to SCOPE's adoption of MapReduce to describe the algorithm (see Section 3.4). Working together with the original designers of the RLSI algorithm, it took us a single man-day to write the code. As we will report in Section 5, MadLINQ is also significantly faster than the MapReduce-based implementation.

```
MadLINQ.For(0, T, 1, i =>
{
  // Update U
  Matrix S = V.Multiply(V.Transpose());
  Matrix R = D.Multiply(V.Transpose());

  // Assume tile size >= K
  MadLINQ.For(0, U.M, 1, m =>
   U[m, 0] = Tile.UpdateU(S[0, 0], R[m, 0]));

  // Update V
  Matrix Phi = U.Transpose().Multiply(D);
  V = U.Transpose()
   .Multiply(U)
   .Add(TiledMatrix<double>.EYE(U.N, lambda2))
   .CholeskySolve(Phi);
});
```

Finally, notice that `Tile.UpdateU` is a user-defined operation on tiles which can be implemented using the extension interface MadLINQ provides.

3.3 Integration with DryadLINQ

We have shown in the previous section how to implement matrix computations in MadLINQ. One strength of our approach is that by embedding the language (and hence the matrix library) in C#, it is natural and easy to inter-operate with other data processing systems such as DryadLINQ. This seamless integration of MadLINQ + DryadLINQ + C# provides a unified and elegant solution to many real-world problems in which certain parts of the computation are naturally handled using relational algebra operators; whereas other parts of the computation require matrix operations. To illustrate these two disparate styles of data analysis/manipulation, consider the following collaborative filtering example. In this example, the input is Netflix data, the output is a recommendation for a movie for each user.

```
// The input datasets
var ratings = PartitionedTable
  .Get<LineRecord>(NetflixRating);

// Step 1: Process the Netflix dataset in DryadLINQ
Matrix R = ratings
  .Select(x => CreateEntry(x))
  .GroupBy(x => x.col)
  .SelectMany((g, i) =>
   g.Select(x => new Entry(x.row, i, x.val)))
  .ToMadLINQ(MovieCnt, UserCnt, tileSize);

// Step 2: Compute the scores of movies for each user
Matrix similarity = R.Multiply(R.Transpose());
Matrix scores = similarity.Multiply(R).Normalize();

// Step 3: Create the result report
var result = scores
  .ToDryadLinq();
  .GroupBy(x => x.col)
  .Select(g => g.OrderBy().Take(5));
```

The above code shows the two systems DryadLINQ and MadLINQ inter-operate, each system doing the part of the computation for which it is suited. The initial data *ratings* is from Netflix and is represented as a text file. There are three steps. In Step 1, DryadLINQ is used to process the input data into the matrix representation accepted by MadLINQ. It boils down to creating matrix R to represent the movie-rating relations. In Step 2, MadLINQ is called to perform the collaborative filtering on matrix R, which is more suitable to do in MadLINQ. In Step 3, after the MadLINQ computation completes, DryadLINQ is used again to create a report that recommends the top 5 movies for each user.

This example highlights MadLINQ's philosophy of preserving a unified programming experience at the surface, while calling into different domain engines to leverage their strengths. Steps 1 and 3 are best handled by relational algebra engines such as DryadLINQ, whereas Step 2 is a linear algebra routine best handled by MadLINQ.

3.4 Alternative using MapReduce

In Section 3.2, we described the programming of matrix algorithms in MadLINQ. It is insightful to compare this to programming the same algorithms in MadReduce. In principle, collaborative filtering (i.e., computing $R \times R^T \times R$ of a matrix R) is sufficiently simple to be expressed in MapReduce. The Apache Mahout [4] project (a comprehensive machine learning package) includes a variant of the algorithm, and also provides an implementation of matrix multiplication. Briefly, a matrix in Mahout is an HDFS file that stores non-zero elements. The file is keyed by the row index, and is a collection of rows. Each row contains a list of tuples, and each tuple is a pair, the column index and the value of the corresponding non-zero entry. In order to apply the MapReduce APIs to perform a matrix multiplication $A \times B$, the mapper takes the i's column of A, multiples it with the i's row of B, and produces a partial matrix. The reducer then reduces on the entry (i, j), aggregates all the partial matrices, and outputs the final matrix. Since the matrix is stored as a set of rows, the first matrix A needs to be transposed first. This is accomplished by another job, whose mapper breaks the list of non-zeros and output tuples that are now keyed by column index, and the reducer aggregates on the column index to produce A^T. Thus, the MapReduce version of the operation $R \times R^T \times R$ used by our CF takes four MapReduce jobs. In our evaluations, we will show that while it performs reasonably well for the multiplication of two sparse matrices (as in $R \times R^T$), MapReduce/Mahout faces severe problems if one of the matrices becomes dense (e.g., the second multiplication). Essentially it requires a different algorithm whose execution plan is difficult to be expressed in MapReduce.

The situation is similar for the RLSI algorithm. Consider $D \times V^T$ (in UpdateU, line number 3 of Fig. 4). Both matrices are big, but D is sparse and V is dense. This turns out to be the most time-consuming step of the algorithm. MadLINQ implements this with a single line: D.Multiply(V.Transpose()). In an implementation using SCOPE, since V^T is too large to fit into memory, following the same procedure as in [26], the authors structured the computation in two MapReduce phases. The first one generates many sparse matrices by multiplying a column of D with a row of V^T, and the second one aggregates them up, which is essentially the same as in the collaborative filtering application and faces similar problems.

4. System Design and Implementation

We first give an overview of MadLINQ's architecture, and then focus on the key features of our design. In Section 4.2, we describe a fully automatic DAG generation scheme for tiled matrix algorithms that uses in-flight symbolic execution to avoid the problem of DAG-size explosion. Section 4.3 introduces our distributed DAG-based execution engine. The engine is non-blocking, and enables *automatic fine-grained pipelining* (FGP) of the computation, thus leveraging extra parallelism. Section 4.4 describes our novel fault-tolerance protocol, which reduces I/O, and handles failures in a highly-efficient way. Finally, we end the section with noteworthy optimizations.

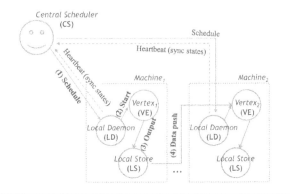

Figure 5. MadLINQ system architecture. The system consists of a Central Scheduler, and a Local Daemon, a Local Store and a Vertex Engine on each compute node.

4.1 System Architecture

As shown in Section 3, MadLINQ programs are written using ordinary C# programs with our embedded language and data types (e.g., Matrix, Tile). The translation of a program into a DAG is discussed in Section 4.2. At runtime, the execution flows into the MadLINQ system. Fig. 5 shows the flow of execution when a job is entered into the MadLINQ system.

The MadLINQ distributed runtime consists of a central scheduler (CS) running on a server node and three processes, a local daemon (LD), a local store (LS), and a vertex engine (VE), all running on the compute nodes in the cluster. The central scheduler receives a job submitted from a client and schedules it on the compute cluster (Step 1). It also monitors the current utilization levels and availabilities of all the compute nodes. On a compute node, the local daemon is responsible for starting the vertex engine (Step 2). It is also responsible for periodically sending progress reports of the vertex execution to CS.

The vertex engine executes the vertex code corresponding to the program DAG. Each compute node is preloaded with the MadLINQ runtime which includes the full set of math libraries by which the actual computation is carried out. We carefully designed the interface such that we can call any of the state-of-art math libraries (e.g., MKL). This is an important design decision because a high-quality, domain-specific math library is orthogonal to MadLINQ's system architecture, but important for its performance.

Finally, the local store manages the output of the vertex (Step 3), and is responsible for pushing the data to a downstream vertex, possibly in a pipelined fashion (Step 4).

CS assigns a static priority to each vertex based on a critical path analysis of the program. It maintains a priority queue of all ready vertices and schedules the vertices based on their priorities. In systems such as Dryad and MapReduce, a vertex is considered to be ready when its parents have produced all the data. We call such execution *staged*. The default execution in MadLINQ is *pipelined*, a vertex is ready

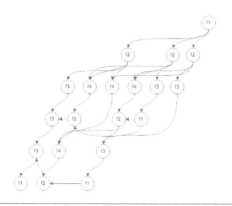

Figure 6. DAG of Cholesky factorization algorithm for a 4×4 tiled matrix (where $f1$ through $f4$ are the tile operators: DPOTRF, DTRSM, DSYRK and DGEMM).

when each input channel has partial results, and it can start executing while consuming additional inputs (Section 4.3).

When scheduling a ready vertex, CS takes into account data locality, assigning the vertex to the machine(s) where its inputs are produced when possible. De(re)-scheduling of a vertex may happen when it is done, crashed during execution, or timed out while waiting for input (e.g., a parent crashed) The local daemon reports back to CS periodically the progress of the running vertices so that CS can make informed scheduling decisions. When a vertex fails, CS runs the fault-tolerance protocol (Section 4.4), fixes its state, and schedules it again.

4.2 DAG Generation and Vertex Initialization

The scheduler keeps in memory the list of running vertices and their immediate children, a subset of these children are also kept in the ready queue. Collectively, they comprise the frontier that the execution is exploring. This frontier is dynamic: as a ready vertex becomes running, its children need to be included in the list. Doing so requires consulting the DAG.

Keeping the DAG in memory can be cumbersome and unscalable. This is especially true when the matrix is big and number of iterations (often nested) is high. If the matrix is divided into $n \times n$ tiles, then the DAG size of multiplication and Choleksy is $O(n^3)$, and for Jacobi-based SVD the DAG size is $O(n^4)$. Therefore, in anticipation of large problem size, we need to deal with the issue of *DAG explosion*.

We *dynamically expand* the DAG through symbolic execution. Given the loop boundaries, we can symbolically execute the program. Each statement in the loop body is decomposed into an expression tree, where the inputs are tiles that are labeled according to iteration number. During the exploration, each operator is uniquely identified by the order it is visited and becomes a vertex. Finally, vertices are connected by data dependencies identified by the label of the tiles. Fig. 6 visualizes the DAG of Cholesky for a matrix divided into 4×4 tiles.

This DAG exploration also performs several additional tasks. First, it discovers and assigns vertex priorities according to their positions in the DAG topology. Second, it identifies the type of computation a vertex is to perform, allowing the vertex engine to call appropriate routine (e.g., addition). Finally, it computes the set of blocks (needed for pipelining, explained shortly) symbolically. Those metadata are needed for scheduling and failure handling.

In the implementation, this is done by abstracting the necessary APIs when we need to consult the DAG. For instance, when adding new vertices to the frontier, GetChild(v) will return the list of child vertices of a given vertex v, which are then initialized and put into the list. A few other APIs return parent vertices, which are needed in handling failures. These APIs are implemented by executing the program symbolically described above. This approach completely removes the need to keep a materialized DAG, with negligible overhead.

4.3 Fine-Grained Pipelining

In many matrix computations, available parallelism of an algorithm fluctuates. In Cholesky factorization, for example, the bulk of parallelism comes from multiplications in the trailing tiles, which reduces quickly in later iterations (see Section 2). When vertex-level parallelism is low and if there are spare resources, pipelining can effectively explore inter-vertex parallelism. Another benefit is that network utilization becomes less bursty. FGP opportunistically exploits such inter-vertex pipelining to improve performance. [2]

Pipelining requires each vertex to consume and produce data at a finer granularity, which we call a *block*. As a trivial example, suppose we are adding two matrices A and B, each is divided into a 4×4 grid, for a total of 16 tiles. Each tile is recursively divided into 16 blocks, then each of the 16 addition vertices can stream in blocks of its corresponding A and B tile, and similarly output C blocks, all in a pipelined fashion.

In the above example, pipelining means applying the tile algorithm at the block level. More specifically, it requires that 1) the vertex computation be expressed as a tile algorithm and 2) the vertex execution engine can perform the computation incrementally, i.e., computing and outputting partial results. For some matrix algorithms, the vertices are themselves tile algorithms. This is true for simple computation such as multiplication, and for some more sophisticated algorithm such as Cholesky as well. If the vertex is not a tile algorithm, its execution falls back to staged execution, exposing the entire tile only upon termination. Additionally, we provide annotation to allow developers to convert to tile algorithm manually; automatically transforming

---

[2] Note that another possible technique to address the parallelization problem is to reduce the tile size, as this allows to decrease the amount of time the computation spends in low parallelism phases. However, this approach has its natural limits, as doing so substantially increases the number of tiles and hence the system overhead since the DAG size is $O(n^3)$.

an algorithm into tile algorithm is an active research area in the HPC community.

When an input arrives, the vertex engine checks if any computation can be done, and if so it calls a math library (e.g., Intel MKL) to carry out the execution. We keep the intermediate results as context for reuse and remove this context immediately after all dependent output blocks have been generated. Conceptually, the local vertex execution is dataflow-driven, and follows the the same symbolic execution framework as in the CS (see Section 4.2).

4.4 Handling Failure

Pipelined DAG execution is not a new idea. However, providing fault-tolerance in pipelined DAG is non-trivial, even when each vertex's computation is deterministic (which is the case for MadLINQ). To see why, consider a long chain of vertices. If any one of these vertices fails, its re-execution will re-compute blocks that its immediate downstream vertex has already consumed. This has the cascading effect of triggering unnecessary computation in all the descendants. For this reason, without careful bookkeeping the overhead can be non-trivial and unbounded.

For this reason, existing solutions such as TCP streaming in Dryad [23] or streaming support in CIEL [29] choose a different strategy. If any vertex fails, the sub-DAG of which the failed vertex is a root is failed together. This is not an appropriate solution for MadLINQ, because the entire program is pipeline-enabled, and the running vertices may indeed be forming a connected sub-DAG. Thus, adopting these existing strategies would mean that we potentially fail all running vertices. The novel contribution of FGP is that we only do a minimal recomputation, by using lightweight dependency tracking. Furthermore, the protocol can withstand an arbitrary number of fail-stop failures. As we will demonstrate later, such capacity can be used to dynamically size resources, which is an important scenario in the Cloud.

The core idea behind FGP's failure handling is simple. Recall that the input to a vertex is always a set of matrix blocks, from which the vertex computes another set of blocks as its output. Our fault-tolerance mechanism depends on the crucial assumption that for any given set of output blocks S we can automatically derive the set of input blocks that are needed to compute S. Such a backward slicing [31] technique is possible in our system because (rather than using the compiler to determine the data slice), we derive the dependency at the time when we perform symbolic DAG generation. As an example, for a 4×4 matrix multiplication, we derive that $C[0,0]$ depends on $A[0,0:3]$ (A's first row) and $B[0:3,0]$ (B's first column) at the time when we symbolically execute the multiplication of C.

This dependency calculation enables us to minimize the recovery cost of a failed vertex by re-computing only the needed blocks. At a high level, the recovery procedure is therefore as follows. A recovering vertex queries its downstream vertices for blocks they still need in order for them to

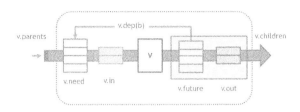

Figure 7. States to describe a vertex for pipelined execution and failure handling.

complete. The union of all blocks needed by its downstream vertices is what the new recovering vertex needs to compute, and from which we apply our dependency analysis to derive the set of input blocks that the recovering vertex needs. The recovering vertex then asks for those input blocks from its upstream vertices. This process can be recursive, in the sense that if the upstream vertex has also crashed or cannot send the missing blocks to this vertex, it too will invoke the same process to request needed blocks from upstream vertices.

We now proceed to give a rigorous description of the FGP protocol. The system-wide invariant is that, as long as 1) there is at least one computing node available and 2) the original input data is available, the execution will terminate correctly.

The states required by the protocol are shown in Fig. 7. $v.in$ specifies the blocks that are available in v's input buffer, $v.need$ specifies the set of blocks that v still needs to complete its computation, $v.future$ identifies the blocks that still need to be computed, and $v.dep()$ is a function that computes the set of input blocks needed for a given set of output blocks. $v.dep()$ is the *inverse* of v's program, and can typically be derived for matrix computation automatically.

Ensuring correct termination can be decomposed into keeping two invariants. The first invariant binds the relationship of buffers inside a vertex. Simply put, what a vertex needs is anything that it needs to produce new blocks, minus what it already has in its input buffer.

(1) $v.need = v.dep(v.future) - v.in$

The second invariant complements the first, and binds the relationship of outwards-facing buffers across dependant vertices. Most importantly, it specifies what $v.future$ really is. In this invariant, $v.out$ is the set of blocks v has computed and made available to the rest of the system. $v.ALL$ is all the blocks that the vertex is to compute in its lifetime (e.g., $C[0:3,0:3]$).

(2) $v.future = v.children.need \cap v.ALL - v.out$

The invariant says that what a vertex needs to produce, is the union of everything to satisfy its children intersected with what this vertex is responsible for (as a child vertex may depend on other vertices), but minus what it has already made available to the children.

During the normal execution of a vertex, the system functions as described in Section 4.3. When a vertex v is initialized in CS using symbolic DAG generation, its $v.ALL$ is computed. Next, $v.need$ is set to $v.dep(v.ALL)$, meaning that it needs all the blocks. The system can schedule any vertex that has data to consume (i.e., $v.need \cap v.parents.out \neq \emptyset$). The vertex then arrives at a computing node, along with $v.need$ and $v.ALL$; $v.in$ and $v.out$ are set to $\emptyset$.

When the vertex is instantiated, it will start exchanging $v.need$ to its parent(s). As blocks arrive, $v.in$ is updated and computation starts. $v.out$ is updated when new outputs are produced. Other fields such as $v.need$ and $v.future$ are updated accordingly.

Active vertices also report $v.out$ back to CS periodically. This allows CS to discover newly enabled vertices, and instruct them where to find their inputs when deployed. More importantly, when failure occurs, CS knows precisely the set of blocks that are now lost. The system restores the required invariants by letting the recovering vertex to query its children for their $need$ set, which is sufficient to compute its own $need$ set using the $v.dep()$ function. Note that the $need$ set is used to request data in normal conditions, and all that is special in failure handling is to set the recovering vertex's various fields appropriately. The process is inherently recursive and converging, and can deal with arbitrary number of failures in arbitrary positions of the DAG.

The same principle is upheld to handle even more complicated cases. For instance, retired vertices (i.e., those who have computed all outputs) are said to be *hibernating* at CS, and in that sense they never truly retire. Also, if any of the child vertices of a retired vertex is requesting blocks that are missing from the system due to failure, the vertex is reactivated since their *future* set is no longer empty.

We also developed a formal specification in TLA+ [24] that significantly increased our confidence of its correctness. The specification is about 200 LoC, and verified with a small DAG using TLC [5].

Our design of FGP is quite general and we believe it is applicable in other contexts as well. For FGP to work, two key conditions must be satisfied. First, as described above we assume that it is possible to infer the set of input blocks that a given output block depends on. When this is impossible, the protocol falls back by assuming any output depends on any input, and thus this particular vertex will be executed in the staged model. Second, we assume that vertex computation is deterministic. Supporting non-determinism can be added by recording the random perturbation as part of the input. We have found that some algorithms require this, e.g., picking a random edge in a graph. These conditions are general and not restrictive to matrix computation, as long as each vertex in the dataflow program can satisfy these two assumptions, it is safe to employ FGP.

4.5 Optimizations

Based on our experience of using the system, we added a number of performance optimizations, and some of the more noticeable ones are described below:

- Pre-loading a ready vertex onto an occupied computing node whose current vertex is about to finish. This prefetches data and helps smoothing network traffic.

- Adding order preference (e.g., row-major, column major or any) when requesting input for a vertex. This is because the pipelined execution is sensitive to the arrival order of input data blocks.

- Auto-switching of block representation depending on sparsity. For sparse matrices, we represent blocks using a compressed-column representation. However, during some intermediate computation blocks may become dense. Therefore, when the number of non-zeros inside a block is larger than a threshold, we switch to dense block representation and invoke the dense math library instead.

5. Evaluation

We present detailed performance results for the applications described in Section 3. We have also implemented a number of additional applications including QR factorization, dense SVD, K-means, PageRank and Betweeness Centrality, but due to space constraints, we can only present results from some representative examples. When possible, we include comparisons against competing alternatives.

We performed the experiments on different computer clusters, all running Windows Server 2008 R2. We use MKL 10.3 which is multi-core-ready to carry out basic matrix operations. Our hardware platform and configurations are typical for Cloud-level offerings: two 1.0TB SATA disks, and 16GB memory, interconnected with 1Gbit Ethernet switches. The CPUs differ slightly, a typical one is dual Intel Xeon CPU L5420 at 2.5GHz, with a total of 8 cores.

5.1 Run Configuration

The run configuration is similar to DryadLINQ. As part of job submission, clients include a configuration file that specifies all the necessary parameters of the matrices, including the location of their tiles, tile and block size. As we also handle sparse matrices (for graph algorithms, for example), block format specification is also included. Choosing the right parameters is a tradeoff between multiple factors:

- Smaller tiles allow higher tile-level parallelism, but increase scheduling overhead. There is also a memory constraint, since even though the vertex engine can perform incremental computation at block granularity, the total working set is typically proportional to the tile size.

- The granularity of computation is a block. Multi-core-ready math libraries such as MKL typically yield better performance for bigger blocks. On the other hand, a smaller block size enables better pipelining. We determine the size of blocks with profiling (for dense matrices).

- For sparse matrices, the block size is determined by the number of non-zeros; we tune it such that this total number is the same as in an appropriate dense block.

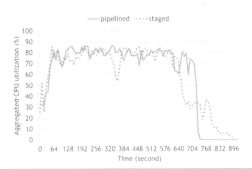

Figure 8. Comparison of aggregated CPU utilization of pipelined and staged executions of Cholesky. 96K × 96K dense matrix, 128 cores (16 nodes).

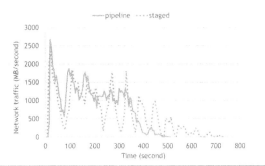

Figure 9. Network traffic comparison for pipelined and staged. Pipelined is more smooth and spread.

5.2 The Effect of Pipelining and Fault Tolerance

We use Cholesky factorization to study the effectiveness of our fine-grained pipelining and fault-tolerance protocol. As described in Section 2, the general pattern is that parallelism fluctuates within an iteration, and the total amount of parallelism decreases with successive outer-loop iterations.

Fig. 8 shows the parallelism curves of two runs, one for the pipelined and another for the staged execution model. The runs are executed on 16 nodes (128 cores) for a problem size of a 96K × 96K dense matrix (roughly 5 billion elements, 36GB), with 8K and 2K as the tile and block size, respectively (364 tile operators, about 167GB intermediate result). The curves show the aggregated CPU utilizations across the entire cluster. Since there is enough parallelism in earlier iterations, both models are equally effective at the beginning, though pipelined is slightly better. As the computation progresses towards later stages, the pipelined model exploits more inter-vertex parallelism and continues to maintain high utilization. In all, the pipelined mode is about 15.9% faster than the staged model.

Pipelining performs better for larger problem sizes and on a larger cluster, as in this case the pipelining can be deeper and there are more spare resources to recruit when vertex-level parallelism is low. For the same problem size on a 256-core cluster, pipelined is 28% faster than staged. One advantage of pipelining is that network traffic is more evenly spread, as blocks start transmitting during the course of a

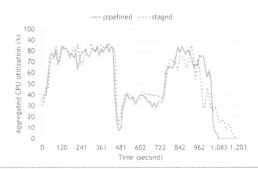

Figure 10. Experiment showing fault-tolerance. We disrupt a run for 5 minutes in the middle of its execution, removing half of the machines and then restoring them. Performance drops, but then recovers accordingly.

vertex's lifetime. Fig. 9 shows the aggregated network traffic volumes of the two runs, it is clear that pipelined behaves in a less bursty pattern.

We tested the fault-tolerance mechanism by killing running processes and deleting generated outputs. Fig. 10 shows the extreme case of simultaneously removing half of the machines altogether, and then adding them back after a window of 5 minutes. This emulates the rapid resource fluctuation that may happen in a Cloud environment. As expected, MadLINQ's performance (as indicated by its overall CPU utilization) degrades after resource removal, and then is quickly restored when those resources return.

We performed numerous experiments against ScaLA-PACK [17], the best known and widely adopted MPI-based solution. ScaLAPACK is a released product running over Windows HPC Server 2008 R2. Each process owns a partition of the matrix, and communicates with each other using MPI. Barriers are used for global synchronization. It calls exactly the same MKL libraries for local computation within a node, as we do in MadLINQ.

The result is shown in Fig. 11, using a dense matrix of 128K × 128K (64GB, intermediate result approximately 375GB). As expected, the performance difference between pipelined and staged widens as the number of machines increases. With 256-cores, pipelined is 16.6% faster than staged; with 512-cores, the gap widens to 31.6%.

The interesting result is that pipelined consistently outperforms ScaLAPACK by an average of 14.4%. The relative performance of MadLINQ's two models against ScaLA-PACK is shown in Fig. 11(b). The gap between pipelined and ScaLAPACK steadily widens as more cores are added, as more resources can be used to fill the valleys. However, with 512-cores, most of the available parallelism is already exploited, and MadLINQ's scheduling overhead somewhat degrades its performance, but still achieves a 10% gain.

Also, despite repeated attempts, ScaLAPACK consistently failed at 32-core because the problem size exceeds the aggregated memory in the cluster. MadLINQ can perform out-of-core computation, and thus removes this constraint and scales easily with different problem sizes; its 32-core

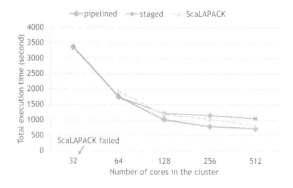

(a) Absolute running time

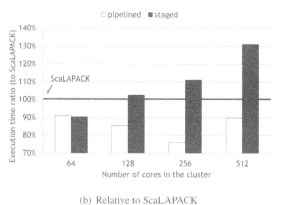

(b) Relative to ScaLAPACK

Figure 11. Comparison of the time and scalability of pipelined and staged executions with ScaLAPACK (Cholesky of a 128K × 128K dense matrix).

performance is roughly two times slower than that of its 64-core run.

The ScaLAPACK experiment is run without adding any checkpointing facility, as turning it on would significantly hurt its performance, thereby drastically improving MadLINQ's advantage. Consequently, these experiments occasionally failed due to jitters in MPI communication. The fact that MadLINQ, currently still a research prototype, supports fault-tolerance by default and yet competes favorably against an industrial-strength product is very encouraging.

5.3 Real World Applications

RLSI: We compare against a SCOPE-based implementation of RLSI, which consists of 1100 LoC and is run on a production cluster of 16 nodes with a sample of real Web data. The most time and space consuming step is to compute $R = D \times V^T$, where D is a matrix of 7M × 2M with 0.005% sparsity (10.5GB), and V^T is 2M × 500 and dense (7.5GB). This step takes around 6000s.

SCOPE requires two MapReduce jobs to compute the step $D \times V^T$ (see Section 3). In comparison, MadLINQ implements this with a single line of code as follows: `D.Multiply(V.Transpose())`. Good performance requires tuning of parameters, and we give some details here. Simple partitioning yields satisfactory results, but the best

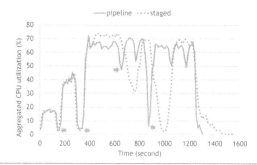

Figure 12. Aggregated CPU utilizations for MCL runs on 64 machines. The valleys correspond to the reduction phase (marked with arrows).

performance is achieved when we partition D into 20 vertical tiles, and V^T into 4 vertical partitions, each of which is then horizontally partitioned into 20 stripes. Such decomposition steps are standard when partitioning for large matrix multiplications. We measured the performance on a 16-node cluster, the result was 1838s, a speedup of more than a factor of 3. Running on a 32-node cluster reduces the time to 1188s. The corresponding numbers for staged is 2053s and 1260s, for 16-node and 32-node runs respectively. This real-world example demonstrates MadLINQ's superior programmability and performance against a MapReduce alternative.

MCL: We use R-MAT [14] to generate a synthetic graph, which models the behavior of several real-world graphs such as the Web graph, small world graphs, and citation graphs. We use the default parameter to generate a graph with half a billion nodes. The node degree ranges between 5 and 50. Thus, after the expansion phase, we choose a pruning threshold such that the average node degree is 50 (about 376GB). The tile size is 32K and the block size is 8K.

With 96 machines, pipelined and staged performs four iterations of MCL for about 1000s and 1172s, respectively. With 64 machines, the number becomes 1300s and 1560s, respectively. The less than perfect scaling is due to the fact that, in each iteration, there is a reduction stage to normalize each column before pruning happens. Fig. 12 shows the two runs' aggregated CPU curves in the case of 64 machines.

We note a few patterns in our results. First, computation progresses in phases. The valleys are the reduction stages, where the degree of parallelism is the lowest. This creates stragglers and resource vacancy, which the pipelined execution effectively exploits. As a result, the valleys of the pipelined run are "thinner". Second, overall utilization rises over time, because the matrix becomes denser over time. This is typical for many iterative graph algorithms, illustrating that a good matrix computation platform must handle both sparse and dense matrices well.

Collaborative Filtering: We evaluate this application with the data set from the Netflix challenge [8]. A 20K × 500K matrix R records user's rating on movies, with $R[i, j]$ being user j's rating on movie i. This matrix has a sparsity of 1.19% (about 2GB). Recall that this is an algorithm where

MadLINQ and DryadLINQ integrate to come up with the final top-5 recommendations to each user (Section 3.3).

The MadLINQ portion first produces a dense $20K \times 20K$ movie *similarity matrix* $R \times R^T$. The resulting matrix multiplied again with R yields the predicted rating of a user over all movies. The step takes 840s on 48 machines. After that, DryadLINQ takes 334s to rank and produce the recommendations using the same cluster.

We compared the performance of $R \times R^T \times R$ using the multiplication provided by Mahout over Hadoop (version 0.020.203.0), running over Windows. The first multiplication ($R \times R^T$) takes approximately 630s, almost twice as much as MadLINQ (347s). The resulting matrix, call it M, is dense. The second multiplication ($M \times R$) therefore has problems to even complete on Hadoop, despite multiple attempts using different configurations. The reason is that the partial matrices (Sec. 3) are dense, and the total working set is so large ($\sim$ 20TB) that I/O thrashing occurs.

To cope with this problem, we divide R into 10 equally-sized matrices of dimension $20K \times 50K$, and multiply M with each of these sub-matrices. Each of these multiplications takes approximately 78 minutes. Thus, $M \times R$ takes a total of 780 minutes. In contrast, MadLINQ's second multiplication is only 9.5 minutes. In performing this step, MadLINQ's optimization of switching between dense and sparse representation transparently is beneficial. Without this optimization, the running time becomes 16 minutes. These numbers are using staged execution.

To make the CF algorithm practical, the implementation in Mahout over Hadoop performs aggressive pruning of M so as to re-sparsify it. This may have an impact on the end result. Whether such an efficiency-vs-accuracy tradeoff is reasonable is not the focus of our study, but it allows the algorithm to terminate in Mahout. We find that matrix multiplication in Mahout is reasonable for sparse matrices, however, as soon as dense matrices are involved, the algorithm needs to be changed altogether. The MapReduce APIs has made it difficult to construct a more efficient execution plan, which would be necessary for this algorithm to be implemented efficiently. In contrast, MadLINQ is both flexible in forming the plan and robust with regard to the density of the matrix.

6. Related Work

Existing domain-specific engines for handling big data have a focus on relational algebra (e.g., MapReduce [19], Hive [3], DryadLINQ [36], Pig Latin [30]), with more recent developments in graph analysis (e.g., Pregel [27], GraphLab [28]). MadLINQ complements these efforts with its focus on linear algebra. Since matrices naturally represent graphs, MadLINQ can also tackle a substantial subset of graph algorithms. Inspired by works such as Combinatorial BLAS [12], we have successfully ported graph algorithms such as BFS, MCL, Betweeness Centrality [12], PageRank, random bipartite graph matching and semi-clustering to MadLINQ. Furthermore, recognizing that a holistic sys-

tem must incorporate multiple domain-specific engines, we demonstrated how to seamlessly integrate MadLINQ with DryadLINQ under the uniform language framework of LINQ.

MadLINQ provides a set of domain-specific constructs and translates a tiled matrix algorithm into the DAG automatically, using in-flight symbolic execution that avoids the DAG explosion problem. Other DAG generation processes like CIEL [29] could in theory be leveraged by MadLINQ, but they are not particularly tailored for the tile algorithms that we focus on.

In terms of system design, our core contribution is the fine-grained pipelined DAG execution engine. Unlike other DAG engines such as Dryad and CIEL, FGP enables fault-tolerant streaming by default. The performance gain of streaming is application dependent, but it is one optimization that simultaneously exploits more parallelism, reduces burstiness of network traffic, and removes the dependency of expensive disk I/O, provided it deals with the complexity of handling failure across vertices. In the pipelined execution, when a failure occurs, all downstream vertices are affected. A conservative approach, adopted for example in Dryad [23] TCP streaming, MapReduce Online [18] and CIEL, is to restart all those nodes and/or throw away useful work. Yet, simply restarting the failed vertices will trigger redundant recomputation in the downstream nodes instead. Alternatively, one can adopt the classical Chandy-Lamport protocol [16] to handle failures in the pipeline. The protocol is general, where the communication can have arbitrary pattern (instead of a DAG) and computation can be non-deterministic (instead of deterministic). However, checkpointing may impose significant runtime overhead for our scenario.

To the best of our knowledge, FGP is the first design that is capable of minimizing recomputation for failure recovery, and is robust against arbitrary failure patterns. Critically, it only requires that data dependencies can be computed or tracked at runtime. In the context of large-scale matrix computation, we have demonstrated this through formal protocol development. Our experiments show that the system can withstand massive resource fluctuation, an important scenario in Cloud computing.

MadLINQ advances the state of the art as a matrix computation platform. Table 1 summarizes existing approaches with regard to the key properties: programmability, execution model, scalability, and failure-handling. We believe that these are important attributes in today's context, where new and experimental algorithms are being developed continuously, and the system needs to deal with large volume of data while relying on unreliable Cloud-level hardware.

HPC Solutions: Matrix computation has been a focus area in the HPC community for many years. LAPACK [7] was developed nearly 20 years ago, and its algorithms are highly tuned for shared-memory and multi-core architectures. ScaLAPACK [17] is its distributed variant and uses an SPMD model, which is problematic in terms of scalabil-

	Programmability	Execution model	Scalability	Failure-handling
ScaLAPACK (HPC Solution)	Grid-based matrix partition; high expressiveness but difficult to program	Bulk Synchronous Parallel (BSP), one process per node, MPI-based communication	Problem size bounded by total memory size; performance bounded by synchronization overhead	Global checkpointing, superstep rollback and recovery, high performance impact
DAGuE (Tiles & DAG)	Tile algorithm; high expressiveness; programmer must annotate data dependencies explicitly	One-level dataflow at tile level	Problem size bounded by total memory size; performance bound by parallelism at tile level	N/A
HAMA (MapReduce)	Tile algorithm; expressiveness constrained by MapReduce abstraction	MapReduce; implicit BSP between map and reduce phases	No constraint on problem size; performance bounded by BSP model	Individual operator roll back at tile granularity
MadLINQ	Tile algorithm in modern language; high expressiveness for experimental algorithms	Dataflow at tile level, with block-level pipelining across tile execution	No constraint of problem size; performance bounded by tile-level parallelism, improved with block-level pipelining	Precise re-computation at block granularity

Table 1. Comparison with alternative approaches and systems.

ity and fault-tolerance: the problem size is constrained by aggregate memory size, and implicit global barrier is executed at each matrix operation. As such, today's HPC solutions often require high-end network support, and are unsuitable for today's Cloud-level hardware. MadLINQ leverages the well-tuned LAPACK for local computation, but replaces its distributed framework with a pipelined DAG execution model. Even at the stage of a research prototype, MadLINQ has demonstrated that it is competitive with ScaLAPACK in terms of performance, while providing a level of fault-resilience that ScaLAPACK is unable to offer.

Tile Algorithms & DAG Execution: Using tile algorithms to derive DAG style execution for matrix computation is not new. For a more complete treatment, we refer readers to recent work such as FLAME [22], PLASMA [6] and DAGuE [9]. DAGuE adds annotations to a tiled matrix algorithm so that the DAG is explicitly embedded along the edges of data inputs and outputs. Vertices are then statically mapped out to a cluster of machines, and the computation is entirely decentralized. As such, this architecture can exploit maximum parallelism by using much smaller tiles. MadLINQ employs a central scheduler so as to deal with failures and resource dynamics, which are not addressed in these systems. The consequence is that tile size cannot be too small, otherwise scheduling overhead can be significant. This design choice, however, leads to reduced vertex level parallelism. We mitigate this by using pipelining at block granularity to exploit inter-vertex parallelism. Finally, MadLINQ removes the need of user annotation altogether by deriving the DAG automatically.

Matrix Algorithms in MapReduce: The wide-spread adoption of MapReduce in dealing with big data presents a recent paradigm shift. Open source projects such as HAMA [32] and PEGASUS [33] have used MapReduce

(or Hadoop) to express matrix algorithms. However, expressing and composing matrix algorithms using the narrow MapReduce APIs is tedious and improvisational. The otherwise straightforward flow of the algorithm needs to be broken down into various map and reduce phases and as a consequence, programming even slightly complex matrix algorithms such as Cholesky requires serious effort (see NMF [26]). The root of the problem is that MapReduce is a subset of relational algebra, and is fundamentally ill-suited to express linear algebra algorithms directly and naturally. Furthermore, solutions such as HAMA are based on the MapReduce abstraction and the execution is bulk synchronous since no reducer can proceed until all mappers complete. In contrast, MadLINQ's engine is fully dataflow-driven (like Dryad), but with the additional ability to perform fault-tolerant pipelining.

7. Discussion and Conclusion

Our original impetus for designing MadLINQ was a demand from our peer researchers in data mining who were unable to find an easy-to-program and scalable matrix computation platform. The system is now actively being used by these and other researchers to develop algorithms such as RLSI. During the course of developing and using the system, we have learned many lessons and identified what we believe to be key avenues for future research:

- **Auto-Tiling**. Currently, a vertex is pipelineable if and only if it represents a tile algorithm. In general, this is not true. For example, our current implementation of SVD is a tile algorithm, but its DAG includes vertices whose operation is not, and thus has to be run in staged mode. Auto-tiling (or blocking) is an important research field in the HPC community, and we will adopt appropriate techniques when available.

- **Dynamic Re-Tiling/Blocking**. As the MCL results indicate, especially for graph algorithms, the nature of the matrices may evolve and require different block and tile size.

- **Sparse Matrices**. Handling sparse matrices well is more difficult than dense matrices, because non-zero distribution can create severe load imbalance.

The current emphasis by the system community on scalable engines such as MapReduce, DryadLINQ and Hive is not accidental. These systems represent and scale-out a subset of the most useful relational algebra APIs. Deeper analysis using linear algebra and graph algorithms, often experimental in nature and operating on large-scale data sets, also need a system that is similarly easy to program, scalable, fault-tolerant and inter-operable. We believe MadLINQ contributes much to fill this vacuum.

Acknowledgements

We thank Cheng Xie, Guowei Liu and Yong He for their help when incubating this project, Jun Xu and Hang Li for the porting of RLSI, Steve Reinhardt for the introduction to Combinatorial BLAS, Jeff Baxter and Zhaoguo Wang on ScaLAPACK and Mahout experiments. We are indebted to our reviewers for their insightful comments on the paper, and particularly to our shepherd Terence Kelly for his feedback and help in writing the final version of this paper.

References

[1] Intel Math Kernel Library. http://software.intel.com/en-us/articles/intel-mkl/

[2] Hadoop project.http://hadoop.apache.org/

[3] HIVE project. http://hadoop.apache.org/hive/

[4] Mahout project. http://mahout.apache.org/

[5] TLC—The TLA+ Model Checker. http://research.microsoft.com/en-us/um/people/lamport/tla/tlc.html

[6] AGULLO, E., DEMMEL, J., DONGARRA, J., ET AL. Numerical linear algebra on emerging architectures: The PLASMA and MAGMA projects. *Journal of Physics: Conference Series 180*, 2009.

[7] ANDERSON, E., BAI, Z., DONGARRA, J., ET AL. LAPACK: A portable linear algebra library for high-performance computers. In *Supercomputing*, 2002.

[8] BENNETT, J., LANNING, S. The Netflix Prize. In *KDD*, 2007.

[9] BOSILCA, G., BOUTEILLER, A., DANALIS, A., ET AL. Dague: A generic distributed dag engine for high performance computing. Tech. Rep. ICL-UT-10-01, EInnovative Computing Laboratory, University of Tennessee, 2010.

[10] BRANDES., U. A faster algorithm for betweenness centrality. *Journal of Mathematical Sociology 25*, 2001.

[11] BREESE, J.S., HECKERMAN, D., KADIE, C., ET AL. Empirical analysis of predictive algorithms for collaborative filtering. In *Conf. on Uncertainty in Artificial Intelligence*, 1998.

[12] BULUÇ, A. Linear algebraic primitives for parallel computing on large graphs. PhD thesis, University of California at Santa Barbara, 2010.

[13] CHAIKEN, R., JENKINS, B., LARSON, P.Å., ET AL. Scope: easy and efficient parallel processing of massive data sets. In *VLDB*, 2008.

[14] CHAKRABARTI, D., ZHAN, Y., FALOUTSOS, C. R-MAT: A recursive model for graph mining. *SIAM Data Mining 6*, 2004.

[15] CHAMBERS, C., RANIWALA, A., PERRY, F., ET AL. Flumejava: easy, efficient data-parallel pipelines. In *PLDI*, 2010.

[16] CHANDY, K., LAMPORT, L. Distributed snapshots: Determining global states of distributed systems. *ACM Transactions on Computer Systems (TOCS) 3*, 1985.

[17] CHOI, J., DONGARRA, J., POZO, R., WALKER, D. Scalapack: A scalable linear algebra library for distributed memory concurrent computers. In *Symposium on the Frontiers of Massively Parallel Computation*, 1992.

[18] CONDIE, T., CONWAY, N., ALVARO, P., ET AL. MapReduce online. In *NSDI*, 2010.

[19] DEAN, J., GHEMAWAT, S. MapReduce: Simplified data processing on large clusters. In *OSDI*, 2004.

[20] FREEMAN, L. A set of measures of centrality based on betweenness. *Sociometry 40*, 1977.

[21] GOLUB, G.H., VAN LOAN, C.F. Matrix computations. Johns Hopkins Univ Pr., 1996.

[22] GUNNELS, J., GUSTAVSON, F., HENRY, G., VAN DE GEIJN, R. Flame: Formal linear algebra methods environment. *ACM Trans. on Math. Software (TOMS) 27*, 2001.

[23] ISARD, M., BUDIU, M., YU, Y., ET AL. Dryad: Distributed data-parallel programs from sequential building blocks. In *EuroSys*, 2007.

[24] LAMPORT, L. Specifying systems: The TLA+ language and tools for hardware and software engineers, 2002.

[25] LAWSON, C., HANSON, R., KINCAID, D., KROGH, F. Basic linear algebra subprograms for Fortran usage. *ACM Trans. on Math. Software (TOMS) 5*, 1979.

[26] LIU, C., YANG, H., FAN, J., ET AL. Distributed nonnegative matrix factorization for web-scale dyadic data analysis on mapreduce. In *WWW*, 2010.

[27] MALEWICZ, G., AUSTERN, M.H., BIK, A.J.C., ET AL. Pregel: a system for large-scale graph processing. In *SIGMOD*, 2010.

[28] LOW, Y., GONZALEZ, J., KYROLA, A., ET AL. Graphlab: A new framework for parallel machine learning. In *Conf. on Uncertainty in Artificial Intelligence*, 2010.

[29] MURRAY, D.G., SCHWARZKOPF, M., SMOWTON, C., ET AL. CIEL: A Universal Execution Engine for Distributed Data-Flow Computing. In *NSDI*, 2011.

[30] OLSTON, C., REED, B., SRIVASTAVA, U., ET AL. Pig Latin: A not-so-foreign language for data processing. In *SIGMOD*, 2008.

[31] SCHOENIG, S., DUCASSÉ, M. A backward slicing algorithm for prolog. *Static Analysis*, 1996.

[32] SEO, S., YOON, E., KIM, J., ET AL. HAMA: An Efficient Matrix Computation with the MapReduce Framework. In *CloudCom*, 2010.

[33] KANG, U., TSOURAKAKIS, C.E., FALOUTSOS, C. PEGASUS: mining peta-scale graphs. *Knowledge and Information Systems 27*, 2011.

[34] VAN DONGEN, S. Graph clustering via a discrete uncoupling process. *SIAM J. Matrix Anal. Appl 30*, 2008.

[35] WANG, Q., XU, J., LI, H., CRASWELL, N. Regularized latent semantic indexing. In *SIGIR*, 2011.

[36] YU, Y., ISARD, M., FETTERLY, D., ET AL. DryadLINQ: A system for general-purpose distributed data-parallel computing using a high-level language. In *OSDI*, 2008.

Jettison: Efficient Idle Desktop Consolidation with Partial VM Migration

Nilton Bila[†], Eyal de Lara[†], Kaustubh Joshi[×], H. Andrés Lagar-Cavilla[*],
Matti Hiltunen[×] and Mahadev Satyanarayanan[‡]

[†]University of Toronto, [×]AT&T Labs Research, [*]GridCentric Inc., [‡]Carnegie Mellon University

Abstract

Idle desktop systems are frequently left powered, often because of applications that maintain network presence or to enable potential remote access. Unfortunately, an idle PC consumes up to 60% of its peak power. Solutions have been proposed that perform consolidation of idle desktop virtual machines. However, desktop VMs are often large requiring gigabytes of memory. Consolidating such VMs, creates bulk network transfers lasting in the order of minutes, and utilizes server memory inefficiently. When multiple VMs migrate simultaneously, each VM's experienced migration latency grows, and this limits the use of VM consolidation to environments in which only a few daily migrations are expected for each VM. This paper introduces *Partial VM Migration,* a technique that transparently migrates only the working set of an idle VM. Jettison, our partial VM migration prototype, can deliver 85% to 104% of the energy savings of full VM migration, while using less than 10% as much network resources, and providing migration latencies that are two to three orders of magnitude smaller.

Categories and Subject Descriptors D.4.7 [*Operating Systems*]: Organization and Design —Distributed systems

General Terms Design, Experimentation, Measurement

Keywords Desktop Virtualization, Cloud Computing, Energy

1. Introduction

Modern offices are crowded with personal computers. Previous studies have shown that office computers are left continuously running, even when idle [8, 19, 25]. These idle times have been shown to add up to close to 12 hours per day, excluding off times [19]. Unfortunately an idle PC consumes close to 60% of the power of a fully utilized system. While modern computers support low power ACPI states [3], the same studies have shown that the main reason these are not used is because of applications that require always-on semantics. Applications such as instant messengers, VoIP clients, and remote desktop access and administration utilities, maintain network presence even when the PC is idle. Remotely waking up the PC on-demand via Wake-on-LAN [5] and similar mechanisms has been shown not to work, as frequent gratuitous network traffic in enterprise environments prevents the PC from sleeping [16, 19].

An attractive solution is to host the user's desktop inside a virtual machine (VM), migrate the VM to a consolidation server when idle, and put the desktop to sleep [13]. The key advantage of this approach is that it does not require changes to applications or special purpose proxies. However, a straightforward implementation requires large network transfers, to migrate memory (and optionally disk) state, which can saturate shared networks in medium to large offices, and utilizes server memory inefficiently.

This paper introduces *Partial VM Migration*, a technique that addresses these challenges. Partial VM migration is based on the observation that an idle desktop, even in spite of background activity, requires only a small fraction of its memory and disk state to function, typically less than 10% of memory and about 1 MiB of disk state. Partial VM migration creates a partial VM on the server, and transfers on-demand only the limited working set that is accessed while the VM is idle. The desktop sleeps when the consolidated partial VM needs no state from it, and wakes up to service on-demand requests. We call these opportune sleeps *microsleeps*. Migrating the VM back to the user's desktop is fast because partial VM migration maintains VM residues on the desktop and transfers only the dirty state created by the partial VM back to the desktop.

Partial VM migration makes energy-oriented desktop consolidation practical. Because its network transfers are small, and partial VMs require only a small fraction of their desktop mode memory footprint, partial VM migration has the benefit that both, the network and server infrastructure, can scale well with the number of users, while providing

---

[*] Andrés participated in this work while employed at AT&T Labs Research.

migration times that are very small. High migration efficiency creates more opportunities for energy savings, because shorter periods of idleness can be targeted. Fine-grain migration also lowers the penalty for poor migration decisions. If an idle user becomes active much sooner than expected, he hardly notices that his VM has migrated. This approach is suitable for personal computers, such as desktops and laptops, which have local execution state, and we refer to these simply as desktops.

Jettison is our desktop based partial VM migration prototype. Our experience with a Jettison deployment shows that significant energy savings are achievable without negative impact on user experience. Within an hour of inactivity, desktops were able to save up to 78% of energy. Experienced migration times were near 4 seconds and migration sizes averaged under 243 MiB for Linux desktop VMs with 4 GiB of nominal memory. Our experiments also show that, in a simulated environment with 500 users, partial VM migration can deliver similar energy savings as full VM migration, while using less than 10% as much network resources, and providing migrations latencies that are three orders of magnitude smaller. The capital investment needed to achieve these energy savings is modest. Even a small private cloud can support a large number of desktop VMs because the VMs migrated there have small network and memory footprints: they only do what is needed to sustain always-on semantics for desktop applications. While our current prototype targets VMs with local storage on the desktop, the approach is equally applicable to enterprise deployments with shared network storage. Similarly, partial VM migration is complementary to solutions like Intelligent Desktop Virtualization (IDV) [6] that simplify desktop management by centralizing it, while supporting local execution. Whereas these approaches concentrate on managing and backing up the VM persistent state, partial VM migration is mainly concerned about migration of run state.

This paper makes five contributions: (i), it shows that the working set of an idle VM is small and consists mostly of memory state (disk is less than 1%); (ii), it shows that migrating a VM in full is unnecessary, and indeed does not scale well for energy oriented idle desktop consolidation; (iii), it shows that on-demand state requests are clustered enough to allow desktops to save energy by sleeping between request bursts; (iv), it shows that partial VM migration can save as much energy as full VM migration while sending less than 10% of the data, with migration latencies that are three orders of magnitude smaller; and (v), it presents a complete architecture used to consolidate idle partial VMs and reintegrate them back to their desktop, when active.

The remainder of the paper is organized as follows. Section 2 motivates the need for partial VM migration, by demonstrating that migrating VMs in full is inadequate for energy oriented consolidation of idle desktop VMs. Section 3 introduces partial VM migration as a technique to

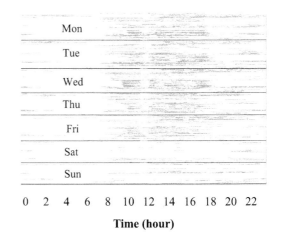

Figure 1. Desktop/laptop usage and idle periods

reduce energy use of idle desktops. Section 4 describes Jettison, our implementation of partial VM migration. Section 5 presents results from a our deployment of Jettison and, by using simulations, Section 6 extends these results for large office environments and evaluates the scalability of our approach. In Section 7, we discuss the sensitivity of our results, the implications of using network accessible shared storage, the implications of our approach to hardware and software reliability, and how our approach fits within the context of virtualization solutions in the market place. Section 8 discusses related work, and Section 9 concludes the paper.

2. Motivation

Our research confirms prior studies (e.g., [19]) that desktops are powered up but idle significant portions of time. Figure 1 illustrates activity traces collected from desktop and laptop machines in a research lab for 500 person days. Each line represents one machine day, with a dot indicating that the machine is in use, and a white space that the machine is idle. The figure shows that, in addition to the overnight and lunch time idle periods, there are numerous significant idle periods that are opportunities for energy savings. However, to take advantage of these periods, the following requirements must be met:

1. Quick resume: To ensure user acceptance, the desktop must be restored in a few seconds when the user resumes their work.

2. Conservation of the network resources: With 100s or 1000s of users in one organization, frequent desktop migrations put significant strain on the network.

3. Cost effective: The extra capital cost incurred by the consolidation servers must be small enough that it does not exceed the savings from reduced energy use.

While prior work (e.g., [13]) proposes desktop consolidation using existing VM technology (live migration [12] and ballooning [23]), we find such techniques fall short in meeting these requirements. We performed experiments to quantify the performance of existing VM technologies on enterprise class hardware[1]. In these experiments, the desktop VM was warmed up through a script that loaded a number of documents and web pages and then idled. After one minute of idleness, the VM was migrated to the consolidation server through a dedicated network switch. The VM used shared storage, provided through Redhat's network block device GNBD, which ensured disk availability upon migration. Each experiment was repeated 5 times and we report the average results. Even though the footprint of the VM was 4 GiB, the script would consistently lead the VM to using only 1.2 GiB of its memory.

Live migration [12] provides an obvious baseline. In our experimental setup, the average latency of live migration is 38.59 seconds, and the average network bandwidth consumed is 4.27 GiB. However, the migration of one VM at a time does not give the full picture of the user experience. Specifically, a "boot storm" occurs when multiple users start work or resume work at the same time or in close proximity. As expected, live migrating multiple VMs out of a single consolidation server concurrently degrades linearly: 4 VMs takes an average of 137 seconds, while 8 take 253 seconds. Staggering the resume times helps, but even with 20 second pause between resumes of 8 VMs still results in average latency of 115.62 seconds. Not only is live migration unable to ensure quick resumes, but it will introduce significant strain on the network (number of migrations times the average VM size) as we will demonstrate in Section 6.

Ballooning is a technique that allows the memory footprint of a VM to be shrunk when desired and thus, using it before consolidations could alleviate some of the disadvantages of live migration. While ballooning is able to shrink the VM footprint, this happens at a considerable expense of time and I/O. In our experiments with Xen's ballooning implementation, our idle VM's footprint reached its saturation point at 423 MiB (swapping turned on to avoid killing any processes), but ballooning took an average of 328.44 seconds to reach this saturation point. In the process, it evicted 275.99 ± 9.25 MiBs of disk cached state and swapped out 449.08 ± 51.55 MiBs of main memory to secondary storage, using the network resources. While the ballooned VMs can be easily migrated—the VMs with 423 MiB footprints were migrated on the average in 4.86 seconds—the memory state swapped out and the cached disk state have to be reconstructed from the shared storage after resume resulting in additional network usage and slowed desktop responsiveness. Thus, while ballooning reduces the VM's footprint on the consolidation server, it fails to significantly reduce network bandwidth. Even if we use local disks instead of shared storage in order to reduce network usage, the ballooning latency

is still prohibitive for our goals and, in this case, the desktops must to be woken up to serve pages being swapped in while the desktop VM executes at the consolidation server.

3. Partial VM Migration

Partial VM migration allows user applications to maintain network presence while the desktop sleeps. It transfers the execution of an idle VM to a consolidation server, and fetches the VM's memory and disk state on-demand. Partial VM migration differs from post-copy VM migration [17] in that the migration is not executed to completion. Instead most of the VM state remains as a residual on the user's desktop in anticipation of a reverse migration. Partial VM migration does not require application modifications, the development of specialized protocol-specific proxies or additional hardware.

When the VM is executing on the desktop, the desktop has all of the VM's state, which provides full system performance to the user. When on the server, only the working set required for idle execution is available there.

By migrating only the limited working set that is accessed while the desktop remains idle, partial VM migration allows for high consolidation ratios on the server, and makes it possible to save energy by migrating often throughout the day without overwhelming the network infrastructure. Similarly, migrating back to the user's desktop is fast because only the dirty state created by the partial VM is reintegrated back into the desktop.

Partial migration leverages two insights. First, the working set of an idle VM is small, often more than an order of magnitude smaller than the total memory allocated to the VM. Second, rather than waiting until all state has been transferred to the server before going to sleep for long durations, the desktop can save energy by microsleeping early and often, whenever the remote partial VM has no outstanding on-demand request for state. Existing desktops can save energy by microsleeping for few tens of seconds. Shorter intervals do not save energy because the transient power to enter and leave sleep state is higher than the idle power of the system. The challenge is to ensure that the desktop microsleeps only when it will save energy. In the next sections, we determine strategies that answer the following questions:

1. When should a desktop microsleep?

2. How can prefetching be used to optimize microsleep opportunities?

We first describe how we migrate idle VM working set on-demand, and describe a deployment of our partial VM migration prototype from which we collected memory and disk access traces for the analysis.

3.1 Working Set Migration

When consolidating a VM from the desktop to the server, partial VM migration transfers memory state only as the VM

[1] Xen VMs with 4 GiB of memory and 12 GiB of disk; Dell Poweredge R610, 24 GiB of RAM, 8 2.3 GHz Xeon cores, Fusion-MPT SAS drives, and a Broadcom NetXtreme II gigabit NIC.

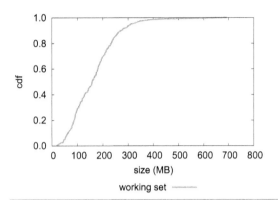

Figure 2. Distribution of working set sizes of idle Linux VMs with 4 GiB of memory.

requires it for its execution. During consolidation, partial VM migration transfers only a VM descriptor, which contains VM configuration (e.g. device listing, memory limit), virtual CPU register state, and page table pages set up by the VM's kernel. The descriptor is used to set up page tables and start the partial VM's execution. As the VM tries to access its pages, it causes faults that are handled by an external process. This process migrates each faulting page from the desktop, on-demand. We refer to these page faults accesses as *remote faults*. Once migrated, future accesses to a page do not result in remote faults. To improve performance, accesses caused by allocations that overwrite whole pages are handled differently. These faults are handled locally by the VM's kernel with no remote fault ensuing.

For VMs with local disk images rather than shared network storage, disk state is also migrated from the desktop on-demand. At consolidation time, only device configuration is transmitted as part of the descriptor. Each first time disk block access results in its migration from the desktop. First block accesses that result in whole block writes are also handled locally by the disk driver.

3.2 State Access Traces

We collected traces of idle VMs memory and disk accesses in a deployment of our prototype implementation of partial VM migration on the desktops of three users over a seven week period. To identify idle periods, we monitored UI activity and if the user was found to be inactive for at least 15 seconds, a 5 second dialog was displayed, warning of an impending VM consolidation. If no response was given, we considered the user idle and the VM was consolidated. Each VM's 12 GiB disk image was stored locally on the desktop.

Figure 2 shows the distribution of working set sizes of the three user VMs over 313 idle periods. These desktop VMs were each allocated 4 GiB of memory and were used as general purpose Linux desktop systems with applications such as Web browsers, document processors and instant messengers. Idle periods occurred throughout the day.

The mean memory working set was only 165.63 MiB with standard deviation of 91.38 MiB. The mean working set

size is barely 4.0% of the VMs allocated memory. The mean size of disk accesses during these idle times was 1.16 MiB with standard deviation of 5.75 MiB. The implications of a small memory and disk footprint are: (i), little state needs to be migrated when consolidating, a benefit in terms of reduced network load; (ii), little state needs to be migrated when resuming, a network benefit, but also, more importantly an improvement of user experience by reducing reintegration latency; and (iii), limited memory needs to be committed to each running VM on the server, a benefit in terms of reduced infrastructure costs.

3.3 When to Microsleep

A desktop system experiences increased power use during transitions to sleep and wake-up. A microsleep will only save energy if it lasts long enough to compensate for the transient energy rise required to enter sleep and wakeup the system to serve a remote fault.

Specifically, the energy use of an idle desktop system is given by:

$$E_i = P_i t_i \tag{1}$$

Where E_i is the energy used in watt hours, P_i is the system's idle power rate and t_i is the idle time in hours.

The energy use of an idle system that microsleeps is:

$$E_\mu = P_i t_{i'} + P_o t_o + P_s t_s + P_r t_r \tag{2}$$

Where $t_{i'}$ is the portion of time the system remains powered, P_o and t_o the power rate and time the system spends entering sleep, P_s and t_s the power rate and time the system spends in sleep, and P_r and t_r the power rate and time the system spends exiting sleep.

Power rates, t_o, and t_r depend only on the desktop's profile. In typical desktops, P_s is often an order of magnitude smaller than P_i, and P_o and P_r are larger than P_i. Then, microsleep can only save energy if t_s is long enough to compensate for increased energy use during t_o and t_r. The shortest interval for which it is energy efficient to microsleep is one in which $E_i = E_\mu$. In such interval the system wastes no time awake, so $t_{i'} = 0$, and the interval is given by:

$$t_b = \frac{-P_s(t_o + t_r) + P_o t_o + P_r t_r}{P_i - P_s} \tag{3}$$

Plugging in our desktop profile from Table 1, we find that, for our systems, $t_b = 32.22$ seconds. Thus, our desktop should microsleep only when there is an expectation that no remote faults will arrive in at least the next 32.22 s.

To determine the likelihood of a fault-free period of at least t_b length, we determine the conditional probability of that the next remote fault will arrive in less than t_b as a function of the *wait time* (t_w), the time interval that has elapsed since the last remote fault arrived at the desktop.

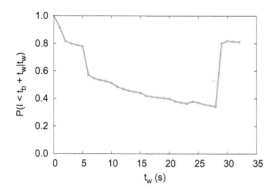

Figure 3. Conditional probability that the next remote fault will arrive in less than 32.22 s as a function of the wait time.

More formally, $p(I < t_b + t_w | t_w)$ is the probability of inter-arrival I being energy inefficient.

Figure 3 plots the conditional probability that the next remote fault will arrive in less than 32.22 s based on remote fault inter-arrival times for the prototype deployment of the previous section. The figure shows that as the wait time increases up to 28 s, the likelihood of seeing the next remote fault in less than 32.22 s decreases rapidly. This is because faults are highly correlated, and indeed more than 99.23% of remote faults occur within one second of previous faults. The implication is that for the vast majority of faults, when the desktop wakes up to service one fault, it will likely be able to service faults that follow immediately, avoiding many inefficient microsleeps. With wait times immediately above 28 s, the probability of seeing a remote fault increases significantly because 60 s inter-arrivals are common, typically because of timer based events.

We determine next the optimal value of wait time, t_w, that minimizes the energy waste as follows:

$$\min E_{waste}(t_w) = t_w E_i + p(I < t_b + t_w | t_w) E_\mu \quad (4)$$

Where E_{waste} is the total energy wasted. To compute E_μ, we assume the worst case, in which a fault occurs immediately after the desktop enters sleep so that $t_s = 0$ and $t_{i'} = 0$.

With our desktops' energy profile, E_{waste} is shown in Figure 4, and it is clear that the energy waste minimizing t_w is 6 seconds.

3.4 State Prefetch

We use prefetching to increase the frequency and length of energy efficient inter-arrivals. Prefetching proactively migrates state to the server and allows faults to be serviced locally on the server, not requiring the desktop to be awake.

As discussed in Section 3.1, most state transfer, hence remote faults, is caused by memory accesses (more than 99%). As a result, we concentrate our efforts on reducing memory faults and allow disk requests to be serviced on-demand, independent of whether storage is local or networked.

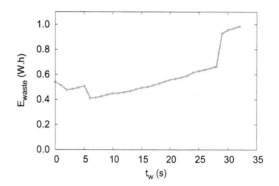

Figure 4. Expected energy waste as a function of sleep timeout (t_w).

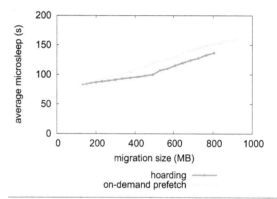

Figure 5. Effect of hoarding and on-demand prefetching on microsleep lengths.

We explored two prefetch strategies. The first, *hoarding*, explores similarity in page frame numbers accessed between different migrations of the same VM. At the time of consolidation, this approach fetches a sequence of pages whose frame numbers were requested in previous instances in which the VM was consolidated. In the second prefetch strategy, *on-demand prefetch*, we exploit spatial locality of page accesses by using a pivot window to prefetch pages whose frame numbers are near a requested page. Both strategies fetch pages into a per VM buffer, either in disk or in a discrete memory location, and pages are only committed to the partial VM's memory when the VM attempts to access them. This approach ensures that prefetching does not grow the memory footprint of an idle VM, and whenever the prefetch buffer is full it can evict pages unlikely to be used.

Figure 5 compares the performance of hoarding and on-demand prefetch per MiB of migrated state. The figure, uses simulation results based on page access traces from a user VM from our deployment that is consolidated 58 times. The primary performance metric is the average length of time of each microsleep. The objective of prefetch is to reduce the number remote faults that interrupt microsleeps. Figure 6 shows the energy savings for the same VM, normalized over the energy the desktop uses during those idle periods when left powered. We compute energy use of the

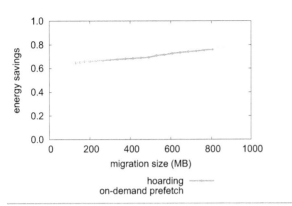

Figure 6. Effect of hoarding and on-demand prefetching on energy savings.

desktop by aggregating energy used over each interval the desktop would be idle, suspending, sleeping and resuming under each prefetch strategy, using Equation 2. For any given migration size, on-demand prefetch increases average microsleep durations faster than hoarding, which result in slightly better energy savings. Migration size is composed of state migrated by the prefetch strategy, and state fetched due to a prefetch cache miss. Our results indicate that on-demand prefetch is better at predicting contiguous sequence of requests. Hoarding can more often miss requests in the middle of a cluster, resulting in extra desktop wake-ups.

We also experimented with an approach that combines hoarding and prefetch, and found it to yield an improvement in energy savings for a given migration size of only 1 to 4% over on-demand prefetch alone. However, an attractive feature of on-demand prefetch is that it does not create bulk network transfers which can quickly congest the network, rather, it amortizes state migration over the duration of consolidation, as state is needed by the VM. Given similar energy savings performance, on-demand prefetch is preferable.

Separately, we also explored maintaining VM residuals on the server and found it to have limited success in reducing remote faults. In our experiments, page content reuse across subsequent consolidations of the same VM, averaged 28%. Fewer than one third of a VM's page requests could be serviced from residuals stored from previous server instances of itself. While we did not explore page content sharing across different VMs, we expect it's effectiveness in reducing remote faults to be no better than with same VM residuals.

For the remainder of the paper we use on-demand prefetch for memory migration and fix the prefetch pivot window size at 20 pages, which we found to deliver the highest savings per MiB. We also fix the prefetch cache at 50 MiB as prefetched pages are commonly used within a short period, and with such buffer we see little re-fetch of evicted pages.

4. Jettison

Our partial consolidation prototype is Jettison. It is implemented on top of the Xen 3.4 hypervisor [10]. Xen is a type

1 hypervisor which runs in the highest processor privilege level and relegates guest domains to lower privilege ones. Xen supports an administrative guest, domain 0 (henceforth dom0) and multiple unprivileged guests, domUs. In our architecture desktop environments are encapsulated in domUs.

Jettison is implemented as modifications to the hypervisor, daemons in dom0, and patches to the domU kernel. Our implementation currently supports paravirtualized guests, and we plan to extend it to also support fully virtualized VMs. In the discussion below, we explain where changes are needed for fully virtualized VMs.

Jettison runs the following components on the dom0 of the desktop system. An *activityMonitor* daemon, responsible for detecting user activity, initiating both consolidation and user-triggered reintegrations, and suspending the desktop system to memory sleep (S3). At present, activityMonitor monitors keyboard and mouse and, after an user configured period of inactivity, provides an on-screen warning for another pre-configured period, before consolidating the VM. Our defaults are 15 and 5 seconds for the inactivity and warning periods, respectively. Only while the VM is consolidated, the desktop runs a *memserv* and a *diskserv* processes, responsible for serving memory pages and disk blocks, respectively, to the server over TCP. memserv, maps all of the consolidated VM's frames with read-only access.

On the consolidation server's dom0, Jettison runs a *remoteWakeup* daemon and two additional processes for each domU. remoteWakeup wakes up a sleeping desktop via Wake-On-LAN [5] whenever remote state is required. A *memtap* process monitors VM page faults, notifies remoteWakeup and issues page requests to memserv running on the desktop and, on response, updates the VM's page frame. memtap maps its VM's frames with write access so it can perform direct updates.

Xen employs a split device model in which a device front end interface runs in the kernel of domU, and a backend, implementing the functionality of the device, runs in dom0. *cownetdisk* is our instantiation of the block device backend for consolidated VMs with desktop local storage. It is based on the blocktap interface [24] and implements a copy-on-write networked disk device. While a VM runs on the server, cownetdisk maintains two sparse virtual disk slices as files in dom0. The bottom slice, the read-only slice, keeps blocks that have only been read by the VM, and the top slice, the dirty slice, maintains all that have been written to. A bitmap is used to identify the valid slice for a block. Read requests for blocks not in the server are fetched from the desktop and placed in the read-only slice. First writes to a block cause the promotion of the block to the dirty slice. Once a block is promoted, all future accesses occur in the top slice. Writes to blocks not present in the server cause a fetch from the desktop first, and an immediate promotion. The exception are whole block writes, which cause only a promotion. On a remote fetch, cownetdisk also notifies remoteWakeup first, to ensure that the desktop is awake.

When to consolidate and reintegrate? The decision to consolidate rests on three conditions: (i) user idleness - the user is not actively engaging the VM, (ii) server capacity - the server has sufficient resources to accommodate the VM, (iii) VM idleness - the VM can execute on the server with sufficient autonomy from the desktop, such that the desktop can sleep and save energy.

We determine user idleness by monitoring keyboard and mouse activity. In the absence of activity, we provide an on-screen warning, that allows the user to cancel consolidation.

On the server we care primarily about memory availability. When deciding to consolidate an idle VM, Jettison checks that the server has enough memory to accommodate it. Because a partial VM requires only a fraction of its nominal memory, we must estimate the size of its working set before migration, and ensure that the server can accommodate it. Initially, we estimate the working set size from the observed sizes in our deployment. This estimate can then be adjusted based on the VM's previous history on the server. The median working set size of our VMs was 157.87 MiB. If during server-side execution, the VM requires less memory, some, though minimal, server memory is left un-utilized. If the VM requires more memory than estimated, and the server has enough free memory, it allocates it as needed. If not, the server evicts the VM back to its desktop.

Consolidating a VM to the server is only feasible when it allows its desktop to sleep long enough to conserve energy. This requires that the VM is accessing minimal amount of disk and memory state resident on the desktop. While the VM runs on the desktop, we monitor it's I/O and CPU usage. Xen already maintains these statistics, which we can access to determine that the VM is idle. We can determine memory usage periodically via the hypervisor's *dirty state tracking* mechanism. Xen can initially make all pages of a VM read-only and, an attempt by the VM to make a write is trapped by the hypervisor, which sets a dirty bit for the page.

The decision to reintegrate a VM to the desktop is symmetrical to that of consolidating it to the server. It hinges on failures to meet idleness and server capacity conditions. That is, either the user becomes active, the VM becomes active and requires a large amount of state from the desktop, or the server's capacity is exceeded.

What happens during consolidation? On the desktop, the execution of the VM is halted and our dom0 tools generate a VM descriptor and all memory state of the VM remains in core. The descriptor contains VM configuration metadata, such as device configuration, VCPU register state, page table pages, and configuration pages shared between the domain and hypervisor. The largest component of the descriptor are the page table pages. The descriptor is migrated to the server which creates a new domain and begins its execution.

On the desktop, a diskserv and a memserv processes are instantiated and device backends are disconnected from the halted VM. Whenever these state servers receive a request, they notify the activityMonitor so it knows not to schedule an immediate sleep of the desktop.

As the VM begins execution on the server, it faults on page accesses. These faults generate an interrupt handled by the hypervisor. In turn, using an event channel, Xen's inter-domain communication interface, the hypervisor notifies the memtap process of the fault and suspends the faulting VCPU. When memtap has received the page and updated the VM's frame, it notifies the hypervisor via the same event channel. The hypervisor then re-schedules the faulting VCPU for execution.

What happens during reintegration? When the VM resumes execution on the desktop, for example, because the user has returned, any state that was modified while it ran on the server needs to be integrated into the desktop state. Because the desktop contains all of the VM's state and, only a small fraction of it has become stale, we only need to migrate back the new state. For this, we use the disk and memory dirty state tracking mechanisms described above. When the VM is reintegrated, only pages and disk blocks marked as dirty are migrated to the desktop.

On the consolidation server, the VM is halted and our dom0 tools map in dirty memory frames and VCPU register state, and send their contents to the desktop. The dirty disk slice, if any, is also sent. On the desktop, the VM's memory frames are mapped with write permission by our dom0 tools, which update them with received dirty state. In parallel, the dirty disk slice is merged with local disk. Once all state has been updated, device backends are started and the VM is allowed to begin execution.

Network Migration is supported within LAN environments where both the desktop and the server are in the same Layer 2 broadcast domain. In these environments, because Jettison VMs rely on host network bridging and maintain the same MAC address across hosts, they continue to receive network packets that are destined to them after migration. This allows existing connections to remain active, with minimal latencies during migration. When the desktop and server connect via a Layer 3 or above network device, the device must ensure that both are in the same broadcast domain. For example, a router must include both the desktop's and the server's subnets within the same Virtual LAN.

Dynamic Memory Allocation is achieved by allocating on-demand the underlying pages of memory of a consolidated VM. For paravirtualized guests, we realize on-demand allocations through the concept of a "ghost MFN". Xen uses two complementary concepts to address a page frame. Machine frame number (MFN) refers to the machine address of the frame, as viewed by the MMU. Physical frame numbers (PFNs) are indirect addresses given to the paravirtualized VM kernel to refer to the real MFNs. PFNs give the VM the illusion of having access to a contiguous address space. A ghost MFN has the property of serving as a place-holder that encodes the PFN that it backs, and a flag indicating absence of actual allocation. The ghost MFN is placed in lieu of an allocated MFN in the page tables, and the PFN-to-MFN translation table that each Xen paravirtual guest maintains. The first guest access to the PFN triggers a shadow page fault in the hypervisor, which is trapped and handled by allocating the real MFN to replace the ghost. We limit fragmentation of the hosts free page heap by increasing the granularity of requested memory chunks to 2MiB at a time, while still replacing ghost MFNs one at a time.

While we have not implemented dynamic memory allocation and remote fault handling for fully virtualized guests, known as hardware assisted VMs (HVMs), we plan to use Xen's built-in populate-on-demand (PoD) mechanism to do both. PoD maps PFNs to MFNs on-demand for HVMs, by faulting on first access to each page. This mechanism is used to boot HVMs with lower memory commitments than their maximum reservation, *maximum*. PoD allocates a preset *target* memory to a per-guest cache, and maps pages to the guest's memory on-demand. When the cache runs out of pages, PoD scans the memory of the guest for zero pages, unmaps and returns them to the cache. For our purposes, we will modify the PoD cache so it starts with a chunk-size of memory, and when it runs out of pages, instead of scanning for zero pages, it gets additional allocation chunks from the hypervisor, as we do for our ghost MFN implementation.

We note that in both approaches, the faults used to allocate memory on-demand are the same we use to fetch missing state on-demand. That is, when a fault occurs, first, we commit the backing page to the VM, and then notify memtap to fetch the content from the desktop.

5. Prototype Evaluation

We evaluated the performance of Jettison with a deployment that involved four users and lasted 6 days. We use the results of this deployment to answer the following questions:

1. How much energy is saved by partial VM migration?

2. Does microsleeping save energy?

3. How much state needs to be migrated to the consolidation server to run an idle VM?

4. How much data needs to be migrated back to the desktop when reintegrating the VM?

5. How long does it take to migrate a consolidated VM back to the desktop?

5.1 Experimental Setup

Our deployments employed desktop systems and a consolidation server. When the users were active, VMs ran on the desktops. When inactive the VMs migrated to the server.

State	Time (s)	Power (W)
Suspend	8.38 (0.22)	107.90 (1.77)
Resume	8.58 (0.85)	121.72 (24.52)
Idle	N/A	61.40 (0.03)
Sleep (S3)	N/A	1.95 (0.02)
Network	N/A	136.63 (2.81)

Table 1. Power profile of Dell Studio XPS 7100 Desktop.

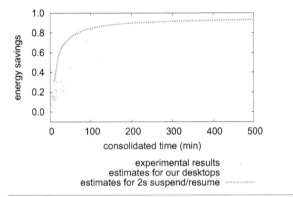

Figure 7. Desktop energy savings.

Each VM was configured with 4 GiB of memory and 12 GiB of disk. The VMs ran Linux with the GNOME desktop configured with Mozilla Firefox and Thunderbird, OpenOffice.org, Pidgin IM client, OpenSSH, among others. Background IM and e-mail traffic was often present, including occasional delivery of messages. Some of our users used the IM client to connect to Google Talk and used Thunderbird for e-mail, while others used web based Gmail and chat. Our VMs were also accessible via SSH, and some users reported downloading documents from their consolidated VMs from home. Such activities, did not require VM reintegration because they did not cause high I/O activity or significant growth of VM memory.

The desktops were Dell Studio XPS 7100 systems, with a 3 GHz quad-core AMD Phenom™ II X4 945 processor and 6 GiB of RAM. Table 1 presents the desktop's power profile obtained with a GW Instek GPM-8212 power meter. These numbers are comparable to those of other published systems [8, 13]. The server was a Sun Fire X2250 system with two quad-core 3 GHz Intel Xeon® CPUs and 16 GiB of memory. It's idle power averaged 150.70 W. The desktops connected to the server over a GigE switch shared with approximately 100 other hosts. We measured the effective throughput between the desktops and servers to be 813.44 Mbps. Power use of the desktops during the deployment was measured with Watts up? PRO power meters.

5.2 Energy Savings

Figure 7 shows energy savings experienced by desktop users during the deployment. Energy savings are normalized over the energy these desktops spend if left powered during those idle periods. The figure also shows two estimates. First, it shows finer grained estimates of expected energy savings for

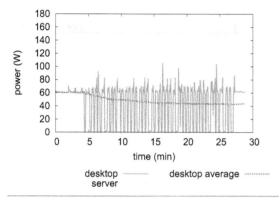

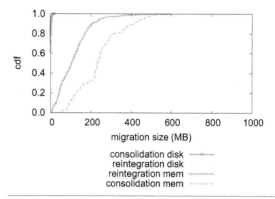

Figure 8. Power usage of a desktop and server during partial migration. The figure shows a reduction in the average energy use over time.

Figure 9. Distribution of migration sizes for VMs with 4 GiB of memory. Plot order matches legend top to bottom.

the desktops used in the deployment over varying lengths of consolidation time. Second, similar estimates for a desktop with similar profile characteristic as those in the deployment, except for having faster suspend and resume times of 2 seconds rather than nearly 8.5 seconds of our systems. These estimates were computed from memory access traces, as described in Section 3.4. The estimates match our experimental data well.

The experimental results show that our users were able to see reductions on their desktop energy use from as short idle periods as 4 minutes. While in short idle times of under 10 minutes we see savings of 7% to 16%, in longer idle times the savings were significant. In idle times of 67 minutes, we see 78% savings and, in idle times of 308 minutes, we see even higher savings of 91%.

In too short idle times, the energy expended by the desktop going to sleep and waking up is not outweighed by the energy savings of the short microsleeps available. The reason is that the desktops we use have very slow suspend and resume times (nearly 8.5 seconds). We note, however, that recent laptops have demonstrated short resume times, such as nearly 2 seconds in both the Macbook Air [2] and Acer Aspire S3 [1]. We argue that with approaches such as Context-Aware Selective Resume [26] that initialize only the necessary devices on wake-up, desktops can achieve fast suspends and resumes that are comparable to those of optimized laptops. The estimates for a desktop with 2-second suspend and resume in Figure 7 shows that, faster transitions lead to higher savings in short idle times. Intervals under 10 minutes would see savings that are closer to 30%.

Figure 8 shows detailed power usage of one desktop and the consolidation server over a 30 minute period in which the VM is consolidated to the server for 25 minutes. The figure shows the power usage patterns as the desktop performs microsleeps. At 1 minute and 57 seconds the VM begins migration to the server. This is represented by the first spike in power use in both the desktop and server. As the server runs the VM we note, two additional spikes, as batches of pages

are fetched for the VM. From 4 minutes and 21 seconds, the desktop performs a series of microsleeps until VM resume time. While initially, the energy use of the desktop nominally exceeds its idle use, as soon as the first microsleeps take place, the average energy use of the desktop drops below, and it continues to drop over the course of the idle period. As a result, the average power use of the desktop over the idle period drops from 61.4 W to 43.8 W, a savings of 28.8%. The energy savings of the desktop and the length of each microsleep increase over time.

While the server adds to energy use over an environment in which no consolidation is performed, it is worth noting that with our VM's working set sizes, each server is capable of hosting at least 98 VMs, so it's power use per VM amounts to less than 2 W. This power can be driven further down by increasing only the memory capacity of the server.

5.3 Network Load

Figure 9 shows the distribution of disk and memory state migrated during consolidation and resume stages. The results show that partial VM migration makes frugal use of the network. Overall, the mean amount of memory migrated (including data migrated by on-demand prefetching) to the consolidation server was 242.23 MiB, a mere 6% of the VMs' nominal memory. The average disk state migrated to the consolidation server was much smaller at 0.50 MiB. Similarly, on average, each VM migrates 114.68 MiB of memory and 6.81 MiB of disk state back to the desktop; confirming that VMs do not generate much dirty state while idle. This dirty state is generated by all processes that run in the VM independent of user activity, including always-on applications, but also tasks that run periodically, such as OS daemons and user tasks (e.g. browser JavaScript).

5.4 Migration Latencies

User perceived latency is important because it directly affects the user's experience, and his willingness to accept any approach that relies on migration. Of particular importance is reintegration latency, the time it takes for a consolidated

VM to migrate to the desktop and resume execution there, on user request.

Our experiments show that the time to migrate a VM back to the user's desktop is small. On average, users can expect their VMs to reintegrate in 4.11 seconds. Similarly, the average time to consolidate a VM is 3.78 seconds. These results exclude the desktop hardware suspend and resume times, found in Table 1.

5.5 Summary

Our evaluation shows that partial migration is able to achieve significant energy savings while generating only minimal loads on the network and providing low migration latencies to the user. These benefits are made possible by migrating barely more than the working set of idle VMs, and by taking advantage of microsleeps, short sleep times in which the desktop's attention is not required.

6. Scalability and Comparison with Full VM Migration

Next, we extrapolate the benefits of partial migration for settings with hundreds of desktops using user-idleness traces collected from real users in an office environment. We address the following questions: (i) How does partial migration compare against full migration in terms of network usage, overall energy savings, and the desktop reintegration latency experienced by users? (ii) Do the techniques scale with the number of desktops? (iii) Can they weather "boot storms" present in actual usage patterns? and most importantly, (iv) Do the energy savings exceed the capital costs required to deploy each technique?

Simulation Environment.   Our evaluation uses simulation driven by real user traces collected using a Mac OS X based tracker that runs on a desktop and tracks whether the user is active every 5 seconds. Users are said to be inactive if they are not using the keyboard or mouse, and no program (e.g., a video player) has disabled the OS screen-saver timer. We deployed the tracker for 4 months at an industrial research lab on 22 researchers' primary work Macs including both desktops and laptops. The machines had user-controlled software environments - there were no corporate lockdowns in place. We collected 2086 person day traces from which a sample of 500 are shown in Figure 1. Of the full traces, 1542 days were weekdays and 544 were weekends. Because a number of traces were from laptops that users take home, usage patterns in the evenings and nights were heavier than would be expected of office desktops. Furthermore, since the lab has flexible work hours, the data does not show tightly synchronized boot storms at the beginning of the workday - the most highly correlated period of inactivity was the lunch hour. Therefore, we expect this dataset to provide fewer sleep opportunities, but a somewhat friendlier environment for migration than a traditional office environment.

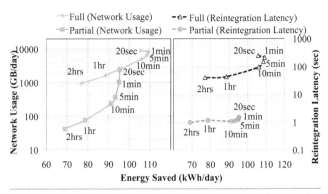

Figure 10. Energy savings in kW-h per day vs. reintegration latency and network utilization for 100 desktops and varying idle timeout values.

The traces were fed into a simulator that simulates consolidation and reintegration activity over the course of a single day for a given number of users (traces) and a given value of the idle timeout, the time of user inactivity the system waits before consolidating a VM. Because of qualitatively different user behavior on the weekends, we ran simulations using weekday and weekend data separately. In the interest of space, we report only on weekday results unless otherwise stated. The simulations assume a shared GigE network, desktop VMs with 4 GiB of RAM, and the same energy profile as the desktops used in our experiments (Table 1). The simulator takes into account network contention due to concurrent VM migrations when computing consolidation and reintegration latencies. It also takes into account energy use during migrations and desktop sleep periods when computing energy savings. We bias the results in favor of full migration by ignoring iterative pre-copy rounds or disk accesses, and assuming exactly a 4 GiB network transfer per migration for both, consolidation and reintegration. Finally we assume that full migration saves 100% of the desktop's idle power when the VM executes on the server,

For partial migration, we used the distributions of VM memory and disk migration sizes for consolidations and reintegrations shown in Figure 9. Even though partial migration consolidations create network traffic on-demand, we assumed bulk transfers on consolidations for ease of simulation. This creates more network congestion and biases results against partial migration. To estimate energy savings for partial migration while accounting for the energy costs of consolidation, reintegration and servicing of faults, we scale the time the VM remains on the server by a factor obtained from Figure 7 that estimates the savings as a function of consolidation time for our desktops.

Is Partial VM Migration a Real Improvement?   Section 5 suggests that when compared to full migration, partial migration significantly improves the network load and user-perceived reintegration latency at the expense of reduced energy savings. The question then arises whether full migration can be made competitive simply by increasing the idle timeout to migrate less aggressively, thus reducing network load and improving reintegration latencies, but reducing sleep opportunities and energy savings. Figure 10 shows that the answer to this question is an emphatic no. It shows a scatter-plot of energy savings per day against network load (left graph), and energy savings per day against reintegration latency (right graph) for different values of idle timeout in an office with 100 desktops. While partial migration does not match the highest energy savings possible using full migration in this setting (although it gets to within 85%), for an equal amount of energy saved, it has over an order of magnitude lower network load and reintegration latency.

The graphs also show that for both full and partial migration, there is a sweet-spot between 5-10 min for the idle timeout. Higher values significantly reduce energy savings, while lower values dramatically increase network load and reintegration latency without increasing energy savings much. For full migration, energy savings actually reduce for small idle timeouts because the aggressive migrations entailed lead to a lot of energy wasted in aborted migrations and oscillations between the desktop and consolidation server. Similar graphs for 10 to 500 desktops show that an idle timeout between 5 and 10 min provided the best balance of energy savings and resource usage across the board.

Scaling with Number of Desktops. Next, we show how the benefits of partial migration scale with the number of users. We use an idle timeout of 5 min for these experiments.

Figure 11(a) shows an over two orders of magnitude reintegration latency advantage for partial migration at 100 users that grows to three orders of magnitude at 500 users. Increased congestion and boot storms cause the performance of full migration to degrade with scale. In contrast, the latency of partial migration remains very stable. We contend that even at 100 users, the 151 s reintegration latency of full migration will be intolerable for users. Das et al. [13] propose using a remote desktop solution to provide immediate reintegration access to users to mask long reintegration latencies of full migration. However, remote desktop access has many limitations, such as the inability to seamlessly access local devices such as graphics cards, and the reliance on the performance of an overburdened network that is the cause of the long reintegration latencies in the first place. We show that partial migration offers a superior alternative.

Figure 11(b) shows that network utilization of partial migration is an order of magnitude lower than full migration, and remains low even as the number of users grows. Due to the fast consolidation and reintegration times, there are few aborted migrations. Aborted full migrations result from long migration times that increase with network congestion, and reduce successful attempts, and ultimately energy savings. The y2 axis of the figure shows the average daily network utilization in terms of total network capacity. Full migration quickly dominates the network (65% utilization at 100 users)

and, as a result often requires dedicated network infrastructure to prevent interfering with other applications.

Cost Effectiveness. Figure 11(c) shows the overall energy savings in kWh per day for partial and full migration for both the weekday and weekend datasets. The y2 axis shows the corresponding annualized energy savings using the average July 2011 US price of electricity of USD 0.1058 per kWh [2]. As the number of desktops increase, partial migration becomes more efficient than full migration (85% of full migration at 10 users to 104% at 500 users) because the large consolidation times for full migration on an increasingly congested network significantly reduce sleep time opportunities. Weekends are better, but weekdays have significant savings as well - with idle timeout of 5 minutes, VMs spend an average of 76% of a weekday on the server. With at least 100 desktops, energy savings increase almost linearly with the number of desktops, at a rate of USD 37.35 and 33.95 per desktop per year for partial and full migration, respectively.

We can compare these savings to the yearly depreciation costs for the consolidation servers to determine whether the schemes can pay for themselves. The question we ask is: assuming a 3 year depreciation window, can each migration scheme justify the purchase of a server with energy savings alone? We assume a server with 16 GiB of memory, similar to our testbed system. Since fully migrated idle VMs are memory constrained on the server side, we assume 4 4 GiB VMs on a single server giving us a break-even server budget of USD 33.95×4 VMs $\times 3$ years, or USD 407.40. In comparison, the results from Section 5 show that we can fit 98 partial VMs on a 16 GiB server when using partial migration, giving partial migration a budget of 37.35×98 VMs $\times 3$ years, or USD 10,980.90. To put these numbers in context, we priced the SunFire X2250 server used in our testbed at USD 6099.[3] In conclusion, given existing server and electricity prices a large consolidation ratio is required to make consolidation of idle desktop VMs cost effective, and partial VM migration is able to provide this high consolidation.

7. Discussion

We discuss next the sensitivity of our results, how our approach fits in the contexts of shared storage and virtualization infrastructures, and the implications of our approach to hardware reliability and software behaviour.

Sensitivity of Results. Our experimental use of Jettison was limited to a Linux desktop based research environment and our results demonstrate the benefits of partial VM migration in this type of environment. While we cannot speculate about the system's behaviour under a different OS or different office scenarios, we hope that the applications we use, many of them available across platforms, exhibit sim-

---

[2] US Energy Information Administration: http://www.eia.gov/electricity/
[3] https://shop.oracle.com

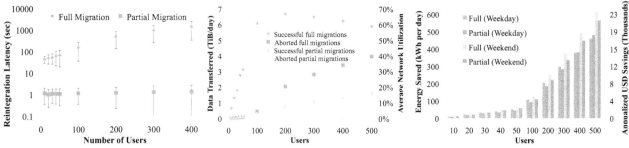

(a) Reintegration latency as desktops increase. The error bars show the standard deviations.

(b) Network load. Aborted migrations occur when a new migrations overrides an ongoing one.

(c) Total energy savings in kWh and USD.

Figure 11. Performance of partial migration and full migration as the number of desktops grow.

ilar behaviours in other OSes. We expect to support other guest OSes after implementing the HVM support discussed in Section 4. In our current prototype, the only function that required domU kernel modification was the optional fetch avoidance for whole page allocations described in Section 3.1. On average, this optimization reduced the fraction of the working set fetched remotely by 9.06 MiB from 165.63 MiB to 156.57 MiB. Similarly, our study did not quantify the energy savings in a laptop computer, however, given their similarity to desktop energy profiles, with more than an order of magnitude gap between idle and sleep power, we expect the savings to be comparable to our desktop results. For example, Agarwal et al. [8] found idle and sleep power of three laptop models to be 16.0 W and 0.74 W, 27.4 W and 1.15 W, and 29.7 W and 0.55 W, respectively.

Storage Placement. As described in Section 1, partial VM migration is data placement agnostic. Disk state can be placed either in network servers or locally on the desktops. The benefit of partial VM migration is in reducing migration of run state and, as we have shown in Section 3 more than 99% of state accessed by idle VMs is memory (165.63 MiB), while disk represents less than 1% (1.16 MiB). An environment with shared network storage reduces the number of faults that must be serviced from the desktop, and potentially increase the energy savings with partial VM migration, though minimally. In our deployment, we used desktop local storage, which supports legacy environments where shared storage is not always available.

The semantics of failure of a consolidated VM on storage consistency is similar under both scenarios, and is based on checkpointing. When a VM is consolidated, memory and disk state is checkpointed on the desktop. Disk changes made by the partial VM are stored in the per disk dirty slice held as a file in the server. If a failure occurs on the server, Jettison resumes the VM from checkpointed state on the desktop. The benefit of this approach is that in case of server failure, the desktop resumes from consistent disk and memory state. The disadvantage is that disk state that was written on the server and that may otherwise be useful can be lost. In cases of server-side failures which do not corrupt the host's file system and from which the host can recover,

for example by rebooting, the dirty slice may still be recovered, though this is something we have not implemented. Presently, we have implemented the server-side disk writes buffering, which enables desktop recovery from checkpoint, only for the local disk driver. Adding a similar function to shared storage drivers is left for future work.

Virtualization Context. Virtual Desktop Infrastructure (VDI) has emerged in the past decade as a means to simplify desktop management. It consolidates desktop VMs permanently on shared servers and provides remote access to desktop clients. Full time conversion to VDI can help reducing idle energy use, by powering off idle client devices. However, the pace of adoption of VDI remains slow [15], and full fledged desktops continue to outsell thin clients used in VDI. These thick clients will remain in use for years to come. Our approach provides the energy savings benefits of virtual machine consolidation without incurring costs of full VDI deployment. Our infrastructure requirements are modest because servers need only host idle VMs. In addition, partial VM migration provides support for clients that leverage local hardware resources, such as 3D acceleration.

Partial VM migration can be used with the Intelligent Desktop Virtualization (IDV) model [6] to simplify desktop management. IDV manages desktops centrally while executing them locally on desktops. Partial VM migration VMs can be based off a single golden OS image that resides on a shared server, with user state placed on separate image layers. Like VDI, this approach allows administrators to perform administrative tasks such as software upgrades on a single master image.

Reliability Implications. Our use of microsleeps leads to two concerns. First, frequent power state transitions may lead to reduced life span of hardware components. And second, slow wake up times reduce responsiveness of applications during remote faults, and for networked applications this may cause unintended side-effects on connections.

The potential impact on the life span of system components may arise particularly because on system wake up, current desktops power up all devices, independent of whether they are required. For most instances of system wake up in partial VM migration, the majority of devices is not needed. Indeed, most desktop wake ups require only access to CPU, memory and network card.

This problem can be mitigated with the Context-Aware Selective Resume approach proposed by Wright et al. [26]. That paper demonstrates that the majority of resume time is spent on OS and BIOS re-initialization, and shows that an approach that bypasses most devices and, in fact, does not re-initialize the entire OS on wake-ups but only the components necessary to, for example read memory and access the network, may reduce resume and suspend times by up to 87%.

In terms of software reliability, the desktop applications we used were able to content gracefully with the increased latency required to fulfill a remote fault when the desktop is microsleeping. In our experience, applications that rely on TCP and do not expect real time network performance can function reliably even during short absences of an end point. For example, the default Linux configuration for TCP allows for retries for up to 13 to 30 minutes, which has proven far more than sufficient to deal with the 8 to 17 seconds remote fault latency, in the worst case, in our usage of the system.

8.   Related Work

Although VM consolidation is one of the oldest ideas in cloud computing, previous work has focused on coarse-grain migration of VM memory state. Once the decision to migrate a VM has been made, the migration is executed to completion. Live migration [12] allows execution to begin at the destination before state is fully transferred from the source, but the transfer is completed in the background. After completion, no residual VM state is retained on the source machine in anticipation of a future reverse migration. This stateless model makes sense in the context of large public clouds, where all machines are viewed as a common pool. In our use case, however, a user is typically associated with a specific desktop. Preserving migrated state in anticipation of a reverse migration is likely to have high payoff and, indeed, our work shows that it does.

Enterprise energy savings through desktop consolidation in a private cloud has been previously explored in the context of LiteGreen [13]. However, the consolidation technique used there is the coarse-grain migration approach described in the previous paragraph. While LiteGreen shows significant energy savings, we expect many advantages with fine-grain migration. As discussed, these advantages include the ability to target shorter periods of idleness, a smaller private cloud, and greater tolerance of unpredictable user behavior.

More broadly, there has been extensive previous work on understanding the potential for energy savings from desktop computing infrastructure. Modern computers ship with built-in mechanisms to reduce the power usage of idle systems by entering low power sleep states [3] . However, recent studies have found that users are reluctant to put their idle systems in low power states. Nedevschi et al. [19] find that desktop systems remain powered but idle for an average of 12 hours daily. Webber et al. [25] find that 60% of corporate desktops remain powered overnight. It is conjectured that people refuse to put their system to sleep either for the off-chance they may require remote access, run background applications (IM, e-mail), among other uses [8], or because many idle periods are short, often interspersed with active periods [13]. While there have been approaches to support remote access [4, 5, 7, 21], they do not support always-on application semantics. Support for always-on applications have been proposed [8, 9, 16, 19, 22] either through remote proxies or specialized hardware. These approaches require developers to re-engineer most applications to support bimodal operation, transferring control and state between the full-fledged application and its proxied instance. Alternatively, thin clients [20] allow users to run low power clients, which waste little power when idle. However, thin clients remain unpopular due to poor interactive performance, lacking crispness in response and local hardware acceleration. Also, thin clients require fully-provisioned cloud infrastructure that is capable of supporting their peak collective load.

Exploiting short opportunities for sleep while a host is waiting for work is also explored in Catnap [14]. Catnap exploits the bandwidth difference between WLAN interface of end hosts and the WAN link to allow idle end hosts to sleep during network downloads while content is buffered in network proxies. That approach is focused on energy reduction in ongoing network transfers and not in providing continued execution of desktop applications during sleep.

In the data center, SnowFlock [18] has demonstrated the benefits of on-demand state migration to instantiate stateful worker replicas of cloud VMs. Our work has shown that on-demand migration is suitable for reducing energy use of idle desktops with our support of host sleep, the working set of an idle desktop VM is small and consists mostly of memory, on-demand migration scales better than full VM migration in shared office networks, and provides a means to reintegrate a partial VM state back to its origin.

In previous workshop paper [11], we proposed Partial VM migration. That work, however, only estimated the migration size and used simulation to estimate energy savings. In contrast, this paper presents a working implementation and an evaluation with a real deployment.

9.   Conclusion

This work introduces *fine-grain migration of VM state with long-term residues at endpoints*. An important use of this capability is for energy savings through partial consolidation of idle desktops in the private cloud of an enterprise to support applications with always-on network semantics. When the user is inactive partial VM migration transfers only the working set of the idle VM for execution on the consolidation server, and puts the desktop to sleep. When the user becomes active, it migrates only the changed state back to the desktop. It is based on the observation that idle desktops, in spite of background activity access only a small fraction of their memory and disk state, typically less than 10% for memory and about 1 MiB for disk. It migrates state on-demand and allows the desktop to microsleep when not serving requests. Partial VM migration provides significant energy savings with the dual benefits that network and server infrastructure can scale well with the number of users, and migration latencies are very small. We show that a desktop can achieve energy savings of 78% in an hour of consolidation and up to 91% in longer periods, while maintaining latencies of about 4 s. We show that in small to medium offices, partial migration provides energy savings that are competitive with full VM migration (85% of full migration at 10 users to 104% at 500 users), while providing migration latencies that are two to three orders of magnitude smaller, and network utilization that is an order of magnitude lower.

Acknowledgments

We thank Vidur Taneja for his early assistance exploring on-demand prefetching of pages. We thank our shepherd Orran Krieger and the anonymous EuroSys'12 reviewers for helping improve the quality of the final version of this paper. This research was funded in part by the National Science and Engineering Research Council of Canada (NSERC) under grant number 261545-3. Satyanarayanan was supported in this research by the National Science Foundation (NSF) under grant number CNS-0833882.

References

[1] Acer Aspire S3. http://us.acer.com/ac/en/US/content/series/aspiresseries.

[2] Macbook Air. http://www.apple.com/macbookair/performance.html.

[3] Advanced configuration and power interface specification. http://www.acpi.info/DOWNLOADS/ACPIspec10b.pdf, Feb 1999.

[4] Intel® Centrino® mobile technology wake on wireless LAN (WoWLAN) feature: Technical brief. http://www.intel.com/network/connectivity/resources/doc_library/tech_brief/wowlan_tech_brief.pdf, 2006.

[5] Wake on LAN technology. http://www.liebsoft.com/pdfs/Wake_On_LAN.pdf, Jun 2006.

[6] Vision paper: Intelligent desktop virtualization. http://goo.gl/MNmEa, Oct 2011.

[7] Y. Agarwal, R. Chandra, A. Wolman, P. Bahl, K. Chin, and R. Gupta. Wireless wakeups revisited: Energy management for voip over wi-fi smartphones. In *MobiSys '07*, Jun 2007.

[8] Y. Agarwal, S. Hodges, J. Scott, R. Chandra, P. Bahl, and R. Gupta. Somniloquy: Augmenting network interfaces to reduce pc energy usage. In *NSDI '09*, Apr 2009.

[9] Y. Agarwal, S. Savage, and R. Gupta. Sleepserver: A software-only approach for reducing the energy consumption of pcs within enterprise environments. In *USENIX ATC '10*, Jun 2010.

[10] P. Barham, B. Dragovic, K. Fraser, S. Hand, T. Harris, A. Ho, R. Neugebauer, I. Pratt, and A. Warfield. Xen and the art of virtualization. In *SOSP '03*, Oct 2003.

[11] N. Bila, E. de Lara, M. Hiltunen, H. A. L.-C. Kaustubh Joshi, and M. Satyanarayanan. The Case for Energy-Oriented Partial Desktop Migration. In *HotCloud '10*, Jun 2010.

[12] C. Clark, K. Fraser, S. Hand, J. G. Hansen, E. Jul, C. Limpach, I. Pratt, and A. Warfield. Live migration of virtual machines. In *NSDI'05*, May 2005.

[13] T. Das, P. Padala, V. N. Padmanabhan, R. Ramjee, and K. G. Shin. LiteGreen: Saving energy in networked desktops using virtualization. In *2010 USENIX ATC*, Jun 2010.

[14] F. R. Dogar, P. Steenkiste, and K. Papagiannaki. Catnap: Exploiting high bandwidth wireless interfaces to save energy for mobile devices. In *MobiSys 2010*, Jun 2010.

[15] K. Fogarty. The year of the virtual desktop fails to materialize–again. http://www.cio.com/article/691303/The_Year_of_the_Virtual_Desktop_Fails_to_Materialize_Again, Oct 2011.

[16] C. Gunaratne, K. Christensen, and B. Nordman. Managing energy consumption costs in desktop pcs and lan switches with proxying, split tcp connections, and scaling of link speed. *IJNM*, 15(5):297–310, Sep 2005.

[17] M. R. Hines, U. Deshpande, and K. Gopalan. Post-copy live migration of virtual machines. In *VEE 2009*, Mar 2009.

[18] H. A. Lagar-Cavilla, J. A. Whitney, A. M. Scannell, P. Patchin, S. M. Rumble, E. de Lara, M. Brudno, and M. Satyanarayanan. Snowflock: rapid virtual machine cloning for cloud computing. In *EuroSys '09*, Mar 2009.

[19] S. Nedevschi, J. Chandrashekar, J. Liu, B. Nordman, S. Ratnasamy, and N. Taf. Skilled in the art of being idle: Reducing energy waste in networked systems. In *NSDI '09*, Apr 2009.

[20] T. Richardson, Q. Stafford-Fraser, K. Wood, and A. Hopper. Virtual Network Computing. *IEEE Internet Computing*, 2(1), Jan/Feb. 1998.

[21] E. Shih, P. Bahl, and M. J. Sinclair. Wake on wireless: An event driven energy saving strategy for battery operated devices. In *MobiCom 2002*, Sep 2002.

[22] J. Sorber, N. Banerjee, M. D. Corner, and S. Rollins. Turducken: Hierarchical power management for mobile devices. In *MobiSys '05*, Jun 2005.

[23] C. A. Waldspurger. Memory Resource Management in VMWare ESX Server. In *OSDI '02*, Dec 2002.

[24] A. Warfield, S. Hand, K. Fraser, and T. Deegan. Facilitating the development of soft devices. In *USENIX ATC '05*, Jun 2005.

[25] C. A. Webber, J. A. Robertson, M. C. McWhinney, R. E. Brown, M. J. Pinckard, and J. F. Busch. After-hours power status of office equipment in the usa. *Energy*, 31(14):2487–2502, Nov 2006.

[26] E. J. Wright, E. de Lara, and A. Goel. Vision: The case for context-aware selective resume. In *MCS 2011*, Jun 2011.

Practical TDMA for Datacenter Ethernet

Bhanu C. Vattikonda, George Porter, Amin Vahdat, Alex C. Snoeren

Department of Computer Science and Engineering
University of California, San Diego
{bvattikonda, gmporter, vahdat, snoeren}@cs.ucsd.edu

Abstract

Cloud computing is placing increasingly stringent demands on datacenter networks. Applications like MapReduce and Hadoop demand high bisection bandwidth to support their all-to-all shuffle communication phases. Conversely, Web services often rely on deep chains of relatively lightweight RPCs. While HPC vendors market niche hardware solutions, current approaches to providing high-bandwidth and low-latency communication in the datacenter exhibit significant inefficiencies on commodity Ethernet hardware.

We propose addressing these challenges by leveraging the tightly coupled nature of the datacenter environment to apply time-division multiple access (TDMA). We design and implement a TDMA MAC layer for commodity Ethernet hardware that allows end hosts to dispense with TCP's reliability and congestion control. We evaluate the practicality of our approach and find that TDMA slots as short as 100s of microseconds are possible. We show that partitioning link bandwidth and switch buffer space to flows in a TDMA fashion can result in higher bandwidth for MapReduce shuffle workloads, lower latency for RPC workloads in the presence of background traffic, and more efficient operation in highly dynamic and hybrid optical/electrical networks.

Categories and Subject Descriptors C.2.1 [*Computer-Communication Networks*]: Network Architecture and Design—Network communications.

General Terms Performance, Measurement, Experimentation.

Keywords Datacenter, TDMA, Ethernet.

1. Introduction

The size, scale, and ubiquity of datacenter applications are growing at a rapid pace, placing increasingly stringent demands on the underlying network layer. Datacenter networks have unique requirements and characteristics compared to wide-area or enterprise environments: Today's datacenter network architects must balance applications' demands for low one-way latencies (sometimes measured in 10s of microseconds or less), high bandwidth utilization—i.e., 10 Gbps at the top-of-rack switch and increasingly in end hosts—and congestion-free operation to avoid unanticipated queuing delays. This goal is complicated by the dynamic nature of the traffic patterns and even topology within some datacenters. A flow's path, and the available bandwidth along that path, can change on very fine timescales [4].

The applications that must be supported in datacenter environments can have drastically varying requirements. On one hand, data-intensive scalable computing (DISC) systems like MapReduce [9], Hadoop, and TritonSort [21] can place significant demands on a network's capacity. DISC deployments are often bottlenecked by their all-to-all shuffle phases, in which large amounts of state must be transferred from each node to every other node. On the other hand, modern Web services are increasingly structured as a set of hierarchical components that must pass a series of small, inter-dependent RPCs between them in order to construct a response to incoming requests [18]. The overall throughput of these so-called Partition/Aggregate workloads [2] is frequently gated by the latency of the slowest constituent RPC. Similarly, structured stores like BigTable [6] or their front-ends (e.g., Memcached) require highly parallel access to a large number of content nodes to persist state across a number of machines, or to reconstruct state that is distributed through the datacenter. In these latter cases, low-latency access between clients and their servers is critical for good application performance.

While hardware vendors have long offered boutique link layers to address extreme application demands, the cost advantages of Ethernet continue to win out in the vast majority of deployments. Moreover, Ethernet is increasingly capable, pushing toward 40- and even 100-Gbps link bandwidths. Switch vendors have also begun to offer lower-latency switches supporting cut-through forwarding along a single network hop. Recent proposals for datacenter design have suggested leveraging this increasing hardware performance—even including optical interconnects—through fine-grained, dynamic path selection [10, 26]. In these environments, TCP transport becomes a major barrier to low-latency, high-throughput intercommunication. Indeed, Facebook reportedly eschews TCP in favor of a custom UDP transport layer [22], and the RAMCloud prototype dispenses with Ethernet entirely (in favor of Infiniband) due to its poor end-to-end latency [16].

We argue that these datacenter communication patterns look less like the traditional wide-area workloads TCP was designed to handle, and instead resemble a much more tightly coupled communication network: the back-plane of a large supercomputer. We seek to provide support for high-bandwidth and low latency—specifically all-to-all bulk transfers and scatter-gather type RPCs—in this much more controlled environment, where one can forego the distributed nature of TCP's control loop. In order to dispense with TCP, however, one must either replace its reliability and congestion control functionality, or remove the need for it. Here, we seek to eliminate the potential for congestion, and, therefore, queuing delay and packet loss. To do so, we impose a time-division multiple access (TDMA) MAC layer on a commodity Ethernet network that ensures end hosts have exclusive access to the path they are assigned at any point in time.

In our approach, we deploy a logically centralized link scheduler that allocates links exclusively to individual sender-receiver pairs on a time-shared basis. In this way, link bandwidth and switch buffer space is exclusively assigned to a particular flow, ensuring that in-network queuing and congestion is minimized or, ideally, eliminated. As such, our approach is a good fit for cut-through switching fabrics, which only work with minimal buffering, as well as future generations of hybrid datacenter optical circuit switches [10, 24, 26] which have no buffering. Our technique works with commodity Ethernet NICs and switching hardware. It does not require modifications to the network switches, and only modest software changes to end hosts. Because we do not require time synchronization among the end hosts, our design has the potential to scale across multiple racks and even entire datacenters. Instead, our centralized controller explicitly schedules end host NIC transmissions through the standardized IEEE 802.3x and 802.1Qbb protocols. A small change to these protocols could allow our approach to scale to an even larger number of end hosts.

In this paper, we evaluate the practicality of implementing TDMA on commodity datacenter hardware. The contributions of our work include 1) a TDMA-based Ethernet MAC protocol that ensures fine-grained and exclusive access to links and buffers along datacenter network paths, 2) a

reduction in the completion times of bulk all-to-all transfers by approximately 15% compared to TCP, 3) a 3× reduction in latency for RPC-like traffic, and 4) increased TCP throughput in dynamic network and traffic environments.

2. Related work

We are far from the first to suggest providing stronger guarantees on Ethernet. There have been a variety of proposals to adapt Ethernet for use in industrial automation as a replacement for traditional fieldbus technologies. These efforts are far too vast to survey here[1]; we simply observe that they are driven by the need to provide real-time guarantees and expect to be deployed in tightly time-synchronized environments that employ real-time operating systems. For example, FTT-Ethernet [19] and RTL-TEP [1] both extend real-time operating systems to build TDMA schedules in an Ethernet environment. RTL-TEP further leverages time-triggered Ethernet (TT-Ethernet), a protocol that has gone through a variety of incarnations. Modern implementations of both TT-Ethernet [13] and FTT-Ethernet [23] require modified switching hardware. In contrast to these real-time Ethernet (RTE) proposals, we do not require the use of real-time operating systems or modified hardware, nor do we presume tight time synchronization.

The IETF developed Integrated Services [5] to provide guaranteed bandwidth to individual flows, as well as controlled load for queue-sensitive applications. IntServ relies on a per-connection, end-host-originated reservation packet, or RSVP packet [30], to signal end-host requirements, and support from the switches to manage their buffers accordingly. Our work differs in that end hosts signal their demand and receive buffer capacity to a logically centralized controller, which explicitly schedules end-host NICs on a per-flow basis, leaving the network switches unmodified.

Our observation that the traffic patterns seen in datacenter networks differ greatly from wide-area traffic is well known, and many researchers have attempted to improve TCP to better support this new environment. One problem that has received a great deal of attention is incast. Incast occurs when switch buffers overflow in time-spans too quick for TCP to react to, and several proposals have been made to avoid incast [2, 7, 20, 25, 28]. TDMA, on the other hand, can be used to address a spectrum of potentially complimentary issues. In particular, end hosts might still choose to employ a modified TCP during their assigned time slots. While we have not yet explored these enhanced TCPs, we show in Section 6.4 that our TDMA layer can improve the performance of regular TCP in certain, non-incast scenarios.

One limitation of a TDMA MAC is that the benefits can only be enjoyed when all of the end hosts respect the schedule. Hence, datacenter operators may not want to deploy

---

[1] http://www.real-time-ethernet.de/ provides a nice compendium of many of them.

TDMA network-wide. Several proposals have been made for ways of carving up the network into different virtual networks, each with their own properties, protocols, and behaviors. Notable examples of this approach to partitioning include VINI [3], OpenFlow [17], and Onix [14]. Webb *et al.* [27] introduce topology switching to allow applications to deploy individual routing tasks at small time scales. This work complements ours, as it enables datacenter operators to employ TDMA on only a portion of their network.

3. Motivation and challenges

A primary contribution of this work is evaluating the feasibility of deploying a TDMA MAC layer over commodity Ethernet switches and end hosts. In this section we describe how a TDMA MAC layer could improve the performance of applications in today's datacenters and leverage future technologies like hybrid packet-circuit switched networks.

3.1 Motivation

The TCP transport protocol has adapted to decades of changes in underlying network technologies, from wide-area fiber optics, to satellite links, to the mobile Web, and to consumer broadband. However, in certain environments, such as sensor networks, alternative transports have emerged to better suit the particular characteristics of these networks. Already the datacenter is becoming such a network.

3.1.1 Supporting high-performance applications

TCP was initially applied to problems of moving data from one network to another, connecting clients to servers, or in some cases servers to each other. Contrast that with MapReduce and Hadoop deployments [29] and Memcached installations (e.g., at Facebook), which provide a datacenter-wide distributed memory for multiple applications. The traffic patterns of these distributed applications look less like traditional TCP traffic, and increasingly resemble a much more tightly coupled communication network. Recent experiences with the incast problem show that the parallel nature of scatter-gather type problems (e.g., distributed search index queries), leads to packet loss in the network. [2, 7, 20, 25, 28] When a single query is farmed out to a large set of servers, which all respond within a short time period (often within microseconds of each other), those packets overflow in-network switch buffers before TCP can detect and respond to this temporary congestion. Here a more proactive, rather than reactive, approach to managing in-network switch buffers and end hosts would alleviate this problem.

One critical aspect of gather-scatter workloads is that they are typically characterized by a large number of peer nodes. In a large Memcached scenario, parallel requests are sent to each of the server nodes, which return partial results, which the client aggregates together to obtain the final result returned to the user. The latency imposed by these lookups can easily be dominated by the variance of response time seen by the sub-requests. So while a service might be built for an average response time of 10 milliseconds, if half of the requests finish in 5 ms, and the other half finish in 15 ms, the net result is a 15-ms response time.

3.1.2 Supporting dynamic network topologies

Datacenters increasingly employ new and custom topologies to support dynamic traffic patterns. We see the adoption of several new technologies as a challenge for current transport protocols. As bandwidth requirements increase, relying on multiple network paths has become a common way of increasing network capacity. Commodity switches now support hashing traffic at a flow-level across multiple parallel data paths. A key way to provide network operators with more flexibility in allocating traffic to links is supporting finer-grained allocation of flows to links. This promises to improve link (and network) utilization. At the same time, a single TCP connection migrating from one link to another might experience a rapidly changing set of network conditions.

The demand for fine-grained control led to the development of software-defined network controllers, including OpenFlow [17]. Through OpenFlow, novel network designs can be built within a logically centralized network controller, leaving data path forwarding to the switches and routers spread throughout the network. As the latency for reconfiguring the network controller shrinks, network paths might be reconfigured on very small timescales. This will pose a challenge to TCP, since its round-trip time and available throughput estimates might change due to policy changes in the network, rather than just due to physical link failures and other more infrequent events.

Another scenario in which flow paths change rapidly arises due to network designs that propose to include optical circuit switches within datacenters. The advantages of optical switches include lower energy, lower price and lower cabling complexity as compared to electrical options. These benefits currently come at the cost of higher switching times, but they are rapidly decreasing. Technologies as DLP-based wavelength selective switches can be reconfigured in 10s to 100s of microseconds [15], at which point it will no longer be possible to choose circuit configurations by reacting to network observations [4]. Instead, the set of switch configurations will have to be programmed in advance for a period of time. In this model, if the end hosts and/or switches can be informed of the switch schedule, they can coordinate the transmission of packets to make use of the circuit when it becomes available to them. Our TDMA mechanism would naturally enable this type of microsecond-granularity interconnect architecture.

3.2 Challenges

As a starting point, we assume that a datacenter operator either deploys TDMA throughout their entire network, or that they rely on OpenFlow or some other isolation technology to carve out a portion of their network to devote to TDMA. Within the portion of the network dedicated to TDMA, we rely upon a centralized controller to compute and distribute a schedule that specifies an assignment of slots to individual end hosts. Each slot represents permission for a host to send to a particular destination: when a host is assigned to a slot, it can communicate with that destination at full link capacity and be guaranteed not to experience any cross traffic, either on the links or at the switches.

The feasibility of our proposed approach depends on how effectively one can schedule Ethernet transmissions. Clearly the overhead of per-packet polling is too high, so end hosts must be in charge of scheduling individual packet transmissions. It is an open question, however, what else should be managed by the end hosts, versus what can— or needs to be—controlled in a centralized fashion. The answer depends upon the following features of commodity hardware:

1. The (in)ability of end-host clocks to stay synchronized;

2. The effectiveness with which an external entity can signal end hosts to begin or cease transmitting or, alternatively, the precision with which end hosts can keep time; and

3. The variability in packet propagation times as they traverse the network, including multiple switches.

Here, we set out to answer these questions empirically by evaluating the behavior of Ethernet devices in our testbed. (Results with other Ethernet NICs from different manufacturers are similar.) The results show that end-host clocks very quickly go out of sync; hence, we cannot rely entirely on end hosts to schedule Ethernet transmissions. On the other hand, we find that existing Ethernet signaling mechanisms provide an effective means for a centralized fabric manager to control end hosts' Ethernet transmissions in order to enforce a TDMA schedule.

3.2.1 End-host clock skew

The most basic of all questions revolves around how time synchronization should be established. In particular, a straightforward approach would synchronize end-host clocks at coarse timescales (e.g., through NTP), and rely upon the end hosts themselves to manage slot timing. In this model, the only centralized task would be to periodically broadcast the schedule of slots; end hosts would send data at the appropriate times.

The feasibility of such an approach hinges on how well different machines' clocks are able to stay in sync. Previous studies in the enterprise and wide area have found significant inter-host skew [8, 12], but one might conjecture that the shared power and thermal context of a datacenter reduces the sources of variance. We measure the drift between machines in our testbed (described in Section 6) by having the nodes each send packets to the same destination at pre-determined

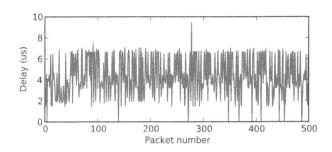

Figure 1. Delay in responding to 802.3x pause frames when transmitting 64-byte packets.

intervals, and examine the differences in arrival times of the subsequent packets. At the beginning of the experiment the destination broadcasts a "sync" packet to all the senders to initialize their clocks to within a few microseconds.

We find that the individual nodes in our testbed rapidly drift apart from each other, and, in as little as 20 seconds, some of the senders are as much as 2 ms out of sync; i.e., in just one second senders can be out of sync by 100 μs. Given that a minimum-sized (64-byte) frame takes only 0.05 μs to transmit at 10 Gbps, it becomes clear that end hosts need to be resynchronized on the order of every few milliseconds to prevent packet collisions. Conversely, it appears possible for end hosts to operate independently for 100s of microseconds without ill effect from clock skew. Hence, we consider a design where an external entity starts and stops transmissions on that timescale, but allows the end hosts to manage individual packet transmissions.

3.2.2 Pause frame handling

Of course, it is difficult for application-level software on today's end hosts to react to network packets in less than a few 10s of microseconds [16], so signaling every 100 μs seems impractical—at least at the application level.

Luckily, the Ethernet specification includes a host of signaling mechanisms that can be leveraged to control the end hosts' access to the Ethernet channel, many offered under the banner of datacenter bridging (DCB) [11]. One of the oldest, the 802.3x flow-control protocol, has long been implemented by Ethernet NICs. 802.3x was originally designed to enable flow control at layer 2: When the receiver detects that it is becoming overloaded, it sends a link-local pause frame to the sender, with a configurable pause time payload. This pause time is a 16-bit value that represents the number of 512-bit times that the sender should pause for, and during that time, no traffic will be sent by the sender. On a 10-Gbps link, a single bit-time is about 51 ns, therefore the maximum pause time that can be expressed is about 3.4 ms.

To understand the granularity with which we can control end-host traffic, we measure how quickly an Ethernet sender responds to 802.3x pause frames. We set up an experiment in which a single sender sends minimum-size (64-byte) packets to a receiver as fast as possible. The receiver periodically

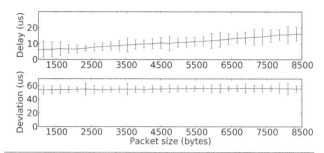

Figure 2. Average delay before pausing and deviation from the requested 3.4-ms interval as a function of the size of packets being sent by sender.

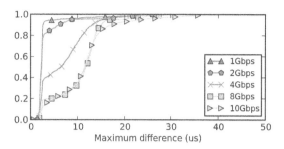

Figure 3. CDF of difference of inter-packet arrival of two pause packets for various host sending rates.

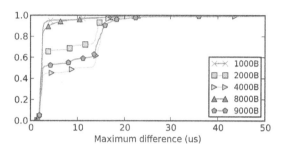

Figure 4. CDF of difference of inter-packet arrival of the control packets for various data packet sizes.

sends pause frames to the sender for the full pause amount (3.4 ms), and we measure the lag between when the pause frame is sent and when the packets stop arriving. As shown in Figure 1, The pause frame mechanism engages quite rapidly in our NICs, generally reacting between 2–6 μs after the frame was transmitted. Of course, the absolute delay is less important than the variance, which is similarly small.

The 802.3x specification requires that a sender defer subsequent transmissions upon receipt of a pause frame, but does not insist that it abort any current frame transmission. Hence, the delay before pausing increases linearly with the packet size at the sender as shown in the top portion of Figure 2. It is not clear, however, how well commodity NICs respect the requested pause time. The bottom portion of Figure 2 shows the average deviation in microseconds from the requested interval (3.4 ms in this experiment). While constant with respect to the sender's packet size (implying the NIC properly accounts for the time spent finishing the transmission), it is significant. Hence, in our design we do not rely on the end host to "time out." Instead, we send a subsequent pause frame to explicitly resume transmission as explained in the next section.

3.2.3 Synchronized pause frame reception

Enforcing TDMA slots with 802.3x pause frames simplifies the design of the end hosts, which can now become entirely reactive. However, such a design hinges on our ability to transmit (receive) pause frames to (at) the end hosts simultaneously. In particular, to prevent end hosts from sending during another's slot, the difference in receive (and processing) time for pause frames must be small across a wide set of nodes. The previous experiments show that the delay variation at an individual host is small (on the order of 5 μs or less), so the remaining question is how tightly can one synchronize the delivery of pause frames to a large number of end hosts.

Because our end host clocks are not synchronized with enough precision to make this measurement directly, we instead indirectly measure the level of synchronization by measuring the difference in arrival times of a pair of control packets at 24 distinct receivers. In this experiment, we con-

nect all the hosts to a single switch and a control host sends control packets serially to all of the other hosts.[2] To simulate the TDMA scenario where these pause packets represent the end of a slot, we have the hosts generate traffic of varying intensity to other end hosts. By comparing the difference in perceived gap between the pair of control packets at each end host, we factor out any systemic propagation delay.

The cumulative distribution function (CDF) of the inter-packet arrival times of the control packets at the end hosts for various packet sizes and sending rates of the traffic being generated are shown in Figures 3 and 4, respectively. The inter-host variation is on the order of 10–15 μs for the vast majority of packet pairs, and rarely more than 20 μs. These values guide our selection of guard times as described in Section 4.

Of course, one might worry that the story changes as the topology gets more complicated. We repeat the experiments with a multi-hop topology consisting of a single root switch and three leaf switches. Hosts are spread across the leaf switches, resulting in a 3-hop path between sets of end hosts. The results are almost indistinguishable from the single-hop case, giving us confidence that we can control a reasonable number of end hosts (at least a few racks' worth) in a centralized fashion—at least when the controller has symmetric connectivity to all end hosts, as would be the case if it was attached to the core of a hierarchical switching

---

[2] While it is not clear that 802.3x pause frames were intended to be forwarded, in our experience switches do so when appropriately addressed.

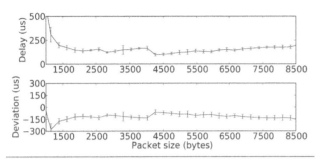

Figure 5. Average delay before pausing and deviation from the requested interval using PFC code as a function of the size of packets being sent.

topology or we attach the controller to each of the leaf switches.

3.2.4 Traffic differentiation

While 802.3x pause frames are supported by most Ethernet cards, they unfortunately pause all traffic on the sender, making them less useful for our purposes, as we wish to selectively pause (and unpause) flows targeting various destinations. For traffic patterns in which a sender concurrently sends to multiple destinations, we require a more expressive pause mechanism that can pause at a flow-level granularity. One candidate within the DCB suite is the 802.1Qbb priority-based flow control (PFC) format, which supports 8 traffic classes. By sending an 802.1Qbb PFC pause frame, arbitrary subsets of these traffic classes can be paused. While 802.1Qbb flow control is supported by a wide range of modern Ethernet products (e.g., Cisco and Juniper equipment), the 10-Gbps NICs in our testbed do not naively support PFC frames. Hence, we implement support in software.

While we have no reason to believe native 802.1Qbb PFC processing will differ substantially from 802.3x pause frame handling when implemented on the NIC, our user-level software implementation is substantially more coarse grained. To lower the latency we rely on the kernel-bypass network interface provided by our Myricom hardware. Figure 5 shows the response time of PFC frames as seen by the application-layer (c.f. the 802.3x performance in Figure 2). Here we see that the average delay in responding to PFC frames is an order of magnitude higher than before, at approximately 100-200 μs for most packet sizes. Fortunately, the variation in this delay remains low. Hence, we can still use a centralized controller to enforce slot times; the end hosts' slots will just systematically lag the controller.

3.2.5 Alternative signaling mechanisms

While our design leverages the performance and pervasiveness of Ethernet Priority Flow Control, there are a variety of other signaling mechanisms that might be employed to control end host transmissions within any given datacenter, some more portable than others. As long as the operating

system or hypervisor can enqueue packets for different destinations into distinct transmit queues (e.g., by employing Linux NetFilter rules that create a queue per IP destination), a NIC could use its own proprietary mechanisms to communicate with the controller to determine when to drain each queue. For example, we are exploring modifying the firmware in our Myricom testbed hardware to generate and respond to a custom pause-frame format which would provide hardware support for a much larger set of traffic classes than 802.11Qbb.

4. Design

We now discuss the design of our proposed TDMA system. Due to the fundamental challenges involved in tightly time-synchronizing end hosts as discussed in Section 3, we choose to centralize the control at a network-wide *fabric manager* that signals the end hosts when it is time for them to send. For their part, end hosts simply send traffic (at line rate) to the indicated (set of) destination(s) when signaled by the controller, and remain quiet at all other times. We do not modify the network switches in any way. The fabric manager is responsible for learning about demand, scheduling flows, and notifying end hosts when and to whom to send data.

At a high-level, the fabric manager leads the network through a sequence of *rounds*, where each round consists of the following logical steps.

1. Hosts communicate their demand to the fabric manager on a per-destination basis.

2. The fabric manager aggregates these individual reports into a network-wide picture of total system demand for the upcoming round.

3. The fabric manager computes a communication pattern for the next round, dividing the round into fixed-size *slots*, during which each link is occupied by non-competing flows (i.e., no link is oversubscribed). We call this assignment of source/destination flows to slots a *schedule*.

4. At the start of a round, the fabric manager informs each of the end hosts of (their portion of) the schedule for the round, and causes them to stop sending traffic, in effect muting the hosts.

5. At the start of each TDMA slot—as determined by the clock at the fabric manager—the fabric manager sends an "unpause" packet to each host that is scheduled to transmit in that slot. This packet encodes the destination of flows that should be transmitted in the slot. At the end of the slot, the fabric manager sends a "pause" packet to the host indicating that it should stop sending packets.

For efficiency reasons, several of these steps are pipelined and run in parallel with previous rounds. We now describe some of the components of our design.

4.1 Demand estimation

In our proposed design, each round consists of a set of fixed-sized slots, each assigned to a sender-destination pair. The optimal size of the slots depends on the aggregate network demand for that round—slots should be as large as possible without leaving any dead time—and the number of slots assigned to each host depends on the demand at each end host. Estimating future demand is obviously a challenging task. An optimal solution would instrument applications to report demand, in much the same way as applications are occasionally annotated with prefetching hints. Such an expectation seems impractical, however.

We seek to simplify the prediction task by keeping round size small, so each end host needs only report demand over a short time period, e.g., 10 ms. At that timescale, our experience shows that it is possible to extract the necessary demand information from the operating system itself rather than the applications—at least for large transfers. For example, demand can be collected by analyzing the size of socket buffers, an approach also employed by other datacenter networking proposals like c-Through [26].

It is much more challenging, however, to estimate the demand for short flows in an application-transparent fashion. If multiple short flows make up part of a larger session, it may be possible to predict demand for the session in aggregate. For cases where demand estimation is fundamentally challenging—namely short flows to unpredictable destinations—it may instead be better to handle them outside of the TDMA process. For example, one might employ a network virtualization technology to reserve some amount of bandwidth for short flows that would not be subject to TDMA. Because short flows require only a small share of the fabric bandwidth, the impact on overall efficiency would be limited. One could then mark the short flows with special tags (QoS bits, VLAN tags, etc.) and handle their forwarding differently. We have not yet implemented such a facility in our prototype.

For TDMA traffic, demand can be signaled out of band, or a (very short) slot can be scheduled in each round to allow the fabric manager to collect demand from each host. Our current prototype uses explicit out of band demand signaling; we defer a more thorough exploration of demand estimation and communication to future work.

4.2 Flow control

Demand estimation is only half the story, however. An important responsibility of a network transport is ensuring that a sender does not overrun a receiver with more data than it can handle. This process is called flow control. Because nodes send traffic to their assigned destinations during the appropriate slot, it is important that those sending hosts are assured that the destinations are prepared to receive that data. In TCP this is done in-band by indicating the size of the receive buffer in ACK packets. However, in our approach we do not presume that there are packets to be sent directly from the receiver to the sender. Instead, we leverage the demand estimation subsystem described above. In particular, demand reports also include the sizes of receive buffers at each end host in addition to send buffers. In this way, the fabric manager has all the information it needs to avoid scheduling slots that would cause the receiver to drop incoming data due to a buffer overflow. While the buffer sizes will vary during the course of a round—resulting in potentially suboptimal scheduling—the schedule will never assign a slot where there is insufficient demand or receive buffer. We limit the potential inefficiency resulting from our periodic buffer updates by keeping the rounds as short as practical.

4.3 Scheduling

In a traditional switched Ethernet network, end hosts opportunistically send data when it becomes available, and indirectly coordinate amongst themselves by probing the properties of the source-destination path to detect contention for resources. For example, TCP uses packet drops and increases in the network round-trip time (resulting from queuing at switches) as indications of congestion. The collection of end hosts then attempt to coordinate to arrive at an efficient allocation of network resources. In our centralized model, the scheduler has all the information it needs to compute an optimal schedule. What aspects it should optimize for—e.g., throughput, fairness, latency, etc.—depends greatly on the requirements of the applications being supported. Indeed, we expect that a real deployment would likely seek to optimize for different metrics as circumstances vary.

Hence, we do not advocate for a particular scheduling algorithm in this work; we limit our focus to making it practical to carry out a given TDMA schedule on commodity Ethernet. Our initial design computes weighted round-robin schedules, where each host is assigned a slot in a fixed order before being assigned a new slot in the round. The delay between slots for any particular sender is therefore bounded.

A particular challenge occurs when multiple senders have data to send to the same destination, but none of them have sufficient data to fill an entire slot themselves. Alternatives include using a smaller slot size, or combining multiple senders in one slot. Slot sizes are bounded below by practical constraints. Due to the bursty nature of (even paced) transmissions on commodity NICs, however, combining multiple senders into one slot can potentially oversubscribe links at small timescales, which requires buffering at the switch. Again, we defer this complexity to future work and focus on schedules that assign slots exclusively to individual senders.

This issue becomes even more complex in networks with mixed host link rates, such as those with some hosts that have gigabit Ethernet NICs and others with 10-Gbps NICs. In such a network, a fixed-size slot assigned to a 10-Gbps transmitter will exceed the capacity of a 1-Gbps receiver to receive traffic in the same slot. One alternative is to share the slot at the transmitter among destinations (for example, ten

1-Gbps receivers). Another is to buffer traffic at the switch. We could leverage our flow control mechanism to ensure a switch was prepared to buffer a slot's worth of traffic at 10 Gbps for an outgoing port, and then schedule that port to drain the queue for the next 9 slots. We have not yet incorporated either of these possibilities into our prototype.

4.4 Scale

Perhaps the most daunting challenge facing a centralized design comes from the need to ensure that pause packets from the controller arrive in close proximity at the nodes, especially when the network can have an arbitrary topology. In the ideal case, the fabric manager is connected to the same switch as the hosts it controls, but such a topology obviously constrains the size of the deployment to the number of hosts that can be connected to a single switch. While that suffices for, say, a single rack, multi-rack deployments would likely require the system to function with end hosts that are connected to disparate switches.

While the function of the scheduler is logically centralized, the actual implementation can of course be physically distributed. Hence, one approach is to send pause frames not from one fabric manager, but instead from multiple slave controllers that are located close to the end hosts they control, but are themselves synchronized through additional means such as GPS-enabled NICs.

We have not yet implemented such a hierarchical design in our prototype. Instead, we scale by employing a single physical controller with multiple NICs that are connected directly to distinct edge switches. Using separate threads to send pause frames from each NIC attached to the controller, we control hosts connected to each edge switch in a manner which resembles separate slave controllers with synchronized clocks. So far, we have tested up to 24 hosts per switch; using our current topology and 8 NICs in a single, centralized controller, the approach would scale to 384 hosts. Multiple such controllers which have hardware synchronize clocks would need to be deployed to achieve scalability to thousands of end hosts. So long as each switch is at the same distance to the end hosts being controlled, this approach can work for arbitrary topologies.

In a large-scale installation, these two techniques can be combined. I.e., multiple physical controllers can coordinate to drive a large number of hosts, where each controller is directly connected to multiple switches. The scale of this approach is bounded by the number of NICs a controller can hold, the number of ports on each switch, and the ability to tightly time synchronize each slave controller—although the latter is easily done by connecting all the slave controllers to a control switch and triggering the transmission of pause frames using a link-layer broadcast frame.

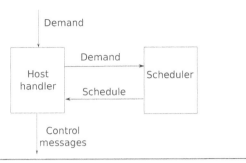

Figure 6. The main components of the fabric manager

5. Implementation

Our prototype implementation consists of a centralized, multi-core fabric manager that communicates with application-level TDMA agents at the end hosts that monitor and communicate demand as well as schedule transmission. Slots are coordinated through 802.1Qbb PFC pause frames.

5.1 PFC message format

Unlike the original use case for Ethernet PFC, our system does not use these frames to pause individual flows, but rather the converse: we pause all flows except the one(s) that are assigned to a particular slot. Unfortunately, the priority flow control format currently being defined in the IEEE 802.1Qbb group allows for only 8 different classes of flows. To support our TDMA-based scheduling, one has to either classify all the flows from a host into these 8 classes or perform dynamic re-mapping of flows to classes within a round. While either solution is workable, in the interest of expediency (since we implement PFC support in software anyway) we simply extend the PFC format to support a larger number of classes.

In our experiments that use fewer than 8 hosts, we use the unmodified frame format; for larger deployments we modify the PFC format to support a 11-bit class field, rather than the 3-bit field dictated by the 802.1Qbb specification. We remark, however, that since the PFC frames are only acted upon by their destination, the fabric manager can reuse PFC classes across different nodes, as long as those classes are not reused on the same link. Thus, the pause frame does not need enough classes to support all the flows in the datacenter, but rather only the flows on a single link.

5.2 Fabric manager

The fabric manager has two components as shown in Figure 6. One component is the Host Handler and other component is Scheduler. All the tasks of interacting with the hosts are done by the host handler while the actual scheduling is done by the Scheduler component. The Scheduler is a pluggable module depending on the underlying network topology and the desired scheduling algorithm.

The fabric manager needs to be aware of both the sending demand from each end host to calculate slot assignments, as well as the receiving capacity to support flow control. The role of the Host Handler is to receive the above mentioned demand and capacity information from the end hosts and share it with the Scheduler. End hosts send their demand to the Host Handler out-of-band in our implementation, and that demand is used by the Scheduler for the next round of slot assignments. The slot assignments are sent back to the end hosts by the Host Handler. During each round the Host Handler sends extended PFC packet frames to each of the end hosts to instigate the start and stop of each TDMA slot.

5.2.1 Host Handler

The Host Handler is implemented in two threads, each pinned to their own core so as to reduce processing latency. The first thread handles receiving demand and capacity information from the hosts, and the second is responsible for sending control packets to the end hosts. The actual demand analysis is performed by the scheduler, described next.

Once the new schedule is available, a control thread sends the pause frames to the end hosts to control the destination to which each host sends data. The control packet destined for each host specifies the class of traffic which the host can send (the unpaused class). In our testbed, the fabric manager is connected to each edge switch to reduce the variance in sending the PFC packet frames to the end hosts. When the pause frames are scheduled to be sent to the end hosts, the controller sends the pause frames to the end hosts one after the other. The pause frames are sent to all the hosts under a switch before moving on to the next switch. The order of the switches and the order of hosts under a switch changes in a round robin fashion.

5.2.2 Scheduler

The scheduler identifies the flows that are going to be scheduled in each slot. It does this with the goal of achieving high overall bandwidth and fairness among hosts with the constraint that no two source-destination flows use the same link at the same time. This ensures that each sender has unrestricted access to its own network path for the duration of the slot. The scheduler updates the demand state information whenever it receives demand information from the Host Handler and periodically computes the schedule and forwards it back to the Host Handler. The scheduler is pluggable, supporting different implementations. It is invoked for each round, parameterized with the current demand and capacity information obtained during the previous set of rounds.

In our implementation we employ a round-robin scheduler that leverages some simplifying assumptions about common network topologies (namely that they are trees) in order to compute the schedule for the next round during the current round. The computational complexity of this task scales as a function of both the size of the network and the communication pattern between the hosts. At some point, the time required to collect demand and compute the

next schedule may become a limiting factor for round size. Developing a scheduler that can compute a schedule for arbitrary topologies in an efficient manner remains an open problem.

5.3 End hosts

As discussed previously, the NICs in our experimental testbed do not naively support PFC, and thus we handle these control packets at user-level. We rely on a kernel-bypass, user-level NIC firmware to reduce latency on processing PFC packets by eliminating the kernel overhead. We are able to read packets off the wire and process them in user space in about 5 μs.

5.3.1 End-host controller

We separate the implementation of the controller into distinct processes for control, sending and receiving. This is based on our observation that the responsiveness of the control system to control packets has greater variance if the sending and receiving is done in the same process using separate threads. This was true even if we pinned the threads to separate cores. Thus, our implementation has the separate processes implementing our service communicate through shared memory. The control packets arriving at the end hosts specify which class of traffic (e.g., source-destination pair) should be sent during a slot. Hosts receive the flow-to-priority class mapping out of band. The control process handles the PFC message and informs the sending process of the destination to which data can be sent.

5.3.2 Sender and receiver

The sending process sends data to the appropriate destination during the assigned slot. If this host is not scheduled in a particular slot then the sending process remains quiescent. To simplify sending applications, we present an API similar to TCP in that it copies data from the application into a send buffer. This buffer is drained when the sending process gets a slot assignment and sent to the destination as raw Ethernet frames. We use indexed queues so that performing these data transfers are constant-time operations. The receiving process receives the incoming data and copies the data into receive buffers. The application then reads the data from the receive buffer pool through a corresponding API. As before, these are constant time operations.

5.4 Guard times

As detailed in Section 3.2, end host timing and pause frame processing is far from perfect. Moreover, at high overall network utilization, small variances in packet arrival times can cause some in-network switch buffering, resulting in inband control packets getting delayed, which further reduces the precision of our signaling protocol. We mitigate this phenomenon by introducing guard times between slots. These are "safety buffers" that ensure that small discrepancies in synchronization do not cause slot boundaries to be violated.

We have empirically determined (based largely on the experiments in Section 3.2) on our testbed hardware that that a guard time of 15 μs is sufficient to separate slots. This guard time is independent of the slot time and depends on the variance in the control packet processing time at the hosts and the in-network buffer lengths. The cost of the guard time is of course best amortized by introducing large slot times; however, there is a trade-off between the slot time and how well dynamic traffic changes are supported.

We implement guard times by first sending a pause frame to stop all the flows in the network followed 15 μs later by the PFC packet frame that unpauses the appropriate traffic class at each host for the next slot. The 15-μs pause in the system is enough to absorb variances in end host transmission timing and drain any in-network buffers; hence, our PFC frames reach the hosts with greater precision.

6. Evaluation

We now evaluate our TDMA-based system in several scenarios on a modest-sized testbed consisting of quad-core Xeon servers running Linux 2.6.32.8 outfitted with two 10GE Myricom NICs. The hosts are connected together using Cisco Nexus 5000 series switches in varying topologies as described below. In summary, our prototype TDMA scheme 1) achieves about 15% shorter finish times than TCP for all-to-all transfers in different topologies, 2) can achieve 3× lower RTTs for small flows (e.g., Partition/Aggregate workloads) in the presence of long data transfers, 3) achieves higher throughput for transfer patterns where lack of coordination between the flows dramatically hurts TCP performance, and 4) can improve TCP performance in rapidly changing network topologies.

6.1 All-to-all transfer

First, we consider the time it takes to do an all-to-all transfer (i.e., the MapReduce shuffle) in different topologies. Due do the lack of coordination between TCP flows without TDMA, some flows finish ahead of others. This can be problematic in situations when progress cannot be made until all the transfers are complete.

6.1.1 Non-blocking topology

In our first all-to-all transfer experiment, we connect 24 hosts to the same switch and transfer 10 GB to each other. Ideally, such a transfer would finish in 184 seconds. The top portion of Figure 7 shows the performance of a TCP all-to-all transfer in this set up. The figure plots the progress of each flow with time. We see that some flows finish early at the expense of other flows, and, hence, the overall transfer takes substantially more time than necessary, completing in 225 seconds.

Contrast that with bottom portion of Figure 7, which similarly plots the progress of the hosts while running our TDMA prototype. Due to the limitation of our end

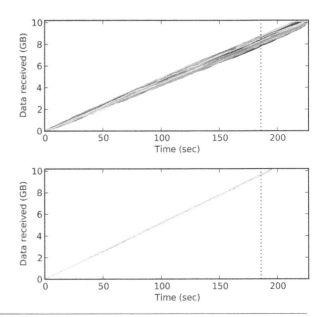

Figure 7. 10-GB all-to-all transfer between 24 hosts connected to the same switch. TCP over regular Ethernet takes $225s$ (top) to finish while the TDMA based system takes $194s$ to finish (bottom).

host networking stack, we do not use a TCP stack in our experiments. Instead, raw Ethernet frames are transferred between the end hosts. The TDMA system employs an empirically chosen slot time of 300 μs (and guard times of 15μs). The finish time of the overall transfer of the same size, 194 seconds, is about 15% better than the corresponding TCP finish time and only 5% slower than ideal (due almost entirely to the guard band). The better finish time is achieved by ensuring that the flows are well coordinated and finish at the same time effectively using the available bandwidth.

6.1.2 Multi-hop topology

The non-blocking case is admittedly fairly trivial. Here, we consider spreading the 24 hosts across three separate switches (8 hosts per switch) and connect these three switches to a fourth aggregation switch. We implement this topology with two physical switches by using VLANs to create logical switches. We then perform the same set of experiments as before. The top and bottom portions of Figure 8 show the results for TCP and TDMA, respectively. The finish times are 1225 seconds for TCP and 1075 seconds for TDMA, compared to the optimal completion time of 1024 seconds. As we describe in Section 4.4 the controller has 3 NICs each of which is connected directly to the edge switches. This configuration allows us to send pause frames to the end hosts with the same precision that we achieve in the non-blocking scenario. We use the same TDMA slot settings as described previously, but our scheduler takes advantage of the higher bandwidth between two hosts on the same switch. Thus, the flows between hosts in the same

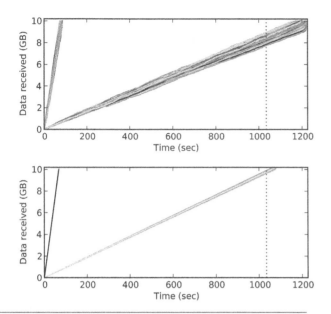

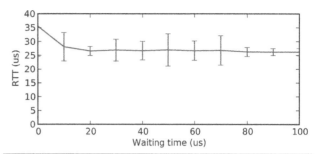

Figure 10. RTT between two hosts as a function of the time in the round when the ping is sent

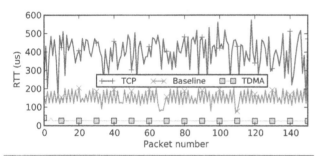

Figure 8. 10-GB all-to-all transfer between 24 hosts in a tree topology. TCP over regular Ethernet takes 1225s (top) to finish while the TDMA based system takes 1075s to finish (bottom).

Figure 9. Hosts in the TDMA system have a 3x lower RTT than hosts in the presence of other TCP flows

switch finish earlier than the flows that go across switches, just as with TCP.

6.2 Managing delay

In a TDMA based system, the send times of hosts are controlled by a central manager. But, when the hosts get to send data they have unrestricted access to the network. This should mean that when a host has access to the channel it should experience very low latency to the destination host even in the presence of other large flows (that are assigned other slots). On the other hand, in a typical datacenter environment, TCP flows occupy the buffers in the switches increasing the latency for short flows—a key challenge facing applications that use the Partition/Aggregate model and require dependably low latency.

To illustrate this, we show that in the presence of long-lived TCP flows the RTT between hosts increases. We use the same 24-node, four-switch tree topology as before. We call the hosts connected to each of the edge switches a *pod*. A host each in pod 0 and pod 2 sends a long-lived TCP flow to a host in pod 1. While these flows are present we send a UDP-based ping from a host in pod 0 to a different host in pod 1. The host which receives the ping immediately responds and we measure the RTT between the hosts. This RTT is shown with the TCP line in Figure 9. As expected, the RTT is high and variable due to the queue occupancy at the switch caused by the TCP cross traffic.

In contrast, in our TDMA-based system (where neither UDP nor TCP is employed) the switch buffers are empty during the slots assigned to the ping traffic resulting in a stable, low RTT. Since the host sending ping gets access to the channel for the entire slot, it can choose to send the ping at any time during the slot. Depending on when the ping is sent, it provides more time for the few buffers still in the switch to be emptied and hence achieve lower RTT. We show this in Figure 10. While we do not show it here due to lack of space, the average of 26 μs compares favorably with the RTT measurement in the absence of any traffic.

The reduced RTT is due to two factors, 1) usage of low-level kernel bypass at the end hosts and 2) near-zero buffer occupancy in the switches. To separate the two effects—as the former does not require TDMA—we measure RTT between the hosts in the testbed using UDP-based ping in the absence of other traffic and plot this as "baseline" in Figure 9. This shows that the TDMA system would achieve a 95th percentile RTT of 170 μs even without the kernel bypass, which is still over a 3× reduction.

The overhead of the TDMA approach is that when sending a ping, the hosts transmitting bulk data have to be de-scheduled and, hence, the long-lived flows could take longer to finish depending on the choice of schedule. For this experiment, we send a ping packet once every 30 ms, that is, once every 100 TDMA slots. Thus, we see about a 1% hit in the transfer time of the large flows.

6.3 Traffic oscillation

The lack of coordination amongst TCP flows can have a large impact on the performance of a network. To illustrate this we run an experiment in which each host sends a fixed-

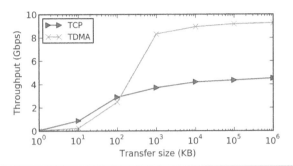

Figure 11. Throughput of the TCP system and TDMA system for round robin transfers with varying unit transfer size

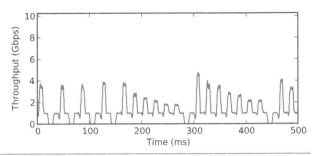

Figure 12. Bandwidth seen by the receiver in case of regular TCP adapting to changing link capacities.

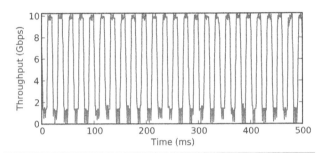

Figure 13. Bandwidth seen by the receiver when the TCP flow is controlled by TDMA.

sized block of data to a neighbor and once that transfer is finished, it moves on to the next neighbor. In the end we measure the average throughput achieved at each host. In a non-blocking scenario, if the hosts are perfectly synchronized then they should be able to communicate at link speed because at any point of time a link is used by a single flow.

Figure 11 shows that this is not the case with TCP regardless of block size. TCP achieves a best performance of about 4.5 Gbps on links which have 10 Gbps capacity. The TDMA-based system on the other hand can control the access to the links in a fine-grained manner and achieve higher throughput. The performance of our TDMA system begins to suffer as the unit transfer size desired is smaller than the amount of data that can be transferred in a TDMA slot (at 10 Gbps a 300-μs slot can accommodate 375 KB of data).

6.4 Dynamic network configurations

TCP is fundamentally reactive and takes a few RTTs to adapt to changes in the network. This can lead to very inefficient performance in scenarios where the link bandwidth fluctuates rapidly. A TDMA-based system, on the other, can avoid this through explicit scheduling. Here we evaluate the potential benefits of employing our TDMA *underneath* TCP in these environments using our pause-frame approach.

We emulate an extreme version of the optical/electrical link flapping scenario found in Helios [10] and c-through [26] by transferring data between two end hosts while a host between them acts as a switch. The host in the middle has two NICs, one connected to each of the other hosts. It forwards the packets that it receives on one NIC out the other NIC. We use the Myricom sniffer API which lets us receive the packet with very low latency in user space and send it out at varying rates. We oscillate the forwarding rate (link capacity) between 10 Gbps and 1 Gbps every 10 ms. The choice of oscillation interval is based upon an estimate of the time that TCP would take to adapt to the changing link capacities in the system: The RTT, including application reception and processing, is about 250 μs. Thus, TCP should take about 8 ms to ramp up from 1 Gbps to 10 Gbps.

Figure 12 shows the performance of TCP over regular Ethernet in the above scenario. Every 500μs we plot the average bandwidth seen at the receiver over the preceding 2.5 ms for a period of 500 ms. TCP does not ramp up quickly enough to realize the 10 Gbps bandwidth before being throttled back to 1 Gbps. Moreover, TCP frequently drops to below 1 Gbps due to packet losses during the switch-over.

We can use our TDMA system to vary each end host's access to the channel. When the rate enforced is 10 Gbps the host is scheduled every slot; it is scheduled only $\frac{1}{10}$th of the time when the rate being enforced is 1 Gbps. Figure 13 plots the performance of TCP when such rate limiting is done using 802.3x pause frames. In this the host acting as the switch also functions as the fabric manager, scheduling the TCP flow using 802.3x pause frames.

6.5 Overhead of control traffic

While the precise overhead of control traffic is dependent on the strategy used for demand collection from the end hosts, it is dominated by the pause frames sent by the fabric manager to end hosts–demand is signalled only once per round, but pause frames are sent per slot. We send two pause frames for each TDMA slot to each end host which is about 3 Mbps per host. Half of this traffic (the pause frames that re-enable sending) is sent during the guard slot which means that the effective overhead of control traffic is about 1.5 Mbps or 0.015% of the link capacity.

7. Conclusion and future work

In this work, we propose to adapt an old approach to a new domain by deploying a TDMA-based MAC layer across an Ethernet datacenter network. Our approach, which does not require changes to network switches, relies on using link-layer flow control protocols to explicitly signal end hosts when to send packets. Our initial results show that the reduced in-network queuing and contention for buffer resources result in better performance for all-to-all transfer workloads and lower latency for request-response type workloads. Significant work remains, however, to evaluate how effectively a centralized scheduler can estimate demand and compute efficient slot assignments for real applications on arbitrary topologies. For example, we expect that some workloads–particularly those made up of unpredictable short flows, may be better serviced outside of the TDMA process. Moreover, while our system architecture should, in principle, allow the scheduler to react to switch, node, and link failures, we defer the evaluation of such a system to future work.

Acknowledgments

This work was funded in part by the National Science Foundation through grants CNS-0917339, CNS-0923523, and ERC-0812072. Portions of our experimental testbed were generously donated by Myricom and Cisco. We thank the anonymous reviewers and our shepherd, Jon Crowcroft, for their detailed feedback which helped us significantly improve the paper.

References

[1] J. A. Alegre, J. V. Sala, S. Péres, and J. Vila. RTL-TEP: An Ethernet protocol based on TDMA. In M. L. Chavez, editor, *Fieldbus Systems and Their Applications 2005: Proceedings of the 6th IFAC International Conference*, Nov. 2005.

[2] M. Alizadeh, A. Greenberg, D. A. Maltz, J. Padhye, P. Patel, B. Prabhakar, S. Sengupta, and M. Sridharan. Data center TCP (DCTCP). In *ACM SIGCOMM*, pages 63–74, Aug. 2010.

[3] A. Bavier, N. Feamster, M. Huang, L. Peterson, and J. Rexford. In VINI veritas: realistic and controlled network experimentation. ACM SIGCOMM, pages 3–14, Sept. 2006.

[4] H. H. Bazzaz, M. Tewari, G. Wang, G. Porter, T. S. E. Ng, D. G. Andersen, M. Kaminsky, M. A. Kozuch, and A. Vahdat. Switching the optical divide: Fundamental challenges for hybrid electrical/optical datacenter networks. In *ACM SOCC*, Oct. 2011.

[5] R. Braden, D. Clark, and S. Shenker. Integrated Services in the Internet Architecture: an Overview. RFC 1633, June 1994.

[6] F. Chang, J. Dean, S. Ghemawat, W. C. Hsieh, D. A. Wallach, M. Burrows, T. Chandra, A. Fikes, and R. E. Gruber. Bigtable: A Distributed Storage System for Structured Data. *ACM Trans. Comput. Syst.*, 26:4:1–4:26, June 2008.

[7] Y. Chen, R. Griffith, J. Liu, R. H. Katz, and A. D. Joseph. Understanding TCP incast throughput collapse in datacenter networks. In *WREN*, pages 73–82, 2009.

[8] Y.-C. Cheng, J. Bellardo, P. Benkö, A. C. Snoeren, G. M. Voelker, and S. Savage. Jigsaw: Solving the puzzle of enterprise 802.11 analysis. In *ACM SIGCOMM*, Sept. 2006.

[9] J. Dean and S. Ghemawat. MapReduce: simplified data processing on large clusters. In *USENIX OSDI*, Dec. 2004.

[10] N. Farrington, G. Porter, S. Radhakrishnan, H. H. Bazzaz, V. Subramanya, Y. Fainman, G. Papen, and A. Vahdat. Helios: a hybrid electrical/optical switch architecture for modular data centers. In *ACM SIGCOMM*, pages 339–350, Aug. 2010.

[11] Juniper Networks. Opportunities and challenges with the convergence of data center networks. Technical report, 2011.

[12] T. Kohno, A. Brodio, and kc claffy. Remote Physical Device Fingerprinting. In *Proceedings of the IEEE Symposium and Security and Privacy*, Oakland, CA, May 2005.

[13] H. Kopetz, A. Ademaj, P. Grillinger, and K. Steinhammer. The time-triggered Ethernet (TTE) design. In *IEEE Int'l Symp. on Object-oriented Real-time Distributed Comp.*, May 2005.

[14] T. Koponen, M. Casado, N. Gude, J. Stribling, L. Poutievski, M. Zhu, R. Ramanathan, Y. Iwata, H. Inoue, T. Hama, and S. Shenker. Onix: a distributed control platform for large-scale production networks. USENIX OSDI, Oct. 2010.

[15] Nistica, Inc. http://www.nistica.com/.

[16] D. Ongaro, S. M. Rumble, R. Stutsman, J. Ousterhout, and M. Rosenblum. Fast crash recovery in RAMCloud. In *ACM SOSP*, pages 29–41, Oct. 2012.

[17] OpenFlow. http://www.openflow.org.

[18] J. Ousterhout, P. Agrawal, D. Erickson, C. Kozyrakis, J. Leverich, D. Mazières, S. Mitra, A. Narayanan, G. Parulkar, M. Rosenblum, S. M. Rumble, E. Stratmann, and R. Stutsman. The case for RAMClouds: Scalable high-performance storage entirely in DRAM. *ACM SIGOPS OSR*, 43(4), Dec. 2009.

[19] P. Pedreiras, L. Almeida, and P. Gai. The FTT-Ethernet protocol: Merging flexibility, timeliness and efficiency. In *Euromicro Conference on Real-Time Systems*, June 2002.

[20] A. Phanishayee, E. Krevat, V. Vasudevan, D. G. Andersen, G. R. Ganger, G. A. Gibson, and S. Seshan. Measurement and analysis of TCP throughput collapse in cluster-based storage systems. USENIX FAST, Feb. 2008.

[21] A. Rasmussen, G. Porter, M. Conley, H. V. Madhyastha, R. N. Mysore, A. Pucher, and A. Vahdat. Tritonsort: A balanced large-scale sorting system. In *USENIX NSDI*, Mar. 2011.

[22] J. Rothschild. High performance at massive scale lessons learned at facebook. http://video-jsoe.ucsd.edu/asx/JeffRothschildFacebook.asx, Oct. 2009.

[23] R. Santos, A. Vieira, P. Pedreiras, A. Oliveira, L. Almeida, R. Marau, and T. Nolte. Flexible, efficient and robust real-time communication with server-based Ethernet switching. In *IEEE Workshop on Factory Comm. Systems*, May 2010.

[24] A. Singla, A. Singh, K. Ramachandran, L. Xu, and Y. Zhang. Proteus: a topology malleable data center network. In *ACM HotNets*, Oct. 2010.

[25] V. Vasudevan, A. Phanishayee, H. Shah, E. Krevat, D. G. Andersen, G. R. Ganger, G. A. Gibson, and B. Mueller. Safe and effective fine-grained TCP retransmissions for datacenter

communication. In *ACM SIGCOMM*, pages 303–314, Aug. 2009.

[26] G. Wang, D. G. Andersen, M. Kaminsky, K. Papagiannaki, T. E. Ng, M. Kozuch, and M. Ryan. c-Through: part-time optics in data centers. In *ACM SIGCOMM*, Aug. 2010.

[27] K. Webb, A. C. Snoeren, and K. Yocum. Topology switching for data center networks. In *USENIX Hot-ICE*, Mar. 2011.

[28] H. Wu, Z. Feng, C. Guo, and Y. Zhang. ICTCP: Incast congestion control for TCP in data center networks. In *ACM CoNEXT*, Dec. 2010.

[29] Scaling Hadoop to 4000 nodes at Yahoo! `http://developer.yahoo.net/blogs/hadoop/2008/09/scaling_hadoop_to_4000_nodes_a.html`.

[30] L. Zhang, S. Deering, D. Estrin, S. Shenker, and D. Zappala. RSVP: A new resource reservation protocol. *IEEE Communications*, 40(5):116–127, May 2002.

Scalable Testing of File System Checkers

João Carreira[†§], Rodrigo Rodrigues[†], George Candea[‡], Rupak Majumdar[†]

[†]Max Planck Institute for Software Systems (MPI-SWS),
[§]Instituto Superior Técnico, and [‡]École Polytechnique Fédérale de Lausanne (EPFL)

Abstract

File system checkers (like e2fsck) are critical, complex, and hard to develop, and developers today rely on hand-written tests to exercise this intricate code. Test suites for file system checkers take a lot of effort to develop and require careful reasoning to cover a sufficiently comprehensive set of inputs and recovery mechanisms. We present a tool and methodology for testing file system checkers that reduces the need for a specification of the recovery process and the development of a test suite. Our methodology splits the correctness of the checker into two objectives: consistency and completeness of recovery. For each objective, we leverage either the file system checker code itself or a comparison among the outputs of multiple checkers to extract an implicit specification of correct behavior. Our methodology is embodied in a testing tool called SWIFT, which uses a mix of symbolic and concrete execution; it introduces two new techniques: a specific concretization strategy and a corruption model that leverages test suites of file system checkers. We used SWIFT to test the file system checkers of ext2, ext3, ext4, ReiserFS, and Minix; we found bugs in all checkers, including cases leading to data loss. Additionally, we automatically generated test suites achieving code coverage on par with manually constructed test suites shipped with the checkers.

Categories and Subject Descriptors   D.2.4 [*Software Engineering*]: Software/Program Verification — *reliability, validation*;   D.4.5 [*Operating Systems*]: Reliability — *verification*

Keywords   testing, file system checker, symbolic execution

1. Introduction

Modern storage systems are complex and diverse, and can fail in multiple ways, such as physical failures or software

EuroSys'12,   April 10–13, 2012, Bern, Switzerland.

or firmware bugs [10, 12, 13, 15, 16]. For example, Bairavasundaram et al. have observed $400,000$ instances of checksum mismatches (i.e., instances when reads returned incorrect data) in a period of 41 months, in a set of 1.53 million disks [2]. While many failures manifest as system crashes, the more pernicious bugs in the storage stack can lead to the corruption of file system structures, where there is no immediate observable "crash," but key system invariants are violated, leading to an eventual crash or data loss many operations later.

Owing to the reality of storage failures, developers of file systems ship a recovery tool, known as a file system checker, with each file system. The file system checker is responsible for checking the integrity and consistency of the on-disk data structures of a specific file system and, in case of data corruption, for recovering the disk data to a "consistent" state usable by the file system code.

Although file system checkers are an essential tool, their recovery behaviors are complex, hard to get correct, and hard to test [8, 9]. Developers have to consider potentially every possible corruption, every disk state, and low-level language subtleties. Moreover, the correct behavior of a file system checker is usually poorly specified. While, in principle, one can formulate the file system invariants in a declarative language [9], in practice, the correctness of file system checkers is checked with respect to a test suite provided by the developer, which checks for specific violations of the intended behavior. Developing good test suites requires significant manual effort, yet may still end up testing only a small fraction of the possible behaviors. In particular, there may be bugs in the recovery code for corruption and recovery scenarios that are not tested (and perhaps not envisioned when designing the test suite).

We present an automatic tool-supported methodology for the systematic testing of file system checkers without manual specifications or system invariants or test suites. Our methodology checks for two properties of the checker: *consistency* and *completeness*. Consistency is the property that the output of the checker and the final disk state are coherent, i.e., an indication of success or failure to recover a disk should leave the disk respectively in a consistent or irrecoverable state. Completeness is the property that the checker recovers a maximal amount of information. The key technical problem is that determining the notion of consistent state and complete recovery without explicit specifications of the behavior of the file system and the file system checker is hard. Our methodology addresses this problem based on two insights.

First, even though we do not have explicit invariants, we can use the checking logic in the file system checker as a proxy for correctness. This is because the logic that verifies whether a disk is consistent is simpler and more mature than the recovery logic, and therefore we can use this verification logic to determine whether the outcome of a recovery matches the actions and the degree of success that the recovery reported. To give a simple example, when a first run of the checker returns that the disk has been recovered to a consistent state, we can then use the file system checker's own consistency verification logic to test whether this state is indeed consistent. Thus, we avoid the problem of inferring a specification of consistency by focusing on the *internal* consistency of the checker.

Second, in order to assess the completeness of a checker, we run checkers for different file systems on semantically equivalent file system images and compare results for the same corruption of this state. Different checkers share a common specification for the recovery of file systems. Even though specific on-disk representations of the file system can vary, checkers operate on semantically equivalent data structures and have access to the same information, and so they should be able to perform the same recoveries. Consequently, differences in the recoveries performed by different file system checkers on the same semantic file system under the same corruption scenario are likely due to incompleteness in one of the checkers. Thus, we avoid the problem of inferring a specification of completeness by focusing on *relative* completeness between different checkers.

In summary, both parts of our methodology reduce the problems of checker consistency and checker completeness to the problem of state space exploration of checker *compositions*. In the first case, we compose the same checker sequentially and compare results; in the second case, we compose two or more different checker implementations in parallel and compare results.

We developed SWIFT (Scalable and Wide Fsck Testing), a system that implements the aforementioned methodology and allows developers to test file system checkers. SWIFT uses S^2E [6], a full-system symbolic execution engine for binaries, as a basic path exploration tool to explore the execution of file system checkers under different data corruption instances. SWIFT is able to systematically explore the recovery code of file system checkers and find bugs that are hard to detect with classic testing methodologies.

We used SWIFT to test e2fsck (ext2–4), reiserfsck (ReiserFS) and fsck.minix (Minix). SWIFT found bugs in all three checkers, including cases that lead to loss of data and incorrect recoveries. Additionally, SWIFT achieves code coverage on par with manual tests, but with much less effort.

The rest of the paper is structured as follows: §2 surveys the related work, §3 provides background on symbolic execution and S^2E, §4 presents our methodology for testing file system checkers, §5 describes SWIFT, the system that instantiates this methodology, §6 presents our evaluation of SWIFT, and §7 concludes.

2. Related Work

File System Testers. Model checking and symbolic execution have already been used in the past to systematically test file systems. EXPLODE [17] is a tool for end-to-end testing of real storage stack systems based on enumerative model checking. EXPLODE exhaustively explores all states of a storage system by systematically invoking file system operations, injecting crashes in the system, exploring all choices of a program at specific points, and checking each state against specific properties of the correctness of the system. The developer provides a *checker* program, which is responsible for systematically invoking system specific operations, injecting crashes and checking assertions on the system state. FiSC [19] applies this idea to file systems, and checks disk data against a model describing the data that is expected to be stored. In contrast to SWIFT, these tools are not symbolic, do not explore the recovery behavior of file system checkers, and require a human-provided specification to check the correctness of the code.

Yang et al. proposed a system for testing disk mount mechanisms [18]. During the mount of a disk, file system code must check if the disk data is consistent and if all the invariants of the file system hold. Since these invariants can be complex and depend on a high number of values, mount code is hard to test and exercise. In order to test this code, the authors proposed using symbolic execution to systematically explore the code of the *mount* function of different file systems. As multiple paths are explored, pluggable pieces of code (property checkers) check for specific bugs, such as null pointer accesses. However, bugs that lead to latent file system data or metadata errors may not be caught.

In contrast to all of the above, we focus on testing file system checkers, and we look for problems that manifest in subtle ways, such as latent bugs, without requiring hand-written specifications of correctness properties. This is achieved by looking for inconsistencies that are internal to the checker or incompleteness relative to other checkers.

Leveraging code diversity. The idea of using different implementations of similar systems has been proposed in the context of replicated file systems for tolerating correlated faults [1, 14], and also for verifying the equivalence of coreutils tools [4]. In our work, we leverage this idea to test one aspect of the specification of file system checkers, namely the completeness property.

Corruption model Bairavasundaram et al. proposed *type aware pointer corruption* (TAPC) to explore how file systems react to corrupt block pointers [3]. The proposed methodology consists of creating different instances of block pointer corruptions and observing how the file system behaves in those cases. The systematic introduction of data corruption faces an explosion problem: it is not possible to explore all possible cases of corruption. TAPC addresses this problem by assuming that the behavior of the system being tested only depends on the type of the pointer that has been corrupted and on the type of the block where the pointer points to after corruption. SWIFT makes use of a corruption model, and TAPC could have been used for this purpose. However, we decided to use different models that enable a larger corruption space. Some of the bugs that SWIFT uncovered cannot be found using TAPC.

Declarative Specifications Gunawi et al. have proposed SQCK [9], a file system checker based on a declarative query language. The reason for using a declarative language is that declarative queries are a good match for file system cross-checks and repairs. While this is a promising approach to improve the reliability of file system checkers, it requires rewriting the checker code itself (and moves inconsistency and incompleteness issues to the declarative specification). In contrast, we aim to improve the reliability of the large code base of existing file system checkers.

3. Symbolic Execution and S^2E

SWIFT relies on symbolic execution to systematically explore the recovery behavior of file system checkers. Symbolic execution [7, 11] is a technique that allows the exploration of non-redundant paths of code. To achieve this, input data is initially marked as "symbolic," that is, instead of assigning concrete values to inputs, the symbolic execution engine represents each input with a symbolic constant that represents all possible values allowed for that input.

The symbolic execution engine executes the program on the symbolic input, and maintains a symbolic store that maps program variables to symbolic expressions defined over the symbolic inputs. The symbolic store is updated on each assignment statement. For example, if the program has an input x that is represented using the symbolic constant α_x, and the program performs the assignment $y = x + 5$, the symbolic store maintains the mapping $[x \mapsto \alpha_x, y \mapsto \alpha_x + 5]$.

In addition to the symbolic store, the symbolic execution engine maintains a path constraint that represents constraints on the inputs in order for the current path to be executed. Initially, the path constraint is *true*, indicating that there are no constraints on the inputs. When a conditional instruction that depends on symbolic data is executed, the system execution may be forked in two feasible paths. In the then-branch, the condition is marked as true (by conjoining the conditional with the current path constraint), and in the else-branch, it is marked as false (by conjoining the negation of the conditional with the current path constraint). For example, if the conditional is $y > 0$ and the symbolic store is as above, the then-branch of the conditional adds the constraint $\alpha_x + 5 > 0$ to the path constraint and the else-branch adds the constraint $\alpha_x + 5 \leq 0$. This constrains the input values that can cause execution to go down the then- or else-branch. As the code in each path is explored and execution is forked, input data is progressively constrained along each individual path and paths through the system are explored. When a path is fully executed, a constraint solver is used to find concrete inputs that satisfy the path constraints that were collected along that path. Any concrete input satisfying the path constraint is guaranteed to execute the program along that path. Symbolic execution continues until all paths of the program are covered (or some user-provided coverage goal or resource bound is met).

SWIFT uses S^2E [6], an in-vivo symbolic execution engine. Testing using in-vivo symbolic execution enables us to use a real software stack, without having to model the environment in which the target code runs. For improved scalability, S^2E combines symbolic execution with the concrete execution of certain sections of the code, by converting symbolic data into concrete data upon entering those sections, and judiciously converting back to symbolic upon leaving, in such a way that execution consistency is preserved. S^2E operates directly on binaries, and therefore it does not require access to the source code of the software being analyzed.

4. Methodology

4.1 Overview

Our methodology checks for two aspects of the specification of a file system checker. The first aspect, which we call *consistency*, is the property that the output of the checker and the final disk state are coherent, namely that a successful recovery should not lead to a corrupt disk, and a run of the checker that ends with an error code should produce a disk that is consistent with the error code. The second part, which we call *completeness*, is the property that a checker should recover as much information as reasonably possible from a corrupt disk.

If there was a full specification of the layout of a file system, one could check consistency by exploring the set of possible behaviors of the checker and verify that, when run from an arbitrary disk state, the checker either returns success and a disk state satisfying the specification, or returns an error code with the disk state satisfying the conditions implied by the error code. Similarly, if there was a full specification of recovery behavior, one could check completeness by verifying that the checker conforms to the recovery specification. In practice, file system layouts and file system checkers do not come with full specifications, therefore the developers of the file system checker construct a partial specification in the form of a test suite.

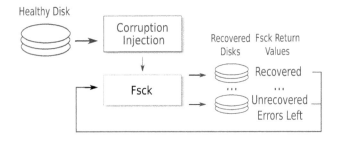

Healthy Disk

Figure 1. Finding fsck recovery inconsistencies.

First Execution Result	Second Execution Result
Disk is consistent	Disk is consistent
Uncorrected errors left	Uncorrected errors left
Recovered but uncorrected errors left	Uncorrected errors left
All errors corrected	Disk is consistent
Operational Error	Operational Error

Table 1. List of correct results fsck should output when run consecutively on the same disk.

Our goal is to provide a methodology and a tool to *systematically* test the implementations of file system checkers, *without* manually provided behavioral specifications and with minimal manual effort. Our methodology has three parts.

First, we expect a *corruption model* that systematically injects data corruption to disks. Our methodology is parametrized by a user-provided corruption model, and the depth and complexity of the corruption model influences the coverage of recovery behaviors. This is, in essence, a specification of what failures are of interest. In § 5 we present two methods for the systematic and symbolic injection of data corruption.

Second, we perform the systematic exploration of checker code (for each given corruption scenario) using symbolic execution [4–7]. This enables us to systematically explore a large number of paths through the checker code, and, when problems are found, to generate an input disk image that triggers the problematic path.

Third, we check the consistency and completeness of checkers using a *composition* of checkers, that is, by using the file system checker code itself as a specification, as follows.

We check consistency using sequential self-composition. This means that we take a corrupt disk and perform two consecutive runs of a checker on this disk. If the outcomes of the two runs are not coherent with each other, then we can be sure that some erroneous behavior occurred. This happens, for instance, if the second run needs to recover a disk that was successfully recovered in the first run. Thus, we can check for inconsistent behaviors by running the checker twice in succession and comparing the two results.

We check completeness using parallel composition of multiple file system checkers. That is, we run different implementations of file system checkers (possibly for different file systems) and compare their results when started with the same semantic state (i.e., a logical representation of the file system state that abstracts away the differences in the data and metadata physical layout) and the same data corruption. While different file systems may be represented differently on-disk, we use the fact that one can relatively simply specify the common data structures used in a file system (inodes, data blocks, etc.) and describe a corruption purely as muta-

tions on these data structures. Assuming that correlated bugs are less likely, this detects sources of incompleteness where one checker cannot recover some information but the other can.

4.2 Checking Consistency

Our approach to check consistency, depicted in Figure 1, works as follows.

A healthy disk is fed to our testing system. Using a corruption model, we systematically introduce corruption (in the form of unconstrained symbolic values) in this disk. We call this a symbolic corrupt disk, i.e., a disk that contains symbolic values, thus encoding any possible values for the bytes that are marked as symbolic.

Next, we symbolically execute the checker under test to recover from this corruption, if possible. This leads to multiple recovered disks and, for each recovery, the checker returns a numeric value indicating whether it was able to recover the disk and, if so, whether the recovery was partial or complete. Afterwards, we run the checker a second time on the recovered disk to determine whether the consistency property is met.

To exemplify how the second run checks the correctness of the first one, if the first checker execution completely recovers the disk data, the second run must indicate a fully consistent disk. If not, then it is likely that the recovery performed in the first execution is not correct, e.g., a set of recoveries performed in the second execution were missed by the first one, or the first recovery has introduced inconsistencies. A complete list of the expected outcomes of the sequential composition of checker executions is shown in Table 1. A deviation from these outcomes signals the existence of a bug in the checker; this process does not generate any false positives. Once a positive is flagged, the developer obtains a bug-triggering input that (s)he can use to manually inspect the cause of the bug. Note that we cannot exclude that the bug can be in the checking logic to verify if recovery is needed (that implies the specification we use).

The effectiveness of this phase in terms of not having any false negatives, relies on two assumptions: first, that the code for checking whether recovery is needed is correct, and, second, that an execution that outputs that the disk is initially consistent does not modify the file system state. We expect these assumptions to be commonly met in practice because of the following intuition: Since the code that checks

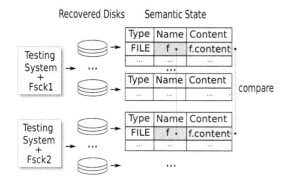

Figure 2. Assessing the completeness of recoveries.

Field	Description
Number of blocks	Number of used blocks
Number of free blocks	Number of unused blocks
Block size	Size of the block used by the file system
State of the file system	Value indicating if the file system is valid or not
Magic file system value	Value indicating which file system and version are being used
Symbolic link data	Path to the file that the symbolic link points to
Directory entries	< Name, Inode number> pairs
Data block pointers	Pointers stored in data blocks and inodes
VFS file attributes	File attributes exposed by the VFS layer (see Table 3)

Table 2. List of fields shared by modern file systems. The term "symbolic" is used above in the sense of symbolic (soft) links in file systems, which differs somewhat from the use of this term in the rest of the paper.

whether on-disk file system data structures need recovery is frequently executed, and also given its relative simplicity, we expect this checking logic to be mature and to be a good specification of a consistent disk. In contrast, recovery code often depends on intricate failure conditions and complex correction decisions, and thus this code is more likely to be fragile.

4.3 Checking Completeness

Even though the disk recovered by a file system checker may be consistent, a checker may not have done as good a job as it could have, i.e., may not have recovered the disk to a state that is as close to the pre-corruption state as possible. For instance, data or metadata may have been lost in the process, files or directories may have been relocated, or the checker may have not used all the available data redundancy during the recovery process and thus missed opportunities for recovery.

In order to assess the completeness of file system checker recoveries, we compare the contents from different disks resulting from the execution of different file system checkers. The idea is that file system checkers should be able to arrive at the same logical contents for the file system after recovering from corruption in equivalent fields. Note that it is only possible to use this strategy if file systems have common data structures that can be used to produce equivalent corruption scenarios. In practice, we expect this to be feasible for a large class of file systems that have similar organization strategies and use similar data structures, e.g., inode-based designs.

The second part of the methodology is depicted in more detail in Figure 2. We start with two or more healthy disks, formatted with different file systems and containing the same logical data (i.e., having identical file system entries). We use the corruption model to introduce semantically equivalent corruptions in each disk image. To ensure semantically equivalent corruptions, the corruption model introduces symbolic values in fields which are common to both disk data structures (see Table 2).

For each corrupted disk, we execute the corresponding file system checker symbolically to recover from the injected corruption. Then, for each recovery path and the corresponding recovered disk, we assemble a logical representation of the data stored in the disk (i.e., the set of file system entries it contains) using file system operations. Finally, we perform an all-to-all comparison among the logical representations of the recovered data in the various file systems and various recovery paths (but for the same corruption). Mismatches in the logical data contained in different recovered disks indicate that the different file system checkers performed different recoveries, and might be caused by a bug.

Unlike checking consistency, this approach is subject to false positives. Since different file systems may have different levels of on-disk redundancy, some file system checkers may be able to recover more information than others. Thus, the developer needs to manually inspect the bugs found by this part of our methodology in order to separate mismatches caused by a bug in the checker from those resulting from the file system's design.

Moreover, our approach does not pinpoint which of the file system checkers whose recoveries are being compared has a bug. However, we have found it easy to discover through manual inspection which of the file system checkers has performed an incorrect recovery. It is possible that a majority voting mechanism could be used to isolate the buggy file system checker from a set of three or more file system checkers being compared (akin to BASE [14] and EnvyFS [1]), but we did not explore this approach.

5. SWIFT

We now describe SWIFT (Scalable and Wide Fsck Testing), a testing tool that implements our methodology. As illustrated in Figure 3, SWIFT has three phases: processing a description of which fields are considered to be sources of corruption, systematically exploring paths in the checker code, and using these path traces to find inconsistent recoveries and instances of data loss or missed recovery opportunities.

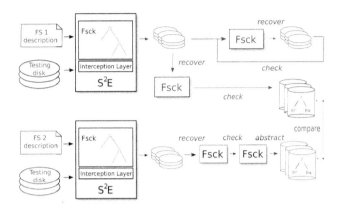

Figure 3. Overview of SWIFT's testing process.

Field	Description
Path name	Path to the file
Type	Type of the file (e.g., directory)
Permissions	Read, write and execute permissions of the file
Number of hard links	Number of links to this file
User ID of owner	Identification number for the file's user owner
Group ID of owner	Identification number for the file's group owner
Total size	Size of the file
File content	Content of the file (in case of regular files)

Table 3. List of files attributes accessible with VFS.

5.1 System Overview

Checking consistency. For this phase, the input to SWIFT is a file system and file system checker under test, an initial healthy disk, and a description of the corruption model. An example of a corruption model is a list of file system fields that can be mutated. SWIFT introduces a symbolic input according to each entry in the corruption model (e.g., in one file system field at a time), and runs S^2E to explore file system checker executions for each symbolic input. The symbolic execution of these paths will lead to checking and possibly recovering from the corruption that was injected. Moreover, each of these paths leads to S^2E generating a disk trace — a concrete corrupt disk that can be used as an input to exercise that path in the checker code. Once corruption in all fields has been explored, the disk traces generated by the path exploration phase are used to test the consistency of the checker. To this end, SWIFT uses the file system checker to recover each concrete disk in the set of disk traces two consecutive times. On each recovery, SWIFT records the value returned by the fsck. At the end, SWIFT checks these values, looking for incorrect recoveries. Sequences of executions whose return values deviate from the set of "good" cases that are listed in Table 1 are marked as buggy cases.

Checking completeness. For checking completeness, the input to SWIFT is two or more file systems and their corresponding checkers, a semantic description of the initial file system data, and a description of the corruption model. The corruption model marks fields shared by the file systems as symbolic. For each symbolic input, SWIFT runs S^2E to generate disk traces for each file system checker. For each field that is analyzed (as described in Section 4.3), SWIFT runs the recovery code on each disk in the set of disk traces (corresponding to the various recovery paths) and builds a logical representation of the data contained in it using the data and metadata accessible through VFS operations (see

Table 3). Then, SWIFT compares all the logical disk contents across all the file system checkers being compared and all recovery paths, but for the same corrupted field. Finally, mismatches between these representations are flagged. In order to make the logical comparison agnostic to the order in which these entries were returned by the VFS calls, SWIFT sorts the directory entries that are read.

Output. Since SWIFT starts from a real disk to exercise recovery code, and the output of S^2E is a set of concrete disks that lead to different execution paths, SWIFT can output, upon finding a potential bug, the corresponding concrete disk that triggers the identified problem. Developers can then use this disk image to replay the bug and manually find its root cause.

5.2 Initial Disk

To explore diverse recovery behaviors, we have to create an initial disk that uses many features of the file system. Otherwise, the execution of the checker under test will be confined to a small subset of recoveries. We developed a generic file system content for the testing disk, taking into account the data structures that specific file systems use to organize their data and metadata. This disk not only contains all types of entries, but also exercises specific layouts that stem from certain file system design features. For instance, our testing disk contains 100 small files in a directory to force specific file systems (e.g., ReiserFS) to use a multi-level tree with internal and leaf nodes. The resulting testing disk layout is depicted in Figure 4 and described in Table 4.

5.3 Corruption Model

The set of possible disk corruptions, file system structures, and file system fields is prohibitively large. Fortunately, many of the possible corruptions exercise the same fsck recovery code mechanisms (e.g., the same corrupt field in inodes of the same type is recovered in the same way).

To systematically explore corruption instances, and given that we are not aware of any existing studies for real disk corruption, we experimented with two simple methods for injecting data corruption in a disk. In the first method, the corruption that is injected in the disk is based on the fields of the data structures used by file systems. In the second method, the injection of corruption is guided by existing file system checker test suites. While we believe that more so-

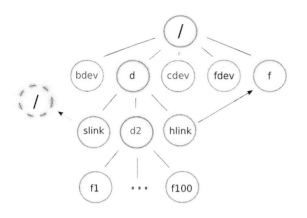

Figure 4. Semantic representation of the data stored in SWIFT's generic test disk. The meaning of the nodes is explained in Table 4.

Item	Type	Description
/	Directory	
/bdev	Block device	
/d	Directory	
/cdev	Char device	
/fdev	FIFO Device	
/f	Regular File	File with 278 1Kb blocks
/d/slink	Symbolic link	Link to root directory
/d/hlink	Hard link	Link to /f
/d/d2	Directory	
/d/f1...f100	Regular file	100 empty files

Table 4. Description of the contents of the test disk.

phisticated models could help the productivity of our testing tool, we leave the task of finding such models to future work. We also note that even with these simple models our methodology is effective.

5.3.1 Corruption of Fields

Most file system checker recovery mechanisms target specific file system fields and data structures. Thus, we have developed and implemented a corruption model that is aware of the position of file system fields in the disk and that can selectively corrupt them. While developing this model we tried to exhaustively consider the different types of structures used by modern file systems. Moreover, we analyzed the list of recoveries performed by different file system checkers, namely e2fsck and xfs_fsck, whose description is provided by developers along with the source code, and asked the question "Is our corruption model able to exercise these recovery mechanisms?" We eventually converged onto a model that encompasses a wide set of corruption cases.

Table 5 shows the fields our model considers as possible sources of corruption. The first column describes the on-disk

Disk Data Structure	Fields
Superblock	All fields
Group Descriptor	All fields
Inode Bitmap	All bits of used blocks and one bit of an unused block
Block Bitmap	All bits of used blocks and one bit of an unused block
Metadata	For each inode type: 1. all non-pointer fields 2. one direct block pointer 3. one indirect block pointer 4. one double indirect block pointer All fields of reserved inodes
Data	Directory entries (root and one other directory): 1. Directory entry (e.g., inode number, file name) to itself 2. Directory entry to parent 3. Directory entry to another Data pointers: 1. One direct pointer stored in an indirect block 2. One indirect pointer stored in a double indirect block Symbolic links: 1. One symbolic link path name
Journal Superblock	All fields
Journal Commit Record	All fields
Journal Revoke Record	All fields

Table 5. Corruption model. This table shows the fields and respective data structures considered to be possible sources of corruption.

file system data structure, while the second column identifies the specific field(s) in that structure. This corruption model targets inode-based file systems. Thus, this model considers the most common structures in this family of file systems, such as superblock, inode bitmap, block bitmap, metadata (inodes) and data (data blocks). We additionally considered some more modern features (e.g., related to journaling).

We consider all the fields in each one of these structures as possible sources of corruption. However, in order to achieve scalability, we apply some simplifications. In the case of bitmaps, our model only considers one bit from the set of bits indicating unused blocks or inodes. Our model considers only one pointer of each type (direct, indirect, and double indirect), and inode fields are considered once for each type of inode. Finally, we only consider corruption in one field at a time, similar to single-event upset models in VLSI-CAD. While silent data corruption may affect several fields of the file system disk data structures, we believe that considering only one field at a time is a good compromise between the large number of possible corruptions and the efficiency of our testing methodology. Additionally, in this way, the developer is able to direct the execution of the file system checker towards specific recovery mechanisms.

Since our corruption model targets inode-based file systems, it can be used to test most of the currently used file system checkers. However, some file system checkers may not implement some of the structures outlined, or may use additional structures not captured by it. In particular, many modern file systems provide more advanced features, such as indexed directory entries. To allow for capturing these

```
<FileSystem name="Ext4">
  <AddStructure name="Superblock">
    <Field name="s_inodes_count" position="0h"
                                 size="4"/>
    <Field name="s_blocks_count_lo" position="4h"
                                 size="4"/>
    <Field name="s_r_blocks_count_lo" position="8h"
                                 size="4"/>
    <Field name="s_free_blocks_count_lo" position="Ch"
                                 size="4"/>
  </AddStructure>
  <AddStructure name="Inode">
    <Field name="i_mode" position="0h" size="2"/>
    <Field name="i_uid" position="2h" size="2"/>
    <Field name="i_size" position="4h" size="4"/>
    <Field name="i_atime" position="8h" size="4"/>
    <Field name="i_ctime" position="Ch" size="4"/>
  </AddStructure>
  <AddStructure name="DirEntry">
    <Field name="inode_nr" position="0" size="4"/>
    <Field name="rec_len" position="4" size="2"/>
    <Field name="name_len" position="6" size="2"/>
    <Field name="entry_name" position="8" size="1"/>
  </AddStructure>
  <AddTest>
    <TestStructure name="Superblock"
        startPosition="1024"/>
    <TestStructure name="Inode" startPosition="49300h"
                    description="journal inode"/>
  </AddTest>
</FileSystem>
```

Figure 5. Test description for an ext4 disk. Some structures and fields are omitted for clarity.

```
char* disk_data; // disk data
char* test_disk; // disk file path
int symb_pos; // position of the symbolic field
int symb_size; // size of the field
char buffer[4096];

int open(const char * pathname, int flags, mode_t mode) {
    int fd = _open(pathname, flags, mode);

    // not opening the test disk
    if (strcmp(pathname, test_disk) != 0)
        return fd;

    isTestDisk[fd] = 1;
    s2e_make_symbolic(disk_data + symb_pos,
                              symb_size, "disk");
    return fd;
}

ssize_t read(int fd, void *buf, size_t count) {
    // check if we are reading our test disk
    if (isTestDisk[fd] == 1) {
        // get seek position
        off64_t seek = _lseek64(fd, 0, SEEK_CUR);
        // get number of bytes read
        int readRet = _read(fd, buffer, count);
        memcpy(buf, disk_data + seek, readRet);
        return readRet;
    } else {
        // delegate operation to the 'real' file system
        return _read(fd, buf, count);
    }
}
```

Figure 6. Simplified interception layer for the `open` and `read` file system operations.

features, developers can easily extend the model by editing the corresponding XML-based description of the possible sources of corruption and their respective positions on the disk. An example of such a description is depicted in Figure 5. In this description, the developer defines disk data structures (e.g., an inode), using `AddStructure`. These structures contain file systems fields, their names, relative positions and sizes.

5.3.2 Corruption Using Fsck Test Suites

One limitation of the above corruption model is that it considers that corruptions do not span more than one file system field, which is important to keep the number of scenarios being tested within a reasonable bound. Ideally, we would like to additionally test more intricate cases of corruption that exercise more complex recovery mechanisms, but doing so in a scalable way is challenging.

To address this, we use the file system checker test suites to drive the exploration of recovery paths towards recoveries that are harder to exercise, while maintaining the scalability of our methodology. When available, test suites can be a good vehicle for exercising recoveries, because they make use of the knowledge of the developers about the file system, the checker and real data corruptions. In addition, test suites tend to be developed over a long period of time and, as they mature, they explore more intricate cases of data corruption.

In this work we focus on the test suite of e2fsck, since it was the only system we tested that provided a test suite along with the checker. In this suite, each test consists of one

corrupt disk and the expected output from recovering it. Our corruption model uses the test suite in the following way. For each test, we run e2fsck on the test disk and record which bytes of the disk are changed during the recovery. Then, we run SWIFT, considering these bytes as possible sources of corruption, thus exploring multiple fault scenarios for the same set of bytes. As our results will highlight, this latter corruption model proved more effective than the individual field model in uncovering incorrect recoveries.

5.4 Generating Symbolic Input

To explore recoveries of on-disk data corruption, we invoke the file system checker inside S^2E on the testing disk. However, this execution must differ from a normal fsck execution, because the data that is read from the testing disk must be in memory and must contain a mix of concrete and symbolic values, the latter being marked through an invocation of S^2E's `s2e_make_symbolic` function.

To feed symbolic disk data to a file system checker in a transparent way, we have developed an interception layer, as depicted in Figure 6. This layer is compiled in Linux as a shared library and is used to intercept functions that handle file system operations provided by the *libc* library. The role of the layer is to load the test disk contents into memory and replace portions of the data read from disk with symbolic values by calling the `s2e_make_symbolic` function. Then, when the checker invokes a *read()* call, instead of accessing

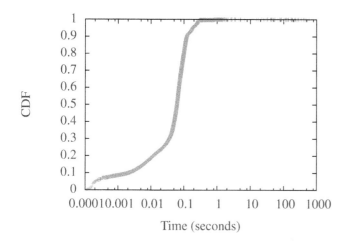

Figure 7. CDF of the solving time for a sample set of constraint expressions generated during our tests.

the disk contents, the mix of concrete and symbolic data is read from memory. The behavior of the *write()* method is not changed, since code running on S^2E can handle symbolic values transparently.

5.5 Improving Scalability: A Concretization Strategy

S^2E relies indirectly on a constraint solver to solve constraint expressions during the exploration of paths. Most of the constraint solver queries are issued in two situations: when a path is forked and when a symbolic value is concretized in order to simplify a symbolic memory address access.

Figure 7 shows the distribution of constraint solving times. While most of the queries can be solved by the constraint solver in less than 1 second, a small fraction of the queries takes a considerable amount of time. These queries can hurt the performance of the path exploration and slow down the rate of explored paths. In order to solve this problem, symbolic execution systems allow developers to set a timeout on the constraint solving process. This way, whenever a constraint solving query takes more than a specified amount of time, the constraint solving process is canceled and the respective path is discarded. This approach is far from ideal: discarding a path wastes the time that was spent executing the code that led to that path and solving previous constraint queries. Moreover, constraints that may be hard to solve by the constraint solver may also be harder to reason about by the developer, and thus can arguably be more likely to exercise corner cases of the file system checker.

In order to decrease the number of paths that are discarded this way, we introduce the following optimization: Whenever a constraint query times out during a path fork, we partially concretize the constraint expression of the path, i.e., find a set of values for a subset of the variables in the constraint expression of the path that satisfy these constraints.

The idea is that, by concretizing a subset of the symbolic bytes of the path's constraint expression, we can simplify the constraint expression, thus transforming it into an expression that can be solved more efficiently.

The subset of bytes concretized can be chosen according to different strategies. One possibility is to choose the bytes according to the order in which they appear in the constraint expression. Another possibility is to concretize the symbolic bytes that occur more often in a constraint expression. Finally, a third strategy can pick the symbolic bytes to concretize that appear in arithmetic expressions.

In this work we only evaluate the first strategy. Our strategy allows the developer to decide the fraction of the bytes that is concretized, i.e., the developer has, at compile time, the ability to decide if the constraint expression should be fully or only partially concretized. We leave the evaluation of the remaining strategies to future work.

6. Evaluation

We used SWIFT to check the consistency and completeness of three file system checkers: e2fsck 1.41.14, reiserfsck 3.6.21 and fsck.minix 2.17.2. These file system checkers are used to check the integrity of ext2 through ext4, ReiserFS and the MINIX file system, respectively. Both e2fsck and reiserfsck are modern and reasonably sized file system checkers: $18,046$ and $8,125$ lines of code, respectively. Fsck.minix is a small but mature file system checker with $1,156$ lines of code.

To implement our first corruption model that tests the corruption of individual fields, we developed a test description for each one of these file system checkers, as described in Section 5.3.1. Table 6 summarizes the complexity of these three descriptions. For the second corruption model, SWIFT collects the bytes changed during the recovery of the disk that is provided by each test, as described in Section 5.3.2.

Fsck	# Data Structures	# Fields	LoC
e2fsck	13	233	323
reiserfsck	10	63	128
fsck.minix (V1)	4	28	63
fsck.minix (V2)	4	31	72

Table 6. Size of the test descriptions developed for each file system checker.

In order to execute the file system checkers being tested, we had to provide command-line arguments they support (as summarized in Table 7). An interesting case was reiserfsck, which provides one argument to check the consistency and three other arguments that enable different recovery mechanisms. As a result, to test the reiserfsck file system checker, we invoke it three times in the first execution, one for each command-line argument, to test all recovery mechanisms.

When testing individual field corruption, we let SWIFT perform the code exploration for 1,000 seconds for each field

Fsck	Bug Type	Description
e2fsck	Wrong return type	e2fsck incorrectly flags a disk as recovered in the first execution
e2fsck	Unrecoverable field is recovered	Corrupt *s_wtime* field is recovered despite being considered unrecoverable
e2fsck	Cloning of blocks	Wrong recovery leads to unnecessary cloning of blocks
e2fsck	Recovery fails to recover	Recovery of inconsistent resize inode leaves inode in an inconsistent state
e2fsck	Journal backup mismatch	Recovery may create mismatches between the journal inode and its backups
reiserfsck	Infinite Loop	Corruption in entry key leads to an infinite loop
reiserfsck	Segmentation fault	Corruption in the size field of a child pointer leads to a segmentation fault
fsck.minix	Data Loss	Wrong inode number in . entry of root inode makes all data unreachable
fsck.minix	Segmentation fault	Bug detecting double indirect pointer leads to segmentation fault
fsck.minix	Segmentation fault	Loop in the file system leads to an infinite loop and segmentation fault

Table 8. List of bugs found when testing the consistency of recoveries.

Command-Line Invocation	Description
e2fsck -fy test_disk	Performs all the possible recoveries
reiserfsck -fy --rebuild-sb test_disk	Recovers the superblock
reiserfsck -fy --fix-fixable test_disk	Recovers cases of corruption which do not involve the file system tree
reiserfsck -f --rebuild-tree test_disk	Recovers the file system tree
reiserfsck --check test_disk	Checks the consistency of the file system
fsck.minix -fa test_disk	Performs all automatic repairs
fsck.minix -f test_disk	Checks the consistency of the file system

Table 7. List of command-line arguments used while testing e2fsck, reiserfsck and fsck.minix.

Bug	Description
Deleted inode is treated as an orphan inode	e2fsck uses *s_wtime* and *s_mtime* to determine if an orphan inode release has been missed. Corruption in these fields can make e2fsck consider an inode as regular in the first execution and as an orphan inode in the second execution.
salvage_directory recovers file	e2fsck is unable to detect corruption in ext4's i_mode field. When recovering a file as if it was a directory, the recovery is unable to leave the disk in a consistent state.

Table 9. Some of the bugs found by SWIFT using the corruption model based on e2fsck's test suite.

indicated in the test description. When using the test suite, we configure SWIFT to use 1,000 seconds for each test. All the experiments run on an Intel 2.66GHz Xeon CPU using 48GB of RAM, and we run S^2E with 8 threads.

To understand what was the cause for incorrect recoveries, we manually analyzed as many buggy paths as time permitted.

6.1 Checking the Consistency of Recoveries

We start by reporting several bugs we found using each of the corruption models. Our findings are summarized in Table 8.

6.1.1 Corruption of individual fields

Overall, using the individual field corruption model, our tests found buggy paths in all three file system checkers. We manually analyzed a subset of the paths that SWIFT flagged as buggy. This analysis revealed 5, 2 and 3 bugs in e2fsck, reiserfsck and fsck.minix, respectively. These include instances of infinite loops and segmentation faults, even though SWIFT does not directly target this type of bugs.

To give an example of an inconsistent recovery that our methodology detected, in one case, when the disk contains two duplicate files, e2fsck outputs a message indicating that this error was found and fixed. However, e2fsck fails to rename one of the duplicate files in the first execution of e2fsck. Only a second execution fixes this problem. The rea-

son for this bug is that the check that detects this inconsistency and the code that recovers it have different assumptions about the order of files in the same directory. While the former is always able to detect the duplicate files by using a hash of file names in a dictionary, the latter assumes that the files are ordered alphabetically in a directory, and thus fails to detect some instances of duplicate files.

Another interesting finding is that e2fsck does not check the values stored in the main superblock against the values stored in the backup superblocks before using them. This makes e2fsck blindly trust corrupt values, which leads to incorrect recoveries.

6.1.2 Corruption Using Test Suites

Using SWIFT along with the test suite of e2fsck, we found more than 6,000 paths that lead to incorrect recoveries, compared to less than 200 with the previous corruption model (though this model leads to about twice the exploration time). While this is an encouragingly positive result, especially since this part of the methodology does not lead to false positives, the same bug may trigger incorrect recoveries in tens or hundreds of paths. We were unable to manually analyze *all* these recoveries to understand the bugs that lead to them, and so we show in Table 9 only a partial list of bugs that we found during our tests.

The first bug was found while exploring e2fsck recoveries on a disk containing orphan inodes. Orphan inodes are inodes that are deleted while the corresponding file is still open. In order to delete the file once it is closed, ext4 stores the inode in a special linked list, the orphan inode list. When

248

e2fsck is invoked, it checks for the presence of inodes in this list. In order to identify inodes in the orphan inode list, e2fsck relies on the *s_wtime* and *s_mtime* fields. When one of these fields is corrupt, e2fsck may wrongly identify a normal inode as orphan. When e2fsck is invoked the first time, e2fsck recovers a disk containing a list of orphan inodes successfully. When e2fsck recovers the disk, it overwrites the previously mentioned time fields. As a result, when e2fsck is invoked again, an inode is identified as being orphan and the execution of e2fsck aborts.

Finally, the second bug is an example of a recovery that fails to leave the file system in a consistent state. When a file is mistakenly identified as being a directory, its contents are blindly considered by e2fsck to be directory entries. In one of the cases found by SWIFT, e2fsck invokes the `salvage_directory` function in order to recover the contents of the directory. When this function finds a directory entry with a size of 8 bytes, the entry is considered to be a 'hole' in the directory data and the remaining contents are moved 8 bytes to the left, thus overwriting this space. However, e2fsck does not realize that the data moved to this space does not contain valid directory entries. Thus, repeated executions of e2fsck lead to multiple recoveries of this data.

Both bugs presented above support our idea that the test suites of file system checkers allow us to perform more complex tests that would not be possible with the corruption model presented in Section 5.3.1. For instance, test suites provided by e2fsck exercise specific features of the file system, such as orphan inodes, that require an advanced knowledge of the file system being tested.

6.2 Checking the Completeness of Recoveries

In order to check the completeness of the recoveries performed by e2fsck and reiserfsck, we first identified the fields that are used by both ext4 and ReiserFS (shown in Table 10). Next, we used the disk traces produced during the exploration of corruption of those fields in both file systems to compare the logical representations of the data after recovery, as described in Section 4.3.

SWIFT was able to reveal a situation in which a wrong file type (symbolic link type) makes e2fsck erase a regular file, thus losing data, whereas reiserfsck was able to restore the type of the file to the correct value. In this case, the e2fsck recovery works as follows: e2fsck looks at the size of the file data, wrongly considered as being a symbolic link, and is able to detect an inconsistency, since in this specific case the file data occupies more than one file system block and symbolic links can only use one block of data. Once the file system checker detects this inconsistency, it clears the inode and the pointers to the data of the file. In this situation, e2fsck ignores the file type value that is stored in the directory entry that leads to this file. Therefore, this is a case where e2fsck does not use all the information available in the disk.

ext4 field	ReiserFS field	Description
s_blocks_count_lo	s_block_count	Number of blocks
free_blocks_count_lo	s_free_blocks	Number of free blocks
s_log_block_size	s_blocksize	Size of the block
s_state	s_umount_state	State indicating whether the disk needs to be checked/recovered
magic_string	s_magic	Magic value identifying the file system
Block bitmap	Block bitmap	Block bitmap
i_mode	sd_mode	Type and permissions of a file
i_links_count	sd_nlink	Number of hard links pointing to file
i_uid	sd_uid	User ID
i_gid	sd_gid	Group ID
i_size	sd_size	Size of file
i_atime	sd_atime	Access time
i_mtime	sd_mtime	Modification time
i_ctime	sd_ctime	Creation time
i_dtime	sd_dtime	Deletion time
i_blocks_lo	sd_blocks	Number of blocks of the file
direct data pointer (i_block)	direct data pointer	Pointer to data
indirect data pointer (i_block)	indirect data pointer	Pointer pointing to data pointers
double indirect data pointer (i_block)	double indirect data pointer	Pointer pointing to pointers to data pointers

Table 10. Fields in common between Ext4 and ReiserFS.

6.3 Efficiency and Scalability

In this section we evaluate the efficiency and scalability of SWIFT. Efficiency refers to the execution time of the tests performed by the system, and scalability refers to the number and diversity of recovery behaviors of the file system checkers that are tested.

In Table 11 we show the execution time, number of paths, and paths flagged as executing inconsistent recoveries for the tests of the three file system checkers considered in this work. This table shows that SWIFT is able to find numerous instances of wrong recoveries. Even though the testing process can take up to several hours, we consider this a small price to pay given the significantly lower effort required of the tester, when compared to traditional approaches.

In order to evaluate the ability of SWIFT to explore a comprehensive set of recovery behaviors of a file system checker, we measured the statement coverage obtained during the path exploration phase of the tests we performed. In Figure 8 we show how the statement coverage of e2fsck and fsck.minix, using corruption on individual fields, varies over the course of the testing process. Moreover, in Figure 9 we show the statement coverage of reiserfsck, for the three different command-line arguments.

In the first graph, we can observe that applying SWIFT to the e2fsck file system checker led to a lower code coverage than that obtained with the e2fsck test suite. This has

Fsck	Exploration Time (hours)	# Paths Explored	# Paths with Bugs
e2fsck (individual field corruption model)	9.5	50064	193
e2fsck (test suite corruption model)	21	163288	6305
reiserfsck	37	27636	3
fsck.minix	11.5	22488	229

Table 11. Summary of the exploration phase of the different file system checkers.

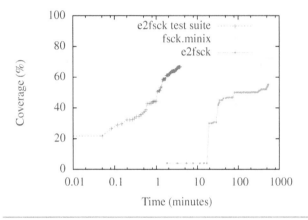

Figure 8. Comparison between the statement coverage of SWIFT applied to e2fsck and fsck.minix, and the coverage achieved by the original test suite of e2fsck.

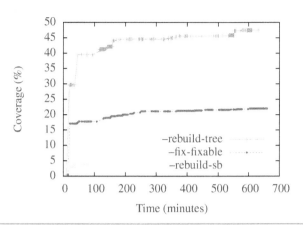

Figure 9. Statement coverage of the three tests of reiserfsck. In total, SWIFT achieved 62.3% code coverage.

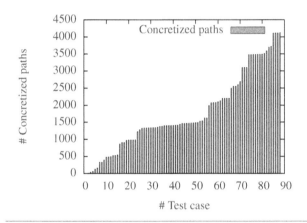

Figure 10. Number of paths concretized during the SWIFT tests using the e2fsck suite. SWIFT explored a total of 163288 paths.

to do with the fact that the test suite of e2fsck makes use of different disks, which have diverse configurations of the file system being used and make use of specific file systems data structures that go beyond the simple corruption model used by SWIFT. For instance, one of the tests contains a separate file with journal data in order to exercise the file system checker code that replays the journal. These results are nonetheless positive for SWIFT, given the relatively short testing period, and the fact that, unlike the test suite of e2fsck, our tests require little advanced knowledge about file system checkers and file systems.

Figure 9 shows three lines, one for each command-line argument used in each test of reiserfsck. The three arguments exercise considerably different amounts of code, which translates into different values for the statement coverage. In total, our tests of the reiserfsck file system checker exercised 62.3% of the code.

In both graphs we can observe long periods of time during which the statement coverage does not change. These periods of time exist because some of the corruptions injected

by SWIFT are not checked and recovered by the file system checker, and thus do not lead to the exploration of new code. One can also observe moments during which the coverage of the file system checker abruptly increases. This usually occurs when SWIFT starts exploring corruption on a new field that is checked and recovered by the file system checker.

To conclude, it is worth noting that not only SWIFT does not require deep knowledge of the file system code, but once disk traces have been generated by SWIFT, they can be subsequently reused as regression tests.

6.4 Optimizations - Concretization Strategy

Next, we evaluate the concretization strategy described in Section 5.5, aimed at making SWIFT discard a smaller number of paths than using the original timeout-based strategy.

In Figure 10 we show the evolution of the cumulative number of paths that were not discarded due to the concretization of path constraints, and would have been discarded otherwise. During the execution of SWIFT using the test suite of e2fsck, SWIFT was able to continue the execution of around 4,000 paths that would have been discarded if we had not used our strategy. From this set, SWIFT completely explored 283 paths during the symbolic execution phase. From these, SWIFT marked 3 paths as buggy.

7. Conclusion

In this paper we presented a methodology for testing file system checkers. Our methodology builds upon two insights. First, we can use the file system checker itself to check the consistency of its recoveries. Second, we can use different file system checkers to check the completeness of recoveries. Based on these two ideas, we provide a testing methodology that requires minimal effort from the tester and no formally written specification of the file system checker.

We implemented SWIFT, a system that implements our methodology. Our experimental evaluation shows that SWIFT can find bugs in real, widely used, file system checkers. SWIFT found cases of bugs in which the file system checker fails to use all available redundancy to perform recovery, as well as cases that lead to the loss of data. SWIFT is able to achieve code coverage levels comparable to that obtained with manual tests.

Acknowledgements

We thank the anonymous reviewers, the members of the sysnets group at MPI-SWS, and our shepherd, Leendert van Doorn, for valuable feedback. We are indebted to Vitaly Chipounov for tirelessly helping us with our use of S^2E.

References

[1] BAIRAVASUNDARAM, L., SUNDARARAMAN, S., ARPACI-DUSSEAU, A., AND ARPACI-DUSSEAU, R. Tolerating File-System Mistakes with EnvyFS. In *USENIX Annual Technical Conference '09* (2009), USENIX.

[2] BAIRAVASUNDARAM, L. N., ARPACI-DUSSEAU, A. C., ARPACI-DUSSEAU, R. H., GOODSON, G. R., AND SCHROEDER, B. An analysis of data corruption in the storage stack. *ACM Transactions on Storage 4* (November 2008).

[3] BAIRAVASUNDARAM, L. N., RUNGTA, M., AGRAWA, N., ARPACI-DUSSEAU, A. C., ARPACI-DUSSEAU, R. H., AND SWIFT, M. M. Analyzing the effects of disk-pointer corruption. In *DSN '08: Dependable Systems and Networks* (2008), IEEE Press.

[4] CADAR, C., DUNBAR, D., AND ENGLER, D. KLEE : Unassisted and Automatic Generation of High-Coverage Tests for Complex Systems Programs. In *OSDI '08: Operating systems design and implementation* (2008), USENIX.

[5] CADAR, C., AND ENGLER, D. Execution Generated Test Cases: How to Make Systems Code Crash Itself. In *SPIN '05: Model Checking Software* (2005), vol. 3639 of *Lecture Notes in Computer Science*, Springer.

[6] CHIPOUNOV, V., KUZNETSOV, V., AND CANDEA, G. S2E: A platform for in-vivo multi-path analysis of software systems. In *ASPLOS '11: Architectural Support for Programming Languages and Operating Systems* (2011), ACM.

[7] GODEFROID, P., KLARLUND, N., AND SEN, K. DART: directed automated random testing. In *PLDI '05: Programming language design and implementation* (2005), ACM.

[8] GUNAWI, H., DO, T., JOSHI, P., ALVARO, P., HELLERSTEIN, J., ARPACI-DUSSEAU, A., ARPACI-DUSSEAU, R., SEN, K., AND BORTHAKUR, D. FATE and DESTINI: A framework for cloud recovery testing. In *NSDI '11: Networked Systems Design and Implementation* (2011), USENIX.

[9] GUNAWI, H. S., RAJIMWALE, A., ARPACI-DUSSEAU, A. C., AND ARPACI-DUSSEAU, R. H. SQCK: a declarative file system checker. In *OSDI '08: Operating Systems Design and Implementation* (2008), USENIX.

[10] JIANG, W., HU, C., ZHOU, Y., AND KANEVSKY, A. Are disks the dominant contributor for storage failures?: a comprehensive study of storage subsystem failure characteristics. In *FAST '08: File and Storage Technologies* (2008), USENIX.

[11] KING, J. Symbolic execution and program testing. *Commun. ACM 19* (July 1976).

[12] PANZER-STEINDEL, B. Data integrity. `http://indico.cern.ch/getFile.py/access?contribId=3&sessionId=0&resId=1&materialId=paper&confId=13797`, 2007.

[13] PINHEIRO, E., WEBER, W.-D., AND BARROSO, L. A. Failure trends in a large disk drive population. In *FAST '07: File and Storage Technologies* (2007), USENIX.

[14] RODRIGUES, R., CASTRO, M., AND LISKOV, B. BASE: Using abstraction to improve fault tolerance. In *SOSP '01: Symposium on Operating Systems Principles* (2001), ACM.

[15] SCHROEDER, B., DAMOURAS, S., AND GILL, P. Understanding latent sector errors and how to protect against them. *ACM Transactions on Storage 6* (2010).

[16] TALAGALA, N., AND PATTERSON, D. An analysis of error behavior in a large storage system. Tech. Rep. UCB/CSD-99-1042, EECS Department, University of California, Berkeley, Feb 1999.

[17] YANG, J., SAR, C., AND ENGLER, D. EXPLODE: a lightweight, general system for finding serious storage system errors. In *OSDI '06: Operating systems design and implementation* (2006), USENIX Association.

[18] YANG, J., SAR, C., TWOHEY, P., CADAR, C., AND ENGLER, D. Automatically generating malicious disks using symbolic execution. In *S&P '06: IEEE Symposium on Security and Privacy* (2006).

[19] YANG, J., TWOHEY, P., ENGLER, D., AND MUSUVATHI, M. Using model checking to find serious file system errors. *ACM Transactions on Computer Systems 24*, 4 (2006).

ΔFTL: Improving SSD Lifetime via Exploiting Content Locality

Guanying Wu and Xubin He

Department of Electrical and Computer Engineering
Virginia Commonwealth University, Richmond, VA 23284, USA
{wug, xhe2}@vcu.edu

Abstract

NAND flash-based SSDs suffer from limited lifetime due to the fact that NAND flash can only be programmed or erased for limited times. Among various approaches to address this problem, we propose to reduce the number of writes to the flash via exploiting the content locality between the write data and its corresponding old version in the flash. This content locality means, the new version, i.e., the content of a new write request, shares some extent of similarity with its old version. The information redundancy existing in the difference (delta) between the new and old data leads to a small compression ratio. The key idea of our approach, named ΔFTL (Delta Flash Translation Layer), is to store this compressed delta in the SSD, instead of the original new data, in order to reduce the number of writes committed to the flash. This write reduction further extends the lifetime of SSDs due to less frequent garbage collection process, which is a significant write amplification factor in SSDs. Experimental results based on our ΔFTL prototype show that ΔFTL can significantly reduce the number of writes and garbage collection operations and thus improve SSD lifetime at a cost of trivial overhead on read latency performance.

Categories and Subject Descriptors C.4 [*PERFORMANCE OF SYSTEMS*]: Reliability, availability, and serviceability

General Terms Design, Reliability, Performance

Keywords SSD, Lifetime, NAND flash, Reliability, FTL

1. Introduction

Solid state drives (SSDs) exhibit good performance, particularly for random workloads, compared to traditional hard drives (HDDs). From a reliability standpoint, SSDs have no moving parts, no mechanical wear-out, and are silent and resistant to heat and shock. However, the limited lifetime of SSDs is a major drawback that hinders their deployment in reliability sensitive environments [3, 5]. As pointed out in [5], "endurance and retention (of SSDs) is not yet proven in the field" and integrating SSDs into commercial systems is "painfully slow". The reliability problem of SSDs mainly comes from the following facts. Flash memory must be erased before it can be written and it may only be programmed/erased for a limited times (5K to 100K) [10]. In addition, the out-of-place writes result in invalid pages to be discarded by garbage collection (GC). Extra writes are introduced in GC operations to move valid pages to a clean block [2] which further aggravates the lifetime problem of SSDs.

Existing approaches for this problem mainly focus on two perspectives: 1) to prevent early defects of flash blocks by wear-leveling techniques [6, 38]; 2) to reduce the number of write operations on the flash. For the later, various techniques are proposed including in-drive buffer management schemes [16, 18, 22, 48] to exploit the temporal or spatial locality; FTLs (Flash Translation Layer) [12, 17, 23, 24] to optimize the mapping policies or garbage collection schemes to reduce the write-amplification factor; or data deduplication [7, 11] to eliminate writes of existing content in the drive.

In this paper, we aim to efficiently solve this lifetime issue from a different aspect. We propose a new FTL scheme, ΔFTL, to reduce the write count via exploiting the content locality. The content locality has been observed and exploited in memory systems [13], file systems [8], and block devices [32, 49, 50]. Content locality means data blocks, either blocks at distinct locations or created at different time, share *similar contents*. We exploit the content locality that exists between the new (the content of update write) and the old version of page data mapped to the same logical address. This content locality implies the new version resembles the old to some extend, so that the difference (*delta*) between them can be compressed compactly. Instead of storing new data in its original form in the flash, ΔFTL stores the compressed deltas to reduce the number of writes.

EuroSys'12, April 10–13, 2012, Bern, Switzerland.
Copyright © 2012 ACM 978-1-4503-1223-3/12/04... $10.00

Research contributions:

- We propose a novel FTL scheme, ΔFTL to extend SSD lifetime via exploiting the content locality. We describe how ΔFTL functionality can be achieved from the data structures and algorithms that enhance the regular page-mapping FTL.

- We propose techniques to alleviate the potential performance overheads of ΔFTL.

- We model ΔFTL's performance on extending SSD's lifetime via analytical discussions and outline the workload characteristics favored by ΔFTL.

- We evaluate the performance of ΔFTL under real-world workloads via simulation experiments. Results show that ΔFTL significantly extends SSD's lifetime by reducing the number of garbage collection operations at a cost of trivial overhead on read latency performance. Specifically, ΔFTL results in 33% to 58% of the baseline garbage collection operations; and the read latency is only increased by approximately 5%.

The rest of the paper is organized as follows: Section 2 gives an introduction to NAND flash-based SSDs and a brief survey of techniques to extent SSD's lifetime as well as techniques to leverage the content locality. In Section 3, we discuss the design of ΔFTL in detail. Analytical modeling of ΔFTL's performance for SSD lifetime enhancement is expanded in Section 4. The performance evaluation under real-world workloads is given in Section 5. We conclude this paper and outline the future work in Section 6.

2. Background and Related Work

2.1 NAND Flash-based SSDs

The NAND flash by itself exhibits relatively poor performance [46, 47]. The high performance of an SSD comes from leveraging a hierarchy of parallelism. At the lowest level is the *page*, which is the basic unit of I/O read and write requests in SSDs. Erase operations operate at the *block* level, which are sequential groups of pages. A typical value for the size of a block is 64 or 128 pages. Further up the hierarchy is the plane, and on a single die there could be several planes. Planes operate semi-independently, offering potential speed-ups if data is striped across several planes. Additionally, certain copy operations can operate between planes without crossing the I/O pins. An upper level of abstraction, the chip interfaces, free the SSD controller from the analog processes of the basic operations, i.e., read, program, and erase, with a set of defined commands. NAND interface standards includes ONFI [34], BA-NAND [34], OneNAND [36], LBA-NAND [42], etc. SSDs hides the underlying details of the chip interfaces and exports the storage space as a standard block-level disk via a software layer called *Flash Translation Layer* (FTL). FTL is a key component of an SSD in that it not only is

responsible for managing the "logical to physical" address mapping but also works as a flash memory allocator, wear-leveler, and garbage collection engine. The mapping policy is mostly related to our work in this paper. The mapping policies of FTLs can be classified into two types: page-level mapping [2, 12], where a logical page can be placed onto any physical page; or block-level mapping [17, 23, 24], where the logical page LBA is translated to a physical block address and the offset of that page in the block. Page-level mapping is believed to be popular in modern SSD design [7, 11]. In this paper, our design augments the regular page-mapping FTL to support the delta-encoding of the newly written data.

2.2 Extending SSD's Lifetime

To extend the lifetime of SSDs, many designs have been proposed in the literature such as FTLs, cache schemes, hybrid storage materials, etc.

FTLs: For block-level mapping, several FTL schemes have been proposed to use a number of physical blocks to log the updates. Examples include FAST [24], BAST [23], SAST [17], and LAST [25]. The garbage collection of these schemes involves three types of merge operations, *full*, *partial*, and *switch* merge. The block-level mapping FTL schemes leverage the spatial or temporal locality in write workloads to reduce the overhead introduced in the merge operations. For page level mapping, DFTL [12] is proposed to cache the frequently used mapping table in the in-drive SRAM so as to improve the address translation performance as well as reduce the mapping table updates in the flash; μ-FTL [27] adopts the μ-tree on the mapping table to reduce the memory footprint. Two-level FTL [45] is proposed to dynamically switch between page-level and block-level mapping. Content-aware FTLs (CAFTL) [7, 11] implement the deduplication technique as FTL in SSDs to eliminate contents that are "exactly" the same across the entire drive. CAFTL requires complicated FTL design and implementation, e.g., a large finger-print store to facilitate content lookup and multi-layer mapping tables to locate logical addresses associated to the same content. Due to the limited computation power of the micro-processor inside SSDs, the complexity of deduplication via CAFTL is a major concern. On the other hand, our ΔFTL focuses on leveraging the similarity existing among old and new versions of data at the same logical address (as opposed to the entire drive), which brings a lightweight FTL design and implementation.

Cache schemes: A few in-drive cache schemes like BPLRU [22], FAB [16], CLC [18], and BPAC [48] are proposed to improve the sequentiality of the write workload sent to the FTL, so as to reduce the merge operation overhead on the FTLs. CFLRU [35] which works as an OS level scheduling policy, chooses to prioritize the clean cache elements when doing replacements so that the write operations can be reduced or avoided. Taking advantage of fast sequential performance of HDDs, Griffin [39] and I-CASH [49] are proposed to extend the SSD lifetime by caching SSDs with HDDs.

Heterogeneous material: Utilizing advantages of PCRAM, such as the in-place update ability and faster access, Sun *et al.* [41] describe a hybrid architecture to log the updates on PCRAM for flash. FlexFS [26], on the other hand, combines MLC and SLC as trading off the capacity and erase cycle.

Wear-leveling Techniques: Dynamic wear-leveling techniques, such as [38], try to recycle blocks of small erase counts. To address the problem of blocks containing cold data, static wear-leveling techniques [6] try to evenly distribute the wear over the entire SSD.

2.3 Exploiting the Content Locality

The content locality implies that the data in the system share similarity with each other. Such similarity can be exploited to reduce the memory or storage usage by delta-encoding the difference between the selected data and its reference. Content locality has been leveraged in various level of the system. In virtual machine environments, VMs share a significant number of *identical* pages in the memory, which can be deduplicated to reduce the memory system pressure. Difference engine [13] improves the performance over deduplication by detecting the *nearly* identical pages and coalesce them via in-core compression [30] into much smaller memory footprint. Difference engine detects similar pages based on hashes of several chucks of each page: hash collisions are considered as a sign of similarity. Different from difference engine, GLIMPSE [31] and DERD system [8] work on the file system to leverage similarity across files; the similarity detection method adopted in these techniques is based on Rabin fingerprints over chunks at multiple offsets in a file. In the block device level, Peabody [32] and TRAP-Array [50] are proposed to reduce the space overhead of storage system backup, recovery, and rollback via exploiting the content locality between the previous (old) version of data and the current (new) version. Peabody mainly focuses on eliminating duplicated writes, i.e., the update write contains the same data as the corresponding old version (silent write) or sectors at different location (coalesced sectors). On the other hand, TRAP-Array reduces the storage usage of data backup by logging the compressed XORs (delta) of successive writes to each data block. The intensive content locality in the block I/O workloads produces a small compression ratio on such deltas and TRAP-Array is significantly space-efficient compared to traditional approaches. I-CASH [49] takes the advantage of content locality existing across the entire drive to reduce the number of writes in the SSDs. I-CASH stores only the reference blocks on the SSDs while logs the delta in the HDDs.

Our approach ΔFTL is mostly similar to the idea of TRAP-Array [50] , which exploits the content locality

between new and old version. The major differences are: 1) ΔFTL aims at reducing the number of program/erase (**P/E**) operations committed to the flash memory so as to extend SSD's lifetime, instead of reducing storage space usage involved in data backup or recovery. Technically, the history data are backed up in TRAP-Array while they are considered "invalid" and discarded in ΔFTL; 2) ΔFTL is an embedded software in the SSD to manage the allocation and de-allocation of flash space, which requires relative complex data structures and algorithms that are "flash-aware". It also requires that the computation complexity should be kept minimum due to limited micro-processor capability.

3. Design of ΔFTL

In this section, we first outline the architecture of ΔFTL and then depict its major components in detail.

3.1 Overview

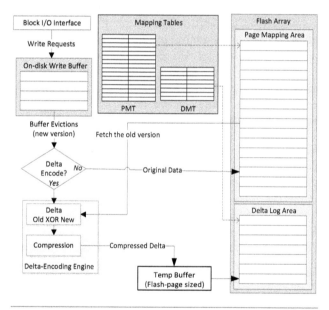

Figure 1. ΔFTL Overview

ΔFTL is designed as a flash management scheme that can store the write data in form of compressed deltas on the flash. Instead of devising from scratch, ΔFTL is rather an enhancement to the framework of the popular page-mapping FTL like DFTL [12]. Figure 1 gives an overview of ΔFTL and unveils its major differences from a regular page-mapping FTL:

- First, ΔFTL has a dedicated area, *Delta Log Area* (DLA), for logging the compressed deltas.

- Second, the compressed deltas must be associated with their corresponding old versions to retrieve the data. An extra mapping table, *Delta Mapping Table* (DMT), collaborates with *Page Mapping Table* (PMT) to achieve this functionality.

- Third, ΔFTL has a *Delta-encoding Engine* to derive and then compress the delta between the write buffer evictions and their old version on the flash. We have a set of dispatching rules (Section 3.2) determining whether a write request is stored in its original form or in its "delta-XOR-old" form. For the first case, the data is written to a flash page in page mapping area in its original form. For the later case, the delta-encoding engine derives and then compresses the delta between old and new. The compressed deltas are buffered in a flash-page-sized *Temp Buffer* until the buffer is full. Then, the content of the temp buffer is committed to a flash page in delta log area.

Details of the data structures and algorithms to implement ΔFTL are given in the following subsections.

3.2 Dispatching Policy: Delta Encode?

The content locality between the new and old data allows us to compress the delta, which has rich information redundancy, to a compact form. Writing the compressed deltas rather than the original data, would indeed reduce the number of flash writes. However, delta-encoding all data indiscriminately would cause overheads. First, if a page is stored in "delta-XOR-old" form, this page actually requires storage space for both delta and the old page, compared to only one flash page if in the original form. The extra space is provided by the over-provisioning area of the drive [2]. To make a trade-off between the over-provisioning resource and the number of writes, ΔFTL favors the data that are overwritten frequently. This policy can be interpreted intuitively with a simple example: in a workload, page data A is only overwritten once while B is overwritten 4 times. Assuming the compression ratio is 0.25, delta-encoding A would reduce the number of write by $3/4$ page (compared to the baseline which would take one page write) at a cost of $1/4$ page in the over-provision space. Delta-encoding B, on the other hand, reduces the number of write by $4 * (3/4) = 3$ pages at the same cost of space. Clearly, we would achieve better performance/cost ratio with such write "hot" data rather than the cold ones. The approach taken by ΔFTL to differentiate hot data from cold ones is discussed in Section 3.5.2. Second, fulfilling a read request targeting a page in "delta-XOR-old" form requires two flash page reads. This may have reverse impact on the read latency. To alleviate this overhead, ΔFTL avoids delta-encoding pages that are read intensive. If a page in "delta-XOR-old" form is found read intensive, ΔFTL will merge it to the original form to avoid the reading overhead. Again, the detailed approach is discussed in Section 3.5.2 in detail and evaluated in Section 5. Third, the delta-encoding process involves operations to fetch the old, derive delta, and compress delta. This extra time may potentially add overhead to the write performance (discussed in Section 3.3.2). ΔFTL must cease delta-encoding if it would

Temp Buffer (Flash page sized)

Figure 2. ΔFTL Temp Buffer

degrade the write performance. To summarize, ΔFTL delta-encodes data that are *write-hot* but *read-cold* while ensuring the write performance is not degraded.

3.3 Write Buffer and Delta-encoding

The in-drive write buffer resides in the volatile memory (SRAM or DRAM) managed by an SSD's internal controller and shares a significant portion of it [16, 18, 22]. The write buffer absorbs repeated writes and improves the spatial locality of the output workload from it. We concentrate our effort on FTL design, which services write buffer's outputs, and adopt simple buffer management schemes like FIFO or SLRU [19] that are usual in disk drives. When buffer eviction occurs, the evicted write pages are dispatched according to our dispatching policy discussed above to either ΔFTL's *Delta-encoding Engine* or directly to the page mapping area. Delta-encoding engine takes the new version of the page data (i.e., the evicted page) and the corresponding old version in page mapping area, as its inputs. It derives the delta by XOR the new and old version and then compress the delta. The compressed delta are buffered in *Temp Buffer*. *Temp Buffer* is of the same size as a flash page. Its content will be committed to delta log area once it is full or there is no space for the next compressed delta. Splitting a compressed delta on two flash pages would involve in unnecessary complications for our design. Storing multiple deltas in one flash page requires meta-data, like LPA (logical page address) and the offset of each delta (as shown in Figure 2) in the page, to associate them with their old versions and locate the exact positions. The meta-data is stored at the MSB part of a page instead of attached after the deltas, for the purpose of fast retrieval. This is because the flash read operation always buses out the content of a page from its beginning [34]. The content of temp buffer described here is essentially what we have in flash pages of delta log area. Delta-encoding engine demands the computation power of SSD's internal micro-processor and would introduce overhead for write requests. We discuss the delta-encoding latency in Section 3.3.1 and the approach adopted by ΔFTL to control the overhead in Section 3.3.2.

3.3.1 Delta-encoding Latency

Delta-encoding involves two steps: to derive delta (XOR the new and old versions) and to compress it. Among many data compression algorithms, the lightweight ones are favorable for ΔFTL due to the limited computation power of the SSD's internal micro-processor. We investigate the latency of a few candidates, including Bzip2 [37], LZO [33],

Table 1. Delta-encoding Latency

Frequency(MHz)	304	619	934
Compression(μs)	89.5	44.0	29.1
Decompression(μs)	22.2	10.9	7.2

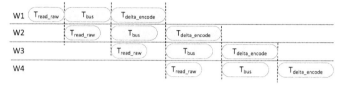

Figure 3. ΔFTL Delta-encoding Timeline

Table 2. List of Symbols

Symbols	Description
n	Number of pending write pages
P_c	Probability of compressible writes
R_c	Average compression ratio
T_{write}	Time for page write
T_{read_raw}	Time for raw flash read access
T_{bus}	Time for transferring a page via bus
T_{erase}	Time to erase a block
T_{delta_encode}	Time for delta-encoding a page
B_s	Block size (pages/block)
N	Total Number of page writes in the workload
T	Data blocks containing invalid pages (baseline)
t	Data blocks containing invalid pages (ΔFTL's PMA)
PE_{gc}	The number of P/E operations done in GC
F_{gc}	GC frequency
OH_{gc}	Average GC overhead
G_{gc}	Average GC gain (number of invalid pages reclaimed)
S_{cons}	Consumption speed of available clean blocks

Table 3. Flash Access Latency

Parameter	Value
Flash Read/Write/Erase	$25\mu s/200\mu s/1.5ms$
Bus Transfer Time	$40\mu s$

LZF [28], Snappy [9], and Xdelta [30], by emulating the execution of them on the ARM platform: the source codes are cross-compiled and run on the *SimpleScalar-ARM* simulator [29]. The simulator is an extension to SimpleScalar supporting ARM7 [4] architecture and we configured a processor similar to ARM®Cortex R4 [1], which inherits ARM7 architecture. For each algorithm, the number of CPU cycles is reported and the latency is then estimated by dividing the cycle number by the CPU frequency. We select LZF (LZF1X-1) from the candidates because. it makes a good trade-off between speed and compression performance, plus a compact executable size. The average number of CPU cycles for LZF to compress and decompress a 4KB page is about 27212 and 6737, respectively. According to Cortex R4's write paper, it can run at a frequency from 304MHz to 934MHz. The latency values in μs are listed in Table 1. An intermediate frequency value (619MHz) is included along with the other two to represent three classes of micro-processors in SSDs.

3.3.2 Discussion: Write Performance Overhead

ΔFTL's delta-encoding is a two-step procedure. First, delta-encoding engine fetches the old version from the page mapping area. Second, the delta between the old and new data are derived and compressed. The first step consists of raw flash access and bus transmission, which exclusively occupy the flash chip and the bus to the micro-processor, respectively. The second step occupies exclusively the micro-processor to perform the computations. Naturally, these three elements, the flash chip, the bus, and micro-processor, forms a simple pipeline, where the delta-encoding procedures of a serial of write requests could be overlapped. An example of four writes is demonstrated in Figure 3, where T_{delta_encode} is the longest phase. This is true for a micro-processor of 304MHz or 619MHz assuming T_{read_raw} and T_{bus} take $25\mu s$ and $40\mu s$ (Table 3), respectively. A list of symbols used in this section is summarized in Table 2. For an analytical view of the write overhead, we assume there is a total number of n write requests pending for a chip. Among these requests, the percentage that is considered *compressible* according to

our dispatching policy is P_c and the average compression ratio is R_c. The delta-encoding procedure for these n requests takes a total time of: $MAX(T_{read\_raw}, T_{bus}, T_{delta\_encode}) * n * P_c$ The number of page writes committed to the flash is the sum of original data writes and compressed delta writes: $(1 - P_c) * n + P_c * n * R_c$. For the baseline, which always outputs the data in their original form, the page write total is n. We define that the write overhead exists if ΔFTL's write routine takes more time than the baseline. Thus, there is *no* overhead if the following expression is true:

$$MAX(T_{read\_raw}, T_{bus}, T_{delta\_encode}) * n * P_c + \\ ((1 - P_c) * n + P_c * n * R_c) * T_{write} < n * T_{write} \quad (1)$$

Expression 1 can be simplified to:

$$1 - Rc > \frac{MAX(T_{read\_raw}, T_{bus}, T_{delta\_encode})}{T_{write}} \quad (2)$$

Substituting the numerical values in Table 1 and Table 3, the right side of Expression 2 is 0.45, 0.22, and 0.20, for micro-processor running at 304, 619, and 934MHz, respectively. Therefore, the viable range of R_c should be smaller than 0.55, 0.78, and 0.80. Clearly, high performance micro-processor would impose a less restricted constraint on R_c. If R_c is out of the viable range due to weak content locality in the workload, in order to eliminate the write overhead, ΔFTL must switch to the baseline mode where the delta-encoding procedure is bypassed.

3.4 Flash Allocation

ΔFTL's flash allocation scheme is an enhancement to the regular page mapping FTL scheme with a number of flash blocks dedicated to store the compressed deltas. These blocks are referred to as *Delta Log Area* (DLA). Similar to page mapping area (PMA), we allocate a clean block for DLA so long as the previous active block is full [2]. The garbage collection policy will be discussed in Section 3.6. DLA cooperates with PMA to render the latest version of one data page if it is stored as *delta-XOR-old* form. Obviously, read requests for such data page would suffer from the overhead of fetching two flash pages. To alleviate this problem, we keep the track of the read access popularity of each delta. If one delta is found read-popular, it is merged with the corresponding old version and the result (data in its original form) is stored in PMA. Furthermore, as discussed in Section 3.2, write-cold data should not be delta-encoded in order to save the over-provisioning space. Considering the temporal locality of a page may last for only a period in the workload, if a page previously considered write-hot is no longer demonstrating its temporal locality, this page should be transformed to its original form from its delta-XOR-old form. ΔFTL periodically scans the write-cold pages and merges them to PMA from DLA if needed.

3.5 Mapping Table

The flash management scheme discussed above requires ΔFTL to associate each valid delta in DLA with its old version in PMA. ΔFTL adopts two mapping tables for this purpose: *Page Mapping Table* (PMT) and *Delta Mapping Table* (DMT). Page mapping table is the primary table indexed by logical page address (LPA) of 32bits. For each LPA, PMT maps it to a physical page address (PPA) in page mapping area, either the corresponding data page is stored as its original form or in delta-XOR-old form. For the later case, the PPA points to the old version. PMT differentiates this two cases by prefixing a flag bit to the 31bits PPA (which can address 8TB storage space assuming a 4KB page size). As demonstrated in Figure 4: if the flag bit is "1", which means this page is stored in delta-XOR-old form, we use the PPA (of the old version) to consult the delta mapping table and find out on which physical page the corresponding delta resides. Otherwise, the PPA in this page mapping table entry points to the original form of the page. DMT does not maintain the offset information of each delta in the flash page; we locate the exact position with the metadata prefixed in the page (Figure 2).

3.5.1 Store Mapping Tables On the Flash

ΔFTL stores both mapping tables on the flash and keeps an *journal* of update records for each table. The updates are first buffered in the in-drive RAM and when they grow up to a full page, these records are flushed to the journal on the flash. In case of power failure, a built-in capacitor or battery in the SSD (e.g., a SuperCap [43]) may provide the power to flush the un-synchronized records to the flash. The journals are merged with the tables periodically.

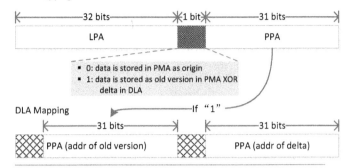

Figure 4. ΔFTL Mapping Entry

3.5.2 Cache Mapping Table In the RAM

ΔFTL adopts the same idea of caching popular table entries in the RAM as DFTL [12], as shown in Figure 5(a). The cache is managed using *segment LRU* scheme (SLRU) [19]. Different from two separate tables on the flash, the mapping entries for data either in the original form or delta-XOR-old form are included in one SLRU list. For look-up efficiency, we have all entries indexed by the LPA. Particularly, entries for data in delta-XOR-old form associate the LPA with PPA of old version and PPA of delta, as demonstrated in Figure 5(b). When we have an address look-up miss in the mapping table cache and the target page is in delta-XOR-old form, both on-flash tables are consulted and we merge the information together to an entry as shown in Figure 5(b). As discussed in Section 3.4, the capability of differentiating write-hot and read-hot data is critical to ΔFTL. We have to avoid delta-encoding the write-cold or read-hot data and merge the delta and old version of one page if it is found read-hot or found no longer write-hot. To keep the track of read/write access frequency, we associate each mapping entry in the cache with an *access count*. If the mapping entry of a page is found having a read-access (or write-access) count larger or equal to a predefined threshold, we consider this page read-hot (or write-hot) and vice versa. In our prototyping implementation (discussed in Section 5), we set this threshold as 2 and it captures the temporal locality for both read and writes successfully in our experiments. This information is forwarded to the dispatching policy module to guide the destination of a write request. In addition, merge operations take place if needed.

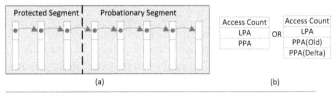

Figure 5. ΔFTL Buffered Mapping Entry

3.6 Garbage Collection

Overwrite operations causes invalidation of old data, which the garbage collection engine is required to discard when clean flash blocks are short. GC engine copies the valid data on the victim block to a clean one and erase the victim thereafter. ΔFTL selects victim blocks based on a simple "greedy" policy, i.e., blocks having the most number of invalid data result in the least number of valid data copy operations and the most clean space reclaimed [21]. ΔFTL's GC victim selection policy does not differentiate blocks from page mapping area or delta log area. In delta log area, the deltas becomes *invalid* in the following scenarios:

- If there is a new write considered not compressible (the latest version will be dispatched to PMA), according to the dispatching policy, the corresponding delta of this request and the old version in PMA become invalid.

- If the new write is compressible and thus a new delta for the same LPA is to be logged in DLA, the old delta becomes invalid.

- If this delta is merged with the old version in PMA, either due to read-hot or write-cold, it is invalidated.

- If there is a TRIM[1] command indicating that a page is no longer in use, the corresponding delta and the old version in PMA are invalidated.

For any case, ΔFTL maintains the information about the invalidation of the deltas for GC engine to select the victims. In order to facilitate the merging operations, when a block is selected as GC victim, the GC engine will consult the mapping table for information about the access frequency of the valid pages in the block. The GC engine will conduct necessary merging operations while it is moving the valid pages to the new position. For example, for a victim block in PMA, GC engine finds out a valid page is associated with a delta which is read-hot, then this page will be merged with the delta and mark the delta as invalidated.

4. Discussion: SSD Lifetime Extension of ΔFTL

Analytical discussion about ΔFTL's performance on SSD lifetime extension is given in this section. In this paper, we use the number of program and erase operations executed to service the write requests as the metric to evaluate the lifetime of SSDs. This is a common practice in most existing related work targeting SSD lifetime improvement [7, 12, 39, 49]. This is because the estimation of SSDs' lifetime is very challenging due to many complicated factors that would affect the actual number of write requests an SSD could handle before failure,

---

[1] The TRIM [44] command informs a SSD which pages of data are no longer considered in use and can be marked as invalid. Such pages are reclaimed so as to reduce the no-in-place-write overhead caused by subsequent overwrites.

including implementation details the device manufacturers would not unveil. On the other hand, comparing the P/E counts resulted from our approach to the baseline is relatively a more practical metric for the purpose of performance evaluation. Write amplification is a well-known problem for SSDs: due to the out-of-place-update feature of NAND flash, the SSDs have to take multiple flash write operations (and even erase operations) in order to fulfill one write request. There are a few factors that would affect the write amplification, e.g., the write buffer, garbage collection, wear leveling, etc [15]. We focus on garbage collection for our discussion, providing that the other factors are the same for ΔFTL and the regular page mapping FTLs. We breakdown the total number of P/E operations into two parts: the **foreground** writes issued from the write buffer (for the baseline) or ΔFTL's dispatcher and delta-encoding engine; the **background** page writes and block erase operations involved in GC processes. Symbols introduced in this section are listed in Table 2.

4.1 Foreground Page Writes

Assuming for one workload, there is a total number of N page writes issued from the write buffer. The baseline has N foreground page writes while ΔFTL has $(1 - P_c) * N + P_c * N * R_c$ (as discussed in Section 3.3.2). ΔFTL would resemble the baseline if P_c (percentage of compressible writes) approaches 0 or R_c (average compression ratio of compressible writes) approaches 1, which means the temporal locality or content locality is weak in the workload.

4.2 GC Caused P/E Operations

The P/E operations caused by GC processes is essentially determined by the frequency of GC and the average overhead of each GC, which can be expressed as:

$$PE_{gc} \propto F_{gc} * OH_{gc} \qquad (3)$$

GC process is triggered when clean flash blocks are short in the drive. Thus, the GC frequency is proportional to *the consumption speed of clean space* and inversely proportional to *the average number of clean space reclaimed of each GC* (GC gain):

$$F_{gc} \propto \frac{S_{cons}}{G_{gc}} \qquad (4)$$

Consumption Speed is actually determined by the number of foreground page writes (N for the baseline). *GC Gain* is determined by the average number of invalid pages on each GC victim block.

4.2.1 GC P/E of The Baseline

First, let's consider the baseline. Assuming for the given workload, all write requests are overwrites to existing data in the drive, then N page writes invalidate a total number of N

existing pages. If these N invalid pages spread over T data blocks, the average number of invalid pages (thus GC Gain) on GC victim blocks is N/T. Substituting into Expression 4, we have the following expression for the baseline:

$$F_{gc} \propto \frac{N}{N/T} = T \qquad (5)$$

For each GC, we have to copy the valid pages (assuming there are B_s pages/block, we have $B_s - N/T$ valid pages on each victim block on average) and erase the victim block. Substituting into Expression 3, we have:

$$PE_{gc} \propto T * (Erase + Program * (B_s - N/T)) \qquad (6)$$

4.2.2 GC P/E of ΔFTL

Now let's consider ΔFTL's performance. Among N page writes issued from the write buffer, $(1 - P_c) * N$ pages are committed in PMA causing the same number of flash pages in PMA to be invalidated. Assuming there are t blocks containing invalid pages caused by those writes in PMA, we apparently have $t \leq T$. The average number of invalid pages in PMA is then $(1 - P_c) * N/t$. On the other hand, $P_c * N * R_c$ pages containing compressed deltas are committed to DLA. Recall that there are three scenarios where the deltas in DLA get invalidated (Section 3.6). Omitting the last scenario which is rare compared to the first two, the number of deltas invalidated is determined by the *overwrite rate* (P_{ow}) of deltas committed to DLA: while we assume in the workload all writes are overwrites to existing data in the drive, this *overwrite rate* here defines the percentage of deltas that are overwritten by the subsequent writes in the workload. For example, no matter the subsequent writes are incompressible and committed to PMA or otherwise, the corresponding delta gets invalidated. The average invalid space (in the term of pages) of victim block in DLA is thus $P_{ow} * B_s$. Substituting these numbers to Expression 4: If the average GC gain in PMA outnumbers that in DLA, we have:

$$F_{gc} \propto \frac{(1 - P_c + P_c R_c)N}{(1 - P_c)N/t} = t(1 + \frac{P_c R_c}{1 - P_c}) \qquad (7)$$

Otherwise, we have:

$$F_{gc} \propto \frac{(1 - P_c + P_c R_c)N}{P_{ow} B_s} \qquad (8)$$

Substituting Expression 7 and 8 to Expression 3, we have for GC introduced P/E:

$$PE_{gc} \propto t(1 + \frac{P_c R_c}{1 - P_c}) * \\ (Erase + Program * (B_s - (1 - P_c)N/t)) \qquad (9)$$

or:

$$PE_{gc} \propto \frac{(1 - P_c + P_c R_c)N}{P_{ow} B_s} * \\ (T_{erase} + T_{write} * B_s(1 - P_{ow})) \qquad (10)$$

4.3 Summary

From above discussions, we observe that ΔFTL favors the disk I/O workloads that demonstrate: (i) High content locality that results in small R_c; (ii) High temporal locality for writes that results in large P_c and P_{ow}. Such workload characteristics are widely present in various OLTP applications such as TPC-C, TPC-W, etc [20, 40, 49, 50].

5. Performance Evaluation

We have implemented and evaluated our design of ΔFTL based on a series of comprehensive trace-driven simulation experiments. In this section, we present the experimental results comparing ΔFTL with the page mapping FTL as the baseline. In Section 4, the total number of P/E operations are broken down to foreground writes and GC introduced P/E's for intuitive analytical discussions. Essentially, the number of foreground writes and the efficiency of GC are reflected by the number of GC operations. Thus, in this section we use the number of GC operations as the major metric to evaluate ΔFTL's performance on extending SSD's lifetime. In addition, we evaluate the overheads ΔFTL may potentially introduce, including read and write performance. Particularly, read/write performance is measured in terms of response time.

5.1 Simulation Tool and SSD Configurations

ΔFTL is a device-level software in the SSD controller. We have implemented it (as well as the baseline page mapping FTL) in an SSD simulator based on the Microsoft Research SSD extension [2] for DiskSim 4.0. The simulated SSD is configured as follows: there are 16 flash chips, each of which owns a dedicated channel to the flash controller. Each chip has four planes that are organized in a RAID-0 fashion; the size of one plane is 1GB assuming the flash is used as 2-bit MLC (page size is 4KB). To maximize the concurrency, each individual plane has its own allocation pool [2]. The garbage collection processes are executed in the background so as to minimizing the interference upon the foreground requests. In addition, the percentage of flash space over-provisioning is set as 30%, which doubles the value suggested in [2]. Considering the limited working-set size of the workloads used in this paper, 30% over-provisioning is believed to be sufficient to avoid garbage collection processes to be executed too frequently. The garbage collection threshold is set as 10%, which means if the clean space goes below 10% of the exported space, the garbage collection processes are triggered. Due to negligible impact that the write buffer size has on ΔFTL's performance compared to the baseline, we only report the results with buffer size of 64MB. The SSD is connected to the host via a PCI-E bus of 2.0 GB/s. In addition, the physical operating parameters of the flash memory are summarized in Table 3.

5.2 Workloads

We choose 6 popular disk I/O traces for the simulation experiments. *Financial 1* and *Financial 2* (F1, F2) [40] were obtained from OLTP applications running at two large financial institutions; the *Display Ads Platform and payload servers* (DAP-PS) and *MSN storage metadata* (MSN-CFS) traces were from the Production Windows Servers and described in [20] (MSN-CFS trace contains I/O requests on multiple disks and we only use one of them); the *Cello99* [14] trace pool is collected from the "Cello" server that runs HP-UX 10.20. Because the entire *Cello99* is huge, we randomly use one day traces (07/17/99) of two disks (Disk 3 and Disk 8). Table 4 summarizes the traces we use in our simulation.

Table 4. Disk Traces Information

	Reads(10^6)	Read %	Writes	Write %	Duration(h)
F1	1.23	23.2	4.07	76.8	12
F2	3.04	82.3	0.65	17.7	12
C3	0.75	35.3	1.37	64.7	24
C8	0.56	27.4	1.48	72.6	24
DAP	0.61	56.2	0.47	43.8	24
MSN	0.82	75.0	0.27	25.0	6

5.3 Emulating the Content Locality

As pointed out in [7, 8, 32, 50], the content locality of a workload is application specific and different applications may result in distinctive extent of content locality. In this paper, instead of focusing on only the workloads possessing intensive content locality, we aim at exploring the performance of ΔFTL under diverse situations. As discussed in Section 4, the content locality as well as temporal locality are leading factors that have significant impact on ΔFTL's performance. In our trace-driven simulation, we explore various temporal locality characteristics via 6 disk I/O traces; on the other hand, we emulate the content locality by assigning randomized compression ratio values to the write requests in the traces. The compression ratio values follows Gaussian distribution, of which the average equals R_c. Referring to the values of R_c reported in [50] (0.05 to 0.25) and in [32] (0.17 to 0.6), we evaluate three levels of content locality in our experiments, having $R_c = 0.50, 0.35$, and 0.20 to represent low, medium, and high content locality, respectively. In the rest of this section, we present the experimental results under 6 traces and three levels of content locality, comparing ΔFTL with the baseline.

5.4 Experimental Results

To verify the performance of ΔFTL, we measure the number of garbage collection operations and foreground writes, the write latency, and overhead on read latency.

5.4.1 Number of Garbage Collection Operations and Foreground Writes

First, we evaluate the number of garbage collection operations as the metric for ΔFTL's performance on extending SSD lifetime. Due to the large range of the numerical values of the experimental results, we normalize them to the corresponding results of the baseline as shown in Figure 6. Clearly, ΔFTL significantly reduces the GC count compared to the baseline: ΔFTL results in only 58%, 46%, and 33% of the baseline GC count on average, for $R_c = 0.50, 0.35, 0.20$ respectively. ΔFTL's maximum performance gain (22% of baseline) is achieved with C3 trace when $R_c = 0.20$; the minimum (82%) is with F1, $R_c = 0.50$. We may observe from the results that the performance gain is proportional to the content locality, which is represented by the average compression ratio R_c; in addition, ΔFTL performs relatively poorer with two traces F1 and F2, compared to the rests. In order to interpret our findings, we examine two factors that determine the GC count: the consumption speed of clean space (S_{cons}, Expression 4) and the speed of clean space reclaiming, i.e., the average GC gain (G_{gc}). **Consumption Speed:** As

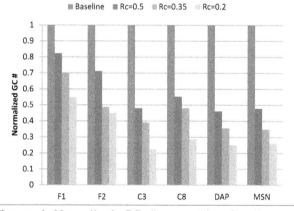

Figure 6. Normalized GC #: comparing baseline and ΔFTL; smaller # implies longer SSD lifetime.

discussed in Section 4, the consumption speed is determined by the number of foreground flash page writes. We plot the normalized number of foreground writes in Figure 7. As seen in the figure, the results are proportional to R_c as well; F1 and F2 produce more foreground writes than the others, which result in larger GC counts as shown in Figure 6. If there are N writes in the baseline, ΔFTL would have $(1 - P_c + P_c * R_c) * N$. The foreground write counts are reversely proportional to R_c (self-explained in Figure 7) as well as P_c. So, what does P_c look like? Recall in Section 3.2 that P_c is determined by the dispatching rules, which favor write-hot and read-cold data. The access frequency characteristics, i.e., the temporal locality, is workload-specific, which means the P_c values should be different among traces but not affected by R_c. This point is justified clearly in Figure 8, which plots the ratio of DLA

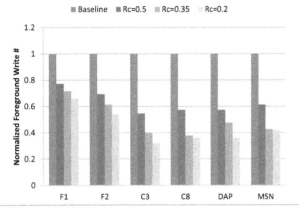

Figure 7. Normalized foreground write #: comparing baseline and ΔFTL; smaller # implies: a) larger P_c and b) lower consumption speed of clean flash space.

writes (P_c) out of the total foreground writes. We may also verify that the foreground write counts (Figure 7) are reversely proportional to P_c: F1 and F2 have the least P_c values among all traces and they produce the most number of foreground writes; this trend can be also observed with other traces. **Garbage collection gain** is another factor that

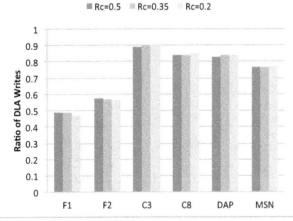

Figure 8. Ratio of DLA writes (P_c).

determines GC count. Figure 9 plots the average GC gain in terms of the number of invalid pages reclaimed. GC gain ranges from 14 (C8, baseline) to 54 (F2, $R_c = 0.20$). F1 and F2 outperform the other traces on the average GC gain. However, comparing to the baseline performance, ΔFTL actually does not improve much with F1 and F2: we normalize each trace's results with its individual baseline in Figure 10. ΔFTL even degrades average GC gain with F1 and F2 when $R_c = 0.50$. This also complies with the GC count results shown in Figure 6, where ΔFTL achieves poorer performance gain with F1 and F2 compared to the others. The reason why ΔFTL does not improve GC gain significantly over the baseline with F1 and F2 is: compared to the other traces, F1 and F2 result in larger invalid page counts in blocks of PMA, which makes ΔFTL's GC engine

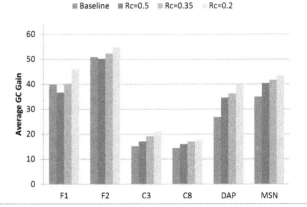

Figure 9. Average GC gain (number of invalid pages reclaimed): comparing baseline and ΔFTL; smaller # implies lower GC efficiency on reclaiming flash space.

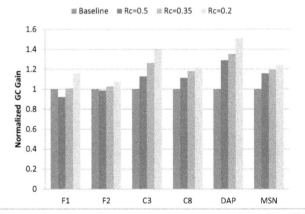

Figure 10. Normalized average GC gain (number of invalid pages reclaimed): comparing baseline and ΔFTL.

to choose more PMA blocks as GC victims than DLA blocks. Thus, the average GC gain performance of ΔFTL resembles the baseline. To the contrary, ΔFTL benefits from the relative higher temporal locality of write requests in the DLA than in the PMA, under the other 4 traces. This is the reason why ΔFTL outperforms the baseline with these traces. In order to verify this point, we collect the number of GC executed in DLA and plot the ratio over the total in Figure 11: the majority of the total GC operations lies in PMA for F1 and F2 and in DLA for the rest.

5.4.2 Write Performance

In ΔFTL, the delta-encoding procedure in servicing a write request may cause overhead on write latency if R_c is out of the viable range (Section 3.3.2). R_c values adopted in our simulation experiments ensures there is no write overhead. ΔFTL significantly reduces the foreground write counts, and the write latency performance also benefits from this. As shown in Figure 12, ΔFTL reduces the average write latency by 36%, 47%, and 51% when $R_c = 0.50, 0.35, 0.20$, respectively.

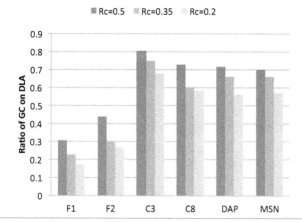

Figure 11. Ratio of GC executed in DLA.

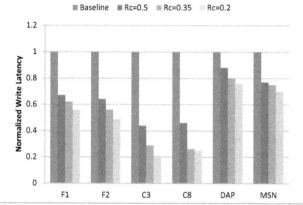

Figure 12. Normalized write latency performance: comparing baseline and ΔFTL.

5.4.3 Garbage Collection Overhead

The GC operation involves copying the valid data from the victim block to a clean block and erasing the victim block. The GC overhead, i.e., the time for a GC operation, may potentially hinder the foreground requests to be serviced. We evaluate the average GC overhead of ΔFTL and compare the results to the baseline in Figure 13. We observe that ΔFTL does not significantly increase the GC overhead under most cases.

5.4.4 Overhead on Read Performance

ΔFTL reduces the write latency significantly and therefore alleviates the chip contention between the read and write requests, resulting less queuing delay for the reads. Under intensive workloads, the effective read latency (considering queuing delay on the device side) is reduced in Delta-FTL. However, ΔFTL inevitably introduces overhead on the raw read latency (despite queuing delay) when the target page is delta-encoded. Fulfilling such a read request requires two flash read operations. To overcome this potential overhead, ΔFTL delta-encodes only the write-hot and read-cold data and merges DLA pages to their original form if they are

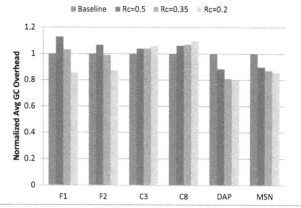

Figure 13. Normalized average GC overhead.

found read-hot. To evaluate the effectiveness of our approach, we collect the raw read latency values reported by the simulator and demonstrate the results in Figure 14. Compared to the baseline (normalized to 1), ΔFTL's impact on the read performance is trivial: the read latency is increased by 5.3%, 5.4%, and 5.6% on average[2] when $R_c = 0.50, 0.35, 0.20$, respectively. The maximum (F2, $R_c = 0.50$) is 10.7%. To summarize, our experimental

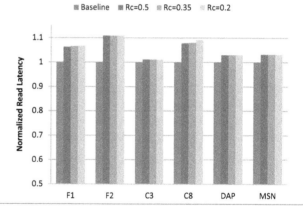

Figure 14. Normalized read latency performance: comparing baseline and ΔFTL.

results verify that ΔFTL significantly reduces the GC count and thus extends SSDs' lifetime at a cost of trivial overhead on read performance.

6. Conclusions and Future Work

The limited lifetime impedes NAND flash-based SSDs from wide deployment in reliability-sensitive environments. In this paper, we have proposed a solution, ΔFTL, to alleviate this problem. ΔFTL extends SSDs' lifetime by reducing the number of program/erase operations for servicing the disk I/O requests. By leveraging the content locality existing between the new data and its old version,

---

[2] x% read latency overhead implies that x% of the requested pages are delta-encoded, which would double the raw latency compared to non-delta-encoded pages.

ΔFTL stores the new data in the flash in the form of compressed delta. We have presented the design of ΔFTL in detail including the data structures, algorithms, and overhead control approaches in this paper. ΔFTL is prototyped and evaluated via simulation. Our trace-driven experiments demonstrate that ΔFTL significantly extends SSD's lifetime by reducing the number of garbage collection operations at a cost of trivial overhead on read latency performance. Specifically, ΔFTL results in 33% to 58% of the baseline garbage collection operations, while the read latency is only increased by approximately 5%.

Our future work will explore the integration of deduplication to ΔFTL to further improve the lifetime of SSDs. The major technical challenge is to alleviate the pressure of computation and space complexity introduced by the need of managing the mapping of logical addresses to the contents.

Acknowledgments

We thank our shepherd Steven Gribble and anonymous reviewers for their feedback. This research is sponsored in part by the U.S. National Science Foundation (NSF) under grants CCF-1102605 and CCF-1102624. Any opinions, findings, and conclusions or recommendations expressed in this material are those of the author(s) and do not necessarily reflect the views of the funding agency.

References

[1] ARM Cortex R4. www.arm.com/files/pdf/Cortex-R4-white-paper.pdf.

[2] N. Agrawal, V. Prabhakaran, T. Wobber, J. D. Davis, M. Manasse, and R. Panigrahy. Design Tradeoffs for SSD Performance. In *USENIX ATC*, Boston, Massachusetts, USA, 2008.

[3] D. Andersen and S. Swanson. Rethinking flash in the data center. *IEEE Micro*, 30(4):52–54, 2010.

[4] ARM®. Arm7. http://www.arm.com/products/processors/classic/arm7/index.php.

[5] L. A. Barroso. Warehouse-scale Computing. In *Keynote in the SIGMOD10 conference*, 2010.

[6] Y.-H. Chang, J.-W. Hsieh, and T.-W. Kuo. Endurance enhancement of flash-memory storage systems: An efficient static wear leveling design. In *DAC*, San Diego, CA, USA, June 2007.

[7] F. Chen, T. Luo, and X. Zhang. CAFTL: A content-aware flash translation layer enhancing the lifespan of flash memory based solid state drives. In *Proceedings of FAST'2011*.

[8] F. Douglis and A. Iyengar. Application-specific delta-encoding via resemblance detection. In *Proceedings of the USENIX ATC*, pages 1–23, 2003.

[9] Google. Snappy. http://code.google.com/p/snappy/.

[10] L. Grupp, A. Caulfield, J. Coburn, S. Swanson, E. Yaakobi, P. Siegel, and J. Wolf. Characterizing flash memory: anomalies, observations, and applications. In *Proceedings*

of the 42nd Annual IEEE/ACM International Symposium on Microarchitecture, pages 24–33. ACM, 2009.

[11] A. Gupta, R. Pisolkar, B. Urgaonkar, and A. Sivasubramaniam. Leveraging value locality in optimizing NAND flash-based SSDs. In *Proceedings of FAST'2011*.

[12] A. Gupta, Y. Kim, and B. Urgaonkar. DFTL: a flash translation layer employing demand-based selective caching of page-level address mappings. In *ASPLOS '09*, 2009.

[13] D. Gupta, S. Lee, M. Vrable, S. Savage, A. Snoeren, G. Varghese, G. Voelker, and A. Vahdat. Difference engine: Harnessing memory redundancy in virtual machines. *Communications of the ACM*, 53(10):85–93, 2010.

[14] Hewlett-Packard Laboratories. cello99 traces. http://tesla.hpl.hp.com/opensource/.

[15] X. Hu, E. Eleftheriou, R. Haas, I. Iliadis, and R. Pletka. Write amplification analysis in flash-based solid state drives. In *Proceedings of SYSTOR09*, page 10. ACM, 2009.

[16] H. Jo, J. Kang, S. Park, J. Kim, and J. Lee. FAB: flash-aware buffer management policy for portable media players. *IEEE Transactions on Consumer Electronics*, 52(2):485–493, 2006.

[17] J. U. Kang, H. Jo, J. S. Kim, and J. Lee. A superblock-based flash translation layer for nand flash memory. In *International Conference on Embedded Software*, 2006.

[18] S. Kang, S. Park, H. Jung, H. Shim, and J. Cha. Performance Trade-Offs in Using NVRAM Write Buffer for Flash Memory-Based Storage Devices. *IEEE Transactions on Computers*, 58(6):744–758, 2009.

[19] R. Karedla, J. S. Love, and B. G. Wherry. Caching strategies to improve disk system performance. *IEEE Computer*, 27(3): 38–46, March 1994.

[20] S. Kavalanekar, B. Worthington, Q. Zhang, and V. Sharda. Characterization of storage workload traces from production windows servers. In *IISWC*, 2008.

[21] A. Kawaguchi, S. Nishioka, and H. Motoda. A flash-memory based file system. In *Proceedings of the USENIX 1995 Technical Conference*, pages 13–13. USENIX Association, 1995.

[22] H. Kim and S. Ahn. BPLRU: A Buffer Management Scheme for Improving Random Writes in Flash Storage Abstract. In *Proceedings of FAST*, 2008.

[23] J. Kim, J. M. Kim, S. Noh, S. L. Min, and Y. Cho. A space-efficient flash translation layer for Compact Flash Systems. *IEEE Transactions on Consumer Electronics*, 48(2):366–375, 2002.

[24] S. Lee, D. Park, T. Chung, D. Lee, S. Park, and H. Song. FAST: An FTL Scheme with Fully Associative Sector Translations. In *UKC*, August 2005.

[25] S. Lee, D. Shin, Y. Kim, and J. Kim. LAST: locality-aware sector translation for NAND flash memory-based storage systems. *SIGOPS*, 42(6), 2008.

[26] S. Lee, K. Ha, K. Zhang, J. Kim, and J. Kim. FlexFS: A Flexible Flash File System for MLC NAND Flash Memory. In *USENIX ATC*, June 2009.

[27] Y.-G. Lee, D. Jung, D. Kang, and J.-S. Kim. uFTL: a memory-efficient flash translation layer supporting multiple mapping granularities. In *EMSOFT*, 2008.

[28] M. Lehmann. Lzf. http://oldhome.schmorp.de/marc/liblzf.html.

[29] S. LLC. Simplescalar/arm. http://www.simplescalar.com/v4test.html.

[30] J. MacDonald. xdelta. http://xdelta.org.

[31] U. Manber and S. Wu. Glimpse: A tool to search through entire file systems. In *Usenix Winter 1994 Technical Conference*, pages 23–32, 1994.

[32] C. Morrey III and D. Grunwald. Peabody: The time travelling disk. In *Proceedings of MSST 2003*, pages 241–253. IEEE.

[33] M. Oberhumer. Lzo. http://www.oberhumer.com/opensource/lzo.

[34] ONFI, 2010. http://onfi.org/.

[35] S. Park, D. Jung, J. Kang, J. Kim, and J. Lee. CFLRU: a replacement algorithm for flash memory. In *Proceedings of CASES'2006*, pages 234–241, 2006.

[36] Samsung, 2010. http://www.samsung.com/global/business/semiconductor/products/fusionmemory/Products-OneNAND.html.

[37] J. Seward. The bzip2 and libbzip2 official home page. 2002. http://sources.redhat.com/bzip2.

[38] SiliconSystems. Increasing flash solid state disk reliability. *Technical report*, 2005.

[39] G. Soundararajan, V. Prabhakaran, M. Balakrishnan, and T. Wobber. Extending SSD Lifetimes with Disk-Based Write Caches. In *Proceedings of FAST*. USENIX, Feb 2010.

[40] Storage Performance Council. SPC trace file format specification. http://traces.cs.umass.edu/index.php/Storage/Storage.

[41] G. Sun, Y. Joo, Y. Chen, D. Niu, Y. Xie, Y. Chen, and H. Li. A hybrid solid-state storage architecture for the performance, energy consumption, and lifetime improvement. In *Proceedings of HPCA-16*, pages 141–153. IEEE, Jan 2010.

[42] Toshiba. http://www.toshiba.com/taec/news/press-releases/2006/memy-06-337.jsp, 2010.

[43] wikipedia. Battery or super cap, 2010. http://en.wikipedia.org/wiki/Solid-state-drive#Battery_or_SuperCap.

[44] wikipedia. TRIM, 2012. http://en.wikipedia.org/wiki/TRIM.

[45] C.-H. Wu and T.-W. Kuo. An adaptive two-level management for the flash translation layer in embedded systems. In *Proceedings of ICCAD '06*, 2006.

[46] G. Wu and X. He. Reducing SSD Read Latency via NAND Flash Program and Erase Suspension. In *Proceedings of FAST'2012*.

[47] G. Wu, X. He, N. Xie, and T. Zhang. DiffECC: Improving SSD Read Performance Using Differentiated Error Correction Coding Schemes. In *MASCOTS*, pages 57–66, 2010.

[48] G. Wu, X. He, and B. Eckart. An Adaptive Write Buffer Management Scheme for Flash-Based SSDs. *ACM Transactions on Storage*, 8(1), 2012.

[49] Q. Yang and J. Ren. I-CASH: Intelligently Coupled Array of SSD and HDD. In *Proceedings of HPCA 2011*, pages 278–289. IEEE.

[50] Q. Yang, W. Xiao, and J. Ren. TRAP-Array: A disk array architecture providing timely recovery to any point-in-time. *ACM SIGARCH Computer Architecture News*, 34(2):289–301, 2006.

FlashTier: A Lightweight, Consistent and Durable Storage Cache

Mohit Saxena, Michael M. Swift and Yiying Zhang

University of Wisconsin-Madison

{msaxena,swift,yyzhang}@cs.wisc.edu

Abstract

The availability of high-speed solid-state storage has introduced a new tier into the storage hierarchy. Low-latency and high-IOPS solid-state drives (SSDs) cache data in front of high-capacity disks. However, most existing SSDs are designed to be a drop-in disk replacement, and hence are mismatched for use as a cache.

This paper describes *FlashTier*, a system architecture built upon *solid-state cache* (SSC), a flash device with an interface designed for caching. Management software at the operating system block layer directs caching. The FlashTier design addresses three limitations of using traditional SSDs for caching. First, FlashTier provides a unified logical address space to reduce the cost of cache block management within both the OS and the SSD. Second, FlashTier provides cache consistency guarantees allowing the cached data to be used following a crash. Finally, FlashTier leverages cache behavior to silently evict data blocks during garbage collection to improve performance of the SSC.

We have implemented an SSC simulator and a cache manager in Linux. In trace-based experiments, we show that FlashTier reduces address translation space by 60% and silent eviction improves performance by up to 167%. Furthermore, FlashTier can recover from the crash of a 100 GB cache in only 2.4 seconds.

Categories and Subject Descriptors D.4.2 [*Operating Systems*]: Storage Management; C.4 [*Computer Systems Organization*]: Performance of Systems

Keywords Solid-State Cache, Device Interface, Consistency, Durability

1. Introduction

Solid-state drives (SSDs) composed of multiple flash memory chips are often deployed as a cache in front of cheap and slow disks [9, 22]. This provides the performance of flash with the cost of disk for large data sets, and is actively used by Facebook and others to provide low-latency access to petabytes of data [10, 32, 36]. Many vendors sell dedicated caching products that pair an SSD with proprietary software that runs in the OS to migrate data between the SSD and disks [12, 19, 30] to improve storage performance.

Building a cache upon a standard SSD, though, is hindered by the narrow block interface and internal block management of SSDs, which are designed to serve as a disk replacement [1, 34, 39]. Caches have at least three different behaviors that distinguish them from general-purpose storage. First, data in a cache may be present elsewhere in the system, and hence need not be durable. Thus, caches have more flexibility in how they manage data than a device dedicated to storing data persistently. Second, a cache stores data from a separate address space, the disks', rather than at native addresses. Thus, using a standard SSD as a cache requires an additional step to map block addresses from the disk into SSD addresses for the cache. If the cache has to survive crashes, this map must be persistent. Third, the consistency requirements for caches differ from storage devices. A cache must ensure it never returns stale data, but can also return nothing if the data is not present. In contrast, a storage device provides ordering guarantees on when writes become durable.

This paper describes *FlashTier*, a system that explores the opportunities for tightly integrating solid-state caching devices into the storage hierarchy. First, we investigate how small changes to the interface and internal block management of conventional SSDs can result in a much more effective caching device, a *solid-state cache*. Second, we investigate how such a dedicated caching device changes *cache managers*, the software component responsible for migrating data between the flash caching tier and disk storage. This design provides a clean separation between the caching device and its internal structures, the system software managing the cache, and the disks storing data.

FlashTier exploits the three features of caching workloads to improve over SSD-based caches. First, FlashTier provides a *unified address space* that allows data to be written to the SSC at its disk address. This removes the need for a separate table mapping disk addresses to SSD addresses. In addition,

| Device | Access Latency | | Capacity | Price | Endurance |
	Read	Write	Bytes	$/GB	Erase Cycles
DRAM	50 ns	50 ns	8-16 GB	$15	∞
Flash	40-100 μs	60-200 μs	TB	$3	10^4
Disk	500-5000 μs	500-5000 μs	TB	$0.3	∞

Table 1. Device Attributes: Price, performance and endurance of DRAM, Flash SSDs and Disk. (GB: gigabyte, TB: terabyte).

an SSC uses internal data structures tuned for large, sparse address spaces to maintain the mapping of block number to physical location in flash.

Second, FlashTier provides *cache consistency guarantees* to ensure correctness following a power failure or system crash. It provides separate guarantees for clean and dirty data to support both write-through and write-back caching. In both cases, it guarantees that stale data will never be returned. Furthermore, FlashTier introduces new operations in the device interface to manage cache contents and direct eviction policies. FlashTier ensures that internal SSC metadata is always persistent and recoverable after a crash, allowing cache contents to be used after a failure.

Finally, FlashTier leverages its status as a cache to reduce the cost of garbage collection. Unlike a storage device, which promises to never lose data, a cache can evict blocks when space is needed. For example, flash must be erased before being written, requiring a garbage collection step to create free blocks. An SSD must copy live data from blocks before erasing them, requiring additional space for live data and time to write the data. In contrast, an SSC may instead *silently evict* the data, freeing more space faster.

We implemented an SSC simulator and a cache manager for Linux and evaluate FlashTier on four different storage traces. We measure the cost and benefits of each of our design techniques. Our results show that:

- FlashTier reduces total memory usage by more than 60% compared to existing systems using an SSD cache.

- FlashTier's free space management improves performance by up to 167% and requires up to 57% fewer erase cycles than an SSD cache.

- After a crash, FlashTier can recover a 100 GB cache in less than 2.4 seconds, much faster than existing systems providing consistency on an SSD cache.

The remainder of the paper is structured as follows. Section 2 describes our caching workload characteristics and motivates FlashTier. Section 3 presents an overview of FlashTier design, followed by a detailed description in Section 4 and 5. We evaluate FlashTier design techniques in Section 6, and finish with related work and conclusions.

2. Motivation

Flash is an attractive technology for caching because its price and performance are between DRAM and disk: about five times cheaper than DRAM and an order of magni-

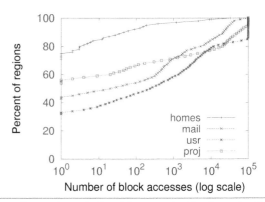

Figure 1. Logical Block Addresses Distribution: The distribution of unique block accesses across 100,000 4 KB block regions of the disk address space.

tude (or more) faster than disk (see Table 1). Furthermore, its persistence enables cache contents to survive crashes or power failures, and hence can improve cold-start performance. As a result, SSD-backed caching is popular in many environments including workstations, virtualized enterprise servers, database backends, and network disk storage [22, 29, 30, 36, 37].

Flash has two characteristics that require special management to achieve high reliability and performance. First, flash does not support *in-place writes*. Instead, a block of flash must be *erased* (a lengthy operation) before it can be written. Second, to support writing a block multiple times, flash devices use *address mapping* to translate block addresses received from a host into physical locations in flash. This mapping allows a block to be written out-of-place to a pre-erased block rather than erasing and rewriting in-place. As a result, SSDs employ *garbage collection* to compact data and provide free, erased blocks for upcoming writes.

The motivation for FlashTier is the observation that caching and storage have different behavior and different requirements. We next study three aspects of caching behavior to distinguish it from general-purpose storage. Our study uses traces from two different sets of production systems downstream of an active page cache over 1-3 week periods [24, 27]. These systems have different I/O workloads that consist of a file server (*homes* workload), an email server (*mail* workload) and file servers from a small enterprise data center hosting user home and project directories (*usr* and *proj*). Table 3 summarizes the workload statistics. Trends observed across all these workloads directly motivate our design for FlashTier.

Address Space Density. A hard disk or SSD exposes an address space of the same size as its capacity. As a result, a mostly full disk will have a dense address space, because there is valid data at most addresses. In contrast, a cache stores only *hot data* that is currently in use. Thus, out of the terabytes of storage, a cache may only contain a few gigabytes. However, that data may be at addresses that range over the full set of possible disk addresses.

Figure 1 shows the density of requests to 100,000-block regions of the disk address space. To emulate the effect of caching, we use only the top 25% most-accessed blocks from each trace (those likely to be cached). Across all four traces, more than 55% of the regions get less than 1% of their blocks referenced, and only 25% of the regions get more than 10%. These results motivate a change in how mapping information is stored within an SSC as compared to an SSD: while an SSD should optimize for a *dense address space*, where most addresses contain data, an SSC storing only active data should instead optimize for a *sparse address space*.

Persistence and Cache Consistency. Disk caches are most effective when they offload workloads that perform poorly, such as random reads and writes. However, large caches and poor disk performance for such workloads result in exceedingly long cache warming periods. For example, filling a 100 GB cache from a 500 IOPS disk system takes over 14 hours. Thus, caching data persistently across system restarts can greatly improve cache effectiveness.

On an SSD-backed cache, maintaining cached data persistently requires storing cache metadata, such as the state of every cached block and the mapping of disk blocks to flash blocks. On a clean shutdown, this can be written back at low cost. However, to make cached data *durable* so that it can survive crash failure, is much more expensive. Cache metadata must be persisted on every update, for example when updating or invalidating a block in the cache. These writes degrade performance, and hence many caches do not provide crash recovery [5, 14], and discard all cached data after a crash.

A hard disk or SSD provides crash recovery with simple consistency guarantees to the operating system: barriers ensure that preceding requests complete before subsequent ones are initiated. For example, a barrier can ensure that a journal commit record only reaches disk *after* the journal entries [7]. However, barriers provide ordering between requests to a single device, and do not address consistency between data on different devices. For example, a write sent both to a disk and a cache may complete on just one of the two devices, but the combined system must remain consistent.

Thus, the guarantee a cache makes is semantically different than ordering: a cache should never return stale data, and should never lose dirty data. However, within this guarantee, the cache has freedom to relax other guarantees, such as the persistence of clean data.

Wear Management. A major challenge with using SSDs as a disk cache is their limited write endurance: a single MLC flash cell can only be erased 10,000 times. In addition, garbage collection is often a contributor to wear, as live data must be copied to make free blocks available. A recent study

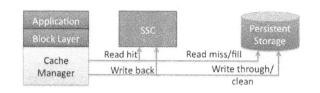

Figure 2. FlashTier Data Path: A cache manager forwards block read/write requests to disk and solid-state cache.

showed that more than 70% of the erasures on a full SSD were due to garbage collection [8].

Furthermore, caching workloads are often more intensive than regular storage workloads: a cache stores a greater fraction of hot blocks, which are written frequently, as compared to a general storage workload. In looking at the top 25% most frequently referenced blocks in two write-intensive storage traces, we find that the average writes per block is 4 times greater than for the trace as a whole, indicating that caching workloads are likely to place greater durability demands on the device. Second, caches operate at full capacity while storage devices tend to be partially filled. At full capacity, there is more demand for garbage collection. This can hurt reliability by copying data more frequently to make empty blocks [16, 18].

3. Design Overview

FlashTier is a block-level caching system, suitable for use below a file system, virtual memory manager, or database. A *cache manager* interposes above the disk device driver in the operating system to send requests to the either the flash device or the disk, while a *solid-state cache (SSC)* stores and assists in managing cached data. Figure 2 shows the flow of read and write requests from the application to SSC and disk-storage tiers from the cache manager.

3.1 Cache Management

The cache manager receives requests from the block layer and decides whether to consult the cache on reads, and whether to cache data on writes. On a cache miss, the manager sends the request to the disk tier, and it may optionally store the returned data in the SSC.

FlashTier supports two modes of usage: *write-through* and *write-back*. In write-through mode, the cache manager writes data to the disk and populates the cache either on read requests or at the same time as writing to disk. In this mode, the SSC contains only clean data, and is best for read-heavy workloads, where there is little benefit to caching writes, and when the cache is not considered reliable, as in a client-side cache for networked storage. In this mode, the cache manager consults the SSC on every read request. If the data is not present, the SSC returns an error, and the cache manager fetches the data from disk. On a write, the cache manager must either evict the old data from the SSC or write the new data to it.

In write-back mode, the cache manager may write to the SSC without updating the disk. Thus, the cache may contain dirty data that is later evicted by writing it back to the disk. This complicates cache management, but performs better with write-heavy workloads and local disks. In this mode, the cache manager must actively manage the contents of the cache to ensure there is space for new data. The cache manager maintains a table of dirty cached blocks to track which data is in the cache and ensure there is enough space in the cache for incoming writes. The manager has two options to make free space: it can evict a block, which guarantees that subsequent reads to the block will fail, and allows the manager to direct future reads of the block to disk. Or, the manager notifies the SSC that the block is clean, which then allows the SSC to evict the block in the future. In the latter case, the manager can still consult the cache on reads and must evict/overwrite the block on writes if it still exists in the cache.

3.2 Addressing

With an SSD-backed cache, the manager must maintain a *mapping table* to store the block's location on the SSD. The table is indexed by logical block number (LBN), and can be used to quickly test whether block is in the cache. In addition, the manager must track free space and evict data from the SSD when additional space is needed. It does this by removing the old mapping from the mapping table, inserting a mapping for a new LBN with the same SSD address, and then writing the new data to the SSD.

In contrast, an SSC does not have its own set of addresses. Instead, it exposes a *unified address space*: the cache manager can write to an SSC using logical block numbers (or disk addresses), and the SSC internally maps those addresses to physical locations in flash. As flash devices already maintain a mapping table to support garbage collection, this change does not introduce new overheads. Thus the cache manager in FlashTier no longer needs to store the mapping table persistently, because this functionality is provided by the SSC.

The large address space raises the new possibility that cache does not have capacity to store the data, which means the cache manager must ensure not to write too much data or the SSC must evict data to make space.

3.3 Space Management

As a cache is much smaller than the disks that it caches, it requires mechanisms and policies to manage its contents. For write-through caching, the data is clean, so the SSC may silently evict data to make space. With write-back caching, though, there may be a mix of clean and dirty data in the SSC. An SSC exposes three mechanisms to cache managers for managing the cached data: *evict*, which forces out a block; *clean*, which indicates the data is clean and can be evicted by the SSC, and *exists*, which tests for the presence of a block and is used during recovery. As described above,

for write-through caching all data is clean, whereas with write-back caching, the cache manager must explicitly clean blocks after writing them back to disk.

The ability to evict data can greatly simplify space management within the SSC. Flash drives use garbage collection to compact data and create freshly erased blocks to receive new writes, and may relocate data to perform wear leveling, which ensures that erases are spread evenly across the physical flash cells. This has two costs. First, copying data for garbage collection or for wear leveling reduces performance, as creating a single free block may require reading and writing multiple blocks for compaction. Second, an SSD may copy and compact data that is never referenced again. An SSC, in contrast, can evict data rather than copying it. This speeds garbage collection, which can now erase clean blocks without copying their live data because clean cache blocks are also available in disk. If the data is not later referenced, this has little impact on performance. If the data is referenced later, then it must be re-fetched from disk and cached again.

Finally, a cache does not require overprovisioned blocks to make free space available. Most SSDs reserve 5-20% of their capacity to create free erased blocks to accept writes. However, because an SSC does not promise a fixed capacity, it can flexibly dedicate space either to data, to reduce miss rates, or to the log, to accept writes.

3.4 Crash Behavior

Flash storage is persistent, and in many cases it would be beneficial to retain data across system crashes. For large caches in particular, a durable cache can avoid an extended warm-up period where all data must be fetched from disks. However, to be usable after a crash, the cache must retain the metadata mapping disk blocks to flash blocks, and must guarantee correctness by never returning stale data. This can be slow, as it requires synchronous metadata writes when modifying the cache. As a result, many SSD-backed caches, such as Solaris L2ARC and NetApp Mercury, must be reset after a crash [5, 14].

The challenge in surviving crashes in an SSD-backed cache is that the mapping must be persisted along with cached data, and the consistency between the two must also be guaranteed. This can greatly slow cache updates, as replacing a block requires writes to: (i) remove the old block from the mapping, (ii) write the new data, and (iii) add the new data to the mapping.

3.5 Guarantees

FlashTier provides consistency and durability guarantees over cached data in order to allow caches to survive a system crash. The system distinguishes *dirty data*, for which the newest copy of the data may only be present in the cache, from *clean data*, for which the underlying disk also has the latest value.

1. A read following a write of dirty data will return that data.

2. A read following a write of clean data will return *either* that data or a not-present error.

3. A read following an eviction will return a not-present error.

The first guarantee ensures that dirty data is durable and will not be lost in a crash. The second guarantee ensures that it is *always* safe for the cache manager to consult the cache for data, as it must either return the newest copy or an error. Finally, the last guarantee ensures that the cache manager can invalidate data in the cache and force subsequent requests to consult the disk. Implementing these guarantees within the SSC is much simpler than providing them in the cache manager, as a flash device can use internal transaction mechanisms to make all three writes at once [33, 34].

4. System Design

FlashTier has three design goals to address the limitations of caching on SSDs:

- *Address space management* to unify address space translation and block state between the OS and SSC, and optimize for sparseness of cached blocks.

- *Free space management* to improve cache write performance by silently evicting data rather than copying it within the SSC.

- *Consistent interface* to provide consistent reads after cache writes and eviction, and make both clean and dirty data as well as the address mapping durable across a system crash or reboot.

This section discusses the design of FlashTier's address space management, block interface and consistency guarantees of SSC, and free space management.

4.1 Unified Address Space

FlashTier unifies the address space and cache block state split between the cache manager running on host and firmware in SSC. Unlike past work on virtual addressing in SSDs [21], the address space in an SSC may be very sparse because caching occurs at the block level.

Sparse Mapping. The SSC optimizes for sparseness in the blocks it caches with a *sparse hash map* data structure, developed at Google [13]. This structure provides high performance and low space overhead for sparse hash keys. In contrast to the mapping structure used by Facebook's Flash-Cache, it is fully associative and thus must encode the complete block address for lookups.

The map is a hash table with t buckets divided into t/M groups of M buckets each. Each group is stored sparsely as an array that holds values for allocated block addresses and an occupancy bitmap of size M, with one bit for each bucket. A bit at location i is set to 1 if and only if bucket i is non-empty. A lookup for bucket i calculates the value location

from the number of 1s in the bitmap before location i. We set M to 32 buckets per group, which reduces the overhead of bitmap to just 3.5 bits per key, or approximately 8.4 bytes per occupied entry for 64-bit memory pointers [13]. The runtime of all operations on the hash map is bounded by the constant M, and typically there are no more than 4-5 probes per lookup.

The SSC keeps the entire mapping in its memory. However, the SSC maps a fixed portion of the flash blocks at a 4 KB page granularity and the rest at the granularity of an 256 KB erase block, similar to hybrid FTL mapping mechanisms [18, 25]. The mapping data structure supports lookup, insert and remove operations for a given key-value pair. Lookups return the physical flash page number for the logical block address in a request. The physical page number addresses the internal hierarchy of the SSC arranged as flash package, die, plane, block and page. Inserts either add a new entry or overwrite an existing entry in the hash map. For a remove operation, an invalid or unallocated bucket results in reclaiming memory and the occupancy bitmap is updated accordingly. Therefore, the size of the sparse hash map grows with the actual number of entries, unlike a linear table indexed by a logical or physical address.

Block State. In addition to the logical-to-physical map, the SSC maintains additional data for internal operations, such as the state of all flash blocks for garbage collection and usage statistics to guide wear-leveling and eviction policies. This information is accessed by physical address only, and therefore can be stored in the out-of-band (OOB) area of each flash page. This is a small area (64–224 bytes) associated with each page [6] that can be written at the same time as data. To support fast address translation for physical addresses when garbage collecting or evicting data, the SSC also maintains a reverse map, stored in the OOB area of each page and updates it on writes. With each block-level map entry in device memory, the SSC also stores a dirty-block bitmap recording which pages within the erase block contain dirty data.

4.2 Consistent Cache Interface

FlashTier provides a consistent cache interface that reflects the needs of a cache to (i) persist cached data across a system reboot or crash, and (ii) never return stale data because of an inconsistent mapping. Most SSDs provide the read-/write interface of disks, augmented with a *trim* command to inform the SSD that data need not be saved during garbage collection. However, the existing interface is insufficient for SSD caches because it leaves undefined what data is returned when reading an address that has been written or evicted [28]. An SSC, in contrast, provides an interface with precise guarantees over consistency of both cached data and mapping information. The SSC interface is a small extension to the standard SATA/SCSI read/write/trim commands.

4.2.1 Interface

FlashTier's interface consists of six operations:

write-dirty	Insert new block or update existing block with dirty data.
write-clean	Insert new block or update existing block with clean data.
read	Read block if present or return error.
evict	Evict block immediately.
clean	Allow future eviction of block.
exists	Test for presence of dirty blocks.

We next describe these operations and their usage by the cache manager in more detail.

Writes. FlashTier provides two write commands to support write-through and write-back caching. For write-back caching, the *write-dirty* operation guarantees that data is durable before returning. This command is similar to a standard SSD write, and causes the SSC also update the mapping, set the dirty bit on the block and save the mapping to flash using logging. The operation returns only when the data and mapping are durable in order to provide a consistency guarantee.

The *write-clean* command writes data and marks the block as clean, so it can be evicted if space is needed. This operation is intended for write-through caching and when fetching a block into the cache on a miss. The guarantee of *write-clean* is that a subsequent read will return either the new data or a not-present error, and hence the SSC must ensure that data and metadata writes are properly ordered. Unlike *write-dirty*, this operation can be buffered; if the power fails before the write is durable, the effect is the same as if the SSC silently evicted the data. However, if the write replaces previous data at the same address, the mapping change must be durable before the SSC completes the request.

Reads. A read operation looks up the requested block in the device map. If it is present it returns the data, and otherwise returns an error. The ability to return errors from reads serves three purposes. First, it allows the cache manager to request any block, without knowing if it is cached. This means that the manager need not track the state of all cached blocks precisely; approximation structures such as a Bloom Filter can be used safely to prevent reads that miss in the SSC. Second, it allows the SSC to manage space internally by evicting data. Subsequent reads of evicted data return an error. Finally, it simplifies the consistency guarantee: after a block is written with *write-clean*, the cache can still return an error on reads. This may occur if a crash occurred after the write but before the data reached flash.

Eviction. FlashTier also provides a new *evict* interface to provide a well-defined read-after-evict semantics. After issuing this request, the cache manager knows that the cache cannot contain the block, and hence is free to write updated versions to disk. As part of the eviction, the SSC removes the forward and reverse mappings for the logical and physical pages from the hash maps and increments the number of invalid pages in the erase block. The durability guarantee of *evict* is similar to *write-dirty*: the SSC ensures the eviction is durable before completing the request.

Explicit eviction is used to invalidate cached data when writes are sent only to the disk. In addition, it allows the cache manager to precisely control the contents of the SSC. The cache manager can leave data dirty and explicitly evict selected victim blocks. Our implementation, however, does not use this policy.

Block cleaning. A cache manager indicates that a block is clean and may be evicted with the *clean* command. It updates the block metadata to indicate that the contents are clean, but does not touch the data or mapping. The operation is asynchronous, after a crash cleaned blocks may return to their dirty state.

A write-back cache manager can use *clean* to manage the capacity of the cache: the manager can clean blocks that are unlikely to be accessed to make space for new writes. However, until the space is actually needed, the data remains cached and can still be accessed. This is similar to the management of free pages by operating systems, where page contents remain usable until they are rewritten.

***Testing with* exists.** The *exists* operation allows the the cache manager to query the state of a range of cached blocks. The cache manager passes a block range, and the SSC returns the dirty bitmaps from mappings within the range. As this information is stored in the SSC's memory, the operation does not have to scan flash. The returned data includes a single bit for each block in the requested range that, if set, indicates the block is present and dirty. If the block is not present or clean, the bit is cleared. While this version of *exists* returns only dirty blocks, it could be extended to return additional per-block metadata, such as access time or frequency, to help manage cache contents.

This operation is used by the cache manager for recovering the list of dirty blocks after a crash. It scans the entire disk address space to learn which blocks are dirty in the cache so it can later write them back to disk.

4.2.2 Persistence

SSCs rely on a combination of logging, checkpoints, and out-of-band writes to persist its internal data. Logging allows low-latency writes to data distributed throughout memory, while checkpointing provides fast recovery times by keeping the log short. Out-of-band writes provide a low-latency means to write metadata near its associated data.

Logging. An SSC uses an operation log to persist changes to the sparse hash map. A log record consists of a monotonically increasing log sequence number, the logical and physical block addresses, and an identifier indicating whether this is a page-level or block-level mapping.

For operations that may be buffered, such as *clean* and *write-clean*, an SSC uses asynchronous group commit [17] to flush the log records from device memory to flash device periodically. For operations with immediate consistency guarantees, such as *write-dirty* and *evict*, the log is flushed as part of the operation using a synchronous commit. For example, when updating a block with *write-dirty*, the SSC will create a log record invalidating the old mapping of block number to physical flash address and a log record inserting the new mapping for the new block address. These are flushed using an atomic-write primitive [33] to ensure that transient states exposing stale or invalid data are not possible.

Checkpointing.   To ensure faster recovery and small log size, SSCs checkpoint the mapping data structure periodically so that the log size is less than a fixed fraction of the size of checkpoint. This limits the cost of checkpoints, while ensuring logs do not grow too long. It only checkpoints the forward mappings because of the high degree of sparseness in the logical address space. The reverse map used for invalidation operations and the free list of blocks are clustered on flash and written in-place using out-of-band updates to individual flash pages. FlashTier maintains two checkpoints on dedicated regions spread across different planes of the SSC that bypass address translation.

Recovery.   The recovery operation reconstructs the different mappings in device memory after a power failure or reboot. It first computes the difference between the sequence number of the most recent committed log record and the log sequence number corresponding to the beginning of the most recent checkpoint. It then loads the mapping checkpoint and replays the log records falling in the range of the computed difference. The SSC performs roll-forward recovery for both the page-level and block-level maps, and reconstructs the reverse-mapping table from the forward tables.

4.3   Free Space Management

FlashTier provides high write performance by leveraging the semantics of caches for garbage collection. SSDs use garbage collection to compact data and create free erased blocks. Internally, flash is organized as a set of *erase blocks*, which contain a number of pages, typically 64. Garbage collection coalesces the live data from multiple blocks and erases blocks that have no valid data. If garbage collection is performed frequently, it can lead to *write amplification*, where data written once must be copied multiple times, which hurts performance and reduces the lifetime of the drive [16, 18].

The hybrid flash translation layer in modern SSDs separates the drive into data blocks and log blocks. New data is written to the log and then merged into data blocks with garbage collection. The data blocks are managed with block-level translations (256 KB) while the log blocks use finer-grained 4 KB translations. Any update to a data block is per-

formed by first writing to a log block, and later doing a *full merge* that creates a new data block by merging the old data block with the log blocks containing overwrites to the data block.

Silent eviction.   SSCs leverage the behavior of caches by evicting data when possible rather than copying it as part of garbage collection. FlashTier implements a *silent eviction* mechanism by integrating cache replacement with garbage collection. The garbage collector selects a flash plane to clean and then selects the top-k victim blocks based on a policy described below. It then removes the mappings for any valid pages within the victim blocks, and erases the victim blocks. Unlike garbage collection, FlashTier does not incur any copy overhead for rewriting the valid pages.

When using silent eviction, an SSC will only consider blocks written with *write-clean* or explicitly cleaned. If there are not enough candidate blocks to provide free space, it reverts to regular garbage collection. Neither *evict* nor *clean* operations trigger silent eviction; they instead update metadata indicating a block is a candidate for eviction during the next collection cycle.

Policies.   We have implemented two policies to select victim blocks for eviction. Both policies only apply silent eviction to data blocks. The first policy, *SE-Util* selects the erase bock with the smallest number of valid pages (*i.e.*, lowest utilization). This minimizes the number of valid pages purged, although it may evict recently referenced data. This policy only creates erased *data blocks* and not log blocks, which still must use normal garbage collection.

The second policy, *SE-Merge* uses the same policy for selecting candidate victims (utilization), but allows the erased blocks to be used for either data or logging. This allows the number of log blocks to increase, which reduces garbage collection costs: with more log blocks, garbage collection of them is less frequent, and there may be fewer valid pages in each log block. However, this approach increases memory usage to store fine-grained translations for each block in the log. With *SE-Merge*, new data blocks are created via switch merges, which convert a sequentially written log block into a data block without copying data.

4.4   Cache Manager

The cache manager is based on Facebook's FlashCache for Linux [10]. It provides support for both write-back and write-through caching modes and implements a recovery mechanism to enable cache use after a crash.

The write-through policy consults the cache on every read. As read misses require only access to the in-memory mapping, these incur little delay. The cache manager, fetches the data from the disk on a miss and writes it to the SSC with *write-clean*. Similarly, the cache manager sends new data from writes both to the disk and to the SSC with *write-clean*. As all data is clean, the manager never sends any *clean* requests. We optimize the design for memory consumption assuming a high hit rate: the manager stores no data about cached blocks, and consults the cache on every request. An alternative design would be to store more information about which blocks are cached in order to avoid the SSC on most cache misses.

The write-back mode differs on the write path and in cache management; reads are handled similarly to write-through caching. On a write, the cache manager use *write-dirty* to write the data to the SSC only. The cache manager maintains an in-memory table of cached dirty blocks. Using its table, the manager can detect when the percentage of dirty blocks within the SSC exceeds a set threshold, and if so issues *clean* commands for LRU blocks. Within the set of LRU blocks, the cache manager prioritizes cleaning of contiguous dirty blocks, which can be merged together for writing to disk. The cache manager then removes the state of the clean block from its table.

The dirty-block table is stored as a linear hash table containing metadata about each dirty block. The metadata consists of an 8-byte associated disk block number, an optional 8-byte checksum, two 2-byte indexes to the previous and next blocks in the LRU cache replacement list, and a 2-byte block state, for a total of 14-22 bytes.

After a failure, a write-through cache manager may immediately begin using the SSC. It maintains no transient in-memory state, and the cache-consistency guarantees ensure it is safe to use all data in the SSC. Similarly, a write-back cache manager can also start using the cache immediately, but must eventually repopulate the dirty-block table in order to manage cache space. The cache manager scans the entire disk address space with *exists*. This operation can overlap normal activity and thus does not delay recovery.

5. Implementation

The implementation of FlashTier entails three components: the cache manager, an SSC functional emulator, and an SSC timing simulator. The first two are Linux kernel modules (kernel 2.6.33), and the simulator models the time for the completion of each request.

We base the cache manager on Facebook's FlashCache [10]. We modify its code to implement the cache policies described in the previous section. In addition, we added a trace-replay framework invokable from user-space with direct I/O calls to evaluate performance.

We base the SSC simulator on FlashSim [23]. The simulator provides support for an SSD controller, and a hierarchy of NAND-flash packages, planes, dies, blocks and pages. We enhance the simulator to support page-level and hybrid mapping with different mapping data structures for address translation and block state, write-ahead logging with synchronous and asynchronous group commit support for insert and remove operations on mapping, periodic checkpointing from device memory to a dedicated flash region, and a roll-forward recovery logic to reconstruct the mapping and block state. We have two basic configurations of the simulator, targeting the two silent eviction policies. The first configuration (termed *SSC* in the evaluation) uses the *SE-Util* policy and statically reserves a portion of the flash for log blocks and provisions enough memory to map these with page-level mappings. The second configuration, *SSC-R*, uses the *SE-Merge* policy and allows the fraction of log blocks to vary based on workload but must reserve memory capacity for the maximum fraction at page level. In our tests, we fix log blocks at 7% of capacity for SSC and allow the fraction to range from 0-20% for SSC-R.

We implemented our own FTL that is similar to the FAST FTL [25]. We integrate silent eviction with background and foreground garbage collection for data blocks, and with merge operations for *SE-Merge* when recycling log blocks [16]. We also implement inter-plane copy of valid pages for garbage collection (where pages collected from one plane are written to another) to balance the number of free blocks across all planes. The simulator also tracks the utilization of each block for the silent eviction policies.

The SSC emulator is implemented as a block device and uses the same code for SSC logic as the simulator. In order to emulate large caches efficiently (much larger than DRAM), it stores the metadata of all cached blocks in memory but discards data on writes and returns fake data on reads, similar to David [2].

6. Evaluation

We compare the cost and benefits of FlashTier's design components against traditional caching on SSDs and focus on three key questions:

- What are the benefits of providing a sparse unified cache address space for FlashTier?

- What is the cost of providing cache consistency and recovery guarantees in FlashTier?

- What are the benefits of silent eviction for free space management and write performance in FlashTier?

We describe our methods and present a summary of our results before answering these questions in detail.

6.1 Methods

We emulate an SSC with the parameters in Table 2, which are taken from the latencies of the third generation Intel 300 series SSD [20]. We scale the size of each plane to vary the SSD capacity. On the SSD, we over provision by 7% of the capacity for garbage collection. The SSC does not require over provisioning, because it does not promise a fixed-size address space. The performance numbers are not parameters but rather are the measured output of the SSC timing simulator, and reflect performance on an empty SSD/SSC. Other mainstream SSDs documented to perform better rely on deduplication or compression, which are orthogonal to our design [31].

Page read/write	65/85 μs	Block erase	1000 μs
Bus control delay	2 μs	Control delay	10 μs
Flash planes	10	Erase block/plane	256
Pages/erase block	64	Page size	4096 bytes
Seq. Read	585 MB/sec	Rand. Read	149,700 IOPS
Seq. Write	124 MB/sec	Rand. Write	15,300 IOPS

Table 2. Emulation parameters.

Workload	Range	Unique Blocks	Total Ops.	% Writes
homes	532 GB	1,684,407	17,836,701	95.9
mail	277 GB	15,136,141	462,082,021	88.5
usr	530 GB	99,450,142	116,060,427	5.9
proj	816 GB	107,509,907	311,253,714	14.2

Table 3. Workload Characteristics: All requests are sector-aligned and 4,096 bytes.

We compare the FlashTier system against the *Native* system, which uses uses the unmodified Facebook FlashCache cache manager and the FlashSim SSD simulator. We experiment with both write-through and write-back modes of caching. The write-back cache manager stores its metadata on the SSD, so it can recover after a crash, while the write-through cache manager cannot.

We use four real-world traces with the characteristics shown in Table 3. These traces were collected on systems with different I/O workloads that consist of a departmental email server (*mail* workload), and file server (*homes* workload) [24]; and a small enterprise data center hosting user home directories (*usr* workload) and project directories (*proj* workload) [27]. Workload duration varies from 1 week (*usr* and *proj*) to 3 weeks (*homes* and *mail*). The range of logical block addresses is large and sparsely accessed, which helps evaluate the memory consumption for address translation. The traces also have different mixes of reads and writes (the first two are write heavy and the latter two are read heavy) to let us analyze the performance impact of the SSC interface and silent eviction mechanisms. To keep replay times short, we use only the first 20 million requests from the *mail* workload, and the first 100 million requests from *usr* and *proj* workloads.

6.2 System Comparison

FlashTier improves on caching with an SSD by improving performance, reducing memory consumption, and reducing wear on the device. We begin with a high-level comparison of FlashTier and SSD caching, and in the following sections provide a detailed analysis of FlashTier's behavior.

Performance. Figure 3 shows the performance of the two FlashTier configurations with SSC and SSC-R in write-back and write-through modes relative to the native system with an SSD cache in write-back mode. For the write-intensive *homes* and *mail* workloads, the FlashTier system with SSC outperforms the native system by 59-128% in write-back mode and 38-79% in write-through mode. With SSC-R, the FlashTier system outperforms the native system by 101-

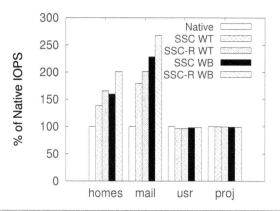

Figure 3. **Application Performance**: The performance of write-through and write-back FlashTier systems normalized to native write-back performance. We do not include native write-through because it does not implement durability.

167% in write-back mode and by 65-102% in write-through mode. The write-back systems improve the performance of cache writes, and hence perform best on these workloads.

For the read-intensive *usr* and *proj* workloads, the native system performs almost identical to the FlashTier system. The performance gain comes largely from garbage collection, as we describe in Section 6.5, which is offset by the cost of FlashTier's consistency guarantees, which are described in Section 6.4.

Memory consumption. Table 4 compares the memory usage on the device for the native system and FlashTier. Overall, Flashtier with the SSC consumes 11% more device memory and with SSC-R consumes 160% more. However, both FlashTier configurations consume 89% less host memory. We describe these results more in Section 6.3.

Wearout. For Figure 3, we also compare the number of erases and the wear differential (indicating a skewed write pattern) between the native and FlashTier systems. Overall, on the write-intensive *homes* and *mail* workloads, FlashTier with SSC performs 45% fewer erases, and with SSC-R performs 57% fewer. On the read-intensive *usr* and *proj* workloads, the SSC configuration performs 3% fewer erases and 6% fewer with SSC-R. The silent-eviction policy accounts for much of the difference in wear: in write-heavy workloads it reduces the number of erases but in read-heavy workloads may evict useful data that has to be written again. We describe these results more in Section 6.5.

6.3 FlashTier Address Space Management

In this section, we evaluate the device and cache manager memory consumption from using a single sparse address space to maintain mapping information and block state.

Device memory usage. Table 4 compares the memory usage on the device for the native system and FlashTier. The native system SSD stores a dense mapping translating from

Workload	Size GB	SSD	SSC	SSC-R	Native	FTCM
		Device (MB)			Host (MB)	
homes	1.6	1.13	1.33	3.07	8.83	0.96
mail	14.4	10.3	12.1	27.4	79.3	8.66
usr	94.8	66.8	71.1	174	521	56.9
proj	102	72.1	78.2	189	564	61.5
proj-50	205	144	152	374	1,128	123

Table 4. Memory Consumption: Total size of cached data, and host and device memory usage for Native and FlashTier systems for different traces. FTCM: write-back FlashTier Cache Manager.

SSD logical block address space to physical flash addresses. The FlashTier system stores a sparse mapping from disk logical block addresses to physical flash addresses using a sparse hash map. Both systems use a hybrid layer mapping (HLM) mixing translations for entire erase blocks with per-page translations. We evaluate both SSC and SSC-R configurations.

For this test, both SSD and SSC map 93% of the cache using 256 KB blocks and the remaining 7% is mapped using 4 KB pages. SSC-R stores page-level mappings for a total of 20% for reserved space. As described earlier in Section 4.3, SSC-R can reduce the garbage collection cost by using the *SE-Merge* policy to increase the percentage of log blocks. In addition to the target physical address, both SSC configurations store an eight-byte dirty-page bitmap with each block-level map entry in device memory. This map encodes which pages within the erase block are dirty.

We measure the device memory usage as we scale the cache size to accommodate the 25% most popular blocks from each of the workloads, and top 50% for *proj-50*. The SSD averages 2.8 bytes/block, while the SSC averages 3.1 and SSC-R averages 7.4 (due to its extra page-level mappings). The *homes* trace has the lowest density, which leads to the highest overhead (3.36 bytes/bock for SSC and 7.7 for SSC-R), while the *proj-50* trace has the highest density, which leads to lower overhead (2.9 and 7.3 bytes/block).

Across all cache sizes from 1.6 GB to 205 GB, the sparse hash map in SSC consumes only 5–17% more memory than SSD. For a cache size as large as 205 GB for *proj-50*, SSC consumes no more than 152 MB of device memory, which is comparable to the memory requirements of an SSD. The performance advantages of the SSC-R configuration comes at the cost of doubling the required device memory, but is still only 374 MB for a 205 GB cache.

The average latencies for remove and lookup operations are less than 0.8 μs for both SSD and SSC mappings. For inserts, the sparse hash map in SSC is 90% slower than SSD due to the rehashing operations. However, these latencies are much smaller than the bus control and data delays and thus have little impact on the total time to service a request.

Host memory usage. The cache manager requires memory to store information about cached blocks. In write-through mode, the FlashTier cache manager requires no per-block state, so its memory usage is effectively zero, while the

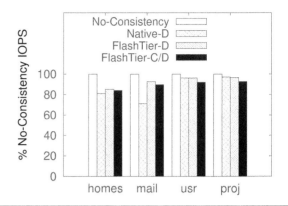

Figure 4. Consistency Cost: No-consistency system does not provide any consistency guarantees for cached data or metadata. Native-D and FlashTier-D systems only provide consistency for dirty data. FlashTier-C/D provides consistency for both clean and dirty data.

native system uses the same amount of memory for both write-back and write-through. Table 4 compares the cache-manager memory usage in write-back mode for native and FlashTier configured with a dirty percentage threshold of 20% of the cache size (above this threshold the cache manager will clean blocks).

Overall, the FlashTier cache manager consumes less than 11% of the native cache manager. The native system requires 22 bytes/block for a disk block number, checksum, LRU indexes and block state. The FlashTier system stores a similar amount of data (without the Flash address) for dirty blocks, but nothing for clean blocks. Thus, the FlashTier system consumes only 2.4 bytes/block, an 89% reduction. For a cache size of 205 GB, the savings with FlashTier cache manager are more than 1 GB of host memory.

Overall, the SSC provides a 78% reduction in total memory usage for the device and host combined. These savings come from the unification of address space and metadata across the cache manager and SSC. Even with the additional memory used for the SSC-R device, it reduces total memory use by 60%. For systems that rely on host memory to store mappings, such as FusionIO devices [11], these savings are immediately realizable.

6.4 FlashTier Consistency

In this section, we evaluate the cost of crash consistency and recovery by measuring the overhead of logging, checkpointing and the time to recover. On a system with non-volatile memory or that can flush RAM contents to flash on a power failure, consistency imposes no performance cost because there is no need to write logs or checkpoints.

Consistency cost. We first measure the performance cost of FlashTier's consistency guarantees by comparing against a baseline *no-consistency* system that does not make the mapping persistent. Figure 4 compares the throughput of FlashTier with the SSC configuration and the native system, which implements consistency guarantees by writing back mapping metadata, normalized to the no-consistency system. For FlashTier, we configure group commit to flush the log buffer every 10,000 write operations or when a synchronous operation occurs. In addition, the SSC writes a checkpoint if the log size exceeds two-thirds of the checkpoint size or after 1 million writes, whichever occurs earlier. This limits both the number of log records flushed on a commit and the log size replayed on recovery. For the native system, we assume that consistency for mapping information is provided by out-of-band (OOB) writes to per-page metadata without any additional cost [16].

As the native system does not provide persistence in write-through mode, we only evaluate write-back caching. For efficiency, the native system (Native-D) only saves metadata for dirty blocks at runtime, and loses clean blocks across unclean shutdowns or crash failures. It only saves metadata for clean blocks at shutdown. For comparison with such a system, we show two FlashTier configurations: FlashTier-D, which relaxes consistency for clean blocks by buffering log records for *write-clean*, and FlashTier-C/D, which persists both clean and dirty blocks using synchronous logging.

For the write-intensive *homes* and *mail* workloads, the extra metadata writes by the native cache manager to persist block state reduce performance by 18-29% compared to the no-consistency system. The *mail* workload has 1.5x more metadata writes per second than *homes*, therefore, incurs more overhead for consistency. The overhead of consistency for persisting clean and dirty blocks in both FlashTier systems is lower than the native system, at 8-15% for FlashTier-D and 11-16% for FlashTier-C/D. This overhead stems mainly from synchronous logging for insert/remove operations from *write-dirty* (inserts) and *write-clean* (removes from overwrite). The *homes* workload has two-thirds fewer *write-clean* operations than *mail*, and hence there is a small performance difference between the two FlashTier configurations.

For read-intensive *usr* and *proj* workloads, the cost of consistency is low for the native system at 2-5%. The native system does not incur any synchronous metadata updates when adding clean pages from a miss and batches sequential metadata updates. The FlashTier-D system performs identical to the native system because the majority of log records can be buffered for *write-clean*. The FlashTier-C/D system's overhead is only slightly higher at 7%, because clean writes following a miss also require synchronous logging.

We also analyze the average request response time for both the systems. For write-intensive workloads *homes* and *mail*, the native system increases response time by 24-37% because of frequent small metadata writes. Both FlashTier configurations increase response time less, by 18-32%, due to logging updates to the map. For read-intensive workloads, the average response time is dominated by the read latencies of the flash medium. The native and FlashTier systems incur

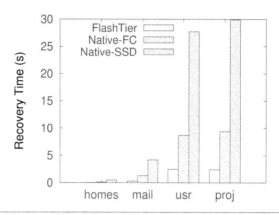

Figure 5. **Recovery Time**: Native-FC accounts for only recovering FlashCache cache manager state. Native-SSD accounts for only recovering the SSD mapping.

a 3-5% increase in average response times for these workloads respectively. Overall, the extra cost of consistency for the request response time is less than 26 μs for all workloads with FlashTier.

Recovery time. Figure 5 compares the time for recovering after a crash. The mapping and cache sizes for each workload are shown in Table 4.

For FlashTier, the only recovery is to reload the mapping and block state into device memory. The cache manager metadata can be read later. FlashTier recovers the mapping by replaying the log on the most recent checkpoint. It recovers the cache manager state in write-back mode using *exists* operations. This is only needed for space management, and thus can be deferred without incurring any start up latency. In contrast, for the native system *both* the cache manager and SSD must reload mapping metadata.

Most SSDs store the logical-to-physical map in the OOB area of a physical page. We assume that writing to the OOB is free, as it can be overlapped with regular writes and hence has little impact on write performance. After a power failure, however, these entries must be read to reconstruct the mapping [16], which requires scanning the whole SSD in the worst case. We estimate the best case performance for recovering using an OOB scan by reading just enough OOB area to equal the size of the mapping table.

The recovery times for FlashTier vary from 34 ms for a small cache (*homes*) to 2.4 seconds for *proj* with a 102 GB cache. In contrast, recovering the cache manager state alone for the native system is much slower than FlashTier and takes from 133 ms for *homes* to 9.4 seconds for *proj*. Recovering the mapping in the native system is slowest because scanning the OOB areas require reading many separate locations on the SSD. It takes from 468 ms for *homes* to 30 seconds for *proj*.

6.5 FlashTier Silent Eviction

In this section, we evaluate the impact of silent eviction on caching performance and wear management. We com-

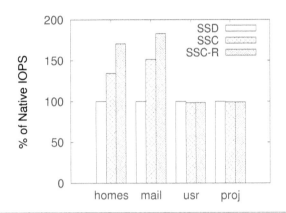

Figure 6. Garbage Collection Performance: Comparing the impact of garbage collection on caching performance for different workloads on SSD, SSC and SSC-R devices.

pare the behavior of caching on three devices: SSD, SSC and SSC-R, which use garbage collection and silent eviction with SE-Util and SE-Merge policies. For all traces, we replay the trace on a cache sized according to Table 4. To warm the cache, we replay the first 15% of the trace before gathering statistics, which also ensures there are no available erased blocks. To isolate the performance effects of silent eviction, we disabled logging and checkpointing for these tests and use only write-through caching, in which the SSC is entirely responsible for replacement.

Garbage Collection. Figure 6 shows the performance impact of silent eviction policies on SSC and SSC-R. We focus on the write-intensive *homes* and *mail* workloads, as the other two workloads have few evictions. On these workloads, the Flashtier system with SSC outperforms the native SSD by 34-52%, and SSC-R by 71-83%. This improvement comes from the reduction in time spent for garbage collection because silent eviction avoids reading and rewriting data. This is evidenced by the difference in write amplification, shown in Table 5. For example, on *homes*, the native system writes each block an additional 2.3 times due to garbage collection. In contrast, with SSC the block is written an additional 1.84 times, and with SSC-R, only 1.3 more times. The difference between the two policies comes from the additional availability of log blocks in SSC-R. As described in Section 4.3, having more log blocks improves performance for write-intensive workloads by delaying garbage collection and eviction, and decreasing the number of valid blocks that are discarded by eviction. The performance on *mail* is better than *homes* because the trace has 3 times more overwrites per disk block, and hence more nearly empty erase blocks to evict.

Cache Misses. The time spent satisfying reads is similar in all three configurations across all four traces. As *usr* and *proj* are predominantly reads, the total execution times for

these traces is also similar across devices. For these traces, the miss rate, as shown in Table 5, increases negligibly.

On the write-intensive workloads, the FlashTier device has to impose its policy on what to replace when making space for new writes. Hence, there is a larger increase in miss rate, but in the worst case, for *homes*, is less than 2.5 percentage points. This increase occurs because the SSC eviction policy relies on erase-block utilization rather than recency, and thus evicts blocks that were later referenced and caused a miss. For SSC-R, though, the extra log blocks again help performance by reducing the number of valid pages evicted, and the miss rate increases by only 1.5 percentage points on this trace. As described above, this improved performance comes at the cost of more device memory for page-level mappings. Overall, both silent eviction policies keep useful data in the cache and greatly increase the performance for recycling blocks.

Wear Management. In addition to improving performance, silent eviction can also improve reliability by decreasing the number of blocks erased for merge operations. Table 5 shows the total number of erase operations and the maximum wear difference (indicating that some blocks may wear out before others) between any two blocks over the execution of different workloads on SSD, SSC and SSC-R.

For the write-intensive *homes* and *mail* workloads, the total number of erases reduce for SSC and SSC-R. In addition, they are also more uniformly distributed for both SSC and SSC-R. We find that most erases on SSD are during garbage collection of *data blocks* for copying valid pages to free log blocks, and during full merge operations for recycling *log blocks*. While SSC only reduces the number of copy operations by evicting the data instead, SSC-R provides more log blocks. This reduces the total number of full merge operations by replacing them with switch merges, in which a full log block is made into a data block. On these traces, SSC and SSC-R reduce the total number of erases by an average of 26% and 35%, and the overhead of copying valid pages by an average of 32% and 52% respectively, as compared to the SSD.

For the read-intensive *usr* and *proj* workloads, most blocks are read-only, so the total number of erases and wear difference is lower for all three devices. The SSC increases erases by an average of 5%, because it evicts data that must later be brought back in and rewritten. However the low write rate for these traces makes reliability less of a concern. For SSC-R, the number of erases decrease by an average of 2%, again from reducing the number of merge operations.

Both SSC and SSC-R greatly improve performance and on important write-intensive workloads, also decrease the write amplification and the resulting erases. Overall, the SSC-R configuration performs better, has a lower miss rate, and better reliability and wear-leveling achieved through increased memory consumption and a better replacement policy.

Workload	Erases			Wear Diff.			Write Amp.			Miss Rate		
	SSD	SSC	SSC-R	SSD	SSC	SSC-R	SSD	SSC	SSC-R	SSD	SSC	SSC-R
homes	878,395	829,356	617,298	3,094	864	431	2.30	1.84	1.30	10.4	12.8	11.9
mail	880,710	637,089	525,954	1,044	757	181	1.96	1.08	0.77	15.6	16.9	16.5
usr	339,198	369,842	325,272	219	237	122	1.23	1.30	1.18	10.6	10.9	10.8
proj	164,807	166,712	164,527	41	226	17	1.03	1.04	1.02	9.77	9.82	9.80

Table 5. Wear Distribution: For each workload, the total number of erase operations, the maximum wear difference between blocks, the write amplification, and the cache miss rate is shown for SSD, SSC and SSC-R.

7. Related Work

The FlashTier design draws on past work investigating the use of solid-state memory for caching and hybrid systems.

SSD Caches. Guided by the price, power and performance of flash, cache management on flash SSDs has been proposed for fast access to disk storage. Windows and Solaris have software cache managers that use USB flash drives and solid-state disks as read-optimized disk caches managed by the file system [3, 14]. Oracle has a write-through flash cache for databases [32] and Facebook has started the deployment of their in-house write-back cache manager to expand the OS cache for managing large amounts of data on their Timeline SQL servers [10, 36]. Storage vendors have also proposed the use of local SSDs as write-through caches to centrally-managed storage shared across virtual machine servers [5, 29]. However, all these software-only systems are still limited by the narrow storage interface, multiple levels of address space, and free space management within SSDs designed for persistent storage. In contrast, FlashTier provides a novel consistent interface, unified address space, and silent eviction mechanism within the SSC to match the requirements of a cache, yet maintaining complete portability for applications by operating at block layer.

Hybrid Systems. SSD vendors have recently proposed new flash caching products, which cache most-frequently accessed reads and write I/O requests to disk [12, 30]. Flash-Cache [22] and the flash-based disk cache [35] also propose specialized hardware for caching. Hybrid drives [4] provision small amounts of flash caches within a hard disk for improved performance. Similar to these systems, FlashTier allows custom control of the device over free space and wear management designed for the purpose of caching. In addition, FlashTier also provides a consistent interface to persist both clean and dirty data. Such an interface also cleanly separates the responsibilities of the cache manager, the SSC and disk, unlike hybrid drives, which incorporate all three in a single device. The FlashTier approach provides more flexibility to the OS and applications for informed caching.

Informed Caching. Past proposals for multi-level caches have argued for informed and exclusive cache interfaces to provide a single, large unified cache in the context of storage arrays [38, 40]. Recent work on storage tiering and differentiated storage services has further proposed to classify I/O and use different policies for cache allocation and eviction

on SSD caches based on the information available to the OS and applications [15, 26]. However, all these systems are still limited by the narrow storage interface of SSDs, which restricts the semantic information about blocks available to the cache. The SSC interface bridges this gap by exposing primitives to the OS for guiding cache allocation on writing clean and dirty data, and an explicit *evict* operation for invalidating cached data.

Storage Interfaces. Recent work on a new nameless-write SSD interface and virtualized flash storage for file systems have argued for removing the costs of indirection within SSDs by exposing physical flash addresses to the OS [41], providing caching support [28], and completely delegating block allocation to the SSD [21]. Similar to these systems, FlashTier unifies multiple levels of address space, and provides more control over block management to the SSC. In contrast, FlashTier is the first system to provide internal flash management and a novel device interface to match the requirements of caching. Furthermore, the SSC provides a virtualized address space using disk logical block addresses, and keeps its interface grounded within the SATA read-/write/trim space without requiring migration callbacks from the device into the OS like these systems.

8. Conclusions

Flash caching promises an inexpensive boost to storage performance. However, traditional SSDs are designed to be a drop-in disk replacement and do not leverage the unique behavior of caching workloads, such as a large, sparse address space and clean data that can safely be lost. In this paper, we describe FlashTier, a system architecture that provides a new flash device, the SSC, which has an interface designed for caching. FlashTier provides memory-efficient address space management, improved performance and cache consistency to quickly recover cached data following a crash. As new non-volatile memory technologies become available, such as phase-change and storage-class memory, it will be important to revisit the interface and abstraction that best match the requirements of their memory tiers.

Acknowledgements

This work is supported in part by National Science Foundation (NSF) grant CNS-0834473. We would like to thank our shepherd Andrew Warfield for his valuable feedback. Swift has a significant financial interest in Microsoft.

References

[1] N. Agrawal, V. Prabhakaran, T. Wobber, J. Davis, M. Manasse, and R. Panigrahy. Design tradeoffs for ssd performance. In *USENIX*, 2008.

[2] N. Agrawal, L. Arulraj, A. C. Arpaci-Dusseau, and R. H. Arpaci-Dusseau. Emulating Goliath storage systems with David. In *FAST*, 2011.

[3] T. Archer. MSDN Blog: Microsoft ReadyBoost., 2006. http://blogs.msdn.com/tomarcher/archive/2006/06/02/615199.aspx.

[4] T. Bisson. Reducing hybrid disk write latency with flash-backed io requests. In *MASCOTS*, 2007.

[5] S. Byan, J. Lentini, L. Pabon, C. Small, and M. W. Storer. Mercury: host-side flash caching for the datacenter. In *FAST Poster*, 2011.

[6] F. Chen, T. Luo, and X. Zhang. CAFTL: A content-aware flash translation layer enhancing the lifespan of flash memory based solid state drives. In *FAST*, 2011.

[7] J. Corbet. Barriers and journaling filesystems, May 2008. http://lwn.net/Articles/283161/.

[8] S. Doyle and A. Narayan. Enterprise solid state drive endurance. In *Intel IDF*, 2010.

[9] EMC. Fully Automated Storage Tiering (FAST) Cache. http://www.emc.com/about/glossary/fast-cache.htm.

[10] Facebook Inc. Facebook FlashCache. https://github.com/facebook/flashcache.

[11] FusionIO Inc. ioXtreme PCI-e SSD Datasheet. http://www.fusionio.com/ioxtreme/PDFs/ioXtremeDS_v.9.pdf, .

[12] FusionIO Inc. directCache. http://www.fusionio.com/data-sheets/directcache, .

[13] Google Inc. Google Sparse Hash. http://goog-sparsehash.sourceforge.net.

[14] B. Gregg. Sun Blog: Solaris L2ARC Cache., July 2008. http://blogs.sun.com/brendan/entry/test.

[15] J. Guerra, H. Pucha, J. Glider, W. Belluomini, and R. Rangaswami. Cost effective storage using extent based dynamic tiering. In *FAST*, 2011.

[16] A. Gupta, Y. Kim, and B. Urgaonkar. DFTL: a flash translation layer employing demand-based selective caching of page-level address mappings. In *ASPLOS*, 2009.

[17] P. Helland, H. Sammer, J. Lyon, R. Carr, and P. Garrett. Group commit timers and high-volume transaction systems. In *Tandem TR 88.1*, 1988.

[18] Intel Corp. Understanding the flash translation layer (ftl) specification, Dec. 1998. Application Note AP-684.

[19] Intel Corp. Intel Smart Response Technology. http://download.intel.com/design/flash/nand/325554.pdf, 2011.

[20] Intel Corp. Intel 300 series SSD. http://ark.intel.com/products/family/56542/Intel-SSD-300-Family.

[21] W. K. Josephson, L. A. Bongo, D. Flynn, and K. Li. DFS: a file system for virtualized flash storage. In *FAST*, 2010.

[22] T. Kgil and T. N. Mudge. Flashcache: A nand flash memory file cache for low power web servers. In *CASES*, 2006.

[23] Y. Kim, B. Tauras, A. Gupta, and B. Urgaonkar. FlashSim: A simulator for nand flash-based solid-state drives. *Advances in System Simulation, International Conference on*, 0:125–131, 2009.

[24] R. Koller and R. Rangaswami. I/O deduplication: Utilizing content similarity to improve I/O performance. In *FAST*, 2010.

[25] S.-W. Lee, D.-J. Park, T.-S. Chung, D.-H. Lee, S. Park, and H.-J. Song. A log buffer-based flash translation layer using fully-associative sector translation. *ACM Trans. Embed. Comput. Syst*, 6(3), July 2007.

[26] M. Mesnier, J. B. Akers, F. Chen, and T. Luo. Differentiated storage services. In *SOSP*, 2011.

[27] D. Narayanan, A. Donnelly, and A. Rowstron. Write Off-loading: Practical power management for enterprise storage. In *FAST*, 2008.

[28] D. Nellans, M. Zappe, J. Axboe, and D. Flynn. ptrim() + exists(): Exposing new FTL primitives to applications. In *NVMW*, 2011.

[29] NetApp Inc. Flash Cache for Enterprise. http://www.netapp.com/us/products/storage-systems/flash-cache.

[30] OCZ Technologies. Synapse Cache SSD. http://www.ocztechnology.com/ocz-synapse-cache-sata-iii-2-5-ssd.html.

[31] OCZ Technologies. Vertex 3 SSD. http://www.ocztechnology.com/ocz-vertex-3-sata-iii-2-5-ssd.html.

[32] Oracle Corp. Oracle Database Smart Flash Cache. http://www.oracle.com/technetwork/articles/systems-hardware-architecture/oracle-db-smart-flash-cache-175588.pdf.

[33] X. Ouyang, D. Nellans, R. Wipfel, D. Flynn, and D.K.Panda. Beyond block i/o: Rethinking traditional storage primitives. In *HPCA*, pages 301 –311, feb. 2011.

[34] V. Prabhakaran, T. Rodeheffer, and L. Zhou. Transactional flash. In *OSDI*, 2008.

[35] D. Roberts, T. Kgil, and T. Mudge. Integrating NAND flash devices onto servers. *CACM*, 52(4):98–106, Apr. 2009.

[36] Ryan Mack. Building Facebook Timeline: Scaling up to hold your life story. http://www.facebook.com/note.php?note_id=10150468255628920.

[37] M. Saxena and M. M. Swift. FlashVM: Virtual Memory Management on Flash. In *Usenix ATC*, 2010.

[38] T. M. Wong and J. Wilkes. My cache or yours? Making storage more exclusive. In *Usenix ATC*, 2002.

[39] M. Wu and W. Zwaenepoel. eNVy: A non-volatile, main memory storage system. In *ASPLOS-VI*, 1994.

[40] G. Yadgar, M. Factor, and A. Schuster. Karma: Know-it-all replacement for a multilevel cache. In *FAST*, 2007.

[41] Y. Zhang, L. P. Arulraj, A. Arpaci-Dusseau, and R. Arpaci-Dusseau. De-indirection for flash-based ssds with nameless writes. In *FAST*, 2012.

Fast Black-Box Testing of System Recovery Code

Radu Banabic   George Candea

School of Computer and Communication Sciences
École Polytechnique Fédérale de Lausanne (EPFL), Switzerland
{radu.banabic,george.candea}@epfl.ch

Abstract

Fault injection—a key technique for testing the robustness of software systems—ends up rarely being used in practice, because it is labor-intensive and one needs to choose between performing random injections (which leads to poor coverage and low representativeness) or systematic testing (which takes a long time to wade through large fault spaces). As a result, testers of systems with high reliability requirements, such as MySQL, perform fault injection in an ad-hoc manner, using explicitly-coded injection statements in the base source code and manual triggering of failures.

This paper introduces AFEX, a technique and tool for automating the entire fault injection process, from choosing the faults to inject, to setting up the environment, performing the injections, and finally characterizing the results of the tests (e.g., in terms of impact, coverage, and redundancy). The AFEX approach uses a metric-driven search algorithm that aims to maximize the number of bugs discovered in a fixed amount of time. We applied AFEX to real-world systems—MySQL, Apache httpd, UNIX utilities, and MongoDB—and it uncovered new bugs automatically in considerably less time than other black-box approaches.

Categories and Subject Descriptors   D.2.5 [*Software Engineering*]: Testing and Debugging—Error handling and recovery

Keywords   fault injection; testing; automated testing

1.   Introduction

Fault injection is a form of testing that consists of introducing faults in a system under test, with the goal of exercising the system's error-handling code paths. Fault injection is crucial to system testing, especially as increasingly more general-purpose systems (e.g., databases, backup software, Web servers) are used in business-critical settings.

These systems are often "black boxes," in that the tester has no (or little) knowledge of the internals, either because the software is closed source (e.g., commercial application servers) or because the system is just too complicated to understand (e.g., MySQL has over 1 million lines of code). Even when the internals are reasonably well understood, every major upgrade renders parts of this knowledge obsolete.

Engineers who employ fault injection to test these systems often do so in an ad-hoc manner, such as pulling out network cables or unplugging hard drives. These actions are typically dictated by the intersection of what is believed might happen in production and what testers can actually control or directly simulate. Such ad-hoc approaches are typically based on a poor understanding of the space of possible faults and lead to poor-coverage testing. Recent tools, like LFI [16], improve the state of the art by offering the ability to simulate a wide variety of fine-grained faults that occur in a program's environment and become visible to applications through the application–library interface. Such tools offer developers better control over fault injection.

However, with fine-grain control comes the necessity to make hard choices, because these tools offer developers a vast universe of possible fault scenarios. There exist three degrees of freedom: *what* fault to inject (e.g., read() call fails with EINTR), *where* to inject it (e.g., in the logging subsystem), and *when* to do so (e.g., while the DBMS is flushing the log to disk) [17]. Poor choices can cause test suites to miss important aspects of the tested system's behavior. Ideally, a tool could automatically identify the "interesting" faults and test the system; the human would then only need to describe the fault space and provide one or more generic fault injectors like LFI. Such an automated tool would then find a small set of high-impact fault injection tests that are good at breaking or validating the target system.

One way to avoid making the hard choices, yet still have automated testing, is to perform brute-force exhaustive testing, such as using large clusters to try out all combinations of faults that the available injectors can simulate—this approach will certainly find the faults that cause most damage. Alas, the universe of possible faults is typically overwhelming: even in our small scale evaluation on MySQL, the fault space consisted of more than 2 million possibilities for injecting a single fault. Exploring such fault spaces exhaustively requires many CPU-years, followed by substantial amounts of human labor to sift through the results. A commonly employed alternative is to not inject all faults, but only a randomly selected subset: the fault space can be uniformly sampled, and tests can be stopped whenever time runs out. However, random injection achieves poor coverage, and the chances of finding the high impact faults is low.

We propose an approach in which still a subset of the fault space is sampled, but this sampling is guided. We observe that the universe of faults often has an inherent *structure*, which both random and exhaustive testing are oblivious to, and that exploiting this structure can improve the efficiency of finding high impact faults. Since this structure is hard to identify and specify a priori, it needs to be *inferred*.

We describe AFEX, a cluster-based parallel testing system that uses a fitness-guided feedback-based algorithm to search for high-impact faults in spaces with unknown structure. It uses the effect of previously injected faults to dynamically learn the space's structure and choose new faults for subsequent tests. The search process continues until a specific target is reached, such as a given level of code coverage, a threshold on the faults' impact level (e.g., "find 3 disk faults that hang the DBMS"), or a time limit. Upon completion, AFEX analyzes the injected faults for redundancy, clusters and categorizes them, and then ranks them by severity to make it easier for developers to analyze. AFEX is also capable of leveraging domain-specific knowledge, whenever humans have such knowledge and can suitably encode it; in §7 we show how such knowledge can be provided to AFEX and the influence it has on the speed and quality of the search.

Our paper advances the state of the art in two ways: an adaptive algorithm for *finding high value faults*, and a technique for automatic *categorization and ranking* of faults in a set based on their degree of redundancy and reproducibility in testing. We embody these ideas in an extensible system that can automatically test real-world software with fault injection scenarios of arbitrary complexity.

The rest of the paper presents background and definitions (§2), the fault exploration algorithm (§3), trade-offs developers can make when using AFEX (§4), techniques for measuring result quality (§5), the AFEX prototype (§6), and an evaluation of its scalability and effectiveness on MySQL, Apache httpd, UNIX utilities, and MongoDB (§7). We close with related work (§8) and conclusions (§9).

2. Definitions

We start by defining three concepts that are central to this paper: fault space, fault impact, and fault space structure.

Fault Space A fault space is a concise description of the failures that a fault injector can simulate in a target system's environment. A fault injection tool T defines implicitly a fault space by virtue of the possible values its parameters can take. For example, a library-level fault injector can inject a variety of faults at the application–library interface—the library call in which to inject, the error code to inject, and the call number at which to inject represent three axes describing the universe of library-level faults injectable by T. We think of a fault space as a hyperspace, in which a point represents a fault defined by a combination of parameters that, when passed to tool T, will cause that fault to be simulated in the target system's environment. This hyperspace may have holes, corresponding to invalid combinations of parameters to T.

We define the attributes of a fault ϕ to be the parameters to tool T that cause ϕ to be injected. If Φ is the space of possible faults, then fault $\phi \in \Phi$ is a vector of attributes $< \alpha_1, ..., \alpha_N >$ where α_i is the value of the fault's i-th attribute. For example, in the universe of failed calls made by a program to POSIX library functions, the return of error code -1 by the 5-th call to `close` would be represented as $\phi = <$ close$, 5, -1 >$. The values of fault attributes are taken from the finite sets $A_1, ..., A_N$, meaning that, for any fault $\phi = < \alpha_1, ..., \alpha_N > \in \Phi$, the attribute value $\alpha_i \in A_i$.

In order to lay out the values contained in each A_i along an axis, we assume the existence of a total order $\prec_i$ on each set A_i, so that we can refer to attribute values by their index in the corresponding order. In the case of $\phi = <$ close$, 5, -1 >$, we can assume A_1 is ordered as (open, close, read, write, ...), A_2 as $(1, 2, 3, ...)$, and A_3 as $(-1, 0, ...)$. If there is no intrinsic total order, then we can pick a convenient one (e.g., group POSIX functions by functionality: file, networking, memory, etc.), or simply choose an arbitrary one.

We now define a *fault space* Φ to be spanned by axes $X_1, X_2, ...X_N$, meaning $\Phi = X_1 \times X_2 \times .. \times X_N$, where each axis X_i is a totally ordered set with elements from A_i and order $\prec_i$. A fault space represents all possible combinations of values from sets $A_1, ..., A_N$, along with the total order on each such set. Using the example shown above, the space of failed calls to POSIX functions is spanned by three axes, one for call types $X_1 :$ (open $\prec$ close $\prec$ ...), one for the index of the call made by the caller program to the failed function $X_2 : (1 \prec 2 \prec ...)$, and one for the return value of the POSIX function $X_3 : (-1 \prec 0 \prec ...)$. This enables us to represent fault $\phi = <$ close$, 5, -1 >$ as $\phi = < 2, 5, 1 >$, because the index of close on axis X_1 under order $\prec_1$ is 2, the index of 5 on X_2 under $\prec_2$ is 5, and the index of -1 on X_3 under $\prec_3$ is 1. A fault space can have holes corresponding to invalid faults, such as close returning 1.

Impact Metric Our proposed approach uses the effect of past injected faults to guide the search for new, higher impact faults. Therefore, we need an *impact metric* that quantifies the change effected by an injected fault in the target system's behavior (e.g., the change in number of requests per second served by Apache when random TCP packets are dropped). Conceptually, an impact metric is a function

$I_S : \Phi \to \mathbb{R}$ that maps a fault ϕ in the fault space Φ to a measure of the impact that fault ϕ has on system S. Since Φ is a hyperspace, I_S defines a hypersurface. The (adversarial) goal of a tester employing fault injection is to find peaks on this hypersurface, i.e., find those faults that have the largest impact on the behavior of the system under test. Since testing is often a race against time, the tester needs to find as many such peaks as possible in the allotted time budget.

Fault Space Structure We observe empirically that, often, there are some patterns in the distribution of fault impact over the fault space, as suggested by Fig. 1, which shows the impact of library-level faults on the `ls` utility in UNIX. The structure that emerges from these patterns is caused by structure and modularity in the underlying code of the system being tested. Engler et al. [9] made a similar observation of bug patterns, which emerge due to implementation-based correlations between bodies of code. When viewing the fault space as a search space, this structure can help make the search more efficient than random sampling; in the next section we draw an analogy between fault space exploration and the Battleship game.

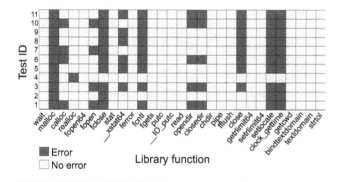

■ Error
□ No error
Test ID
Library function

Figure 1. Part of the fault space created by LFI [16] for the `ls` utility. The horizontal axis represents functions in the C standard library that fail, and the vertical axis represents the tests in the default test suite for this utility. A point (x, y) in the plot is black if failing the first call to function x while running test y leads to a test failure, and is gray otherwise.

To characterize the structure of a fault space, we use a *relative linear density* metric ρ as follows: given a fault $\phi = <\alpha_1^0, ..., \alpha_k^0, ..., \alpha_N^0>$, the relative linear density at ϕ along an axis X_k is the average impact of faults $\phi' = <\alpha_1^0, ..., \alpha_k, ..., \alpha_N^0>$ with the same attributes as ϕ except along axis X_k, scaled by the average impact of all faults in the space. Specifically, $\rho_\phi^k = \frac{avg[\, I_S(<\alpha_1^0,...,\alpha_k,...,\alpha_N^0>),\, \alpha_k \in X_k\,]}{avg[\, I_S(\phi_x),\, \phi_x \in \Phi\,]}$. If $\rho_\phi^k > 1$, walking from ϕ along the X_k axis will encounter more high-impact faults than along a random direction. In practice, it is advantageous to compute ρ_ϕ over only a small vicinity of ϕ, instead of the entire fault space. This vicinity is a subspace containing all faults within distance D of ϕ, i.e., all faults ϕ'' s.t. $\delta(\phi, \phi'') \leq D$. Distance $\delta : \Phi \times \Phi \to \mathbb{N}$

is a Manhattan (or city-block) distance [6], i.e., the shortest distance between fault ϕ and ϕ'' when traveling along Φ's coordinate axes. $\delta(\phi, \phi'')$ gives the smallest number of increments/decrements of attribute indices that would turn ϕ into ϕ''. Thus, the D-vicinity of ϕ consists of all faults that can be obtained from ϕ with no more than D increments/decrements of ϕ's attributes $\alpha_j, 1 \leq j \leq N$.

To illustrate, consider fault $\phi = <$ fclose, $7 >$ in Fig. 1, and its 4-vicinity (the faults within a distance $\delta \leq 4$). If the impact corresponding to a black square is 1, and to a gray one is 0, then the relative linear density at ϕ along the vertical axis is $\rho_\phi^2 = 2.27$. This means that walking in the vertical direction is more likely to encounter faults that cause test errors than walking in the horizontal direction or diagonally. In other words, exploration along the vertical axis is expected to be more rewarding than random exploration.

3. Fault Exploration

Fault exploration "navigates" a fault space in search of faults that have high impact on the system being tested. Visiting a point in the fault space incurs a certain cost corresponding to the generation of a test, its execution, and the subsequent measurement of the impact. Thus, ideally, one would aim to visit as few points as possible before finding a desired fault.

Exhaustive exploration (as used for instance by Gunawi et al. [11]) iterates through every point in the fault space by generating all combinations of attribute values, and then evaluates the impact of the corresponding faults. This method is complete, but inefficient and, thus, prohibitively slow for large fault spaces. Alternatively, random exploration [1] constructs random combinations of attribute values and evaluates the corresponding points in the fault space. When the fault space has no structure, random sampling of the space is no less efficient than any other form of sampling. However, if structure is present (i.e., the relative linear density is non-uniformly distributed over the fault space), then there exist more efficient search algorithms.

Fitness-guided Exploration We propose a fitness-guided algorithm for searching the fault space. This algorithm uses the impact metric I_S as a measure of a fault's "fitness," in essence steering the search process toward finding "ridges" on the hypersurface defined by (Φ, I_S) and then following these ridges to the peaks representing high-impact faults. Exploring a structured fault space like the one in Fig. 1 is analogous to playing Battleship, a board game involving two players, each with a grid. Before play begins, each player arranges a number of ships secretly on his/her own grid. After the ships have been positioned, one player announces a target square in the opponent's grid that is to be shot at; if a ship occupies that square, then it takes a hit. Players take turns and, when all of a ship's squares have been hit, the ship is sunk. A typical strategy is to start by shooting randomly until a target is hit, and then fire in the neighborhood of that target to guess the orientation of the ship and sink it.

Similarly, the AFEX algorithm exploits structure to avoid sampling faults that are unlikely to be interesting, and instead focus on those that are near other faults with high impact. For example, if a developer has a poor understanding of how some I/O library works, then there is perhaps a higher likelihood for bugs to lurk in the code that calls that library than in code that does not. Once AFEX finds a call to the I/O library whose failure causes, say, data corruption, it will eventually focus on failing other calls to that same library, persisting for as long as it improves the achieved fault impact. Note that the AFEX algorithm focuses on related but distinct bugs, rather than on multiple instances of the same bug. If the fault space definition contains duplicates (i.e., different points in the fault space expose the same bug), then AFEX's clustering discovers and avoids the duplicates (§5).

Another perspective on AFEX is that impact-guided exploration merely generates a priority in which tests should be executed—if each fault in Φ corresponds to a test, the question is which tests to run first. AFEX both generates the tests and executes them; to construct new tests, it mutates previous high-impact tests in ways that AFEX believes will further increase their impact. It also avoids re-executing any tests that have already been executed in the past. Since it does not discard any tests, rather only prioritizes their execution, AFEX's coverage of the fault space increases proportionally to the allocated time budget.

Our proposed exploration algorithm is similar to the Battleship strategy mentioned earlier, except it is fully automated, so there are no human decisions or actions in the critical path. AFEX consists of the following steps:

1. Generate an initial batch of tests randomly, execute the tests, and evaluate their impact
2. Choose a previously executed high-impact test ϕ
3. Modify one of ϕ's attributes (injection parameters) to obtain a new test ϕ'
4. Execute ϕ' and evaluate its impact
5. Repeat step 2

In order to decide which test attribute to mutate, we could rely on the linear density metric to suggest the highest-reward axis. However, given that the fault space is not known a priori, we instead compute dynamically a sensitivity (described later) based on the historical benefit of choosing one dimension vs. another. This sensitivity calculation steers the search to align with the fault space structure observed thus far, in much the same way a Battleship player infers the orientation of her opponent's battleships.

When deciding by how much to mutate an attribute (i.e., the magnitude of the increment), we choose a value according to a Gaussian distribution, rather than a static value, in order to keep the algorithm robust. This distribution favors ϕ's closest neighbors without completely dismissing points that are further away. By changing the standard deviation of

Data: $Q_{priority}$: priority queue of high-fitness fault injection tests (already executed)
$Q_{pending}$: queue of tests awaiting execution
History: set of all previously executed tests
Sensitivity: vector of N sensitivity values, one for each test attribute $\alpha_1, ... \alpha_N$

1 **foreach** *fault injection test* $\phi_x \in Q_{priority}$ **do**
2     $testProbs[\phi_x] := assignProbability(\phi_x, fitness)$
3 **end**
4 $\phi := sample(Q_{priority}, testProbs)$
5 $attributeProbs := normalize(Sensitivity)$
6 $\alpha_i := sample(\{\alpha_1, ..., \alpha_N\}, attributeProbs)$
7 $oldValue := \phi.\alpha_i$ // remember that oldValue $\in A_i$
8 $\sigma := chooseStdDev(\phi, A_i)$
9 $newValue := sample(A_i, Gaussian(oldValue, \sigma))$
10 $\phi' := clone(\phi)$
11 $\phi'.\alpha_i := newValue$
12 **if** $\phi' \notin History \land \phi' \notin Q_{priority}$ **then**
13     $Q_{pending} := Q_{pending} \cup \phi'$
14 **end**

Algorithm 1: Fitness-guided generation of the next test. Execution of tests, computation of fitness and sensitivity, and aging occur outside this algorithm.

the Gaussian distribution, we can control the amount of bias the algorithm has in favor of nearby points.

Finally, we use an "aging" mechanism among the previously executed tests: the fitness of a test is initially equal to its impact, but then decreases over time. Once the fitness of old tests drops below a threshold, they are retired and can never have offspring. The purpose of this aging mechanism is to encourage improvements in test coverage concomitantly with improvements in impact—without aging, the exploration algorithm may get stuck in a high-impact vicinity, despite not finding any new high-impact faults. In the extreme, discovering a massive-impact "outlier" fault with no serious faults in its vicinity would cause an AFEX with no aging to waste time exploring exhaustively that vicinity.

Algorithm 1 embodies steps 2–3 of the AFEX algorithm. We now describe Algorithm 1 in more detail.

Choosing Which Test to Mutate The algorithm uses three queues: a priority queue $Q_{priority}$ of already executed high-impact tests, a queue $Q_{pending}$ of test cases that have been generated but not yet executed, and a set *History* containing all previously executed tests. Once a test in $Q_{pending}$ is executed and its impact is evaluated, it gets moved to $Q_{priority}$. $Q_{priority}$ has a limited size; whenever the limit is reached, a test case is dropped from the queue, sampled with a probability inversely proportional to its fitness (tests with low fitness have a higher probability of being dropped). As a result, the average fitness of tests in $Q_{priority}$ increases over time. When old test cases are retired from $Q_{priority}$, they go into *History*.

This history set helps AFEX avoid redundant re-execution of already evaluated tests.

On lines 1–4, AFEX picks a parent test ϕ from $Q_{priority}$, to mutate into offspring ϕ'. Instead of always picking the highest fitness test, AFEX samples $Q_{priority}$ with a probability proportional to fitness—highest fitness tests are favored, but others still have a non-zero chance to be picked.

Mutating the Test   The new test ϕ' is obtained from parent test ϕ by modifying one of ϕ's attributes.

On lines 5–6, we choose the fault/test attribute α_i with a probability proportional to axis X_i's normalized sensitivity. We use *sensitivity* to capture the history of fitness gain: the sensitivity of each axis X_i of the fault space reflects the historical benefit of modifying attribute α_i when generating a new test. This sensitivity is directly related to relative linear density (from §2): the inherent structure of the system under test makes mutations along one axis to be more likely to produce high-impact faults than along others. In other words, if there is structure in the fault space, the sensitivity biases future mutations to occur along high-density axes. Given a value n, the sensitivity of X_i is computed by summing the fitness value of the previous n test cases in which attribute α_i was mutated. This sum helps detect "impact ridges" present in the currently sampled vicinity: if X_i's density is high, then we expect this sum of previous fitness values—the sensitivity to mutations along X_i—to be high as well, otherwise not. Our use of sensitivity is similar to the fitness-gain computation in Fitnex [27], since it essentially corresponds to betting on choices that have proven to be good in the past.

Sensitivity guides the choice of *which* fault attribute to mutate; next we describe *how* to mutate the chosen attribute in order to obtain a new fault injection test.

On lines 7–9, we use a discrete approximation of a Gaussian probability distribution to choose a new value for the test attribute to be mutated. This distribution is centered at *oldValue* and has standard deviation σ. The chosen standard deviation is proportional to the number of values the α_i attribute can take, i.e., to the cardinality of set A_i. For the evaluation in this paper, we chose $\sigma = \frac{1}{5} \cdot |A_i|$. σ can also be computed dynamically, based on the evolution of tests in the currently explored vicinity within the fault space—we leave the pursuit of this alternative to future work.

Our use of a Gaussian distribution implicitly assumes that there is some similarity between neighboring values of a test attribute. This similarity of course depends on the meaning of attributes (i.e., parameters to a fault injector) and on the way the human tester describes them in the fault space. In our experience, many parameters to fault injectors do have such similarity and, by using the Gaussian distribution, we can make use of this particularity to further improve on the naive method of randomly chosing a new attribute value. Revisiting the example from §2, it is not surprising that there is correlation between library functions (e.g., close is related to open), call numbers (e.g., successive calls from a program to a given function are likely to do similar things), or even tests from a suite (e.g., they are often grouped by functionality). Profiling tools, like LibTrac [5], can be used to discover such correlation when defining the fault space.

Finally, Algorithm 1 produces ϕ' by cloning ϕ and replacing attribute α_i with the new value (lines 10–11). If ϕ' has not been executed before, it goes on $Q_{pending}$ (lines 12–14).

Alternative Algorithms   The goal of building AFEX was to have an automated general-purpose fault exploration system that is not tied to any particular fault injection tool. AFEX is tool-independent—we evaluate it using library-level fault injection tools, but believe it to be equally suitable to other kinds of fault injection, such as flipping bits in data structures [26] or injecting human errors [13].

In an earlier version of our system, we employed a genetic algorithm [24], but abandoned it, because we found it inefficient. AFEX aims to optimize for "ridges" on the fault-impact hypersurface, and this makes global optimization algorithms (such as genetic algorithms) difficult to apply. The algorithm we present here is, in essence, a variation of stochastic beam search [24]—parallel hill-climbing with a common pool of candidate states—enhanced with sensitivity analysis and Gaussian value selection.

4.   Developer Trade-Offs in AFEX

Leveraging Domain Knowledge   By default, AFEX works in pure black-box mode, in that it has no a priori knowledge of the specifics of the system under test or its environment. This makes AFEX a good fit for generic testing, such as that done in a certification service [8].

However, developers often have significant amounts of domain knowledge about the system or its environment, and this could enable them to reduce the fault space explored by AFEX, thus speeding up exploration. For example, when using a library-level fault injector and an application known to use only blocking I/O with no timeouts, it makes sense to exclude EAGAIN from the set of possible values of the errno attribute of faults injected in read. AFEX can accept domain knowledge about the system under test, the fault space, and/or the tested system's environment; we evaluate in §7.5 the benefit of doing so.

AFEX can also benefit from static analysis tools, which provide a complementary method for detecting vulnerable injection points (LFI's callsite analyzer [17] is such a tool). For example, AFEX can use the results of the static analysis in the initial generation phase of test candidates. By starting off with highly relevant tests from the beginning, AFEX can quickly learn the structure of the fault space, which is likely to boost its efficiency. This increase in efficiency can manifest as finding high impact faults sooner, as well as finding additional faults that were not suggested by the static analysis. For example, we show in §7.1 how AFEX finds bugs in the Apache HTTP server and MySQL, both of which have already been analyzed by the Reasoning service [2].

Injection Point Precision An injection point is the location in the execution of a program where a fault is to be injected. Even though AFEX has no knowledge of how injection points are defined, this does affect its accuracy and speed.

In our evaluation we use LFI [16], a library fault injection tool that allows the developer to fine-tune the definition of an injection point according to their own needs. Since we aim to maximize the accuracy of our evaluation, we define an injection point as the tuple ⟨ *testID, functionName, callNumber* ⟩. *testID* identifies a test from the test suite of the target system (in essence specifying one execution path, modulo non-determinism), *functionName* identifies the called library function in which to inject an error, and *callNumber* identifies the cardinality of the call to that library function that should fail. This level of precision ensures that injection points are unique on each tested execution path, and all possible library-level faults can be explored. However, this produces a large fault space, and introduces the possibility of test redundancy (we will show how AFEX explores this space efficiently in §7.1 and mitigates redundancy in §7.4).

A simple way to define an injection point is via the callsite, i.e., file and line number where the program is to encounter a fault (e.g., failed call to a library or system call, memory operation). Since the same callsite may be reached on different paths by the system under test, this definition is relatively broad. A more accurate definition is the "failure ID" described by Gunawi et al. [11], which associates a stack trace and domain-specific data (e.g., function arguments or state of system under test) to the definition of the injection point. This definition is more tightly related to an individual execution path and offers more precision. However, unlike the 3-tuple definition we use in our evaluation, failure IDs ignore loops and can lead to missed bugs.

5. Quantifying Result Quality

In addition to automatically finding high-impact faults, AFEX also quantifies the level of confidence users can have in its results. We consider three aspects of interest to practitioners: cutting through redundant tests (i.e., identifying equivalence classes of redundant faults within the result set), assessing the precision of our impact assessment, and identifying which faults are representative and practically relevant.

Redundancy Clusters One measure of result quality is whether the different faults generated by AFEX exercise diverse system behaviors—if two faults exercise the same code path in the target system, it is sufficient to test with only one of the faults. Being a black-box testing system, AFEX cannot rely on source code to identify redundant faults.

AFEX computes clusters (equivalence classes) of closely related faults as follows: While executing a test that injects fault ϕ, AFEX captures the stack trace corresponding to ϕ's injection point. Subsequently, it compares the stack traces of all injected faults by computing the edit distance between every pair of stack traces (specifically, we use the Levenshtein distance [14]). Any two faults for which the distance is below a threshold end up in the same cluster. In §7.4 we evaluate the efficiency of this technique in avoiding test redundancy. In choosing this approach, we were inspired by the work of Liblit and Aiken on identifying which parts of a program led to a particular bug manifestation [15].

Besides helping developers to analyze fault exploration results, redundancy clusters are also used online by AFEX itself, in a feedback loop, to steer fault exploration away from test scenarios that trigger manifestations of the same underlying bug. This improves the efficiency of exploration.

Impact Precision Impact precision indicates, for a given fault ϕ, how likely it is to consistently have the same impact on the system under test S. To obtain it, AFEX runs the same test n times (with n configured by the developer) and computes the variance $Var(I_S(\phi))$ of ϕ's impact across the n trials. The impact precision is $\frac{1}{Var(I_S(\phi))}$, and AFEX reports it with each fault in the result set. The higher the precision, the more likely it is that re-injecting ϕ will result in the same impact that AFEX measured. In other words, a high value for impact precision suggest that the system's response to that fault in that environment is likely to be deterministic. Developers may find it easier, for example, to focus on debugging high-precision (thus reproducible) failure scenarios.

Practical Relevance The final quality metric employed by AFEX is a measure of each fault's representativeness and, thus, practical relevance. Using published studies [4, 25] or proprietary studies of the particular environments where a system will be deployed, developers can associate with each class of faults a probability of it occurring in practice. Using such statistical models of faults, AFEX can automatically associate with each generated fault a probability of it occurring in the target environment. This enables developers to better choose which failure scenarios to debug first.

6. AFEX Prototype

We built a prototype that embodies the techniques presented in this paper. The user provides AFEX with a description of the explorable fault space Φ, dictated by the available fault injectors, along with scripts that start/stop/measure the system under test S. AFEX automatically generates tests that inject faults from Φ and evaluates their quality. Our prototype is a parallel system that runs on clusters of computers, thus taking advantage of the parallelism inherent in AFEX.

The core of AFEX consists of an explorer and a set of node managers, as shown in Fig. 2. The explorer receives as input a fault space description and an exploration target (e.g., find the top-10 highest impact faults), and produces a set of fault injection tests that satisfy this target. AFEX synthesizes configuration files for each injection tool and instructs the various node managers to proceed with the injection of the corresponding faults. The managers then report to the explorer the results of the injections, and, based on this, the explorer decides which faults from Φ to inject next.

Each of the managers is associated with several fault injectors and sensors. One manager is in charge of all tests on one physical machine. When the manager receives a fault scenario from the explorer (e.g., "inject an EINTR error in the third read socket call, and an ENOMEM error in the seventh malloc call"), it breaks the scenario down into atomic faults and instructs the corresponding injectors to perform the injection. The sensors are instructed to run the developer-provided workload scripts (e.g., a benchmark) and perform measurements, which are then reported back to the manager. The manager aggregates these measurements into a single impact value and returns it to the explorer.

The goal of a sequence of such injections—a fault exploration session—is to produce a set of faults that satisfy a given criterion. For example, AFEX can be used to find combinations of faults that cause a database system to lose or corrupt data. As another example, one could obtain the top-50 worst faults performance-wise (i.e., faults that affect system performance the most). Prior to AFEX, this kind of test generation involved significant amounts of human labor.

To further help developers, AFEX presents the faults it found as a map, clustered by the degree of redundancy with respect to code these faults exercise in the target S. For each fault in the result set, AFEX provides a generated script that can run the test and replay the injection. Representatives of each redundancy cluster can thus be directly assembled into (or inserted into existing) regression test suites.

6.1 Architecture

Since tests are independent of each other, AFEX enjoys "embarrassing parallelism." Node managers need not talk to each other, only the explorer communicates with node managers. Given that the explorer's workload (i.e., selecting the next test) is significantly less than that of the managers (i.e., actually executing and evaluating the test), the system has no problematic bottleneck for clusters of dozens of nodes, maybe even larger. In this section, we provide more details on our prototype's two main components, the explorer and the node manager.

Explorer   The AFEX explorer is the main control point in the exploration process. It receives the fault space description and the search target, and then searches the fault space for tests to put in the result set. The explorer can navigate the fault space in three ways: using the fitness-guided Algorithm 1, exhaustive search, or random search.

Node Manager   The node manager coordinates all tasks on a physical machine. It contains a set of plugins that convert fault descriptions from the AFEX-internal representation to concrete configuration files and parameters for the injectors and sensors. Each plugin, in essence, adapts a subspace of the fault space to the particulars of its associated injector.

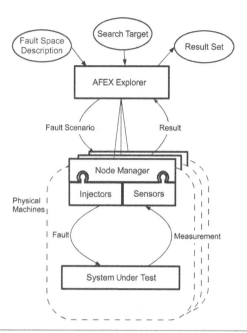

Figure 2. AFEX prototype architecture: an explorer coordinates multiple managers, which in turn coordinate the injection of faults and measurement of the injections' impact on the system under test.

The actual execution of tests on the system S is done via three user-provided scripts: A startup script prepares the environment (setting up workload generators, necessary environment variables, etc.). A test script starts up S and signals the injectors and sensors to proceed; they in turn will report results to the manager. A cleanup script shuts S down after the test and removes all side effects of the test.

6.2 Input

AFEX takes as input descriptions of the fault spaces to be explored, sensor plugins to measure impact metrics (which AFEX then uses to guide fault exploration), and search targets describing what the user wants to search for, in the form of thresholds on the impact metrics.

Fault Description Language   The language for describing fault spaces must be expressive enough to allow the definition of complex fault spaces, but succinct and easy to use and understand. Fig. 3 shows the grammar of the fault space description language used in AFEX.

Fault spaces are described as a Cartesian product of sets, intervals, and unions of subspaces (subtypes). Subspaces are separated by ";". Sets are defined with "{ }". Intervals are defined using "[ ]" or "< >". The difference between these two is that, during fault selection, intervals marked with "[ ]" are sampled for a single number, while intervals marked with "< >" are sampled for entire sub-intervals (we say < 5,10 > is a sub-interval of < 1, 50 >).

```
syntax       = {space};
space        = (subtype | parameter )+";";
subtype      = identifier;
parameter    = identifier ":"
( "{" identifier ( "," identifier )+ "}" |
  "[" number "," number "]"              |
  "<" number "," number ">"
);
identifier   = letter ( letter | digit | "_" )*;
number       = (digit)+;
```

Figure 3. AFEX fault space description language.

```
function   : { malloc, calloc, realloc }
errno      : { ENOMEM }
retval     : { 0 }
callNumber : [ 1 , 100 ] ;

function   : { read }
errno      : { EINTR }
retVal     : { -1 }
callNumber : [ 1 , 50 ] ;
```

Figure 4. Example of a fault space description.

```
function malloc errno ENOMEM retval 0
callNumber 23
```

Figure 5. Example of a fault scenario description.

Fig. 4 shows an example representing the fault space for a library fault injection tool. This fault space is a union of two hyperspaces, separated by ";". The injection can take place in any of the first 100 calls to memory allocation, or in any of the first 50 calls to read. One possible fault injection scenario the explorer may sample from this fault space is shown in Fig. 5. This scenario would be sent by the explorer to a node manager for execution and evaluation.

6.3 Output

AFEX's output consists of a set of faults that satisfy the search target, a characterization of the quality of this fault set, and generated test cases that inject the faults of the result set into the system under test S and measure their impact on S. In addition to these, AFEX also reports operational aspects, such as a synopsis of the search algorithms used, injectors used, CPU/memory/network resources used, exploration time, number of explored faults, etc.

Quality Characterization: The quality characterization provides developers with additional information about the tests, in order to help guide their attention toward the most relevant ones. The two main quality metrics are redundancy and repeatability/precision, described earlier in §5. AFEX aims to provide a confidence characterization, similar to what a Web search engine user would like to get with her search results: which of the returned pages have the same (or similar) content. A practical relevance evaluation of the fault set is optionally available if the developer can provide the corresponding statistical model (§5).

Test Suites: AFEX automatically generates test cases that can directly reproduce each fault injection and the observed impact on the system. Each test case consists of a set of configuration files for the system under test, configuration of the fault injector(s), a script that starts the system and launches the fault injector(s), and finally a script that generates workload on the system and measures the faults' impact. We find these generated test scripts to save considerable human time in constructing regression test suites.

6.4 Extensibility and Control

The AFEX system was designed to be flexible and extensible. It can be augmented with new fault injectors, new sensors and impact metrics, custom search algorithms, and new result-quality metrics.

We present below the steps needed to use AFEX on a new system under test S. In our evaluation, adapting AFEX for use on a new target S took on the order of hours.

1. *Write fault injection plugins.* These are small Java code snippets required to wrap each fault injector tool to be used (~150 lines of code).

2. *Choose fault space.* The developer must write a fault space descriptor file (using the language specified in Fig. 3). We found that the simplest way to come up with this description is to analyze the target system S with a tracer like *ltrace*, or to use a static analysis tool, such as the profiler that ships with LFI [17].

3. *Design impact metric.* The impact metric guides the exploration algorithm. The easiest way to design the metric is to allocate scores to each event of interest, such as 1 point for each newly covered basic block, 10 points for each hang bug found, 20 points for each crash, etc.

4. *Provide domain knowledge.* Optionally, the developer can give AFEX domain knowledge in various ways. For example, if the system under test is to be deployed in a production environment with highly reliable storage, it may make sense to provide a fault relevance model in which I/O faults are deemed less relevant (since they are less likely to occur in practice), unless they have catastrophic impact on S. This will discouraging AFEX from exploring faults of little interest.

5. *Write test scripts.* Developers must provide three scripts: startup, test, and cleanup. These are simple scripts and can be written in any scripting language supported on the worker nodes.

6. *Select search target.* The tester can choose to stop the tests after some specified amount of time, after a number of tests executed, or after a given threshold is met in terms of code coverage, bugs found, etc.

7. *Run AFEX.* AFEX is now ready to start. It provides progress metrics in a log, so that developers can follow its execution, if they wish to do so.

8. *Analyze results.* AFEX produces tables with measurements for each test (fitness, quality characterization, etc.), and it identifies a representative test for each redundancy cluster (as described in §5). AFEX also creates a folder for each test, containing logs, core dumps, or any other output produced during the test.

7. Evaluation

In this section, we address the following questions about the AFEX prototype: Does it find bugs in real-world systems (§7.1)? How efficient is AFEX exploration compared to random and exhaustive search (§7.2)? To what extent does fault space structure improve AFEX's efficiency (§7.3)? Can AFEX leverage result-quality metrics to improve its search efficiency (§7.4)? To what extent can system-specific knowledge aid AFEX (§7.5)? How does AFEX's usefulness vary across different stages of system development (§7.6)? How well does the AFEX prototype scale (§7.7)?

Evaluation Targets Most of our experiments focus on three real-world code bases: the MySQL 5.1.44 database management system, the Apache httpd 2.3.8 Web server, and the coreutils 8.1 suite of UNIX utilities. These systems range from large ($> 10^6$ lines of code in MySQL) to small ($\sim 10^3$ lines of code per UNIX utility). We used AFEX to find new bugs in MySQL and Apache httpd, both mature systems considered to be highly reliable. The UNIX utilities, being small yet still real-world, allow us to closer examine various details of AFEX and show how the various ideas described in the paper come together into a fitness-guided exploration framework that is significantly more efficient than random exploration, while still requiring no source code access. We also report measurements on the MongoDB NoSQL database, versions 0.8 and 2.0.

Fault Space Definition Methodology AFEX can explore both single-fault and multi-fault scenarios, but we limit our evaluation to only single-fault scenarios, which offer sufficient opportunity to examine all aspects of our system. Even this seemingly simple setup produces fault spaces with more than 2 million faults, which are infeasible to explore with brute-force approaches.

Our fault space is defined by the fault injection tools we use, along with profiling tools and, for some specific experiments, general knowledge of the system under test. We use the LFI library-level fault injector [16] and focus on injecting error returns into calls made to functions in the standard C library, libc.so. This library is the principal way for UNIX programs to interact with their environment, so we can use LFI to simulate a wide variety of faults in the file system, network, and memory. To define the fault space, we first run the default test suites that ship with our test targets,

and use the ltrace library-call tracer to identify the calls that our target makes to libc and count how many times each libc function is called. We then use LFI's callsite analyzer, applied to the libc.so binary, to obtain a fault profile for each libc function, indicating its possible error return values and associated errno codes.

We use this methodology to define a fault space for the UNIX coreutils that is defined by three axes: X_{test} corresponds to the tests in the coreutils test suite, with $X_{test} = (1, ..., 29)$. X_{func} corresponds to a subset of libc functions used during these tests, and their index values give us $X_{func} = (1, ..., 19)$. Finally, X_{call} corresponds to the call number at which we want to inject a fault (e.g., the n-th call to malloc). In order to keep the fault space small enough for exhaustive search to be feasible (which allows us to obtain baseline measurements for comparison), we restrict these values to $X_{call} = (0, 1, 2)$, where 0 means no injection, and 1 or 2 correspond to the first or second call, respectively. The size of the resulting fault space $\Phi_{coreutils}$ is $29 \times 19 \times 3 = 1,653$ faults. To measure the impact of an injected fault, we use a combination of code coverage and exit code of the test suite. This encourages AFEX to both inject faults that cause the default test suite to fail and to cover as much code as possible.

For the MySQL experiments, we use the same methodology to obtain a fault space with the same axes, except that $X_{test} = (1, ..., 1147)$ and $X_{call} = (1, ..., 100)$, which gives us a fault space Φ_{MySQL} with 2,179,300 faults. If we assume that, on average, a test takes 1 minute, exploring this fault space exhaustively would take on the order of 4 CPU-*years*. MySQL therefore is a good example of why leveraging fault space structure is important. We use a similar impact metric to that in coreutils, but we also factor in crashes, which we consider to be worth emphasizing in the case of MySQL.

For the Apache httpd experiments, we have the same fault space axes, but $X_{test} = (1, ..., 58)$ and $X_{call} = (1, ..., 10)$, for a fault space Φ_{Apache} of 11,020 possible faults.

Metrics To assess efficiency of exploration, we count the number of failing tests from the X_{test} axis and analyze the generated coredumps. While imperfect, this metric has the benefit of being objective. Once fault injection becomes more widely adopted in test suites, we expect developers to write fault injection-oriented assertions, such as "under no circumstances should a file transfer be only partially completed when the system stops," in which case one can count the number of failed assertions.

Experimental Platform The experiments reported in §7.1 and §7.3–§7.5 ran on an Intel quad-core 2.4GHz CPU with 4GB RAM and 7200rpm HDD. The experiments in §7.2 ran on 5 small Amazon EC2 instances [3], the ones reported in §7.6 on a quad-core Intel 2.3GHz CPU with 16GB RAM and Intel SSD, and the ones reported in §7.7 on a range of 1–14 small Amazon EC2 instances.

7.1 Effectiveness of Search

In this section, we show that AFEX can be used to successfully test the recovery code of large, production-grade software, such as MySQL and the Apache httpd server, with minimal human effort and no access to source code. After running for 24 hours on a small desktop computer, AFEX found 2 new bugs in MySQL and 1 new bug in Apache httpd.

MySQL After exploring the Φ_{MySQL} fault space for 24 hours, AFEX found 464 fault injection scenarios that cause MySQL to crash. By analyzing the generated core dumps, we found two new bugs in MySQL. The results are summarized in Table 1. Comparison to exhaustive search is impractical, as it would take multiple CPU-years to explore all of Φ_{MySQL}.

	MySQL test suite	Fitness-guided	Random
Coverage	54.10%	52.15%	53.14%
# failed tests	0	1,681	575
# crashes	0	464	51

Table 1. Comparison of the effectiveness of fitness-guided fault search vs. random search vs. MySQL's own test suite.

We find that AFEX's fitness-guided fault search is able to find almost $3\times$ as many failed tests as random exploration, and cause more than $9\times$ as many crashes. Of course, not all these crashes are indicative of bugs—many of them result from MySQL aborting the current operation due to the injected fault. The random approach produces slightly higher general code coverage, but spot checks suggest that the *recovery* code coverage obtained by fitness-guided search is better. Unfortunately, it is impractical to estimate recovery code coverage, because this entails manually identifying each block of recovery code in MySQL. We now describe briefly the two bugs found by AFEX.

The first one [20] is an example of buggy error recovery code—the irony of recovery code is that it is hard to test, yet, when it gets to run in production, it cannot afford to fail. Since MySQL places great emphasis on data integrity, it has a significant amount of recovery code that provides graceful handling of I/O faults. However, in the code snippet shown in Fig. 6, the recovery code itself has a bug that leads to an abort. It occurs in a function that performs a series of file operations, any of which could fail. There is a single block of error recovery code (starting at line mi_create.c:836) to which all file operations in this function jump whenever they fail. The recovery code performs some cleanup, including releasing the THR_LOCK_myisam lock (on line 837), and then returns an error return code up the stack. However, if it is the call to my_close (on line 831) that fails, say due to an I/O error, then the recovery code will end up unlocking THR_LOCK_myisam twice and crashing.

The second MySQL bug is a crash that happens when a read from errmsg.sys fails. This bug is a new manifestation

```
mi_create.c
...
830: pthread_mutex_unlock(&THR_LOCK_myisam);
831: if (my_close(file,MYF(0)))
     goto err;
...
836: err:
837:    pthread_mutex_unlock(&THR_LOCK_myisam);
```

Figure 6. Buggy recovery code in MySQL.

of a previously discovered bug [19] that was supposedly fixed. MySQL has recovery code that checks whether the read from errmsg.sys was successful or not, and it correctly logs any encountered error if the read fails. However, after completing this recovery, regardless of whether the read succeeded or not, MySQL proceeds to use a data structure that should have been initialized by that read. This leads to MySQL crashing.

It is worth noting that MySQL does use an (admittedly ad-hoc) method for fault injection testing. The code has macros that override return values and errno codes after calls to libc, in order to simulate faults. These macros are enabled by recompiling MySQL with debug options. However, doing fault injection this way is laborious, because the macros need to be manually placed in each location where a fault is to be injected, and the specifics of the injected fault need to be hardcoded. This explains, in part, why MySQL developers appear to have lacked the human resources to test the scenarios that AFEX uncovered. It also argues for why AFEX-style automated fault exploration is useful, in addition to the fact that AFEX allows even testers unfamiliar with the internal workings of MySQL—such as ourselves—to productively test the server in black-box mode.

Apache httpd We let AFEX explore the Φ_{Apache} fault space of 11,020 possible faults, and we stopped exploration after having executed 1,000 tests. Using fitness-guided exploration, AFEX found 246 scenarios that crash the server; upon closer inspection, we discovered one new bug.

Table 2 summarizes the results. When limited to 1,000 samplings of Φ_{Apache}, AFEX finds $3\times$ more faults that fail Apache tests and almost $12\times$ more tests that crash Apache, compared to random exploration. It finds 27 manifestations of the bug in Figure 7, while random exploration finds none.

	Fitness-guided	Random
# failed tests	736	238
# crashes	246	21

Table 2. Effectiveness of fitness-guided fault search vs. random search for 1,000 test iterations (Apache httpd).

An industrial strength Web server is expected to run under high load, when it becomes more susceptible to running out of memory, and so it aims to handle such errors gracefully. Thus, not surprisingly, Apache httpd has extensive checking code for error conditions like NULL returns from malloc throughout its code base. The recovery code for an out-of-memory error generally logs the error and shuts down the server. Nevertheless, AFEX found a malloc failure scenario that is incorrectly handled by Apache and causes it to crash with no information on why. Fig. 7 shows the code.

```
config.c
...
578: ap_module_short_names[m->module_index]
                        = strdup(sym_name);
579: ap_module_short_names[m->module_index][len]
                        = '\0';
```

Figure 7. Missing recovery code in Apache httpd.

What the Apache developer missed is that strdup itself uses malloc, and can thus incur an out-of-memory error that is propagated up to the Apache code. When this happens, the code on line config.c:579 dereferences the NULL pointer, triggers a segmentation fault, and the server crashes without invoking the recovery code that would log the cause of the error. As a result, operators and technical support will have a hard time understanding what happened.

This bug illustrates the need for black-box fault injection techniques: an error behavior in a third-party library causes the calling code to fail, because it does not check the return value. Such problems are hard to detect with source code analysis tools, since the fault occurs not in the test system's code but in the third-party library, and such libraries are often closed-source or even obfuscated.

The MySQL and Apache experiments in this section show that automatic fault injection can test real systems and find bugs, with minimal human intervention and minimal system-specific knowledge. We now evaluate the efficiency of this automated process.

7.2 Efficiency of Search

To evaluate efficiency, we compare fitness-based exploration not only to random search but also to exhaustive search. In order for this to be feasible, we let AFEX test a couple UNIX coreutils, i.e., explore the $\Phi_{coreutils}$ fault space (1,653 faults). This is small enough to provide us an exhaustive-search baseline, yet large enough to show meaningful results.

First, we evaluate how efficiently can AFEX find interesting fault injection scenarios. We let AFEX run for 250 test iterations, in both fitness-guided and random mode, on the ln and mv coreutils. These are utilities that call a large number of library functions. We report in the first two columns of Table 3 how many of the tests in the test suite failed due to fault injection. These results show that, given a fixed time budget, AFEX is 2.3× more efficient at finding failed tests (i.e., high-impact fault injections) than random exploration. Exhaustive exploration finds 2.77× more failed tests than fitness-guided search, but takes 6.61× more time (each test takes roughly the same amount of time, and ~90% of the

	Fitness-guided	Random	Exhaustive
Code coverage	36.14%	35.84%	36.17%
# tests executed	250	250	1,653
# failed tests	74	32	205

Table 3. Coreutils: Efficiency of fitness-guided vs. random exploration for a fixed number (250) of faults sampled from the fault space. For comparison, we also show the results for exhaustive exploration (all 1,653 faults sampled).

time in each test iteration is taken up by our coverage computation, which is independent of injected fault or workload).

Fitness-guided exploration is efficient at covering error recovery code. Consider the following: running the entire coreutils test suite without fault injection obtains 35.53% code coverage, while running additionally with exhaustive fault exploration (third column of Table 3) obtains 36.17% coverage; this leads us to conclude that roughly 0.64% of the code performs recovery. Fitness-guided exploration with 250 iterations (i.e., 15% of the fault space) covers 0.61% additional code, meaning that it covers 95% of the recovery code while sampling only 15% of the fault space.

Code coverage clearly is not a good metric for measuring the quality of reliability testing: even though all three searches achieve similar code coverage, the number of failed tests in the default test suite differs by up to 6×.

In Fig. 8 we show the number of failed tests induced by injecting faults found via fitness-guided vs. random exploration. As the number of iterations increases, the difference between the rates of finding high-impact faults increases as well: the fitness-guided algorithm becomes more efficient, as it starts inferring (and taking advantage of) the structure of the fault space. We now analyze this effect further.

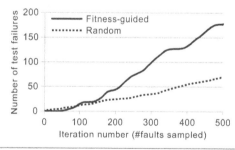

Figure 8. Number of test-failure-inducing fault injections for fitness-guided vs. random exploration.

7.3 Benefits of Fault Space Structure

To assess how much AFEX leverages the structure of the fault space, we evaluate its efficiency when one of the fault space dimensions is randomized, i.e., the values along that X_i are shuffled, thus eliminating any structure it had. If the efficiency of AFEX is hurt by such randomization, then it means that the structure along that dimension had been suitably exploited by AFEX. We perform this experiment on Apache httpd with Φ_{Apache}.

The results are summarized in Table 4: the randomization of each axis results in a reduction in overall impact. For example, 25% of the faults injected by AFEX with the original structure of Φ_{Apache} led to crashes; randomizing X_{test} causes this number to drop to 22%, randomizing X_{func} makes it drop to 13%, and randomizing X_{call} makes it drop to 17%. The last column, random search, is equivalent to randomizing all three dimensions. This is clear evidence that AFEX takes substantial advantage of whatever fault space structure it can find in each dimension in order to improve its efficiency.

	Original structure	Rand. X_{test}	Rand. X_{func}	Rand. X_{call}	Random search
# failed tests	73%	59%	43%	48%	23%
# crashes	25%	22%	13%	17%	2%

Table 4. Efficiency of AFEX in the face of structure loss, when shuffling the values of one dimension of the fault space (Apache httpd). Percentages represent the fraction of injected faults that cause a test in Apache's test suite to fail, respectively crash (thus, 25% crashes means that 25% of all injections led to Apache crashing).

Additionally, in the MySQL experiments of §7.1, we inspected the evolution of the sensitivity parameter (described in §3) and the choice of test scenarios, in order to see what structure AFEX infers in the Φ_{MySQL} fault space. The sensitivity of X_{func} converges to 0.1, while that of X_{test} and X_{call} both converge to 0.4 for MySQL. Table 4 suggests that Φ_{Apache} is different from Φ_{MySQL}: randomizing X_{func}, which was the least sensitive dimension in the case of MySQL, causes the largest drop in number of crashes, which means that for Φ_{Apache} it is actually the most sensitive dimension.

7.4 Benefits of Result-Quality Feedback

Another source of improvement in efficiency is the use of immediate feedback on the quality of a candidate fault relative to those obtained so far. AFEX aims to generate a result set that corresponds as closely as possible to the search target, and it continuously monitors the quality of this result set. One important dimension of this assessment is the degree of redundancy. In this section, we show how AFEX automatically derives redundancy clusters and uses these online, in a feedback loop, to increase its exploration efficiency.

As mentioned in §5, AFEX uses the Levenshtein edit distance for redundancy detection. In this experiment, we compare the stack traces at the injection points in the Apache tests, cluster them, and tie the outcome into a feedback loop: When evaluating the fitness of a candidate injection scenario, AFEX computes the edit distance between that scenario and all previous tests, and uses this value to weigh the fitness on a linear scale (100% similarity ends up zero-ing the fitness, while 0% similarity leaves the fitness unmodified).

The results are shown in Table 5. Even though the use of the feedback loop produces fewer failed tests overall, the search target is more closely reached: fitness-guided exploration with feedback produces about 40% more "unique" failures (i.e., the stack traces at the injection points are distinct) than fitness-guided exploration without feedback, and 75% more "unique" crashes. Of course, the method is not 100% accurate, since injecting a fault with the same call stack at the injection point can still trigger different behavior (e.g., depending on the inputs, the system under test may or may not use a NULL pointer generated by an out-of-memory error), but it still suggests improved efficiency.

	Fitness-guided	Fitness-guided with feedback	Random search
# failed tests	736	512	238
# unique failures	249	348	190
# unique crashes	4	7	2

Table 5. Number of unique failures/crashes (distinct stack traces at injection point) found by 1,000 tests (Apache).

Having assessed AFEX's properties when operating with no human assistance, we now turn our attention to evaluating the benefits of human-provided system-specific knowledge.

7.5 Benefits of System-Specific Knowledge

So far, we used AFEX purely in black-box mode, with no information about the system being tested. We now construct an experiment to evaluate how much benefit AFEX can obtain from knowledge of the tested system and environment.

We choose as search target finding all out-of-memory scenarios that cause the ln and mv coreutils to fail. Based on an exhaustive exploration of $\Phi_{coreutils}$, we know there are 28 such scenarios for these two utilities. Our goal is to count how many samplings of the fault space are required by the AFEX explorer to find these 28 faults.

	Fitness-guided	Exhaustive	Random
Black-box AFEX	417	1,653	836
Trimmed fault space	213	783	391
Trim + Env. model	103	783	391

Table 6. Number of samples (injection tests) needed to find all 28 malloc faults in $\Phi_{coreutils}$ that cause ln and mv to fail, for various levels of system-specific knowledge.

Table 6 shows the results for three different levels of system-specific knowledge. First, we run AFEX in its default black-box mode; this constitutes the baseline. Then we trim the fault space by reducing X_{func} to contain only the 9 libc functions that we know these two coreutils call—this reduces the search space. Next, we also add knowledge about the environment in the form of a statistical environment model, which specifies that malloc has a relative probability of failing of 40%, all file-related operations (fopen, read, etc.) have a combined weight of 50%, and opendir, chdir a combined weight of 10%. We use this model to weigh the measured impact of each test according to how likely it is to have occurred in the modeled environment.

The results show that trimming the fault space improves AFEX's efficiency by almost 2×, and adding the environment model further doubles efficiency—AFEX is able to reach the search target more than 4× faster than without this knowledge. Furthermore, compared to uninformed random search, leveraging this domain-specific knowledge helps AFEX be more than 8× faster, and compared to uninformed exhaustive search more than 16× faster.

7.6 Efficiency in Different Development Stages

So far, we have evaluated AFEX only on mature software; we now look at whether AFEX's effectiveness is affected by the maturity of the code base or not. For this, we evaluate AFEX on the MongoDB DBMS, looking at two different stages of development that are roughly 3 years apart: version 0.8 (pre-production) and version 2.0 (industrial strength production release). We ask AFEX to find faults that cause the tests in MongoDB's test suite to fail, and we expose both versions to identical setup and workloads. We let AFEX sample the fault space 250 times and compare its efficiency to 250 random samplings. The results are shown in Figure 9.

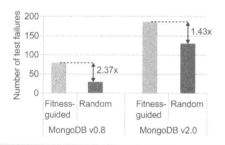

Figure 9. Changes in AFEX efficiency from pre-production MongoDB to industrial strength MongoDB.

For early versions of the software, AFEX is more efficient at discovering high-impact faults: compared to random search, AFEX finds 2.37× more faults that cause test failures; this efficiency drops in the industrial strength version to 1.43×. What may seem at first surprising is that AFEX causes more failures in v2.0 than in v0.8—this is due to increased complexity of the software and heavier interaction with the environment, which offers more opportunities for failure. Ironically, AFEX found an injection scenario that crashes v2.0, but did not find any way to crash v0.8. More features appear to indeed come at the cost of reliability.

7.7 Scalability

We have run AFEX on up to 14 nodes in Amazon EC2 [3], and verified that the number of tests performed scales linearly, with virtually no overhead. This is not surprising. We

believe AFEX can scale much further, due to its embarrassing parallelism. In isolation, the AFEX explorer can generate 8,500 tests per second on a Xeon E5405 processor at 2GHz, which suggests that it could easily keep a cluster of several thousand node managers 100% busy.

8. Related Work

Pacheco [22] presents a technique that selects from a large set of test inputs a small subset likely to reveal faults in the software under test. This work focuses on finding software flaws in normal operation of software, different from our goal of finding weak points by injecting faults.

In our work we leverage the impact of previous injections to guide the exploration of the fault space. This impact is expressed using various metrics, and there is extensive prior work that has used metrics to characterize the effect of failures. Hariri et al. [12] present an agent-based framework that quantifies how attacks and faults impact network performance and services, discovers attack points, and examines how critical network components behave during an attack. Nagaraja et al. [21] propose a two-phase methodology for quantifying the performability of cluster-based Internet services, combining fault impact measurements with the expected fault load in a production environment.

Gunawi et al. [11] describe a framework for systematically injecting sequences of faults in a system under test. The authors present Failure IDs as a means of identifying injection points and describe a method for systematically generating injection sequences on the fly. The framework presented by Gunawi et al. takes an exhaustive exploration approach. An important merit of their method, however, is the means through which the fault space is automatically generated.

KLEE [7], a well-known symbolic execution tool, also has an optional fault injection operation mode. The approach in KLEE is again an example of exhaustive exploration. An important advantage of symbolic execution is that it allows fine-grain control on the execution paths through the system under test. We expect AFEX would benefit from the power of symbolic execution, allowing more control on the system under test, but at the cost of a significantly larger exploration space.

Godefroid et al. [10] and Pacheco et al. [23] introduce search algorithms for maximizing code coverage by generating input based on execution feedback. As suggested by our usage scenarios, we target finding errors at higher level (integration level).

McMinn surveyed various approaches towards the use of metaheuristic search techniques in software testing [18]. This survey covers various heuristics, such as Genetic Algorithms or Simulated Annealing, and various test techniques, from white box to black box testing. The survey relates to exploring the control flow graph of a program, rather than fault injection in particular.

9. Conclusion

We presented a set of techniques for enabling automated fault injection-based testing of software systems. Our main contribution is a fitness-driven fault exploration algorithm that is able to efficiently explore the fault space of a system under test, finding high-impact faults significantly faster than random exploration. We also show how to categorize the found faults into equivalence classes, such that the human effort required to analyze them is reduced. We implemented our ideas in the AFEX prototype, which found new bugs in real systems like MySQL and Apache httpd with minimal human intervention and no access to source code.

Acknowledgments

We thank the anonymous reviewers, our shepherd Dawson Engler, and the members of DSLAB for their valuable feedback on earlier versions of this paper. We are indebted to IBM and Google for their generous support of our work.

References

[1] Random fault injection in linux kernel. `http://lwn.net/Articles/209292/`.

[2] Reasoning software inspection services. `http://reasoning.com/index.html`.

[3] Amazon EC2. `http://aws.amazon.com/ec2`.

[4] L. N. Bairavasundaram, G. Goodson, B. Schroeder, A. C. Arpaci-Dusseau, and R. H. Arpaci-Dusseau. An analysis of data corruption in the storage stack. In *USENIX Conf. on File and Storage Technologies*, 2008.

[5] E. Bisolfati, P. D. Marinescu, and G. Candea. Studying application–library interaction and behavior with LibTrac. In *Intl. Conf. on Dependable Systems and Networks*, 2010.

[6] P. E. Black, editor. *Dictionary of Algorithms and Data Structures*, chapter Manhattan distance. U.S. National Institute of Standards and Technology, 2006. `http://www.nist.gov/dads/HTML/manhattanDistance.html`.

[7] C. Cadar, D. Dunbar, and D. R. Engler. KLEE: Unassisted and automatic generation of high-coverage tests for complex systems programs. In *Symp. on Operating Sys. Design and Implem.*, 2008.

[8] G. Candea, S. Bucur, and C. Zamfir. Automated software testing as a service. In *Symp. on Cloud Computing*, 2010.

[9] D. Engler, D. Y. Chen, S. Hallem, A. Chou, and B. Chelf. Bugs as deviant behavior: A general approach to inferring errors in systems code. In *Symp. on Operating Systems Principles*, 2001.

[10] P. Godefroid, M. Y. Levin, and D. Molnar. Automated whitebox fuzz testing. In *Network and Distributed System Security Symp.*, 2008.

[11] H. Gunawi, T. Do, P. Joshi, P. Alvaro, J. Hellerstein, A. Arpaci-Dusseau, R. Arpaci-Dusseau, K. Sen, and D. Borthakur. Fate and destini: A framework for cloud recovery testing. In *Symp. on Networked Systems Design and Implem.*, 2011.

[12] S. Hariri, G. Qu, T. Dharmagadda, M. Ramkishore, and C. S. Raghavendra. Impact analysis of faults and attacks in large-scale networks. *IEEE Security & Privacy*, 2003.

[13] L. Keller, P. Upadhyaya, and G. Candea. ConfErr: A tool for assessing resilience to human configuration errors. In *Intl. Conf. on Dependable Systems and Networks*, 2008.

[14] V. I. Levenshtein. Binary codes capable of correcting deletions, insertions, and reversals. *Soviet Physics – Doklady*, 10, 1966.

[15] B. Liblit, M. Naik, A. X. Zheng, A. Aiken, and M. I. Jordan. Scalable statistical bug isolation. In *Intl. Conf. on Programming Language Design and Implem.*, 2005.

[16] P. D. Marinescu and G. Candea. LFI: A practical and general library-level fault injector. In *Intl. Conf. on Dependable Systems and Networks*, 2009.

[17] P. D. Marinescu and G. Candea. Efficient testing of recovery code using fault injection. *ACM Transactions on Computer Systems*, 29(4), Dec. 2011.

[18] P. McMinn. Search-based software test data generation: A survey. *Intl. Journal on Software Testing, Verification and Reliability*, 14:105–156, 2004.

[19] Crash due to missing errmsg.sys. `http://bugs.mysql.com/bug.php?id=25097`, 2006.

[20] Crash due to double unlock. `http://bugs.mysql.com/bug.php?id=53268`, 2010.

[21] K. Nagaraja, X. Li, R. Bianchini, R. P. Martin, and T. D. Nguyen. Using Fault Injection and Modeling to Evaluate the Performability of Cluster-Based Services. *USENIX Symp. on Internet Technologies and Systems*, 2003.

[22] C. Pacheco. *Eclat: Automatic Generation and Classification of Test Inputs*. PhD thesis, Springer, 2005.

[23] C. Pacheco, S. K. Lahiri, M. D. Ernst, and T. Ball. Feedback-directed random test generation. In *Intl. Conf. on Software Engineering*, 2007.

[24] S. Russell and P. Norvig. *Artificial Intelligence: A Modern Approach*. Prentice-Hall, 1995.

[25] M. Sullivan and R. Chillarege. Software defects and their impact on system availability – a study of field failures in operating systems. In *Intl. Symp. on Fault-Tolerant Computing*, 1991.

[26] T. K. Tsai and R. K. Iyer. Measuring fault tolerance with the FTAPE fault injection tool. In *Intl. Conf. on Modelling Techniques and Tools for Computer Performance Evaluation*, 1995.

[27] T. Xie, N. Tillmann, P. de Halleux, and W. Schulte. Fitness-guided path exploration in dynamic symbolic execution. In *Intl. Conf. on Dependable Systems and Networks*, 2009.

CheapBFT: Resource-efficient Byzantine Fault Tolerance[*]

Rüdiger Kapitza[1]   Johannes Behl[2]   Christian Cachin[3]   Tobias Distler[2]   Simon Kuhnle[2]

Seyed Vahid Mohammadi[4]   Wolfgang Schröder-Preikschat[2]   Klaus Stengel[2]

[1]TU Braunschweig   [2]Friedrich–Alexander University Erlangen–Nuremberg
[3]IBM Research – Zurich   [4]KTH – Royal Institute of Technology

Abstract

One of the main reasons why Byzantine fault-tolerant (BFT) systems are not widely used lies in their high resource consumption: $3f + 1$ replicas are necessary to tolerate only f faults. Recent works have been able to reduce the minimum number of replicas to $2f + 1$ by relying on a trusted subsystem that prevents a replica from making conflicting statements to other replicas without being detected. Nevertheless, having been designed with the focus on fault handling, these systems still employ a majority of replicas during normal-case operation for seemingly redundant work. Furthermore, the trusted subsystems available trade off performance for security; that is, they either achieve high throughput or they come with a small trusted computing base.

This paper presents CheapBFT, a BFT system that, for the first time, tolerates that *all but one* of the replicas active in normal-case operation become faulty. CheapBFT runs a composite agreement protocol and exploits passive replication to save resources; in the absence of faults, it requires that only $f + 1$ replicas actively agree on client requests and execute them. In case of suspected faulty behavior, CheapBFT triggers a transition protocol that activates f extra passive replicas and brings all non-faulty replicas into a consistent state again. This approach, for example, allows the system to safely switch to another, more resilient agreement protocol. CheapBFT relies on an FPGA-based trusted subsystem for the authentication of protocol messages that provides high performance and comprises a small trusted computing base.

Categories and Subject Descriptors D.4.7 [*Organization and Design*]: Distributed Systems; C.4 [*Performance of Systems*]: Fault Tolerance

General Terms Design, Performance, Reliability

Keywords Byzantine Failures; Resource Efficiency

1. Introduction

In an ongoing process, conventional computing infrastructure is increasingly replaced by services accessible over the Internet. On the one hand, this development is convenient for both users and providers as availability increases while provisioning costs decrease. On the other hand, it makes our society more and more dependent on the well-functioning of these services, which becomes evident when services fail or deliver faulty results to users.

Today, the fault-tolerance techniques applied in practice are almost solely dedicated to handling crash-stop failures, for example, by employing replication. Apart from that, only specific techniques are used to selectively address the most common or most severe non-crash faults, for example, by using checksums to detect bit flips. In consequence, a wide spectrum of threats remains largely unaddressed, including software bugs, spurious hardware errors, viruses, and intrusions. Handling such arbitrary faults in a generic fashion requires Byzantine fault tolerance (BFT).

In the past, Byzantine fault-tolerant systems have mainly been considered of theoretical interest. However, numerous research efforts in recent years have contributed to making BFT systems practical: their performance has become much better [4, 9, 17, 18], the number of required replicas has been reduced [8, 33, 34], and methods for adding diversity and for realizing intrinsically different replicas with varying attack surfaces have been introduced [3, 24]. Therefore, a debate has been started lately on why, despite all this progress, industry is reluctant to actually exploit the available research [6, 19]. A key outcome of this debate is that economical reasons, mainly the systems' high resource demand, prevent current BFT systems from being widely used. Based on this assessment, our work aims at building resource-efficient BFT systems.

Traditional BFT systems, like PBFT [4], require $3f + 1$ replicas to tolerate up to f faults. By separating request ordering (i.e., the *agreement stage*) from request process-

---

[*] This work was partially supported by the European Union's Seventh Framework Programme (FP7/2007-2013) under grant agreement no. 257243 (TClouds project: http://www.tclouds-project.eu/) and by the German Research Council (DFG) under grant no. KA 3171/1.

ing (i. e., the *execution stage*), the number of execution replicas can be reduced to $2f + 1$ [34]. Nevertheless, $3f + 1$ replicas still need to take part in the agreement of requests. To further decrease the number of replicas, systems with a hybrid fault model have been proposed that consist of *untrusted* parts that may fail arbitrarily and *trusted* parts which are assumed to only fail by crashing [5, 8, 21, 23, 30, 31, 33]. Applying this approach, virtualization-based BFT systems can be built that comprise only $f + 1$ execution replicas [33]. Other systems [5, 8, 30, 31] make use of a hybrid fault model to reduce the number of replicas at both stages to $2f + 1$ by relying on a trusted subsystem to prevent *equivocation*; that is, the ability of a replica to make conflicting statements.

Although they reduce the provisioning costs for BFT, these state-of-the-art systems have a major disadvantage: they either require a large trusted computing base, which includes the complete virtualization layer [23, 30, 33], for example, or they rely on trusted subsystems for authenticating messages, such as a trusted platform module (TPM) or a smart card [21, 31]. These subsystems impose a major performance bottleneck, however. To address these issues, we present *CheapBFT*, a resource-efficient BFT system that relies on a novel FPGA-based trusted subsystem called *CASH*. Our current implementation of CASH is able to authenticate more than 17,500 messages per second and has a small trusted computing base of only about 21,500 lines of code.

In addition, CheapBFT advances the state of the art in resource-efficient BFT systems by running a composite agreement protocol that requires only $f + 1$ actively participating replicas for agreeing on requests during normal-case operation. The agreement protocol of CheapBFT consists of three subprotocols: the normal-case protocol *CheapTiny*, the transition protocol *CheapSwitch*, and the fall-back protocol *MinBFT* [31]. During normal-case operation, Cheap-Tiny makes use of passive replication to save resources; it is the first Byzantine fault-tolerant agreement protocol that requires only $f + 1$ *active* replicas. However, CheapTiny is not able to tolerate faults, so that in case of suspected or detected faulty behavior of replicas, CheapBFT runs CheapSwitch to bring all non-faulty replicas into a consistent state. Having completed CheapSwitch, the replicas temporarily execute the MinBFT protocol, which involves $2f + 1$ active replicas (i. e., it can tolerate up to f faults), before eventually switching back to CheapTiny.

The particular contributions of this paper are:

- To present and evaluate the CASH subsystem (Section 2). CASH prevents equivocation and is used by CheapBFT for message authentication and verification.

- To describe CheapBFT's normal-case agreement protocol CheapTiny, which uses passive replication to save resources (Section 4). CheapTiny works together with the novel transition protocol CheapSwitch, which allows to abort CheapTiny in favor of a more resilient protocol when faults have been suspected or detected (Section 5).

- To evaluate CheapBFT and related BFT systems with different workloads and a Byzantine fault-tolerant variant of the ZooKeeper [16] coordination service (Section 7).

In addition, Section 3 provides an overview of CheapBFT and its system model. Section 6 outlines the integration of MinBFT [31]. Section 8 discusses design decisions, Section 9 presents related work, and Section 10 concludes.

2. Preventing Equivocation

Our proposal of a resource-efficient BFT system is based on a trusted subsystem that prevents *equivocation*; that is, the ability of a node to make conflicting statements to different participants in a distributed protocol. In this section, we give background information on why preventing equivocation allows one to reduce the minimum number of replicas in a BFT system from $3f + 1$ to $2f + 1$. Furthermore, we present and evaluate CheapBFT's FPGA-based CASH subsystem used for message authentication and verification.

2.1 From $3f + 1$ Replicas to $2f + 1$ Replicas

In traditional BFT protocols like PBFT [4], a dedicated replica, the *leader*, proposes the order in which to execute requests. As a malicious leader may send conflicting proposals to different replicas (equivocation), the protocol requires an additional communication round to ensure that all non-faulty replicas act on the same proposal. In this round, each non-faulty replica echoes the proposal it has received from the leader by broadcasting it to all other replicas, enabling all non-faulty replicas to confirm the proposal.

In recent years, alternative solutions have been introduced to prevent equivocation, which eliminate the need for the additional round of communication [31] and/or reduce the minimum number of replicas in a BFT system from $3f + 1$ to $2f + 1$ [5, 8, 31]. Chun et al. [5], for example, present an attested append-only memory (A2M) that provides a trusted log for recording the messages transmitted in a protocol. As every replica may access the log independently to validate the messages, non-faulty replicas are able to detect when a leader sends conflicting proposals.

Levin et al. [21] show that it is sufficient for a trusted subsystem to provide a monotonically increasing counter. In their approach, the subsystem securely assigns a unique counter value to each message and guarantees that it will never bind the same counter value to a different message. Hence, when a replica receives a message, it can be sure that no other replica ever sees a message with the same counter value but different content. As each non-faulty replica validates that the sequence of counter values of messages received from another replica does not contain gaps, malicious replicas cannot equivocate messages. Levin et al. used the trusted counter to build A2M, from which a BFT system with $2f + 1$ replicas has been realized.

We propose CheapBFT, a system with only $f + 1$ active replicas, built directly from the trusted counter. In the following, we present the trusted counter service in CheapBFT.

2.2 The CASH Subsystem

The *CASH* (*C*ounter *A*ssignment *S*ervice in *H*ardware) subsystem is used by CheapBFT for message authentication and verification. To prevent equivocation, we require each replica to comprise a trusted CASH subsystem; it is initialized with a secret key and uniquely identified by a subsystem id, which corresponds to the replica that hosts the subsystem. The secret key is shared among the subsystems of all replicas. Apart from the secret key, the internal state of a subsystem as well as the algorithm used to authenticate messages may be known publicly.

For now, we assume that the secret key is manually installed before system startup. In a future version, every CASH subsystem would maintain a private key and expose the corresponding public key. A shared secret key for every protocol instance may be generated during initialization, encrypted under the public key of every subsystem, and transported securely to every replica.

2.2.1 Trusted Counter Service

CASH prevents equivocation by issuing *message certificates* for protocol messages. A message certificate is a cryptographically protected proof that a certain CASH instance has bound a unique counter value to a message. It comprises the id of the subsystem that issued the certificate, the counter value assigned, and a message authentication code (MAC) generated with the secret key. Note that CASH only needs symmetric-key cryptographic operations for message authentication and verification, which are much faster than public-key operations.

The basic version of CASH provides functions for creating (*createMC*) and verifying (*checkMC*) message certificates (see Figure 1). When called with a message m, the *createMC* function increments the local counter and uses the secret key K to generate a MAC a covering the local subsystem id S, the current counter value c, and the message (L. 7-8). The message certificate mc is then created by appending S, c, and a (L. 9). To attest a certificate issued by another subsystem s, the *checkMC* function verifies the certificate's MAC and uses a function $isNext()$ to validate that the sequence of messages the local subsystem has received from subsystem s contains no gaps (L. 14). Internally, the $isNext()$ function keeps track of the latest counter values of all subsystems and is therefore able to decide whether a counter value c_s assigned to a message is the next in line for subsystem s. If this is the case, the $isNext()$ function increments the counter corresponding to subsystem s and returns success; otherwise, the counter remains unchanged.

To support distinct counter instances in a protocol and several concurrent protocols, the full version of CASH supports multiple counters, each specified by a different *counter name*. All counters to be used have to be provisioned during initialization. In the counter implementation, the name becomes a part of the argument passed to the MAC for the cre-

```
1   upon initialization do
2       K := secret key;
3       S := local subsystem id;
4       c := 0;

6   upon call createMC(m) do
7       c := c + 1;
8       a := MAC(K, S‖c‖m);
9       mc := (S, c, a);
10      return mc;

12  upon call checkMC(mc, m) do
13      (s, c_s, a) := mc;
14      if MAC(K, s‖c_s‖m) = a and isNext(s, c_s) do
15          return TRUE;
16      else
17          return FALSE;
```

Figure 1. Implementation of CASH's trusted counter.

ation and verification of message certificates. In the remainder of this paper, the counter name is written as a subscript to CASH operations (e. g., $createMC_c$ for counter c).

Furthermore, CASH provides operations for verifying a certificate without checking the correspondence of the counter values and without the side-effect of incrementing the counter in $isNext()$; there are also administrative operations for reading the subsystem id, the configured counter names, and the values of all internal counters. These operations are omitted from Figure 1. There are no means for the host system to modify subsystem id, counter names, or counter values after the initialization stage.

2.2.2 Implementation

We developed CASH to meet the following design goals:

- **Minimal trusted computing base**: The code size of CASH must be small to reduce the probability of program errors that could be exploited by attackers. Given its limited functionality, there is no need to trust an entire (hardened) Linux kernel [8] or hypervisor [23].

- **High performance**: As every interaction between replicas involves authenticated messages, we require CASH to handle thousands of messages per second. Therefore, the use of trusted platform modules or smart cards is not an option, as on such systems a single authentication operation takes more than 100 milliseconds [21, 31].

Our implementation of CASH is based on a commodity Xilinx Spartan-3 XC3S1500 FPGA mounted on a dedicated PCI card. Both the program code and the secret key are stored on the FPGA and cannot be accessed or modified by the operating system of the host machine. The only way to reprogram the subsystem is by attaching an FPGA programmer, which requires physical access to the machine.

As depicted in Figure 2, applications communicate with the FPGA via a character device (i. e., /dev/cash). To authenticate a message, for example, the application first writes

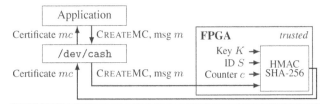

Figure 2. Creation of a message certificate mc for a message m using the FPGA-based trusted CASH subsystem.

both a CREATEMC op code and the message to the device, and then retrieves the message certificate as soon it becomes available. Our current prototype uses an HMAC-SHA-256 for the authentication of messages.

2.2.3 Integration with CheapBFT

In CheapBFT, replicas use the CASH subsystem to authenticate all messages intended for other replicas. However, this does not apply to messages sent to clients, as those messages are not subject to equivocation. To authenticate a message, a replica first calculates a hash of the message and then passes the hash to CASH's *createMC* function. Creating a message certificate for the message hash instead of the full message increases the throughput of the subsystem, especially for large messages, as less data has to be transferred to the FPGA. To verify a message received from another replica, a replica calls the *checkMC* function of its local CASH instance, passing the message certificate received as well as a hash of the message. Note that, for simplicity, we omit the use of this hash in the description of CheapBFT.

2.2.4 Performance Evaluation

We evaluate the performance of the CASH subsystem integrated with an 8-core machine (2.3 GHz, 8 GB RAM) and compare CASH with three other subsystems that provide the same service of assigning counter values to messages:

- **SoftLib** is a library that performs message authentication and verification completely in software. As it runs in the same process as the replica and therefore does not require any additional communication, we consider its overhead to be minimal. Note, however, that it is not feasible to use SoftLib in a BFT setting with $2f + 1$ replicas because trusting SoftLib would imply trusting the whole replica.

- **SSL** is a local OpenSSL server running in a separate process on the replica host. Like SoftLib, we evaluate SSL only for comparison, as it would also not be safe to use this subsystem in a BFT system with $2f + 1$ replicas.

- **VM-SSL** is a variant of SSL, in which the OpenSSL server runs in a Xen domain on the same host, similar to the approach used in [30]. Relying on VM-SSL requires one to trust that the hypervisor enforces isolation.

In this experiment, we measure the time it takes each subsystem variant to create certificates for messages of different sizes, which includes computing a SHA-256 hash (32 bytes)

Subsystem	Message size			
	32 B (no hashing)	32 B	1 KB	4 KB
VM-SSL	1013	1014	1015	1014
SSL	67	69	86	139
SoftLib	4	4	17	55
CASH	57	58	77	131

(a) Creation overhead for a certificate depending on message size.

Subsystem	Message size			
	32 B (no hashing)	32 B	1 KB	4 KB
VM-SSL	1013	1013	1013	1012
SSL	67	69	87	140
SoftLib	4	4	17	55
CASH	60	62	80	134

(b) Verification overhead for a certificate depending on message size.

Table 1. Overhead (in microseconds) for creating and verifying a message certificate in different subsystems.

over a message and then authenticating only the hash, not the full message (see Section 2.2.3). In addition, we evaluate the verification of message certificates. Table 1 presents the results for message authentication and verification for the four subsystems evaluated. The first set of values excludes the computation of the message hash and only reports the times it takes the subsystems to authenticate/verify a hash. With all four trusted counter service implementations only relying on symmetric-key cryptographic operations, the results in Tables 1a and 1b show a similar picture.

In the VM-SSL subsystem, the overhead for communication with the virtual machine dominates the authentication process and leads to results of more than a millisecond, independent of message size. Executing the same binary as VM-SSL but requiring only local socket communication, SSL achieves a performance in the microseconds range. In SoftLib, which does not involve any inter-process communication, the processing time significantly increases with message size. In our CASH subsystem, creating a certificate for a message hash takes 57 microseconds, which is mainly due to the costs for communication with the FPGA. As a result, CASH is able to authenticate more than 17,500 messages per second. Depending on the message size, computing the hash adds up 1 to 74 microseconds per operation; however, as hash creation is done in software, this can be done in parallel with the FPGA authenticating another message hash. The results in Table 1b show that in CASH the verification of a certificate for a message hash takes about 5% longer than its creation. This is due to the fact that in order to check a certificate, the FPGA not only has to recompute the certificate but also needs to perform a comparison.

Note that we did not evaluate a subsystem based on a trusted platform module (TPM), as the TPMs currently available only allow a single increment operation every 3.5 seconds to protect their internal counter from burning out too soon [31]. A TPM implementation based on reconfigurable hardware that could be adapted to overcome this issue did not reach the prototype status due to hardware limitations [11]. Alternative implementations either perform substantial parts in software, which makes them comparable to the software-based systems we presented, or suffer from the same problems as commodity solutions [1, 12].

Furthermore, we did not measure the performance of a smart-card-based subsystem: in [21], Levin et al. report a single authentication operation with 3-DES to take 129 milliseconds, and the verification operation to take 86 milliseconds using a smart card. This is orders of magnitude slower than the performance of CASH.

2.2.5 Trusted Computing Base

Besides performance, the complexity of a trusted subsystem is crucial: the more complex a subsystem, the more likely it is to fail in an arbitrary way, for example, due to an attacker exploiting a vulnerability. In consequence, to justify the assumption of the subsystem being trusted, it is essential to minimize its trusted computing base.

Table 2 outlines that the basic counter logic and the routines necessary to create and check message certificates are similar in complexity for both SSL variants and CASH. However, the software-based isolation and execution substrate for SSL and VM-SSL are clearly larger albeit we use the conservative values presented by Steinberg and Kauer [26]. In contrast, the trusted computing base of a TPM is rather small: based on the TPM emulator implementation of Strasser and Stamer [28], we estimate its size to be about 20 KLOC, which is only slightly smaller than the trusted computing base of CASH. For a smartcard-based solution, we assume similar values for the counter logic and certificate handling as for CASH. In addition some runtime support has to be accounted.

Going one step beyond approximating code complexity, it has to be noted that FPGAs, as used by CASH, per se are less resilient to single event upsets (e. g., bit flips caused by radiation) compared to dedicated hardware. However, fault-tolerance schemes can be applied that enable the use of FPGAs even in the space and nuclear sector [27]. Regarding code generation and the verifiability of code, similar tool chains can be used for CASH and building TPMs. Accordingly, their trustworthiness should be comparable.

In summary, our CASH subsystem comprises a small trusted computing base, which is comparable in size to the trusted computing base of a TPM, and similarly resilient to faults, while providing a much higher performance than readily available TPM implementations (see Section 2.2.4).

3. CheapBFT

This section presents our system model and gives an overview of the composite agreement protocol used in Cheap-BFT to save resources during normal-case operation; the subprotocols are detailed in Sections 4 to 6.

Subsystem	Components	KLOC	Total
SSL	Linux	200.0	
	Counter logic	0.3	
	Cryptographic functions	0.4	**200.7**
VM-SSL	Virtualization	100.0	**300.7**
CASH	PCI core	18.5	
	Counter logic	2.2	
	Cryptographic functions	0.8	**21.5**

Table 2. Size comparison of the trusted computing bases of different subsystems in thousands of lines of code.

3.1 System Model

We assume the system model used for most BFT systems based on state-machine replication [4, 17, 18, 29–31, 34] according to which up to f replicas and an unlimited number of clients may fail arbitrarily (i. e., exhibit Byzantine faults). Every replica hosts a trusted CASH subsystem with its subsystem id set to the replica's identity. The trusted CASH subsystem may fail only by crashing and its key remains secret even at Byzantine replicas. As discussed in Section 2.2.2, this implies that an attacker cannot gain physical access to a replica. In accordance with other BFT systems, we assume that replicas only process requests of authenticated clients and ignore any messages sent by other clients.

The network used for communication between clients and replicas may drop messages, delay them, or deliver them out of order. However, for simplicity, we use the abstraction of FIFO channels, assumed to be provided by a lower layer, in the description of the CheapBFT protocols. For authenticating point-to-point messages where needed, the operations of CASH are invoked. Our system is safe in an asynchronous environment; to guarantee liveness, we require the network and processes to be partially synchronous.

3.2 Resource-efficient Replication

CheapBFT has been designed with a focus on saving resources. Compared with BFT systems like PBFT [4, 17, 18, 29, 34], it achieves better resource efficiency thanks to two major design changes: First, each CheapBFT replica has a small trusted CASH subsystem that prevents equivocation (see Section 2); this not only allows us to reduce the minimum number of replicas from $3f + 1$ to $2f + 1$ but also minimizes the number of protocol messages [5, 8, 21, 30, 31, 34]. Second, CheapBFT uses a composite agreement protocol that saves resources during normal-case operation by supporting *passive replication*.

In traditional BFT systems [4, 17, 18, 29], all (non-faulty) replicas participate in both the agreement and the execution of requests. As recent work has shown [9, 33], in the absence of faults, it is sufficient to actually process a request on only $f + 1$ replicas as long as it is guaranteed that all other replicas are able to safely obtain changes to the application state. In CheapBFT, we take this idea even further and propose

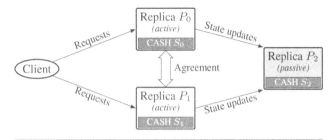

Figure 3. CheapBFT architecture with two active replicas and a passive replica ($f = 1$) for normal-case operation.

our CheapTiny protocol, in which only $f + 1$ *active* replicas take part in the agreement stage during normal-case operation (see Figure 3). The other f replicas remain *passive*, that is, they neither agree on requests nor execute requests. Instead, passive replicas modify their states by processing validated *state updates* provided by the active replicas. This approach minimizes not only the number of executions but also the number of protocol messages.

3.3 Fault Handling

With only $f + 1$ replicas actively participating in the protocol, CheapTiny is not able to tolerate faults. Therefore, in case of suspected or detected faulty behavior of one or more active replicas, CheapBFT abandons CheapTiny in favor of a more resilient protocol. The current CheapBFT prototype relies on MinBFT [31] for this purpose, but we could have selected other BFT protocols (e. g., A2M-PBFT-EA [5]) that make use of $2f + 1$ replicas to tolerate f faults.

During the protocol switch to MinBFT, CheapBFT runs the CheapSwitch transition protocol to ensure that replicas start the new MinBFT protocol instance in a consistent state. The main task of non-faulty replicas in CheapSwitch is to agree on a CheapTiny *abort history*. An abort history is a list of protocol messages that indicates the status of pending requests and therefore allows the remaining non-faulty replicas to safely continue agreement. In contrast to Abstract [14], which relies on a similar technique to change protocols, an abort history in CheapBFT can be verified to be correct even if it has only been provided by a single replica.

4. Normal-case Protocol: CheapTiny

CheapTiny is the default protocol of CheapBFT and designed to save resources in the absence of faults by making use of passive replication. It comprises a total of four phases of communication (see Figure 4), which resemble the phases in PBFT [4]. However, as CheapBFT replicas rely on a trusted subsystem to prevent equivocation, the CheapTiny protocol does not require a pre-prepare phase.

4.1 Client

During normal-case operation, clients in CheapBFT behave similar to clients in other BFT state-machine-replication protocols: Upon each new request, a client sends a

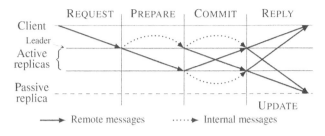

Figure 4. CheapTiny protocol messages exchanged between a client, two active replicas, and a passive replica ($f = 1$).

$\langle \text{REQUEST}, m \rangle$ message authenticated by the client's key to the leader; m is a request object containing the id of the client, the command to be executed, as well as a client-specific sequence number that is used by the replicas to ensure exactly-once semantics. After sending the request, the client waits until it has received $f + 1$ matching replies from different replicas, which form a proof for the correctness of the reply in the presence of at most f faults.

4.2 Replica

Taking up the separation introduced by Yin et al. [34], the internal architecture of an active CheapBFT replica can be logically divided into two stages: the *agreement stage* establishes a stable total order on client requests, whereas the *execution stage* is responsible for processing requests and for providing state updates to passive replicas. Note that as passive replicas do not take part in the agreement of requests, they also do not execute the CheapTiny agreement stage.

Both stages draw on the CASH subsystem to authenticate messages intended for other replicas. To decouple agreement messages from state updates, a replica uses two trusted counters, called ag and up.

4.2.1 Agreement Stage

During protocol initialization, each replica is assigned a unique id (see Figure 5, L. 2). Furthermore, a set of $f + 1$ active replicas is selected in a deterministic way. The active replica with the lowest id becomes the leader (L. 3-5). Similarly to other PBFT-inspired agreement protocols, the leader in CheapTiny is responsible for proposing the order in which requests from clients are to be executed. When all $f + 1$ active replicas have accepted a proposed request, the request becomes *committed* and can be processed safely.

When the leader receives a client request, it first verifies the authenticity of the request (omitted in Figure 5). If the request is valid and originates from an authenticated client, the leader then broadcasts a $\langle \text{PREPARE}, m, mc_L \rangle$ message to all active replicas (L. 7-9). The PREPARE contains the client request m and a message certificate mc_L issued by the local trusted CASH subsystem. The certificate uses the agreement-stage-specific counter ag and contains the leader's identity in the form of the subsystem id.

```
 1  upon initialization do
 2     P := local replica id;
 3     active := {p_0, p_1, ... p_f};
 4     passive := {p_{f+1}, p_{f+2}, ..., p_{2f}};
 5     leader := select_leader(active);

 7  upon receiving ⟨REQUEST, m⟩ such that P = leader do
 8     mc_L := createMC_ag(m);
 9     send ⟨PREPARE, m, mc_L⟩ to all in active;

11  upon receiving ⟨PREPARE, m, mc_L⟩ such that
          (mc_L = (leader, ·, ·)) and checkMC_ag(mc_L, m) do
12     mc_P := createMC_ag(m||mc_L);
13     send ⟨COMMIT, m, mc_L, mc_P⟩ to all in active;

15  upon receiving C := { ⟨COMMIT, m, mc_L, mc_p⟩ with
          mc_p = (p, ·, ·) from every p in active such that
          checkMC_ag(mc_p, m||mc_L) and all m are equal } do
16     execute(m, C);
```

Figure 5. CheapTiny agreement protocol for active replicas.

```
 1  upon call execute(m, C) do
 2     (r, u) := process(m);
 3     uc_P := createMC_up(r||u||C);
 4     send ⟨UPDATE, r, u, C, uc_P⟩ to all in passive;
 5     send ⟨REPLY, P, r⟩ to client;
```

Figure 6. CheapTiny execution-stage protocol run by active replicas to execute requests and distribute state updates.

```
 1  upon receiving {
          ⟨UPDATE, r, u, C, uc_p⟩ with uc_p = (p, ·, ·)
          from every p in active
          such that checkMC_up(uc_p, r||u||C)
          and all r are equal and all u are equal
       } do
 2     process(u);
```

Figure 7. CheapTiny execution-stage protocol run by passive replicas to process updates provided by active replicas.

Upon receiving a PREPARE (L. 11), an active replica asks CASH to verify that it originates from the leader, that the message certificate is valid, and that the PREPARE is the next message sent by the leader, as indicated by the assigned counter value. This procedure guarantees that the replica only accepts the PREPARE if the sequence of messages received from the leader contains no gaps. If the message certificate has been successfully verified, the replica sends a ⟨COMMIT, m, mc_L, mc_P⟩ message to all active replicas (L. 13). As part of the COMMIT, the replica propagates its own message certificate mc_P for the request m, which is created by authenticating the concatenation of m and the leader's certificate mc_L (L. 12). Note that issuing a combined certificate for m and mc_L helps replicas determine the status of pending requests in case of a protocol abort, as the certificate is a proof that the replica has received and accepted both m and mc_L (see Section 5.3).

When an active replica receives a COMMIT message, it extracts the sender p from mc_p and verifies that the message certificate mc_p is valid (L. 15). As soon as the replica has obtained a set C of f + 1 valid COMMITs for the same request m (one from each active replica, as determined by the subsystem id found in the message certificates), the request is committed and the replica forwards m to the execution stage (L. 15-16). Because of our assumption of FIFO channels and because of the fact that COMMITs from all f + 1 active replicas have to be available, CheapTiny guarantees that requests are committed in the order proposed by the leader without explicit use of a sequence number.

4.2.2 Execution Stage

Processing a request m in CheapBFT requires the application to provide two objects (see Figure 6, L. 2): a reply r intended for the client and a state update u that reflects the changes to the application state caused by the execution of m. Having processed a request, an active replica asks the CASH subsystem to create an update certificate uc_P for the concatenation of r, u, and the set of COMMITs C confirming that m has been committed (L. 3). The update certificate is generated using the counter up, which is dedicated to the execution stage. Next, the active replica sends an ⟨UPDATE, r, u, C, uc_P⟩ message to all passive replicas (L. 4), and finally forwards the reply to the client (L. 5).

Upon receiving an UPDATE, a passive replica confirms that the update certificate is correct and that its assigned counter value indicates no gaps (see Figure 7, L. 1). When the replica has received f + 1 matching UPDATEs from all active replicas for the same reply and state update, the replica adjusts its application state by processing the state update (L. 1-2).

4.2.3 Checkpoints and Garbage Collection

In case of a protocol switch, active replicas must be able to provide an abort history indicating the agreement status of pending requests (see Section 5). Therefore, an active replica logs all protocol messages sent to other replicas (omitted in Figures 5 and 6). To prevent a replica from running out of memory, CheapTiny makes use of periodic protocol checkpoints that allow a replica to truncate its message log.

A non-faulty active replica creates a new checkpoint after the execution of every kth request; k is a system-wide constant (e.g., 200). Having distributed the UPDATE for a request q that triggered a checkpoint, the replica first creates an application snapshot. Next, the replica sends a ⟨CHECKPOINT, ash_q, cc_ag, cc_up⟩ message to all (active and passive) replicas, which includes a digest of the application snapshot ash_q and two checkpoint certificates, cc_ag and cc_up, issued under the two CASH counters ag and up.

Upon receiving a CHECKPOINT, a replica verifies that its certificates are correct and that the counter values assigned are both in line with expectations. A checkpoint becomes stable as soon as a replica has obtained matching checkpoints from all $f + 1$ active replicas. In this case, an active replica discards all requests up to request q as well as all corresponding PREPARE, COMMIT, and UPDATE messages.

4.2.4 Optimizations

CheapTiny allows to apply most of the standard optimizations used in Byzantine fault-tolerant protocols related to PBFT [4]. In particular, this includes batching, which makes it possible to agree on multiple requests (combined in a batch) within a single round of agreement. In the following, we want to emphasize two additional optimizations to reduce communication costs.

***Implicit Leader* COMMIT**　In the protocol description in Figure 4, the leader sends a COMMIT to all active replicas after having received its own (internal) PREPARE. As this COMMIT carries no additional information, the leader's PREPARE and COMMIT can be merged into a single message that is distributed upon receiving a request; that is, all replicas treat a PREPARE from the leader as an implicit COMMIT.

Use of Hashes PBFT reduces communication costs by selecting one replica for each request to send a full reply. All other replicas only provide a hash of the reply that allows the client to prove the result correct. The same approach can be implemented in CheapTiny. Furthermore, only a single active replica in CheapTiny needs to include a full state update in its UPDATE for the passive replicas.

5. Transition Protocol: CheapSwitch

CheapTiny is optimized to save resources during normal-case operation. However, the subprotocol is not able to make progress in the presence of suspected or detected faulty behavior of replicas. In such cases, CheapBFT falls back to the MinBFT protocol, which relies on $2f + 1$ active replicas and can therefore tolerate up to f faults. In this section, we present the CheapSwitch transition protocol responsible for the safe protocol switch.

5.1 Initiating a Protocol Switch

In CheapBFT, all nodes are eligible to request the abortion of the CheapTiny protocol. There are two scenarios that trigger a protocol switch:

- A client asks for a protocol switch in case the active replicas fail to provide $f + 1$ matching replies to a request within a certain period of time.

- A replica demands to abort CheapTiny if it suspects or detects that another replica does not behave according to the protocol specification, for example, by sending a false message certificate, or by not providing a valid checkpoint or state update in a timely manner.

In these cases, the node requesting the protocol switch sends a ⟨PANIC⟩ message to all (active and passive) replicas (see Figure 8). The replicas react by rebroadcasting the message

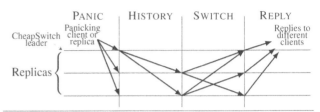

Figure 8. CheapSwitch protocol messages exchanged between clients and replicas during protocol switch ($f = 1$).

to ensure that all replicas are notified (omitted in Figure 8). Furthermore, upon receiving a PANIC, a non-faulty active replica stops to send CheapTiny protocol messages and waits for the leader of the new CheapSwitch protocol instance to distribute an abort history. The CheapSwitch leader is chosen deterministically as the active replica with the lowest id apart from the leader of the previous CheapTiny protocol.

5.2 Creating an Abort History

An abort history is used by non-faulty replicas to safely end the active CheapTiny instance during a protocol switch. It comprises the CHECKPOINTs of all active replicas proving that the latest checkpoint has become stable, as well as a set of CheapTiny protocol messages that provide replicas with information about the status of pending requests. We distinguish three status categories:

- **Decided**: The request has been committed prior to the protocol abort. The leader proves this by including the corresponding UPDATE (which comprises the set of $f + 1$ COMMITs from all active replicas) in the history.

- **Potentially decided**: The request has not been committed, but prior to the protocol abort, the leader has received a valid PREPARE for the request and has therefore sent out a corresponding COMMIT. Accordingly, the request may have been committed on some active replicas. In this case, the leader includes its own COMMIT in the history.

- **Undecided**: The leader has received a request and/or a PREPARE for a request, but has not yet sent a COMMIT. As a result, the request cannot have been committed on any non-faulty replica. In this case, the leader includes the request in the abort history.

When creating the abort history, the leader of the Cheap-Switch protocol instance has to consider the status of all requests that are not covered by the latest stable checkpoint. When a history h is complete, the leader asks the CASH subsystem for two history certificates $hc_{L,ag}$ and $hc_{L,up}$, authenticated by *both* counters. Then it sends a ⟨HISTORY, h, $hc_{L,ag}$, $hc_{L,up}$⟩ message to all replicas.

5.3 Validating an Abort History

When a replica receives an abort history from the leader of the CheapSwitch instance, it verifies that the history is correct. An abort history is deemed to be correct by a correct replica when all of the following four criteria hold:

- Both history certificates verify correctly.

- The CHECKPOINTs contained in the abort history prove that the latest checkpoint has become stable.

- Using only information contained in the abort history, the replica can reconstruct *the complete sequence* of authenticated protocol messages that the CheapSwitch leader has sent in CheapTiny since the latest checkpoint.

- The reconstructed sequence of messages does not violate the CheapTiny protocol specification.

Note that although an abort history is issued by only a single replica (i. e., the new leader), all other replicas are able to verify its correctness independently: each UPDATE contains the $f + 1$ COMMIT certificates that prove a request to be decided; each COMMIT in turn comprises a certificate that proves that the old leader has sent a PREPARE for the request (see Section 4.2). As replicas verify that all these certificates are valid and that the sequence of messages sent by the leader has no gaps, a malicious leader cannot modify or invent authenticated protocol messages and include them in the history without being detected. As a result, it is safe to use a correct abort history to get replicas into a consistent state (see Section 5.4).

Figure 9 shows an example of an abort history deemed to be correct, containing the proof CHK that the latest checkpoint has become stable, UPDATEs for three decided requests a, b, and c, and a COMMIT for a potentially decided request d. After verifying that all certificates are correct, a replica ensures that the messages in the history do not violate the protocol specification (e. g., the UPDATE for request a must comprise $f + 1$ matching COMMITs for a). Finally, a replica checks that the abort history proves the complete sequence of messages sent by the leader since the latest checkpoint; that is, the history must contain an authenticated message for every counter value of both the agreement-stage counter ag as well as the execution-stage counter up, starting from the counter values assigned to the last checkpoint and ending with the counter values assigned to the abort history.

The requirement to report a complete sequence of messages prevents equivocation by a malicious leader. In particular, a malicious leader cannot send inconsistent authenticated abort histories to different replicas without being detected: in order to create diverging histories that are both deemed to be correct, the leader would be forced to include the first authenticated history into all other histories. Furthermore, the complete message sequence ensures that all decided or potentially decided requests are included in the history: if a malicious leader, for example, sends a COMMIT for a request e after having created the history, all non-faulty replicas will detect the gap in the sequence of agreement counter values (caused by the history) and ignore the

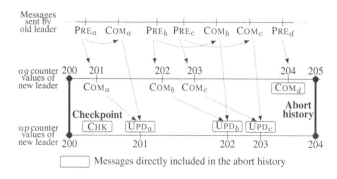

Figure 9. Dependencies of UPDATE (UPD$_*$) and COMMIT (COM$_*$) messages contained in a correct CheapTiny abort history for four requests a, b, c, and d ($f = 1$).

COMMIT. As a result, it is impossible for e to have been decided in the old CheapTiny instance. This property depends critically on the trusted counter.

5.4 Processing an Abort History

Having concluded that an abort history is correct, a replica sends a $\langle$SWITCH, hh, $hc_{L,ag}$, $hc_{L,up}$, $hc_{P,ag}$, $hc_{P,up}\rangle$ message to all other replicas (see Figure 8); hh is a hash of the abort history, $hc_{L,ag}$ and $hc_{L,up}$ are the leader's history certificates, and $hc_{P,ag}$ and $hc_{P,up}$ are history certificates issued by the replica and generated with the agreement-stage counter and the update-stage counter, respectively. Note that a SWITCH is to a HISTORY what a COMMIT is to a PREPARE. When a replica has obtained a correct history and f matching SWITCH messages from different replicas, the history becomes stable. In this case, a replica processes the abort history, taking into account its local state.

First, a replica executes all decided requests that have not yet been processed locally, retaining the order determined by the history, and sends the replies back to the respective clients. Former passive replicas only execute a decided request if they have not yet processed the corresponding state update. Next, a replica executes all unprocessed potentially decided requests as well as all undecided requests from the history. This is safe, as both categories of requests have been implicitly decided by $f + 1$ replicas accepting the abort history. Having processed the history, all non-faulty replicas are in a consistent state and therefore able to safely switch to the new MinBFT protocol instance.

5.5 Handling Faults

If an abort history does not become stable within a certain period of time after having received a PANIC, a replica suspects the leader of the CheapSwitch protocol to be faulty. As a consequence, a new instance of the CheapSwitch protocol is started, whose leader is chosen deterministically as the active replica with the smallest id that has not already been leader in an immediately preceding CheapSwitch instance. If these options have all been exploited the leader of the last

CheapTiny protocol instance is chosen. To this end, the suspecting replica sends a $\langle \text{SKIP}, p_{NL}, sc_{P,ag}, sc_{P,up}\rangle$ message to all replicas, where p_{NL} denotes the replica that will now become the leader; $sc_{P,ag}$ and $sc_{P,up}$ are two skip certificates authenticated by both trusted counters ag and up, respectively. Upon obtaining $f + 1$ matching SKIPs with correct certificates, p_{NL} becomes the new leader and reacts by creating and distributing its own abort history.

The abort history provided by the new leader may differ from the old leader's abort history. However, as non-faulty replicas only accept an abort history from a new leader after having received at least $f + 1$ SKIPs proving a leader change, it is impossible that a non-faulty replica has already processed the abort history of the old leader.

Consider two abort histories h_0 and h_1 that are both deemed to be correct, but are provided by different replicas P_0 and P_1. Note that the extent to which they can differ is limited. Making use of the trusted CASH subsystem guarantees that the order (as indicated by the counter values assigned) of authenticated messages that are included in both h_0 and h_1 is identical across both histories. However, h_0 may contain messages that are not in h_1, and vice versa, for example, because one of the replicas has already received $f + 1$ COMMITs for a request, but the other replica has not yet done so. As a result, both histories may report a slightly different status for each pending request: In h_0, for example, a request may have already been decided, whereas in h_1 its is reported to be potentially decided. Also, a request may be potentially decided in one history and undecided in the other.

However, if both histories are deemed to be correct, h_0 will never report a request to be decided that is undecided in h_1. This is based on the fact that for the request to become decided on P_0, P_1 must have provided an authenticated COMMIT for the request. Therefore, P_1 is forced to include this COMMIT in h_1 to create a correct history, which upgrades the status of the request to potentially decided (see Section 5.2). In consequence, it is safe to complete the CheapSwitch protocol by processing any correct abort history available, as long as all replicas process the same history, because all correct histories contain all requests that have become decided on at least one non-faulty replica.

It is possible that the abort history eventually processed does not contain all undecided requests, for example, because the CheapSwitch leader may not have seen all PREPAREs distributed by the CheapTiny leader. Therefore, a client retransmits its request if it is not able to obtain a stable result after having demanded a protocol switch. All requests that are not executed prior to or during the CheapSwitch run are handled by the following MinBFT instance.

6. Fall-back Protocol: MinBFT

After completing CheapSwitch, a replica is properly initialized to run the MinBFT protocol [31]. In contrast to CheapTiny, all $2f + 1$ replicas in MinBFT are active, which al-

lows the protocol to tolerate up to f faults. However, as we expect permanent replica faults to be rare [9, 14, 33], the protocol switch to MinBFT will in most cases be performed to make progress in the presence of temporary faults or periods of asynchrony. To address this issue, CheapBFT executes MinBFT for only a limited period of time and then switches back to CheapTiny, similarly to the approach proposed by Guerraoui et al. in [14].

6.1 Protocol

In MinBFT, all replicas actively participate in the agreement of requests. Apart from that, the protocol steps are similar to CheapTiny: when the leader receives a client request, it sends a PREPARE to all other replicas, which in turn respond by multicasting COMMITs, including the PREPARE certificate. Upon receiving $f + 1$ matching COMMITs, a replica processes the request and sends a reply back to the client. Similar to CheapTiny, replicas in MinBFT authenticate all agreement-stage messages using the CASH subsystem and only accept message sequences that contain no gaps and are verified to be correct. Furthermore, MinBFT also relies on stable checkpoints to garbage collect message logs.

6.2 Protocol Switch

In CheapBFT, an instance of the MinBFT protocol runs only a predefined number of agreement rounds x. When the xth request becomes committed, a non-faulty replica switches back to the CheapTiny protocol and handles all subsequent requests. Note that if the problem that led to the start of MinBFT has not yet been removed, the CheapTiny fault-handling mechanism ensures that the CheapSwitch transition protocol will be triggered once again, eventually initializing a new instance of MinBFT. This new instance uses a higher value for x to account for the prolonged period of asynchrony or faults.

7. Evaluation

In this section, we evaluate the performance and resource consumption of CheapBFT. Our test setting comprises a replica cluster of 8-core machines (2.3 GHz, 8 GB RAM) and a client cluster of 12-core machines (2.4 GHz, 24 GB RAM) that are all connected with switched Gigabit Ethernet.

We have implemented CheapBFT by adapting the BFT-SMaRt library [2]. Our CheapBFT implementation reuses BFT-SMaRt's communication layer but provides its own composite agreement protocol. Furthermore, CheapBFT relies on the CASH subsystem to authenticate and verify messages. In addition to CheapBFT and BFT-SMaRt, we evaluate an implementation of plain MinBFT [31]; note that to enable a protocol comparison the MinBFT implementation also uses our CASH subsystem. All of the following experiments are conducted with system configurations that are able to tolerate a single Byzantine fault (i. e., BFT-SMaRt: four replicas, MinBFT and CheapBFT: three replicas). In all cases, the maximum request-batch size is set to 20.

7.1 Normal-case Operation

We evaluate BFT-SMaRt, MinBFT, and CheapBFT during normal-case operation using a micro benchmark in which clients continuously send empty requests to replicas; each client waits to receive an empty reply before sending a subsequent request. In the CheapBFT configuration, each client request triggers an empty update. Between test runs, we vary the number of clients from 5 to 400 to increase load and measure the average response time of an operation. With no execution overhead and only small messages to be sent, the focus of the benchmark lies on the throughput of the agreement protocols inside BFT-SMaRt, MinBFT, and CheapBFT.

The performance results in Figure 10a show that requiring only four instead of five communication steps and only $2f + 1$ instead of $3f + 1$ agreement replicas, MinBFT achieves a significantly higher throughput than BFT-SMaRt. With only the $f + 1$ active replicas taking part in the agreement of requests, a CheapBFT replica needs to handle fewer protocol messages than a MinBFT replica. As a result, CheapBFT is able to process more than 72,000 requests per second, an increase of 14% over MinBFT.

Besides performance, we evaluate the CPU and network usage of BFT-SMaRt, MinBFT, and CheapBFT. In order to be able to directly compare the three systems, we aggregate the resource consumption of all replicas in a system and normalize the respective value at maximum throughput to a throughput of 10,000 requests per second (see Figure 10b). Compared to MinBFT, CheapBFT requires 24% less CPU, which is mainly due to the fact that a passive replica does not participate in the agreement protocol and neither processes client requests nor sends replies. CheapBFT replicas also send 31% less data than MinBFT replicas over the network, as the simplified agreement protocol of CheapBFT results in a reduced number of messages. Compared to BFT-SMaRt, the resource savings of CheapBFT add up to 37% (CPU) and 58% (network).

We also evaluate the three BFT systems in an experiment in which clients send empty requests and receive replies of 4 kilobyte size. Note that in this scenario, as discussed in Section 4.2.4, only a single replica responds with the actual full reply while all other replicas only provide a reply hash to the client. Figure 11 shows the results for performance and resource usage for this experiment. In contrast to the previous benchmark, this benchmark is dominated by the overhead for reply transmission: as full replies constitute the majority of network traffic, CheapBFT replicas only send 2% less data than MinBFT replicas and 8% less data than BFT-SMaRt replicas over the network. Furthermore, the need to provide a passive replica with reply hashes reduces the CPU savings of CheapBFT to 7% compared to MinBFT and 20% compared to BFT-SMaRt.

In our third micro-benchmark experiment, clients send requests of 4 kilobyte size and receive empty replies; Figure 12 reports the corresponding performance and resource-usage

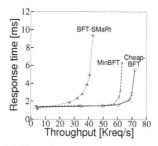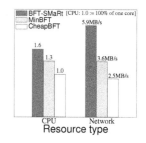

(a) Throughput vs. response time for an increasing number of clients.   (b) Average resource usage per 10 Kreq/s normalized by throughput.

Figure 10. Performance and resource-usage results for a micro benchmark with empty requests and empty replies.

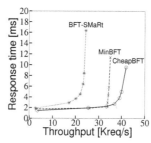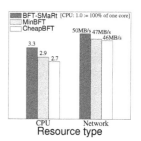

(a) Throughput vs. response time for an increasing number of clients.   (b) Average resource usage per 10 Kreq/s normalized by throughput.

Figure 11. Performance and resource-usage results for a micro benchmark with empty requests and 4 kilobyte replies.

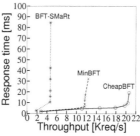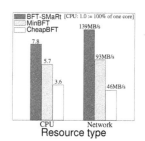

(a) Throughput vs. response time for an increasing number of clients.   (b) Average resource usage per 10 Kreq/s normalized by throughput.

Figure 12. Performance and resource-usage results for a micro benchmark with 4 kilobyte requests and empty replies.

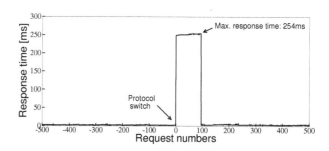

Figure 13. Response time development of CheapBFT during a protocol switch from CheapTiny to MinBFT.

results for this experiment. For such a workload, transmitting requests to active replicas is the decisive factor influencing both performance and resource consumption. With the size of requests being much larger than the size of other protocol messages exchanged between replicas, compared to BFT-SMaRt, CheapBFT replicas need to send 67% less data over the network (50% less data compared to MinBFT). In addition, CheapBFT consumes 54% less CPU than BFT-SMaRt and 37% less CPU than MinBFT.

7.2 Protocol Switch

To evaluate the impact of a fault on the performance of CheapBFT, we execute a protocol switch from CheapTiny to MinBFT during a micro benchmark run with 100 clients; the checkpoint interval is set to 200 requests. In this experiment, we trigger the protocol switch shortly before a checkpoint becomes stable in CheapTiny to evaluate the worst-case overhead caused by an abort history of maximum size. Figure 13 shows the response times of 1,000 requests handled by CheapBFT around the time the replicas run the CheapSwitch transition protocol. While verifying and processing the abort history, replicas are not able to execute requests, which leads to a temporary service disruption of max. 254 milliseconds. After the protocol switch is complete, the response times drop back to the normal level for MinBFT.

7.3 ZooKeeper Use Case

ZooKeeper [16] is a crash-tolerant coordination service used in large-scale distributed systems for crucial tasks like leader election, synchronization, and failure detection. This section presents an evaluation of a ZooKeeper-like BFT service that rely on BFT-SMaRt, MinBFT, and CheapBFT for fault-tolerant request dissemination, respectively.

ZooKeeper allows clients to store and retrieve (usually small) chunks of information in data nodes, which are managed in a hierarchical tree structure. We evaluate the three implementations for different mixes of read and write operations. In all cases, 1,000 clients repeatedly access different data nodes, reading and writing data chunks of random sizes between one byte and two kilobytes. Figure 14 presents the performance and resource-usage results for this experiment.

The results show that with the execution stage (i.e., the ZooKeeper application) performing actual work (and not just sending replies as in the micro-benchmark experiments of Section 7.1), the impact of the agreement protocol on system performance is reduced. In consequence, all three ZooKeeper implementations provide similar throughput for write-heavy workloads. However, the resource footprints significantly differ between variants: in comparison to the MinBFT-based ZooKeeper, the replicas in the CheapBFT-based variant save 7-12% CPU and send 12-20% less data over the network. Compared to the BFT-SMaRt implementation, the resource savings of the CheapBFT-based ZooKeeper add up to 23-42% (CPU) and 27-43% (network).

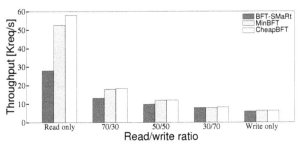

(a) Realized throughput for 1,000 clients.

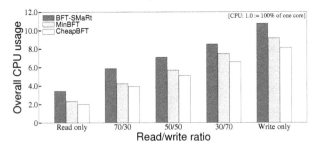

(b) CPU usage per 10 Kreq/s normalized by throughput.

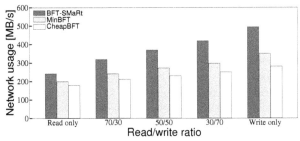

(c) Network transfer volume per 10 Kreq/s normalized by throughput.

Figure 14. Performance and resource-usage results for different BFT variants of our ZooKeeper service for workloads comprising different mixes of read and write operations.

8. Discussion

As described in Section 5.1, the first PANIC received by a replica triggers the abort of the CheapTiny protocol. In consequence, a single faulty client is able to force a protocol switch, even if all replicas are correct and the network delivers messages in time. In general, we expect such faulty behavior to be rare, as only authenticated clients get access to the system (see Section 3.1). Nevertheless, if an authenticated client repeatedly panics, human intervention may be necessary to revoke the access permissions of the client. However, even if it takes some time to remove the client from the system, unnecessary switches to the MinBFT protocol only increase the resource consumption of CheapBFT but do not compromise safety.

Having completed the CheapSwitch transition protocol, all non-faulty replicas are in a consistent state. Following this, the default procedure in CheapBFT is to run the MinBFT protocol for a certain number of requests before switching back to CheapTiny (see Section 6.2). The rationale of this approach is to handle temporary faults and/or short periods of asynchrony which usually affect only a number of subsequent requests. Note that in case such situations are not characteristic for the particular use-case scenario, different strategies of how to remedy them may be applied. In fact, if faults are typically limited to single requests, for example, it might even make sense to directly start a new instance of CheapTiny after CheapSwitch has been completed.

CheapTiny has a low resource footprint, however, the resource usage is asymmetrically distributed over active and passive replicas. Accordingly, the active replicas, especially the leader, can turn into a bottleneck under high load. This issue can be solved by dynamically alternating the leader role between the active replicas similar to Aardvark [7] and Spinning [29]. Furthermore, one could dynamically assign the role of passive and active replicas thereby distributing the load of agreement and execution over all nodes.

9. Related Work

Reducing the overhead is a key step to make BFT systems applicable to real-world use cases. Most optimized BFT systems introduced so far have focused on improving time and communication delays, however, and still need $3f + 1$ nodes that actually run agreement as well as execution stage [14, 18]. Note that this is the same as in the pioneering work of Castro and Liskov [4]. The high resource demand of BFT was first addressed by Yin et al. [34] with their separation of agreement and execution that enables the system to run on only $2f + 1$ execution nodes. In a next step, systems were subdivided in trusted and untrusted components for preventing equivocation; based on a trusted subsystem, these protocols need only $2f + 1$ replicas during the agreement and execution stages [5, 8, 23]. The trusted subsystems may become as large as a complete virtual machine and its virtualization layer [8, 23], or may be as small as the trusted counter abstraction [30, 31].

Subsequently, Wood et al. [33] presented ZZ, a system that constrains the execution component to $f + 1$ nodes and starts new replicas on demand. However, it requires $3f + 1$ nodes for the agreement task and relies on a trusted hypervisor and a machine-management system. In a previous work, we increased throughput by partitioning request execution among replicas [9]. Here, a system relies on a selector component that is co-located with each replica, and no additional trust assumptions are imposed. Moreover, we introduced passive execution nodes in SPARE [10]; these nodes passively obtain state updates and can be activated rapidly. The system uses a trusted group communication, a virtualization layer, and reliable means to detect node crashes. Of all these works, CheapBFT is the first BFT system that limits the execution *and* agreement components for all requests to only $f + 1$ replicas, whereas only f passive replicas witness progress during normal-case operation. Furthermore, it relies only on a lightweight trusted counter abstraction.

The idea of witnesses has mainly been explored in the context of the fail-stop fault model so far [22]. In this regard, CheapBFT is conceptually related to the Cheap Paxos protocol [20], in which $f + 1$ main processors perform agreement and can invoke the services of up to f auxiliary processors. In case of processor crashes, the auxiliary processors take part in the agreement protocol and support the reconfiguration of the main processor set.

Related to our approach, Guerraoui et al. [14] have proposed to optimistically employ a very efficient but less robust protocol and to resort to a more resilient algorithm if needed. CheapBFT builds on this work and is the first to exploit this approach for changing the number of nodes actively involved (rather than only for changing the protocol), with the goal of reducing the system's resource demand.

PeerReview [15] omits replication at all by enabling accountability. It needs a sufficient number of witnesses for discovering actions of faulty nodes and, more importantly, may detect faults only *after* they have occurred. This is an interesting and orthogonal approach to ours, which aims at tolerating faults. Several other recent works aim at verifying services and computations provided by a single, potentially faulty entity, ranging from database executions [32] and storage integrity [25] to group collaboration [13].

10. Conclusion

CheapBFT is the first Byzantine fault-tolerant system to use $f + 1$ active replicas for both agreement and execution during normal-case operation. As a result, it offers resource savings compared with traditional BFT systems. In case of suspected or detected faults, replicas run a transition protocol that safely brings all non-faulty replicas into a consistent state and allows the system to switch to a more resilient agreement protocol. CheapBFT relies on the CASH subsystem for message authentication and verification, which advances the state of the art by achieving high performance while comprising a small trusted computing base.

Acknowledgments

We thank the anonymous reviewers for their comments and our shepherd, Eric Jul, for his guidance. Furthermore, we are grateful to Michael Gernoth and Christian Spann for technical support, and to Alysson Bessani, Allen Clement as well as Marco Vukolić for interesting discussions and helpful comments on drafts of the paper.

References

[1] S. Berger, R. Cáceres, K. A. Goldman, R. Perez, R. Sailer, and L. van Doorn. vTPM: Virtualizing the trusted platform module. In *Proceedings of the 15th USENIX Security Symposium*, pages 305–320, 2006.

[2] BFT-SMaRt. http://code.google.com/p/bft-smart/.

[3] C. Cachin. Distributing trust on the Internet. In *Proceedings of the Conference on Dependable Systems and Networks*, pages 183–192, 2001.

[4] M. Castro and B. Liskov. Practical Byzantine fault tolerance and proactive recovery. *ACM Transactions on Computer Systems*, 20(4):398–461, 2002.

[5] B.-G. Chun, P. Maniatis, S. Shenker, and J. Kubiatowicz. Attested append-only memory: Making adversaries stick to their word. In *Proceedings of 21st Symposium on Operating Systems Principles*, pages 189–204, 2007.

[6] A. Clement, M. Marchetti, E. Wong, L. Alvisi, and M. Dahlin. BFT: The time is now. In *Proceedings of the 2nd Workshop on Large-Scale Distributed Systems and Middleware*, pages 1–4, 2008.

[7] A. Clement, E. Wong, L. Alvisi, M. Dahlin, and M. Marchetti. Making Byzantine fault tolerant systems tolerate Byzantine faults. In *Proceedings of the 6th Symposium on Networked Systems Design and Implementation*, pages 153–168, 2009.

[8] M. Correia, N. F. Neves, and P. Veríssimo. How to tolerate half less one Byzantine nodes in practical distributed systems. In *Proceedings of the 23rd Symposium on Reliable Distributed Systems*, pages 174–183, 2004.

[9] T. Distler and R. Kapitza. Increasing performance in Byzantine fault-tolerant systems with on-demand replica consistency. In *Proceedings of the 6th EuroSys Conference*, pages 91–105, 2011.

[10] T. Distler, R. Kapitza, I. Popov, H. P. Reiser, and W. Schröder-Preikschat. SPARE: Replicas on hold. In *Proceedings of the 18th Network and Distributed System Security Symposium*, pages 407–420, 2011.

[11] T. Eisenbarth, T. Güneysu, C. Paar, A.-R. Sadeghi, D. Schellekens, and M. Wolf. Reconfigurable trusted computing in hardware. In *Proceedings of the 2007 Workshop on Scalable Trusted Computing*, pages 15–20, 2007.

[12] P. England and J. Loeser. Para-virtualized TPM sharing. In *Proceedings of the 1st International Conference on Trusted Computing and Trust in Information Technologies*, pages 119–132, 2008.

[13] A. J. Feldman, W. P. Zeller, M. J. Freedman, and E. W. Felten. SPORC: Group collaboration using untrusted cloud resources. In *Proceedings of the 9th Symposium on Operating Systems Design and Implementation*, pages 337–350, 2010.

[14] R. Guerraoui, N. Knežević, V. Quéma, and M. Vukolić. The next 700 BFT protocols. In *Proceedings of the 5th EuroSys Conference*, pages 363–376, 2010.

[15] A. Haeberlen, P. Kouznetsov, and P. Druschel. PeerReview: Practical accountability for distributed systems. In *Proceedings of the 21st Symposium on Operating Systems Principles*, pages 175–188, 2007.

[16] P. Hunt, M. Konar, F. P. Junqueira, and B. Reed. ZooKeeper: Wait-free coordination for Internet-scale systems. In *Proceedings of the 2010 USENIX Annual Technical Conference*, pages 145–158, 2010.

[17] R. Kotla and M. Dahlin. High throughput Byzantine fault tolerance. In *Proceedings of the 2004 Conference on Dependable Systems and Networks*, pages 575–584, 2004.

[18] R. Kotla, L. Alvisi, M. Dahlin, A. Clement, and E. Wong. Zyzzyva: Speculative Byzantine fault tolerance. *ACM Transactions on Computer Systems*, 27(4):1–39, 2009.

[19] P. Kuznetsov and R. Rodrigues. BFTW3: Why? When? Where? Workshop on the theory and practice of Byzantine fault tolerance. *SIGACT News*, 40(4):82–86, 2009.

[20] L. Lamport and M. Massa. Cheap Paxos. In *Proceedings of the Conference on Dependable Systems and Networks*, pages 307–314, 2004.

[21] D. Levin, J. R. Douceur, J. R. Lorch, and T. Moscibroda. TrInc: Small trusted hardware for large distributed systems. In *Proceedings of the 6th Symposium on Networked Systems Design and Implementation*, pages 1–14, 2009.

[22] J.-F. Paris. Voting with witnesses: A consistency scheme for replicated files. In *Proceedings of the 6th Int'l Conference on Distributed Computing Systems*, pages 606–612, 1986.

[23] H. P. Reiser and R. Kapitza. Hypervisor-based efficient proactive recovery. In *Proceedings of the 26th Symposium on Reliable Distributed Systems*, pages 83–92, 2007.

[24] F. B. Schneider and L. Zhou. Implementing trustworthy services using replicated state machines. *IEEE Security & Privacy Magazine*, 3:34–43, 2005.

[25] A. Shraer, C. Cachin, A. Cidon, I. Keidar, Y. Michalevsky, and D. Shaket. Venus: Verification for untrusted cloud storage. In *Proceedings of the 2010 Workshop on Cloud Computing Security*, pages 19–30, 2010.

[26] U. Steinberg and B. Kauer. NOVA: A microhypervisor-based secure virtualization architecture. In *Proceedings of the 5th EuroSys Conference*, pages 209–222, 2010.

[27] E. Stott, P. Sedcole, and P. Cheung. Fault tolerance and reliability in field-programmable gate arrays. *IET Computers & Digital Techniques*, 4(3):196–210, 2010.

[28] M. Strasser and H. Stamer. A software-based trusted platform module emulator. In *Proceedings of the 1st International Conference on Trusted Computing and Trust in Information Technologies*, pages 33–47, 2008.

[29] G. S. Veronese, M. Correia, A. N. Bessani, and L. C. Lung. Spin one's wheels? Byzantine fault tolerance with a spinning primary. In *Proceedings of the 28th Symposium on Reliable Distributed Systems*, pages 135–144, 2009.

[30] G. S. Veronese, M. Correia, A. N. Bessani, and L. C. Lung. EBAWA: Efficient Byzantine agreement for wide-area networks. In *Proceedings of the 12th Symposium on High-Assurance Systems Engineering*, pages 10–19, 2010.

[31] G. S. Veronese, M. Correia, A. N. Bessani, L. C. Lung, and P. Veríssimo. Efficient Byzantine fault tolerance. *IEEE Transactions on Computers*, 2011.

[32] P. Williams, R. Sion, and D. Shasha. The blind stone tablet: Outsourcing durability to untrusted parties. In *Proceedings of the 16th Network and Distributed System Security Symposium*, 2009.

[33] T. Wood, R. Singh, A. Venkataramani, P. Shenoy, and E. Cecchet. ZZ and the art of practical BFT execution. In *Proceedings of the 6th EuroSys Conference*, pages 123–138, 2011.

[34] J. Yin, J.-P. Martin, A. Venkataramani, L. Alvisi, and M. Dahlin. Separating agreement from execution for Byzantine fault tolerant services. In *Proceedings of the 19th Symposium on Operating Systems Principles*, pages 253–267, 2003.

Canal: Scaling Social Network-Based Sybil Tolerance Schemes

Bimal Viswanath

MPI-SWS

bviswana@mpi-sws.org

Mainack Mondal

MPI-SWS

mainack@mpi-sws.org

Krishna P. Gummadi

MPI-SWS

gummadi@mpi-sws.org

Alan Mislove

Northeastern University

amislove@ccs.neu.edu

Ansley Post

MPI-SWS

abpost@mpi-sws.org

Abstract

There has been a flurry of research on leveraging social networks to defend against multiple identity, or Sybil, attacks. A series of recent works does not try to explicitly identify Sybil identities and, instead, bounds the impact that Sybil identities can have. We call these approaches *Sybil tolerance*; they have shown to be effective in applications including reputation systems, spam protection, online auctions, and content rating systems. All of these approaches use a social network as a credit network, rendering multiple identities ineffective to an attacker without a commensurate increase in social links to honest users (which are assumed to be hard to obtain). Unfortunately, a hurdle to practical adoption is that Sybil tolerance relies on computationally expensive network analysis, thereby limiting widespread deployment.

To address this problem, we first demonstrate that despite their differences, all proposed Sybil tolerance systems work by conducting payments over credit networks. These payments require max flow computations on a social network graph, and lead to poor scalability. We then present *Canal*, a system that uses landmark routing-based techniques to efficiently approximate credit payments over large networks. Through an evaluation on real-world data, we show that Canal provides up to a three-order-of-magnitude speedup while maintaining safety and accuracy, even when applied to social networks with millions of nodes and hundreds of millions of edges. Finally, we demonstrate that Canal can be easily plugged into existing Sybil tolerance schemes, enabling them to be deployed in an online fashion in real-world systems.

Categories and Subject Descriptors C.4 [*Performance of Systems*]: Design studies; C.2.0 [*Computer-Communication Networks*]: General—Security and protection

General Terms Algorithms, Design, Performance, Security

Keywords Sybil attacks; social networks; sybil tolerance; social network-based Sybil defense; credit networks

1. Introduction

Multiple identity attacks—commonly known as Sybil attacks [10]—are known to be a fundamental problem in many distributed systems. In a Sybil attack, a malicious user creates multiple identities and takes advantage of these identities to attack the system. For example, in social networking sites like Digg or YouTube, where content is rated based on user feedback, an attacker can create multiple identities and cast multiple votes, thereby manipulating content popularity. Recent studies have shown that Sybil attacks are becoming more widespread [42], affecting news aggregators like Digg [35], microblogs like Twitter [46], and review sites like TripAdvisor [33].

Recently, a series of schemes have been proposed that defend against Sybil attacks by leveraging social networks [24, 29, 34, 35]. These schemes are based on the assumption that, although an attacker can create an arbitrary number of Sybil identities, she cannot establish an arbitrarily large number of social connections to non-Sybil identities. In contrast to previous social network-based Sybil detection, e.g. [6, 44, 45], the schemes we consider do not explicitly identify Sybil identities in the network but, instead, bound the impact that Sybil identities can have. This approach is called *Sybil tolerance* [39]; these schemes have been shown to be effective in applications including reputation systems [9], spam protection [24], online auctions [29], and content rating systems [35].

We demonstrate that despite their differences, all of these schemes work by assigning credit values to links in a social network, and then conducting payments between nodes in the network. Effectively, these schemes are using *credit networks* [5, 12] as a basis for Sybil tolerance.[1] Unfortunately, these schemes do not scale well to large social networks. Finding routes for credit payments can be reduced to determining the maximum flow [11] between nodes in the network; doing this over large graphs is known to be expensive [13], and existing techniques for pre-calculating [14] the maximum flow are not directly applicable since the credit network is constantly changing. This serves as a practical deployment barrier, and to the best of our knowledge, none of these Sybil tolerance schemes have been deployed in a real-world system.

In this paper, we address this situation and scale Sybil tolerance schemes to extremely large graphs. We build Canal, a system that can efficiently approximate credit payments over large, dynamic networks. Canal trades accuracy for speed; we demonstrate that Canal's approximation rarely impacts users and does not change the Sybil tolerance properties of the application or benefit malicious users. We show that Canal can be directly plugged into existing Sybil tolerance schemes, and would reduce the credit payment latency from multiple seconds to a few hundred microseconds.

In more detail, Canal uses a novel landmark routing-based algorithm, routing credit payments via landmark nodes [36]. Canal consists of two components: a set of *universe creator* processes, which continually select new landmarks, and a set of *path stitcher* processes, which continually process incoming credit payment requests. Since the credit network is constantly changing (due to credit movements, as well as new identities and social links), Canal continually calculates new landmarks in parallel with making flow calculations. We design Canal to naturally take advantage of multiple cores and machines, enabling Canal to run over social networks that cannot be stored on a single machine.

We evaluate Canal on real-world networks at scale. We first demonstrate that Canal's approximation provides a dramatic speedup in the processing of credit payments, enabling Canal to be run in an online fashion. We then show that the approximation that Canal uses rarely impacts users, and that users eventually receive the same total available credit in Canal as they would in an exact system. Finally, we re-run the experimental setup of two previously proposed Sybil tolerance schemes, and demonstrate that using Canal would provide up to a 2,329-fold speedup in runtime while maintaining over 94% accuracy. This shows that existing schemes can naturally leverage Canal, and that Canal enables new

schemes to be designed to inherit the benefits of credit networks.

The remainder of this paper is organized as follows. Section 2 provides background on the Sybil tolerance schemes we consider, and Section 3 provides background on the credit networks that underlie these schemes. Section 4 describes the design of Canal. Section 5 provides Canal microbenchmarks on real-world graph data, and Section 6 evaluates the performance of Canal when applied to real-world Sybil tolerance schemes. Section 7 concludes.

2. Background and related work

In this section, we give a brief overview of the prior work on social network-based Sybil defenses, with the goal of placing the contributions of this paper into context. A more extensive background is provided in [39]; we review the details relevant to Canal here. For the remainder of this paper, we consider *identity-based* systems where each user is intended to have a single identity and is expected to use the identity when interacting with other users in the system. In such systems, we call a user with multiple identities a *Sybil user* and each identity she uses a *Sybil identity*.

We divide the related work on Sybil defense into three classes, discussed in the sections below: Sybil prevention, Sybil detection, and Sybil tolerance.

2.1 Sybil prevention

Traditional defenses against Sybil attacks rely on either trusting central authorities or tying identities to resources that are hard to forge or obtain in abundance, preventing a user from creating many Sybil identities in the first place. We term these approaches *Sybil prevention*. For instance, systems like Cyworld [4] require users to present verified identities, such as passports or social security numbers, when creating new accounts. Other approaches include solving memory or CPU-intensive crypto-puzzles before granting access to system services [1–3, 41].

2.2 Sybil detection

Researchers have also explored allowing Sybil identities to be created but later detecting the identities and preventing them from interacting with other users (e.g., banning those identities) [32]. We term these approaches *Sybil detection*.

Recently, researchers have explored analyzing the structure of the social network as a mechanism for Sybil detection [6, 20, 30, 34, 44, 45]. To identify Sybils, all social network-based Sybil detection schemes make two common assumptions [43]:

1. Although an attacker can create an arbitrary number of Sybil identities in the social network, she cannot establish an arbitrary number of social connections to non-Sybil identities.

---

[1] Credit networks are a concept borrowed from the electronic commerce community. Credit networks provide a way to model trust between identities in a distributed system and leverage it as a payment infrastructure for transactions between arbitrary identities, even in the absence of a central trusted bank and common currency.

2. The non-Sybil region of the network is densely connected (or fast-mixing [25]), meaning random walks in the non-Sybil region quickly reach a stationary distribution.

The first assumption concerns how the Sybil and non-Sybil identities are connected and is necessary in order for the schemes to be able to leverage the social network; if it were not assumed, the attacker could establish social network links at will. While this assumption may not hold on all online social networks, recent work suggests that there are social networks where this assumption holds true [28]. The second assumption concerns the internal structure of the non-Sybil region and is necessary for these schemes to locate the boundary between the non-Sybil region and the Sybil region. If the second assumption did not to hold (implying small cuts existed within the non-Sybil region), the honest identities on either sides of cuts are likely be blocked from interacting with each other [40].[2]

2.3 Sybil tolerance

More recently, a series of schemes has taken an alternate approach to defend against Sybils. Instead of trying to explicitly label identities as Sybil or non-Sybil, these schemes are designed to limit the impact that a malicious user can have on others, regardless of the number of identities the malicious user possesses. We refer to these schemes as *Sybil tolerance* [39]. Sybil tolerance schemes make the same assumption 1 from Section 2.2, but avoid making assumption 2. Instead, they require more information about the system to which they are applied: In addition to the social network, these schemes also take as input the interactions between users. By doing so, they are able to allow or deny individual interactions, and reason about the impact (in terms of interactions) that identities have on one another.

The result is that the guarantees of Sybil tolerance are expressed in terms of interactions that are allowed. To compare, Sybil detection schemes reason only about identities (i.e., they reason about identities being *admitted*, and express their guarantees in terms of the number of Sybil identities admitted), while Sybil tolerance schemes reason about interactions (i.e., they decide whether certain interactions are allowed or denied). Thus, in a Sybil tolerance scheme, a certain pair of identities may be allowed to participate in certain interactions and not others, and may be allowed to interact at certain times and not others (all depending on the state of the system).

We now provide a brief overview of three example Sybil tolerance schemes. It is important to note that other Sybil

tolerance schemes exist [9, 27], but we only discuss the three below for brevity.

Ostra [24]   is targeted at countering unwanted communication (i.e., spam). Ostra assumes the existence of a social network, and assigns credit values to the links. When a user wishes to send a message to another user, Ostra locates a path with available credit from the source to the destination. If such a path is found, credit is "paid" from each user to the next along the path, and the credit is refunded if the message is not marked as spam. If no path can be found, the message is blocked from being sent.

SumUp [35]   is designed to prevent users with multiple identities from manipulating object ratings in content sharing systems like Digg. SumUp assumes the existence of a social network and selects a trusted vote collector. SumUp then assigns weights to the links around the vote collector by handing out "tokens" (causing the links around the vote collector to be more highly weighted; links farther away are assigned weight 1). Finally, to vote, each voting identity must find a path with credit between himself and the vote collector and consume a credit along that path; if no such path can be found, the vote is discarded.

Bazaar [29]   provides stronger user reputations in online marketplaces like eBay. To do so, Bazaar creates a transaction network (akin to a social network) by linking pairs of identities that have successfully completed a transaction; the weight of each link is the dollar value of the transaction. When a new transaction is about to take place, Bazaar compares the value of the new transaction to the max flow between the buyer and seller. If sufficient flow is found, credit totaling the value of the transaction is removed between the buyer and seller, and is added back if the transaction is later reported to not be fraudulent. Otherwise, if sufficient flow is not found, the new transaction is denied.

Unfortunately, these schemes all tend to require significant computational resources in order to locate paths for credit payments. For example, on average, Bazaar takes over 6 seconds of CPU time to determine whether sufficient flow exists on a network with 5.5 M links [29], and Ostra requires over 35 milliseconds on a network with 3.4 M links [24]. Given that both of these are intended to be run in an online fashion, Bazaar would require an average of 6 seconds of CPU time for every bid on a marketplace like eBay, and Ostra would require an average of 35 milliseconds of additional CPU time for every message sent. Both of these represent substantial computational resource investments. With ever-larger and denser networks being created, it is unsurprising that—to the best of our knowledge—none of these schemes have been deployed in a real-world system.

The underlying reason for this high computation time is that these systems are required to check for credits on all possible paths, requiring one or more breadth-first-searches (BFSs) over the graph, with $O(E)$ cost per BFS.

---

[2] Researchers have begun to explore whether the second assumption holds in practice. Unfortunately, recent work [26] demonstrates that the mixing time for many real-world networks is substantially higher than was previously thought, suggesting that the networks are actually *not* fast mixing. Additionally, another study [19] demonstrates that in real-world social networks, identities in the periphery are often organized into densely connected clusters that connect to the rest of the network via a small cut.

Figure 1. Simple credit network between two nodes A and B, with credit available c_{ab} and c_{ba} shown. In this example, A has 5 credits available from B, and B has 2 credits available from A.

3. Sybil tolerance and credit networks

We now show that Sybil tolerance schemes are all effectively using *credit networks*. We first give a brief overview of credit networks before describing how existing systems are leveraging them internally.

3.1 Credit networks

Credit networks [5, 12] were first introduced in the electronic commerce community in order to build transitive trust protocols in an environment where there is only pairwise trust between accounts and there are no central trusted entities. In a credit network, identities (nodes) trust each other by offering pairwise credit (links) up to a certain limit. Nodes can use the credit to pay for services they receive from each other. The credit network could also be used as a payment infrastructure between nodes that do not directly extend credit to each other. Nodes can route credit payments to a remote node via network paths that traverse over links where credits are available (see Figures 1 and 2).

Formally, a *credit network* is a directed graph $G = (V, E)$ where V is the set of nodes and E is the set of labeled edges. Each directed edge $(a, b) \in E$ is labeled with a dynamic scalar value c_{ab}, called the *available credit*, and is initialized to C_{ab}. Intuitively, C_{ab} represents the initial credit allocation that b gives to a, and c_{ab} represents the amount of unconsumed credit that b has extended to a. Note that $c_{ab} \geq 0$ at all times.

Payments between two nodes in a credit network are contingent upon the availability of credit along network paths connecting the nodes. If a node a wishes to pay node b a total of c credits, then a path

$$a \to u_1 \to ... \to u_n \to b$$

(which could just be $a \to b$) must exist where c credits are available on each (i, j) link (i.e., $c_{ij} \geq c$). If so, the credit available on each directed edge c_{ij} on the path from a to b is decreased by c. As a result of this action, each node "pays" c credits to its successor on the path to b.

It is not necessary to find a single path with available credit along each edge; instead, the payment could be split across multiple paths. For example, consider the network shown in Figure 3. In this scenario, node A could pay 4 credits to node E by paying 2 credits along $A \to B \to C \to E$ and 2 credits along $A \to B \to D \to E$.

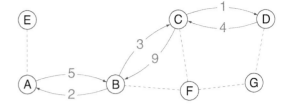

Figure 2. More complex credit network, with credit available (c_{ij}) shown for each link. In this example, A can pay 1 credit to D along the path $A \to B \to C \to D$. After paying the credit, the values on these links would be 4, 2, and 0, respectively. Note that, for simplicity, the links not on this path are only shown as dashed lines.

3.2 Sybil tolerant nature of available credit

Credit networks have been shown to be naturally tolerant to Sybil attacks [31]. In brief, we assume that an attacker is allowed to create as many identities as she wishes and manipulate the available credit on links between identities she owns. However, the attacker is able to establish only a limited number of links to non-malicious users (by assumption 1 in Section 2.2), and she can not manipulate the credit available to him on these links.

As shown in Figure 4, the total amount of available credit to the malicious user is the sum of the available credit on her links to other users. An attacker with an arbitrary number of Sybil identities has exactly the same available credit as the attacker with just one identity; in this case, the relevant set of edges is the cut between the subgraph consisting of the attacker's Sybil identities and the rest of the network. Any available credit on edges between the attacker's Sybil identities does not matter, because it does not enable ad-

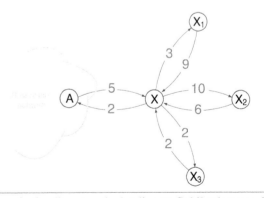

Figure 4. Credit networks leading to Sybil tolerance. User X can create any number of identities (X_1, X_2, X_3) and arbitrarily assign the credit available between them. However, if X wishes to pay credits from any of these identities to another identity in the rest of the network, the credits must be debited from X's single valid link to A. Thus, the multiple identities do not enable any additional available credit with nodes in the rest of the network.

Figure 3. The (a) initial and (b) final state of the credit network with a credit payment along multiple paths. A pays 4 credits to E: 2 credits are paid along the path $A \to B \to C \to E$ and 2 credits are paid along the path $A \to B \to D \to E$.

ditional payments to legitimate nodes. Moreover, collusion between malicious users does not enable the users to access more available credit together than they could separately.

Thus, available credit in a credit network is resilient to Sybil attacks.

3.3 Credit networks in existing systems

We now briefly discuss how the three example schemes discussed in Section 2.3 all work by essentially performing payments over credit networks. First, we note that each of the schemes internally uses a credit network: In Ostra and SumUp, the credit network is based on an externally provided social network, and in Bazaar, the credit network (called the *risk network*) is constructed from the feedback on prior transactions. Second, we observe that each scheme assigns available credit to links: In Ostra, the initial available credit is statically defined by the system operator, in SumUp, the credit is assigned by a token distribution mechanism, and in Bazaar, the credit is increased after each successful transaction.

Third, we observe that these schemes work by *paying credits* along paths between identities. In Ostra, a sender must first pay a receiver one credit before sending a message; if the sender is out of credit, the message is not delivered.[3] Similarly, in SumUp, each voter must pay one credit to the vote collector; if no path exists between the voter and vote collector with available credit, the vote is not counted. Finally, in Bazaar, when a transaction is about to occur, the system insists that the buyer pay the seller a number of credits corresponding to the new transaction value; if the sufficient available credit does not exist, the transaction is blocked.[4]

3.4 Computation speed of credit payments

The high computation time that Sybil tolerance schemes experience is explained by the use of credit payments over social networks. First, we observe that performing a credit payment involves searching for one or more paths with avail-

able credit between two nodes; this is essentially the maximum flow problem [11], which is known to be a computationally expensive operation. The most efficient algorithms for the maximum flow problem run in $O(V^3)$ [13] or $O(V^2 \log(E))$ [8] time. Second, techniques that precalculate the all-pairs maximum flow (e.g., Gomory-Hu trees [14]) cannot be applied to Sybil tolerance schemes, as these techniques assume a static network and impose a large, upfront pre-calculation cost of $|V| - 1$ maximum flow computations. Credit networks are constantly changing due to credit manipulations as well as new users and links; performing $|V| - 1$ maximum flow computations for every change in the credit network is impractical. Additionally, algorithms [17] that dynamically maintain a Gomory-Hu tree when the edge capacities increase or decrease often end up being expensive as well, requiring several maximum flow computations for each edge capacity update.

4. Canal design

We now detail the design of Canal, first giving a high-level overview of the model and goals of Canal before detailing the internal design.

4.1 Model and goals

Canal is designed to run alongside an existing Sybil tolerance scheme, providing two services: (a) maintaining the state of the credit network and (b) conducting credit payments. Canal is built to provide these services in a much faster manner than current implementations. We assume that Canal is run by the same organization that runs the Sybil tolerance scheme (alleviating concerns about Canal having access to potentially private social network data).

In order for existing Sybil tolerance systems like Bazaar and SumUp to take advantage of Canal, they need only allow Canal to store the credit network and replace any internal logic for conducting payments with calls into Canal. To avoid having to rebuild existing systems from scratch, Canal exports an API which can be easily used by existing Sybil tolerant applications. The API includes methods to initialize and add links to the credit network, but we are primarily concerned with the method

```
boolean payment(a,b,c)
```

---

[3] In Ostra, when a sender pays a credit to a receiver, a credit is debited from the sender–receiver path and, at the same time, *added* to the reverse path. Doing so allows Ostra to ensure liveness (as there is always credit available in the system).

[4] In Bazaar, this credit payment is undone if the transaction turns out not to be fraudulent.

that attempts a payment of c credits from identity a to identity b, and returns whether or not the payment could be made.

Canal responds to payment requests using an approximation that only considers a subset of the paths that exist when handling payments. As a result, Canal may not be able to find paths with available credit between a pair of users even though such paths exist. However, Canal will never find paths that do not exist or paths that do exist but do not have any available credit. Thus, Canal can suffer from *false negatives* (i.e., a payment is denied even though paths with available credit exist) but does not suffer from *false positives* (i.e., a payment is allowed even though sufficient credit is not actually available).

4.2 Design challenges

In order for Canal to be used in a real-world application, it has to overcome several challenges:

- *Latency:* Sybil tolerance schemes make user-visible decisions based on whether credit payments can be made. Thus, they will be practically deployable only if the Canal processing time is very fast (preferably in the order of a few milliseconds).

- *Efficiency:* Sybil tolerance schemes often have to process large numbers of payments in a short period of time; Canal must be deployable with reasonable computational resources.

- *Scalability:* Sybil tolerance schemes are designed to be run on very large social networks. Canal should support credit networks with hundreds of millions of links or more.

- *Accuracy:* Canal trades off accuracy for speed. The error introduced should not impact the Sybil tolerance guarantees, and should rarely impact users.

- *Dynamicity:* The credit network is constantly changing, due to payments being processed and changes to the social network. Canal should be able to support such a rapidly changing credit network.

4.3 Using landmark routing

Canal speeds up payments using a landmark routing-based technique. Historically, landmark routing [36] has enabled paths to be found between any pair of nodes via certain specific nodes (called landmarks). To do so, each node determines its path to the landmark; to route between a pair of non-landmark nodes, we need only have each route to the landmark. This is effectively *stitching* a path together out of two paths, and the stitched path may be longer than the shortest path (this is particularly likely when the landmark is located far away from the two nodes).

Canal's selection of landmark nodes is driven by three concerns, discussed in detail in the subsections below: First, we wish to be able to find short paths between nodes, but we are not required to use the absolute shortest path (Sybil tol-

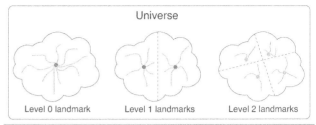

Figure 5. Diagram of a 2-level landmark universe, consisting of multiple levels of landmarks. Each level i has 2^i landmarks. Paths can be found using landmark routing; all nodes share a level 0 landmark, and closer nodes share landmarks at multiple levels (resulting in shorter paths). The landmarks at lower levels induce partitions on the network (indicated by dashed lines).

erance systems are designed so that *any* payment path will do, but shorter paths often result in greater efficiency). Second, landmark routing is not typically designed for dynamic graphs (the paths to the landmark are generally treated as static; if the credit network is changing, Canal needs to update the paths to the landmarks). Third, we may need to conduct payments that require multiple paths (the credit available on any single path may not be sufficient).

4.3.1 Finding short paths

Recent work has designed landmark routing techniques for accurately finding shortest paths in large networks [16]; we leverage this existing work to efficiently find short paths. Instead of using a single landmark, Canal uses a *landmark universe* with multiple *levels*. At each level i, there are 2^i landmarks selected randomly; each node finds a path to the closest landmark at each level. Thus, if there are k levels, there are a total of $2^{k+1} - 1$ landmarks, and each node has paths to k of these landmarks (one at each level). Furthermore, we refer to a universe with k levels as a k-level landmark universe. A diagram of a landmark universe is shown in Figure 5.

Using a landmark universe enables Canal to find short paths. To see why, first consider a payment request between two nodes who are on opposite sides of the network (i.e., two nodes who have a relatively large shortest path length). For this pair of nodes, the only landmark they are likely to share is the level 0 landmark[5] (since they are far away, they are likely to have paths to two *different* level 1 landmarks, and two different level 2 landmarks, etc). Now consider the case of a payment request between two nodes who are close in the network. For this pair of nodes, there is likely to be a number of landmarks shared between them (since they are close in the network). By stitching a path between these nodes via one of the higher-level landmarks, we are likely to find a short path. A full explanation is available in [7, 16].

---

[5] Note that any pair of nodes is guaranteed to share at least one landmark in a given universe (the level 0 landmark), although the stitched path via that landmark is not guaranteed to have credit.

It is important to note that Canal's correctness guarantees are not affected if a Sybil node is selected as a landmark. On the other hand, Sybil landmarks may affect the liveness of paths stitched via that landmark, as links near the landmark may not have credit. As a result, a Sybil landmark may not be useful for routing credit payments. Since Canal typically uses hundreds of landmarks at any time, Sybil landmarks rarely impact Canal's ability to route credit payments.

In Section 5, we show how the deployer of Canal can select the level k of each universe. Higher values of k allow shorter paths to be located, but introduce an exponentially increasing number of landmarks (and corresponding overhead). In practice, setting k to 5 works well on the social networks we use to evaluate Canal.

4.3.2 Handling dynamic credit networks

We observe that, due to the rapidly changing nature of the credit network, any existing landmark data may quickly become stale. For example, as new links are introduced into the credit network, paths may exist that are not reflected in the landmark universe. Similarly, as credit payments are processed, paths near lower-level landmarks are likely to become congested and may run out of available credit (since a disproportionate number of credit payments will be routed via these landmarks); this would prevent Canal from finding available credit that may exist via other potential landmarks.

Canal addresses this issue by continually constructing landmark universes as it is running, replacing an old universe whenever a new one is created. This serves two purposes. First, continually constructing universes enables Canal to incorporate changes in the credit network into the landmark path data. Second, continually constructing universes ensures that any node is only a landmark for a short period of time, reducing the likelihood that the paths around the landmark would become congested with credit payments.

4.3.3 Finding multiple paths

We noted above that Canal may need to conduct payments that require multiple paths (i.e., in the example in Figure 3, suppose A wishes to pay 5 credits to E). In particular, we would like to be able to locate *disjoint* paths, as this increases our likelihood of finding the necessary available credit.

Canal addresses this issue by keeping a queue of recent landmark universes available. As new landmark universes are generated, they are added to the end of the queue and the oldest existing landmark universe is discarded. Keeping a set of universes available enables Canal to find paths between pairs of nodes via the landmarks that exist in different universes. By configuring the number of landmark universes that are stored in the queue, Canal can control the maximum number of paths that can be used at once for a credit payment.

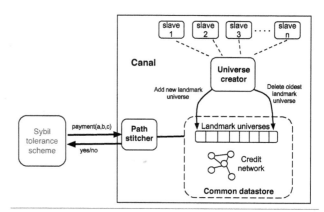

Figure 6. Canal system design.

4.4 Canal components

Figure 6 gives a high level view of Canal system design. There are three main components in Canal: a common datastore, *universe creator* processes, and *path stitcher* processes. The common datastore serves as a location to store the landmark universes and the credit network. The universe creator processes continually generate new landmark universes as described above, and the path stitcher processes respond to payment requests by the Sybil tolerance scheme. In the rest of this section, we will discuss in detail the design of each component.

4.4.1 Common datastore

The common datastore serves as the repository for the state of the credit network as well as the landmark universes. The credit network is stored as a hash table of links, with each link stored with its current available credit. Because multiple processes will be manipulating the values on the credit network, each link also contains a shared/exclusive lock that processes must obtain before reading/writing the credit value. When a new link is added to the credit network, its lock and credit available are first initialized before it is inserted into the credit network hash table.

The landmark universes are stored using a linked list, with a global pointer to the head of the landmark universe list and each landmark universe pointing to the next. Since multiple processes will be scanning the landmark universe list, the pointers are also protected with read/write locks which processes obtain before following or changing a pointer.

The landmark universes themselves are represented as a series of *landmark maps* with one landmark map for each level in the landmark universe. Each landmark map contains tuples

```
(node, landmark, next_hop)
```

with one entry for each node in the network. The `landmark` represents the given node's landmark at this level, and the `next_hop` represents the node's next hop towards this landmark. By recursively following the `next_hops`, each node can reconstruct its path to the landmark. Thus, in a k-level landmark universe, there are k landmark maps, each with an entry for all nodes in the network. Thus, each landmark universe requires $O(n \cdot k)$ space, where n is the number of nodes in the credit network.

4.4.2 Universe creator processes

We now describe the design of the universe creator processes, which construct new landmark universes. Assume that Canal is configured to construct k-level landmark universes. The universe creator processes all continually construct landmark universes using the following approach, taken from [16].

1. Randomly select k random node sets of sizes $2^0, 2^1, 2^2, 2^3, \ldots 2^k$ respectively, from the network. Let the selected sets be denoted by $V_0, V_1, V_2, \ldots V_k$. These sets contain the new landmarks at each level.

2. For each set V_i, and every node $u \in V$, calculate the shortest path from u to each of the landmark nodes in each set V_i. This is done by having the processes perform BFSs from each landmark in V_i.

3. Finally, using the BFSs, construct the landmark map for level V_i by select the closest landmark node in V_i and the next hop for all nodes.

In Canal, we speed up this universe creator process using three techniques: First, Canal exploits the fact that conducting the BFSs from the new landmarks can be parallelized. We configure the BFSs to be conducted in parallel by a set of slave threads. Second, to make sure that we only find paths with available credit, we design the BFS algorithm to only consider edges with available credit. This allows newly constructed landmark universes to "route around" links which have no available credit (and cannot be used for payments).

Third, the process of selecting the closest landmark at a given level for all nodes (step 3 above) can be broken down into a series of *merges* that can easily be parallelized as well.[6] Let us consider the 2^i BFSs that are conducted when constructing the landmark map for level V_i. Note that these BFSs are completed at different times by different processes. The landmark map is constructed by taking the first BFS and creating an entry for every node in the landmark map pointing to the landmark at the root of the BFS. Then, as subsequent BFSs complete, they are merged into the landmark map by scanning over the existing landmark map, and changing any tuples where the node is closer to the new landmark than to any landmark previously merged. In fact, multiple landmark maps can be merged together in the same manner, allowing all of the processes to contribute to constructing the landmark map.

Once the new landmark universe is constructed, it is added on to the end of landmark universe list in the common datastore. At the same time, the oldest landmark universe is removed from the front of the list and discarded. This ensures that landmarks are only "active" for a short period of time, reducing the likelihood that they will become hotspots in the network (Section 5 shows this happens rarely).

4.4.3 Path stitcher processes

Finally, we describe the design of the path stitcher processes, which respond to `payment` requests from the Sybil tolerance scheme. Let us suppose that a path stitcher process has received a request to pay c credits from node a to b. At a high level, the path stitcher process walks down the landmark universe list, looking for paths with available credit between a and b using the landmarks in each universe. As soon as the path stitcher process has found paths with a total of c available credits, it returns a successful result. Otherwise, if the path stitcher process reaches the end of the universe list without finding a total of c credits, it returns an unsuccessful result.

To find paths with available credit in a single k-level landmark universe, the path stitcher process executes the following algorithm:

1. Scan the k landmark maps and collect the set of common landmarks between a and b. Note that there is guaranteed to be at least one common landmark (at level 0).

2. For each shared landmark, use the `next_hop` in the landmark map to "stitch" together a path via the landmark.

3. Refine the path by (a) eliminating any cycles and (b) performing path *short-cutting*. To perform short-cutting, we traverse the path up to the landmark node and see if there is a link from any of these nodes to a node lying in the path after the landmark node. If so, we short-circuit the path by using that link to create a shorter path between a and b.

This process results in up to L paths between a and b, where L is the number of common landmarks in this universe.[7]

Next, the path stitcher process pays as much credit as possible along each path. For each path, the path stitcher process walks the path, obtaining the lock on each link of the path, temporarily lowering the credit available to 0, and then releasing the lock. Once the end of the path has been reached, the path stitcher calculates the maximum credit available on the entire path (determined by the link with the minimal credit available); let this be C. Then, the path stitcher process walks the path once more, locking each link and resetting the credit available to be its previous value minus C. This effects a removal of C credits along the entire path.

Once sufficient credit has been removed to meet the original `payment` request, the path stitcher process returns a suc-

---

[6] Our current implementation does not support the parallel BFS merge feature. We plan to incorporate this in the future.

[7] There could be potentially fewer resulting paths, as some of the paths may end up duplicated (e.g., if a path happens to cross two landmarks). This happens rarely in practice.

Network	Nodes	Links	Avg. degree	Avg. max flow time (s)
Renren [18]	33 K	1.4 M	21.1	0.352
Facebook [38]	63 K	1.6 M	25.7	0.445
YouTube [23]	1.1 M	5.8 M	5.2	2.91
Flickr [22]	1.6 M	30 M	18.8	15.2
Orkut [23]	3.1 M	234 M	76.3	220

Table 1. Statistics of the networks we evaluate Canal on. Also included is the average time for completing a max flow computation.

cessful result. However, if the end of the universe list is reached without enough credit being found, the path stitcher process first replaces any credit removed before returning an unsuccessful result.

The path stitching process is fast, since the landmark paths are all pre-computed; the path stitcher process simply walks the paths and removes available credit. Additionally, the path stitcher processes only ever hold a single link lock at a given time, ensuring that Canal is deadlock-free. Finally, the memory requirements of the path stitcher process is low, as it only needs to temporarily store the paths where it has removed credit.

4.5 Implementation

Our implementation of Canal is written in 2,269 lines of C++ (excluding publicly available libraries). The current implementation is designed to be run on a single machine, and uses Pthreads for the universe creator and path stitcher processes and Pthread locks to protect shared data. Our implementation is written so that the deployer can specify the number of universe creator and path stitcher processes to use; the tradeoff depends on the number of incoming payment requests that the deployer wishes to process (since more path stitcher processes allows a higher throughput, assuming CPU resources are available). We demonstrate in Section 5 that our single-machine implementation is able to support graphs with over 220 million edges. It is important to note while our current implementation runs on a single machine, we have designed Canal to be implementable across a cluster of machines. Doing so would allow Canal to be deployed on credit networks that are too large to fit in a single machine's memory. Canal can be implemented using graph parallel processing platforms [15, 21] that automatically distribute the graph state (our credit network) across multiple machines. This would mean that the Canal common datastore would be distributed across multiple machines and the universe creator processes would be using distributed graph processing algorithms. Existing graph parallel processing platforms follow the bulk synchronous parallel (BSP) model [37] and the challenge would be to minimize the global communication between the processes and the barrier synchronization cost associated with BSP algorithms. Additionally, a distributed implementation would likely re-

Renren	Facebook	YouTube	Flickr	Orkut
225	292	4,131	13,296	41,787

Table 2. Time in milliseconds to calculate a level-0 landmark universe with one universe creator process for various datasets.

quire transactional updates to the common datastore to properly handle node failures. However, we leave a full implementation of a distributed version of Canal to future work.

5. Canal microbenchmarks

In this section, we explore a number of Canal microbenchmarks before exploring how Canal performs alongside Sybil tolerance schemes in the following section. Here, we center our evaluation around five questions:

- What is the memory overhead of landmark universes?
- How expensive are landmark universes to compute?
- What is the response time for payment requests?
- Do nodes receive all of their available credits over time?
- Do "hotspots" in the network form around landmarks?

5.1 Experimental setup

We evaluate Canal on five real-world social networks of varying size, shown in Table 1. These networks are some of the largest publicly available social network data sets, and cover a wide number of nodes (33 K to 3.1 M) and edges (1.4 M to 234 M).

We run our experiments on machines with dual 12-core Intel Xeon X5650 2.66 GHz processors and 48 GB of RAM. In many of the experiments, we vary two key parameters of Canal: the universe level, and the size of the universe list (i.e., the number of universes that are cached). Unless otherwise stated, each experiment is the average of five random trials.

For reference, the final column in Table 1 shows the average time to compute max flow[8] between 50 random pairs of nodes in these networks; this further emphasizes the computational expense of conducting credit payments on large networks. Even for networks with only a few million links, the computation time can quickly become multiple seconds.

5.2 Memory and compute time of landmark universes

Canal has a certain fixed memory requirement to hold the credit network and edge locks in memory. For example, Orkut, the largest graph we consider, requires almost 20 GB of memory for storing the graph state. However, Canal also requires memory for storing the landmark universes; the amount depends on the universe level and size of the universe list. Figure 7 plots the memory size for a single

---

[8] We use the push-relabel algorithm [13] for computing max flow.

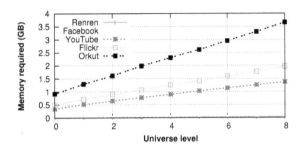

Figure 7. Memory requirements of different universe levels. The memory required increases linearly with the universe level.

landmark universe of different levels for each of the five networks we consider (multiple landmark universes simply require multiples of this size). We observe that the memory size increases linearly with the landmark universe level, and that the sizes allow multiple landmark universes to be kept in memory on our test machine.

We now turn to examine how quickly landmark universes can be created. Table 2 presents the time required to construct a level-0 landmark universe with a single universe creator process; this follows the general trends of the max flow results in Table 1, but is sometimes higher due to Canal's use of per-link locks.

However, in Canal, we can take advantage of multiple cores to conduct landmark universe creation in parallel. Figures 8 and 9 present the speedup (relative to creating a landmark universe with a single universe creator process) and absolute time, respectively, when creating different levels of universes with 22 universe creator processes. We observe that higher level universes enable a greater level of parallelism, meaning Canal is more efficient at creating higher level landmark universes.

5.3 Latency of payment requests

Next, we examine the latency of processing payment requests in Canal. For this experiment, we select 5,000 random pairs of nodes in each network, and issue a payment request between each pair of nodes for one credit. We then record the

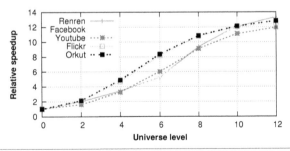

Figure 8. Landmark universe creation time speedup, relative to a single universe creator process, for Canal configured with 22 universe creator processes.

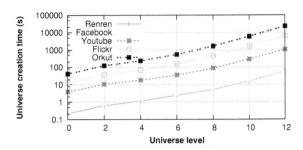

Figure 9. Graph showing the absolute landmark universe creation time as we increase the number of universe levels, for Canal configured with 22 universe creator processes.

latency of the response from Canal. To see how the latency scales with the payment size, we then repeat this experiment by pushing five units of credit. We use 8 level-5 landmark universes, and the credit network is initialized to have one available credit per link.

Table 3 presents the results for the five networks. We observe that both the median and 95th percentile latency for pushing one credit is below 1 millisecond for all networks, and the latency for pushing five credits is below 2.5 milliseconds for all networks. This represents a substantial speedup, as existing systems often take multiple seconds to determine if sufficient available credit is present in the credit network [24, 29].

5.4 Do nodes eventually receive all available credit?

Recall that, at any particular moment, Canal can only use a subset of the paths with available credit between two nodes (in particular, it can only use the paths via their common landmarks). However, if available credit along some of these paths is used up, Canal will disregard the exhausted links when constructing new landmark universes. Thus, even though a node only has access to a subset of its available credit at any one time, it will eventually receive more of its credit as new landmark universes are created. We now explore *how long* it takes for a node to access all of its available credit.

To do so, we pick 50 random pairs of nodes with degree greater than 10 (so that there is significant available credit between them) and the credit network is initialized to have

Network	1 credit		5 credits	
	Median	**95th P.**	**Median**	**95th P.**
Renren	0.04	0.09	0.40	0.64
Facebook	0.04	0.13	0.52	0.74
YouTube	0.14	0.59	1.3	2.3
Flickr	0.17	0.51	1.3	2.0
Orkut	0.34	0.83	0.89	1.9

Table 3. Median and 95th percentile time in milliseconds taken by Canal to respond to a payment requests pushing a one unit and five units of credit.

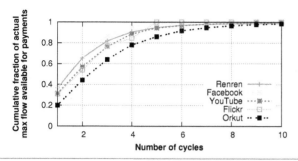

Figure 10. Cumulative fraction of actual max flow that is available for payments in Canal, for increasing cycles of landmark universe creation. We observe that nodes can quickly access all of their available credit.

one available credit per link. We then conduct a number of *cycles*, where each cycle consists of constructing a new set of 8 level-5 landmark universes and then making the largest payment possible between each pair of nodes (meaning we use up all of the available credit between the two nodes). Over time, we expect that the total payments will approach the actual max flow in the credit network between each pair of nodes.

Figure 10 presents the results of this experiment, showing the cumulative fraction of the actual max flow in the credit network that is used for payments. As expected, we see that the total payments asymptotically approach the actual max flow. More importantly, we observe that it does so very quickly: For example, node pairs in each dataset can achieve between 80% and 95% of their actual max flow in just 4 cycles. This indicates that even though Canal only has access to a subset of paths at any one time, nodes do eventually receive all of their available credit, even over short time windows.

5.5 Do landmarks lead to hotspots?

Our final microbenchmark concerns whether or not landmarks in Canal end up becoming "hotspots." To explore this effect, we again select 5,000 random pairs of nodes and have each pair of nodes pay one credit between each other. We

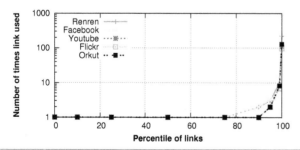

Figure 11. Distribution of the number of times links are used when processing 5,000 random credit payments. For all networks, the 99th percentile links are used fewer than 14 times.

Category	Nodes	Links
Clothes	1.3 M	5.5 M
Home	1.3 M	4.5 M
Collectables	419 K	1.2 M
Electronics	600 K	1.5 M
Computing	626 K	1.7 M

Table 4. Size statistics of the different categories of risk networks used in evaluating Canal implementation of Bazaar.

then count the total number of times each link in the network was used in transferring a credit. If hotspots form, we would expect to see a number of links used many times. For this experiment, we configure Canal to have 8 level-5 landmark universes.

The results of this experiment are shown in Figure 11. We plot the number of times a link is used versus percentile of links, and find that almost all links are used only once, and very few links are used many times. For example, the 90th percentile link is used no more than twice in all networks, and the 99th percentile link is used no more than 14 times.

6. Applying Canal to Sybil tolerance systems

The second half of our evaluation considers the impact that Canal would have on previously proposed Sybil tolerance schemes. In particular, we integrate Canal into both Bazaar [29] and Ostra [24]. We then recreate the original evaluation of these schemes and measure the speedup that these schemes observe when running with Canal, as well as the resulting impact on accuracy (in terms of false negatives).

6.1 Bazaar

Recall that Bazaar is designed to strengthen user reputations in online marketplaces like eBay. We replace the storage of the credit network (called the *risk network* in Bazaar) and max flow calculation components with Canal, and re-perform the same evaluation as in the original paper. Bazaar was originally evaluated using a 90-day trace of five of the largest categories on the UK eBay site, and we use the same dataset to evaluate accuracy and speed up of our implementation compared to the original one. The five categories range in size from 419 K users to 1.3 M users, and from 1.2 M links to 5.5 M links as shown in Table 4.

Table 5 presents the latency for credit network `payment` transactions for the original implementation of Bazaar and for Bazaar augmented with Canal. We make a number of interesting observations. First, we observe that the median latency for transactions is below 200 microseconds for all categories, and the 95th percentile latency is below 4 milliseconds. This low latency enables Bazaar to be used in an online fashion. Second, when compared to the latency of the original Bazaar implementation, we observe speedups of be-

Category	Orig. Avg.	Canal		Relative Speedup
		Med	95th P.	
Clothes	6,290	0.2	3.4	2,329 ×
Home	5,340	0.1	3.4	785 ×
Collectables	1,180	0.08	2.0	1,404 ×
Electronics	1,660	0.09	2.70	1,522 ×
Computing	1,410	0.1	2.56	1,084 ×

Table 5. Time in milliseconds required to process credit network transactions in Bazaar with Canal with 30 level-2 landmark universes. Also included is the original processing time from the Bazaar paper and the relative speedup. We observe speedups between 785-fold and 2,329-fold.

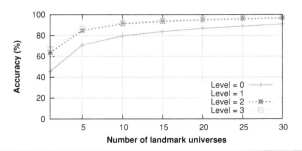

Figure 12. Accuracy of Bazaar with Canal for the Home category, for varying numbers of landmark universes and universe levels. Over 95% accuracy can be achieved with 20 level-3 landmark universes.

tween 785-fold and 2,329-fold. This underscores the impact of Canal on Sybil tolerance systems like Bazaar.

However, this reduction in latency comes at the cost of accuracy. Since Canal can only look for credit on a subset of paths, it may be unable to find sufficient available credit between a buyer–seller pair, thereby wrongly flagging a transaction as fraudulent. To determine how often this occurs, we calculate the fraction of the transactions for which the original Bazaar implementation found sufficient available credit, but Canal was unable to.

The results of this experiment are presented in Table 6, for a configuration with 30 level-3 landmark universes. We observe that Canal provides between 94% and 98% accuracy in all categories, meaning that at least 94% of the time, Canal is able to find sufficient available credit when the original Bazaar implementation did as well. We further explore the sensitivity of Canal's accuracy to configuration parameters in Figure 12, where we vary the number of landmark universes and the level of each universe for the Home category. We observe that accuracy over 95% can be achieved with 20 level-3 landmark universes, suggesting that even a modest number of landmark universes is likely to be sufficient to deploy Canal in practice.

6.2 Ostra

Next, we explore integrating Canal into Ostra [24], a system designed to prevent unwanted communication. Ostra was

Category	Accuracy
Clothes	94.2%
Home	97.0%
Collectables	97.6%
Electronics	95.4%
Computing	95.9%

Table 6. Accuracy of Bazaar implementation using Canal in each category, relative to the original Bazaar implementation. Canal provides high accuracy for Bazaar, implying that users are rarely impacted by the approximate available credit that Canal finds.

originally evaluated on a social network derived from largest strongly connected component of YouTube network [23]; this network consists of 446 K nodes and 3.4 M links [24]. A synthetic communication trace was generated using statistics of a real email trace. We re-run the original Ostra experiments using the same input data, and evaluate accuracy and speed up of our implementation compared to the original one. We use a configuration of Ostra with 128 randomly selected nodes as spammers in the system (each of whom tries to send 500 spam messages), with a credit limit of 3 on every link, and with a 1% false email classification probability by good users.

We first examine the speedup that is observed with Canal deployed to Ostra. Presented in Table 7, the results show that if Ostra were to use Canal, the average time taken to find a path with available credit would drop from 35.4 milliseconds to 190 microseconds (a relative speedup of over 186 times). We observe a lower speedup when Canal is applied to Ostra, compared to Bazaar, for two reasons: First, Ostra requires only a single path for every transaction, while Bazaar generally requires the use of multiple paths, and second, the attacker strength is lower for Ostra (just 128 attackers each attempting to send 500 messages).

We now examine the accuracy that Canal provides when deployed with Ostra. Similar to the evaluation with Bazaar, we calculate the fraction of transactions for which the original version of Ostra was able to find a path with available credit, but Canal is not. The results of this experiment for different configurations of the number of landmark universes and the universe level is presented in Figure 13. We see that

Original Avg.	Canal		Relative Speedup
	Median	95th Percentile	
35.4	0.05	1.4	186 ×

Table 7. Time in milliseconds required to process a credit network transaction in Ostra in Canal with 30 level-3 landmark universes. Also included is the original processing time from the Ostra paper and the relative speedup.

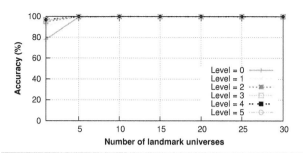

Figure 13. Accuracy of the Ostra implementation using Canal, for varying numbers of landmark universes and universe levels. Over 99% accuracy can be achieved once 5 landmark universes are used.

Canal provides over 99% accuracy once at least five landmark universes are used.

6.3 Summary

Overall, the results in this section demonstrate that Canal can be easily integrated into existing Sybil tolerance schemes. Moreover, the results show that implementations of both Ostra and Bazaar with Canal achieve significant speedup while providing an approximation that only rarely impacts the credit available to users. Given the previous high computation cost of these systems, Canal opens the door for schemes like Ostra, Bazaar, and SumUp to be deployed in real systems, with on-demand computations done over highly-dynamic credit networks.

7. Conclusion

We have presented Canal, a system that can efficiently and accurately transfer credit payments over large credit networks. Canal is designed to complement existing Sybil tolerance schemes such as Ostra [24], SumUp [35], Trust-Davis [9], and Bazaar [29]. We argued that these schemes are all based on computing payments over credit networks, a computation that requires computing max-flow over a graph, that leads to significant computational complexity and makes them impractical to deploy on real-world sites. With Canal, these schemes see a dramatic speedup, making them practical for real-world use.

An evaluation demonstrated that Canal's approximation rarely impacts honest users and does not allow malicious users to obtain any additional credit. Furthermore, Canal is able to perform payment calculations in under a few millisecond on graphs with hundreds of millions of links, a massive speedup when compared to existing approaches. Finally, we demonstrated that, were existing Sybil tolerance schemes to use Canal, the time necessary to process credit payments would be reduced by multiple orders of magnitude while achieving over 94% accuracy.

Acknowledgements

We thank the anonymous reviewers, Allen Clement, Peter Druschel, and our shepherd, Emin Gün Sirer, for their helpful comments. This research was supported in part by NSF grant IIS-0964465, a Google Research Award, and an Amazon Web Services in Education Grant.

References

[1] M. Abadi, M. Burrows, M. Manasse, and T. Wobber. Moderately hard, memory-bound functions. In *ACM Transactions on Internet Technology*, volume 5, pages 299–314, 2005.

[2] N. Borisov. Computational puzzles as Sybil defenses. In *Proceedings of the 6th IEEE International Conference on Peer-to-Peer Computing (IEEE P2P'06)*, 2006.

[3] M. Castro, P. Druschel, A. Ganesh, A. Rowstron, and D. S. Wallach. Secure routing for structured peer-to-peer overlay networks. In *SIGOPS Operating Systems Review*, volume 36, pages 299–314, 2002.

[4] H. Chun, H. Kwak, Y.-H. Eom, Y.-Y. Ahn, S. Moon, and H. Jeong. Comparison of online social relations in volume vs interaction: A case study of cyworld. In *Proceedings of the 8th ACM/USENIX Internet Measurement Conference (IMC'08)*, 2008.

[5] P. Dandekar, A. Goel, R. Govindan, and I. Post. Liquidity in credit networks: A little trust goes a long way. In *Proceedings of the 12th ACM Conference on Electronic Commerce (EC'11)*, 2011.

[6] G. Danezis and P. Mittal. SybilInfer: Detecting Sybil nodes using social networks. In *Proceedings of the 16th Network and Distributed System Security Symposium (NDSS'09)*, 2009.

[7] A. Das Sarma, S. Gollapudi, M. Najork, and R. Panigrahy. A sketch-based distance oracle for web-scale graphs. In *Proceedings of the 3rd ACM International Conference of Web Search and Data Mining (WSDM'10)*, 2010.

[8] E. A. Dinic. An algorithm for the solution of the max-flow problem with the polynomial estimation. *Doklady Akademii Nauk SSSR*, 194(4), 1970.

[9] D. do B. DeFigueiredo and E. T. Barr. Trustdavis: A non-exploitable online reputation system. In *Proceedings of the 7th IEEE International Conference on E-Commerce Technology (IEEE E-Commerce)*, 2005.

[10] J. Douceur. The Sybil Attack. In *Proceedings of the 1st International Workshop on Peer-to-Peer Systems (IPTPS'02)*, 2002.

[11] L. R. Ford and D. R. Fulkerson. Maximal flow through a network. In *Canadian Journal of Mathematics*, volume 8, pages 399–404.

[12] A. Ghosh, M. Mahdian, D. M. Reeves, D. M. Pennock, and R. Fugger. Mechanism design on trust networks. In *Proceedings of the 3rd International Conference on Internet and Network Economics (WINE'07)*, 2007.

[13] A. V. Goldberg and R. E. Tarjan. A new approach to the maximum flow problem. In *Proceedings of the 18th annual ACM Symposium on Theory of Computing (STOC'86)*, 1986.

[14] R. E. Gomory and T. Hu. Multi-terminal network flows. In *Journal of the Society for Industrial and Applied Mathematics (SIAM)*, volume 9, pages 551–570, 1961.

[15] D. Gregor and A. Lumsdaine. The parallel BGL: A generic library for distributed graph computations. In *Proceedings of*

the Parallel Object-Oriented Scientific Computing (POOSC), 2005.

[16] A. Gubichev, S. Bedathur, S. Seufert, and G. Weikum. Fast and accurate estimation of shortest paths in large graphs. In *Proceedings of the 19th ACM international conference on Information and knowledge management (CIKM'10)*, 2010.

[17] T. Hartmann and D. Wagner. Fully-dynamic cut tree construction. Technical Report 2011.25, Karlsruhe Institute of Technology, 2011.

[18] J. Jiang, C. Wilson, X. Wang, P. Huang, W. Sha, Y. Dai, and B. Y. Zhao. Understanding latent interactions in online social networks. In *Proceedings of the 10th ACM/USENIX Internet Measurement Conference (IMC'10)*, 2010.

[19] J. Leskovec, K. Lang, and M. Mahoney. Empirical comparison of algorithms for network community detection. In *Proceedings of the 19th International World Wide Web Conference (WWW'10)*, 2010.

[20] C. Lesniewski-Laas and M. F. Kaashoek. Whānau: A Sybil-proof distributed hash table. In *Proceedings of the 7th Symposium on Networked Systems Design and Implementation (NSDI'10)*, 2010.

[21] G. Malewicz, M. H. Austern, A. J. Bik, J. C. Dehnert, I. Horn, N. Leiser, and G. Czajkowski. Pregel: A system for large-scale graph processing. In *Proceedings of the International Conference on Management of Data (SIGMOD'10)*, 2010.

[22] A. Mislove, H. S. Koppula, K. P. Gummadi, P. Druschel, and B. Bhattacharjee. Growth of the Flickr social network. In *Proceedings of the 1st ACM SIGCOMM Workshop on Social Networks (WOSN'08)*, 2008.

[23] A. Mislove, M. Marcon, K. P. Gummadi, P. Druschel, and B. Bhattacharjee. Measurement and analysis of online social networks. In *Proceedings of the 7th ACM/USENIX Internet Measurement Conference (IMC'07)*, 2007.

[24] A. Mislove, A. Post, K. P. Gummadi, and P. Druschel. Ostra: Leveraging trust to thwart unwanted communication. In *Proceedings of the 5th Symposium on Networked Systems Design and Implementation (NSDI'08)*, 2008.

[25] M. Mitzenmacher and E. Upfal. *Probability and Computing*. Cambridge University Press, Cambridge, UK, 2005.

[26] A. Mohaisen, A. Yun, and Y. Kim. Measuring the mixing time of social graphs. In *Proceedings of the 10th ACM/USENIX Internet Measurement Conference (IMC'10)*, 2010.

[27] M. Mondal, B. Viswanath, A. Clement, P. Druschel, K. P. Gummadi, A. Mislove, and A. Post. Limiting large-scale crawls of social networking sites. In *Proceedings of the Annual Conference of the ACM Special Interest Group on Data Communication (SIGCOMM'11, poster session)*, 2011.

[28] M. Motoyama, D. McCoy, K. Levchenko, S. Savage, and G. M. Voelker. Dirty jobs: The role of freelance labor in web service abuse. In *Proceedings of the 20th USENIX conference on Security (SEC'11)*, 2011.

[29] A. Post, V. Shah, and A. Mislove. Bazaar: Strengthening user reputations in online marketplaces. In *Proceedings of the 8th Symposium on Networked Systems Design and Implementation (NSDI'11)*, 2011.

[30] D. Quercia and S. Hailes. Sybil attacks against mobile users: Friends and foes to the rescue. In *Proceedings of the 29th Conference on Information Communications (INFO-COM'10)*, 2010.

[31] S. Seuken and D. C. Parkes. On the Sybil-proofness of accounting mechanisms. In *Proceedings of the 6 th Workshop on the Economics of Networks, Systems and Computation (NetEcon'11)*, 2011.

[32] T. Stein, E. Chen, and K. Mangla. Facebook immune system. In *Proceedings of the 4th Workshop on Social Network Systems (SNS'11)*, 2011.

[33] D. Streitfeld. Ferreting out fake reviews online. http://nytimes.com/2011/08/20/technology/finding-fake-reviews-online.html.

[34] N. Tran, J. Li, L. Subramanian, and S. S. Chow. Optimal Sybil-resilient node admission control. In *Proceedings of the 30th Conference on Information Communications (INFO-COM'11)*, 2011.

[35] N. Tran, B. Min, J. Li, and L. Subramanian. Sybil-resilient online content voting. In *Proceedings of the 6th Symposium on Networked Systems Design and Implementation (NSDI'09)*, 2009.

[36] P. Tsuchiya. The landmark hierarchy: A new hierarchy for routing in very large networks. In *Proceedings of the Annual Conference of the ACM Special Interest Group on Data Communication (SIGCOMM'88)*, 1988.

[37] L. G. Valiant. A bridging model for parallel computation. *Communications of the ACM*, 1990.

[38] B. Viswanath, A. Mislove, M. Cha, and K. P. Gummadi. On the evolution of user interaction in Facebook. In *Proceedings of the 2nd ACM SIGCOMM Workshop on Social Networks (WOSN'09)*, 2009.

[39] B. Viswanath, M. Mondal, A. Clement, P. Druschel, K. P. Gummadi, A. Mislove, and A. Post. Exploring the design space of social network-based Sybil defense. In *Proceedings of the 4th International Conference on Communication Systems and Network (COMSNETS'12)*, 2012.

[40] B. Viswanath, A. Post, K. P. Gummadi, and A. Mislove. An analysis of social network-based Sybil defenses. In *Proceedings of the Annual Conference of the ACM Special Interest Group on Data Communication (SIGCOMM'10)*, 2010.

[41] K. Walsh and E. G. Sirer. Experience with a distributed object reputation system for peer-to-peer filesharing. In *Proceedings of the 3rd Symposium on Networked Systems Design and Implementation (NSDI'06)*, 2006.

[42] Z. Yang, C. Wilson, X. Wang, T. Gao, B. Y. Zhao, and Y. Dai. Uncovering social network Sybils in the wild. In *Proceedings of the 11th ACM/USENIX Internet Measurement Conference (IMC'11)*, 2011.

[43] H. Yu. Sybil defenses via social networks: A tutorial and survey. *SIGACT News*, 42(3), 2011.

[44] H. Yu, P. B. Gibbons, M. Kaminsky, and F. Xiao. SybilLimit: A near-optimal social network defense against Sybil attacks. In *Proceedings of the IEEE Symposium on Security and Privacy (IEEE S&P'08)*, 2008.

[45] H. Yu, M. Kaminsky, P. B. Gibbons, and A. Flaxman. Sybil-Guard: Defending against Sybil attacks via social networks. In *Proceedings of the Annual Conference of the ACM Special Interest Group on Data Communication (SIGCOMM'06)*, 2006.

[46] C. M. Zhang and V. Paxson. Detecting and analyzing automated activity on twitter. In *Proceedings of the 12th International Conference on Passive and Active Measurement (PAM'11)*, 2011.

Improving Interrupt Response Time
in a Verifiable Protected Microkernel

Bernard Blackham, Yao Shi and Gernot Heiser

NICTA and University of New South Wales, Sydney, Australia

First.Last@nicta.com.au

Abstract

Many real-time operating systems (RTOSes) offer very small interrupt latencies, in the order of tens or hundreds of cycles. They achieve this by making the RTOS kernel fully preemptible, permitting interrupts at almost any point in execution except for some small critical sections. One drawback of this approach is that it is difficult to reason about or formally model the kernel's behavior for verification, especially when written in a low-level language such as C.

An alternate model for an RTOS kernel is to permit interrupts at specific preemption points only. This controls the possible interleavings and enables the use of techniques such as formal verification or model checking. Although this model cannot (yet) obtain the small interrupt latencies achievable with a fully-preemptible kernel, it can still achieve worst-case latencies in the range of 10,000s to 100,000s of cycles. As modern embedded CPUs enter the 1 GHz range, such latencies become acceptable for more applications, particularly when they come with the additional benefit of simplicity and formal models. This is particularly attractive for protected multitasking microkernels, where the (inherently non-preemptible) kernel entry and exit costs dominate the latencies of many system calls.

This paper explores how to reduce the worst-case interrupt latency in a (mostly) non-preemptible protected kernel, and still maintain the ability to apply formal methods for analysis. We use the formally-verified seL4 microkernel as a case study and demonstrate that it is possible to achieve reasonable response-time guarantees. By combining short predictable interrupt latencies with formal verification, a design such as seL4's creates a compelling platform for building mixed-criticality real-time systems.

EuroSys'12, April 10–13, 2012, Bern, Switzerland.

Categories and Subject Descriptors D.4.7 [*Operating Systems*]: Organization and Design—Real-time systems and embedded systems; D.4.5 [*Operating Systems*]: Reliability—Verification; D.4.8 [*Operating Systems*]: Performance—Modeling and prediction

General Terms Design, Performance, Reliability

Keywords Microkernels, worst-case execution time, hard real-time systems, trusted systems, formal verification

1. Introduction

Hard real-time systems are regularly deployed in critical environments such as cars, aircraft and medical devices. These systems demand both functional correctness as well as precise timing guarantees. A failure to meet either functional or timing requirements may result in catastrophic consequences. As manufacturers strive to gain a competitive advantage by combining both critical and convenience functionality, the overall complexity of devices has increased. Maintaining the stringent demands on safety and reliability of these systems is paramount.

One approach to improve reliability is to physically separate critical subsystems onto separate processors, with minimal interference from other subsystems. Whilst this approach has its benefits, it does not scale to the more complex devices being created today, which would require tens or possibly hundreds of processors, each servicing different subsystems. The added weight, cost and power consumption of these processors are severe drawbacks to this approach. It also provides poor support for (controlled) communication between the otherwise isolated subsystems; in an embedded system, where all subsystems cooperate to achieve the overall system mission, this can result in performance degradation and increased energy use.

An alternative approach is to consolidate multiple subsystems onto a single processor, and use a trustworthy supervisor to provide functional and temporal isolation [Mehnert 2002]. The supervisor also provides controlled communication between selected components. This approach is represented in Figure 1. The supervisor may be a microkernel, hypervisor or protected real-time operating system (RTOS),

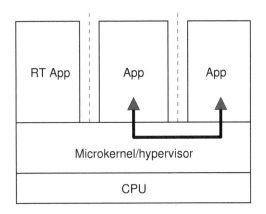

Figure 1. A trustworthy microkernel or hypervisor can be used to provide functional and temporal isolation between distinct components executing on a single processor.

and should have a small trusted code base. The supervisor must be able to provide the required temporal guarantees such that all real-time deadlines can be met, and also protect components from each other.

seL4 [Klein 2009b] is the world's first formally-verified general-purpose operating system kernel. seL4 offers a machine-checked proof that the C implementation adheres to a formal specification of the kernel's behaviour. seL4 is a third-generation microkernel broadly based on the concepts of L4 [Liedtke 1995]. It provides virtual address spaces, threads, inter-process communication and capabilities [Dennis 1966] for managing authority.

We have previously shown that the design of seL4 enables a complete and sound analysis of worst-case interrupt response time [Blackham 2011a]. Combining this with formal verification makes seL4 a compelling platform for building systems with critical hard real-time functionality co-located with other real-time or best-effort components. The size and structure of seL4's code base have also been key ingredients to the successful formal verification of its functional behaviour.

Like most of its predecessor L4 kernels, seL4 disables interrupts throughout kernel execution, except at specific preemption points. This was originally done to optimise average-case performance, at the expense of increased interrupt latency. However, it was also essential to making the formal verification of the functional behaviour of seL4 tractable. As a consequence, seL4 is unable to achieve the very short interrupt latencies of a fully-preemptible kernel (within hundreds of cycles). However, with embedded processor speeds of 1 GHz or higher becoming common-place, many applications on these platforms can tolerate latencies in the tens of thousands, or even hundreds of thousands of cycles. We show that seL4 is able to guarantee worst-case latencies of this magnitude, whilst retaining the ability to offer strong functional guarantees.

Mixed-criticality systems with reasonable latency requirements are therefore well-suited to this model. Some examples include medical implants, or automotive systems for braking or ABS. These devices demand functional and temporal correctness but their required latencies are in the order of milliseconds.

In this paper, we explore the limits of the response time of a verified protected microkernel such as seL4. Previous analyses have been instrumental in the development of seL4's real-time properties [Blackham 2011a;b]. We describe the bottlenecks encountered in achieving suitable real-time performance and the challenges associated with overcoming them. Although re-verification of these changes is ongoing work, it is largely mechanical and similar in nature to other proof maintenance activities over the past two years.

2. Avoiding Preemption in the Kernel

OS kernels are typically developed using either a process-based model or an event-based model supporting multi-threading. In the process-based model, each thread is allocated a dedicated kernel stack. This kernel stack is used for handling requests on behalf of the thread, and implicitly stores the state of any kernel operation in progress through the contents of the call stack and local variables stored on the stack.

A process-based kernel lends itself to being made fully preemptible. With some defensive coding, an interrupt can be permitted almost anywhere in the kernel, allowing for very short interrupt response times.

An event-based kernel uses a single kernel stack to handle requests for all threads on the system. This reduces memory consumption significantly, but changes the way in which preemption can be handled. In the general case, this stack cannot be shared amongst multiple threads as doing so could result in deadlock due to stack blocking. Scheduling disciplines such as the stack resource policy [Baker 1991] are able to re-use stacks and avoid this. However, seL4 is not bound to a specific scheduling discipline – currently, a fixed-priority preemptive scheduler is used, and alternatives are in development.

To preempt threads running on a single kernel stack, preemption points are manually inserted into seL4 to detect and handle pending interrupts. If an interrupt is pending, the state of the current operation must be explicitly saved.

Continuations can be used in an event-based kernel to efficiently represent the saved state of a kernel operation that has blocked or been preempted [Draves 1991]. A continuation specifies (a) the function that a thread should execute when it next runs; and (b) a structure containing any necessary saved state. Using continuations allows a thread to discard its stack whilst it is blocked or preempted.

L4 kernels have traditionally been process-based but not fully preemptible[1]. The process-based kernel had previously been claimed to be more efficient in the presence of frequent context switching [Liedtke 1993], leading to this favoured design. However, experiments on modern ARM hardware have shown a negligible difference between the two models [Warton 2005]. Furthermore, in a microkernel-based system, kernel execution tends to be dominated by fast inter-process communication (IPC) operations; there is little benefit in making the microkernel fully-preemptible, as long as the worst-case latencies of the longer-running operations are kept reasonable through well-placed preemption points.

2.1 Design of seL4

As seL4 is event-based, context switches involve no stack manipulation. This simplifies formal verification, as the seL4 code has a standard procedural control flow like any regular C program. The most common operations in seL4 (IPC) are designed to be short. However, object creation and deletion operations are necessarily longer, as they require iterating over potentially large regions of memory and manipulating complex data structures.

In seL4, a preempted operation is effectively a restartable system call. Interrupts are disabled in hardware during kernel execution, and handled when encountering a preemption point or upon returning to the user. At a preemption point, any necessary state for the preempted operation is saved as seL4 returns up the call stack. The system is left in a state where simply re-executing the original system call will continue the operation.

This is in contrast to using continuations for each thread and maintaining the state of the operation in progress. By not using continuations, the amount of code required is reduced, as the safety checks needed for resuming a preempted operation are similar to those required for starting the operation from scratch; kernel re-entry automatically re-establishes the required invariants. It also simplifies reasoning about the kernel's correctness: it is not necessary to reason about what state a preempted thread is in and whether it was performing an operation, instead it suffices to reason about the state of objects in the system.

This design leads to a small amount of duplicated effort, as the system call must be decoded again each time a preempted operation is resumed. However, the code paths taken are likely to be hot in the CPU's caches. Work on the Fluke kernel demonstrated that these overheads are negligible [Ford 1999].

Incremental Consistency A noteworthy design pattern in seL4 is an idea we call *incremental consistency*: large composite objects are composed of individual components that can be added or deleted one-at-a-time. Specifically, there is always a constant-time operation that will partially construct or deconstruct a large composite object and still maintain a coherent system. In seL4, this is relevant to objects such as address spaces and book-keeping data structures, which commonly pose significant issues in deletion paths.

Although a simple concept, it is not trivial to maintain in a system with complex data structures and intricate dependencies between them. Ensuring that composite objects can be incrementally created and destroyed has benefits for verification and also naturally lends itself to preemption.

2.2 Proof Invariants of seL4

In seL4, consistency of the kernel is defined by a set of formalised invariants on the kernel's state and in turn all objects in the kernel. There are in fact hundreds of invariants and lemmas that are maintained across all seL4 operations. These include:

- *well-formed data structures*: structures such as linked lists are well-formed – i.e., there are no circular links and all back-pointers point to the correct node in doubly-linked lists;

- *object alignment*: all objects in seL4 are aligned to their size, and do not overlap in memory with any other objects;

- *algorithmic invariants*: some optimisations in seL4 depend on specific properties being true, allowing redundant checks to be eliminated;

- *book-keeping invariants*: seL4 maintains a complex data-structure that stores information about what objects exist on the system and who has access to them. The integrity of seL4 depends on the consistency of this information.

The formally-verified seL4 code base proves that all kernel operations will maintain all of the given invariants. Any modifications to seL4 require proving that these invariants still hold, in addition to proving that the code still correctly implements the specification of the kernel. Therefore, for each preemption point that we add to seL4, we must correspondingly update the proof in order to maintain these invariants.

In some cases, it is not possible to maintain all invariants, in which case the invariant may be replaced by a weaker statement. The weakened invariant must be sufficient to satisfy the remainder of the proof over the whole kernel. If an aspect of the proof fails with the weakened invariant, this generally suggests that a bug has been introduced and that extra safety checks may be required in the code.

3. Areas of Improvement

In this section, we look at some of the long-running operations in seL4 and examine how to either add suitable preemption points or replace the operations with better algorithms. Most of these operations, whilst presented in the con-

---

[1] There are some exceptions: the L4-based Fiasco kernel [Hohmuth 2002] is process-based and also preemptible; both OKL4 [Heiser 2010] and seL4 use a single kernel stack and are therefore not fully preemptible.

```
thread_t chooseThread() {
  foreach (prio in priorities) {
    foreach (thread in runQueue[prio]) {
      if (isRunnable(thread))
        return thread;
      else
        schedDequeue(thread);
    }
  }
  return idleThread;
}
```

Figure 2. Pseudo-code of scheduler implementing lazy scheduling.

```
thread_t chooseThread() {
  foreach (prio in priorities) {
    thread = runQueue[prio].head;
    if (thread != NULL)
      return thread;
  }
  return idleThread;
}
```

Figure 3. Pseudo-code of scheduler without lazy scheduling.

text of seL4, are typical of any OS kernel providing abstractions such as protected address spaces, threads and IPC.

There are some operations that may be found in other OS kernels which are not present in seL4. One example is the absence of any memory allocation routines. Almost all allocation policies are delegated to userspace; seL4 provides only the mechanisms required to enforce policies and ensure they are safe (e.g. checking that objects do not overlap) [Elkaduwe 2007]. This design decision removes much of the complexity of a typical allocator from seL4 as well as some potentially long-running operations.

3.1 Removal of Lazy Scheduling

The original version of seL4 featured an optimisation known as *lazy scheduling*. Lazy scheduling attempts to minimise the manipulation of scheduling queues on the critical path of IPC operations [Liedtke 1993], and has traditionally been used in almost all L4 kernels (Fiasco is an exception). It is based on the observation that in L4's synchronous IPC model, threads frequently block while sending a message to another thread, but in many cases the other thread replies quickly. Multiple such ping-pongs can happen on a single time slice, leading to repeated de-queueing and re-queueing of the same thread in the run queue.

Lazy scheduling leaves a thread in the run queue when it executes a blocking IPC operation. When the scheduler is next invoked, it dequeues all threads which are still blocked. Pseudo-code for a scheduler implementing lazy scheduling is shown in Figure 2.

Lazy scheduling can lead to pathological cases where the scheduler must dequeue a large number of blocked threads (theoretically only limited by the amount of memory available for thread control blocks), which obviously leads to horrible worst-case performance. As the scheduler is responsible for determining which thread to run next, it is not feasible or even meaningful to add a preemption point to this potentially long-running operation.

We therefore had to change the scheduling model so that only runnable threads existed on the run queue. In order to maintain the benefits of lazy scheduling, we use a different scheduling trick, (internally known as "Benno scheduling", after the engineer who first implemented it in an earlier version of L4): when a thread is unblocked by an IPC operation and, according to its priority, it is able to execute immediately, we switch directly to it and do not place it into the run queue (as it may block again very soon). The run queue's consistency can be re-established at preemption time, when the preempted thread must be entered in the run queue if it is not already there. This has the same best-case performance as lazy scheduling, but maintains good worst-case performance, as only a single thread (the presently running one) may have to be enqueued lazily.

In this model the implementation of the scheduler is simplified, as it now just chooses the first thread of highest priority, as demonstrated in the pseudo-code listing in Figure 3. There is an existing invariant in the kernel that all runnable threads on the system are either on the run queue or currently executing. This is sufficient for lazy scheduling, but Benno scheduling obviously requires an additional invariant which must be maintained throughout the kernel: that all threads on the scheduler's run queue must be in the runnable state.

This seemingly simple C code change impacts the proof in all functions that alter a thread's state, or modifies the scheduler's run queue. The invariant must be proven true when any thread ceases to be runnable and when any thread is placed onto the run queue.

3.2 Scheduler Bitmaps

We added one more optimisation to the scheduler: a bitmap representing the priorities that contain runnable threads. We make use of ARM's *count leading zeroes* (CLZ) instruction which finds the highest set bit in a 32-bit word, and executes in a single cycle. seL4 supports 256 thread priorities, which we represent using a two-level bitmap. The 256 priorities are divided into 8 "buckets" of 32 priorities each. The top-level bitmap contains 8 bits each representing the existence of runnable threads in any of the 32 priorities within a bucket. Each bucket has a 32-bit word with each bit representing one of the 32 priorities. Using two loads and two CLZ instructions, we can find the highest runnable priority very efficiently, and have thus removed the loop from Figure 3 altogether.

This optimisation technique is commonly found in OS schedulers and has reduced the WCET of seL4 in several cases. However, it introduces yet another invariant to be proven: that the scheduler's bitmap precisely reflects the state of the run queues. As this is an incremental change to the existing scheduler, the re-verification effort is significantly lowered.

3.3 Aborting IPC Operations

Threads in seL4 do not communicate directly with each other; they instead communicate via *endpoints* which act as communication channels between threads. Multiple threads may send or receive messages through an endpoint. Each endpoint maintains a linked list of all threads waiting to send or receive a message. Naturally, this list can grow to an arbitrary length (limited by the number of threads in the system, which is limited by the amount of physical memory that can be used for threads, which in turn is theoretically limited by the size of free physical memory after the kernel boots). The length of this list is not an issue for most operations, as they can manipulate the list in constant time.

The only exception is the operation to delete an endpoint. Deletion must iterate over and dequeue a potentially large number of threads. There is an obvious preemption point in this operation: after each thread is dequeued. This intermediate step is fortunately consistent with all existing invariants, even if the thread performing the deletion operation is itself deleted. Forward progress is ensured by deactivating the endpoint at the beginning of delete operations, so threads (including those just dequeued) cannot attempt another IPC operation on the same endpoint.

The preemption point here is obvious because it is a direct result of the incremental consistency design pattern in seL4. As a result, the impact of these changes on the proof are minimal.

3.4 Aborting Badged IPC Operations

A related real-time challenge in seL4 is the aborting of *badged* IPC operations. Badges are unforgeable tokens (represented as an integer) that server processes may assign to clients. When a client sends a message to the server using a badge, the server can be assured of the authenticity of the client. A server may revoke a specific badge, so that it can ensure that no existing clients have access to that badge. Once revoked, the server may re-issue the badge to a different client, preserving guarantees of authenticity.

In order to revoke a badge, seL4 must first prevent any thread from starting a new IPC operation using the badge, and second ensure that any pending IPC operations using the badge are aborted. It is this second operation which requires a compromise between execution time, memory consumption and ease of verification. The choice of data structure used to store the set of pending IPC operations

(clients and their badges) has a significant impact on all three factors.

For example, a balanced binary-tree structure has very good worst-case and average-case execution time, but requires more work on the verification effort; the invariants involved in self-balancing binary tree structures are more tedious than linear data structures. A hash-table-based data structure may be easier to verify, and has good average-case performance, but raises challenging memory allocation issues in seL4, where memory allocation is handled outside the kernel. It also does not improve worst-case execution time, as a determined adversary could potentially force hash collisions.

Instead, seL4 uses a simple linked list containing the list of waiting threads and their associated badges, as described in Section 3.3. Enqueuing and dequeuing threads are simple $O(1)$ operations. In order to remove all entries with a specific badge, seL4 must iterate over the list; this is a potentially unbounded operation, and so we require a preemption point. Unlike the simple deletion case where we simply restart from the beginning of the list, here we additionally need to store four pieces of information:

1. at what point within the list the operation was preempted, so that we can avoid repeating work and ensure forward progress;
2. a pointer to the last item in the list when the operation commenced, so that new waiting clients do not affect the execution time of the original operation;
3. the badge which is currently being removed from the list, so that if a badge removal operation is preempted and a second operation is started, the first operation can be completed before starting the new one;
4. a pointer to the thread that was performing the badge removal operation when preempted, so that if another thread needs to continue its operation, it can indicate to the original thread that its operation has been completed.

With all this information, we are able to achieve our goal of incremental consistency. The above information is associated with the endpoint object rather than the preempted thread (as would be done in a continuation). In doing so, we can reason simply about the state of objects in our invariants, rather than the state of any preempted thread.

Note that although the preemption point bounds interrupt latency, this approach gives a longer than desirable execution time for the badged abort operation, as every waiting thread must be iterated over, rather than only threads waiting for a specific badge. This has not yet been an issue in real systems, however, should it cause problems then we may replace it with an alternative such as a self-balancing binary tree data structure and undertake the extra verification effort required.

3.5 Object Creation

When objects, such as threads, page tables or memory frames, are created on behalf of the user, their contents must be cleared and/or initialised in order to avoid information leakage. Clearing an object may be a long-running operation, as some kernel objects are megabytes in size (e.g. large memory frames on ARM can be up to 16 MiB; capability tables for managing authority can be of arbitrary size).

The code to clear an object was previously deep inside the object creation path, and replicated for each type of object. Additionally, the code updated some of the kernel's state before objects were cleared, and the rest of the kernel's state after objects were cleared. Adding a preemption point in the middle of clearing an object would therefore leave the kernel in an inconsistent state.

To make clearing of objects preemptible, seL4 required significant restructuring of the object creation paths. We chose to clear out the contents of all objects prior to any other kernel state being modified. The progress of this clearing is stored within the object itself. As clearing is the only long-running aspect of these operations, the remainder of the creation code that manipulates the state of the kernel (e.g. updating the kernel's book-keeping data structures) can be performed in one short, atomic pass.

Page directories (top-level page tables) however pose an added complication. The kernel reserves the top 256 MiB of virtual address space for itself, and is mapped into all address spaces. When a new page directory is created, the kernel mappings for this region must be copied in. This copy operation is embedded deep within the creation path of page directories. There is also an seL4 invariant specifying that all page directories will contain these global mappings – an invariant that must be maintained upon exiting the kernel.

Preempting the global-mapping copy poses significant (though not insurmountable) challenges for verification. Fortunately, on the ARMv6 and ARMv7 architectures, only 1 KiB of the page table needs to be updated. We measured the time taken to copy 1 KiB of memory on our target platform (described in Section 5.1) to be around $20 \mu s$. We decided that $20 \mu s$ would be a tolerable latency (for now), as there were other long-latency issues to tackle first. Therefore we made all other block copy and clearing operations in seL4 preempt at multiples of 1 KiB, as smaller multiples would not improve the worst-case interrupt latency until the global-mapping copy is made preemptible.

3.6 Address Space Management

In a virtual address space, physical memory frames are mapped into page tables or page directories, creating a mapping from virtual address to physical address. In order to support operations on individual frames, seL4 must additionally maintain the inverse information: which address space(s) a frame has been mapped into, and at which address.

In seL4, all objects are represented by one or more capabilities, or *caps*, which encapsulate metadata about the object such as access rights and mapping information. Capabilities form the basic unit of object management and access

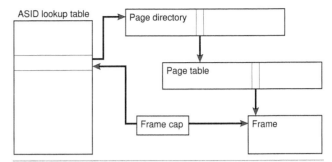

Figure 4. Virtual address spaces managed using ASIDs. Each arrow denotes a reference stored in one object to another.

control in seL4 systems, and a typical system may have tens or hundreds of thousands of caps. As such, the design of seL4 endeavours to keep caps small to minimise memory overhead. seL4 caps are 16 bytes in size: 8 bytes are used for pointers to maintain their position in a "derivation tree", and the other 8 bytes are used for object-specific purposes.

8 bytes of extra information suffices for almost all objects, however caps to physical memory frames are an exception. To support seL4's object deletion model, frames are required to store their physical address, the virtual address at which they are mapped, and the address space into which they are mapped. This, along with some extra bits of metadata, exceeds the 8-byte limit inside a cap.

In order to squeeze this information into 8 bytes, the original seL4 design uses a lookup table to map from an 18-bit index to an actual address space. The index is called an *address space identifier*, or *ASID*, and is small enough to be stored inside a frame cap. The lookup table is stored as a sparse 2-level data structure in order to minimise space usage, with each second level (*ASID pool*) providing entries for 1024 address spaces. The objects and references required for using ASIDs are shown in Figure 4.

Using ASIDs offered the additional benefit of enabling dangling references to safely exist. If frame caps were to store a reference to the address space itself, then when the address space is deleted, all frame caps referring to it would need to be updated to purge this reference. By instead indirecting through the ASID table, the references from each frame cap, whilst stale, are harmless. Any time the ASID stored in a frame cap is used, it can be simply checked that the mapping in the address space (if any still exist) agrees with the frame cap. As a result, deleting an address space in this design simply involves: (a) removing one entry from the ASID lookup table, and (b) invalidating any TLB entries from the address space.

However, the use of ASIDs poses issues for interrupt latency in other areas, such as locating a free ASID to allocate and deleting an ASID pool. Locating a free ASID is difficult to make preemptible – in the common case, a free ASID would be found immediately, but a pathological case may re-

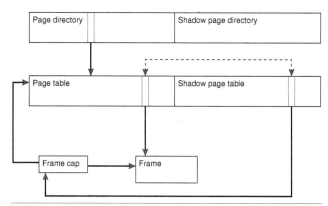

Figure 5. Virtual address spaces managed using shadow page tables. As in Figure 4, each arrow denotes a reference stored in one object to another. The dotted line shows an implicit link by virtue of the shadow being adjacent to the page table itself.

quire searching over 1024 possible ASIDs. Similarly, deleting an ASID pool requires iterating over up to 1024 address spaces. Whilst we could play with the size of these pools to minimise latency, the allocation and deallocation routines are inherently difficult to preempt, and so we decided to seek an alternative to ASIDs.

By removing ASIDs, we needed some other method to prevent dangling references within frame caps. In particular, we needed to store a back-pointer from a virtual address mapping to the frame cap used for the mapping. We chose to store these pointers in a *shadow page table*, mapping from virtual address to frame cap (as opposed to mapping to the frame itself). This effectively doubles the amount of space required for each page table and page directory. We store this data adjacent to the page table in order to facilitate fast lookup from a given page table entry, as shown in Figure 5. Now, all mapping and unmapping operations, along with address space deletion must eagerly update all back-pointers to avoid any dangling references.

This design removes the ability to perform lazy deletion of address spaces, but resolves many of the latency issues surrounding the management of ASID pools. We needed to insert preemption points in the code to delete address spaces, however this is trivial to do and can be done without violating any invariants on the kernel's state. The natural preemption point in the deletion path is to preempt after unmapping each entry in a page table or page directory. To avoid repeating unnecessary work, we also store the index of the lowest mapped entry in the page table and only resume the operation from that point.

We observe that this preemption point is again a direct result of the shadow page table design adhering to the incremental consistency design pattern.

Memory Overhead of Shadow Page Tables The space overhead of shadow page tables might be considered detri-

mental on some systems. We can compare it to an alternative solution, where we utilise a frame table to maintain bookkeeping information about every physical page on the system. This is the approach used by many other operating systems, including Linux.

The frame table incurs a fixed memory overhead and removes the need for shadows. In its simplest form, without support for sharing pages between address spaces (which the shadow page table solution does support), a frame table would require a single pointer to track each frame cap created. On a 32-bit system with 256 MiB of physical memory and 4 KiB frames, the frame table would occupy 256 KiB of memory. On ARMv6 platforms, page directories are 16 KiB and page tables are 1 KiB. A densely-packed page directory covering 256 MiB of virtual address space would use an extra 256 KiB in shadow page tables, and an extra 16 KiB per address space in page directories.

The shadow page table approach is not significantly less space efficient than using a frame table, except when the system uses sparsely-populated page tables. However, this incurs memory overhead already as the page tables themselves are underutilised, as well as the shadows.

4. Cache Pinning

In order to achieve faster interrupt delivery and tighter bounds on the worst-case execution time (WCET) of seL4, we modified seL4 to pin specific cache lines into the L1 caches so that these cache lines would not be evicted. We selected the interrupt delivery path, along with some commonly accessed memory regions to be permanently pinned into the instruction and data caches. The specific lines to pin were chosen based on execution traces of both a typical interrupt delivery, and some worst-case interrupt delivery paths.

As the cache on our target platform (described in Section 5.1) supports locking one or more complete cache ways, we can choose to lock $1/4$, $1/2$ or $3/4$ of the contents of the cache. We selected as much as would fit into $1/4$ of the cache, without resorting to code placement optimisations. A total of 118 instruction cache lines were pinned, along with the first 256 bytes of stack memory and some key data regions.

The benefit of cache pinning on worst-case execution time is shown in Table 1. On the interrupt path, where the pinned cache lines have the greatest benefit, the worst-case execution time is almost halved. On other paths, the gain is less significant but still beneficial.

Of course, these benefits do not come for free; as a portion of the cache has been partitioned for specific code paths, the remainder of the system has less cache for general usage. A system with hard real-time requirements would also need to ensure that all code and data used for deadline-critical tasks are pinned into the cache. Methods to optimally select cache lines to pin for periodic hard real-time task sets have been the subject of previous research [Campoy 2001, Puaut 2002].

Event handler	Without pinning	With pinning	% gain
System call	$421.6\,\mu s$	$378.0\,\mu s$	10%
Undefined instruction	$70.4\,\mu s$	$48.8\,\mu s$	30%
Page fault	$69.0\,\mu s$	$50.1\,\mu s$	27%
Interrupt	$36.2\,\mu s$	$19.5\,\mu s$	46%

Table 1. Improvement in computed worst-case latency by pinning frequently used cache lines into the L1 cache.

Our platform has a 128 KiB unified L2 cache with a hit access latency of 26 cycles (compared with external memory latency of 96 cycles). Our compiled seL4 binary is 36 KiB, and so it would be possible to lock the entire seL4 microkernel into the L2 cache. Doing so would drastically reduce execution time even further, but we have not yet adapted our analysis tools to support this.

5. Analysis Method

After making the changes outlined above, we analysed seL4 to compute a new safe upper bound on its interrupt latency. The analysis was performed on a compiled binary of the kernel and finds the longest paths through the microkernel using a model of the hardware. We also evaluate the overestimation of the analysis by executing the longest paths on real hardware.

5.1 Evaluation Platform

seL4 can run on a variety of ARM-based CPUs, including processors such as the ARM Cortex-A8 which can be clocked at over 1 GHz. However, we were unable to obtain a recent ARM processor (e.g. using the ARMv7 architecture) which also supported cache pinning. In order to gain the benefits of cache pinning, we ran our experiments on a somewhat older processor, the Freescale i.MX31, on a KZM evaluation board. The i.MX31 contains an ARM1136 CPU core with an 8-stage pipeline and is clocked at 532 MHz.

The CPU has split L1 instruction and data caches, each 16 KiB in size and 4-way set-associative. These caches support either round-robin or pseudo-random replacement policies. The caches also provide the ability to select a subset of the four ways for cache replacement, effectively allowing some cache lines to be permanently pinned. Alternately, the caches may also be used as tightly-coupled memory (TCM), providing a region of memory which is guaranteed to accessible in a single cycle.

As our analysis tools do not yet support round-robin replacement (and pseudo-random is not feasible to analyse), we analysed the caches as if they were a direct-mapped cache of the size of one way (4 KiB). This is a pessimistic but sound approximation of the cache's behaviour, as the most recently accessed cache line in any cache set is guaranteed to reside in the cache when next accessed.

The i.MX31 also provides a unified 128 KiB L2 cache which is 8-way set-associative. The KZM board provides 128 MiB of RAM with an access latency of 60 cycles when the L2 cache is disabled, or 96 cycles when the L2 cache is enabled. Due to this significant disparity in memory latency, we analysed the kernel both with the L2 cache enabled and with it disabled.

We disabled the branch predictors of the ARM1136 CPU both on hardware used for measurements and in the static analysis itself, as our analysis tools do not yet model them. Interestingly, using the branch predictor increases the worst-case latency of a branch: with branch predictors enabled, branches on the ARM1136 vary between 0 and 7 cycles, depending on the type of branch and whether or not it is predicted correctly. With the branch predictor disabled, all branches execute in a constant 5 cycles.

The effect of disabling these features on execution time is quantified in Section 6.4.

5.2 Static Analysis for Worst-Case Execution Time

Our analysis to compute the interrupt response time of seL4 is based upon our previous work [Blackham 2011a], to which we refer the reader for more background on the tools used. This section summarises the analysis method and highlights improvements over the previous analysis technique.

We use Chronos 4.2 [Li 2007] to compute the worst-case execution time of seL4 and evaluate our improvements to seL4. We had previously modified Chronos to analyse binaries on the ARMv7 architecture using a model of the Cortex-A8 pipeline. For this analysis we adapted the pipeline model to support the ARM1136 CPU on our target hardware. ARM's documentation of the ARM1136 describes the performance characteristics of the pipeline in detail [ARM 2005].

To analyse the interrupt response time of seL4, we computed upper bounds on the worst-case execution time of all paths through seL4 where interrupts cannot be immediately serviced. These paths begin at one of the kernel's exception vectors: system calls, page faults, undefined instructions or interrupts. A path through the kernel ends when either (a) control is passed back to user and interrupts are re-enabled; or (b) at the start of the kernel's interrupt handler (a pre-empted kernel operation will return up the call stack and then call the kernel's interrupt handler).

After extracting the control flow graph of the kernel, loops and loop nests are automatically identified. We annotate the control flow graph with the upper bound on the number of iterations of all loops. In this analysis, some of these upper bounds are computed automatically (described further in Section 5.3).

The analysis virtually inlines all functions so that function calls in the control flow graph are transformed into simple branches. This enables the static analysis to be aware of the calling context of a function that is called from multiple call sites; the processor's cache will often be in wildly different states depending on the execution history. Unfortunately, this virtual inlining also leads to significant overestimation as described in Section 6.

As Chronos is based on the implicit path enumeration technique (IPET) [Li 1995], the output of Chronos is an integer linear programming (ILP) problem: a set of integer linear equations that represent constraints, and an objective function to be maximised subject to the constraints. The solution to the ILP problem is the worst-case execution time, and is obtained using an off-the-shelf ILP solver.

Additional constraints can be added manually in order to exclude certain infeasible paths. As the analysis only considers the control flow graph, it has no insight into the values of variables in the kernel. Therefore, it may consider paths that are not actually realisable. In order to exclude these paths, we manually added extra constraints to the ILP problem where necessary. These constraints take one of three forms:

- a **conflicts with** b **in** f: specifies that the basic blocks at addresses a and b are mutually exclusive, and will not both execute during an invocation of the function f. If f is invoked multiple times, a and b can each be executed under different invocations.
- a **is consistent with** b **in** f: specifies that the basic blocks at addresses a and b will execute the same number of times during an invocation of the function f.
- a **executes** n **times**: specifies that the basic block at address a will only ever execute at most n times in total in all possible contexts.

It would be possible to transform these extra constraints into *proof obligations* – statements which a verification engineer could be asked to prove formally. This would remove the possibility of human error mistakenly excluding a path which is in fact feasible, resulting in an unsound analysis.

5.3 Computing Loop Bounds

As described in the previous section, our analysis currently requires annotations to specify the iteration counts of each loop in seL4. Many of these annotations can be generated automatically. For example, loops which use explicit counter variables can be easily bounded using static analysis. We have computed the loop bounds automatically for several of the loops in seL4 using program slicing and model checking, thereby reducing the possibility of human error. Our approach shares similarities to previous model-checking techniques to find loop bounds [Rieder 2008] or compute WCET [Metzner 2004]. It operates on unmodified binaries, and is unaffected by compiler optimisations.

First, we obtain the semantics of each individual program instruction using an existing formalisation of the ARMv7 instruction set [Fox 2010]. We transform the program into SSA form [Cytron 1991], and then compute a program slice [Weiser 1984] to identify a subset of instructions which encapsulates the behaviour of the loop. This slice captures the control flow dependencies of the loop, and expresses the semantics of the data flow through the loop. This information is converted into a model in linear temporal logic (LTL). A model checker is used to solve for the maximum execution count of the loop head by using a binary search over the loop count.

Not all loops in seL4 have been analysed successfully yet – due to the lack of pointer analysis support in our tools, we presently are unable to compute the bounds of loops which store and load critical values to and from memory. However, almost all of these accesses are to and from the stack, which in the absence of pointer aliasing (guaranteed by seL4's invariants), can be computed and tracked offline. With some work, we expect that this technique will be able to compute all of the remaining loop bounds in seL4.

There are other types of loops which are difficult to bound – e.g., loops which traverse linked lists. In seL4, linked lists do exist which are bounded only by the size of physical memory. However, all traversals of these lists contain pre-emption points after a fixed number of iterations. Therefore, for interrupt response time analysis, we can simply consider the fixed number of iterations as the upper bound.

5.4 Comparing Analysis with Measurements

The results of our static analysis give an upper bound on the worst-case execution time of kernel operations. However, this upper bound is a pessimistic estimate. In practice, we may never observe latencies near the upper bound for several reasons:

- The conservative nature of our pipeline and cache models means we consider potential worst-case processor states which are impossible to achieve.
- Of the worst-case processor states which are feasible, it may be extremely difficult to manipulate the processor into such a state.
- The worst-case paths found by the analysis may be extremely difficult (but not impossible) to exercise in practice.

In order to gain some insight into how close our upper bounds are, we can try to approximate the worst-case as best we can. We wrote test programs to exercise the longest paths we could find ourselves (guided by the results of the analysis) and ran these on the hardware. Our test programs pollute both the instruction and data caches with dirty cache lines prior to exercising the paths, in order to maximise execution time. We measured the execution time of these paths using the cycle counters available on the ARM1136's performance monitoring unit.

In order to quantify the amount of pessimism introduced by the first two factors alone, we used our static analysis model to compute the execution time of paths that we are able to reproduce, and compared them with real hardware. The results of this are shown in Section 6.2.

Event handler	Before changes; L2 disabled	After changes; L2 disabled			After changes; L2 enabled		
	Computed	Computed	Observed	Ratio	Computed	Observed	Ratio
System call	3851 μs	332.4 μs	101.9 μs	3.26	436.3 μs	80.5 μs	5.42
Undefined instruction	394.5 μs	44.4 μs	42.6 μs	1.04	76.8 μs	43.1 μs	1.78
Page fault	396.1 μs	44.9 μs	42.9 μs	1.05	77.5 μs	41.1 μs	1.89
Interrupt	143.1 μs	23.2 μs	17.7 μs	1.31	44.8 μs	14.3 μs	3.13

Table 2. WCET for each kernel entry-point in seL4, before and after our changes to reduce WCET. Computed results are a safe upper bound on execution time. Observed results are our best-effort attempt at recreating worst-cases on hardware.

6. Results

We first computed the worst-case execution time of our modified seL4 kernel binary using only the loop iteration counts and no other human input. This provided us with an upper bound on the execution time of the kernel of over 600,000 cycles. We converted the solution to a concrete execution trace. However, from looking at these traces it was quickly apparent that the solution was in fact infeasible as the path it took was meaningless – no input could possibly result in execution of the path.

We then added additional constraints of the form described in Section 5.2, in order to eliminate paths that were obviously infeasible. Each of these constraints was derived by observing why a given trace could not be executed. The biggest cause of these infeasible paths was due to the style of coding in seL4, which stems from its functional roots. Many functions in seL4 contain switch statements that select code based on the type of cap passed in, as shown in Figure 6. If `f()` and `g()` both use this style then, due to virtual inlining, much of the inlined copy of `g()` will never be executed, as the return value of `getCapType()` is guaranteed to be the same in both functions.

Our analysis detects the WCET of `g()`, which only occurs for one specific cap type, as contributing to every invocation of `g()` from `f()`. This leads to significant overestimation of the WCET. Based on this, we added several constraints of the form *a is consistent with b*, where *a* and *b* were the blocks corresponding to the same types in `f()` and `g()`.

We added additional constraints until we obtained a path that appeared to be feasible. This path has an execution time estimate of 232,098 cycles with the L2 cache enabled, or 176,851 cycles with the L2 cache disabled. On the 532 MHz i.MX31, this corresponds to an execution time of 436.3 μs with L2 and 332.4 μs without L2.

The full results of the analysis are shown in Table 2. The first column shows the WCET before we modified seL4 as outlined in this paper, making the results comparable to our previous analysis [Blackham 2011a] (the previous analysis was on the OMAP3 platform and thus is not directly comparable). For the system call path, a factor of 11.6 improvement in WCET was observed, largely due to the added preemption points. The other kernel entry points also see a significant improvement because the scheduler bitmaps and the

```
void f(cap_t cap) {
    ...
    switch (getCapType(cap)) {
        case frame_cap:
            ...
            g(cap);
            ...
            break;
        case page_table_cap:
            ...
            g(cap);
            ...
            break;
    ...
```

Figure 6. Example of the coding style used in many seL4 functions. This arises from the use of pattern matching over type constructors in its Haskell specification.

new address-space management techniques remove two potentially long-running loops.

The worst-case interrupt latency of seL4 is the sum of the WCET for the system call path (the longest of all kernel operations), and the interrupt path. This gives an upper bound on the interrupt latency of 481 μs with L2 and 356 μs without.

For all entry points except the system call handler, we were able to construct scenarios that produced execution times that were within 31% of the computed upper bound when the L2 cache was disabled. Enabling the L2 cache increases the amount of pessimism in our upper bounds, and thus the disparity is much higher (e.g. 3.13 for the interrupt path). Recreating the path identified by the system call handler proved to be extremely complicated and our best efforts only achieved a case that was within 5.4 times of our computed upper bound.

6.1 Analysis

The worst-case we detected was a system call performing an atomic two-way (send-receive) IPC operation, using all the features seL4 provides for its IPC, including a full-length message transfer, and granting access rights to objects over IPC. The largest contributing factor to the run-time of this case was address decoding for caps. Recall that caps are

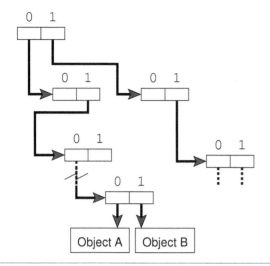

Figure 7. A worst-case address decoding scenario uses a capability space that requires a separate lookup for each bit of an address. Here, a binary address `010...0` would decode to object A, but may need to traverse up to 32 levels of this structure to do so.

essentially pointers to kernel objects with some associated metadata. In seL4, caps have addresses that exist in a 32-bit *capability space*; decoding an address to a kernel object may require traversing up to 32 edges of a directed graph, as shown in Figure 7. In a worst-case IPC, this decoding may need to be performed up to 11 times, each in different capability spaces, leading to a huge number of cache misses. Note that most seL4-based systems would be designed to require at most one or two levels of decoding; it would be highly unusual to encounter anything close to this worst-case capability space on a real system, unless crafted by an adversary.

This worst case demonstrates that our work has been successful in minimising the interrupt latency of the longer running kernel operations, such as object creation and deletion. In previous analyses of seL4, a distinction was made between *open* and *closed* systems, where closed systems permitted only specific IPC operations to avoid long interrupt latencies, and open systems permitted any untrusted code to execute. Our work now eliminates the need for this distinction, as the latencies for the open-system scenarios are no more than that of the closed system.

The atomic send-receive operation exists in seL4 primarily as an optimisation to avoid entering the kernel twice for this common scenario – user-level servers in an event loop will frequently respond to one request and then wait to receive the next. If necessary, the execution time of this operation could be almost halved either by inserting a preemption point between the send and receive phases, or by simply forcing the user to invoke the send and receive phases separately. This latter approach would be detrimental to average-

case throughput. It would be worthwhile to investigate inserting a preemption point here to reduce worst-case latency even further.

Other entry points to the kernel show no unexpected pathological cases; these entry points are largely deterministic and have little branching. Like the IPC operations, the worst case for these require decoding a capability that exists 32 levels deep in the capability space. However only one such capability needs to be decoded in the other exception handlers (to the thread which will handle the exception).

The improvements outlined in this paper do not significantly affect the best- or average-case execution time. This is because IPCs are the most frequent operations in microkernel-based systems. seL4 already provides *fastpaths* to improve the performance of common IPC operations by an order of magnitude – fastpaths are highly-optimised code paths designed to execute a specific operation as quickly as possible. The fastpath performance is not affected by our preemption points. In fact, the IPC fastpath is one of the fastest operations the kernel performs (around 200-250 cycles on the ARM1136) and hence there would be no benefit to making it preemptible.

6.2 Conservatism of Hardware Model

Our hardware model is conservative to guarantee a safe bound on execution time. In order to determine the amount of pessimism this adds to our upper bounds, we computed the execution time of the specific paths we tested in our analysis. We achieved this by adding extra constraints to the ILP problem to force analysis of the desired path. The results are shown in Figure 8. The observed execution times were obtained by taking the maximum of 100,000 executions of each path.

The disparity between the computed and observed time is attributable to both conservatism in our pipeline and cache models of the processor, and the difficultly in forcing a worst-case processor state. Our model of the CPU's caches is very conservative – the hardware's L1 caches are 4-way set-associative and the L2 cache is 8-way set-associative, but because we have not modelled the replacement policy of the caches, we are forced to treat any contention for cache lines within a cache set as a miss. Thus accesses which might not miss the cache on hardware must be assumed to miss in our model unless it was the most recently-used cache line within the cache set.

As the system call path is much longer than the other three paths (by an order of magnitude), there is much more contention within each cache set. Therefore it suffers the most from this conservative model.

6.3 Computation Time

The entire static analysis ran in 65 minutes on an AMD Opteron (Barcelona) system running at 2.1 GHz. We repeated all analysis steps for each entry point – system calls, undefined instructions, page faults and interrupts. The analy-

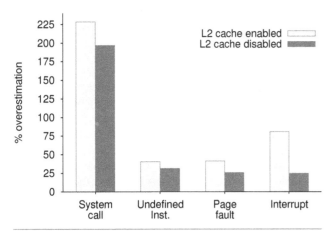

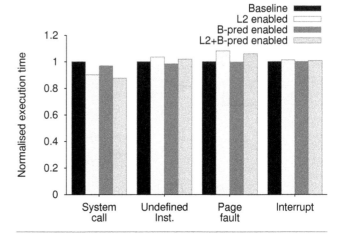

Figure 8. Overestimation of our hardware model for static analysis with the L2 cache enabled and disabled. Each bar corresponds to a realisable path and shows the percentage difference between the observed execution time on hardware and the predicted execution time for the same path.

Figure 9. Effects of enabling L2 cache and/or branch prediction on worst-case observed execution times. Each path is normalised to the baseline execution time (L2 and branch predictors disabled).

sis of the latter three entry points completed within seconds, whilst the analysis of the system call entry point took significantly longer. This is to be expected, as the system call handler is the entry point for the majority of seL4's code.

For the system call handler, the most computationally-intensive step of the analysis was running Chronos, taking 61 minutes. Over half the execution time of Chronos was spent in the address and cache analysis phases – these phases compute worst-case cache hit/miss scenarios for each data load, store and instruction fetch.

We went through numerous iterations of adding additional constraints to the ILP problem in order to exclude infeasible paths, with each iteration taking around an hour to execute. Future work will investigate how to automate the generation of these additional constraints to arrive at a feasible solution sooner.

6.4 Impact of L2 and Branch Predictors

As mentioned in Section 5.1, we disabled the branch predictors on our platform and in our model as we are presently unable to analyse their effect. We also compare the effects of enabling or disabling the L2 cache. Figure 9 shows the impact of enabling these features both individually and together on actual execution time.

It is interesting to note that some of the observed times actually increased when enabling the L2 cache, by up to 8% for the page fault path. This is because the worst case scenarios execute with cold caches that are polluted with data which must first be evicted. Enabling the L2 cache increases the latency of the memory hierarchy – from 60 cycles to 96 cycles for a miss serviced by main memory – which is particularly detrimental to cold-cache performance. The code paths executed in seL4 are typically very short and

non-repetitive, thereby gaining little added benefit from the L2 cache that is not already provided by the L1 caches.

Enabling the branch predictor gave a minor improvement in all test cases. The benefit is minimal again because of the cold-cache nature of these benchmarks; the benefit of the branch predictor barely makes up for the added costs of the initial mispredictions.

Despite these results, the L2 cache and branch predictors greatly improve performance in the average case. Reduced run-time translates directly to increased battery life for hand-held devices such as mobile phones, and so the slightly detrimental effect on interrupt latency is almost certainly worthwhile on such devices.

As noted earlier, it would be possible to lock the entire seL4 microkernel into the L2 cache. This would result in a huge benefit to worst-case interrupt latency of the kernel whilst also reducing non-determinism, resulting in a tighter upper bound.

7. Related work

Ford et al. explore the differences between process-based and event-based kernels, and present the Fluke kernel, which utilises restartable system calls rather than continuations to implement an atomic kernel API [Ford 1999]. They outline the advantages of this model, including ease of userspace checkpointing, process migration and aided reliability. They also measured the overhead of restarting kernel operations to be at most 8% of the cost of the operations themselves.

Several subprojects of Verisoft have attempted to formally verify all or part of different OS kernels. They have verified a very small and simple time-triggered RTOS called OLOS [Daum 2009b], as well as parts of their VAMOS microkernel [Daum 2009a]. These kernels are also based on the event-driven single-kernel-stack model. They are much simpler kernels than seL4 (e.g. VAMOS supports only single-level page tables) and are designed for the formally-verified VAMP processor [Beyer 2006]. Whilst the VAMP processor is a real-world product, it is not widely used.

A related project began to verify the PikeOS RTOS with some progress but the proof has not been completed [Baumann 2010]. PikeOS is a commercial product used in safety-critical real-time systems such as aircraft and medical devices, but there has been no indication of a sound worst-case interrupt latency analysis.

Some progress has been made towards verifying code that executes in the presence of interrupts. Feng et al. have constructed a framework on which to reason about OS code in the presence of interrupts and preemption [Feng 2008]. Gotsman and Yang have also constructed frameworks for verifying preemptible and multiprocessor kernels, and have used theirs to verify an OS scheduler [Gotsman 2011].

We refer the reader to Klein's thorough overview of the state of formal verification of operating systems [Klein 2009a].

Our previous analyses of seL4's response time were performed on older versions of the seL4 kernel and targeted an 800 MHz OMAP3 CPU [Blackham 2011a;b]. In this work, we chose a different platform, the i.MX31, in order to benefit from better cache management. The OMAP3 differs from the i.MX31 in CPU speed, micro-architecture and memory latency. We have repeated our previous analysis on the i.MX31 platform to obtain directly comparable results. The work presented here gives a further factor of 11.6 improvement over our previous analysis when the L2 cache is disabled, and explores the verification implications of adding preemption points to reduce interrupt latency.

8. Conclusions and Future Work

We have explored how to reduce the worst-case interrupt response time of a verified protected microkernel such as seL4. We have added preemption points into some of seL4's operations, and have restructured others in order to remove all non-preemptible long-running operations from the kernel. These improvements have been guided by an analysis of the kernel's worst-case execution time.

From its inception, the design of seL4 was intended to limit interrupt latency to short bounded operations, although this was not true of the original implementation. Using static analysis to compute interrupt latencies, we could systematically validate and improve the design where necessary.

As a verified microkernel, seL4 imposes additional constraints on how preemption may be introduced. We must take care when adding preemption points to ensure that the effort of re-verifying the kernel is minimised. This effort can be reduced by avoiding unnecessary violations of global kernel invariants, and searching for intermediate states that are generally consistent with the kernel's normal execution.

With careful placement of preemption points, we have eliminated large interrupt latencies caused by longer running operations inside seL4. This enables seL4 to host execution of untrusted code, confined by the capabilities given to it, and still safely meet real-time deadlines within 189,117 cycles. On modern embedded hardware this translates to a few hundred microseconds, which is ample for many real-time applications.

There is scope to reduce this even further, which will be the subject of future work. We will also focus on automating the analysis to reduce the level of human intervention required. Of course, we will also have the work ahead of us to verify our improvements to seL4.

We believe an event-based kernel such as seL4 could realistically attain a worst-case interrupt latency of 50,000 cycles (or approximately $100\,\mu s$ on a 500 MHz CPU). Due to its small code size, L2 cache pinning can be very effective at reducing latency for instruction cache misses. Another potential improvement is to remove, or make preemptible, seL4's atomic send-receive IPC operation.

The biggest issue with seL4's design in terms of interrupt latency, is the decision to use a versatile 32-bit capability addressing scheme – each of the 32 bits that need to be decoded can theoretically lead to another cache miss, and decoding several such addresses results in significant interrupt latencies. Practical systems can use the seL4 authority model to prevent this scenario by not allowing an adversary the ability to construct their own capability space.

We have shown that the event-based model of seL4 does not lead to unreasonably large interrupt latencies. It also brings the benefits of reduced kernel complexity. We assert that a process-based kernel without preemption would attain interrupt latencies in the same order of magnitude as the event-based model. A fully-preemptible process-based kernel might attain much smaller latencies, but forgoes the possibility of formal verification.

Verification technology may some day be able to reason about the correctness of fully-preemptible kernels. Until then, a formally-verifiable event-based microkernel such as seL4 provides a very high assurance platform on which safety-critical and real-time systems can be confidently built.

Acknowledgements

Many members of the seL4 team helped to develop the ideas presented in this paper, including Kevin Elphinstone (lead architect), Adrian Danis, Dhammika Elkaduwe, Ben Leslie, Thomas Sewell and Gerwin Klein.

We thank our shepherd, Wolfgang Schröder-Preikschat, for his guidance and valuable feedback, and our anonymous reviewers for their helpful comments.

NICTA is funded by the Australian Government as represented by the Department of Broadband, Communications and the Digital Economy and the Australian Research Council through the ICT Centre of Excellence program.

References

[ARM 2005] *ARM1136JF-S and ARM1136J-S Technical Reference Manual*. ARM Ltd., R1P1 edition, 2005.

[Baker 1991] T. P. Baker. Stack-based scheduling for realtime processes. *J. Real–Time Syst.*, 3(1):67–99, 1991.

[Baumann 2010] Christoph Baumann, Bernhard Beckert, Holger Blasum, and Thorsten Bormer. Ingredients of operating system correctness. In *Emb. World Conf.*, Nuremberg, Germany, Mar 2010.

[Beyer 2006] Sven Beyer, Christian Jacobi, Daniel Kröning, Dirk Leinenbach, and Wolfgang J. Paul. Putting it all together— formal verification of the VAMP. *International Journal on Software Tools for Technology Transfer (STTT)*, 8(4):411–430, 2006.

[Blackham 2011a] Bernard Blackham, Yao Shi, Sudipta Chattopadhyay, Abhik Roychoudhury, and Gernot Heiser. Timing analysis of a protected operating system kernel. In *32nd RTSS*, Vienna, Austria, Nov 2011.

[Blackham 2011b] Bernard Blackham, Yao Shi, and Gernot Heiser. Protected hard real-time: The next frontier. In *2nd APSys*, pages 1:1–1:5, Shanghai, China, Jul 2011.

[Campoy 2001] M. Campoy, A.P. Ivars, and J.V.B. Mataix. Static use of locking caches in multitask preemptive real-time systems. In *Proceedings of IEEE/IEE Real-Time Embedded Systems Workshop*, 2001. Satellite of the IEEE Real-Time Systems Symposium.

[Cytron 1991] Ron Cytron, Jeanne Ferrante, Barry K. Rosen, Mark N. Wegman, and F. Kenneth Zadeck. Efficiently computing static single assignment form and the control dependence graph. *ACM Trans. Progr. Lang. & Syst.*, 13:451–490, October 1991.

[Daum 2009a] Matthias Daum, Jan Dörrenbächer, and Burkhart Wolff. Proving fairness and implementation correctness of a microkernel scheduler. *JAR: Special Issue Operat. Syst. Verification*, 42(2–4):349–388, 2009.

[Daum 2009b] Matthias Daum, Norbert W. Schirmer, and Mareike Schmidt. Implementation correctness of a real-time operating system. In *IEEE Int. Conf. Softw. Engin. & Formal Methods*, pages 23–32, Hanoi, Vietnam, 2009. IEEE Comp. Soc.

[Dennis 1966] Jack B. Dennis and Earl C. Van Horn. Programming semantics for multiprogrammed computations. *CACM*, 9:143–155, 1966.

[Draves 1991] R.P. Draves, Brian N. Bershad, R.F. Rashid, and R.W. Dean. Using continuations to implement thread management and communication in operating systems. In *13th SOSP*, Asilomar, CA, USA, Oct 1991.

[Elkaduwe 2007] Dhammika Elkaduwe, Philip Derrin, and Kevin Elphinstone. A memory allocation model for an embedded microkernel. In *1st MIKES*, pages 28–34, Sydney, Australia, Jan 2007. NICTA.

[Feng 2008] Xingu Feng, Zhong Shao, Yuan Dong, and Yu Guo. Certifying low-level programs with hardware interrupts and preemptive threads. In *PLDI*, pages 170–182, Tucson, AZ, USA, Jun 2008.

[Ford 1999] Brian Ford, Mike Hibler, Jay Lepreau, Roland McGrath, and Patrick Tullmann. Interface and execution models in the Fluke kernel. In *3rd OSDI*, pages 101–115, New Orleans, LA, USA, Feb 1999. USENIX.

[Fox 2010] Anthony Fox and Magnus Myreen. A trustworthy monadic formalization of the ARMv7 instruction set architecture. volume 6172 of *LNCS*, pages 243–258, Edinburgh, UK, Jul 2010. Springer-Verlag.

[Gotsman 2011] Alexey Gotsman and Hongseok Yang. Modular verification of preemptive OS kernels. *16th ICFP*, pages 404–417, 2011.

[Heiser 2010] Gernot Heiser and Ben Leslie. The OKL4 Microvisor: Convergence point of microkernels and hypervisors. In *1st APSys*, pages 19–24, New Delhi, India, Aug 2010.

[Hohmuth 2002] Michael Hohmuth. The Fiasco kernel: System architecture, 2002. Technical Report TUD-FI02-06-Juli-2002.

[Klein 2009a] Gerwin Klein. Operating system verification — an overview. *Sādhanā*, 34(1):27–69, Feb 2009.

[Klein 2009b] Gerwin Klein, Kevin Elphinstone, Gernot Heiser, June Andronick, David Cock, Philip Derrin, Dhammika Elkaduwe, Kai Engelhardt, Rafal Kolanski, Michael Norrish, Thomas Sewell, Harvey Tuch, and Simon Winwood. seL4: Formal verification of an OS kernel. In *22nd SOSP*, pages 207–220, Big Sky, MT, USA, Oct 2009. ACM.

[Li 2007] Xianfeng Li, Yun Liang, Tulika Mitra, and Abhik Roychoudhury. Chronos: A timing analyzer for embedded software. In *Science of Computer Programming, Special issue on Experimental Software and Toolkit*, volume 69(1-3), Dec 2007.

[Li 1995] Yau-Tsun Li, Sharad Malik, and Andrew Wolfe. Efficient microarchitecture modeling and path analysis for real-time software. In *16th RTSS*, pages 298–307, 1995.

[Liedtke 1993] Jochen Liedtke. Improving IPC by kernel design. In *14th SOSP*, pages 175–188, Asheville, NC, USA, Dec 1993.

[Liedtke 1995] Jochen Liedtke. On μ-kernel construction. In *15th SOSP*, pages 237–250, Copper Mountain, CO, USA, Dec 1995.

[Mehnert 2002] Frank Mehnert, Michael Hohmuth, and Hermann Härtig. Cost and benefit of separate address spaces in real-time operating systems. In *23rd RTSS*, Austin, TX, USA, 2002.

[Metzner 2004] Alexander Metzner. Why model checking can improve WCET analysis. In Rajeev Alur and Doron Peled, editors, *Computer Aided Verification*, volume 3114 of *LNCS*, pages 298–301. Springer-Verlag, 2004.

[Puaut 2002] Isabelle Puaut and David Decotigny. Low-complexity algorithms for static cache locking in multitasking hard real-time systems. In *23rd RTSS*, pages 114–123, 2002.

[Rieder 2008] B. Rieder, P. Puschner, and I. Wenzel. Using model checking to derive loop bounds of general loops within ANSI-C applications for measurement based WCET analysis. In *Intelligent Solutions in Embedded Systems, 2008 International Workshop on*, pages 1–7, july 2008.

[Warton 2005] Matthew Warton. Single kernel stack L4. BE thesis, School Comp. Sci. & Engin., University NSW, Sydney 2052, Australia, Nov 2005.

[Weiser 1984] Mark Weiser. Program slicing. *IEEE Trans. Softw. Engin.*, SE-10(4):352–357, Jul 1984.

Improving Network Connection Locality on Multicore Systems

Aleksey Pesterev*   Jacob Strauss†   Nickolai Zeldovich*   Robert T. Morris*

*MIT CSAIL   †Quanta Research Cambridge

{alekseyp, nickolai, rtm}@csail.mit.edu   jacob.strauss@qrclab.com

Abstract

Incoming and outgoing processing for a given TCP connection often execute on different cores: an incoming packet is typically processed on the core that receives the interrupt, while outgoing data processing occurs on the core running the relevant user code. As a result, accesses to read/write connection state (such as TCP control blocks) often involve cache invalidations and data movement between cores' caches. These can take hundreds of processor cycles, enough to significantly reduce performance.

We present a new design, called Affinity-Accept, that causes all processing for a given TCP connection to occur on the same core. Affinity-Accept arranges for the network interface to determine the core on which application processing for each new connection occurs, in a lightweight way; it adjusts the card's choices only in response to imbalances in CPU scheduling. Measurements show that for the Apache web server serving static files on a 48-core AMD system, Affinity-Accept reduces time spent in the TCP stack by 30% and improves overall throughput by 24%.

Categories and Subject Descriptors D.4.7 [*Operating Systems*]: Organization and Design; D.4.8 [*Operating Systems*]: Performance

General Terms Design, Measurement, Performance

Keywords Multi-core, Packet Processing, Cache Misses

1. Introduction

It is well known that a good policy for processing TCP connections on a multiprocessor is to divide the connections among the cores, and to ensure that each connection is handled entirely on one core [18]. This policy eliminates contention for the locks that guard each connection's state in the kernel, and eliminates cache coherence traffic that would be caused if a connection's state were used on multiple cores. The policy is an instance of a more general rule for parallelism: activities on different cores should interact as little as possible. Many server programs are designed to follow this rule. Web servers, for example, typically process a stream of requests from many independent clients. They process the requests concurrently on many cores, and the requests' independence allows them to be processed with little serialization due to shared state, and thus allows for good parallel speedup.

In practice, however, even with independent requests it is difficult to avoid all interactions between activities on different cores. One problem is that the kernel typically serializes processing of new connections on a given TCP port (e.g., the single UNIX `accept()` queue). A second problem is that there may be no way to cause all of the activities related to a given connection to happen on the same core: packet delivery, kernel-level TCP processing, execution of the user process, packet transmission, memory allocation, etc. A third problem is that the connection-on-one-core goal may conflict with other scheduling policies, most notably load balance. Finally, the application's design may not be fully compatible with independent processing of connections.

This paper describes Affinity-Accept, a design that achieves the goal of executing all activity related to a given connection on a single core, and describes an implementation of that design for Linux. The starting point for Affinity-Accept is an Ethernet controller that distributes incoming packets over a set of receive DMA rings, one per core, based on a hash of connection identification fields. New connection requests (SYN packets) are added to per-core queues, protected by per-core locks, so that connection setup can proceed in parallel. Each server process that is waiting for a connection accepts a new connection from its own core's queue, and we assume that the application processes the connection on the same core where it was accepted. Since the Ethernet controller will place subsequent incoming packets for this connection into the DMA ring for the same core, the end effect is that all packet and application processing for this connection will take place on the same core. This minimizes contention for shared cache lines and locks. Affinity-Accept also balances load at multiple time-scales to handle connections with differing processing times as well as persistent imbalances due to unrelated computing activity.

An alternate solution is to use a "smart" Ethernet card with a configurable flow steering table that routes packets to specific cores. The kernel could configure the card to route packets of each new connection to the core running the user

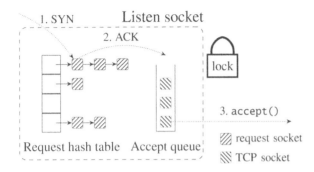

Figure 1: A TCP *listen socket* in Linux is composed of two data structures: the *request hash table*, which holds request sockets, and the *accept queue*, which holds established TCP sockets. The listen socket performs three duties: (1) tracking connection initiation requests on SYN packet reception, (2) storing TCP connections that finished the three-way handshake, and (3) supplying TCP connections to applications on calls to `accept()`.

space application. Unfortunately, this does not work due to limited steering table sizes and the cost of maintaining this table; §7 gives more details.

We present an evaluation on a 48-core Linux server running Apache. First, we show that, independent of Affinity-Accept, splitting up the new connection queue into multiple queues with finer-grained locks improves throughput by 2.8×. Next, we evaluate Affinity-Accept and show that processing each connection on a single core further reduces time spent in the TCP stack by 30% and improves overall throughput by 24%. The main reason for this additional improvement is a reduction in cache misses on connection state written by other cores.

The rest of the paper is organized as follows. §2 describes the problems with connection management in more detail, using Linux as an example. §3 presents the kernel components of Affinity-Accept's design, with application-level considerations in §4, and implementation details in §5. §6 evaluates Affinity-Accept. §7 presents related work and §8 concludes.

2. Connection Processing in Linux

This section provides a brief overview of Linux connection initiation and processing, and describes two problems with parallel connection processing: a single lock per socket and costly accesses to shared cache lines.

2.1 TCP Listen Socket Lock

The Linux kernel represents a TCP port that is waiting for incoming connections with a *TCP listen socket*, shown in Figure 1. To establish a connection on this port the client starts a TCP three-way connection setup handshake by sending a SYN packet to the server. The server responds with a SYN-ACK packet. The client finishes the handshake by returning an ACK packet. A connection that has finished the handshake is called an established connection. A listen socket has two parts to track this handshake protocol: a hash table recording

arrived SYNs for which no ACK has arrived, and an "accept queue" of connections for which the SYN/SYN-ACK/ACK handshake has completed. An arriving SYN creates an entry in the hash table and triggers a SYN-ACK response. An arriving ACK moves the connection from the hash table to the accept queue. An application pulls connections from the accept queue using the `accept()` system call.

Incoming connection processing scales poorly on multicore machines because each TCP port's listen socket has a single hash table and a single accept queue, protected by a single lock. Only one core at a time can process incoming SYN packets, ACK packets (in response to SYN-ACKs), or `accept()` system calls.

Once Linux has set up a TCP connection and an application process has accepted it, further processing scales much better. Per-connection locks allow only one core at a time to manipulate a connection, but in an application with many active connections, this allows for sufficient parallelism. The relatively coarse-grained per-connection locks have low overhead and are easy to reason about [9, 18].

Our approach to increasing parallelism during TCP connection setup is to partition the state of the listen socket in order to allow finer grained locks. §3 describes this design. Locks, however, are not the whole story: there is still the problem of multiple cores sharing an established connection's state, which we discuss next.

2.2 Shared Cache Lines in Packet Processing

The Linux kernel associates a large amount of state with each established TCP connection, and manipulates that state whenever a packet arrives or departs on that connection. The core which manipulates a connection's state in response to incoming packets is determined by where the Ethernet interface (NIC) delivers packets. A different core may execute the application process that reads and writes data on the connection's socket. Thus, for a single connection, different cores often handle incoming packets, outgoing packets, and copy connection data to and from the application.

The result is that cache lines holding a connection's state may frequently move between cores. Each time one core modifies a cache line, the cache coherency hardware must invalidate any other copies of this data. Subsequent reads on other cores pull data out of a remote core's cache. This sharing of cache lines is expensive on a multicore machine because remote accesses are much slower than local accesses.

Processing the same connection on multiple cores also creates memory allocation performance problems. An example is managing buffers for incoming packets. The kernel allocates buffers to hold packets out of a per-core pool. The kernel allocates a buffer on the core that initially receives the packet from the RX DMA ring, and deallocates a buffer on the core that calls `recvmsg()`. With a single core processing a connection, both allocation and deallocation are fast because they access the same local pool. With multiple cores performance suffers because remote deallocation is slower.

3. An Affinity-aware Listen Socket

To solve the connection affinity problem described in the previous section, we propose a new design for a listen socket, called Affinity-Accept. Affinity-Accept's design consists of three parts. As a first step, Affinity-Accept uses the NIC to spread incoming packets among many RX DMA rings, in a way that ensures packets from a single flow always map to the same core (§3.1).

One naïve approach to ensure local packet processing would be to migrate the application-level thread handling the connection to the core where the connection's packets are delivered by the NIC. While this would ensure local processing, thread migration is time-consuming, both because migration requires acquiring scheduler locks, and because the thread will incur cache misses once it starts running on a different core. For short-lived connections, thread migration is not worthwhile. Another approach would be to tell the NIC to redirect the packets for a given flow to a different core. However, a single server may have hundreds of thousands of established TCP connections at a given point in time, likely exceeding the capacity of the NIC's flow steering table. Moreover, the time taken to re-configure the NIC for each flow is also prohibitively high for short-lived connections.

Thus, the second part of Affinity-Accept's design is that instead of forcing specific connections or threads to a particular core, Affinity-Accept arranges for the `accept()` system call to preferentially return local connections to threads running on the local core (§3.2). As long as the NIC's flow steering does not change, and application threads do not migrate to another core, all connection processing will be done locally, with no forcible migration of flows or threads.

Since Affinity-Accept does not use forcible migration to achieve connection affinity, it assumes that the NIC will spread load evenly across cores. However, there are many reasons why some cores may receive more or less load at any given time. Thus, the third part of Affinity-Accept's design is a mechanism to dynamically balance the load offered by the NIC's RX DMA rings to each core, to counteract both short- and long-term variations (§3.3).

3.1 Connection Routing in the NIC

Affinity-Accept assumes that a multi-core machine includes a NIC, such as Intel's 82599 10Gbit Ethernet (IXGBE) card, that exposes multiple hardware DMA rings. Assigning each core one RX and one TX DMA ring spreads the load of processing incoming and outgoing packets among many cores. Additionally, a performance benefit of multiple hardware DMA rings is that cores do not need to synchronize when accessing their own DMA rings.

To solve the connection affinity problem, Affinity-Accept must configure the NIC to route incoming packets from the same connection to the same core. To do this, Affinity-Accept leverages packet routing support in the NIC. The NIC hardware typically hashes each packet's flow identifier

five-tuple (the protocol number, source and destination IP addresses, and source and destination port numbers) and uses the resulting hash value to look up the RX DMA ring where the packet will be placed. Since all packets from a single connection will have the same flow hash values, the NIC will deliver all packets from a single connection into a single DMA ring.

The IXGBE card supports two mechanisms to map flow hash values to RX DMA rings; here, we omit some details for simplicity. The first is called Receive-Side Scaling, or RSS [5]. RSS uses the flow hash value to index a 128-entry table. Each entry in the table is a 4-bit identifier for an RX DMA ring. A limitation of this mechanism is that a 4-bit identifier allows for routing packets to only 16 distinct DMA rings. This is a limitation particular to the IXGBE card; other NICs can route packets to all DMA rings.

The second mechanism supported by IXGBE uses a flow steering table and is called Flow Direction, or FDir [14]. FDir can route packets to 64 distinct DMA rings, and Affinity-Accept uses FDir. FDir works by looking up the flow hash value in a hash table. This hash table resides in the NIC, and the kernel can modify it by issuing special requests to the card. Each entry in the hash table maps a flow's hash value to a 6-bit RX DMA ring identifier. The table is bounded by the size of the NIC's memory, which is also used to hold the NIC's FIFOs; in practice, this means the table can hold anywhere from 8K to 32K flow steering entries.

Affinity-Accept requires the NIC to route every incoming packet to one of the available DMA rings. As described above, FDir can only map specific flows to specific DMA rings, and the FDir table does not have sufficient space to map the hash value for every possible flow's five-tuple. To avoid this problem, we change the NIC's flow hash function to use only a subset of the packet's five-tuple. In particular, we instruct the NIC to hash the low 12 bits of the source port number, resulting in at most 4,096 distinct hash values. Each hash value now represents an entire family of flows, which we call a *flow group*. We then insert FDir hash table entries for each one of these 4,096 flow groups, and map them to RX DMA rings to distribute load between cores. This method frees the kernel from communicating with the NIC on every new connection, and avoids the need for an entry per active connection in the hardware table. As we will describe later, achieving good load balance requires having many more flow groups than cores.

3.2 Accepting Local Connections

In order to efficiently accept local connections, Affinity-Accept must first eliminate the single listen socket lock, shown in Figure 1. The listen socket lock protects two data structures: the request hash table, and the accept queue. To remove the single listen socket lock, we use the well-known technique of splitting a single lock protecting a data structure into many finer-grained locks each protecting a part of the data structure. Affinity-Accept removes the lock by partitioning the accept queue into per-core accept queues, each protected by its own lock, and by using a separate lock to protect each bucket in the request hash table. These changes avoid lock contention on the listen socket. We describe these design decisions in more detail in §5.

To achieve connection affinity, Affinity-Accept modifies the behavior of the `accept()` system call. When an application calls `accept()`, Affinity-Accept returns a connection from the local core's accept queue for the corresponding listen socket, if available. If no local connections are available, `accept()` goes to sleep (as will be described in §3.3, the core first checks other core's queues before going to sleep). When new connections arrive, the network stack wakes up any threads waiting on the local core's accept queue. This allows all connection processing to occur locally.

3.3 Connection Load Balancer

Always accepting connections from the local accept queue, as described in §3.2, addresses the connection affinity problem, but introduces potential load imbalance problems. If one core cannot keep up with incoming connections in its local accept queue, the accept queue will overflow, and the kernel will drop connection requests, adversely affecting the client. However, even when one core is too busy to accept connections, other cores may be idle. An ideal system would offload connections from the local accept queue to other idle cores.

There are two cases for why some cores may be able to process more connections than others. The first is a short-term load spike on one core, perhaps because that core is handling a CPU-intensive request, or an unrelated CPU-intensive process runs on that core. To deal with short-term imbalance, Affinity-Accept performs *connection stealing*, whereby an application thread running on one core accepts incoming connections from another core. Since connection stealing transfers one connection at a time between cores, updating the NIC's flow routing table for each stolen connection would not be worthwhile.

The second case is a longer-term load imbalance, perhaps due to an uneven distribution of flow groups in the NIC, due to unrelated long-running CPU-intensive processes, or due to differences in CPU performance (e.g., some CPUs may be further away from DRAM). In this case, Affinity-Accept's goal is to preserve efficient local processing of connections. Thus, Affinity-Accept must match the load offered to each core (by packets from the NIC's RX DMA rings) to the application's throughput on that core. To do this, Affinity-Accept implements *flow group migration*, in which it changes the assignment of flow groups in the NIC's FDir table (§3.1).

In the rest of this subsection, we first describe connection stealing in §3.3.1, followed by flow group migration in §3.3.2.

3.3.1 Connection Stealing

Affinity-Accept's connection stealing mechanism consists of two parts: the first is the mechanism for stealing a connection from another core, and the second is the logic for determining when stealing should be done, and determining the core from which the connection should be stolen.

Stealing mechanism. When a *stealer* core decides to steal a connection from a *victim* core, it acquires the lock on the victim's local accept queue, and dequeues a connection from it. Once a connection has been stolen, the stealer core executes application code to process the connection, but the victim core still performs processing of incoming packets from the NIC's RX DMA ring. This is because the FDir table in the NIC cannot be updated on a per-flow basis. As a result, the victim core is still responsible for performing some amount of processing on behalf of the stolen connection. Thus, short-term connection stealing temporarily violates Affinity-Accept's goal of connection affinity, in hope of resolving a load imbalance.

Stealing policy. To determine when one core should steal incoming connections from another core, Affinity-Accept designates each core to be either *busy* or *non-busy*. Each core determines its own busy status depending on the length of its local accept queue over time; we will describe this algorithm shortly. Non-busy cores try to steal connections from busy cores, in order to even out the load in the short term. Busy cores never steal connections from other cores.

When an application calls `accept()` on a non-busy core, Affinity-Accept can either choose to dequeue a connection from its local accept queue, or from the accept queue of a busy remote core. When both types of incoming connections are available, Affinity-Accept must maintain efficient local processing of incoming connections, while also handling some connections from remote cores. To do this, Affinity-Accept implements proportional-share scheduling. We find that a ratio of $5 : 1$ between local and remote connections accepted appears to work well for a range of workloads. The overall performance is not significantly affected by the choice of this ratio. Ratios that are too low start to prefer remote connections in favor of local ones, and ratios that are too high do not steal enough connections to resolve a load imbalance.

Each non-busy core uses a simple heuristic to choose from which remote core to steal. Cores are deterministically ordered. Each core keeps a count of the last remote core it stole from, and starts searching for the next busy core one past the last core. Thus, non-busy cores steal in a round-robin fashion from all busy remote cores, achieving fairness and avoiding contention. Unfortunately, round robin does not give preference to any particular remote queue, even if some cores are more busy than others. Investigating this trade-off is left to future work.

Tracking busy cores. An application specifies the maximum accept queue length in the `listen()` system call. Affinity-Accept splits the maximum length evenly across all cores; this length is called the *maximum local accept queue* *length*. Each core tracks the instantaneous length of its local queue which we simply call the local accept queue length.

Each core determines its busy status based on its local accept queue length. Using the max local accept queue length, Affinity-Accept sets high and low watermark values for the queue length. These values determine when a core gets marked as busy, and when a core's busy status is cleared. Once a core's local accept queue length exceeds the high watermark, Affinity-Accept marks the core as busy. Since many applications accept connections in bursts, the length of the accept queue can have significant oscillations. As a result, Affinity-Accept is more cautious about marking cores non-busy: instead of using the instantaneous queue length, it uses a running average. This is done by updating an Exponentially Weighted Moving Average (EWMA) each time a connection is added to the local queue. EWMA's alpha parameter is set to one over twice the max local accept queue length (for example, if an application's max local accept queue length is 64, alpha is set to $1/128$). A small alpha ensures that the EWMA tracks the long term queue length, because the instantaneous queue length oscillates around the average. The work stealer marks a core non-busy when this average drops below the low watermark.

We have experimentally determined that setting the high and low watermarks to be 75% and 10% of the max local accept queue length works well with our hardware; the numbers may need to be adjusted for other hardware. Developers of Apache and lighttpd recommend configuring the accept queue length to 512 or 1024 for machines with a low core count. The length must be adjusted for larger machines. We found a queue length of 64 to 256 per core works well for our benchmarks.

To ensure that finding busy cores does not become a performance bottleneck in itself, Affinity-Accept must allow non-busy cores to efficiently determine which other cores, if any, are currently busy (in order to find potential victims for connection stealing). To achieve this, Affinity-Accept maintains a bit vector for each listen socket, containing one bit per core, which reflects the busy status of that core. With a single read, a core can determine which other cores are busy. If all cores are non-busy, the cache line containing the bit vector will be present in all of the cores' caches. If the server is overloaded and all cores are perpetually busy, this cache line is not read or updated.

Polling. When an application thread calls `accept()`, `poll()`, or `select()` to wait for an incoming connection, Affinity-Accept first scans the local accept queue. If no connections are available, Affinity-Accept looks for available connections in remote busy cores, followed by remote non-busy cores. If no connections are available in any accept queues, the thread goes to sleep.

When new connections are added to an accept queue, Affinity-Accept first tries to wake up local threads waiting for incoming connections. If no threads are waiting locally, the local core checks for waiting threads on any non-busy remote cores, and wakes them up.

To avoid lost wakeups, waiting threads should first add themselves to the local accept queue's wait queue, then check all other cores' accept queues, and then go to sleep. We have not implemented this scheme yet, and rely on timeouts to catch lost wakeups instead.

3.3.2 Flow Group Migration

Connection stealing reduces the user-space load on a busy core, but it neither reduces the load of processing incoming packets nor allows local connection processing of stolen connections. Thus, to address long-term load imbalance, Affinity-Accept migrates flow groups (§3.1) between cores.

To determine when flow group migration should occur, Affinity-Accept uses a simple heuristic based on how often one core has stolen connections from other cores. Every 100*ms*, each non-busy core finds the victim core from which it has stolen the largest number of connections, and migrates one flow group from that core to itself (by reprogramming the NIC's FDir table). In our configuration (4,096 flow groups and 48 cores), stealing one flow group every 100*ms* was sufficient. Busy cores do not migrate additional flow groups to themselves.

4. Connection Affinity in Applications

Applications must adhere to a few practices to realize the full performance gains of Affinity-Accept. This section describes those practices in the context of web servers, but the general principles apply to all types of networking applications.

4.1 Thundering Herd

Some applications serialize calls to `accept()` and `poll()` to avoid the *thundering herd* problem, where a kernel wakes up many threads in response to a single incoming connection. Although all of the newly woken threads would begin running, only one of them would accept a connection. The kernel would then put the remainder back to sleep, wasting cycles in these extra transitions. Historically, applications used to serialize their calls to `accept()` to avoid this problem. However, Linux kernel developers have since changed the `accept()` system call to only wake up one thread. Applications that still serialize calls to `accept()` do so only for legacy reasons.

For Affinity-Accept to work, multiple threads must call `accept()` and `poll()` concurrently on multiple cores. If not, the same scalability problems that manifested due to a single socket lock will appear in the form of user-space serialization. Many web servers use the `poll()` system call to wait for events on the listen socket. The Linux kernel, unfortunately, still wakes up multiple threads that use `poll()` to wait for the same event. Affinity-Accept significantly reduces the thundering herd problem for `poll()` by reducing the number of threads that are awoken. It uses multiple accept queues and only wakes up threads waiting in `poll()` on the local core.

4.2 Application Structure

To get optimal performance with Affinity-Accept, calls to accept(), recvmsg(), and sendmsg() on the same connection must take place on the same core. The architecture of the web server determines whether this happens or not.

An event-driven web server like lighttpd [4] adheres to this guideline. Event-driven servers typically run multiple processes, each running an event loop in a single thread. On calls to accept() the process gets back a connection with an affinity for the local core. Subsequent calls to recvmsg() and sendmsg() therefore also deal with connections that have an affinity for the local core. The designers of such web servers recommend spawning at least two processes per available core [6] to deal with file system I/O blocking a processes and all of its pending requests. If one process blocks, another non-blocked process may be available to run. The Linux process load balancer distributes the multiple processes among the available cores. One potential concern with the process load balancer is that it migrates processes between cores when it detects a load imbalance. All connections the process accepts after the migration would have an affinity to the new core, but existing connections would have affinity for the original core. §6 shows that this is not a problem because the Linux load balancer rarely migrates processes, as long as the load is close to even across all cores.

The Apache [2] web server has more modes of operation than lighttpd, but none of Apache's modes are ideal for Affinity-Accept without additional changes. In "worker" mode, Apache forks multiple processes; each accepts connections in one main thread and spawns multiple threads to process those connections. The problem with using this design with Affinity-Accept is that the scheduler disperses the threads across cores, causing the accept and worker threads to run on different cores. As a result, once the accept thread accepts a new connection, it hands it off to a worker thread that is executing on another core, violating connection affinity.

Apache's "prefork" mode is similar to lighttpd in that it forks multiple processes, each of which accepts and processes a single connection to completion. Prefork does not perform well with Affinity-Accept for two reasons. First, prefork uses many more processes than worker mode, and thus spends more time context-switching between processes. Second, each process allocates memory from the DRAM controller closest to the core on which it was forked, and in prefork mode, Apache initially forks all processes on a single core. Once the processes are moved to another core by the Linux process load balancer, memory operations become more expensive since they require remote DRAM accesses.

The approach we take to evaluate Apache's performance is to use the "worker" mode, but to pin Apache's accept and worker threads to specific cores, which avoids these problems entirely. However, this does require additional setup configuration at startup time to identify the correct number of cores to use, and reduces the number of threads which

the Linux process load balancer can move between cores to address a load imbalance. A better solution would be to add a new kernel interface for specifying groups of threads which the kernel should schedule together on the same core. Designing such an interface is left to future work.

5. Implementation

Affinity-Accept builds upon the Linux 2.6.35 kernel, patched with changes described by Boyd-Wickizer et al [9], and includes the TCP listen socket changes described in §3. Affinity-Accept does not create any new system calls. We added 1,200 lines of code to the base kernel, along with a new kernel module to implement the connection load balancer in about 800 lines of code.

We used the 2.0.84.9 IXGBE driver. We did not use a newer driver (version 3.3.9) because we encountered a 20% performance regression. We modified the driver to add a mode that configures the FDir hardware so that the connection load balancer could migrate connections between cores. We also added an interface to migrate flow groups from one core to another. The changes required about 700 lines of code.

We modified the Apache HTTP Server version 2.2.14 to disable a mutex (described in §4) used to serialize multiple processes on calls to accept() and poll().

5.1 Per-core Accept Queues

One of the challenging aspects of implementing Affinity-Accept was to break up the single lock and accept queue in each listen socket into per-core locks and accept queues. This turned out to be challenging because of the large amount of Linux code that deals with the data structures in question. In particular, Linux uses a single data structure, called a sock, to represent sockets for any protocol (TCP, UDP, etc). Each protocol specializes the sock structure to hold its own additional information for that socket (such as the request hash table and accept queue, for a TCP listen socket). Some functions, especially those in early packet processing stages, manipulate the sock part of the data structure. Other operations are protocol-specific, and use a table of function pointers to invoke protocol-specific handlers. Importantly, socket locking happens on the sock data structure directly, and does not invoke a protocol-specific function pointer; for example, the networking code often grabs the sock lock, calls a protocol-specific function pointer, and then releases the lock. Thus, changing the locking policy on sock objects would require changing the locking policy throughout the entire Linux network stack.

To change the listen socket locking policy without changing the shared networking code that deals with processing sock objects, we *clone* the listen socket. This way, there is a per-core copy of the original listen socket, each protected by its own socket lock. This ensures cores can manipulate their per-core clones in parallel. Most of the existing code does not need to change because it deals with exactly the same type of object as before, and the `sock` locking policy remains the same. Code specific to the listen socket implementation does manipulate state shared by all of the clones (e.g., code in `accept` that performs connection stealing), but such changes are localized to the protocol-specific implementation of the listen socket. Additionally, we modified generic socket code that expects only one socket to be aware of cloned sockets. For example, we aggregate data from all cloned sockets when reporting statistics.

5.2 Fine-grained Request Hash Table Locking

The other data structure protected by the single listen socket lock is the request hash table (Figure 1). One approach to avoid a single lock on the request hash table is to break it up into per-core request hash tables, as with the accept queue above. However, this leads to a subtle problem when flow groups are migrated between cores. Due to flow group migration, a connection's SYN packet could arrive on one core (creating a request socket in its per-core request hash table), and the corresponding ACK packet could arrive on another core. The code to process the ACK would not find the request socket in its local request hash table. The same problem does not occur with established TCP sockets because the kernel maintains a global hash table for established connections, and uses fine-grained locking to avoid contention.

At this point, we are left with two less-than-ideal options: the core that receives an ACK packet could drop it on the floor, breaking the client's connection, or it could scan all other cores' request hash tables looking for the corresponding request socket, which would be time-consuming and interfere with all other cores. Since neither option is appealing, we instead maintain a single request hash table, shared by all clones of a listen socket, and use per-hash-table-bucket locks to avoid lock contention. We have experimentally verified using the benchmark described in §6 that this design incurs at most a 2% performance reduction compared to the per-core request hash table design.

6. Evaluation

In this section we describe the experimental setup (§6.1) and workload (§6.2). Then we show that the listen socket lock in stock Linux is a major scalability bottleneck, and splitting the single lock into many fine grained locks alleviates the problem (§6.3). After removing the lock bottleneck, data sharing is the predominant problem and Affinity-Accept further improves throughput by reducing sharing (§6.4). Clients can experience poor service using Affinity-Accept without a load balancer, and our proposed load balancer addresses this imbalance (§6.5). We end with a characterization of the type of workloads Affinity-Accept helps (§6.6).

6.1 Hardware Setup

We run experiments on two machines. The first is a 48-core machine, with a Tyan Thunder S4985 board and an M4985

	Local Latency (cycles)				Remote Latency (cycles)	
	L1	L2	L3	RAM	L3	RAM
AMD	3	14	28	120	460	500
Intel	4	12	24	90	200	280

Table 1: Access times to different levels of the memory hierarchy. Remote accesses are between two chips farthest on the interconnect.

quad CPU daughterboard. The machine has a total of eight 2.4 GHz 6-core AMD Opteron 8431 chips. Each core has private 64 Kbyte instruction and data caches, and a 512 Kbyte private L2 cache. The cores on each chip share a 6 Mbyte L3 cache, 1 Mbyte of which is used for the HT Assist probe filter [8]. Each chip has 8 Gbytes of local off-chip DRAM. Table 1 shows the access times to different memory levels. The machine has a dual-port Intel 82599 10Gbit Ethernet card, though we use only one port for all experiments. That port connects to an Ethernet switch with a set of load-generating client machines.

The second machine is composed of eight 2.4 GHz 10-core Intel Xeon E7 8870 chips. Each core has a private 32-Kbyte data and instruction cache, and a private 256 Kbyte L2 cache. All 10 cores on one chip share a 30 Mbyte L3 cache. Each chip has 32 Gbytes of local off-chip DRAM. Table 1 shows the memory access times for the Intel machine. The machine is provisioned with two dual-port Intel 82599 10Gbit Ethernet cards. Each port exposes up to 64 hardware DMA rings, which is less than the machine's core count. For experiments that use 64 or fewer cores we use a single port; for experiments with more than 64 cores we add another port from the second card. A second port adds up to 64 more DMA rings and each core can have a private DMA ring.

6.2 Workload

To evaluate the performance of network-heavy applications with and without Affinity-Accept, we measure the rate at which a machine can serve static web content, in terms of HTTP requests per second. This is distinct from connections per second because a single HTTP connection can issue multiple requests.

We profile two web servers, lighttpd [4] and Apache [2], to show that two different architectures work with Affinity-Accept. We use 25 client machines with a total of 54 cores, running the httperf [3] HTTP request generator. A single httperf instance issues many requests in parallel, up to the maximum number of open file descriptors (1024). We run 4 httperf instances per client machine core so that httperf is not limited by file descriptors. Httperf works by generating a target request rate. In all experiments we first search for a request rate that saturates the server and then run the experiment with the discovered rate.

The content is a mix of files inspired by the static parts of the SpecWeb [7] benchmark suite. We do not use SpecWeb directly because it does not sufficiently stress the network stack: some requests involve performing SQL queries or running PHP code, which stresses the disk and CPU more than the network stack. Applications that put less stress on the network stack will see less pronounced improvements with Affinity-Accept. The files served range from 30 bytes to 5,670 bytes. The web server serves 30,000 distinct files, and a client chooses a file to request uniformly over all files.

Unless otherwise stated, in all experiments a client requests a total of 6 files per connection with requests spaced out by think time. First, a client requests one file and waits for 100ms. The client then requests two more files, waits 100ms, requests three more files, and finally closes the connection. §6.6 shows that the results are independent of the think time.

We configure lighttpd with 10 processes per core for a total of 480 processes on the AMD machine. Each process is limited to a maximum of 200 connections. Having several processes handling connections on each core limits the number of broken connection affinities if the Linux scheduler migrates one of the processes to another core, and reduces the number of file descriptors each process must pass to the kernel via `poll()`.

We run Apache in worker mode and spawn one process per core. Each process consists of one thread that only accepts connections and multiple worker threads that process accepted connections. We modify the worker model to pin each process to a separate core. All threads in a process inherit the core affinity of the process, and thus the accept thread and worker threads always run on the same core. A single thread processes one connection at a time from start to finish. We configure Apache with 1,024 worker threads per process, which is enough to keep up with the load and think time.

We use a few different implementations of the listen socket to evaluate our design. We first compare Affinity-Accept to a stock Linux listen socket that we call "Stock-Accept" and then a second intermediate listen socket implementation that we refer to as "Fine-Accept". Fine-Accept is similar to Affinity-Accept, but does not maintain connection affinity to cores. On calls to `accept()`, Fine-Accept dequeues connections out of cloned accept queues in a round-robin fashion. This scheme performs better than Stock-Accept's single accept queue, because with multiple accept queues, each queue is protected by a distinct lock, and multiple connections can be accepted in parallel. The Fine-Accept listen socket does not need a load balancer because accepting connection round-robin is intrinsically load balanced: all queues are serviced equally. In all configurations we use the NIC's FDir hardware to distribute incoming packets among all hardware DMA rings (as described in §3.1) and we configure interrupts so that each core processes its own DMA ring.

6.3 Socket Lock

First, we measure the throughput achieved with the stock Linux listen socket, which uses a single socket lock. The Stock-Accept line in Figure 2 shows the scalability of Apache

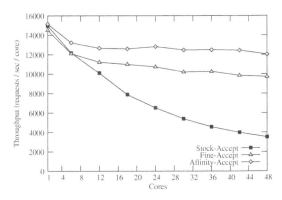

Figure 2: Apache performance with different listen socket implementations on the AMD machine.

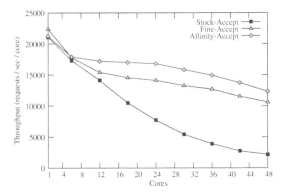

Figure 3: Lighttpd performance with different listen socket implementations on the AMD machine.

on the AMD machine. The number of requests each core can process decreases drastically as the number of cores increases (in fact, the total number of requests handled per second stays about the same, despite the added cores). There is an increasing amount of idle time past 12 cores because the socket lock works in two modes: spinlock mode where the kernel busy loops and mutex mode where the kernel puts the thread to sleep.

To understand the source of this bottleneck, the Stock-Accept row in Table 2 shows the cost of acquiring the socket lock when running Apache on a stock Linux kernel on the AMD machine. The numbers are collected using `lock_stat`, a Linux kernel lock profiler that reports, for all kernel locks, how long each lock is held and the wait time to acquire the lock. Using `lock_stat` incurs substantial overhead due to accounting on each lock operation, and `lock_stat` does not track the wait time to acquire the socket lock in mutex mode; however, the results do give a picture of which locks are contended. Using Stock-Accept, the machine can process a request in 590 μs, 82 μs of which it waits to acquire the listen socket lock in spin mode and at most 320 μs in mutex mode. Close to 70% of the time is spent waiting for another core. Thus, the decline observed for Stock-Accept in Figure 2 is due to contention on the listen socket lock.

Listen Socket	Throughput (requests / sec / core)	Total Time	Idle Time	Non-Idle Time		
				Socket Lock Wait Time	Socket Lock Hold Time	Other Time
Stock-Accept	1,700	590 μs	320 μs	82 μs	25 μs	163 μs
Fine-Accept	5,700	178 μs	8 μs	0 μs	30 μs	140 μs
Affinity-Accept	7,000	144 μs	4 μs	0 μs	17 μs	123 μs

Table 2: The composition of time to process a single request with Apache running on the AMD machine with all 48 cores enabled. These numbers are for a `lock_stat` enabled kernel; as a consequence the throughput numbers, shown in the first column, are lower than in other experiments. The total time to process a request, shown in the second column, is composed of both idle and non-idle time. The idle time is shown in the third column; included in the idle time is the wait time to acquire the socket lock in mutex mode. The last three columns show the composition of active request processing time. The fourth column shows the time the kernel waits to acquire the socket lock in spinlock mode and the fifth column shows the time the socket lock is held once it is acquired. The last column shows the time spent outside the socket lock.

To verify that Apache's thread pinning is not responsible for Affinity-Accept's performance advantage, Figure 3 presents results from the same experiment with lighttpd, which does not pin threads. Affinity-Accept again consistently achieves higher throughput. The downward slope of Affinity-Accept is due to lighttpd's higher performance that saturates the NIC: the NIC hardware is unable to process any additional packets. Additionally the higher request processing rate triggers a scalability limitation in how the kernel tracks reference counts to file objects; we have not yet explored workarounds or solutions for this problem.

The Affinity-Accept line in Figure 2 shows that the scalability of Apache improves when we use the Affinity-Accept listen socket. Part of the performance improvement comes from the reduced socket lock wait time, as shown in Affinity-Accept row of Table 2. Part of the improvement also comes from improved locality, as we evaluate next.

6.4 Cache Line Sharing

To isolate the performance gain of using fine grained locking from gains due to local connection processing, we analyze the performance of Fine-Accept. The Fine-Accept row in Table 2 confirms that Fine-Accept also avoids bottlenecks on the listen socket lock. However, Figures 2 and 3 show that Affinity-Accept consistently outperforms Fine-Accept. This means that local connection processing is important to achieving high throughput, even with fine-grained locking. In case of Apache, Affinity-Accept outperforms Fine-Accept by 24% at 48 cores and in the case of lighttpd by 17%.

Tracking misses. In order to find out why Affinity-Accept outperforms Fine-Accept, we instrumented the kernel to record a number of performance counter events during each type of system call and interrupt. Table 3 shows results of three performance counters (clock cycles, instruction count, and L2 misses) tracking only kernel execution. The table also shows the difference between Fine-Accept and Affinity-Accept. The `softirq_net_rx` kernel entry processes incoming packets. These results show that Fine-Accept uses 40% more clock cycles than Affinity-Accept to do the same amount of work in `softirq_net_rx`. Summing the cycles

Kernel Entry	Cycles		Instructions		L2 Misses	
	Total	Δ	Total	Δ	Total	Δ
`softirq_net_rx`	97k / 69k	28k	33k / 34k	-788	352 / 178	174
`sys_read`	17k / 10k	7k	4k / 4k	260	60 / 31	29
`schedule`	23k / 17k	6k	9k / 8k	450	79 / 38	41
`sys_accept4`	12k / 7k	5k	3k / 2k	666	38 / 19	19
`sys_writev`	15k / 12k	3k	5k / 4k	120	53 / 33	20
`sys_poll`	12k / 9k	3k	4k / 4k	94	39 / 17	22
`sys_shutdown`	8k / 6k	3k	3k / 3k	55	28 / 7	21
`sys_futex`	18k / 16k	3k	8k / 8k	357	56 / 45	11
`sys_close`	5k / 4k	707	2k / 2k	29	12 / 10	2
`softirq_rcu`	714 / 603	111	212 / 204	8	4 / 3	1
`sys_fcntl`	375 / 385	-10	275 / 276	-1	0 / 0	0
`sys_getsockname`	706 / 719	-13	277 / 275	2	1 / 1	0
`sys_epoll_wait`	2k / 2k	-29	568 / 601	-33	3 / 2	1

Table 3: Performance counter results categorized by kernel entry point. System call kernel entry points begin with "sys", and timer and interrupt kernel entry points begin with "softirq". Numbers before and after the slash correspond to Fine-Accept and Affinity-Accept, respectively. Δ reports the difference between Fine-Accept and Affinity-Accept. The kernel processes incoming connection in `softirq_net_rx`.

column over network stack related system calls and interrupts, the improvement from Fine-Accept to Affinity-Accept is 30%. The application level improvement due to Affinity-Accept, however, is not as high at 24%. The is because the machine is doing much more than just processing packets when it runs Apache and lighttpd. Both implementations execute approximately the same number of instructions; thus, the increase is not due to executing more code. The number of L2 misses, however, doubles when using Fine-Accept. These L2 misses indicate that cores need to load more cache lines from either the shared L3, remote caches, or DRAM.

To understand the increase in L2 misses, and in particular, what data structures are contributing to the L2 misses, we use DProf [19]. DProf is a kernel profiling tool that, for a particular workload, profiles the most commonly used data structures and the access patterns to these data structures. Table 4 shows that the most-shared objects are those associated with connection and packet processing. For example the `tcp_sock` data type represents a TCP established socket. Cores share 30% of the bytes that make up this structure.

Data Type	Size of Object (bytes)	% of Object's Cache Lines Shared	% of Object's Bytes Shared	% of Object's Bytes Shared RW	Cycles Accessing Bytes Shared in Fine-Accept, per HTTP Req
tcp_sock	1664	85 / 12	30 / 2	22 / 2	54974 / 30584
sk_buff	512	75 / 25	20 / 2	17 / 2	17586 / 9882
tcp_request_sock	128	100 / 0	22 / 0	12 / 0	5174 / 3278
slab:size-16384	16384	5 / 1	1 / 0	1 / 0	1531 / 1123
slab:size-128	128	100 / 0	9 / 0	9 / 0	1117 / 51
slab:size-1024	1024	38 / 0	4 / 0	4 / 0	882 / 24
slab:size-4096	4096	19 / 5	1 / 0	1 / 0	417 / 136
socket_fd	640	10 / 10	2 / 2	2 / 2	348 / 23
slab:size-192	192	100 / 33	17 / 2	17 / 2	- / -
task_struct	5184	10 / 0	2 / 0	2 / 0	- / -
file	192	100 / 100	8 / 8	8 / 8	- / -

Table 4: DProf results for Fine-Accept, shown before the slash, and Affinity-Accept, shown after the slash. Results for Fine-Accept show that the data types shared across multiple cores are those used by the network stack. The tcp_sock and tcp_request_sock are established and request TCP socket objects respectively. A sk_buff holds packet data and a socket_fd is used to represent an established or listen socket as a file descriptor. Data types that start with "slab" are generic kernel buffers (including packet buffers). Entries with "-" indicate that we did not collect latency data for the data structure.

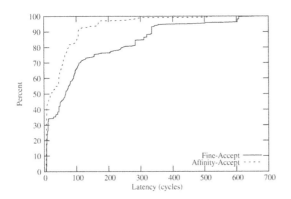

Figure 4: CDF of memory access latencies to shared memory locations reported in the right column of Table 4.

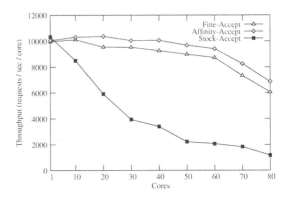

Figure 5: Apache performance with different listen socket implementations on the Intel machine.

Worse yet, these shared bytes are not packed into a few cache lines but spread across the data structure, increasing the number of cache lines that cores need to fetch. For an established socket, cores share 85% of the cache lines.

To get an understanding of how long it takes a core to access shared cache lines, we measure access times for individual load instructions directly. For the top shared data structures, DProf reports all load instructions that access a shared cache line. The set of instructions is bigger for Fine-Accept than for Affinity-Accept because Fine-Accept shares more cache lines. When collecting absolute memory access latencies for Affinity-Accept, we instrument the set of instructions collected from running DProf on Fine-Accept; this ensures that we capture the time to access data that is no longer shared. We measure the access latency by wrapping the load with rdtsc and cpuid instructions. The rdtsc instruction reads a time stamp which the hardware increments on each cycle. We use the cpuid instruction to force in-order execution of the rdtsc and load instructions. The difference between the before and after time stamps is the absolute access latency. The absolute access latency is distinct from the duration a load instruction stalls a core. The core may not

stall at all if it can execute other instructions while waiting for the load to finish. Nevertheless, the measurement is a good indication of from how far away the data is fetched.

The last column in Table 4 shows the total per request absolute latency to access the shared cache lines of each data type. Affinity-Accept reduces the number of cycles needed to access shared cache lines of tcp_sock by more than 50%. We also plot the results as a CDF in Figure 4. Accesses with long latencies are either directed to memory or to remote caches, and the CDF shows that Affinity-Accept considerably reduces long latency memory accesses over Fine-Accept.

The results in Table 4 show that Affinity-Accept removes most of the sharing. The sharing that is left is due to accesses to global data structures. For example, the kernel adds tcp_sock objects to global lists. Multiple cores manipulate these lists and thus modify the cache lines that make up the linked list pointers. The minimal amount of sharing remaining with Affinity-Accept suggests that it will continue to scale better than Fine-Accept as more cores are added.

Intel machine. We also evaluate the performance of Affinity-Accept on a machine with a different architecture. Figure 5 shows the performance of Apache and Figure 6

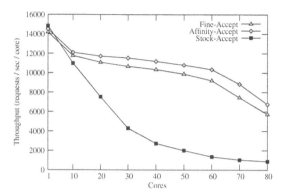

Figure 6: Lighttpd performance with different listen socket implementations on the Intel machine.

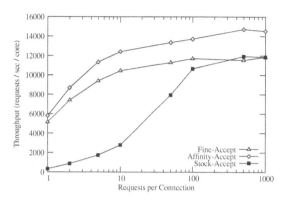

Figure 7: The effect of TCP connection reuse on Apache's throughput running on the AMD machine. The accept rate decreases as clients send more HTTP requests per TCP connection.

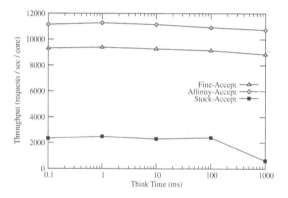

Figure 8: The effect of increasing client think time on Apache's throughput running on the AMD machine.

shows the performance of lighttpd on our Intel system. Affinity-Accept outperforms Fine-Accept by a smaller margin on this system than on the AMD machine. We suspect that this difference is due to faster memory accesses and a faster interconnect.

6.5 Load Balancer

To evaluate the load balancer we want to show two things. First, that without connection stealing, accept queues overflow and affect the performance perceived by clients. Second, that flow group migration reduces the incoming packet load on cores not processing network packets, and speeds up other applications running on these cores.

The first experiment illustrates that the load balancer can deal with cores that suddenly cannot keep up with the incoming load. We test this by running the web server benchmark on all cores but adjusting the load so the server uses only 50% of the CPU time. For each connection, the client terminates the connection after 10 seconds if it gets no response from the server. To reduce the processing capacity of the test machine, we start a build of the Linux kernel using parallel `make` on half of the cores (using `sched_setaffinity()` to limit the cores on which `make` can run). Each client records the time to service each connection, and we compute the median latency.

Running just the web server benchmark yields a median and 90th percentile latency of 200ms with and without the load balancer. This includes both the time to processes the 6 requests, as well as the two 100ms client think times, indicating that request processing takes under 1ms. When `make` is running on half of the cores, the median and 90th percentile latencies jump to 10 seconds in the absence of a load balancer, because the majority of connections time out at the client before they are serviced by the web server. The timeouts are due to accept queue overflows on cores running `make`. Enabling load balancing reduces the median latency to 230ms, and the 90th percentile latency to 480ms. The extra 30ms in median latency is due to the 100% utilization of cores still exclusively running lighttpd, and is a consequence of taking a workload that uses 50% of CPU time on 48 cores and

squeezing it onto 24 cores. If the initial web server utilization is less than 50%, the median latency falls back to 200ms.

The second experiment shows that flow group migration improves non-web server application performance. We run the same experiment as above, with connection stealing enabled, but this time measure the runtime of the kernel compile. As a base line, the compilation takes 125s on 24 cores without the web server running. Adding the web server workload with flow group migration disabled increases the time to 168s. Enabling flow group migration reduces the time to 130s. The extra 5s is due to the time it takes flow group migration to move all flow groups away from the cores running `make`. This migration actually happens twice, because the kernel `make` process has two parallel phases separated by a multi-second serial process. During the break between the two phases, Affinity-Accept migrates flow groups back to the cores that were running `make`.

6.6 Variations to the Workload

The evaluation thus far concentrated on short-lived connections. This section examines the effect of three parameters of the workload on Affinity-Accept performance: accept rate,

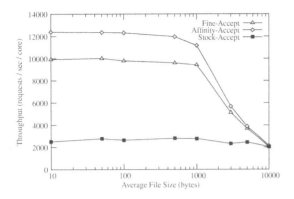

Figure 9: The effect of different average file sizes on Apache's throughput running on the AMD machine. The average file size is of all serviced files.

client think time, and average served file size. All of the experiments in this section were run with all CPUs enabled.

Accept Rate. The first workload variation we consider is HTTP connection reuse. A client can send multiple requests through a single HTTP connection, which reduces the fraction of accepts in the server's total network traffic. In previous experiments the request per connection ratio is fixed to 6; Figure 7 shows the performance of Apache as the number of requests per connection varies. In this example, Apache is configured to permit an unbounded number of requests per connection instead of the default configuration which limits connection reuse. When the number of requests per connection is small, Affinity-Accept and Fine-Accept outperform Stock-Accept as described in the earlier experiments. As connection reuse increases, total throughput increases, as there is less overhead to initiate and tear down connections. Affinity-Accept outperforms Fine-Accept at all measured points. At very high rates of connection reuse (above 5,000 requests per connection), lock contention for the listen socket is no longer a bottleneck for Stock-Accept, and its performance matches that of Fine-Accept.

Figure 7 also shows that Affinity-Accept provides a benefit over Fine-Accept even when accepts are less frequent, since Affinity-Accept reduces data sharing costs after the kernel accepts connections.

Think Time. Figure 8 shows the effect of increasing the lifetime of a connection by adding think time at the client between requests sent over the same TCP connection. This experiment holds connection reuse constant at 6 requests per connection, so it does not vary the fraction of network traffic devoted to connection initiation. It does add a variable amount of client-side think time between subsequent requests on the same connection to increase the total number of active connections that the server must track. The range of think times in the plot covers the range of delays a server might experience in data center or wide area environments, although the pattern of packet arrival would be somewhat different if

the delays were due to propagation delay instead of think time. Beyond the rightmost edge of the plot ($1s$), the server would need more than half a million threads, which our kernel cannot support. Stock-Accept does not perform well in any of these cases due to socket lock contention. Affinity-Accept outperforms Fine-Accept and the two sustain a constant request throughput across a wide range of think times.

This graph also points out the problem with NIC assisted flow redirection. In this experiment at $100ms$ of think time there are more than 50,000 concurrently active connections and at $1s$ of think time more than 300,000 connections. Such a large number of active connections would likely not fit into a current NIC's flow steering table.

Average File Size. Figure 9 shows how file size affects Affinity-Accept. The average file size for previous experiments is around 700 bytes and translates to 4.5 Gbps of traffic at 12,000 requests/second/core. Here we change all files proportionally to increase or decrease the average file size. The performance of Stock-Accept is once again low due to lock contention. At an average file size larger than 1 Kbyte, the NIC's bandwidth saturates for both Fine-Accept and Affinity-Accept; as a consequence, the request rate decreases and server cores experience idle time. The Stock-Accept configuration does not serve enough requests to saturate the NIC, until the average file size reaches about 10 Kbytes.

7. Related Work

There has been previous research that shows processing packets that are part of the same connection on a single core is critical to good networking performance. Nahum et al. [18], Yates et al. [24], Boyd-Wickizer et al. [9], and Willmann et al. [23] all demonstrate that a network stack will scale with the number of cores as long as there are many connections that different cores can processes in parallel. They also show that it is best to process packets of the same connection on the same core to avoid performance issues due to locks and out of order packet processing. We present in detail a method for processing a single connection on the same core. Boyd-Wickizer et al. [9] used an earlier version of this work to get good scalability results from the Linux network stack.

RouteBricks [10] evaluates packet processing and routing schemes on a multicore machine equipped with multiple IXGBE cards. They show that processing a packet exclusively on one core substantially improves performance because it reduces inter-core cache misses and DMA ring locking costs.

Serverswitch [17] applies recent improvements in the programmability of network components to data center networks. Using similar features within future NIC designs could enable a better match between hardware and the needs of systems such as Affinity-Accept.

In addition to network stack organization, there have been attempts to address the connection affinity problem. We describe them in the next two sections.

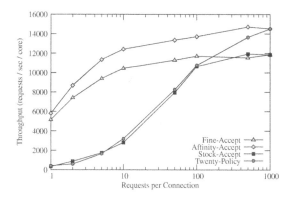

Figure 10: The effect of TCP connection length on Apache's throughput running on the AMD machine. This is a duplicate of Figure 7 but includes "Twenty-Policy": stock Linux with flow steering in hardware.

NIC	HW DMA Rings	RSS DMA Rings	Flow Steering Table (# connections)
Intel [14]	64	16	32K
Chelsio [1]	32 or 64	32 or 64	"tens of thousands"
Solarflare [16]	32	32	8K
Myricom [15]	32	32	-

Table 5: Comparison of features available on modern NICs. Entries with "-" indicate that we could not find information.

7.1 Dealing with Connection Affinity in Hardware

The IXGBE driver authors have tried to use FDir to route incoming packets to the core processing outgoing packets. They do so by updating the FDir hash table on every 20th transmitted packet to route incoming packets to the core calling sendmsg(). We call this scheme "Twenty-Policy" and Figure 10 shows its performance. At 1,000 requests per connection the NIC does a good job of routing packets to the correct core and the performance matches Affinity-Accept. At 500 requests per connection, however, maintaining the hardware table limits performance. Socket lock contention limits performance below 100 requests per connection; the table maintenance problems would still limit performance even if the socket lock were not a bottleneck.

There are a few problems with Twenty-Policy. First, it is expensive to talk to the network card. It takes 10,000 cycles to add an entry into the FDir hash table. The bulk of this cost comes from calculating the hash value, and the table insert takes 600 cycles.

Second, managing the hash table is difficult. The driver cannot remove individual entries from the hash table, because it does not know when connections are no longer active. The driver, instead, flushes the table when it overflows. It takes up to 80,000 cycles ($\sim 40\mu s$) to schedule the kernel to run the flush operation, and 70,000 cycles ($\sim 35\mu s$) to flush the table. The driver halts packet transmissions for the duration of the flush. A rate of 50,000 connections/second and a hash table with 32K entries requires a flush every 0.6 seconds. We have also confirmed that the NIC misses many incoming packets when running in this mode. Although we do not have a concrete reason, we suspect it is because the NIC cannot keep up with the incoming rate while the flush is in progress. The stopped transmission and missed packets cause TCP timeouts and delays, and the end result is poor performance.

Tighter integration with the network stack can reduce many of these costs. This is exactly the approach Accelerated Receive Flow Steering (aRFS) [13] takes. Instead of on every 20th transmitted packet, an aRFS enabled kernel adds a routing entry to the NIC on calls to sendmsg(). To avoid the kernel calculating the connection hash value on a hash table update the NIC reports, in the RX packet descriptor, the hash value of the flow and the network stack stores this value. Unfortunately, the network stack does not notify the driver when a connection is no longer in use so the driver can selectively shoot down connections. Instead, the driver needs to periodically walk the hardware table and query the network stack asking if a connection is still in use. Just as in Twenty-Policy, we see the need for the driver to search for dead connections as a point of inefficiency.

Even with aRFS, flow steering in hardware is still impractical because the third problem is the hard limit on the size of the NIC's table. Table 5 lists the table sizes for different modern 10Gbit NICs. FreeBSD developers, who are also implementing aRFS-like functionality, have raised similar concerns over hardware table sizes [20].

Additionally, currently available 10Gbit NICs provide limited hardware functionality in one way or another. Table 5 summarizes key NIC features. Each card offers either a small number of DMA rings, RSS supported DMA rings, or flow steering entries. For example, using the IXGBE NIC there is no way to spread incoming load among all cores if FDir is also used to route individual connections to particular cores. In this case, we would have to use RSS for load balancing new connections, which only supports 16 DMA rings. It is imperative for NIC manufacturers to grow the number of DMA rings with increasing core counts and provide functionality to all DMA rings.

7.2 Dealing with Connection Affinity in Software

Routing in software is more flexible than routing in hardware. Google's Receive Flow Steering patch [11, 12] for Linux implements flow routing in software. Instead of having the hash table reside in the NIC's memory, the table is in main memory. On each call to sendmsg() the kernel updates the hash table entry with the core number on which sendmsg() executed. The NIC is configured to distribute load equally among a set of cores (the routing cores). Each routing core does the minimum work to extract the information needed to do a lookup in the hash table to find the destination core. The routing core then appends the packet to a destination core's queue (this queue acts like a virtual DMA ring). The destination core processes the packet as if it came directly from the NIC. Unfortunately, routing in software does not perform as well as in hardware: achieving a 40% increase in throughput requires doubling CPU utilization [11]. Our analysis of RFS shows similar results, and points to remote memory deallocation of packet buffers as part of the problem.

The Windows [5], FreeBSD [20], and Solaris [22] kernels have multi-core aware network stacks and support RSS hardware. Both FreeBSD and Solaris have had a form of RFS before Linux. These kernels have the same connection affinity problem as stock Linux: user space and interrupt processing can happen on different cores and lead to cache line sharing. These kernels would benefit from this work.

FlexSC [21] introduces an asynchronous system call interface to the Linux kernel that allows a core other than the local core to execute a system call. With the ability to route system calls to different cores the kernel can execute system calls that touch connection state on the core processing incoming packets. The drawbacks are similar to RFS: cores need to communicate with each other to exchange request and response messages.

8. Conclusion

This paper introduced Affinity-Accept, a new design for operating systems to align all phases of packet processing for an individual network connection onto the same core of a multi-core machine, and implemented this design in Linux. This approach ensures that cores will not suffer from lock contention between cores to modify connection state, as well as long delays to transfer cache lines between cores.

An evaluation of Affinity-Accept shows that on workloads that establish new connections at high rates, such as web servers, these modifications significantly improve application performance on large multi-core machines.

Acknowledgments

This research was supported by NSF awards CNS-0834415 and CNS-0915164, and by Quanta. We thank our shepherd Jeff Mogul and the anonymous reviewers for making suggestions that improved this paper.

References

[1] Chelsio Terminator 4 ASIC. White paper, Chelsio Communications, January 2010. http://chelsio.com/assetlibrary/whitepapers/Chelsio T4 Architecture White Paper.pdf.

[2] Apache HTTP Server, October 2011. http://httpd.apache.org/.

[3] Httperf, October 2011. http://www.hpl.hp.com/research/linux/httperf/.

[4] Lighttpd Server, October 2011. http://www.lighttpd.net/.

[5] Receive Side Scaling, October 2011. http://technet.microsoft.com/en-us/network/dd277646.

[6] SMP and Lighttpd, October 2011. http://redmine.lighttpd.net/wiki/1/Docs:MultiProcessor.

[7] SpecWeb2009, October 2011. http://www.spec.org/web2009/.

[8] AMD, Inc. Six-core AMD opteron processor features. http://www.amd.com/us/products/server/processors/six-core-opteron/Pages/six-core-opteron-key-architectural-features.aspx.

[9] S. Boyd-Wickizer, A. T. Clements, Y. Mao, A. Pesterev, M. F. Kaashoek, R. Morris, and N. Zeldovich. An Analysis of Linux Scalability to Many Cores. In *Proc. OSDI*, 2010.

[10] M. Dobrescu, N. Egi, K. Argyraki, B.-G. Chun, K. Fall, G. Iannaccone, A. Knies, M. Manesh, and S. Ratnasamy. RouteBricks: Exploiting Parallelism To Scale Software Routers. In *Proc. SOSP*, 2009.

[11] T. Herbert. RFS: Receive Flow Steering, October 2011. http://lwn.net/Articles/381955/.

[12] T. Herbert. RPS: Receive Packet Steering, October 2011. http://lwn.net/Articles/361440/.

[13] T. Herbert. aRFS: Accelerated Receive Flow Steering, January 2012. http://lwn.net/Articles/406489/.

[14] Intel. 82599 10 GbE Controller Datasheet, October 2011. http://download.intel.com/design/network/datashts/82599_datasheet.pdf.

[15] Linux 3.2.2 Myricom driver source code, January 2012. drivers/net/ethernet/myricom/myri10ge/myri10ge.c.

[16] Linux 3.2.2 Solarflare driver source code, January 2012. drivers/net/ethernet/sfc/regs.h.

[17] G. Lu, C. Guo, Y. Li, Z. Zhou, T. Yuan, H. Wu, Y. Xiong, R. Gao, and Y. Zhang. ServerSwitch: A Programmable and High Performance Platform for Data Center Networks. In *Proc. NSDI*, 2011.

[18] E. M. Nahum, D. J. Yates, J. F. Kurose, and D. Towsley. Performance issues in parallelized network protocols. In *Proc. OSDI*, 1994.

[19] A. Pesterev, N. Zeldovich, and R. T. Morris. Locating cache performance bottlenecks using data profiling. In *Proc. EuroSys*, 2010.

[20] Robert Watson. Packet Steering in FreeBSD, January 2012. http://freebsd.1045724.n5.nabble.com/Packet-steering-SMP-td4250398.html.

[21] L. Soares and M. Stumm. FlexSC: flexible system call scheduling with exception-less system calls. In *Proc. OSDI*, 2010.

[22] Sunay Tripathi. FireEngine: A new networking architecture for the Solaris operating system. White paper, Sun Microsystems, June 2004.

[23] P. Willmann, S. Rixner, and A. L. Cox. An evaluation of network stack parallelization strategies in modern operating systems. In *Proc. USENIX ATC*, June 2006.

[24] D. J. Yates, E. M. Nahum, J. F. Kurose, and D. Towsley. Networking support for large scale multiprocessor servers. In *Proc. SIGMETRICS*, 1996.

TM²C: a Software Transactional Memory for Many-Cores

Vincent Gramoli

EPFL, Switzerland

vincent.gramoli@epfl.ch

Rachid Guerraoui

EPFL, Switzerland

rachid.guerraoui@epfl.ch

Vasileios Trigonakis

EPFL, Switzerland

vasileios.trigonakis@epfl.ch

Abstract

Transactional memory is an appealing paradigm for concurrent programming. Many software implementations of the paradigm were proposed in the last decades for both shared memory multi-core systems and clusters of distributed machines. However, chip manufacturers have started producing many-core architectures, with low network-on-chip communication latency and limited support for cache-coherence, rendering existing transactional memory implementations inapplicable.

This paper presents TM²C, the first software Transactional Memory protocol for Many-Core systems. TM²C exploits network-on-chip communications to get granted accesses to shared data through efficient message passing. In particular, it allows visible read accesses and hence effective distributed contention management with eager conflict detection.

We also propose FairCM, a companion contention manager that ensures starvation-freedom, which we believe is an important property in many-core systems, as well as an implementation of elastic transactions in these settings. Our evaluation on four benchmarks, i.e., a linked list and a hash table data structures as well as a bank and a MapReduce-like applications, indicates better scalability than locks and up to 20-fold speedup (relative to bare sequential code) when running 24 application cores.

Keywords Transactional Memory; Many-Cores; Concurrent Programming; Contention Management

General Terms Design, Languages, Performance

Categories and Subject Descriptors C.1.4 [*Processor Architectures*]: Parallel Architectures—Distributed architectures; D.1.3 [*Programming Techniques*]: Concurrent Programming

1. Introduction

Although not a silver bullet, Transactional Memory (TM) [20, 39] is an appealing paradigm to leverage the availability of multi-processor systems. TM allows the programmer to define a sequence of commands, called a transaction, and then to execute it atomically. In its software form, called STM, the paradigm can be implemented without requiring any specific hardware support [11, 12], at least in principle. Indeed, this is not entirely true for STMs do typically assume multi-core architectures and rely on an underlying cache-coherent system. Recently, manufacturers have started producing many-core processors [22], with the idea of increasing the number of cores placed on a single die while decreasing their complexity for enhanced energy consumption [6]. Contemporary many-cores consist of up to 100 cores, but they are soon expected to scale up to 1000. In such systems, providing full hardware cache-coherence is not affordable because of memory and time costs [3].

In this many-core context, and since the programming model is message passing, one might be tempted to apply what has been called Distributed Transactional Memory (DTM), namely, implementations of the transaction paradigm on distributed clusters of machines. The communication on such platforms being particularly expensive, classical DTMs try however to enforce as much as possible data and node locality. The setting is fundamentally different from the network-on-chip one of many-cores: messaging latencies among cores (and the memory) differ, but the size of magnitude is insignificant compared to clusters.

Perhaps more importantly, existing DTMs fail to provide strong progress guarantees. We argue that it is particularly important to ensure starvation-freedom in a many-core TM system, so that continuous contention does not repeatedly abort the same transactions. In fact, such systems are usually foreseen to support cloud applications where each individual client request, typically executed on a separate core, must eventually complete. Starvation-freedom ensures that the termination of a client request does not depend on the termination of others and it avoids livelocks.

We present in this paper TM²C, the first TM system tailored for non-coherent many-core processors. TM²C capitalizes the low latency of on-die message passing by being the first starvation-free DTM algorithm. To this end, TM^{2}C exploits visible reads and allows the detection of conflict whenever a transaction attempts to override some data read by another transaction, hence anticipating the conflict resolution, otherwise deferred to the commit phase of the reading transaction. In contrast with many-cores, high latency systems require generally to pipeline asynchronous reads (inherently invisible) to achieve reasonable performance. Visible reads allow us to utilize contention management in a way similar to STMs, yet fully decentralized, to provide starvation-freedom. TM^{2}C comes with FairCM, a companion distributed contention manager that ensures the termination of every transaction and the fair usage of the TM system by each core.

We exploit the large amount of cores by assigning the transactional application and the DTM services of TM^{2}C to different partitions of the cores so that no more than a single task is allocated per core. More precisely, two disjoint groups of cores run each of these two services, respectively. This decoupling benefits the communication load by limiting message exchanges between cores of distinct groups only. In addition and for a particular workload, TM^{2}C reduces communication further by trading read-access requests with a lightweight in-memory read validation to implement a weaker transactional model: elastic transactions [13].

We evaluate TM^{2}C on the Intel®'s Single-chip Cloud Computer (SCC), a non-coherent message passing processor. The SCC is a 48-core experimental processor relying on a 6×4 two-dimensional mesh of tiles (two cores per tile) that is claimed to be "arbitrarily scalable" [29]. On a hash table data structure and a MapReduce example application TM^{2}C performs up to 20 and 27 times better than the corresponding bare (non-transactional) applications running on a single core. We also evaluated the importance of fair contention management by comparing our FairCM scheme with alternative ones on various workloads. Particularly, FairCM performs up to 9 times better than the others on a workload with a single core running long conflict prone transactions. Last but not least, we also elaborate on the portability of TM^{2}C to cache-coherent architectures. We show that TM^{2}C is also efficient on multi-cores and we conjecture on the possible causes of performance difference when running it on multi-cores and many-cores.

The rest of the paper is organized as follows. Section 2 presents the many-core system model. Section 3 presents the services at the core of TM^{2}C and Section 4 describes the contention management policies we applied to TM^{2}C to make it starvation-free. Section 5 presents the results obtained on the Intel®'s SCC and Section 6 illustrates how the elastic transactions benefit TM^{2}C when adequately implemented. Section 7 introduces some preliminary work on porting TM^{2}C on a multi-core and Section 8 discusses privatization and portability. Section 9 positions TM^{2}C to the related work and Section 10 concludes the paper.

2. The Many-Core Model

We consider a *many-core*, a processor that embeds from tens to thousands of simpler cores than a multi-core to maximize overall performance while minimizing energy consumption [6]. The backbone of the many-core is the network-on-chip which interconnects all cores and carries the memory traffic. Every core has a private cache, however, a many-core has either a limited or no hardware cache-coherence at all. Therefore, this on-die interconnection network provides the programmer with efficient message passing. In order to increase the memory bandwidth, a many-core is connected to multiple memory controllers [1]. These controllers comprise both the private and the non-coherent shared memory of the cores.

The system is thus modelled as a fully distributed system whose *nodes*, which represent cores, are fully connected and can communicate with each other using asynchronous messages. We assume that the communication links between nodes are reliable: every message sent is eventually delivered and the links do neither duplicate nor forge new messages. In addition, we assume that nodes are non-faulty in that they respect their code specification but do not crash, and that each of them has a unique identifier. Note also that this model is sufficiently general to capture both homogeneous and heterogeneous many-cores [6].

Our aim is to guarantee that a concurrent program executing in this model is consistent (i.e., safe) and can terminate (i.e., live). To this end, we assume that a concurrent program is correctly written as a transactional program in which regions of sequential code that must appear as atomic are adequately delimited within *transactions* and that there are no infinite loops within a transaction.

Generally, a *Transactional Memory* (TM) protocol is responsible of ensuring the *atomic consistency* (i.e., opacity [15]) of transactions by wrapping all accesses delimited within the transactions and by detecting conflicts. Upon conflict detection a *Contention Manager* (CM) is called to resolve it by possibly aborting, delaying, or resuming the conflicting transactions. Our model is weakly atomic [28] in that transactional accesses are not isolated from non-transactional accesses. We do not support side effects within transactions, yet one could extend our code with irrevocable transactions that ask exclusive accesses to all responsible nodes before executing pessimistically.

As described in the remainder, our TM protocol, namely TM^{2}C, wraps any of the shared memory accesses of a transaction into a communication protocol that requests the access grant for the appropriate memory bytes. Our distributed CM, namely FairCM, assigns a priority to each transaction that totally orders them and eventually rotates the highest priority among all cores. Hence, even if each core executes an infinite amount of transactions our protocol is *starvation-free*: every transaction is guaranteed to terminate.

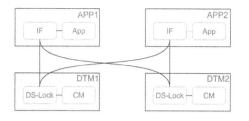

Figure 1. TM²C system's architecture and communication paths.

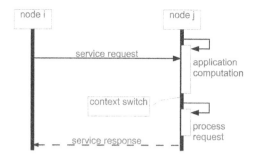

Figure 2. Multitasking – An example where the scheduling of node j affects the execution of node i.

3. TM²C, Transactional Memory for Many-Cores

This section introduces the first *Transactional Memory for Many-Cores* (TM²C). TM²C allows programmers to exploit the inherent parallelism of a many-core through a simple interface. Its main novelty lies in guaranteeing starvation-freedom without the need of an underlying hardware cache-coherence, usually required to handle contention between cores. The immediate benefit is the scalability to foreseeable processors comprising a large number of cores, where a chip-wide coherence is non-affordable due to false conflicts and cache miss overheads. To achieve this result, TM²C exploits the low network-on-chip message latency to implement a distributed contention management arbitrating contention cleverly between cores.

Specifically, TM²C provides two services as depicted in Figure 1: (i) the application service (APP) interfaces the transaction with the application and hosts the transactional runtime; (ii) the Distributed TM (DTM) service grants a data access to the requesting transactions through the distributed locking (DS-Lock) which may call the contention manager (CM) upon conflict detection. First we describe how the two services can be deployed on the nodes, then we detail their roles.

3.1 TM²C Deployment

The application and the DTM services are independent as the former is responsible for executing the transaction by requesting data accesses and the latter is responsible for deciding whether an access can be granted. Both services are fully distributed and could either be deployed on the same cores, all exploiting each core but at different time slots, or deployed on distinct cores, exploiting different cores but at the same time. The former deployment strategy thus leads to multitasking while the latter leads to dedicating roles to cores.

Multitasking. Our initial design used multitasking to allow both the application and the DTM system to run on every core. A user-space library, called libtask, was used for this implementation. We preferred libtask over POSIX threads (pthreads) because it has significantly cheaper context switches. Libtask is a simple coroutine library that gives

the programmer the illusion of threads, but the operating system sees only a single kernel thread. As a result, libtask does not support preemption.

Yet, the multitasking still suffers from an important limitation: the scheduling of node j can potentially affect the execution of node i, where $j \neq i$. One such case is represented in Figure 2. Node j is executing some application code while node i tries to execute a service request that involves node j. The request cannot be served prior to j completing its local computation. Therefore, there is a waiting period that increases the latency of the service operation.

Dedicated service cores. As a many-core provides the application programmer with a large amount of simple cores, assigning a dedicated role to each core better exploits parallelism. As a follow-up to this observation, we engineered a second deployment strategy in which disjoint sets of cores are dedicated to hosting distinct services.

Such a dedicated strategy overcomes the above issue by avoiding timing dependencies between the application and the DTM services. In addition and as depicted in Figure 1, this strategy presents another significant advantage. In fact, the cores running the same service do not need to communicate with each other. This leads to complete decoupling among the DTM cores and the application cores respectively. The advantage is actually twofold. First, the number of messages in the system decreases. Second, the communication paths among the application cores can be exploited by an application that utilizes both the TM²C in addition to direct messaging. Recall that TM²C supports weak atomicity [28], hence the transactionally accessed data should not be concurrently accessed by non-transactional code.

3.2 Distributed Lock Service

The distributed lock (DS-Lock) component is at the heart of the DTM. It provides a service for acquiring multiple-readers/single-writer revocable locks. The operations exposed by the DS-Lock incorporate the transactional semantics, and are thus non-blocking. The transactional semantics comprises of *Read After Write (RAW)*, *Write After Read (WAR)*, and *Write After Write (WAW)* conflicts. Whenever the DS-Lock detects conflicts between two transactions ask-

Algorithm 1 Read-lock acquire operation

```
 1: dsl_read_lock(id, obj):
 2:     enemy_tx ← obj.writer
 3:     if enemy_tx ≠ NULL ∩ enemy_tx ≠ id then
 4:         // if there is a writer different than id, read after write conflict, call CM
 5:         cm ← contention_manager(id, enemy_tx, RAW)
 6:         if cm = RAW then  // CM aborted current transaction
 7:             return RAW
 8:     // no writer, or CM aborted enemy
 9:     add_reader(obj, id)
10:     return NO_CONFLICT
```

ing for conflicting access grants, it calls the contention manager (described in Section 4). The contention manager is responsible for the conflict resolution.

The DS-Lock service is distributed among multiple nodes. Consequently, each node running a part of the DS-Lock service is responsible for controlling the accesses to a partition of the shared memory. In this context, the DS-Lock service is similar to some directory-based cache-coherence solutions [24, 26]. Devising a sophisticated way of allocating the data to the DS-Lock nodes is out of the scope of this work. A memory location, which in the case of TM^2C is a memory byte, is mapped to its responsible DS-Lock node by hashing.

The operations the DS-Lock implements are basically read-lock acquire/release and write-lock acquire/release. Notice that these operations are not explicitly called by the application code. The application calls the read and write wrapper functions which perform the appropriate message passing in order to implicitly trigger the corresponding DS-Lock service operations.

Read-lock acquire/release. The read-lock acquire operation attempts to acquire the read-lock corresponding to the input memory object for the requesting node identifier. It may be unsuccessful due to a RAW conflict. Algorithm 1 illustrates the pseudo-code for this operation. The read-lock release operation removes the corresponding node from the readers set of the memory object.

Write-lock acquire/release. The write-lock acquire operation attempts to acquire the write-lock corresponding to the input memory object for the requesting node identifier. It may be unsuccessful due to a WAW, or a WAR conflict. Algorithm 2 presents the pseudo-code for this operation. The write-lock release operation simply resets the writer of the memory object.

3.3 Transactions

A transaction is a delimited block of sequential code, whose shared accesses are redirected through transaction wrappers. Existing compilers wrap the shared accesses automatically[1]. The programmer could potentially benefit from these compilers as TM^2C respects the simple standard TM inter-

---
[1] The Intel® C/C++ compiler and gcc support it.

Algorithm 2 Write-lock acquire operation

```
 1: dsl_write_lock(id, obj):
 2:     enemy_tx ← obj.writer
 3:     if enemy_tx ≠ NULL ∩ enemy_tx ≠ id then
 4:         // if there is a writer different than id, write after write conflict, call CM
 5:         cm₁ ← contention_manager(id, enemy_tx, WAW)
 6:         if cm₁ = WAW then
 7:             return WAW
 8:     // no writer, or CM aborted enemy
 9:     enemy_list ← obj.readers
10:     if ¬is_empty(enemy_list) then
11:         // write after read conflict, call CM
12:         cm₂ ← contention_manager(id, enemy_list, WAR)
13:         if cm₂ = WAR then
14:             return WAR
15:     // no readers, or CM aborted enemies
16:     obj.writer ← id
17:     return NO_CONFLICT
```

face [23], even though it hides the underlying complex message passing implementation. Using the interface is the only way an application can interact with the DTM system. We discuss further interface extension to support elastic transactions in Section 6.

The interface includes operations to start and commit a transaction, which are the delimiters of the transaction. Start simply creates a new transaction, while commit (`txcommit`) tries to commit a transaction. The commit operation has to acquire the necessary write-locks, persist the changes in the shared memory, and finally release all the acquired locks. The pseudo-code of `txcommit` is depicted in Algorithm 3.

The following paragraphs describe the operations to transactionally read and write from/to a shared memory location.

Algorithm 3 Transaction commit (`txcommit`) operation

```
 1: txcommit():
 2:     tx_metadata ← get_metadata()
 3:     // try to write-lock all objects in the write-buffer
 4:     while (item ← get_item(write_buffer)) ≠ NULL do
 5:         // node responsible for obj locking
 6:         nId ← get_responsible_node(item.obj)
 7:         // similar to an RPC-like call on node nId, but uses message passing
 8:         response ← write_lock(nId, id, tx_metadata, item.obj)
 9:         if response ≠ NO_CONFLICT then
10:             // conflict and CM aborted current
11:             txabort(response)
12:         append(item, writes_locked)
13:     // all locks acquired, persist the write-set to the memory
14:     writeset_persist(writes_locked)
15:     // release all locks and update metadata
16:     wlock_release_all(id, writes_locked)
17:     rlock_release_all(id, read_buffer)
18:     update_metadata(tx_metadata)
```

Algorithm 4 Transactional read (`txread`) operation

```
1: txread(obj):
2:    obj_buf ← get_buffered(obj)
3:    if obj_buf ≠ NULL then
4:        // if memory object is in write or read buffer
5:        return obj.value

6:    // node responsible for obj locking
7:    nId ← get_responsible_node(obj)
8:    tx_metadata ← get_metadata()
9:    // similar to an RPC-like call on node nId, but uses message passing
10:   response ← read_lock(nId, id, tx_metadata, obj)
11:   if response = NO_CONFLICT then // acquired the read-lock
12:       value ← shmem_read(obj)
13:       add_read_buffer(obj, value)
14:       return value
15:   else // else conflict and CM aborted current
16:       txabort(response)
```

Visible reads. The transactional read (`txread`) is the operation used to read a memory object within the context of a transaction. Algorithm 4 contains the pseudo-code describing the steps taken for this operation.

Transactional reads work with early lock acquisition and therefore the system operates with visible reads. Early acquisition suggests that a transaction has to acquire the corresponding read-lock before proceeding to the actual read. The visibility of reads is an outcome of the early acquisition: every transaction is able to "see" the reads of the others because of the read-locks. The motivation behind this design decision is twofold.

Firstly, every many-core processor provides a fast message passing mechanism. Taking this into account, the overhead from performing synchronous read validation is acceptable. On a cluster, the messaging latency is significantly higher, hence such a synchronous solution would be prohibitive. Additionally, visible reads are often cited as problematic for affecting the cache behavior of the system. In TM^{2}C this is not the case due to the message passing. The visibility of reads does not require changing some local memory objects (e.g., locks), but using the locking service to acquire the corresponding locks by communicating with a remote node.

Secondly, visible reads are necessary for contention management. Without the read visibility, the WAR conflict detection is deferred to a validation phase typically before the commit. If a conflict is detected, it is too late to perform conflict resolution, since the writing transaction has already committed the new values.

Deferred writes. Transactional write is the operation used to write to a memory object within the context of a transaction. Transactional writes work with lazy lock acquisition

and deferred writes[2]. Every write operation is buffered and only in the commit phase the actual locks are acquired.

We chose lazy write acquisition for one main reason. If two transactions conflict, one has to be writing on the memory object. Therefore, if a transaction holds a write-lock for a long time, it increases the possibility that a conflict[3] may appear. Lazy write acquisition helps reducing the time that the write-locks are being held. For an experimental comparison of lazy against eager write acquisition see Section 5.2. Moreover, it allows the implementation of write-lock batching: requesting the locks for multiple memory objects in a single message, which can significantly reduce the number of messages.

4. Distributed Contention Management

In this section we present Contention Managers (CMs) that are fully decentralized and ensure transaction termination in the message passing model. Existing contention managers are generally centralized [14, 37, 38] and not applicable to our model as they either rely on a global counter (e.g., Greedy, PublishedTimestamp, Timestamp), randomization (e.g., KinderGarten), or on constantly changing priorities that become inaccurate when conflict resolution gets propagated in an asynchronous system (e.g., Eruption, Karma, Polka).

Our aim is to guarantee starvation-freedom so that each transaction eventually commits, hence precluding situations in which two transactions block each other (*deadlocks*) or where some transactions get repeatedly aborted (*livelocks*). Many-cores are foreseen to support cloud applications where independent client requests may contend on accessing the same service and it is highly desirable that a client request does not get repeatedly restarted because of concurrent requests from other clients. Existing DTMs usually target weaker progress properties than starvation-freedom, like lock-freedom, as it is easier to guarantee that at least one request progresses at any time.

4.1 Preliminaries

Each transaction is assigned a *priority* $\in \mathbb{Z} \times I$ allowing the contention manager to compare concurrent transactions using some identifier in I as a tie-breaker. Upon conflict between multiple transactions, the contention manager compares the priority of the conflicting transactions and aborts all of them but the highest priority one. The status of such an aborting transaction is atomically switched from pending to aborted by the contention manager. An aborted transaction is immediately restarted if not specified otherwise by the contention manager. The transaction's *lifespan* captures the period between the time the transaction starts and the time it commits, be it aborted several times in between.

---

[2] The strategy of deferring writes is also known as write-back.

[3] This conflict can be of type RAW or WAW.

The following property indicates a sufficient set of rules a CM should adhere to provide starvation-freedom on the TM^{2}C system.

PROPERTY 1. *On TM^{2}C, a contention manager satisfying the three following rules:*

a. *the priority of a transaction does not change during its lifespan,*

b. *the priorities define a total order on the set of current transactions and*

c. *the priority of a transaction should be strictly lower than the priority of the preceding committed transaction initialized by the same node*

ensures termination of every transaction.

The intuition of Property 1 is that every CM node has always (upon a conflict) up to date information about the conflicting transactions. Assume that a conflict of transactions t and t' is detected on node i. If t' performed the operation that caused the conflict, then node i has the correct data for t' since they were piggybacked in the request. Moreover, t has earlier performed an operation on node i. Node i has the correct data for t, because t's priority can only change if t has committed (rule *(a)*), in which case it would have already released the lock. Consequently, whenever there is a conflict the CM of the corresponding node will have up-to-date priorities for all the conflicting transactions. This implies that even if there are simultaneous conflicts of two (or more) transactions, the distributed CM will take a coherent decision.

Due to rule *(b)* it is guaranteed that at least one of the i's conflicting transactions, say a transaction on node j, will be able to commit its transaction, thus reducing the priorities of j's next transactions (rule *(c)*). After a finite number of transactions, transactions on j will stop having the highest priority and some other node becomes the highest priority one. This process repeats a finite number of times until node i has the highest priority among the conflicting nodes.

We now consider four contention managers in addition to the default policy, denoted by *no-CM*, that simply consists of aborting and restarting a transaction that detects a conflict. We first present two contention managers that are livelock-prone before presenting two contention managers that ensure starvation-freedom.

4.2 Back-off-Retry

The *Back-off-Retry* contention manager lets the transaction that detects the conflict abort and wait a period of time whose expected duration increases. More precisely, the waiting duration is chosen by tossing an integer that is lower than an upper bound that increases exponentially each time the same transaction aborts. When this transaction commits and a new transaction starts, the upper bound is reset to its initial value. Using TM^{2}C with the Back-off-Retry contention manager may lead to livelock as the same transaction may repeatedly

detect all the conflicts it is involved in, yet in practice transactions often terminate thanks to its randomization.

4.3 Offset-Greedy

We now describe a distributed CM, namely *Offset-Greedy*, as an adaptation of an existing centralized CM, called Greedy [14], to illustrate the difficulty of ensuring starvation-freedom in a distributed system. Greedy prioritizes a transaction using a timestamp, representing the time it started. In case of conflict, the youngest conflicting transactions are aborted in favor of the oldest one.

In a distributed system, the lack of a global clock prevents us from implementing Greedy since different nodes of the system do not have a way of taking consistent timestamps. Typically, the transaction with the most advanced clock may obtain the lower priority even though it starts first.

To bypass this limitation we introduced Offset-Greedy that estimates timestamps based on time offsets. Offset-Greedy takes the following steps whenever a node performs a transactional operation:

1. The transaction uses the node's local clock in order to calculate the time offset since the beginning of the transaction.

2. The transaction sends the request to the responsible DTM node, piggybacking the offset calculated in step 1.

3. The DTM uses the offset from the request and its local clock to estimate the timestamp of the transaction according to its own local clock.

4. The request is normally processed.

However, Offset-Greedy does not guarantee starvation-freedom. Although it ensures rules *(a)* and *(c)* of Property 1, it does not guarantee rule *(b)*. The offset calculation technique does not take into account the message delay in computing the offset. As the DTM load impacts the message delay, nodes may happen obtaining inconsistent views of timestamps. As a result, if a conflict emerges concurrently on the two nodes with inconsistent views, both transactions might abort. This scenario could lead to livelocks, however, we did not experience such an issue in our experiments.

4.4 Wholly

To address the starvation problem of the above contention managers, we propose *Wholly*. Wholly guarantees that the nodes progress altogether. The priority is the inverse of the number of transactions that each application node has already committed. Upon a conflict, the node that has committed the most transactions is aborted. If two nodes have the same number of committed transactions, then their identifiers are used as tie-breakers.

PROPERTY 2. *Wholly guarantees starvation-freedom.*

Property 2 follows from the fact that Wholly satisfies the three rules of Property 1. Wholly clearly ensures rule *(a)*.

The combination of the number of committed transactions and the node identifier (if there is a tie) define a total order on the priorities, thus satisfying rule *(b)*. Finally, Wholly satisfies rule *(c)* because whenever a transaction commits, it reduces its priority. Consequently, according to Property 1, Wholly guarantees the termination of every transaction.

Unfortunately, Wholly does not promote short transactions over longer ones, hence, long transactions may reduce the overall throughput by causing a large amount of aborts due to numerous restarts.

4.5 FairCM

To promote short transactions over longer ones we propose a last contention manager, called *FairCM*, that is fair regarding the effective transactional time of each node. Instead of using the number of committed transactions, FairCM uses the cumulative time spent on successful transaction attempts (in addition to the identifier). So, if a transaction proceeds as follows:

$$\text{Start} \rightarrow \text{Abort}_1 \rightarrow \text{Restart}_1 \rightarrow \text{Abort}_2 \rightarrow \textbf{Restart}_2 \rightarrow \textbf{Commit}$$

then only the duration from **Restart$_2$** to **Commit** will be added to the cumulative time. Upon a conflict, the transaction with the less cumulative time has higher priority. According to Property 3, FairCM guarantees starvation-freedom.

As described in Section 5.3, the particularity of promoting short transactions over longer ones may prove very important for the performance of the system. In particular, when some nodes tend to run long conflict-prone transactions. Without fairness, these nodes would degrade the overall throughput of the system.

PROPERTY 3. *FairCM guarantees starvation-freedom.*

Property 3 follows the exact same reasoning as Wholly's, using the effective transactional time for the priority instead of the number of committed transactions.

5. Evaluating TM^{2}C

In this section we evaluate TM^{2}C on the Intel®'s Single-chip Cloud Computer (SCC) (described in Section 5.1). More precisely, we use TM^{2}C with FairCM, its companion contention manager, to run a concurrent hash table benchmark (Section 5.2), and two concurrent applications: bank (Section 5.3) and MapReduce (Section 5.4). In addition, we compare the obtained performance against the one using Back-off-Retry, Offset-Greedy and Wholly. The elastic transaction evaluation is deferred to Section 6.

5.1 The Target Platform: Intel®'s SCC

The Single-chip Cloud Computer (SCC) [22] is an experimental many-core platform developed by Intel® that embeds 48 non-cache-coherent cores on a single die. Its architecture is designed to "scale, in principle, to 1,000

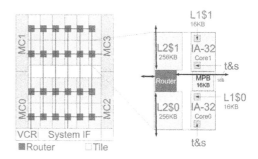

Figure 3. The SCC layout

cores" [29] and represents a 6×4 2D mesh of tiles, each tile comprising two P54C x86 cores. Figure 3 provides an overview of SCC's architecture.

Every core has 32KB of L1 cache (16KB instruction/16KB data), a separate on-tile 256KB L2 cache, and provides one globally accessible atomic test-and-set register. In addition, each tile has 16KB of SRAM, called the Message Passing Buffer (MPB), intended to be used for implementing message passing. Finally, the SCC processor includes 4 DDR3 Memory Controllers (MC), with a default of $4 * 8 = 32$GB of memory. Every core uses a partition of this memory as its local RAM and the remaining can be allocated as shared memory. An important characteristic of the SCC is the lack of any hardware cache-coherence protocol. The coherence of the shared memory and the MPB should be handled by software.

Settings. The SCC has the following five performance settings:

Setting	Tile	Mesh	DRAM
0	533	800	800
1	800	1600	1066
2	800	1600	800
3	800	800	1066
4	800	800	800

The different columns refer to the tile, the mesh, and the memory speed frequency settings (in MHz) respectively. Using a setting other than 0 proved problematic in some cases. Moreover, Intel® recommends using setting 0, consequently the data collected for this section were taken under this setting.

Except for the experiment comparing the multitasking and the dedicated DTM versions, all other measurements used the dedicated DTM TM^{2}C. Specifically, unless explicitly mentioned, the benchmarks use a 24 DTM / 24 application cores setting (the reasoning behind this allocation can be found on Section 5.3).

5.2 Hash Table

The hash table benchmark belongs to the synchrobench suite and supports three operations: a `contains` operation checks if an element exists in the hash table, an `add` inserts an el-

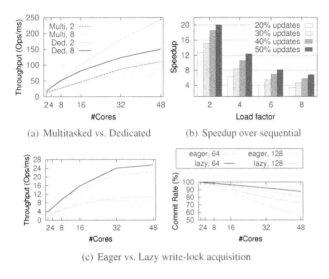

(a) Multitasked vs. Dedicated   (b) Speedup over sequential

(c) Eager vs. Lazy write-lock acquisition

Figure 4. The hash table benchmark

ement in the hash table, and a `remove` deletes an element from the hash table. We designed two versions of the operations, a transactional and a sequential.

All operations are given a random value and the update ratio indicates the amount of operations effectively modifying the hash table, while the failed updates count as read-only transactions. In addition, we tested different load factors that indicate the number of elements divided by the number of buckets.

Deployment strategies. Figure 4(a) indicates the performance of the TM^{2}C deployment strategy against the multitasking strategy as described in Section 3.1: unlike the default strategy that dedicates disjoint sets of nodes to run the application and the DTM, the multitasking strategy runs the application and the DTM on the same nodes. We tested these two deployment strategies for load factors 2 and 8 and update ratio 20%. The results outline the performance benefit of using dedicated cores for the DTM, thus confirming our initial thoughts.

Sequential speedup. Figure 4(b) depicts the improvement of TM^{2}C running the hash table over the bare sequential implementation for 20% to 50% update ratios. The transactional implementation runs on 48 cores, including 24 application cores and 24 DTM cores, and performs up to 20 times faster than its sequential counterpart running on a single core. Interestingly, we notice that the speedup decreases for higher load factors. The reason is that a higher load factor raises the duration of hash table operations, thus increasing the probability of conflicts.

Furthermore, a higher update ratios leads to lower performance, for both the sequential and the TM^{2}C versions. This is due to the additional contention induced by update operations. The performance drops for the sequential version is however more important than for the transactional one.

The initial hash table resides only in one of the four memory controllers of the SCC, thus utilizing 25% of the memory bandwidth. During the benchmark execution, each core adding a new element stores it in its closest memory controller leading to a better balancing of the load as the update ratio increases.

Eager vs. lazy write-lock acquisition. Figure 4(c) corresponds to the throughput and the commit rate of the hash table benchmark using eager and lazy write-lock acquisition. As described in Section 3.3, we decided to use lazy write-lock acquisition on TM^{2}C. With eager acquisition a transaction asks for the write-lock of the memory location on-time, when the transactional write operation is called. For these tests we implemented a fourth operation on the hash table, namely `move`, which removes an element and inserts a new one. We ran our tests with 30% total updates, 20% of which were `move` operations. We picked this workload because it includes some write operations in the middle of the transaction, thus making the two schemes performing differently.

The results follow our expectations: both schemes perform similarly under low contention, however, when the number of conflicts increases, lazy acquisition outperforms eager. Lazy acquisition has the advantage of keeping the write-locks for a smaller amount of time, hence decreasing the number of detected conflicts and increasing the commit rate, as one can notice on the right graph of Figure 4(c).

5.3 Bank

Bank is an application consisting of operations for transferring and computing the balance of bank accounts (1024 accounts, unless specified). It was first used to evaluate shared memory STMs [18] and is especially suited to evaluate the effect of livelocks on performance [17]. We compare TM^{2}C to locks using a single global lock as the SCC provides a limited number of test-and-set registers (one per core) which prevents us from using fine-grained locks. We saw two alternatives to this issue: either implementing lock-striping (medium-grained locks) or a hierarchical form of fine-grained software locks. Yet comparing TM, which is easy-to-use, to these approaches, which are difficult to use in non-cache-coherent machine, is unfair.

Contention management benefits. The left and right graphs of Figure 5(a) illustrate the TM^{2}C's throughput and commit rate, respectively, when each core performs 20% balance operations and 80% transfers with and without CM.

Without any CM, the performance drops because of a livelock. In fact, each balance operation acquires a read-lock on every account thus conflicting with concurrent update transactions. Such conflicts emerge either due to a balance operation (RAW conflict), or due to a transfer operation (WAR conflict). Using any of the four CMs performs and scales significantly better because they avoid livelocks.

Comparing different number of service cores. Due to the reasons described in Section 3.1, dedicating some cores to

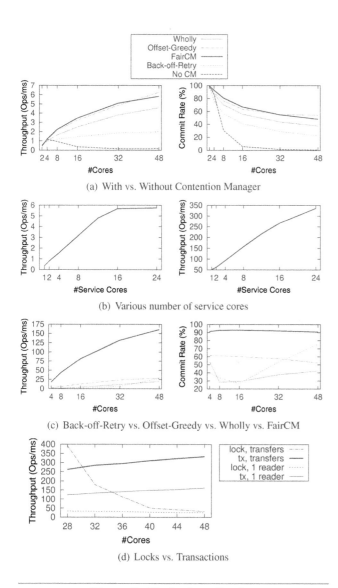

(a) With vs. Without Contention Manager

(b) Various number of service cores

(c) Back-off-Retry vs. Offset-Greedy vs. Wholly vs. FairCM

(d) Locks vs. Transactions

Figure 5. The bank application

host the TM service is advisable on a many-core. This design decision generates the interesting question of how many cores should be allocated for the service. On TM²C this is a system's parameter. We used the bank application to evaluate the performance of TM²C under different number of service cores.

Figure 5(b) depicts the performance of the bank with 20% balance and 80% transfer operations (left) and with 100% transfer operations (right). The label on the x-axis indicates the number of the service cores, all remaining cores are hosting the application.

Both results explain why we selected to dedicate half of the cores for hosting the TM service in most of our experiments. The results are explained as follows. Firstly, bank[4] does not contain any actual local computations since

it consists only of transactional operations. Therefore, the request load produced is very high. Secondly, the message passing on the SCC does not scale particularly well. As an example consider the average latency for a round-trip[5] message. In the case of 2 cores the latency is $5.1\mu s$, while with 48 it increases to $12.4\mu s$ (for more details see Section 7). Consequently, increasing the number of service cores does not entail a linear increase of the system throughput.

Comparing contention managers. Figure 5(c) illustrates in more detail the performance of TM²C when running with each of the four CMs, presented in Section 4. All cores perform transfers, except one which runs balance operations repeatedly.

Offset-Greedy and Wholly exhibit similar performance: the balance and the transfer transactions are prioritized the same, hence the "balance core" degrades the overall throughput. By contrast, FairCM prioritizes the transactions based on the transactional time they consume, therefore the balance operations are significantly more expensive than the transfers. Consequently, FairCM scales well by keeping the abort rate lower than 10%, even for 48 cores, and performs up to 12 and 9 times better than Wholly and Offset-Greedy, respectively.

Back-off-Retry performs similarly to Offset-Greedy and Wholly, but exhibits an interesting behaviour. Up to 16 cores the commit rate drops, but for more than 16 it increases. This is because the core performing balance operations tends to starve. Increasing the number of cores performing transfers, increases the probability that while the "balance core" is scanning the bank will find a RAW conflict. Interestingly, FairCM diminishes the performance of one core to the benefit of the system's throughput by committing 44 balance operations per second as opposed to the 81 of Offset-Greedy. The performance difference of FairCM to the others increases as we increase the number of bank accounts.

Comparing against locks. Figure 5(d) indicates the throughput of the bank implementation based on TM²C and on locks under two different workloads. These experiments use 2048 bank accounts.

The first workload consists in every core executing transfer operations. Up to 28 cores, the lock-based version (lock, transfers) performs better than the transactional version (tx, transfers). This is not surprising as the sequential implementation of a transfer performs only four accesses to the shared memory. However, for more than 28 cores, the performance of the lock-based version degrades due to the contention on the lock, while the transactional version keeps scaling.

The second workload comprises a core that repeatedly performs balance operations, while all others transfer. In this case, the transactional implementation (tx, 1 reader) performs and scales better than the lock-based one (lock, 1 reader), regardless of the number of cores. This is expected

---

[4] The same applies to the hash table and linked list benchmarks.

[5] A round-trip consists in a request followed by a response.

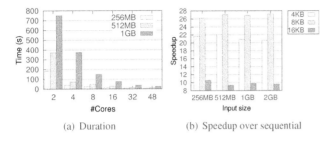

(a) Duration   (b) Speedup over sequential

Figure 6. The MapReduce application

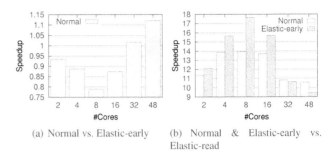

(a) Normal vs. Elastic-early   (b) Normal & Elastic-early vs. Elastic-read

Figure 7. The linked list benchmark

since in the lock-based implementation the core that executes the balance operations delays all other cores from executing the lighter transfer operations, while TM^{2}C handles this case properly.

5.4 MapReduce

To test TM^{2}C under a heterogeneous workload combining transactional and local computations, we developed a MapReduce-like application. The application takes a text file as an input and counts the number of occurrences of each letter in the file. Typical MapReduce implementations use a master node to coordinate the map and reduce phases. TM^{2}C takes here the role of allocating chunks of the file to cores and of updating the total statistics atomically thus removing the need for a master node.

Scalability and sequential speedup. Figure 6(a) indicates the experiment duration as the number of cores increases. Figure 6(b) indicates the speedup of TM^{2}C over the sequential implementation for different chunks sizes (4, 8, and 16 KBytes). Since the transactional load is low, only one core is dedicated to run the DTM service so that the 47 remaining cores run the application. Our evaluation reveals that using an 8KB chunk size leads to the best performance. This can be explained by the L1 cache size of each core. Each core has a 16KB data cache, but since it is shared between the operating system and the application it is not fully available to the latter.

6. Distributed Elastic Transactions on TM^{2}C

The *elastic transaction* model [13] is a variant of the classical transactional model particularly efficient when implementing search structures. Elastic transactions complement the classical transactions and can be optionally used instead to provide higher performance. They ensure atomicity of some high level operations while ignoring their false low level conflicts. An elastic transaction relaxes the atomicity between all the shared read accesses of its read-only prefix by requiring only that consecutive read accesses remain atomic. Consider the following sorted linked list example:

$$\text{head} \rightarrow \boxed{\text{n1}} \rightarrow \boxed{\text{n2}} \rightarrow \boxed{\text{n3}} \rightarrow \boxed{\text{n4}} \rightarrow \text{tail}$$

when a searching transaction reaches node 3, node 1 is no more relevant to the search, because even if it is modified by a concurrent transaction (producing a WAR conflict), the search will not be semantically affected. By ignoring these false conflicts, elastic transactions enable higher concurrency.

6.1 Implementations of the Elastic Transaction Model

The elastic transactional model can be implemented in various ways. We designed two implementations and a linked list data structure to evaluate it.

Our first implementation (elastic-early) employs an explicit `release` action, similar to the one used in DSTM [19], in order to discard a read entry from the transaction read set prior to commit time. In our case, this release action is used by a transaction to release one of its acquired read-locks immediately after acquiring new ones on subsequent data. Using such an early release, we can ensure that only consecutive read accesses are atomic as required by elastic transactions.

Our second implementation (elastic-read) was designed using read-validation. Instead of acquiring the relevant read-locks, the transaction performs read validation. This technique relies on the fact that if a concurrent transaction commits an update, the new value will be visible to a read validation, since the committed transaction can only write new/different values to the altered fields. For example, for the `contains` operation it is important to validate node i after stepping to node $i + 1$. If the value of node i did not change, then the transaction proceeds normally, otherwise it has to be aborted.

6.2 Evaluating the Two Implementations

The linked list benchmark also comes from the synchrobench suite and exports the same operations as the hash table (Section 5.2). We used a 2048 element sorted linked list for this test. Each core performs 20% update operations (`add`, `remove`) and 80% `contains`.

Figure 7(a) depicts the improvement of the elastic-early version over normal transactions. The elastic transactions diminish the abort rate to less than 1%, even for 48 cores, so one would expect a better performance improvement. The

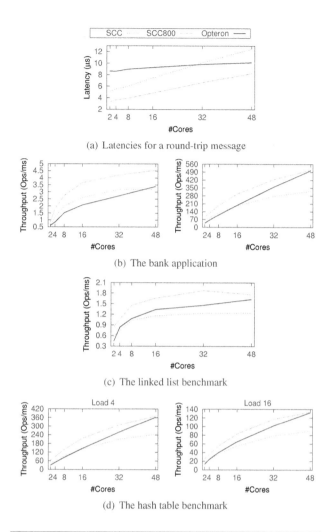

(a) Latencies for a round-trip message

(b) The bank application

(c) The linked list benchmark

(d) The hash table benchmark

Figure 8. TM^{2}C performance on many-core (SC-C/SCC800) vs. multi-core (Opteron)

reason for the limited speedup is that each early release operation requires an extra message to the DTM, thus significantly increasing the communication load of the system and producing extra transactional overheads.

Figure 7(b) depicts the speedup of the elastic-read implementation over the other two. Similarly to the elastic-early, elastic-read diminishes the abort rate. However, elastic-read additionally reduces the number of messages sent by increasing the number of accesses to the shared memory. On the SCC, a memory access is faster than a message delivery, therefore the read validation significantly increases the performance. The speedup drops for more than 8 cores due to memory congestion.

7. TM^{2}C on a Cache-Coherent Multi-Core

In order to verify the portability of TM^{2}C and evaluate its performance and scalability on a different platform we ported it on a cache-coherent multi-core machine.

7.1 Porting TM^{2}C to Multi-cores

The underlying message passing communication paradigm makes TM^{2}C easily portable to different architectures, including multi-core machines with cache-coherence support. We also ported the simple Back-off-Retry contention manager to obtain a common ground for comparison. Like the SCC, our multi-core machine also embeds 48 cores in total. More precisely, it consists of four 2.1 GHz 12-core AMD Opteron[TM] processors and 32 GB of RAM running Linux (Ubuntu 10.04 64 bit, kernel version 2.6.32). The L1 cache size is 128 KB, the L2 cache is 512 KB, and each of the processors has a 12 MB L3 cache. To take benefit of the inherent hardware cache-coherence protocol provided by the multi-core machine, we used a message passing library similar to the one of Barrelfish [3] that translates cache lines into core-to-core communication channels. Additionally, we used the SCC on both its slowest and fastest performance settings (see Section 5.1), yet note that the clock frequencies of the many-core remain more than twice slower than the one of the multi-core.

Figure 8(a) illustrates the latency of message passing in TM^{2}C. Specifically, we use the dedicated service cores (one half dedicated to the DTM, the other half dedicated to the application services) and set each application core to send one million messages evenly distributed to all service cores. Upon reception of a message, a service core responds immediately, without performing any local computation. The results reveal that asynchronous message passing on the SCC does not scale well. This degradation stems from the software-based message passing implementation of the SCC. In order to be able to asynchronously receive messages, a core has to repeatedly poll a flag for any other core to be able to detect any incoming messages. However, the SCC on its fastest setting (SCC800) provides faster message passing than the messaging implementation used on the multi-core.

7.2 Experimental Comparison

We compare TM^{2}C on the multi-core and the many-core using the bank application, the hash table and the linked list benchmarks. On 48 cores, the multi-core and SCC800 performed similarly. SCC800 has slightly faster message passing but the multi-core has significantly faster processing speed. Since our benchmarks make heavy use of the DTM service, messaging is more important than the clock frequency.

We run TM^{2}C on the bank application (Figure 8(b)) under two workloads: the first consists of 20% balance and 80% transfer operations (left graph) and the second contains only transfer operations (right graph). The former workload reveals that the SCC behaves better under heavy contention. The latter, which is a low contention workload, follows the messaging latencies. We also run TM^{2}C both on the linked list (Figure 8(c)) and the hash table (Figure 8(d)) with an initial size of 512 and 10% update ratio. Linked list is another high contention example. In this case, the multi-core performs better relatively to the bank. All operations of the linked list include a sequential search among its elements, creating some hotspots on the first elements. Consequently, caching improves the memory access latencies.

These results are preliminary and a more extensive evaluation is necessary to precisely assess the architectural artifacts that affect the observed performance. Yet, the observed results (in particular on the low contention hash table) confirm the difference of message latencies we observed on both architectures. Finally, a general observation is that TM²C seems to scale almost linearly with the number of application cores on low contended workloads when the message passing scales accordingly, independently from the considered architectures.

8. Discussion

In this section, we discuss a possible extension to support privatization and we elaborate on the portability of TM²C.

Privatization.   The action of making data private to some thread is known as *privatization*. Privatization is appealing when using transactional memory to support legacy code or to avoid the overhead of transactional wrappers when accessing some private data.

The Intel®'s SCC allows the programmer to define barriers that can be employed to guarantee that after some execution point all transactions have completed. Such technique allows to delimit a part of the program where some data is shared among transactions, and a subsequent part where the same data is private to some thread. In TM²C a more generic solution would be to implement barriers using the available message passing paths among the application cores. When the application reaches a barrier it sends a barrier-reached message to all the other application cores and blocks until it receives a message from each of them.

Portability.   As our experience illustrates (see Section 7), TM²C can be ported to platforms providing reliable asynchronous message passing. However, both versions (many-core and multi-core) utilize the existing shared memory of the platform. We have started implementing a Partitioned Global Address Space (PGAS) memory model for TM²C. We expect the benefit from PGAS to be twofold. Firstly, PGAS will increase the portability of the system since message passing will be the only requirement. Towards this direction we are working on implementing a version of TM²C running on clusters. Secondly, PGAS will act as a software-level cache-coherence protocol since the data will be locally cached on the residing node. We anticipate that the data caching will diminish the memory load and increase the performance.

9. Related Work

Transactional memory (TM) was originally proposed to simplify concurrent programming to avoid lock-related issues, like deadlocks [20, 39]. They were dedicated to shared memory systems, all relying on an underlying hardware cache-coherence [35, 36]. More recently, much effort was spent in implementing the TM abstraction on top of clusters of distributed machines, resulting in various distributed transactional memories (DTMs) [5, 25, 27, 33]. This distribution unveiled new research challenges, whose prominent one is possibly to guarantee transaction termination despite message-based synchronization. Our solution is the first to exploit many-cores to provide efficient transactions that are guaranteed to terminate.

A first class of DTMs use a separate centralized service in order to arbitrate contention between transactions. Distributed Multi-Versioning (DMV) [27] is a replicated DTM that exploits multi-version concurrency control to minimize the number of aborts. DMV operates in two different modes. The first mode requires a global token to protect the broadcast of updates in order to keep the memory consistent, but suffers from livelocks. The second mode relies on a centralized master node, which may hamper the scalability by serializing all update transactions, even non-conflicting ones. DiSTM [25] is a framework for prototyping and testing software cache-coherence protocols for TMs. The underlying TCC protocol is described as a decentralized coherence protocol, yet it needs a single master node and a global ticket mechanism.

A second class of DTMs are *control-flow* in that they handle transactions that execute on a distributed set of data. The challenge of such a control-flow technique is to guarantee that the conflict resolution adopted at some place does not contradict another conflict resolution adopted at a remote place. Cluster-TM [5] is a DTM designed for large-scale clusters. It introduces techniques for minimizing the communication among nodes by exploiting data locality. Unfortunately, Cluster-TM suffers from livelock, being unable to guarantee that an issued transaction will eventually commit. Snake D-STM [34] utilizes local contention management where each node takes decision based on local information. Such a local decision does not avoid the creation a global cycle among the aborting relations, also leading to livelocks.

A third class of DTMs are *data-flow* in that they move data among processors executing transactions and rely on an underlying cache-coherence protocol to invalidate distant transactions upon conflict detection. The crux here is rather to ensure that communication asynchrony does not stale contention management. New directory protocols were accordingly designed to move and retrieve data in a cache-coherent way [2, 21, 41] but none of them proposes a full-fledged DTM protocol. Combine [2] guarantees termination of individual move and retrieval operations, not of transactional groups of moves/retrievals, and in a distributed environment the Greedy contention manager needs nodes to synchronize their clock [40]. DecentSTM [4] is another dataflow STM that utilizes consensus on the cached copies but does not guarantee livelock freedom. As opposed to Snake D-STM, the Transactional Forwarding Algorithm (TFA) of RMI-DSTM [32] is a data flow algorithm that relies on an underlying directory protocol. It uses a modification of Lamport's clocks in order to have a synchronized timestamp to be used for object versioning. Although it guarantees strong progressiveness [16], it remains livelock-prone.

Finally and in accordance with [30, 31], there was lately an extensive work towards designing replication techniques for DTMs. To our knowledge, all existing techniques build on top of the Atomic Broadcast [10]; a rather strong and expensive (regarding communication) primitive. D^2STM [9] is a fully replicated fault-tolerant DTM which uses a certification scheme for guaranteeing the consistency among different nodes. D^2STM is also livelock-prone. Asynchronous Lease-Based Replication (ALC) [7] is a certification scheme for replicating STMs. A transaction needs to acquire the leases that correspond to its data-set in order to commit. In case of an abort and retry the transaction keeps the acquired leases, but there is a chance that these data do not coincide with the newly accessed data. For the aforementioned reason, ALC cannot guarantee livelock-freedom since every new transaction run may need a disjoint set of leases, hence it is not guaranteed it will be able to commit. The authors suggest that this problem could be bypassed if all transactions explicitly request for the whole set of leases (sort of a global lock), solution that hinders concurrency. SCert is a complement to ALC replication/certification scheme which inherits ALC's livelock problems [8].

To our knowledge TM^2C is the first TM protocol for many-core systems. It does not require any underlying cache-coherence protocol, thus avoiding data lookup, cache misses and false sharing. It detects conflicts eagerly by exploiting the low network-on-chip latency to rapidly grant shared read accesses to memory bytes. Once granted, the read access becomes visible to other transactions thus allowing conflicts to be detected at read time. Last but not least, all its transactions terminate. Upon conflict detection, any of the three companion contention managers resolve the conflict ensuring that there is no executions in which one transaction may repeatedly abort another.

10. Conclusions

We have proposed TM^2C, the first transactional memory for many-cores, the family of processors that promise to reconcile high performance with low energy consumption at the cost of trading hardware cache-coherence for message passing. TM^2C exports the standard transactional interface hiding the complex underlying on-chip communications from the programmer. It incorporates the first starvation-free distributed contention manager, FairCM, thus preventing continuous contention from repeatedly aborting the same transactions. Moreover, it ascertains the fair usage of the system by every core. We implemented and evaluated TM^2C on the Intel®'s SCC many-core processor, attesting that TM^2C exploits the scalability of many-cores even on irregular applications with many dependencies.

As for future work, we plan to introduce fault-tolerance to TM^2C. Contemporary many-cores consist of less than a hundred cores, thus the non-failure assumption is realistic. However, many-cores are expected to scale in the number of cores, hence on a single many-core node failures should become more frequent.

Another research direction is to automate the selection of the DTM service cores. Currently, the cores that host the TM^2C are statically predetermined. Under heterogeneous workloads it would be preferable for the system to vary the number of service cores depending on the transactional load.

Acknowledgments

We wish to thank our shepherd, Maurice Herlihy, and the anonymous reviewers for their fruitful comments, and the Intel® MARC Community for its support while programming on the SCC. Part of the research leading to these results has received funding from the European Union Seventh Framework Programme (FP7/2007-2013) under grant agreement 248465, the S(o)OS project.

References

[1] Dennis Abts, Natalie D. Enright Jerger, John Kim, Dan Gibson, and Mikko H. Lipasti. Achieving predictable performance through better memory controller placement in many-core cmps. In *ISCA*, pages 451–461, 2009.

[2] Hagit Attiya, Vincent Gramoli, and Alessia Milani. A provably starvation-free distributed directory protocol. In *SSS*, pages 405–419, 2010.

[3] Andrew Baumann, Paul Barham, Pierre-Evariste Dagand, Tim Harris, Rebecca Isaacs, Simon Peter, Timothy Roscoe, Adrian Schupbach, and Akhilesh Singhania. The multikernel: a new OS architecture for scalable multicore systems. In *SOSP*, pages 29–44, 2009.

[4] Annette Bieniusa and Thomas Fuhrmann. Consistency in hindsight: A fully decentralized stm algorithm. In *IPDPS*, pages 1–12, 2010.

[5] Robert Bocchino, Vikram Adve, and Bradford Chamberlain. Software transactional memory for large scale clusters. In *PPoPP*, pages 247–258, 2008.

[6] Shekhar Borkar. Thousand core chips: a technology perspective. In *DAC*, pages 746–749, 2007.

[7] Nuno Carvalho, Paolo Romano, and Luís Rodrigues. Asynchronous lease-based replication of software transactional memory. In *Middleware*, pages 376–396, 2010.

[8] Nuno Carvalho, Paolo Romano, and Luís Rodrigues. SCert: Speculative certification in replicated software transactional memories. In *SYSTOR*, pages 10:1–10:13, 2011.

[9] Maria Couceiro, Paolo Romano, Nuno Carvalho, and Luís Rodrigues. D2STM: Dependable Distributed Software Transactional Memory. In *PRDC*, pages 307–313, 2009.

[10] Xavier Défago, André Schiper, and Péter Urbán. Total order broadcast and multicast algorithms: Taxonomy and survey. *ACM Comput. Surv.*, pages 372–421, 2004.

[11] Dave Dice, Ori Shalev, and Nir Shavit. Transactional Locking II. In *DISC*, pages 194–208, 2006.

[12] Pascal Felber, Christof Fetzer, and Torvald Riegel. Dynamic performance tuning of word-based software transactional memory. In *PPoPP*, pages 237–246, 2008.

[13] Pascal Felber, Vincent Gramoli, and Rachid Guerraoui. Elastic Transactions. *DISC*, pages 93–107, 2009.

[14] Rachid Guerraoui, Maurice Herlihy, and Bastian Pochon. Toward a theory of transactional contention managers. In *PODC*, pages 258–264, 2005.

[15] Rachid Guerraoui and Michal Kapalka. On the correctness of transactional memory. In *PPoPP*, pages 175–184, 2008.

[16] Rachid Guerraoui and Michal Kapalka. The semantics of progress in lock-based transactional memory. In *POPL*, pages 404–415, 2009.

[17] Derin Harmanci, Vincent Gramoli, Pascal Felber, and Christof Fetzer. Extensible transactional memory testbed. *JPDC*, 70(10):1053–1067, 2010.

[18] Maurice Herlihy, Victor Luchangco, and Mark Moir. A flexible framework for implementing software transactional memory. In *OOPSLA*, pages 253–262, 2006.

[19] Maurice Herlihy, Victor Luchangco, Mark Moir, and William Scherer. Software transactional memory for dynamic-sized data structures. In *PODC*, pages 92–101, 2003.

[20] Maurice Herlihy and J. Eliot B. Moss. Transactional memory: architectural support for lock-free data structures. In *ISCA*, pages 289–300, 1993.

[21] Maurice Herlihy and Ye Sun. Distributed transactional memory for metric-space networks. In *DISC*, pages 58–208, 2005.

[22] J. Howard, S. Dighe, Y. Hoskote, S. Vangal, D. Finan, G. Ruhl, D. Jenkins, H. Wilson, N. Borkar, G. Schrom, F. Pailet, S. Jain, T. Jacob, S. Yada, S. Marella, P. Salihundam, V. Erraguntla, M. Konow, M. Riepen, G. Droege, J. Lindemann, M. Gries, T. Apel, K. Henriss, T. Lund-Larsen, S. Steibl, S. Borkar, V. De, R. Van Der Wijngaart, and T. Mattson. A 48-core IA-32 message-passing processor with DVFS in 45nm CMOS. In *ISSCC*, pages 108–109, 2010.

[23] intel. Intel transactional memory abi. http://software.intel.com/file/8097, 2009.

[24] Leonidas Kontothanassis and Michael Scott. Software cache coherence for large scale multiprocessors. In *HPCA*, pages 286–295, 1995.

[25] Christos Kotselidis, Mohammad Ansari, Kim Jarvis, Mikel Luján, Chris Kirkham, and Ian Watson. DiSTM: A Software Transactional Memory Framework for Clusters. In *ICPP*, pages 51–58, 2008.

[26] Daniel Lenoski, James Laudon, Kourosh Gharachorloo, Anoop Gupta, and John Hennessy. The directory-based cache coherence protocol for the DASH multiprocessor. In *ISCA*, pages 148–159, 1990.

[27] Kaloian Manassiev, Madalin Mihailescu, and Cristiana Amza. Exploiting distributed version concurrency in a transactional memory cluster. In *PPoPP*, pages 198–208, 2006.

[28] Milo Martin, Colin Blundell, and E. Lewis. Subtleties of transactional memory atomicity semantics. *IEEE Comput. Archit. Lett.*, 5, 2006.

[29] Timothy G. Mattson, Michael Riepen, Thomas Lehnig, Paul Brett, Werner Haas, Patrick Kennedy, Jason Howard, Sriram Vangal, Nitin Borkar, Greg Ruhl, and Saurabh Dighe. The 48-core SCC processor: the programmer's view. In *SC*, pages 1–11, 2010.

[30] Paolo Romano, Nuno Carvalho, and Luís Rodrigues. Towards distributed software transactional memory systems. In *LADIS*, pages 4:1–4:4, 2008.

[31] Paolo Romano, Luís Rodrigues, Nuno Carvalho, and João Cachopo. Cloud-tm: harnessing the cloud with distributed transactional memories. *SIGOPS Oper. Syst. Rev.*, pages 1–6, 2010.

[32] Mohamed Saad and Binoy Ravindran. Control flow distributed software transactional memory. In *SSS*, 2011.

[33] Mohamed Saad and Binoy Ravindran. Supporting STM in Distributed Systems: Mechanisms and a Java Framework. In *Transact*, 2011.

[34] Mohamed Saad and Binoy Ravindran. Transactional Forwarding Algorithm. Technical report, Virigina Tech, 2011.

[35] Bratin Saha, Ali-Reza Adl-Tabatabai, Anwar Ghuloum, Mohan Rajagopalan, Richard L. Hudson, Leaf Petersen, Vijay Menon, Brian Murphy, Tatiana Shpeisman, Eric Sprangle, Anwar Rohillah, Doug Carmean, and Jesse Fang. Enabling scalability and performance in a large scale CMP environment. In *EuroSys*, pages 73–86, 2007.

[36] Bratin Saha, Ali-Reza Adl-Tabatabai, Richard L. Hudson, Chi Cao Minh, and Benjamin Hertzberg. McRT-STM: a high performance software transactional memory system for a multi-core runtime. In *PPoPP*, pages 187–197, 2006.

[37] William Scherer and Michael Scott. Contention Management in Dynamic Software Transactional Memory. In *CSJP*, 2004.

[38] William Scherer and Michael Scott. Advanced contention management for dynamic software transactional memory. In *PODC*, page 240, 2005.

[39] Nir Shavit and Dan Touitou. Software transactional memory. In *PODC*, pages 204–213, 1995.

[40] Bo Zhang. *On the Design of Contention Managers and Cache-Coherence Protocols for Distributed Transactional Memory*. PhD thesis, Virginia Tech, 2009.

[41] Bo Zhang and Binoy Ravindran. Relay : A Cache-Coherence Protocol for Distributed Transactional Memory. In *OPODIS*, pages 48–53, 2009.

BWS: Balanced Work Stealing for Time-Sharing Multicores

Xiaoning Ding
Intel Labs, Pittsburgh, PA
xiaoning.ding@intel.com

Kaibo Wang
The Ohio State University
wangka@cse.ohio-state.edu

Phillip B. Gibbons
Intel Labs, Pittsburgh, PA
phillip.b.gibbons@intel.com

Xiaodong Zhang
The Ohio State University
zhang@cse.ohio-state.edu

Abstract

Running multithreaded programs in multicore systems has become a common practice for many application domains. Work stealing is a widely-adopted and effective approach for managing and scheduling the concurrent tasks of such programs. Existing work-stealing schedulers, however, are not effective when multiple applications time-share a single multicore—their management of steal-attempting threads often causes unbalanced system effects that hurt both workload throughput and fairness.

In this paper, we present BWS (Balanced Work Stealing), a work-stealing scheduler for time-sharing multicore systems that leverages new, lightweight operating system support. BWS improves system throughput and fairness via two means. First, it monitors and controls the number of awake, steal-attempting threads for each application, so as to balance the costs (resources consumed in steal attempts) and benefits (available tasks get promptly stolen) of such threads. Second, a steal-attempting thread can yield its core directly to a peer thread with an unfinished task, so as to retain the core for that application and put it to better use. We have implemented a prototype of BWS based on Cilk++, a state-of-the-art work-stealing scheduler. Our performance evaluation with various sets of concurrent applications demonstrates the advantages of BWS over Cilk++, with average system throughput increased by 12.5% and average unfairness decreased from 124% to 20%.

Categories and Subject Descriptors D.4.1 [*Operating Systems*]: Process Management—Scheduling; D.3.4 [*Programming Languages*]: Processors—Run-time environments

Keywords work stealing; multicore; time sharing; fairness

1. Introduction

In the multicore era, an application relies on increasing its concurrency level to maximize its performance, which often requires the application to divide its work into small tasks. To efficiently distribute and execute these tasks on multicores, fine-grained task manipulation and scheduling must be adopted [Saha 2007]. A common practice is that the application spawns multiple worker threads (*workers* for brevity) and distributes the tasks dynamically among its workers with a user-level task scheduler.

Work stealing [Blumofe 1994, Burton 1981], as a standard way to distribute tasks among workers, has been widely adopted in both commercial and open-source software and libraries, including Cilk [Blumofe 1995, Frigo 1998] and Cilk++ [Leiserson 2010], Intel Threading Building Blocks (TBB) [Kukanov 2007], Microsoft Task Parallel Library (TPL) in the .NET framework [Leijen 2009], and the Java Fork/Join Framework [Poirier 2011]. In work stealing, workers execute tasks from their local task queue. Any newly spawned tasks are added to the local queue. When a worker runs out of tasks, it steals a task from another worker's queue and executes it. Work stealing has proven to be effective in reducing the complexity of parallel programming, especially for irregular and dynamic computations, and its benefits have been confirmed by several studies [e.g., Navarro 2009, Neill 2009, van Nieuwpoort 2001].

Existing work-stealing schedulers, however, are not effective in the increasingly common setting where multiple applications time-share a single multicore. As our results show, state-of-the-art work-stealing schedulers suffer from both system throughput and fairness problems in such settings. An underlying cause is that the (time-sharing) operating system has little knowledge on the current roles of the threads, such as whether a thread is (i) working on an unfinished task (a *busy worker*), (ii) attempting to steal tasks when available tasks are plentiful (a *useful thief*), or (iii) attempting to steal tasks when available tasks are scarce (a *wasteful thief*). As a result, wasteful thieves can consume resources that should have been used by busy workers or useful thieves. Existing work-stealing schedulers try to mitigate this problem by having wasteful thieves yield their cores spontaneously. However, such yielding often leads to significant unfairness, as a frequently yielding application tends to lose cores to other concurrent applications. Moreover, system throughput suffers as well because the yielded core may fail to go to a busy worker or may be switched back to the wasteful thief prematurely.

In this paper, we present BWS (Balanced Work Stealing), a work-stealing scheduler for time-sharing multicore systems that leverages new, lightweight operating system support. BWS improves both system throughput and fairness using a new approach that minimizes the number of wasteful thieves by putting such thieves into sleep and then waking them up only when they are likely to be useful thieves. (Useful thieves become busy workers as soon as they successfully steal a task.) Moreover, in BWS a wasteful thief can yield its core directly to a busy worker for the same application, so as to retain the core for that application and put it to better use.

We have implemented BWS in Cilk++ and the Linux kernel, and performed extensive experiments with concurrent running benchmarks. Our experiments show that, compared with the original Cilk++, BWS improves average system throughput by 12.5% and reduces average unfairness from 124% to 20%. The experiments also show another benefit of BWS, which is to reduce the performance variation. On average, BWS reduces the performance variation by more than 11% as measured by the coefficient of variation of execution times.

The rest of the paper is organized as follows. Section 2 presents further background on prior work-stealing schedulers and their limitations, and the limitations of current OS support for work stealing. Section 3 and Section 4 describe the design and implementation of BWS, respectively. Section 5 provides a comprehensive evaluation of BWS. Section 6 discusses related work. Finally, Section 7 concludes the paper.

2. Problem: Time-Sharing Work-Stealing Applications

In this section, we first discuss the basics of work stealing in more detail, and then look into the challenges of work stealing in multiprogrammed environments. Next, we describe ABP, a state-of-the-art work stealing scheduler, and discuss its limitations. Finally, we discuss the limitations of current OS support for efficient and fair work stealing.

2.1 Work Stealing Basics

A work-stealing software system provides application developers with a programming interface for specifying parallel tasks over a shared memory. The system handles the tasks as parallel procedure calls, and uses stack frames as the major data structure for bookkeeping task information. To minimize the overhead associated with handling fine-grained

tasks, it uses lazy task creation techniques [Mohr 1991]. We will refer to an application developed and supported by a work-stealing software system as a *work-stealing application*. In practice, such applications span a wide spectrum, including document processing, business intelligence, games and game servers, CAD/CAE tools, media processing, and web search engines.

A *user-level task scheduler* manages tasks and distributes then dynamically among the worker threads (*workers*). It uses a queue to manage the tasks ready to execute for each worker, one queue per worker. During the execution, each worker dequeues the tasks from its queue and executes them. New tasks dynamically generated in the execution (e.g., by a *spawn* or *parallel for* in Cilk++) are enqueued into the worker's task queue. When a worker runs out of tasks, the worker (*thief*) selects another worker (referred to as a *victim*) and tries to steal some tasks from the victim's task queue. If there are available tasks in the victim's queue, the steal is successful, and the thief dequeues some tasks from the victim's queue and continues to process the tasks. Otherwise, the thief selects another victim. Recall from Section 1 that workers processing and generating tasks are *busy workers*, and that we informally distinguish between *useful thieves*, who help distribute tasks promptly whenever there is available parallelism, and *wasteful thieves*, who waste resources on unsuccessful steal attempts.

2.2 Issues of Work Stealing with Multiprogramming

Rapid increases in the number of cores and memory capacity of multicore systems provide a powerful multiprogramming environment for concurrently running multiple jobs and parallel applications. One multiprogramming management option is to time-slice all the cores so that each application is granted a dedicated use of the cores during its scheduling quanta. This approach suffers from low efficiency when some applications can only partially utilize the cores. Similarly, a static partitioning of the cores among the applications (i.e., space-sharing) suffers from the same inefficiencies. Approaches such as process control that dynamically partition the cores among the applications at process granularity [McCann 1993, Tucker 1989] improve upon the static case, but their OS-level mechanisms are slow to react to application phase changes. Moreover, such approaches impose a space-sharing paradigm into standard (time-sharing) operating systems. Thus, work stealing has been advocated as a powerful and effective approach to scheduling in multiprogrammed multicores [Blumofe 1998], where several parallel applications are executed concurrently.

However, early studies on work stealing in multiprogrammed environments demonstrated a tension between how aggressively thieves try to steal work (in order to quickly balance loads) and the wasted resources such steal attempts incur [Blumofe 1998]. In effect, work stealing is a double-edged sword. When a thief cannot obtain tasks quickly, the unsuccessful steals it performs waste computing resources, which could otherwise be used by other threads. More importantly, the execution of thieves may impede the execution of busy workers that would generate new tasks, causing livelock where no workers make useful progress. If unsuccessful steals are not well controlled, applications can easily be slowed down by 15%–350% [Blumofe 1998].

2.3 The ABP Algorithm and its Limitations

To handle the above problems, work-stealing schedulers (e.g., those in Cilk++ and Intel TBB) implement a yielding mechanism, based on the solution proposed by Arora, Blumofe, and Plaxton (referred to herein as **ABP**, and shown in Algorithm 1[1]) [Arora 1998, Blumofe 1998]. When a worker runs out of tasks, it yields its core spontaneously to give way to other threads (line 16). The worker is repeatedly switched back to make steal attempts, and if the attempts fail, the worker yields the core again. It repeats these operations until it successfully steals a task or the computation completes.

Algorithm 1 – ABP Work Stealing Algorithm

```
1:  t : a task
2:  w : current worker
3:  v : a victim worker w selects to steal from
4:
5:  procedure RANDOMSTEAL(w)
6:      Randomly select a worker v as a victim
7:      if w can steal a task t from v then
8:          enqueue t
9:      end if
10: end procedure
11:
12: repeat
13:     if local task queue is not empty then
14:         dequeue a task t and process t
15:     else
16:         yield()
17:         RandomSteal(w)
18:     end if
19: until work is done
```

2.3.1 Drawbacks of ABP

ABP, while the state-of-the-art, suffers from two critical drawbacks for time-sharing multicores: significant unfairness and degraded throughput. Workers in ABP use the *yield* system call to relinquish their cores. *When* they get switched back (i.e., rescheduled by the OS) to continue stealing is determined by OS scheduling policies and the workloads on the system, instead of the availability of tasks ready for steals. If thieves for an application cannot resume steal-

ing when tasks become available (i.e., when they transition from wasteful thieves to useful thieves), the concurrency level of the application is limited. Significant unfairness arises when such limiting of concurrency is applied unevenly across co-running applications. As will be illustrated below and demonstrated in Section 5, such scenarios are common when ABP is used in multiple work-stealing applications co-running on time-sharing multicores. The unfairness also arises when work-stealing applications share the same set of cores with non-work-stealing applications (e.g., pthread applications). In general, the more frequently a work-stealing application yields its cores, the more its execution is delayed.

While *unfairness* arises whenever yielding thieves are not switched back for their work in time, *throughput* is degraded whenever wasteful thieves either (i) fail to yield their cores or (ii) yield their cores but are switched back prematurely. Depending on OS scheduling policies, there are cases in which *yield* calls return without actually relinquishing the cores, for example, when the caller is the only ready thread or the thread with the highest priority on the core. This makes the yielding mechanism ineffective. Because the OS is not aware of whether or not a thread is a wasteful thief, multiple wasteful thieves may be scheduled on the same core. Such thieves yield the core back and forth wasting resources without making progress. If there are suspended threads (perhaps from a different application) that are ready to do useful work, these threads are needlessly delayed, reducing overall system throughput.

2.3.2 Illustrative Examples

We will now provide a quantitative illustration of the above problems using a few representative experiments. We select four benchmarks, BFS, EP, CG, and MM, and run them on a 32-core machine. (Please refer to Section 5 for benchmark description and machine configuration.) In the experiments, we first run each benchmark alone to get its solo-run execution time. Then, we run two benchmarks concurrently to see how much their executions are slowed down due to the co-running. As they may have different execution times, we run each benchmark multiple times so that their executions are fully overlapped.

We first use our results for BFS and EP to illustrate the fairness problem. Compared to the solo-runs, BFS is slowed down significantly by *377%*, while EP is slightly slowed down by *5%*. We define unfairness as the difference between the two slowdowns, in this case 372%. Though BFS creates 32 workers and can achieve a speed up of 21 when it runs alone on the 32 cores, we find that it has only about 5 active workers when it co-runs with EP. This experiment clearly confirms that the actual concurrency levels of work-stealing applications can be seriously limited when they co-run with other applications, because their workers may yield cores prematurely and may not be rescheduled in time.

---

[1] Detailed implementations may vary in different work-stealing software systems. For example, Cilk++ implements the algorithm faithfully, while in Intel TBB a worker yields its core when the number of failed steals exceeds a threshold. Though the implementations may vary, the problems we identify (and address) are the same.

To illustrate the throughput problem, we use our results for CG and MM. After we run each of CG and MM alone to obtain its solo-run execution time, we run them concurrently in two different scenarios. In the first scenario, the number of workers in each application is 32, and in the second scenario, CG has 16 workers and MM has 32 workers. The first scenario represents the case in which the number of thieves in CG is not controlled and its workers may yield cores frequently. The second scenario represents the case in which the number of thieves of CG is under control, and yieldings are less frequent than those in the first scenario. This is because each worker has more work to do and spends a larger proportion of its time working than in the first scenario. We compare the execution times of CG and MM in these two scenarios against their solo-run execution times with 32 workers.

In the first scenario, due to the co-running, the execution time of CG is significantly increased by 144%, while the execution time of MM is increased by only 37%. In the second scenario, the execution time of CG is increased by 97%, and the execution time of MM is increased by 12%. In both scenarios, the execution of CG is delayed by much larger percentages than the execution of MM. This unfairness is caused because the workers in CG yield cores more frequently than the workers in MM. Compare to the first scenario, reducing the number of workers in CG in the second scenario improves the performance of *both* applications. This indicates that in the first scenario, the yielding mechanism is only partially successful in reducing the resource waste caused by steal attempts.

The experiments also show that co-running the two work-stealing applications together may increase the throughput compared to time-slicing all the cores (so that each application gets all the cores during its slice). This is indicated by the slowdowns of the benchmarks being less than 100% in the second scenario, and is consistent with previous studies [Iancu 2010]. We have also co-run CG and MM with a non-yielding work-stealing scheduler, and found that CG was slowed down by more than 600% and MM was slowed down by about 100%. This significant performance degradation confirms the observation in a previous study [Blumofe 1998]. It also demonstrates the need for a work-stealing scheduler that can make efficient use of computing resources on multicores.

2.4 OS Limitations and Insufficient Mechanisms to Support Work Stealing

As discussed above, the OS has little knowledge on the current roles of the threads, such as whether a thread is a busy worker, a useful thief or a wasteful thief. As a result, it may, for example, suspend a busy worker to schedule a wasteful thief. Moreover, it is unable to properly schedule thieves, likely either (i) delaying an application's execution by schedling too few (useful) thieves, or (ii) reducing system throughput by scheduling too many (wasteful) thieves.

Operating systems do provide several mechanisms that could address this lack of user-level information, through its existing API. One type of such mechanisms is policy-based. For example, an application can choose one of a few pre-cooked scheduling algorithms, or a thread can adjust its scheduling priority. However, these mechanisms depend on the scheduling policies hard-coded in the OS, which lack the flexibility to meet the customized scheduling requirements of work-stealing applications.

The other type of mechanisms increases the flexibility by enabling a thread to voluntarily suspend its execution. But, which thread the core will be granted to is still determined by OS scheduling policies. Operating systems usually provide three suspension mechanisms, but none of them can meet the requirements of work-stealing schedulers for fairness and throughput efficiency.

The first suspension mechanism, the *yield* system call, makes its caller thread relinquish its core without blocking. The OS scheduler puts back the caller into a ready thread queue, and makes a rescheduling decision to allow other threads to run. The caller will be rescheduled automatically later by the OS scheduler. The other two suspension mechanisms are sleeping based. A thread can be put into sleep by waiting for a condition denoted by a variable to become true. When the thread sleeps, the core is granted to other threads. When the condition is met, the thread is woken up and put back to the ready thread queue to be scheduled. A thread can also be put into sleep by waiting for a timer to expire.

The above mechanisms incur unfairness when a work-stealing application time-shares the same set of cores with other applications. No matter which of the three suspension mechanisms is used, if the workers relinquish their cores frequently, other applications can take advantage of this and get more chances to run. The problem is more serious if the *yield* mechanism is used, because *yield* indicates that the caller is currently not eager to run and the OS scheduler is usually reluctant to reschedule it very soon. As we have explained, the use of the *yield* system call in work-stealing schedulers also incurs performance concerns, because the *yield* callers may fail to yield their cores, or may be switched back prematurely due to other *yield* calls.

In summary, current operating systems do not provide the mechanisms that can meet the requirements of work-stealing schedulers. This makes work-stealing schedulers unable to effectively address the fairness and throughput issues when they adjust the concurrency levels of work-stealing applications. To solve this problem, we propose a new task scheduling algorithm and new OS support to establish a balanced work-stealing (BWS) system, which will be presented in the next section.

3. The Design of BWS

In this section we describe the design of BWS, including the work-stealing algorithm used in BWS and the new

OS support. Our design is motivated by the considerations and issues outlined in the previous section. Our goals are to maximize throughput and minimize unfairness. We define *unfairness* to be the difference between the larger and smaller slowdowns among co-running applications, where slowdown is relative to the application's performance in isolation.

3.1 BWS Overview

BWS abides by the following three principles in order to minimize the extent that thieves impede busy workers, the resource waste, and the unfairness.

- The *priority principle*. The timeslices that the OS scheduler allocates to a work-stealing application should be used for processing tasks first. Only extra timeslices that are not being used by workers for processing tasks are used for thieves to do work stealing. This is mainly to prevent the execution of thieves from impeding the execution of busy workers. It also helps to put computing resources to best use.

- The *balance principle*. To maintain a high throughput for a work-stealing application, the cost of having steal attempts must be paid in order to quickly distribute dynamically generated tasks. However, the cost must be controlled: too many thieves will not improve application throughput.

- The *efficiency principle*. Both throughput and fairness are improved by having each application running at high parallel efficiency. If an application phase can make highly productive use of additional cores, its concurrency level should be increased in order to acquire more time slices.

At a high level, BWS enforces the *priority principle* by making thieves yield their cores to busy workers. It achieves the *balance principle* by dynamically putting thieves into sleep or waking them up. It realizes the *efficiency principle* by waking up sleeping thieves whenever there are tasks waiting to be stolen, in order to increase the application's concurrency level.

In more detail, the work-stealing algorithm in BWS adjusts the number of sleeping thieves based on how easily thieves can find tasks to steal. When it is easy for thieves to find tasks, more thieves are woken up to maximize throughput. Otherwise, if a thief has performed a number of unsuccessful steals, it puts itself into sleep and relinquishes its core to save computing resources. Every time a thief fails to steal from a victim, it checks the status of the victim. If the victim is working on an unfinished task but is currently preempted, the thief yields its core directly to the victim. Otherwise, the thief tries to steal from another victim.

Our design relies on two operating system features not found in current operating systems, which we now introduce:

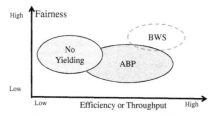

Figure 1. BWS improves both fairness and throughput, compared to current work-stealing implementations

- The OS discloses the running status of the workers to the work-stealing scheduler.

- The OS provides a new yielding facility, which enables a worker to yield its core directly to one of its peer workers.

These are discussed in further detail in Section 4. The first mechanism enables the work-stealing scheduler to find a thread that needs computing resources in a timely manner. The second mechanism enables the above step where a thief yields its core directly to the (busy but preempted) victim.

Note that BWS' use of sleep/wake-up to adjust the number of executing thieves has two key advantages over ABP's use of yield. First, it prevents thieves from being scheduled prematurely. While yielded threads can be switched back at any time, sleeping thieves cannot be switched back as long as they are asleep. Second, because the action of waking-up a thread indicates there are some tasks waiting to be processed by the thread, the thread can be rescheduled at the earliest time supported by the OS scheduler. Thus, awakened thieves can resume stealing promptly to increase the application's concurrency level. Yielded threads, in contrast, have low OS priority to be rescheduled.

Figure 1 depicts a qualitative comparison of BWS, ABP, and a work-stealing scheduler without any yielding mechanism. The X-axis represents how efficiently computing resources are used to execute work-stealing applications. The more efficient, the higher throughput the system will achieve. The Y-axis shows the fairness. With the "No Yielding" scheduler, unsuccessful steals waste computing resources and delay task processing. Thus, the efficiency and system throughput are low. ABP improves efficiency and throughput, but at the cost of fairness. Compared with ABP, BWS addresses the fairness issue, and further improves efficiency and throughput.

3.2 BWS Work Stealing Algorithm

Waking up sleeping thieves requires the involvement of non-sleeping workers to detect the availability of tasks and make wake-up system calls. Busy workers generate new tasks and have the information on whether tasks are available. Thus, an intuitive solution is to have busy workers wake up sleeping workers. However, this violates the work-first principle, because work overhead is increased.[2] To minimize the impact on work overhead, BWS lets thieves wake up sleeping workers.

Algorithm 2 shows the work stealing algorithm. As discussed above, management work is conducted by thieves to minimize the work overhead. Thus, we present only the algorithm for stealing. This algorithm is called whenever the worker's local task queue is empty.

When a thief steals a task successfully, it tries to wake up two sleeping workers (lines 11–15 in Algorithm 2). However, because a thief turns into a busy worker when it gets a task to process, waking up other workers will delay the execution of the task. To minimize the overhead, BWS offloads this management work to other thieves. For this purpose, BWS uses a counter (referred to as the *wake-up counter*) for each worker to bookkeep the number of wake-ups it desires to issue. The actual wake-up operations are to be carried out by other thieves. Thus, this worker starts to process the task immediately after it updates its wake-up counter. When a thief finds a preempted busy worker (lines 18–19), it yields the core to the busy worker.

A thief carries out management work only when it cannot get a task or yield its core to a busy worker (lines 21–40). Specifically, if the victim is a busy worker and the wake-up counter of the victim is greater than 0, it reduces the wake-up counter of the victim by 1 and increases the wake-up counter of itself by 1, implying that it will handle one wake-up operation for the worker. Then, it continues to steal. If the victim a thief tries to steal from is sleeping and the thief has pending wake up operations to process, it wakes up the sleeping worker.

To avoid the high cost associated with global synchronization impacting scalability, workers in BWS function in a peer-to-peer manner. Each thief relies on the information accumulated in its two local counters to determine whether it is a useful thief or a wasteful thief. One is the wake-up counter. The other is the *steal counter*. When a worker becomes a thief, it starts to count how many unsuccessful steals it has made with the steal counter. It is considered to be a useful thief as long as the counter value is below a pre-set threshold. When the counter value exceeds the threshold, it considers whether to sleep. It first checks the wake-up counter. If the wake-up counter is 0, it is considered to be a wasteful thief and is put into sleep. Otherwise, it reduces the wake-up counter by 1 and resets the steal counter. This is to cancel out

---

<hr>

[2] Work overhead measures the overhead spent on task scheduling. It is defined as the ratio between the execution time of a work-stealing application running with a single thread (with the overhead to support task scheduling) and the execution time of its sequential version (without any scheduling overhead) [Frigo 1998]. As a key principle for designing work-stealing schedulers, the work-first principle requires that the scheduling overhead associated with each task (and finally work overhead) be minimized [Frigo 1998]. For example, techniques like lazy task creation [Mohr 1991] have been used to reduce the overhead of task generation to a level similar to that of function calls. The violation of work-first principle causes performance degradation, because tasks in a work-stealing application are usually very small [Kumar 2007, Sanchez 2010].

Algorithm 2 – BWS: Balanced Work Stealing Algorithm

1: **Local Variables:**
2: t : a task
3: n : value of the steal counter of a worker
4: c : value of the wake-up counter of a worker
5: w : current worker
6: v : a victim worker w selects to steal from
7:
8: **procedure** RANDOMSTEAL
9:    **repeat**
10:       Randomly select a worker v as a victim
11:       **if** w can steal a task t from v **then**
12:          enqueue t
13:          $w.c \leftarrow w.c + 2$
14:          reset $w.n$
15:          **return**
16:       **else**
17:          **if** v has an unfinished task **then**
18:             **if** v has been preempted **then**
19:                yield core to v
20:             **else**
21:                **if** $v.c > 0$ **then**
22:                   $v.c \leftarrow v.c - 1$
23:                   $w.c \leftarrow w.c + 1$
24:                **end if**
25:             **end if**
26:          **else**
27:             **if** v is sleeping and $w.c \neq 0$ **then**
28:                wake up v
29:                $w.c \leftarrow w.c - 1$
30:             **end if**
31:          **end if**
32:          $w.n \leftarrow w.n + 1$
33:       **end if**
34:       **if** $w.n > SleepThreshold$ **then**
35:          **if** $w.c = 0$ **then** Sleep
36:          **else**
37:             $w.c \leftarrow w.c - 1$
38:          **end if**
39:          reset $w.n$
40:       **end if**
41:    **until** work is done
42: **end procedure**

---

a wake-up operation, because carrying out both of the wake-up and sleep operations increases the number of unnecessary context switches and incurs unnecessary overhead.

4. The Implementation of BWS

BWS relies on two new OS supporting mechanisms, which require only slight changes to the Linux kernel (about 100 lines of code in two existing files concerned with thread scheduling in Linux kernel 2.6.36). First, BWS needs the

OS to disclose whether a worker is currently running on a core. On current operating systems, an application can only get brief running status of its threads, e.g., whether a thread is sleeping or whether it is terminated. However, whether a thread is currently taking a core and running is not directly disclosed by the OS. To provide the support, we add a new system call, which returns to the calling thread the running status of a peer thread (identified by its thread id) in the same application.

Second, we implement a new yielding support to allow a thread (*yielder*) to yield its core to a designated second thread (*yieldee*) in the same application. When the yielder makes a *yield_to* call (with a thread id argument), it is suspended. The rest of its timeslice is passed to the designated yieldee. Then the yieldee is scheduled immediately on the core that the yielder was running on, using the remaining time-slice offered by the yielder.

With the OS support, we implement a prototype of BWS based on Intel Cilk++ SDK preview (build 8503). The implementation must handle and prevent a special case, in which all the thieves are sleeping, because then parallelism changes in the application would go undetected. To avoid this case in the implementation, BWS uses a thief as a "watchdog", which executes a similar algorithm to Algorithm 2. One difference between the watchdog worker and other thieves is that the watchdog worker does not go to sleep. The other difference is that, when the watchdog worker steals a task, it wakes up sleeping workers itself (instead of relying on other thieves). Before the watchdog worker begins to process the task, it appoints one of the workers it wakes up as the new watchdog worker. Then, it becomes a normal worker.

5. Experiments

With the prototype implementation, we tested the performance of BWS. In this section, we first introduce our experimental setup, then present the experimental results.

5.1 Experimental Setup

We carried out our experiments on a workstation with four 2.26GHz Intel Xeon 7560 processors. Each processor has 8 cores. The memory size is 64GiB. The operating system is 64-bit Ubuntu Linux 10.04LTS. The kernel version is 2.6.36. The kernel parameter sched_compat_yield is set to 1.[3] The *SleepThreshold* is set to 64.

We selected the following benchmarks and measured their execution times in varying scenarios. All the selected

| group 1 | BFS, EP, MM, RayTracer, LOOP |
| group 2 | CG, CLIP, MI |

Table 1. Benchmarks are divided into two groups based on scalability: good (group 1) and fair (group 2).

benchmarks are computation intensive to minimize the performance impact of I/O operations.

- BFS traverses a graph with 10 million nodes using a breadth-first algorithm.

- CG and EP benchmarks were adapted from their OpenMP implementations in the NPB NAS benchmark suite [Jin 1999]. CG finds an estimation of the smallest eigenvalue of a large sparse matrix with a conjugate gradient method. EP computes a large number of gaussian pseudo random numbers with a scheme well suited for parallel computing. The problem size for both benchmarks is class B.

- CLIP executes a parallelized computational geometry algorithm to process a large number of polygon pairs. The algorithm implements a common operation in spatial database systems, which is to compute the areas of the intersection and the union of two polygons [Wang 2011].

- MI implements the matrix inversion algorithm. The size of the matrix is 500×500.

- MM is an example application in the Cilk++ package that multiplies two matrices. The size of each matrix is 1600×1600.

- RayTracer is a 3D renderer that renders an 800×600 image using ray tracing techniques. It casts 4 rays of light from each pixel to generate a vivid 3D world.

- LOOP is a micro-benchmark. It creates 32 threads, each of which performs a busy loop until the main thread notifies them to finish.

The above benchmarks except LOOP were developed with Cilk++. LOOP was developed with pthreads, and is used as a representative of non-work-stealing multi-threaded programs. The computation carried out in LOOP is very simple, in order to minimize the interference from other factors that may affect the performance of co-running applications, such as contention for cache space and memory bandwidth.

Based on the scalability of the benchmarks, we divide them into two groups. In the first group, BFS, EP, MM, RayTracer, and LOOP show good scalability, with speedups exceeding 20 when 32 cores are used. In the second group, CG, CLIP, and MI are not as scalable as those in the first group. Although allocating more cores to each of the benchmarks can improve the performance marginally, the speed-ups are below 16 with 32 cores.

---

[3] With the default Linux kernel configuration, whether a thread calling *yield* can actually yield the core depends on the unfinished time quantums of this thread and other threads co-running with it on the core. Work-stealing applications usually cannot perform well with this configuration, and their performance is similar to that without yielding operations. In the experiments, we changed the configuration to improve the throughput of work-stealing applications with the original Cilk++ and to make the comparison fair.

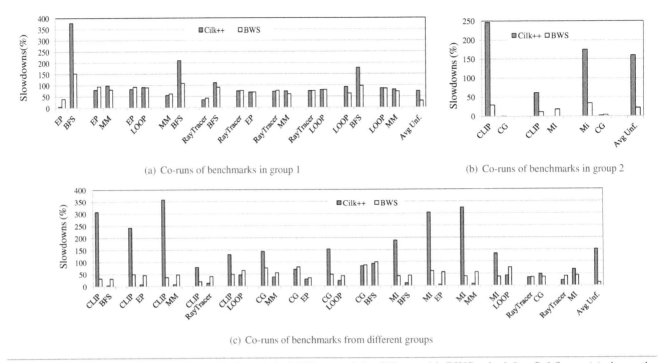

(a) Co-runs of benchmarks in group 1

(b) Co-runs of benchmarks in group 2

(c) Co-runs of benchmarks from different groups

Figure 2. Slowdowns of benchmarks with the original Cilk++ and the Cilk++ with BWS scheduler. Subfigure (a) shows the slowdowns of the benchmarks from group 1 when they co-run, Subfigure (b) shows the slowdowns of the benchmarks from group 2 when they co-run, and Subfigure (c) shows the slowdowns for the co-runs of benchmarks from different groups.

In the experiments, we first run each benchmark alone to get its solo-run execution time, averaged over 5 runs. Then, we run two benchmarks concurrently. As benchmarks have different execution times, we run each benchmark multiple times (between 8 and 100 times, depending on the benchmark's solo-run time) so that their executions are fully overlapped. We call the concurrent executions of two benchmarks a *co-run*. For each benchmark in a co-run, we average its execution times, compare the average execution time (T_c) against its solo-run execution time (T_s), and calculate the slowdown, which is $(T_c - T_s)/T_s$. For each possible combination of two benchmarks, we first co-run the two benchmarks with the original Cilk++ (with ABP). Then we co-run them with the Cilk++ with the BWS scheduler, and compare their slowdowns with the two different systems. We set the number of threads in each benchmark to be 32. As the benchmarks in each combination have the same number of threads, in the ideal case, they show similar slowdowns.

To measure unfairness and performance, we define the unfairness metric and system throughput metric as follows. The unfairness metric is the difference between the larger slowdown and the smaller slowdown between the co-running benchmarks. We use *Weighted-Speedup* to measure system throughputs, which is the sum of the speedups of the benchmarks (i.e. $\Sigma(T_b/T_c)$), where T_b is the execution time of a benchmark in the baseline case [Mutlu 2008, Snavely 2000]. As an example, suppose two benchmarks have the

same solo-run execution time, and when they co-run, each of them is slowed down by 100%. In our setting $T_b = T_s$, so the weighted-speedup throughput of the co-run is $1/2+1/2 = 1$. A throughput of 1 implies that the co-run's throughput is the same as if the benchmarks were run consecutively.

5.2 Performance in Terms of Fairness, Throughput, and Execution Time Variation

In this subsection, we show that the BWS scheduler can effectively achieve both goals of reducing unfairness and improving system throughput. We will also show that BWS can reduce the performance variation of work-stealing applications, as a by-product.

Figure 2 compares the slowdowns of the benchmarks for both the original Cilk++ (with ABP) and the Cilk++ with BWS scheduler. In each subfigure, the last two bars show the average unfairness. As shown in the figure, with the original Cilk++, when two benchmarks co-run, one benchmark may be slowed down by a much larger degree than the other benchmark. Usually, the one that is less scalable shows a larger slowdown. For example, when CLIP and MM co-run, CLIP is slowed down significantly by 358%, while MM is slowed down by only 7%. When MI and EP co-run, MI is slowed down dramatically by 304%, and EP is only slowed down by 5%. The reason is that the workers in the less scalable benchmarks are more likely to run out of tasks and yield their cores. BFS is slowed down by large percents when it co-runs with other benchmarks in group 1. This is because the granularity of the tasks in BFS is very small. Workers in BFS perform steals frequently, and relinquish cores frequently on unsuccessful steals. On average, the unfairness is 73% for benchmark pairs from group 1 (in Figure 2(a)), and 160% for benchmark pairs from group 2 (in Figure 2(b)), and 151% for the remaining benchmark pairs which mix the benchmarks from both groups (in Figure 2(c)).

Our BWS scheduler can avoid the execution of a work-stealing application being excessively delayed. Thus, for each pair of co-running benchmarks, the difference between their slowdowns can be significantly reduced. For example, when CLIP and MM co-run, their slowdowns are 36% and 47%, respectively. When MI and EP co-run, the slowdowns are 61% and 56%, respectively. On average, the BWS scheduler can significantly reduce the unfairness to 30% for benchmark pairs from group 1, to 22% for benchmarks from group 2, and to 13% for the remaining benchmark pairs.

Our BWS scheduler not only improves fairness, but also increases system throughput. Figure 3 shows the throughputs of the co-runs for both the original Cilk++ and the Cilk++ with BWS scheduler. For fair comparison, when we calculate the throughput of a co-run for the two different systems, we use the same baseline, in which each benchmark runs alone with the original Cilk++ for the same amount of time.[4] For the co-runs of the benchmarks from group 1, BWS improves throughput by 4% on average over the original Cilk++. These benchmarks have good scalability, and their workers spend only a small amount of time on stealing with the original Cilk++. Thus, there is only a limited opportunity for BWS to show improvements. In contrast, the benchmarks in group 2 have only fair scalability, and their workers spend more time on stealing than those in group 1. Thus, for the co-runs of these benchmarks, BWS improves throughput by much larger degrees (33% on average). For the co-runs of benchmarks from different groups, BWS improves throughput moderately: the average throughput is 11% higher than that with the original Cilk++.

To understand how BWS improves system throughput and fairness, we have instrumented the OS scheduler to monitor the context switches during the co-runs. We select the co-runs of benchmarks from different groups. For each execution of a benchmark, we collect the number of context switches, as well as the numbers of the following two types of context switches: 1) a *to-thief context switch* that grants the core to a thief, and 2) an *external context switch* that grants the core to a thread from another application.

Compared to the original Cilk++, BWS incurs far fewer context switches. For example, BWS incurs 98% fewer context switches for the co-run of CLIP and MM, and 99%

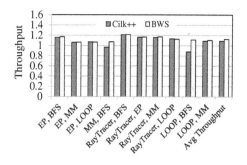

(a) Co-runs of benchmarks in group 1

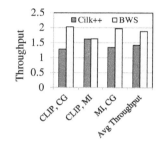

(b) Co-runs of benchmarks in group 2

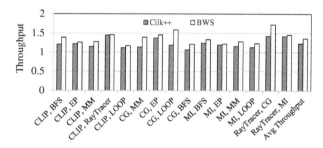

(c) Co-runs of benchmarks from different groups

Figure 3. Throughputs of different co-runs with the original Cilk++ and the Cilk++ with BWS scheduler. Subfigure (a) shows the throughputs of the co-runs with benchmarks from group 1, Subfigure (b) shows the throughputs of the co-runs with benchmarks from group 2, and Subfigure (c) shows the throughputs of the co-runs with benchmarks from different groups.

fewer context switches for the co-run of MI and EP. For most co-runs, the numbers of context switches are reduced by more than 70%.

With the original Cilk++, a significant amount of context switches (93%) are to-thief switches. For example, when CLIP co-runs with MM, 98% of the context switches involving CLIP are to-thief switches, and 99% of the context switches involving MM are to-thief switches. The high percentages of to-thief context switches are caused by scheduling multiple thieves on the same core so the thieves yield the core back and forth quickly. BWS greatly reduces the to-thief context switches. With BWS, only 32% of context switches in the co-runs are to-thief context switches. The

---

[4] Each benchmark has similar solo-run execution times with the two different systems (the difference is less than 5%), except CG and CLIP. With BWS, the solo-run execution time of CG is decreased by 25%, while the solo-run execution time of CLIP is increased by 17%. On average, the benchmark solo-runs are slowed down by 0.4% with BWS, compared with their solo-runs with the original Cilk++.

reduction of context switches and to-thief context switches shows that BWS improves system throughput by preventing thieves from being scheduled prematurely and by having thieves preferentially yield cores to threads that are making progress.

To show how BWS improves fairness, we compare the numbers of external context switches incurred by the original Cilk++ and by BWS. For BFS and the benchmarks in group 2, BWS significantly reduces the number of external context switches by 45%–96%. For example, when MI co-runs with EP, the number of external context switches in each execution of MI is reduced by 80% with BWS. This shows that with BWS, applications in group 2 become less likely to give up cores to their co-running applications, and thus excessive execution delay is avoided. We did not see such an obvious trend for the benchmarks in group 1 (except BFS). While the number of external context switches are reduced for some benchmarks (e.g., MM), the number is increased for others (e.g., EP).

Another important finding is that with the original Cilk++, the benchmarks usually show large performance variations,[5] which are caused by frequent core yieldings across applications. Taking CG as an example, when it co-runs with MM, its execution time varies in a wide range from 35 seconds to 65 seconds. With BWS, its execution time varies in a much smaller range from 23 seconds to 29 seconds.

To monitor the performance variation, for each benchmark in each co-run, we calculate a Coefficient of Variation (CV) of its execution times. For each benchmark, we average its CV values across all the co-runs that include the benchmark, and show the average CV value in Figure 4(a). We also calculate an average CV value and show it in Figure 4(b) for each of the following types of executions.

- Type 1: Executions of a benchmark in group 2 with another benchmark in group 2

- Type 2: Executions of a benchmark in group 2 with a benchmark in group 1

- Type 3: Executions of a benchmark in group 1 with a benchmark in group 2

- Type 4: Executions of a benchmark in group 1 with a benchmark in group 1

As shown in Figure 4(a), with the original Cilk++, benchmarks in group 2 and BFS show larger performance variations than other benchmarks, because their workers yield cores more frequently in the co-runs. Compared to their co-runners, the performance of benchmarks EP, MM, RayTracer, and LOOP changes only slightly across different co-runs.

As shown in Figure 4(b), type 2 executions show the largest performance variations among the four types of exe-

[5] Note that the impact of these variations is minimized in our co-run experiments because each benchmark is run many times in a tight loop.

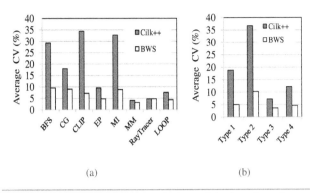

(a)   (b)

Figure 4. Performance variation of the benchmarks

cutions. This is because the benchmarks in group 2 may be slowed down by the largest percentages when they co-run with benchmarks in group 1. Type 3 executions show the smallest performance variations, because the performance of the benchmarks in group 1 is minimally impacted by benchmarks in group 2.

BWS reduces external context switches by letting workers relinquish their cores to their peer workers in the same application. Thus, it reduces the performance variation. For all the benchmarks, it reduces the average CV values to less than 10%. For type 2 executions, it can reduce the average CV value from 37% to 10%.

5.3 Experiments with Alternative Approaches

In Cilk++, a worker yields its core whenever it runs out of local tasks or its steal attempt fails. The execution of a work-stealing application is delayed if its workers relinquish the cores prematurely by this yielding mechanism. Thus, an intuitive proposal to reduce the execution delay is to lower the chance that workers yield their cores prematurely. For example, in Intel TBB, a worker does not yield its core until the number of failed steals exceeds a threshold, which is two times the number of workers. When the threshold is reached, the worker yields its core on each unsuccessful steal. For convenience, we call this method *delay-yielding*. Another method is that a worker yields its core once every time it has conducted a number (e.g., 64 in the experiments below) of failed steals. We call this method *selective-yielding*.

We have implemented these methods into Cilk++, and repeated all the co-runs for each of the methods. The threshold is 64 (i.e. 2×32) for the delay-yielding method. Figure 5 compares the average unfairness and average throughput of the two methods against that of the original Cilk++ and BWS. Compared to the original Cilk++, the two methods can slightly reduce unfairness. However, they undesirably lower system throughput. For example, the selective-yielding method can reduce the average unfairness from 124% to 108%, which is still serious. But it lowers the average throughput by about 8% from 1.2 to 1.1. In contrast, BWS both minimizes unfairness and improves throughput.

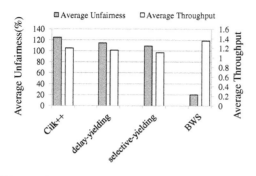

Figure 5. Average unfairness and average throughput for the original Cilk++, two alternative approaches, and BWS

The delay-yielding method or selective-yielding method can only modestly reduce unfairness. There are two reasons. First, the methods still use *yield* calls to relinquish cores. Second, in a work-stealing application, new tasks are dynamically generated by workers processing tasks. Though the methods enable a worker to continue stealing after unsuccessful steal attempts, the worker still may not be able to steal a task before it relinquishes its core if existing tasks are all being processed and new tasks have not been generated. In a multi-programmed environment, workers processing tasks may be preempted. This makes it more difficult for a worker to find a task to steal in a limited number of attempts. In contrast, BWS keeps useful thieves running and only puts wasteful thieves into sleep.

5.4 Parameter Sensitivity

In BWS, *SleepThreshold* is an important parameter. A large threshold value can help reducing unfairness by maintaining the concurrency level of a work-stealing application. However, a large threshold value may increase the resource waste and impact system throughput, because thieves are kept awake for a longer time with a larger threshold value. With the experiments in this subsection, we measure the impact of the threshold value on both fairness and throughput.

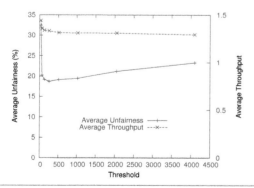

Figure 6. Average unfairness and average throughput achieved by BWS, when varying *SleepThreshold* from 32 to 4096

In the experiments, we vary the value of *SleepThreshold* from 32 to 4096, and execute all the co-runs on the Cilk++ with BWS scheduler. In Figure 6, we show the average unfairness and average throughput of these co-runs. When the threshold is less than 256, increasing the value can effectively reduce unfairness, especially when the threshold is small. For example, increasing the threshold from 32 to 64, the average unfairness value can be reduced from 32% to 20%. But the improved fairness comes at the cost of reducing the throughput from 1.44 to 1.35.

Increasing the threshold from 256 to 4096 both reduces the average throughput from 1.33 to 1.29 and increases the average unfairness from 19% to 23%. The reason that the fairness no longer improves when we increase the threshold beyond 256 is as follows. In some co-runs of benchmarks with different degrees of scalability, the benchmarks with better scalability are slowed down by larger percentages than their co-runners, and the difference between the slowdowns increases with the threshold.

Please note that the average unfairness and average throughput with the original Cilk++ are 124% and 1.20, respectively. Thus, Cilk++ with BWS always performs better than the original Cilk++, no matter which value from 32 to 4096 is chosen for *SleepThreshold*. However, values between 32 and 256 are clearly preferable to larger values.

5.5 Validation of Optimization Techniques

To get good performance, BWS uses a few techniques. One important technique is that the thieves in an application carry out most management work, e.g., inspecting the local data structures of their peer workers to collect information, making scheduling decisions, and waking up sleeping workers. This technique minimizes work overhead. The other critical technique is to keep the solution decentralized to avoid global coordination. Instead of maintaining global information, such as the number of available tasks or the number of busy workers, BWS executes the workers in an application in a peer-to-peer way. The workers accumulate partial information with simple data structures, e.g., wake-up counters and steal counters, and make scheduling decisions based on the information. This makes the solution scalable.

We have designed experiments to validate these optimization techniques. In the first experiment, we run the work-stealing benchmarks with a downgraded BWS, in which busy workers are in charge of waking up sleeping workers. With the downgraded BWS, when a busy worker generates a new task, it wakes up two sleeping workers if there are any, and a thief goes to sleep when its number of unsuccessful steals exceeds a threshold. The work overhead impacts not only the performance of work-stealing appliations when they run concurrently, but also their solo-run performance. Thus, we collect the solo-run execution times of the benchmarks to factor out any interference from co-running. We run each benchmark with 32 workers on 32 cores. Compared to BWS, with the downgraded BWS, the benchmarks are slowed down by 7% on average due to the increased work overhead. Among the benchmarks, MI is slowed down by the largest percentage (35%).

In the second experiment, we show the extent to which collecting global information in a work-stealing application can degrade the performance. We implement and use another work-stealing scheduler, named WSGI (work-stealing with global information), which collects the number of busy workers, the number of non-sleeping thieves, and the number of sleeping thieves. By dynamically putting thieves into sleep or waking up sleeping thieves, WSGI tries to keep a fixed ratio between the number of busy workers and the number of non-sleeping thieves. We set the ratio to 2 in the experiment to guarantee that available tasks can be distributed quickly to thieves [Agrawal 2008]. As we do in the previous experiment, we collect the solo-run execution times of the work-stealing benchmarks on 32 cores, with 32 workers in each benchmark. We compare the execution times against those with BWS. The comparison shows that the benchmarks are 43% slower with WSGI than they are with BWS. Among the benchmarks, CLIP shows the largest slow-down (177%). The performance degradation is due to the contention on the locks protecting the global information. This experiment clear demonstrates the importance of keeping the BWS design decentralized.

6. Related Work

6.1 Work Stealing in Multiprogrammed Environments

To efficiently execute work-stealing applications in multiprogrammed environments, two solutions have been proposed: ABP (as discussed in this paper) and A-Steal. A-Steal [Agrawal 2008] assumes there is a space-sharing OS job scheduler that allocates *disjoint sets of cores to different applications*. Based on whether the cores are efficiently used in one epoch, a work-stealing application requests that the OS job scheduler adjust the number of cores allocated to it for the next epoch. Based on the number of cores the OS grants it, the application in turn adjusts the number of workers it will use in the next epoch, in order to have exactly one worker per allocated core. Similar solutions were also proposed earlier to schedule parallel applications with user-level task scheduling on multiprogrammed multiprocessors [Agrawal 2006, Tucker 1989].

While the ABP solution has the fairness and throughput problems detailed in this paper, A-Steal can hardly be adopted on conventional multicore systems, where operating systems are usually designed for time-sharing the cores among applications. Space-sharing is typically used on batch processing systems. For both high performance and high efficiency, a space-sharing system requires that each application predicts the number of cores it needs and then readily adjusts to the number of cores allocated [McCann 1993, Tucker 1989]. Most applications must be redesigned on conventional systems to meet these requirements. At the same time, accurately predicting the demand for cores can be very challenging, considering various execution dynamics that can affect the demand such as paging, contention, irregularity in computation, etc.

Moreover, A-Steal's epoch-based adjustments work well only when the application's execution phases are much longer than the epoch length, so that the statistics collected in an epoch can be used to predict the number of cores preferred by the application in the next epoch. To amortize overheads, typical epoch lengths in A-Steal are tens to hundreds of milliseconds. However, our experiments show that parallel phases in some work-stealing applications can be as short as hundreds of microseconds. Such applications require much shorter epoch lengths, which may significantly increase the overhead to collect global information on execution efficiency, and thus limit application scalability. BWS does not suffer from these shortcomings.

6.2 System Support for User Level Thread Scheduling

Previous studies have proposed OS support for user level thread scheduling [Anderson 1992, Black 1990, Marsh 1991, Polychronopoulos 1998]. For example, scheduler activations [Anderson 1992] enable user-level thread schedulers to communicate with the OS scheduler via upcalls and downcalls. This provides a user-level thread scheduler with more control over the cores allocated to the application. For example, when a user-level thread is blocked, the user-level thread scheduler can be notified by the OS to perform rescheduling to prevent the kernel thread executing the user-level thread from being blocked. Usually, intensive modifications to the OS must be made to provide the support, and they have not been adopted by mainstream operating systems.[6] We believe that the OS support proposed for BWS, in contrast, are sufficiently lightweight to be adopted into Linux and other mainstream operating systems.

Though the tasks in work-stealing applications are called "threads" in some early articles, they are different from the user-level threads targeted in the above proposals. The granularities of the tasks in work-stealing applications can be very small, e.g., hundreds of CPU cycles. To minimize work overhead, lazy task creation and other similar techniques have been used to make them more like local procedure calls, rather than entities ready to be scheduled like user-level threads [Mohr 1991]. For example, the major data structure for a task is a stack frame. There are neither private stacks, contexts, priorities, nor preemption in scheduling the tasks. At the same time, the fine granularities also dictate that the management costs and scheduling overheads be kept very low. BWS is designed with the full consideration of these features of work-stealing applications, including its OS support, without requiring intensive modifications to the OS kernel.

---

[6] The idea of scheduler activations was once adopted by NetBSD and FreeBSD.

In the Exokernel design, the OS provides applications with a *yield_to* mechanism [Engler 1995], which allows each application to schedule its kernel threads at user level. BWS could exploit this feature.

6.3 Other Related Work

Besides the ABP and A-Steal algorithms, there are other work-stealing algorithms proposed for various purposes such as improved data locality [Acar 2000] and extensions to distributed memory clusters [Blumofe 1997, Dinan 2009]. These studies did not address multiprogramming issues. Hardware support and OS support have been proposed to reduce the overheads of running work-stealing applications [Kumar 2007, Lee 2010, Sanchez 2010], e.g., task stealing overheads; these are orthogonal to BWS.

7. Conclusion

This paper introduced BWS (balanced work stealing), a novel and practical solution for efficiently running work-stealing applications on time-sharing multicores. BWS addresses the fairness and system throughput problems of existing work-stealing approaches via two means. First, it reduces the costs associated with wasteful thieves by putting such thieves into sleep and then waking them up only when they are likely to be useful thieves. Second, it minimizes unfairness by enabling thieves to yield their cores directly to busy workers for the same application, thereby retaining the cores for that application and putting them to better use. BWS reduces scheduling overheads through a decentralized design in which thieves perform scheduling bookkeeping and wake up sleeping workers when appropriate. The design relies on two new system calls added to the OS: one that returns the running status of a peer thread and another that yields the caller's core directly to a peer thread. The required changes to the OS are minimal (100 lines of code in two thread scheduling files in Linux).

Our evaluation with a prototype implementation in Cilk++ and the Linux kernel shows that compared to the original Cilk++, BWS improves average system throughput by 12.5% and reduces average unfairness from 124% to 20%, while also reducing application running time variance. Currently, we are making efforts to merge BWS into production work-stealing libraries and systems.

As part of future work, we intend to extend BWS to improve the fairness and throughput of work-stealing applications in virtualized environments, where physical CPU cores are usually over-committed with multiple virtual cores. Work-stealing applications face similar issues in these environments as they do in multi-programmed environments. Virtual cores running thief threads may impede the execution of other virtual cores doing useful work. However, due to the semantic gap challenge and the simple interface between hypervisor and virtual machines, addressing these issues seems more challenging in virtualized environments than in traditional multiprogrammed environments.

Acknowledgments

We thank Frans Kaashoek for his helpful suggestions as the shepherd for this paper, and the anonymous reviewers for their constructive comments. This research was supported by the National Science Foundation under grants CNS-0834393, CCF-0913150, and CNS-1019343 to the Computing Research Association for the CIFellows Project. Any opinions, findings, and conclusions or recommendations expressed in this material are those of the authors and do not necessarily reflect the views of the National Science Foundation or the Computing Research Association. This work was done under the umbrella of the Intel Science and Technology Center for Cloud Computing.

References

[Acar 2000] Umut A. Acar, Guy E. Blelloch, and Robert D. Blumofe. The data locality of work stealing. In *ACM SPAA '00*, pages 1–12, 2000.

[Agrawal 2006] Kunal Agrawal, Yuxiong He, Wen-Jing Hsu, and Charles E. Leiserson. Adaptive scheduling with parallelism feedback. In *ACM PPoPP '06*, pages 100–109, 2006.

[Agrawal 2008] Kunal Agrawal, Charles E. Leiserson, Yuxiong He, and Wen-Jing Hsu. Adaptive work-stealing with parallelism feedback. *ACM Trans. Comput. Syst.*, 26(3), September 2008.

[Anderson 1992] Thomas E. Anderson, Brian N. Bershad, Edward D. Lazowska, and Henry M. Levy. Scheduler activations: Effective kernel support for the user-level management of parallelism. *ACM Trans. Comput. Syst.*, 10(1):53–79, February 1992.

[Arora 1998] Nimar S. Arora, Robert D. Blumofe, and C. Greg Plaxton. Thread scheduling for multiprogrammed multiprocessors. In *ACM SPAA '98*, pages 119–129, 1998.

[Black 1990] David L. Black. Scheduling support for concurrency and parallelism in the mach operating system. *IEEE Computer*, 23(5):35–43, May 1990.

[Blumofe 1995] Robert D. Blumofe, Christopher F. Joerg, Bradley C. Kuszmaul, Charles E. Leiserson, Keith H. Randall, and Yuli Zhou. Cilk: An efficient multithreaded runtime system. In *ACM PPOPP '95*, pages 207–216, 1995.

[Blumofe 1994] Robert D. Blumofe and Charles E. Leiserson. Scheduling multithreaded computations by work stealing. In *IEEE FOCS '94*, pages 356–368, 1994.

[Blumofe 1997] Robert D. Blumofe and Philip A. Lisiecki. Adaptive and reliable parallel computing on networks of workstations. In *USENIX ATC '97*, pages 133–147, 1997.

[Blumofe 1998] Robert D. Blumofe and Dionisios Papadopoulos. The performance of work stealing in multiprogrammed environments. Technical Report TR-98-13, Department of Computer Science, University of Texas at Austin, 1998.

[Burton 1981] F. Warren Burton and M. Ronan Sleep. Executing functional programs on a virtual tree of processors. In *ACM FPCA '81*, pages 187–194, 1981.

[Dinan 2009] James Dinan, D. Brian Larkins, P. Sadayappan, Sriram Krishnamoorthy, and Jarek Nieplocha. Scalable work stealing. In *ACM SC '09*, pages 53:1–53:11, 2009.

[Engler 1995] Dawson R. Engler, M. Frans Kaashoek, and James O'Toole Jr. Exokernel: An operating system architecture for application-level resource management. In *ACM SOSP '95*, pages 251–266, 1995.

[Frigo 1998] Matteo Frigo, Charles E. Leiserson, and Keith H. Randall. The implementation of the Cilk-5 multithreaded language. In *ACM PLDI '98*, pages 212–223, 1998.

[Iancu 2010] Costin Iancu, Steven Hofmeyr, Filip Blagojevic, and Yili Zheng. Oversubscription on multicore processors. In *IEEE IPDPS '10*, pages 1–11, 2010.

[Jin 1999] Haoqiang Jin, Michael Frumkin, and Jerry Yan. The OpenMP implementation of NAS parallel benchmarks and its performance. Technical Report NAS-99-011, NASA, 1999.

[Kukanov 2007] Alexey Kukanov. The foundations for scalable multi-core software in Intel threading building blocks. *Intel Technology Journal*, 11(4):309–322, November 2007.

[Kumar 2007] Sanjeev Kumar, Christopher J. Hughes, and Anthony Nguyen. Carbon: Architectural support for fine-grained parallelism on chip multiprocessors. In *ACM ISCA '07*, pages 162–173, 2007.

[Lee 2010] I-Ting Angelina Lee, Silas Boyd-Wickizer, Zhiyi Huang, and Charles E. Leiserson. Using memory mapping to support cactus stacks in work-stealing runtime systems. In *ACM PACT '10*, pages 411–420, 2010.

[Leijen 2009] Daan Leijen, Wolfram Schulte, and Sebastian Burckhardt. The design of a task parallel library. In *ACM OOPSLA '09*, pages 227–242, 2009.

[Leiserson 2010] Charles Leiserson. The Cilk++ concurrency platform. *J. Supercomput.*, 51(3):244–257, March 2010.

[Marsh 1991] Brian D. Marsh, Michael L. Scott, Thomas J. LeBlanc, and Evangelos P. Markatos. First-class user-level threads. In *ACM SOSP '91*, pages 110–121, 1991.

[McCann 1993] Cathy McCann, Raj Vaswani, and John Zahorjan. A dynamic processor allocation policy for multiprogrammed shared-memory multiprocessors. *ACM Trans. Comput. Syst.*, 11(2):146–178, May 1993.

[Mohr 1991] E. Mohr, D. A. Kranz, and R. H. Halstead, Jr. Lazy task creation: A technique for increasing the granularity of parallel programs. *IEEE Trans. Parallel Distrib. Syst.*, 2(3):264–280, July 1991.

[Mutlu 2008] Onur Mutlu and Thomas Moscibroda. Parallelism-aware batch scheduling: Enhancing both performance and fairness of shared DRAM systems. In *ACM ISCA '08*, pages 63–74, 2008.

[Navarro 2009] Angeles Navarro, Rafael Asenjo, Siham Tabik, and Călin Caşcaval. Load balancing using work-stealing for pipeline parallelism in emerging applications. In *ACM ICS '09*, pages 517–518, 2009.

[Neill 2009] Daniel Neill and Adam Wierman. On the benefits of work stealing in shared-memory multiprocessors. http://www.cs.cmu.edu/~acw/15740/paper.pdf, 2009.

[Poirier 2011] Yolande Poirier. Java and parallelism computing: An interview with Java developer and researcher Dr. Gilda Garreton. http://www.oracle.com/technetwork/articles/java/gildagarreton-416282.html, 2011.

[Polychronopoulos 1998] Eleftherios D. Polychronopoulos, Xavier Martorell, Dimitrios S. Nikolopoulos, Jesus Labarta, Theodore S. Papatheodorou, and Nacho Navarro. Kernel-level scheduling for the nano-threads programming model. In *ACM ICS '98*, pages 337–344, 1998.

[Saha 2007] Bratin Saha, Ali-Reza Adl-Tabatabai, Anwar M. Ghuloum, et al. Enabling scalability and performance in a large scale CMP environment. In *ACM EuroSys '07*, pages 73–86, 2007.

[Sanchez 2010] Daniel Sanchez, Richard M. Yoo, and Christos Kozyrakis. Flexible architectural support for fine-grain scheduling. In *ACM ASPLOS '10*, pages 311–322, 2010.

[Snavely 2000] Allan Snavely and Dean M. Tullsen. Symbiotic jobscheduling for a simultaneous multithreaded processor. In *ACM ASPLOS '00*, pages 234–244, 2000.

[Tucker 1989] Andrew Tucker and Anoop Gupta. Process control and scheduling issues for multiprogrammed shared-memory multiprocessors. In *ACM SOSP '89*, pages 159–166, 1989.

[van Nieuwpoort 2001] Rob V. van Nieuwpoort, Thilo Kielmann, and Henri E. Bal. Efficient load balancing for wide-area divide-and-conquer applications. In *ACM PPoPP '01*, pages 34–43, 2001.

[Wang 2011] Fusheng Wang, Jun Kong, Lee Cooper, et al. A data model and database for high-resolution pathology analytical image informatics. *J. Pathol. Inform.*, 2:32, July 2011.

Author Index